COSTING

SEVENTH EDITION

COSTING

SEVENTH EDITION

COSTING

SEVENTH EDITION

T. Lucey
MSocSc, FCMA, FCCA, JDipMA

![SOUTH-WESTERN CENGAGE Learning logo]

SOUTH-WESTERN
CENGAGE Learning™

Australia • Brazil • Japan • Korea • Mexico • Singapore • Spain • United Kingdom • United States

SOUTH-WESTERN
CENGAGE Learning™

Costing 7ᵗʰ edition
T. Lucey

Publishing Director: Linden Harris

Publisher: Brendan George

Assistant Editor: Leandra Paoli

Content Project Editor: Dan Benton

Manufacturing Team Lead: Paul Herbert

Production Controller: Eyvett Davis

Marketing Manager: Amanda Cheung

Typesetter: KGL, India

Cover design: Design Deluxe Ltd, Bath, UK

Text design: Design Deluxe Ltd, Bath, UK

For product information and technology assistance, contact
emea.info@cengage.com

For permission to use material from this text or product, and for permission queries,
email **clsuk.permissions@cengage.com**

British Library Cataloguing-in-Publication Data
A catalogue record for this book is available from the British Library.

ISBN: 978-1-84480-943-1

Cengage Learning EMEA
Cheriton House, North Way, Andover
Hampshire SP10 5BE. United Kingdom

Cengage Learning products are represented in Canada by
Nelson Education Ltd.

For your lifelong learning solutions, visit
www.cengage.co.uk

Purchase e-books or e-chapters at:
www.cengagebrain.com

Printed by Zrinski d.d., Croatia
2 3 4 5 6 7 8 9 10 – 12 11 10

ABOUT THE AUTHOR

Terry Lucey has been an accountant and consultant in industry and has had over 20 years' examining and teaching experience at all levels of professional studies and for diploma and degree courses in business studies. He was previously Head of Department of Business Studies at the University of Wolverhampton and Visiting Fellow at Aston Business School, Aston University.

Among his other published works are:

Investment Appraisal: Evaluating Risk and Uncertainty,

Accounting and Computer Systems (co-author),

Quantitative Techniques, Management Information Systems, Management Accounting, First Course in Cost and Management Accounting and several ACCA and CIMA Study and Revision manuals.

CONTENTS

CONTENTS

PREFACE

1. AIMS

This book is designed to provide a thorough understanding of the theory and practice of cost accountancy.

It is particularly relevant for:

a. Students preparing themselves for the examinations of the following bodies; Institute of Chartered Accountants, Chartered Association of Certified Accountants, Chartered Institute of Management Accountants, Chartered Institute of Public Finance and Accountancy and the Association of Accounting Technicians.

b. Students on Foundation Courses in Accounting, Degree and Diploma courses in Accounting and Business Studies and Students on Business/ Technician Education Council (BTEC) courses.

c. Managers and others in industry, commerce, local authorities and similar organisations who wish to gain a working knowledge of the principles and processes of cost accountancy.

2. SCOPE OF THE BOOK

The book comprehensively covers the principles, techniques and methods involved in cost accounting and provides full coverage of the latest professional and college syllabuses. In the first part of the book there is a detailed coverage of the objectives, principles, techniques and methods of cost accounting relating to the analysis and gathering of costs and cost ascertainment. The second part of the book concentrates upon the use of cost information for planning, control and decision-making. At each stage, concepts are illustrated by practical examples and placed into context so that the reader is aware of the importance and relationships of the various aspects of costing. This book does not cover all the more advanced topics contained in some Management Accounting syllabuses. These are covered in the author's book *Management Accounting*, also published by Cengage Learning.

However, because there are many overlaps between Cost and Management Accounting, topics common to both are included in this book. Examples include; budgetary control, standard costing and marginal costing. Whatever the intended final level of study, thorough knowledge of the basics of cost accounting is an essential requirement. This point is stressed again and again in Examiners' Reports.

3. TEACHING APPROACH

The book has been written in a standardised format with numbered paragraphs, end of chapter summaries, and revision exercises at the end of each chapter. This approach has been tested and found effective by thousands of students and the book can be used for independent study or in conjunction with tuition at a college.

4. HOW TO USE THE BOOK EFFECTIVELY

For ease of study the book is divided into self-contained chapters with numbered paragraphs.

In addition each chapter contains a number of exercises with suggested solutions. The solutions are printed immediately below the exercises and you are strongly advised to attempt the exercises *before* looking at the solutions. At appropriate points throughout the book there are Assessment sections. These contain multiple choice and longer questions, both with and without answers. The questions are mainly from past professional examinations and have been selected not merely to repeat the material in the book but to extend knowledge and understanding. They should be considered an integral part of the book. Always make some attempt at the question before working through the solution. The examination questions without answers can be used by lecturers for classwork and assignments when the book is used as a course text or as an extra practice when the book is used for independent study.

5. SEQUENCE OF STUDY

The book should be studied in the sequence of the chapters. The sequence has been arranged so that there is a progressive accumulation of knowledge and any given chapter either includes all the principles necessary or draws upon a previous chapter(s).

6. NOTES TO THE SEVENTH EDITION

The response to this book continues to be extremely encouraging and I would like to express my appreciation for the positive feedback and constructive suggestions received both from tutors and students worldwide. There are numerous detailed revisions throughout the book and it is hoped that this new edition will be found to be of continuing value to students and tutors.

Features of the Seventh Edition:

a. The terminology has been updated throughout and is in accordance with CIMA's *Official Terminology* (2005 Edition).
b. There is a wider selection of multiple choice and longer examination questions drawn from recent professional examinations.
c. There are numerous detailed revisions and extensions of coverage throughout the book.

d. Learning objectives have been set for each chapter which, together with the Assessment sections make the book ideal for use as a course text.

7. FEEDBACK

I would welcome comments and suggestions on the book. Please e-mail these to costing7@hotmail.com or mail them c/o the Accounting Editor at Cengage Learning at the address on page iv. (In the event of the e-mail address given above not working, please e-mail comments to piptel54@aol.com.)

Special assistance to lecturers

A separate Lecturers' Supplement is available free to lecturers who adopt the book as a course text and can be obtained on the companion website (www.cengage.co.uk/lucey7) or by the methods described immediately above.
   The supplement contains:

- Guidance notes on the Case exercises.
- Solutions to all the exercises and examination questions in the book.
- Downloadable copies of key diagrams from the book.
- Four Progress Tests containing Multiple Choice Questions. Each test covers approximately a quarter of the topics in the book.

T. Lucey 2009

ACKNOWLEDGEMENTS

The author would like to express thanks to the following for giving permission to reproduce past examination questions:

Institute of Chartered Accountants in England and Wales (ICAEW)

Chartered Association of Certified Accountants (ACCA)

Chartered Institute of Management Accountants (CIMA)

Chartered Institute of Public Finance and Accountancy (CIPFA)

Association of Accounting Technicians (AAT)

Each question used is cross-referenced to the appropriate Institute or Association and the title of the paper.

Terminology

A major objective of the study of any technical subject, like accounting or cost accounting, is to gain familiarity with the precise definitions of the technical terminology used. The terminology adopted in this book is based on the *Official Terminology* 2005 Edition published by CIMA. Appropriate definitions have been reproduced from the *Terminology*, by kind permission of the Chartered Institute of Management Accountants.

1

What is cost accounting?

1. OBJECTIVES

After studying this chapter you will

- **Be able to define cost accounting**

- **Understand the range of information that could be supplied by the cost accounting system**

- **Know the relationships of cost accounting to management accounting and to financial accounting**

- **Understand how raw data are transformed into information**

- **Have had an introduction to the rest of the book.**

2. COST ACCOUNTING – DEFINITION

Cost Accounting (traditionally termed 'costing') may be defined as:

Gathering of cost information and its attachment to cost objects, the establishment of budgets, standard costs and actual costs of operations, processes, activities or products; and the analysis of variances, profitability or the social use of funds.

Terminology

Detailed explanations of all the terms mentioned and the principles, methods and application of cost accounting form the basis of the subsequent chapters in this book.

3. DEVELOPMENT OF COST ACCOUNTING

Ever since the use of money replaced barter, people have been concerned with costs. However, it was the concentration of manufacturing facilities into

TABLE I.I Examples of cost accounting information and uses

Information provided by Cost Accounting System	Possible uses by Management
Cost per unit of production or service or for a process	As a factor in pricing decisions, production planning and cost control
Cost of running a section, department or factory	Organisational planning, cost control
Wage costs for a unit of production or per period of production	Production planning, decisions on alternative methods, wages cost control
Scrap/Rectification costs	Material cost control, production planning
Cost behaviour with varying levels of activity	Profit planning, make or buy decisions, cost control

Notes:
1. The examples given of uses are not mutually exclusive and it is common to find cost information being used for purposes other than those shown above.
2. The table provides a few examples only. In practice much more information is produced and used.
3. In most cases the usefulness of cost accounting information is enhanced when the actual results and costs are compared to some target or standard figure.

factories which gave impetus to the development of recognisable cost accounting systems. Whilst the early developments were almost entirely related to manufacturing concerns, nowadays cost accounting is used very widely indeed; in hospitals, transport undertakings, local authorities, offices, banks as well as in every manufacturing concern.

4. THE SCOPE OF COST ACCOUNTING

The cost accounting system of any organisation is the foundation of the internal financial information system. Management need a variety of information to plan, to control and to make decisions. Information regarding the financial aspects of performance is provided by the cost accounting system. Examples of the information provided by a typical cost accounting system and how it is used are given in the following table and in the following paragraphs.

5. COST ACCOUNTING AND CONTROL

An important part of the managerial task is to ensure that operations, departments, processes and costs are under control and that the organisation and its constituent parts are working efficiently towards agreed objectives. Although there are numerous other control systems within a typical organisation, for example, Production Control, Quality Control, and Inventory Control, the Cost Accounting system is the key financial control system and monitors the results of all activities and all other control systems. The detailed analysis and location of all expenditure, the calculation of job and product costs, the analysis of losses and scrap, the monitoring of labour and departmental efficiency and the other outputs of the Cost Accounting system provide a sound basis of information for financial control.

6. COST ACCOUNTING AND DECISION MAKING

Decision making is concerned with making a choice between alternatives and frequently an important factor in making that choice is the financial implications of the various alternatives.

Correctly presented cost information can be of great value to management in decision making and accordingly material on short and long term decision making is included later in the book.

Note:
Students should be aware that much of decision making (and planning) is considered to be within the field of Management Accounting rather than Cost Accounting and accordingly, for greater depth and coverage of these topics, students are advised to refer to the author's book *Management Accounting* (Cengage Learning).

7. COST ACCOUNTING AND PLANNING

The analysis and recording of past costs and activities is but one element of cost accounting. Management are also concerned to know what costs will be in the future so that appropriate plans and decisions can be made in good time. Also, having some standard or target against which to compare actual costs greatly assists the control function. The future oriented aspects of cost accounting, namely *budgeting and standard costing,* are dealt with in Chapters 23 to 26.

8. COST ACCOUNTING, ESTIMATING AND PRICING

Pricing decisions are complex and many interacting factors need to be considered including: the type of market in which the firm operates, the degree of competition, demand and the elasticity of demand, the cost structure of the product and firm, the state of the economy and numerous other factors. Pricing is not simply a cost based decision although past costs and expected future costs are factors to be considered in pricing decisions.

9. COST ACCOUNTING MUST BE USEFUL

It cannot be emphasised too strongly that if the information produced by the cost accounting system is not useful for managerial decision making, for control or for planning, then it has no value and should not be prepared. To ensure its usefulness the following questions should be considered:

a. Is the cost accounting system appropriate to the organisation the way services are provided or goods manufactured?

b. Do the reports, statements and analyses produced by the cost accounting system contain the relevant information for the intended purpose?

c. Are the reports and statements produced at appropriate intervals and early enough to be effective?

d. Are they addressed to the person responsible for planning/decision making/control?

e. Is the information produced in a relevant form and to a sufficient degree of accuracy for the intended purpose?

It follows from the above that every cost accounting system will, in certain respects, be unique, because it must be designed to suit the particular organisation, products and processes and personalities involved.

10. COST ACCOUNTING AND MANAGEMENT ACCOUNTING

The definition of management accounting is:

Management accounting is the application of the principles of accounting and financial management to create, protect, preserve and increase value for the stakeholders of for-profit and not-for-profit enterprises in the public and private sectors.

Management accounting is an integral part of management. It requires the identification, generation, presentation, interpretation and use of relevant information to:

– *Inform strategy and decisions and formulate business strategy*
– *Plan long, medium and short-run operations*
– *Determine capital structure and fund that structure*
– *Design reward strategies for executives and shareholders*
– *Inform operational decisions*
– *Control operations and ensure the efficient use of resources*
– *Measure and report financial and non-financial performance to management and other stakeholders*
– *Safeguard tangible and intangible assets*
– *Implement corporate governance procedures, risk management and internal controls.*

Terminology

It will be seen that there are similarities between the objectives of both management and cost accounting and indeed in practice there is no true dividing line. In general, management accounting is wider in scope and uses more advanced techniques.

However, a fundamental requirement for management accounting is the existence of a sound cost accounting system to provide basic data. Without this, sophisticated techniques will be useless.

Both management accounting and cost accounting are in the main concerned with the provision of information (often in great detail) for internal planning, control and decision making purposes with considerable emphasis on the costs of functions, activities, processes, and products.

11. COST ACCOUNTING AND FINANCIAL ACCOUNTING

Financial accounting can be defined as:

Classification and recording of the monetary transactions of an entity with established concepts, principles, accounting standards and legal requirements and their presentation, by means of income statements, balance sheets and cash flow statements during and at the end of an accounting period.

Terminology

Financial accounting originated to fulfil the stewardship function of businesses and this is still an important feature. Most of the external financial aspects of the organisation, eg, dealing with Accounts Payable and Receivable, preparation of Final Accounts etc, are dealt with by the financial accounting system. Of course internal information is also prepared, but in general it can be said that financial accounting presents a broader, more overall view of the organisation with primary emphasis upon classification according to type of transaction (eg, salaries, materials) rather than the cost and management accounting emphasis on functions, activities, products and processes and on internal planning and control information.

Financial accounting statements must conform to legal requirements, for example, Public Limited Companies (PLCs) must produce annual financial statements according to accepted accounting principles. These principles are established by the various regulatory bodies, eg the Accounting Standards Board (ASB) in the UK, the Financial Accounting Standards Board (FASB) in the USA and International Accounting Standards (IASs). The various standards seek to eliminate ambiguity and to give a certain level of uniformity. This enables accounts to be compared on a reasonable basis.

In contrast, cost and management accounts can be devised to suit the requirements of individual organisations and presented in any form which suits management.

12. SUMMARY OF RELATIONSHIPS BETWEEN COST AND MANAGEMENT AND FINANCIAL ACCOUNTING

The objectives of the various facets of accounting have been given above and the differences discussed. However, it must be realised that they all form part of the financial information system of an organisation and in many organisations the various facets are totally integrated with no artificial divisions between them.

13. OVERVIEW OF COST ACCOUNTING

Having defined cost, management and financial accounting and discussed the relationships between them, it is now possible to show more detail of cost accounting. Figure 1.1 summarises the major parts of the cost accounting

FIGURE 1.1   Overview of cost accounting

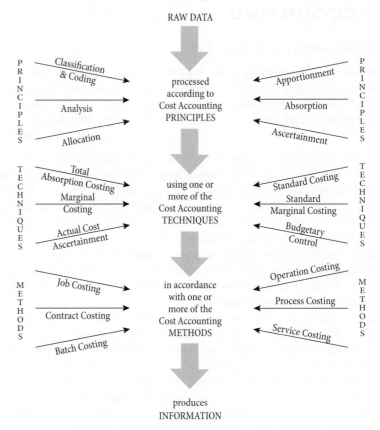

process and shows in diagrammatic form how **data** are transformed into **infor-mation**. The rest of the book provides detailed explanations for each of the elements in the diagram.

14. COST ACCOUNTING AND MANAGEMENT ACCOUNTING – THE FUTURE

Enormous changes are taking place in the way companies are organised and how goods are manufactured or services supplied. Computers are used exten-sively not just for administrative purposes but to plan production, design prod-ucts and to control machines. Production is highly automated, product life cycles are becoming shorter and markets more competitive. In general there is an increasing rate of change which will continue into the foreseeable future.

To deal with this, cost and management accounting (CMA) systems must be flexible and adaptable. Full use must be made of modern information pro-cessing and communications systems and, in addition, the principles and meth-ods of CMA must be continually challenged and updated where necessary to meet current and expected conditions.

Much of cost and management accounting developed in the early part of the last century to meet the requirements of the factories which then existed and the way that products were made. Typically there was a low level of mechanisation, wages were a high proportion of total costs and there was a relatively slow rate of change of methods and products. Contrast this with a modern factory using Just-in-Time (JIT) systems. A JIT system is where production only takes place to meet demand, there are low or zero inventories, and there is an emphasis on perfect quality. Manufacture is highly automated and typically wages may only be 5–10% of total costs. Production is continually changing, there is constant drive for improvement and batch quantities are low because goods are made to meet demand not to move into stock. It is a *demand-pull* system rather than *production-push*.

In addition the service sector has expanded dramatically and manufacturing now accounts for less than 25% of Gross Domestic Product. Service industries also require CMA information so systems, techniques and methods have to be adapted to suit the specific requirements of the enormous variety of service sector organisations. For example the objectives, methods of operations and information requirements of, say, banks, local government and the health service vary greatly yet all need to plan, control and take decisions and consequently need relevant, tailor made information.

In order to provide relevant information the CMA system must take full account of the production system or methods of supplying services and the nature of the organisation. Above all, the greatest care must be taken not to use inappropriate and outmoded principles and techniques which were developed to suit earlier, and now superseded, conditions. As W. Raffish has said, 'It's not that traditional cost accounting doesn't work – it's that the world it was designed for is rapidly disappearing!'

15. SUMMARY

a. Cost accounting is concerned with the ascertainment and control of costs.

b. The purpose of cost accounting is to provide detailed information for control, planning and decision-making.

c. To be of use, cost accounting information must be appropriate, relevant, timely, well presented and sufficiently accurate for the purpose intended.

d. Cost accounting and management accounting are closely related.

e. The emphasis of financial accounting is upon classification by type of transaction and type of expenditure rather than the functional analysis of cost accounting.

f. Cost, financial and management accounting all contribute to the financial information system of an organisation and increasingly in practice are totally integrated.

16. POINTS TO NOTE

a. Cost and financial information is not the only information required for management decision-making, but it is usually an important if not a crucial factor.

b. Decision-making is concerned with the future and with future costs and revenues. Cost accounting, which is based on historical data, can nevertheless provide some guide to future costs and is frequently a critical part of the information upon which a decision is made.

c. Because there is no real dividing line between cost and management accounting, many of the topics introduced in this book, particularly in the latter part, are equally relevant to students studying costing or management accountancy.

d. Cost and management accountancy is essentially for internal purposes. Financial accountancy is for stewardship purposes and is the basis of external reporting.

e. Not all of the cost accounting principles, techniques and methods described in this book will be applicable to a given firm. Some of the principles, techniques and methods are the basis of regularly produced information, whilst others may only be used in providing information for 'one off' decisions.

f. The increasing emphasis on cost effectiveness, 'value for money' and the growth of competition means that costing is being applied ever more widely. Local authorities use cost accounting principles for many of their services as well as for their own internal administration. Transport undertakings, in both the public and private sectors, monitor costs and services in a detailed fashion. Hospitals, banks, water authorities, colleges and universities and numerous other non-manufacturing organisations rely heavily on their cost accounting systems to monitor costs, control activities and to provide information for decision-making.

Accordingly, throughout the book examples are given of cost accounting applications and problems drawn from a wide range of service organisation as well as from the manufacturing sector, which has been the traditional home of cost accounting.

Author's Note

Before tackling the Self-Testing Questions for the first time the reader is advised to read para. 4 of the Preface which explains the purpose behind each type of question.

Student self-testing

Exercises (answers below)

1. Most of the applications of cost accounting appear to relate to manufacturing companies. Can cost accounting be applied in other organisations? If so, give six examples of organisations where cost accounting could usefully be employed.

2. For each of the six examples of organisations given in question 1 give an example of assistance that a cost accounting system could provide.

Solutions to exercises

1. Hospitals
   Transport undertakings
   Departmental stores
   Banks
   Colleges
   Power generation

2. Typical examples include:

Hospitals	– Budgetary control
	– Cost ascertainment eg, cost per patient per night
Transport undertakings	– Cost ascertainment eg, cost per tonne mile or cost per passenger mile
	– Cost control of running costs
Departmental stores	– Operating statements of departmental efficiency and profitability
	– Stock turnover and other efficiency ratios
Banks	– Branch operating statements
Colleges	– Cost control
	– Cost ascertainment eg, cost per full-time equivalent student
Power generation	– Cost ascertainment
	– Plant operating statements

2

The framework of cost accounting

2. A COST

This may be defined as:

> **Cost** *As a noun-The amount of cash or cash equivalent or the fair value of other consideration given to acquire an asset at the time of its acquisition or construction (IAS 16).*
>
> *Terminology*

Note:
IAS means International Accounting Standard

The word 'cost' may also be used as a verb. In which case it can be defined thus:

> *To ascertain the cost of a specified thing or activity. The word cost can rarely stand alone and should be qualified as to its nature and limitations.*
>
> *Terminology*

It will be clear from a study of these definitions that they relate to *past costs* which are the basis of cost ascertainment. At the simplest level, cost includes two components, quantity used and price, ie,

$$\text{cost} = \text{quantity used} \times \text{price}$$

3. COST OBJECT

A cost object is any item, process or activity for which a separate measurement of cost is required. Examples include: the cost of manufacturing a component or product, the cost of operating a department, the cost of dealing with an enquiry at a call centre, the cost of an operation at a hospital or indeed the cost of running the whole hospital. When an individual unit cost is required it is normal to refer to *cost units*.

4. COST UNITS

Costs are always related to some object or function or service. For example, the cost of a car, a haircut, a ton of coal etc. Such units are known as *cost units* and can be formally defined as

A unit of product or service in relation to which costs are ascertained.
Terminology

The cost unit to be used in any given situation is that which is most relevant to the purpose of the cost ascertainment exercise. This means that in any one organisation numerous cost units may be used for particular parts of the organisation or for differing purposes.

For example, in a factory manufacturing typewriters the following cost units might be used for different purposes in the cost accounting system.

Cost Unit	Used for
a typewriter	production cost ascertainment
kilowatt-hours	electricity cost ascertainment
computer minutes of operation	computer running cost ascertainment
tonne-miles	transport cost ascertainment
canteen meals	catering cost ascertainment

Cost units may be *units of production*, eg tonnes of cement, typewriters, gallons of beer, or *units of service,* eg consulting hours, number of invoices processed, patient nights, kilowatt-hours, etc. They may be *identical* units as in the above examples, or they may be dissimilar as in a jobbing engineering factory where the cost unit will be the job or batch, each of which will be costed individually.

5. DIRECT COSTS

Costs may be classified in numerous ways, but a fundamental and important method of classification is into *direct* and *indirect costs*. Direct costs (comprising direct material costs, direct wages cost and direct expenses) are those costs which can be directly identified with a job, batch, product or service. Typical examples are:

Direct materials   The raw materials used in a product, bought in parts and assemblies incorporated into the finished product.

Direct wages or *Direct labour cost*	The remuneration paid to production workers for work directly related to production, the salaries directly attributable to a saleable service (audit clerks' salaries for example).
Direct expenses	Expenses incurred specifically for a particular product, job, batch or service; royalties paid per unit for a copyright design, plant or tool hire charges for a particular job or batch.

It follows therefore that direct costs do not have to be spread between various categories because the whole cost can be attributed directly to a production unit or saleable service.

The total of direct costs is known as *prime cost*, ie:

direct material + direct labour + direct expenses = prime cost

Invariably when direct costs are mentioned, the costing of production cost units is involved. Technically this need not be so, but unless the context of the question clearly points to some other conclusion, any reference to direct costs should be taken to refer to production costs units.

6. INDIRECT COSTS

All material, labour and expense costs which cannot be identified as direct costs are termed *indirect costs*. The three elements of indirect costs; indirect materials, indirect labour and indirect expenses are collectively known as **overheads**. Typical examples of indirect costs in the production area are the following:

INDIRECT MATERIALS	Lubricating oil, stationery, consumable materials, maintenance materials, spare parts for machinery, etc
INDIRECT LABOUR	Factory supervision, maintenance wages, storemen's wages, etc
INDIRECT EXPENSES	Rent and rates for the factory, plant insurance, etc
INDIRECT MATERIAL + INDIRECT LABOUR + INDIRECT EXPENSES = OVERHEADS	

Note:

In practice overheads are usually separated in categories such as Production Overheads, Administration Overheads, Selling Overheads. The above are examples of Production Overheads.

It must be emphasised that the choice of cost object determines what can be classified as a direct or indirect cost. For example in a manufacturing firm the cost object may be to find the cost of running the Inspection Department. In which case the salaries of the inspectors would be a direct cost. However if the cost object was to find a unit component cost then the inspector's salaries would be an indirect cost because they cannot be directly identified with an individual component. The more costs that can be classed as direct, the more accurate will be the cost assignment.

7. COST BUILD-UP

Having defined direct and indirect costs, the framework of cost build-up can be shown thus:

DIRECT MATERIAL		INDIRECT MATERIAL
+		+
DIRECT LABOUR = PRIME COST		INDIRECT LABOUR = OVERHEADS
+		+
DIRECT EXPENSE		INDIRECT EXPENSE
	PRIME COST + OVERHEADS = TOTAL COST	

Note:
The above shows cost ascertainment at its most basic. Additional refinements are dealt with later in the book.

8. CONVERSION COST

This is the term used to describe the costs of converting purchased materials into finished or semi-finished products.

It is thus total production cost minus initial material input costs, ie, the sum of, direct wages, direct expenses and absorbed production overhead. The above is the definition given in Terminology, but students should be aware that alternative interpretations exist. For example, economists define conversion cost as total cost less material costs, ie, all overheads are included, not just production overheads. Alternatively, the term conversion cost is sometimes used to describe the cost of converting materials from one stage of manufacture to the next stage which need not be the finished state.

9. ADDED VALUE OR VALUE ADDED

This can be defined as:

> *Sales value less the cost of purchased materials and services. This represents the worth of an alteration in form, location or availability of a product or service.*
> *Terminology*

It will be seen that added value is equivalent to the economist's conversion cost plus profit. Added value is an important concept and considerable research has been undertaken into methods of incorporating added value concepts into internal and external accounting statements. Added value helps to highlight the relative efficiency of the firm without the analysis being obscured by external input costs which are largely uncontrollable.

10. THE BUILD-UP OF OVERHEADS

Overheads invariably include a large number of types of indirect costs so that the build-up of overheads is a more complicated process than the calculation of prime cost which merely consists of direct costs clearly related to the cost unit being produced. To understand how overheads are derived, three further definitions are required, ie, *cost centre, cost allocation*, and *cost apportionment*.

11. COST CENTRE

This can be defined as:

A production or service location, function, activity or item of equipment for which costs are accumulated.

Typical examples of cost centres are: The Plating shop, The Works Office, The 1,000 ton Power Press, The Milling Machines (consisting of 20 similar machines), Sales Representatives, Invoicing Section, Inspection, etc.

In practice a cost centre is simply a method by which costs are gathered together, according to their incidence, usually by means of cost centre codes. Thus a purchase of copy paper for use in the Invoicing Section would have a code representing say Office sundries – 457, and a code representing the Invoicing section as a cost centre, say 303, and would be coded:

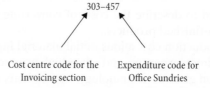

Similarly another purchase of copy paper but for use in Data Processing (cost centre code 106) would be coded:

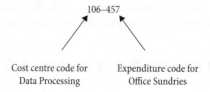

12. COST ALLOCATION

This can be defined as:

To assign a whole item of cost, or of revenue, to a single cost unit, centre, account or time period.

Terminology

The key part of this definition is 'whole item'. Where a cost, without division or splitting, can be clearly identified with a cost centre or cost unit, then it can be allocated (via the cost accounting coding system) to that cost centre or cost unit. It follows that direct costs can be allocated to particular cost units or groups of particular cost units, but cost allocation can, of course, apply equally to indirect costs. The examples shown in Para. 11 are examples of cost allocation of a material cost which would be classed as indirect if the cost object was the product cost.

13. COST APPORTIONMENT

Frequently it is not possible to identify a discrete item of cost with a cost centre and it is necessary to split a cost over several cost centres on some agreed basis. A classic example is that of Rates which are levied upon the premises as a whole, but which, for internal cost ascertainment purposes, need to be shared or apportioned between the cost centres. The basis normally used for Rates being the floor area occupied by the various cost centres. The formal definition of cost apportionment is

> *To spread revenues or costs over two or more cost units, centres, accounts or time periods. This may also be referred to as 'indirect allocation'.*
>
> *Terminology*

The basis upon which the apportionment is made varies from cost to cost. The basis chosen should produce, as far as possible, a fair and equitable share of the common cost for each of the receiving cost centres. The choice of an appropriate basis is a matter of judgement to suit the particular circumstances of the organisation and wherever possible there should be a cost/cause relationship.

Conventional bases used are as follows:

Basis	Costs which may be apportioned on this basis
Floor Area	Rates, Rent, Heating, Cleaning, Lighting, Building Depreciation
Volume or Space Occupied	Heating, Lighting, Building Depreciation
Number of Employees in each Cost Centre	Canteen, Welfare, Personnel, General Administration, Industrial Relations, Safety
Book (or Replacement) Value of Plant, Equipment, Premises, etc	Insurance, Depreciation
Stores Requisitions	Store-Keeping
Weight of Materials	Store-Keeping, Materials Handling

The process of apportionment is an essential part of the build-up of overheads, because many indirect costs apply to numerous cost centres rather than just to one.

Note:
Although cost apportionment is a normal part of the cost ascertainment process, it must be realised that it is a convention only and costs so apportioned are not verifiable.

14. OVERHEAD ABSORPTION

Direct costs, by definition, are readily identifiable traceable to cost objects or cost units, but overheads, which are often considerable, cannot be related directly, but nevertheless form part of the total cost of a product or service.

Accordingly overheads must be shared out in some equitable fashion among all of the cost units produced or services supplied.

Conventionally the process by which this is done is known as *overhead absorption* or *overhead recovery*. Typically an overhead absorption rate, based on factors such as direct machine or labour hours is calculated and the overheads 'shared out' over the cost objects concerned according to the number of machine or labour hours involved.

15. THE CONVENTIONAL BUILD-UP OF TOTAL COST

Having now defined the basic terminology of cost units, cost centres, cost allocation, cost apportionment and overhead absorption, the framework of conventional cost ascertainment is shown in Figure 2.1. The diagram illustrates total cost build-up in a typical manufacturing concern. However, using conventional methods, as explained in the previous paragraphs, similar steps would be taken if a unit of service was being costed.

16. ACTIVITY BASED COSTING (ABC)

The approach to cost ascertainment outlined above is what may be termed the *traditional approach.* This is widely used and must be thoroughly understood by students.

FIGURE 2.1   The conventional build-up of total costs

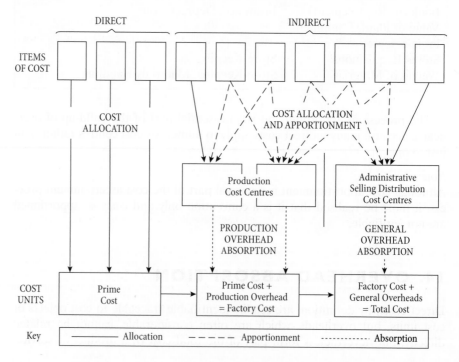

ABC is a more recent approach to product costing, pioneered by Professors Kaplan and Cooper of Harvard University. ABC is an attempt to reflect more accurately in product costs those activities which influence the level of support overheads. Support overheads include such items as Inspection, Despatch, Production Planning, Set-up, Tooling and similar costs.

Traditionally all overheads were absorbed on production volume, as measured by labour or machine hours. This means that high volume standardised products would be charged with most overheads and short run production with lower overheads in spite of the fact that short run production causes more set-ups, retooling, production planning and thereby generates more support overhead costs. Thus, traditional volume related overhead absorption tends to over-cost products made in *long runs* and *undercost* products made in *short runs.*

ABC seeks to overcome this problem by relating support overheads to products, not by production volume, but by a number of specific factors known as *cost drivers.* A cost driver is an activity which causes cost. The formal definition is as follows:

> **Cost driver** *Factor influencing the level of cost. Often used in the context of ABC to denote the factor which links activity resource consumption to product outputs, for example the number of purchase orders would be a cost driver for procurement cost.*
>
> *Terminology*

Table 2.1 shows some typical cost drivers and the costs which the activity influences (or drives).

ABC seeks to deal with the fact that many overhead costs vary not with the *volume* of items produced but with the *range* of the items, ie, the complexity of the production processes. Using ABC a product cost consists of its direct costs plus a share of overheads related to the number of cost driver units the production causes. Direct costs are dealt with in the same way as in traditional systems. Support overheads are collected into what are termed *cost pools,* cost driver rates calculated and the overheads charged (or traced) to the product depending on the product's usage of the particular support activity. The formal definition is:

> **Cost pool** *Grouping of costs relating to a particular activity in an activity-based costing system.*
>
> *Terminology*

In traditional systems overheads are collected via cost centres which tend to be based on departments and sections. In ABC systems overheads are

TABLE 2.1

Examples of cost drivers	Typical costs influenced or 'driven' by cost driver
Number of production runs	Inspection, production planning & scheduling, set-up, tooling
Number of despatches	Despatch department, invoicing etc
Number of purchase orders	Purchasing department, stock-holding etc
Number of engineering changes	Technical department, production planning, stock-holding etc

FIGURE 2.2 Outline of activity-based costing

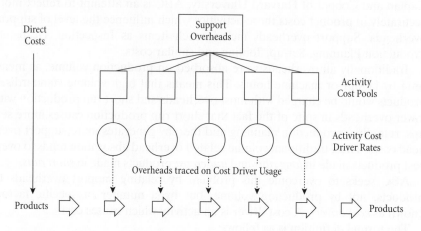

grouped according to the activity performed not by conventional departments. For example, if there were people dealing with Order Handling in three departments; Sales, Production Planning, and Accounts then their costs would be placed in the Order Handling Pool.

Figure 2.2 shows the outline of ABC which should be compared with the more traditional approach shown in Figure 2.1.

It will be seen from the diagrams that there are considerable similarities between the two systems. In both systems, direct costs go straight to the product and overheads are charged or 'traced' to the product using a two stage process. It is in the second stage of the overhead attribution process that differences arise.

In a traditional system, overheads would be charged to products using at the most two absorption bases (labour hours and/or machine hours). On the other hand, ABC systems use many drivers as absorption bases (eg number of set-ups, number of orders, number of despatches and so on). Because of this, it is claimed that the use of ABC and several cost driver rates produces more realistic product or service costs, especially where support overheads are high.

In outline an ABC system is developed and used as follows:

Step 1 Identify the main activities in the organisation. Examples include: materials handling, purchasing, reception, despatch, machining, assembly and so on.

Step 2 Identify the factors which determine the costs of an activity. These are known as *cost drivers*. Examples include: number of purchase orders, number of orders delivered, number of set-ups and so on.

Step 3 Collect the costs of each activity. These are known as *cost pools*.

Step 4 Charge support overheads to products on the basis of their usage of the activity, expressed in terms of the chosen cost driver(s). For example, if the total costs of Purchasing were £200,000 and there were 1,000 Purchase orders (the chosen cost driver), products would be charged £200 for each purchase order. Thus a batch generating three purchase orders would be charged 3 × £200 = £600 for Purchasing overheads.

The use of ABC also requires a change in the way overheads are classified. This is described later in the book when overheads are covered in detail.

17. ACTIVITY BASED ACCOUNTING (ABA)

Activity Based Costing, described above, is but one part of what is a new approach to internal accounting. This approach focuses on analysing, recording, controlling and reporting on the costs and wider performance of *activities* rather than the traditional narrow emphasis on merely the costs of departments and cost centres.

Activity based accounting includes: Activity Based Costing (for product costing), Activity Based Budgeting or Activity Cost Management (for cost planning and control) and Activity Performance Measurement (for performance monitoring using both financial and non-financial indicators). All of these approaches are covered in detail later in the book.

ABA is not merely a new technical system. It has strong behavioural influences and is being widely used to promote cost reduction and increase efficiency. For example, Tektronik designed its ABC system to encourage designers to use existing standard parts in new products rather than designing new components or using unique bought in parts. Rexel Engineering's activity based system focuses attention on value added and non-value added activities with the objective of being able to make specific, guided cost reductions rather than blanket overhead cuts which could damage operations. In general, activity based systems encourage continuous improvement rather than just report on the cost of past operations. It is because of this that their use is becoming more widespread and many leading organisations already use some form of activity based accounting. Examples include; IBM, British Telecom, ICI, Hewlett-Packard, Kodak, Lever Brothers, Johnson Paints, British Airways, Coca-Cola, Lucas and so on.

18. ENHANCING THE VALUE OF INFORMATION

Whatever type of information is produced within the organisation, whether it is a product cost, a lead time, quality statistics or any other item its value is enhance when a relevant comparison can be made. The comparison may be against an internal standard or budget using the well developed cost accounting techniques of standard costing and budgetary control, which are dealt with in detail later in the book, or by the procedure known as *benchmarking*.

The formal definition is:

Benchmarking *Establishment through data gathering of targets and comparators that permit relative levels of performance (and particularly areas of under-performance) to be identified. Adoption of best practices should improve performance.*

Internal benchmarking – comparing one operating unit or function with another within the same industry.

Functional benchmarking – comparing internal functions with those of the best external practitioners regardless of their industry (also known as operational or generic benchmarking).

Competitive benchmarking – in which information is gathered about direct competitors through techniques such as reverse engineering.

FIGURE 2.3 Benchmarking at Nestlé UK

Good Food Good Life

Benchmarking at Nestlé UK

"Nestlé HR uses **benchmarking** to bring the outside world into our business. We regularly exchange data on policies, benefits and conditions with other companies within our sector. These exchanges ensure we remain aware of trends and stay competitive. We use a variety of approaches for benchmarking salary levels within the market, including membership of pay and benefits clubs, collaboration with other company surveys, use of Internet pay data and "one off" job salary matches. Where we have the need for specific measures, for example the overall ratio of HR to business heads or costs of payroll per payslip, then we initiate an exchange with companies that we want to benchmark against.

In my experience, most organisations are very open to these exchanges so long as the data is not business critical or commercially sensitive. We also use benchmarking at the feasibility stages of major projects to gain understanding as to how and why other organisations have made similar changes. You can learn a lot from seeing a change live in another setting, including the benefit of hindsight. It's useful to hear "what I would do differently if I had the time again". It is rare that you will copy the benchmark examples, but it does allow you to refine your own thinking to produce a better proposal to fit your own organisational culture and setting.

We benchmarked with four other organisations that had already made the change to a Shared Services model before we made our own changes within HR. This gave us a better understanding of the implications of the changes to the business as well as to HR itself, provided measures of performance and gave us some real life examples of success.

I see benchmarking as part of our day to day business activity. It's about learning, comparison and exchange of experience. If you don't know how you stand up against the outside world, then you can't really expect to grow and improve."

Nigel Holt
Nestlé UK Group Reward and HR Process Manager

Strategic benchmarking – type of competitive benchmarking aimed at strategic action and organisational change.

Terminology

It will be seen that benchmarking is a broad, forward looking process designed to improve performance across the organisation from the operational to the strategic level. Although accounting information is an important aspect of benchmarking many other facets of the organisation are equally vital. These include performance statistics relating to production, marketing, quality, service, human resources and so on. Benchmarking is widely used across both the private and public sectors. As an example, Nestlé are enthusiastic users.

19. SUMMARY

a. A cost object is any item or activity for which a separate measurement of cost is required. When referring to units of production or saleable service the term *cost unit* is normally used.

b. Direct costs are those which are readily identifiable to a cost unit. Direct labour, Direct Materials and Direct Expenses form Prime Cost.

c. Conversion cost is the cost of converting materials into products. Added value is the increase in market value of a product less bought out materials and services, ie, it includes profit unlike conversion cost.

d. All costs not identifiable as direct are termed Indirect Costs. Indirect Labour, Indirect Material and Indirect Expenses are collectively known as Overheads.

e. Cost centres may be physical locations, items of equipment, groups of personnel, etc. They are a method of gathering indirect costs via the coding system of the firm.

f. Cost allocation is the *allotment of whole items* of cost. Cost apportionment is the *sharing of a common cost* among cost centres.

g. Overhead absorption (or recovery) is the process by which overheads are included in the cost of cost units, ie, Prime Cost plus overheads absorbed = Total Cost.

h. Activity Based Costing (ABC) attributes support overhead costs (eg set-up, planning, despatch, purchasing) to products or product lines using cost drivers, ie, the activities which cause the cost. The costs of support activities are separately identified and collected in *cost pools* from which cost driver rates are collected.

i. Traditional product costing and ABC treat Direct costs and some Production Overheads (eg power costs) in the same way. The treatment of support overheads differs. Traditionally, all were absorbed on production volume whereas ABC uses a range of cost drivers to attribute various support overheads to the product or the product line.

j. ABC is one facet of Activity Based Accounting (ABA). ABA also includes Activity Based Budgeting or Activity Cost Management and Activity Performance Measurement using both financial and non-financial indicators.

20. POINTS TO NOTE

a. The word cost is rarely used on its own. It is invariably qualified in some way, eg Prime Cost, Factory Cost, Indirect Cost, etc.

b. The process of apportionment is sometimes known as *pro-rating costs*. Although many of the bases used, eg Rates apportioned on floor area, appear sensible, it must be realised that the whole process of apportionment is merely a convention. It is not possible to verify that apportioned costs are correct.

c. Alternative names for overheads include *burden* and *on-cost*, but students are recommended always to use the term overheads.

d. Cost accounting is a tool for practical purposes and a common-sense view should be taken over each factor. For example, some costs, although direct, may be of such small value that they may be classified as indirect and included in production overheads. An example of this might be paint used to stencil a number on a machine tool. The effort required to establish how much paint is used on each machine would not be worthwhile.

e. On occasions it may be possible to classify a cost normally regarded as indirect as a direct cost and this should be done whenever possible. An example of this is commission paid to an agent or salesman to gain a particular job where the job is classed as the cost unit.

f. The ascertainment of product cost relies on clear identification of the product or service. In manufacturing companies this is usually self-evident but in many service organisations the problem is more complex. For example, a major clearing bank defined well over 150 products/services which it supplied. Many of these were interrelated and many shared common facilities. In such circumstances product cost ascertainment becomes a difficult operation containing many subjective judgements.

Student self-testing

Exercises (answers below)

1. Give five examples (other than those in the chapter) of each of the following:
   a. Cost units in manufacturing firms
   b. Cost units in service firms

2. Your Managing Director has asked you to consider changing all the firm's cost accounting reports to include the added value of the products. How would you deal with this request and what advantages (if any) might accrue from this practice?

3. From a costing viewpoint what are the effects of the increasing automation of manufacturing facilities?

Solutions to exercises

1. a. Litres of paint
      Thousands of washers
      Tyres
      Garden Forks
      Metres of cloth

   b. Hours of chargeable work (for example, architects, accountants)
      Area ploughed (contract farm work)
      Kilograms plated or printed
      Sets repaired (service contractors)
      Tonnage transported

2. Added value is the increase in market value of the product brought about by the organisation itself, ie, it excludes bought out materials and services. To deal with the requirement that a statement of added value should be included in cost accounting reports it would be necessary to classify (and code accordingly) all expenditures as to whether they are bought or not. In addition, if statements of added value are required at all intermediate processing points (ie before final sale) then a notional sales value would have to be imputed for each stage and process of manufacture. Clearly, this would be an onerous, subjective procedure which would have little to commend it.

However, the calculation of added value at the final stage of external sales could be done relatively easily and would provide a clear statement of the efficiency of the organisation to produce profits without the largely uncontrollable influences of bought in goods and services.

3. The main effect from a costing viewpoint of increasing automation are:

    a. reduction in direct labour costs per unit;

    b. increase in overhead costs caused by purchasing, maintaining, depreciating and operating expensive equipment;

    c. change in cost structures; reducing variable costs and increasing fixed costs. Generally this has the effect of raising a firm's break-even point;

    d. usually greater throughput and thus reduced costs per unit;

    e. makes labour hours increasingly unsuitable as an overhead absorption base; machine hours are likely to be more appropriate;

    f. fewer production workers and more support staff.

The preceding chapters of this book have explained how the major elements of cost – materials, labour and overheads – are used in cost ascertainment. Students should now be aware of the broad framework of basic cost accounting and have a grasp of fundamental terminology.

The succeeding seven chapters explain in detail the make-up of the cost elements and explain the various cost accounting problems associated with each element. Fundamental to accounting (and production control, inventory control, administration, data processing, etc) are the processes of classification and coding. Accordingly the first chapter of this section deals with these processes.

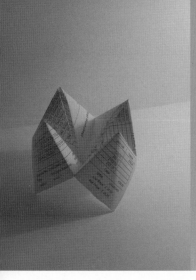

3

Classification and coding

2. CLASSIFICATION

Before any attempts can be made to collect, analyse and control costs, it is essential that all items (labour, material, overheads, etc) can be precisely classified and also that their destination in the costing system (direct to cost units or indirectly to cost centres) can be identified. Classification is the process of arranging items into groups according to their degree of similarity and is formally defined as:

> *The arrangement of items in logical groups having regard to their nature (subjective classification) or purpose (objective classification).*
>
> *Terminology*

The first part of this definition relates to the nature of expenditure, eg expenditure on raw materials and the latter part indicates where the expenditure is to be charged, eg in the case of raw materials, direct to the cost unit.

3. CLASSIFICATION AND OBJECTIVES

The way items are classified must be related to the objectives of the systems using the classification. For examples, the classification of materials must aid all the systems involved with materials and these would typically include: purchasing, storage, stock control, production control, inspection, as well as the costing and accounting systems. Examples of the material classifications which would be found in a typical manufacturing company are the following:

a. Raw materials, ie, bought in material which is used in the manufacture of the product. According to the organisation, raw materials could be further classified into steel, timber, etc, etc.

b. Components and sub-assemblies, ie, bought in components and sub-assemblies which are incorporated in the product.

c. Work-in-progress, ie, partly completed assemblies and products incorporating raw materials and/or sub-assemblies.

d. Consumable materials, ie, materials used in the operation of the factory and during production which do not appear in the product, eg cleaning rags, detergents, etc.

e. Maintenance materials, ie, materials of all types used in maintaining machinery, buildings and vehicles, eg spare parts, lubricating oils and greases, cement, etc.

f. Office materials, ie, materials used in offices, eg stationery, discs, etc.

g. Tools, ie, jigs, tools, fixtures, clamps, etc.

Notes:
1. The above classifications are not exhaustive and others are frequently found.

2. Invariably there are sub-divisions within the above broad classifications. The extent of sub-division depends on the requirements of material control in all its facets.

4. CODING

A code is defined as,

> *A system of symbols designed to be applied to a classified set of items, to give a brief accurate reference facilitating entry, collation and analysis.*
>
> *Terminology*

It will be seen from the above definition that coding is the way that the classification system is applied, ie, *items are classified, then coded*. The importance of well designed coding systems cannot be over-emphasised. Coding is important with normal accounting systems, but becomes vital with computerised systems. Accordingly an understanding of coding systems is vital to accountants. Coding is necessary:

a. To identify uniquely items, materials and parts which cannot be done from descriptions.

b. To avoid ambiguity which would arise from using descriptions.

c. To aid processing, particularly important with computer based systems.

d. To reduce data storage. In the majority of cases a code is much shorter than a description.

5. FEATURES OF GOOD CODING SYSTEMS

a. *Uniqueness* – each item should have one, and only one, code.

b. *Clear symbolisation* – codes should consist of either all numeric or all alphabetic characters. In general, particularly with computer based systems, numeric codes would be preferred. Also, the use of numerous strokes, dashes, colons or brackets should be avoided. The following would be an example of bad notation,

$$56 - 503/291 : 8$$

c. *Distinctiveness* – codes which represent different items should, so far as practicable, look distinctive. Errors may occur if virtually identical codes describe different items. For example, if a code for raw materials was 9-3816 and a code for a bought in component was 7-3816, confusion may occur even though the codes are unique.

d. *Brevity* – codes should be as brief as possible consistent with meeting the requirements of the classification system. In general it has been found that seven digits is the maximum number of digits which can be reliably remembered.

e. *Uniformity* – codes should be equal length and of the same structure. This makes it easy to see whether any characters are missing. Having fixed length codes also considerably facilitates processing.

f. *Exhaustivity* – the coding structure should be exhaustive which means that it should encompass the full range of the classification as it exists and, of equal importance, be able to cope with new items as they arise. This latter point is a major practical problem when designing coding systems.

g. *Non-ambiguity* – the notation used for the coding system should avoid ambiguity. If there is a mixed alpha/numeric system, the letters I and O should not be used because of possible confusion with the numerals 1 and 0 (zero). In addition, when an all alphabetic system is used, the letters I, Q, S and G are most similar to other letters and numerals and should be avoided where possible.

h. *Significance* – Where possible the coding should be significant. This means that the actual code should signify something about the item being coded. For example, part of the code for vehicle tyres could indicate the actual size of the tyre. Thus a code for a 165 × 13 tyre would include 165.

i. *Mnemonic* – On occasions when an alphabetic system is used the actual code is derived from the item's description or name. Most people are probably familiar with the letter code used by airlines to denote various airports, for example:

LHR stands for London Heathrow
LGW stands for London Gatwick

6. PRACTICAL ASPECTS OF CODING SYSTEMS

The previous paragraph has explained various features of coding systems. To implement coding systems which are useful, various practical matters need to be considered.

a. For most data processing purposes a 'closed notation' is preferable, ie, all codes should be of the same length. This effectively means sacrificing some of expansibility which is possible using an expansible notation such as the Universal Decimal Classification used for book classification in libraries. This system is capable of indefinite expansion, but each sub-division requires extra digit(s) and is less suitable for accounts purposes.

b. Because of the need to introduce new items from time to time, most coding systems used for costing purposes are forms of block coding. An example of this is the following:

Item	Block assigned
Raw material	1000–2999
Work in progress	3000–3999
Indirect materials	4000–4999

This system allows, within limits, new items to be introduced into the correct block without destroying the coding structure.

c. *Indexing* – Ideally a code should be self indexing, as for example names in alphabetical order, but this is rarely possible. Accordingly a clear index or coding list should be readily available.

d. *Centralised control* – Depending on the particular circumstances new codes should only be issued centrally. It should not be possible for branches, junior staff, etc, to introduce a new code into the system.

e. *Check digit verification* – Because of the supreme importance of correct identification through the code number, particularly using computers, many important code numbers; account numbers, part numbers etc, have an extra digit suffixed which makes them self checking and guards against many of the common coding errors, eg transposition, incorrect character(s), character(s) missing etc. The most common method used is termed Modulus 11 check digit verification.

f. *Code layouts* – Although there is the general need to keep codes as brief as possible, the requirements of particular systems often mean that codes are unavoidably lengthy. Experience would indicate that lengthy codes are better remembered and transcribed if they are grouped or subdivided into threes.

For example, $658-291-204$ is better than 658291204.

g. *Pre-printing* – Wherever possible, codes should be pre-printed on forms so that errors are reduced.

7. TYPES OF CODING SYSTEMS

The best coding systems, whether for manual or computer use, are those which are simple to understand, flexible and capable of expansion. At the design stage it is important to look ahead and to try to allow for growth, both in volume and diversity. Some of the main types of coding systems are:

Group classification codes

These are codes where a specified digit, usually the first, indicates the items classification. For example:

7XXX	represents Hexagon bars
8XXX	represents Round bars
9XXX	represents Square bars

where XXX represents other digits.

Hierarchical codes

These are developments of group classification codes where each digit represents a classification. Each digit to the right represents a smaller and smaller sub-classification. Probably the best known example of a hierarchical code is the Universal Decimal code used in libraries. This is extremely flexible and can incorporate numerous sub-classifications within the primary one at the expense of having variable length codes.

However for business and accounting purposes, codes of a standard length are preferable. Hierarchical coding can still be used in these circumstances albeit with some potential loss of detail. For example:

6	represents Screws
62	represents Countersunk screws
63	represents Round-headed screws
621	represents Countersunk slotted screws
622	represents Countersunk star screws
. . . .	etc

up to the agreed length of code.

Significant digit codes

These are codes where some of the digits are part of the description of the item being coded. For example:

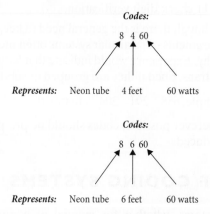

The use of significant digit codes enables the description of an item to be largely derived from its code. In practice the various systems may be mixed to provide one that suits the organisation's requirements. For accounting purposes the most common system is some form of hierarchical coding. This is developed into a published 'Chart of Accounts' which specifies the various expenditure headings.

In addition, for cost accounting purposes, there must be a set of cost centre codes which specify the location or use of the expenditure. Sometimes the type of expenditure and its location or use are combined into one code, sometimes there are two separate codes.

8. SUMMARY

a. Accurate classification of all items is a vital prerequisite to any form of analysis and control.

b. Classification is the process of grouping together items which are similar.

c. The classification system must meet the objectives of all the systems which may use the classifications.

d. Coding is the way that the classification system is applied.

e. The features of good coding systems include; uniqueness, distinctiveness, exhaustiveness, unambiguousness, brevity and uniformity.

f. To ensure that coding systems actually work in practice, care should be taken over the need to allow space for expansion, indexing, central control, self-checking codes, code layouts and pre-printing.

g. Coding systems may be of various types including; Group Classification Codes, Hierarchical Codes, Significant Digit Codes or some combination.

9. POINTS TO NOTE

a. Most coding systems used in accounting are composite systems. Typically they might contain two sections, the first section indicating the nature of the expenditure (termed subjective classification) and the second section indicating the cost centre or cost unit to be charged (termed objective classification).

For example:

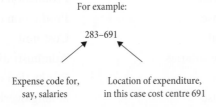

283–691

| Expense code for, | Location of expenditure, |
| say, salaries | in this case cost centre 691 |

b. The Financial Accounting System would be concerned with the subjective classification of an item and not the location of the expenditure, the objective classification.

Student self-testing

Exercises (answers below)

1. The following are items of cost and expenditure in a manufacturing company:
   a. Wages paid to fork-lift truck drivers
   b. Finance Director's salary
   c. Depreciation of production machinery
   d. Heating of factory
   e. Small tools used in the Production Dept.
   f. Repairs to machinery
   g. Steel used in the product
   h. Wages of personnel department staff
   i. Chargehand's wages
   j. Sales advertising
   k. Wages of production workers
   l. Overtime payments made to production workers.

   You are required to give the subjective classification and the likely objective classification for each item.

2. Devise a simple block coding system and code each of the items in question A3.1 in respect of the nature of the item and where it will be charged.

3. Give five likely effects of incorrectly coding a payment of direct wages as indirect.

Solutions to exercises

1. | Subjective Classification | Likely Objective Classification |
   |---|---|
   | a. Indirect wages | Production overheads |
   | b. Administrative salaries | Administrative overheads |
   | c. Indirect expense | Production overheads |
   | d. Indirect expense | Production overheads |
   | e. Indirect materials | Production overheads |
   | f. Indirect expense | Production overheads |
   | g. Direct materials | Cost unit |
   | h. Administrative salaries | Administrative overheads |
   | i. Indirect wages | Production overheads |
   | j. Indirect expense | Selling overheads |
   | k. Direct wages | Cost unit |
   | l. Indirect wages | Production overheads |

2. Possible Block Coding System.

Direct Materials	1000–1100
Indirect Materials	1101–1200
Direct Wages	1201–1300
Direct Expenses	1301–1400
Indirect Wages	1401–1500
Indirect Expenses	1501–1600
Salaries	1601–1700
Cost Centre Codes	
Direct to cost unit	100
Production Cost Centres	101–200
Admin Cost Centres	201–300
S & D Cost Centres	301–400

Using the above simple system the items could be coded as follows:

a. 1410–120 (and other CCs as appropriate)

b. 1637–212

c. 1506–101 (and other CCs as appropriate)

d. 1530–101 (and other CCs as appropriate)

e. 1146–101 (and other CCs as appropriate)

f. 1545– appropriate CC in range 101–200

g. 1120–100

h. 1642–250

i. 1420–101(and other CCs as appropriate)

j. 1570–301

k. 1201–100

l. 1405–101 (and other CCs as appropriate)

3. Five likely effects of incorrectly coding direct wages as indirect:

a. Direct wages will be understated; indirect wages (thus overheads) will be overstated.

b. Predetermined overhead absorption rates will be incorrect.

c. Job and product costs will be incorrect.

d. If substantial, stock valuations will be incorrect.

e. If prices are based on recorded costs then they will be incorrect and thus the firm will lose profits or orders.

4

Materials: Purchasing, reception and storage

1. OBJECTIVES

After studying this chapter you will

- Understand the principles of materials control
- Be able to describe the main purchasing procedures
- Know the elements of storekeeping and stocktaking
- Understand the advantages and disadvantages of centralised stores
- Be able to describe the main features of JIT production and purchasing.

2. THE ESSENTIALS OF MATERIALS CONTROL

From a cost accounting viewpoint the essentials of materials control prior to actual use in production can be summarised as follows:

a. Materials of the appropriate quality and specification should be purchased only when required and appropriately authorised.

b. The suppliers chosen should represent an appropriate balance between quality, price and delivery.

c. Materials should be properly received and inspected.

d. Appropriate storage facilities should be provided and stock levels physically checked on a regular basis.

e. Direct materials used in production should be charged to production on an appropriate and consistent pricing basis.

f. Indirect materials used in production and non production departments should be appropriately charged to the correct cost centre and included in the overheads of the cost centre.

g. The documentation, accounting systems and controls at each stage should be well designed and effective.

h. Stocktaking must be well organised to ensure that stock quantities on hand are available when required.

3. THE MATERIAL CONTROL PROCESS

Figure 4.1 shows the elements of the material control process (prior to actual production material control).

The important features of purchasing, receipt, storage and issue are dealt with below while inventory control and materials costing are dealt with in subsequent chapters.

4. PURCHASING

Because such a large proportion of a firm's costs are represented by bought in materials and services, the purchasing function is of great importance and has become highly specialised. The responsibility of the purchasing function includes price, quality and delivery all of which are crucial factors. Late or non-delivery, poor and substandard materials, incorrect specifications, etc are all likely to have at least as great an impact on profitability as paying an unnecessarily high price. The avoidance of production delays, excessive scrap caused by incorrect materials and the avoidance of excessive stocks are among the aims of an efficient purchasing function. Frequently the purchasing function of a group or of a firm with numerous branches is centralised.

This has many advantages including: larger quantity discounts, uniform standards, possibility of more continuous supplies in difficult times, etc, but there may be disadvantages such as longer response times; some lack of flexibility in catering for specialised needs and general remoteness from the scene of operations.

FIGURE 4.1   The material control process

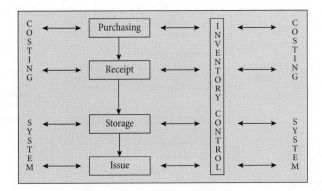

5. PURCHASING PROCEDURES

Although the exact system obviously varies from firm to firm, Figure 4.2 is typical.

Notes to Figure 4.2:

a. Although the diagram shows each of the originating sources producing a Purchase Requisition, frequently Production and Inventory Control may produce a schedule of requirements (often computer based) specifying delivery dates and call off rates.

b. The Purchase Order is the basis of the legal contract between the firm and the supplier and should unambiguously define the required goods or services. Virtually all organisations refuse to recognise an invoice from a supplier which is not covered by a purchase order. The issue of Purchase Orders must be closely controlled and signing restricted to a few senior people.

FIGURE 4.2 Outline of purchasing procedures

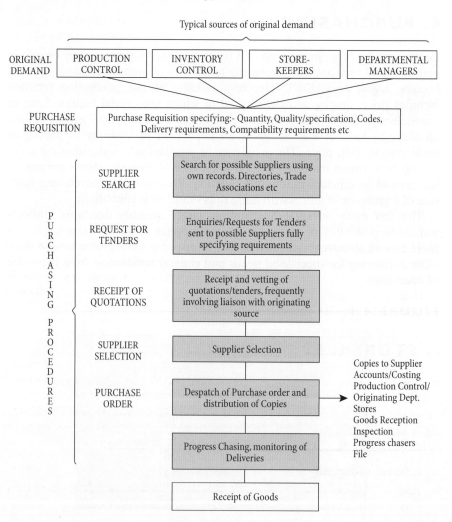

FIGURE 4.3   Reception and inspection procedures

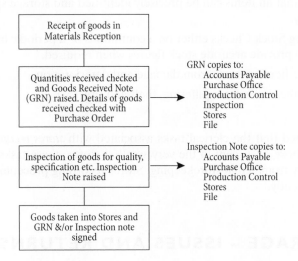

c. Progress chasing is shown as a purchasing procedure which it frequently is. However, it is sometimes the responsibility of Production Control and Works Administration.

6. RECEPTION AND INSPECTION PROCEDURES

Again, while details vary, Figure 4.3 shows a typical position.

Notes to Figure 4.3:

a. The Goods Received Note (GRN) is an important document and is necessary so that the Supplier's invoice can be verified and passed for payment usually by the Purchase Department.

b. The usual procedure for passing the supplier's invoice includes: checks that items invoiced were as ordered (from Purchase Order) and as received (from GRN), verification of price, discounts and credit terms (from Purchase Order), coding of invoice both for type of expenditure and place to be charged.

7. STOREKEEPING

It is salutary to compare the controls and checks on a petty cash float of a few hundred pounds with the frequently haphazard procedures used in many stores containing hundreds of thousands of pounds worth of stock. Storekeeping is an important function and can make a substantial contribution to efficient operations. Storekeeping includes the following activities:

a. Efficient and speedy issue of required materials, tools etc.

b. Receipt of parts and materials from Goods Reception (ie, external items) and from Production (ie, internal items).

c. Organising storage in logical sequences, thus ensuring items can be found speedily, that all items can be precisely identified and storage space is used effectively.

d. Organising Stock Checks either on a continuous or a periodic basis so as to be able to provide accurate stock figures when required.

e. Protecting items in store from damage and deterioration.

f. Securing the stores from pilfering, theft and fire.

Note:

It will be noted that the clerical tasks associated with *stores recording* are not mentioned above as, except in the very smallest stores, these tasks are carried out separately from actual storekeeping. Stores recording procedures are dealt with subsequently.

8. STORAGE – ISSUES AND RETURNS

The issue of materials must be appropriately authorised and amount issued recorded so that the appropriate charge can be made to production or to the receiving cost centre. The usual way this is done is by a *materials requisition* (MR).

An MR would contain:

Quantity – Part No – Description – Job or Centre to be charged – Authorisation

On presenting an MR to the storeman, it would be checked for correctness and authorisation and if satisfactory, the issue would be made. The MR would be retained by stores who would insert date of issue and forward the MR to Stores Records (for updating the Stock Records) and thence to the Cost Department (for pricing and charging). The storeman must ensure that the MR is amended when the issue cannot be made exactly as the original request, eg where only a part issue is made or an alternative material is acceptable when that originally requested is unavailable. The procedure for goods returned to store is similar to that outlined above except that the document involved is termed a *material return note* and, of course, the goods are taken into stores rather than issued.

9. STORAGE – STOCKTAKING

There are two approaches to the task of stocktaking – Periodic (usually annual) and Continuous.

Periodic stocktaking

The objective of periodic stocktaking is to find out the physical quantities of materials of all types (raw materials, finished goods, W-I-P etc) at a given date. This is a substantial task even in a modest organisation and becomes a difficult if not impossible task in a large firm. The following factors need to be considered:

a. Adequate numbers of staff should be available who should receive clear and precise instructions on the procedures.

b. Ideally the stocktake should be done at a weekend or overnight so as not to interfere with production.

c. The stocktake should be organised into clearly defined physical areas and the checkers should count or estimate all materials in the area.

d. Adequate technical assistance should be available to identify materials, part nos etc. Far greater errors are possible because of wrong classification than wrong counting.

e. Great care should be taken to ensure that only valid stock items are included and that all valid items are checked.

f. The completed stock sheets should have random, independent checks to verify their correctness.

g. The quantities of each type of material should be checked against the stock record to expose any gross errors which may be due to stocktaking errors or faults or errors in the recording system. Small discrepancies are inevitable.

h. The pricing and extension of the Stock Sheets, where done manually, should be closely controlled. Frequently the pricing and value calculations are done by computer, the only action necessary being to input quantities and stock and part numbers.

Continuous stocktaking

To avoid some of the disruptions caused by periodic stocktaking and to be able to use better trained staff, many organisations operate a system whereby a proportion of stock is checked daily so that over the year all stock is checked at least once and many items, particularly the major value or fast moving items, would be checked several times. Where continuous stocktaking is adopted, it is invariably carried out by staff independent from the storekeepers.

Note:
Continuous stocktaking is absolutely essential when an organisation uses what is known as the *Perpetual Inventory System.* This is a stock recording system whereby the stock balance is shown on the record *after every stock movement,* either issue or receipt. With this system the balances on the stock record represent the stock on hand and balances would be used in monthly and annual accounts as the closing stock. Continuous stocktaking is necessary to ensure that the perpetual inventory system is functioning correctly and that minor stock discrepancies are corrected.

10. STORAGE – CENTRALISATION VS. DECENTRALISATION

There is no conclusive answer as to whether there should be a centralised stores or several stores situated in branches or departments. Each system has its advantages and disadvantages which are given below.

Advantages of Centralisation

a. Lower stock on average.

b. Less risk of duplication.

c. Higher quality staff may be usefully employed to specialise in various aspects of storekeeping.

d. Closer control is possible on a central site.

e. Possibly more security from pilferage.

f. Some aspects of paperwork may be reduced, eg, purchase requisitions.

g. Stocktaking is facilitated.

h. Likelihood that more advanced equipment will be viable, eg, materials handling, visual displays.

Disadvantages of Centralisation

a. Less convenient for outlying branches/departments.

b. Possible loss of local knowledge.

c. Longer delays possible in obtaining materials.

d. Greater internal/external transport costs in fetching and carrying materials.

11. CHANGES IN PRODUCTION AND PURCHASING SYSTEMS

There are a number of changes taking place in industry which are altering dramatically the way that products are made and production is organised. These changes naturally influence supporting activities such as purchasing and storage. Several of the more important developments are outlined below. These include: Just-in-Time Purchasing, Just-in-Time Production and Materials Requirements Planning.

12. JUST-IN-TIME (JIT) SYSTEMS

JIT systems were developed in Japan, notably at Toyota, and are considered as one of the main contributions to Japanese manufacturing success.

The aim of JIT systems is to produce the required items, of high quality, exactly at the time they are required. JIT systems are characterised by the pursuit of excellence at all stages with a climate of continuous improvement.

A JIT environment is characterised by:

- a move towards zero inventory
- elimination of non-value added activities
- an emphasis on perfect quality, ie, zero defects
- short set-ups
- a move towards a batch size of one
- 100% on-time deliveries

- a constant drive for improvement
- demand-pull manufacture.

It is this latter characteristic which gives rise to the name of Just-in-Time. Production only takes place when there is actual customer demand for the product so JIT works on a *pull-through* basis which means that products are not made to go into stock. Contrast this with the traditional manufacturing approach of *production-push* where products are made in large batches and move into stock.

The formal definition is:

> ***Just-in-time (JIT)*** *– System whose objective is to produce or to procure products or components as they are required by a customer or for use, rather than for stock. Just-in-time pull system which responds to demand, in contrast to a push system in which stocks act as buffers between the different elements of the system such as purchasing, production and sales.*
>
> *Terminology*

There are two aspects to JIT systems: JIT Purchasing and JIT Production.

13. JIT PURCHASING

This seeks to match the usage of materials with the delivery of materials from external suppliers. This means that material stocks can be kept at near-zero levels.

For JIT purchasing to work requires the following:

a. Confidence that suppliers will deliver exactly on time.
b. That suppliers will deliver materials of 100% quality so that there will be no rejects, returns and consequent production delays.

The reliability of suppliers is all-important and JIT purchasing means that the company must build up close working relationships with their suppliers. This is usually achieved by doing more business with fewer suppliers and placing long term purchasing orders in order that the supplier has assured sales and can plan to meet the demand.

14. JIT PRODUCTION

JIT production works on a demand-pull basis and seeks to eliminate all waste and activities which does not add value to the product. As an example, consider the lead times associated with making and selling a product. These include:

- Inspection time
- Transport time
- Queuing time
- Storage time
- Processing time

Of these, only processing time adds value to the product whereas all the others add cost, but not value. The ideal for JIT systems is to convert materials to finished products with a lead time equal to processing time so eliminating all activities which do not add value. A way of emphasising the importance of reducing throughput time is to express the above lead times as follows:

> Throughput time = Value-added time + Non-value added time

The JIT pull system means that components are not made until requested by the next process. The usual way this is done is by monitoring parts consumption at each stage and using a system of markers (known as kanbans) which authorise production and movement to the process which requires the parts. A consequence of this is that there may be idle time at certain work stations but this is considered preferable to adding to work-in-progress inventory.

Poor and uncertain quality is a prime source of delays hence the drive in JIT systems for zero defects and Total Quality Control (TQC). When quality is poor, higher WIP is needed to protect production from delays caused by defective parts. Higher inventory is also required when there are long set-up and changeover times. Accordingly there is continual pressure in JIT systems to reduce set-up times and eventually eliminate them so that the optimal batch size can become one. With a batch size of one, the work can flow smoothly to the next stage without the need to store it and schedule the next machine to accept the item.

15. JIT PRODUCTION IMPLICATIONS

To operate JIT manufacturing successfully and achieve the targets of low inventories and on-time deliveries means that:

a. The production processes must be shortened and simplified. Each product family is made in a work cell based on flowline principles. The JIT system increases the variety and complexity within work cells. These contain groups of dissimilar machines which thus requires workers to be more flexible and adaptable.

b. Using JIT the emphasis is on 'doing the job right the first time' thus avoiding defects and reworking. JIT systems require quality awareness programmes, statistical checks on output quality and continual worker training.

c. Factory layouts must be changed to reduce movement. Traditionally machines were grouped by function; all the drilling machines together, the grinding machines and so on. This meant a part had to travel long distances moving from one area of the factory to another often stopping along the way in a storage area. All these are non-value added activities which have to be reduced or eliminated.

d. There must be full employee involvement. As an example it has been reported that the 60,000 employees of Toyota produced a total of

2.6 million improvement suggestions per annum. In most cases, after line management approval, the working groups simply get on with implementing their ideas. Arguably one of the most important behavioural implications of JIT is that the status quo is continually challenged and there is a never ending search for improvements.

e. Traditional WIP and Raw Material Stocks acted as a buffer against late material deliveries or production problems. As these stocks disappear or decline when using JIT, guaranteed deliveries become of increasing importance. During the UK fuel protests, in September 2000, deliveries were disrupted to many factories causing lay-offs and major losses of production in those organisations using JIT production methods.

16. BENEFITS AND PROBLEMS FROM USING JIT

Successful users of JIT systems are making substantial savings. These arise from numerous areas:

a. Lower investment required in all forms of inventory.

b. Space savings from the reduction in inventory and improved layouts.

c. Greater customer satisfaction resulting from higher quality better deliveries and greater product variety.

d. The buffers provided by traditional inventories masked other areas of waste and inefficiency. Examples include: co-ordination and work flow problems, bottlenecks, supplier unreliability and so on. Elimination of these problems improves performance dramatically.

e. The flexibility of JIT and the ability to supply small batches enables companies to respond more quickly to market changes and to be able to satisfy market niches.

As would be expected there are often problems in implementing JIT systems. JIT does not necessarily reduce inventories in total. One firm may reduce their inventory but this is often at the expense of others in the supply chain. Component and material suppliers need to keep stocks in case of rush orders because there are usually penalty clauses in the event of late delivery.

Frequently there are environmental problems arising from the increased number of truck journeys between suppliers and factories. This factor led General Motors in the USA to introduce 'consolidation centres' to reduce the number journeys.

Reliability of suppliers, with regard to quality and delivery, is often hard to achieve and shortcomings increase vulnerability in that any natural or man made disaster (floods, fire, strikes, etc) which cuts off the supply of critical materials to an assembly process can shut down a manufacturing operation in a matter of hours. For example, strikes in the USA have caused major shutdowns in both Ford and General Motors in the past.

17. MATERIALS REQUIREMENT PLANNING (MRP)

MRP is a computerised information, planning and control system which has the objective of maintaining a smooth production flow.

This is formally defined thus:

MRP (Materials Requirement Planning) – System that converts a production schedule into a listing of the materials and components required to meet that schedule, so that adequate stock levels are maintained and items are available when required.

Terminology

It is concerned with:

- maximising the efficiency in the timing of orders for raw materials or parts that are placed with external suppliers;
- efficient scheduling of the manufacture and assembly of the final product.

The operation of an MRP System requires the following:

a. A master production schedule showing the quantities and timings required for the finished product(s).

b. A Bill of Materials (BOM) which shows the breakdown of each finished product into sub-assemblies components and raw materials.

c. An Inventory file containing the balance on hand, scheduled receipts and numbers already allocated for each sub-assembly, component and type of raw material.

d. A parts manufacturing and purchasing file containing lead times of all purchased items and lead times and production sequences of all sub-assemblies and components produced internally.

MRP has evolved into MRPII which integrates material resource planning, into a single manufacturing control system.

MRP(Manufacturing Resource Planning) – Expansion of materials requirements planning (MRP) to give a broader approach than MRP to the planning and scheduling of resources, embracing areas such as finance, logistics, engineering and marketing.

Terminology

18. SUMMARY

a. The material control process includes: Purchasing, Receipt, Storage and Issue, Inventory Control, and associated costing procedures.

b. The purchasing function is very important and aims for an appropriate balance of price, quality and delivery.

c. The Purchase Requisition giving precise details of quantity required, specification, delivery, etc initiates the main purchasing procedures.

d. The main purchasing procedures are: supplier search, supplier selection, ordering and processing deliveries.

e. Goods must be properly received, inspected and a Goods Received Note (GRN) raised.

f. The GRN is an important document which is used in the supplier invoice approval procedure.

g. Storekeeping involves issue and receipt of materials, storage space organisation, protection of materials from deterioration, stocktaking, etc.

h. Items should not be issued from stores unless covered by a Materials Requisition (MR).

i. The MR is used for amending the stock records and for charging the issue direct to production or to a particular cost centre.

j. Stocktaking is carried out on a Periodic (usually annual) or Continuous basis. Continuous stocktaking is essential for Perpetual Inventory systems.

k. Centralised stores have the advantage of lower stocks, better facilities and staff and some administrative savings, but may cause inconvenience and delays.

l. The newer production systems such as Just-in-Time and Materials Requirements Planning are radically altering traditional approaches to manufacturing, purchasing and storage. Manufacture and purchasing take place only when required, stocks are reduced or eliminated, there is a continual drive for improvement and zero defects.

m. JIT systems rely on timely, scheduled deliveries of raw materials and supplies. Weather, industrial or traffic problems can cause major disruptions.

19. POINTS TO NOTE

a. Many variations exist on the basic systems outlined in this chapter. In particular where there is continuous or assembly line operation, purchasing procedures are often integrated with production control and deliveries are received continuously, frequently directly to the production floor. Whatever the system, adequate, well designed controls are essential.

b. Because there is no clear advantage one way or the other, many organisations have a large central store supported by a number of smaller outlying stores.

c. The process of Continuous Stocktaking is sometimes known as Stock Audit.

d. Where a substantial quantity of items are required from stores say, for a particular job, the issue may be authorised by a Bill of Materials or Requirements Schedule, detailing all the items required rather than individual material Requisitions. Frequently the Requirements Schedules are computer produced and the items required would be listed in the most economical sequence for the storemen, ie, in location sequence or 'Picking order'.

Student self-testing

Exercises (answers below)

1. Invariably goods, services and the supply of materials are obtained by the use of a Purchase Order. Design the layout of a Purchase Order, showing what essential information the order should contain.

2. Give six advantages of continuous stocktaking.

3. Give five reasons why stocktaking errors occur.

4. Give five differences between JIT Purchasing and conventional purchasing.

Solutions to exercises

1. Purchase order

PURCHASE ORDER

No. A 62912

From:

ACME MACHINES PLC
CROWN WORKS, LEGGE STREET
BURNTCHESTER B56 7LO

To: BRIGHTSTAR LTD 47 ASLOW STREET HAMTON HT5 9TD	DELIVERY ADDRESS: No. 2 GATE CROWN WORKS

Please supply the following in accordance with our
Standard Conditions of Purchase printed overleaf.

Quantity	Description	Price
25,000	Components to Drawing 85212 as quoted 5/10/-4 Your ref 59529 Delivery: To schedule attached	£1.75 each

for ACME MACHINING PLC
PURCHASING OFFICE

OUR ORDER NO. MUST BE QUOTED ON ALL COMMUNICATIONS

---

2. Six advantages of Continuous Stocktaking:

   a. Continuous Stocktaking avoids the disruption caused by the large, annual stocktake.

   b. Regular checking is likely to produce more accurate stock figures.

   c. Discrepancies, losses, deterioration, etc will be discovered earlier.

   d. Stock figures for interim operating statements and profit and loss accounts are readily available.

   e. Better quality staff can be employed who will gain experience and expertise which would not be possible with annual stocktaking.

   f. The continuous presence of independent stock checkers may reduce pilferage and losses.

3. Five reasons for stock-taking errors:

   a. Errors in weighing, counting or measuring.

   b. Part number errors.

   c. Omitting whole groups of stock or including more than once.

   d. Calculation errors on stock sheets.

   e. Poor writing, illegible figures causing misreading.

4. Differences of JIT. Purchasing to conventional purchasing.

   a. Deliveries in accordance to Production Schedules not bulk deliveries moving into storage.

   b. Likely to be fewer suppliers.

   c. Usually no incoming quality checks which therefore must be done at the suppliers.

   d. Components/materials delivered in production convenient form, eg on pallets, in packages, etc sometimes directly onto the production floor.

   e. Much closer liaison between Purchaser and Supplier.

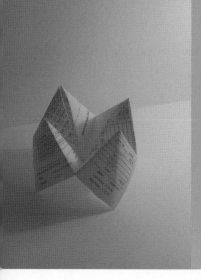

5

Materials: Stock recording and inventory control

I. OBJECTIVES

After studying this chapter you will

● **Understand the objectives and principles of stock recording**

● **Have been introduced to Inventory Control**

● **Know how to calculate the Economic Order Quantity (EOQ).**

2. STOCK RECORDING

However sophisticated the Inventory or Stock Control system is in the firm, a basic prerequisite is that stock movements (issue and receipt) are accurately recorded. In addition the stock record typically shows various control levels which relate to the Inventory Control system and which are explained later in this chapter. In some firms several stock records may be kept regarding a particular materials, but this practice can introduce errors and discrepancies and has little to commend it.

The most frequently encountered records of stocks in manual systems are *Bin Cards* and *Stock Record Cards*.

3. BIN CARDS

Where found, these are attached to or adjacent to the actual materials and the entries made at the time of issue either by the storeman or a stores clerk. They show only basic information relating to physical movements. A typical layout of a Bin Card is shown in Figure 5.1.

Notes:
a. The reference column would be used for inserting the GRN or Material Requisition number.

FIGURE 5.1 Bin card

Bin Card				
Part No .... Location				
Date	Reference	Receipts	Issues	Balance

b. The use of Bin cards is declining partly because of the difficulty of keeping them up to date and partly because of the increasing integration of stock recording and inventory control procedures, frequently using computers.

4. STOCK RECORD CARDS

To obtain a full picture of the stock position of an item it is necessary to know not only the physical stock balance, but also the Free Stock Balance. This is defined as:

> Free stock balance = Physical stock + outstanding replenishment orders
> – unfulfilled requirements or allocations

The free stock balance is a notional, not physical stock and is the key figure in Inventory Control. It is necessary to know *physical stock* for issue purposes, for stocktaking, and for controlling maximum and minimum stock levels and it is necessary to know the *free stock* position for replenishment ordering (these points are expanded below under Inventory Control). A typical Stock Record Card is shown in Figure 5.2.

Notes:
a. The entries in the Ref (Reference) columns would be Receipts (GRN No), Issues (Material Requisition No), Allocations (Job No or Customer's Order No) and Orders (Purchase Order No).
b. The above illustration shows a card for a manual or mechanised system, but even when the Stock Record is computerised, the same type of information is normally included in the computer file.

5. PERPETUAL INVENTORY SYSTEM

This system, mentioned in the previous chapter, simply means that after each issue or receipt the physical balance is calculated. The total of the balances

FIGURE 5.2   Stock record card

				Stock Record Card											

Stock Record Card

Material/Item Description ....
Material Item Code ....
Stores Location Ref ....
Special Requirements ....

Control Quantities

Maximum Level ....
Minimum Level ....
Re-order Level ....
Re-order Quantity ....

Receipts				Issues				Physical Stock	Allocations			Orders			Free Stock Balance
Date	Ref	Qty	Price	Date	Ref	Qty	Price		Date	Ref	Qty	Date	Ref	Qty	

represent the stock on hand and the system avoids the necessity for wholesale, periodic stocktaking. Instead, a continuous stocktaking system must be operated to ensure that the records accurately reflect actual stocks.

If the records are to be relied upon at all times, stock discrepancies must be investigated immediately and appropriate corrections made either to the system or to the record or both. Typical causes of discrepancies between actual stocks and recorded stocks are the following:

a. Errors caused by incorrect recording and calculation.

b. Incorrect coding causing the wrong part to be issued and/or wrong card to be altered.

c. Under or over issues not noted.

d. Parts and materials returned to stores and not documented.

e. Shrinkage, pilferage, evaporation, losses due to breaking bulk, etc.

f. Loss or non-use of GRNs, material requisitions and other appropriate documentation.

6. INVENTORY CONTROL

(This subject is covered in greater depth in *Quantitative Techniques*, T. Lucey, Cengage Learning.) This can be defined as the system used in a firm to control the firm's investment in stock. This includes; the recording and monitoring of stock levels, forecasting future demands and deciding when and how many to order. The overall objective of inventory control is to minimise, in total, the costs associated with stock. These costs can be categorised into three groups:

Carrying costs

a. Interest on capital invested in stocks.

b. Storage charges (rent, lighting, heating, refrigeration and air conditioning).

c. Stores staffing, equipment, maintenance and running costs.

d. Material handling costs.

e. Audit, stocktaking, stock recording costs.

f. Insurance and security.

g. Deterioration and obsolescence.

h. Pilferage, evaporation and vermin damage.

Costs of obtaining Stock

(frequently known as ordering costs)

a. Clerical and administrative costs of Purchasing, Accounting and Goods Reception.

b. Transport Costs.

c. Where goods are manufactured internally, the set-up and tooling costs associated with each production run plus the planning, production control costs associated with the internal order.

Costs of being without Stock (Stockout costs)

a. Lost contribution through the lost sale caused by the Stockout.

b. Loss of future sales because customers may go elsewhere.

c. Cost of production stoppages caused by stockouts of W-I-P and raw materials.

d. Extra costs associated with urgent, often small quantity, replenishment orders.

Some of the above items may be difficult to quantify, particularly stockout costs, but nevertheless may be of considerable importance. The avoidance of stockout costs is the basic reason why stocks are held in the first place.

7. INVENTORY CONTROL TERMINOLOGY

Some common inventory control items are defined and illustrated in Figure 5.3.

a. *Lead or procurement time.* The period of time between ordering (externally or internally) and replenishment, ie when the goods are available for use.

b. *Economic Ordering Quantity (EOQ) or Economic Batch Quantity (EBQ).* This is a calculated reorder quantity which minimises the balance of cost between carrying costs and ordering costs.

c. *Buffer Stock or Minimum Stock or Safety Stock.* A stock allowance to cover errors in forecasting the lead time or the demand during the lead time.

d. *Maximum Level.* A stock level calculated as the maximum desirable which is used as an indicator to management to show when stocks have risen too high.

e. *Reorder Level.* The level of stock (usually free stock) at which a further replenishment order should be placed. The recorder level is dependent on the lead time and the rate of demand during the lead time.

f. *Reorder Quantity.* The quantity of the replenishment order – frequently, but not always, the EOQ.

FIGURE 5.3   Stock terminology illustrated

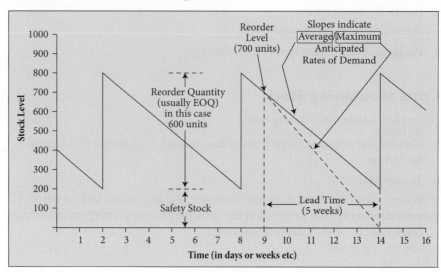

Figure 5.3 shows a simple stock position with the following assumptions and values:

Regular rate of demand of l00 units per week
Fixed lead time of 5 weeks
Reorder quantity 600 units
Maximum rate of demand 140 units per week
Safety stock 200 units
Reorder level 700 units

Notes:
a. It will be seen that the 200 safety stock is necessary to cope with periods of maximum demand during the lead time.
b. With constant rates of demand, as shown, the average stock is the safety stock plus $\frac{1}{2}$ reorder quantity, ie, in example above:

$$\text{average stock} = 200 + \frac{1}{2}\,(600)$$
$$= \textbf{500 units}$$

8. CALCULATING CONTROL LEVELS

Typical methods of calculating the major control levels: Reorder Level, Minimum Level, and Maximum Level, are illustrated below using the following data:

Average usage	100 units per day
Minimum usage	60 units per day
Maximum usage	130 units per day
Lead time	20–26 days
EOQ (previously calculated)	4,000 units

$$\text{Reorder level} = \text{Maximum usage} \times \text{maximum lead time}$$
$$= 130 \times 26$$
$$= \textbf{3,380 units}$$

$$\text{Minimum level} = \text{Reorder level} - \text{average usage in average lead time}$$
$$= 3,380 - (100 \times 23)$$
$$= 3,380 - 2,300$$
$$= \textbf{1,080 units}$$

$$\text{Maximum level} = \text{Reorder level} + \text{EOQ}$$
$$- \text{minimum anticipated usage in minimum lead time}$$
$$= 3,380 + 4,000 - (60 \times 20)$$
$$= \textbf{6,180 units}$$

Notes:

a. These are the normal control levels encountered in basic inventory control systems. Each time an entry is made, a comparison would be made between actual stock and the control level.

b. Reorder level is a definite action level; maximum and minimum levels are levels at which management would be warned that a potential danger may occur.

c. The minimum level is set so that management are warned when usage is above average and buffer stock is being used. There may be no danger, but the situation needs watching.

d. The maximum level is set so that management will be warned when demand is the minimum anticipated and consequently stock may rise above maximum intended.

e. The calculation of control levels is done relatively infrequently in manual systems, but in a computer based system calculations would take place automatically to reflect current and forecast future conditions.

9. ECONOMIC ORDERING QUANTITY (EOQ)

It will be recalled from paragraph 7 that the EOQ is a calculated order quantity which minimises the balance of cost between ordering and carrying costs. To be able to calculate a basic EOQ certain assumptions are necessary.

a. That there is a known, constant stockholding cost.

b. That there is a known, constant ordering cost.

c. That rates of demand are known.

d. That there is a known, constant price per unit.

e. That replenishment is made instantaneously, ie the whole batch is delivered at once.

The above assumptions are wide ranging and it is unlikely that all could be made in practice. Nevertheless the EOQ calculation is a useful starting point in establishing an appropriate reorder quantity.

The EOQ formula is given below and its derivation given in *Quantitative Techniques*, Cengage Learning.

$$\text{EOQ} = \sqrt{\frac{2.C_o.D}{C_c}}$$

where : C_o = Ordering cost per order
D = Demand per annum
C_c = Carrying cost per item per annum

Example

Find the EOQ where the forecasted demand is 1,000 units per month, the ordering cost is £350 per order, the units cost £8 each and it is estimated that carrying costs are 15% per annum.

$$\text{Here} : C_0 = £350$$
$$D = 1,000 \times 12$$
$$= 12,000 \text{ units per annum}$$
$$C_c = £8 \times 15\%$$
$$= £1.2 \text{ per item per annum}$$
$$\text{Thus} : \text{EOQ} = \sqrt{\frac{2 \times 350 \times 12,000}{1.2}}$$
$$= \textbf{2,646 units}$$

Notes:

a. It will be seen that it is necessary to bring the factors involved to the correct time scale.

b. The EOQ formula given above is for replenishment in one batch. Where replenishment takes place gradually, for example where the items are manufactured internally and placed into stock as they are made, the formula changes slightly as follows:

$$\textbf{EOQ (with gradual replenishment)} = \sqrt{\frac{2.C_o.D}{C_c\left(1 - \dfrac{D}{R}\right)}}$$

where : R = Replenishment rate per annum.

10. SUMMARY

a. The two most common stock records found in traditional systems are the Bin Card, and Stock Record Card (or its computer equivalent).

b. The bin card, where used, shows Issues, Receipts and Physical Balance.

c. As well as physical information the Stock Record Card shows the Free Stock balance and the major control levels; Reorder level, Maximum level, and Minimum level.

d. The perpetual inventory system means that after each stock movement the balance on hand is calculated. To ensure that the records keep in line with actual stocks, continuous stocktaking is carried out.

e. Inventory control is the system used in a firm to control the investment in stocks and has the overall objective of minimising in total the three costs associated with stocks: carrying costs, ordering costs and stockout costs.

f. Reorder level is an action point, maximum and minimum levels are management indicators.

g. The EOQ is a calculated order quantity to minimise the balance of ordering and carrying costs and the basic formula is:

$$EOQ = \sqrt{\frac{2.C_o.D}{C_c}}$$

I I. POINTS TO NOTE

a. Keeping stock records aligned with actual stocks is a major practical problem which is rarely solved completely successfully.

b. The inventory control system described in this chapter is the Reorder Level System, sometimes known as the Two Bin System.

c. An alternative control system is known as the Periodic Review System where all stock levels are reviewed at fixed intervals and replenishment orders issued. These orders would be based on estimated usage, lead time, etc and would not be the EOQ used in the Reorder Level System.

d. The newer approaches to production, such as Just-in-Time, challenge the philosophy behind the traditional EOQ approach. Just-in-Time systems seek to eliminate stocks entirely and where possible, move towards a batch size of one. This applies especially to Work-in-Progress stocks. In effect the JIT philosophy does not accept that ordering cost and holding costs are fixed. JIT systems continually seek to reduce both costs. In particular because of the close links with suppliers, ordering costs reduce dramatically and thus the EOQ and total annual costs are reduced. When ordering costs are low and holding costs are high the resulting EOQ drives firms to consider adopting JIT systems.

Student self-testing

Exercises (answers below)

1. An investigation into stores procedures and record keeping showed that for Part No. Y292 the physical stock differed from the Bin Card and also from the Record Card kept in the works office which did not agree with the Bin Card. Give reasons for the differences.

2. What is the relationship between Perpetual Inventory Systems and Continuous Stocktaking?

3. What is the Economic Order Quantity when demand is 25 per working day, ordering costs are £150 per order, the items cost £3 each and carrying costs are 12% per year? There are 250 working days in a year.

Solutions to exercises

1. The situation described in the question is a common one where several records exist relating to the same item. Typical of the reasons are the following:

   a. Errors in entering, totalling or sub-totalling.

   b. Delays in entering up the different records so that at any time they will show different balances.

   c. Loss of source documents, eg Goods Inwards Notes, Material Requisitions, etc.

   d. Errors in source documents either of quantities or part numbers.

   e. Errors in physical issues of receipts.

   f. Deliberate falsification perhaps to hide fraud.

   g. Theft or breakage of materials and parts which is not recorded.

   h. Stores transfers or goods returned not recorded.

2. The Perpetual Inventory System is a system of recording stocks so that the balance of stock is always available from the records whether manually maintained or by computer. To ensure that the stock balance is as accurate as possible the actual stock levels should be checked frequently, particularly for fast moving items, and discrepancies investigated using the procedures of Continuous Stocktaking.

3. Demand p.a. $= 25 \times 250 = 6,250$

$$\text{EOQ} = \sqrt{\frac{2.C_o.D}{C_c}}$$

$$= \sqrt{\frac{2 \times 150 \times 6,250}{3 \times 0.12}}$$

$$= 2,282$$

6

Materials: Pricing issues and stocks

2. ACCURATE RECORDING

There is little point in detailed analysis of pricing systems for charging purposes unless the basic records are accurate and up to date. The system of issues, job recording, scrap records, material returns, material transfers, defective material returns, inspection records, etc, etc must be continually monitored to ensure its relevance and accuracy.

3. OBJECTIVES OF MATERIAL PRICING

There are two main objectives of material pricing:

a. To charge to production on a consistent and realistic basis the cost of materials used.

b. To provide a satisfactory basis of valuation for inventory on hand.

These objectives should be achieved by a materials pricing system which is the simplest effective one and which is administratively realistic.

4. PROBLEMS OF MATERIALS PRICING

In practice the problem of pricing material issues, which thus determine product costs, is complicated by several factors:

a. Rapidly changing prices for bought in materials and components.
b. The stock of any given material is usually made up of several deliveries which may have been made at different prices.
c. The frequent impossibility (and undesirability from a cost accounting viewpoint) of identifying items with their delivery consignment.
d. The sensitivity of profit calculations to the pricing method adopted particularly where materials form a large part of total cost.

No one pricing method has all the advantages and it is necessary to use the most appropriate system to fulfil the requirements of a particular situation. The features of the various pricing systems are described below.

5. GENERAL FEATURES OF PRICING SYSTEMS

In manual systems when an issue is made from Stores, the Materials Requisition would be passed to the Cost Department to be priced and extended for appropriate ledger entries to be made. At the simplest these entries would be:

Debit

Work-in-Progress Control A/C
(for direct material issues)

or

Overhead Control A/C
(for indirect material issues)

Credit

Stores Ledger Control A/C

To be able to use some of the pricing systems described below (eg, the FIFO and LIFO methods) the stock recording system has to be comprehensive enough not only to record overall quantities and prices, but also the number or quantity received in any one batch. This is so that issues can be nominally identified against batches which is necessary to establish the appropriate price to be charged.

6. FIRST IN FIRST OUT (FIFO)

Using this method issues are priced at the price of the oldest batch in stock until all units of the batch have been issued when the price of the next oldest is used and so on.

Characteristics

a. It is an actual cost system and represents historical cost.

b. It is a good representation of sound storekeeping practice whereby oldest items are issued first.

c. Because it is an actual cost system unrealised profits or losses do not arise.

d. The stock valuation is based on the more recently acquired materials and thus more nearly approaches current market values.

e. The FIFO system is acceptable to the Inland Revenue and is acceptable according to SSAP 9 (Stocks and Work-in-Progress) and IAS 2.

f. Product costs, being based on the oldest material prices, lag behind current conditions.

   In periods of rising prices (inflation) product costs are understated and profits over-stated; in periods of falling prices (deflation) product costs are overstated and profits understated.

g. Because of the necessity to keep track of each batch, the system is administratively clumsy.

h. Renders cost comparison between jobs difficult because the material issue price may vary from batch to batch even with issues made on the same day.

7. LAST IN FIRST OUT (LIFO)

Using this method, issues are charged out at the price of the most recent batch received and continue to be charged thus until a new batch is received.

Characteristics

a. It is an actual cost system.

b. LIFO will frequently result in many batches being only partly charged to production where a subsequent batch is received.

c. Product costs will tend to be based fairly closely on current prices and will therefore be more realistic. It approximates economic cost.

d. Stocks are valued at the oldest prices.

e. The LIFO system is generally not acceptable to the Inland Revenue and is not recommended by SSAP 9.

f. Administratively clumsy.

g. Renders cost comparison between jobs difficult.

h. In periods of rising prices LIFO, by keeping down disclosed profits, provides a hedge against inflation.

8. AVERAGE PRICE METHOD

The average price method is a perpetual weighted average system where the issue price is recalculated after each receipt taking into account both quantities and money value.

Characteristics

a. Although realistic, it is not an actual buying in price, except by coincidence.

b. The average price method is acceptable to the Inland Revenue and is one of the methods recommended by SSAP 9, and IAS 2.

c. It is less complicated to administer than LIFO and FIFO.

d. It has an effect on product costs and stock valuation somewhere between the LIFO and FIFO systems.

e. The average price method makes cost comparison between jobs using similar materials somewhat easier.

f. With constantly fluctuating purchase prices, the average price method is likely to give more satisfactory results than LIFO or FIFO as it will tend to even out the price fluctuations.

g. Because it is based on actual costs, no unrealised stock profits and losses occur.

Note:

A variant of the average price method is the periodic average price method. Instead of calculating a new average price on each delivery, the average price is based on the total purchases for the period. This price is then applied to all issues for the period.

9. SPECIFIC OR UNIT PRICE

Where the item issued can be identified with the relevant invoice, the actual cost can be charged. This is usually only possible with special purpose items bought for a particular job.

10. STANDARD PRICE

This is defined as:

> *A predetermined price fixed on the basis of a specification of a product or service and of all factors affecting that price.*
>
> *Terminology*

In effect a standard or planned price is an average price predicted for a future period and all issues/returns would be made at the standard price for the period concerned.

Characteristics

a. Not an actual cost, therefore stock profits and losses may arise.

b. Administratively simple. Only quantities issued and received need be recorded, not the money values as they are predetermined.

c. Very real practical difficulty in establishing an acceptable and realistic standard price; particularly in volatile conditions.

d. If a realistic standard price can be established, some guidance to purchasing efficiency may be obtained.

e. Because material price variations are eliminated, manufacturing cost comparisons can be made more easily.

Note:
A standard issue price for materials may be used even where the firm does not use a full standard costing system – described in Chapter 23 onwards.

11. REPLACEMENT PRICE

A typical example of this method, sometimes known as the market price method, charges out issues at the buying in price on the day of issue. There are many variants to this system. For example, buying in prices may be established by means of a price index or actual prices updated on a monthly basis.

Characteristics

a. Not an actual cost price, therefore stock profits and losses may occur.

b. Issues would be priced at up to date values.

c. Major administrative problem in keeping replacement prices up to date.

d. Replacement pricing is more frequently used with estimating rather than normal stock issues.

e. Not acceptable to Inland Revenue.

f. Makes cost comparison between jobs difficult.

12. BASE STOCK METHOD

Although not strictly a method of valuing issues it is included in this section for completeness. The method assumes that initial purchases were to provide a buffer or base stock and that this base stock should appear in all subsequent stock valuations at its original value. Issues would be valued by one of the methods described earlier in this chapter. The base stock method would result in stock values which were totally unrealistic and its use is not recommended.

13. COMPARISON OF PRICING METHODS

Because of the effect on product costs and stock valuations, there is a need for an organisation to be consistent in its issue pricing methods. Apart from specific or unit prices all the methods are merely conventions, each with advantages and disadvantages. Provided that the system is used consistently and suits the operating conditions of the firm, any of the system could be used. However, because of SSAP and IAS recommendations and the Inland Revenue, the use of the FIFO or the Average price systems appear to be most common.

Based on the stores data below, issue prices using the FIFO, LIFO, Average Price and Standard Price systems are shown in the following accounts.

Stores data for part no 10x for October where the standard price is £4.50 per unit

Date	Receipts	Purchase Price	Issues
1/10	150 units	£4.00	
5/10	100 units	£4.50	
6/10			80 units
12/10			100 units
20/10	90 units	£4.80	
24/10			80 units

Stores Ledger Account using the Average Price Method

Receipt date	GRN No.	Qty	Price £	Total £	Issue date	Mat'l req	Issue details £		Balance (memo only) £	
1/10	5,832	150	4.00	600					150 @ 4.00	600
5/10	6,291	100	4.50	450					250 @ 4.20*	1,050
					6/10	257	80 @ 4.20	336	170 @ 4.20	714
					12/10	492	100 @ 4.20	420		
20/10	7,057	90	4.80	432					70 @ 4.20	294
					24/10	794	80 @ 4.5375	363	160 @ 4.5375†	726
									80 @ 4.5375	363
					Bal c/f	80		363		
		340		1,482		340		1,482		

Average Price calculations

*

	150	units	@	£4	=	£600
plus	100	units	@	£4.5	=	450
	=250	units			=	£1,050

$\therefore$ average price $= £\dfrac{1,050}{250} = £4.20$

†

	70	units	@	£4.2	=	£294
plus	90	units	@	£4.80	=	432
=	160	units			=	£726

$\therefore$ average price $= £\dfrac{726}{160} = £4.5375$

Note:
If the Periodic Average Price had been used, the issue price for all issues in the period would be:

$$\frac{(150 \times £4 + 100 \times £4.50 + 90 \times £4.80)}{340} = £4.359$$

Using this price for all the issues in the period produces a Closing Stock Value of £348.66.

Stores Ledger Account using the Standard Price Method

Receipt date	GRN No.	Qty	Price £	Total £	Issue date	Mat'l req	Issue details £		Balance (memo only) £	
1/10	5,832	150	4.50	675						
5/10	6,291	100	4.50	450					150 @ 4.50	675
					6/10	257	80 @ 4.50	360	250 @ 4.50	1,125
					12/10	492	100 @ 4.50	450	170 @ 4.50	765
20/10	7,057	90	4.50	405					70 @ 4.50	315
					24/10	794	80 @ 4.50	360	160 @ 4.50	720
						Bal c/f	80	360	80 @ 4.50	360
		340		1,530			340	1,530		

Notes:

a. The account using standard prices is shown fully completed for illustration purposes only. If the standard price method was to be used then quantities only need to be recorded thus saving clerical work.

b. It will be noted that receipts, issues and balances are all at standard price. The gain/loss on purchasing would be written off elsewhere in the accounts, the stores ledger being entirely at standard price.

Stores Ledger Account using the FIFO Method

Receipt date	GRN No.	Qty	Price £	Total £	Issue date	Mat'l req	Issue details £		Balance (memo only) £	
1/10	5,832	150	4.00	600					150 @ 4.00	600
5/10	6,291	100	4.50	450					150 @ 4.00 .... 100 @ 4.50	1,050
					6/10	257	80 @ 4.00	320	70 @ 4.00 .... 100 @ 4.50	730
					12/10	492	70 @ 4.00 .... 30 @ 4.50	415	70 @ 4.50	315
20/10	7,057	90	4.80	432					70 @ 4.50 90 @ 4.80	747
					24/10	794	70 @ 4.50 .... 10 @ 4.80	363	80 @ 4.80	384
						Bal c/f	80 @ 4.80	384		
		340		1,482			340	1,482		

Note:

a. Using the FIFO system the closing stock is valued at the latest price(s) of receipt.

Stores Ledger Account using the LIFO Method

Receipt date	GRN No.	Qty	Price £	Total £	Issue date	Mat'l req	Issue details £		Balance (memo only) £	
1/10	5,832	150	4.00	600					150 @ 4.00	600
5/10	6,291	100	4.50	450					150 @ 4.00 100 @ 4.50	 1,050
					6/10	257	80 @ 4.50	360	150 @ 4.00 20 @ 4.50	 690
					12/10	492	20 @ 4.50 80 @ 4.00	 410	70 @ 4.00	280
20/10	7,057	90	4.80	432					70 @ 4.00 90 @ 4.80	 712
					24/10	794	80 @ 4.80	384	70 @ 4.00 10 @ 4.80	 328
						Bal c/f	80	328		
		340		1,482			340	1,482		

Note:
Using the LIFO system may mean that some of a batch in a clerical sense, is unused and theoretically could get carried forward indefinitely.

As a consequence the closing stock may include the remnants of several batches. For example in this case the closing stock includes 70 from the earliest batch and 10 from the latest batch.

It will be seen that the various pricing systems produce issue prices ranging from £4 to £4.8 and closing stock valuations ranging from £328 to £384.

14. STOCK VALUATION

The application of any of the issue pricing methods automatically results in a closing stock valuation of the particular item in the stores ledger. The summation of the individual items, ie the balance on the Stores Ledger Control Account, represents a valuation of closing stock. Invariably this valuation is used for operating statements and internal management accounts. In addition this valuation is frequently the basis of stock valuation for use in the financial accounts, but on occasion some adjustment to the figure is made. The general rule of stock valuation for financial accounting purposes is the lower of cost or net realisable value.

15. WHAT PURCHASE PRICE TO USE?

So far the last three chapters have conveniently assumed that there is a clear-cut purchase price which is entered in the cost accounts and which forms the basis of pricing issues and stocks. In practice this is not always the case and various charges, taxes and discounts may create some ambiguity. A number of the more commonly encountered complications are dealt with below.

a. *Value Added Tax (VAT)*
   Most of the goods and services supplied to a typical organisation have an additional charge (currently at $17\frac{1}{2}\%$) levied on the value of the goods or services and this appears on invoices. This tax charge is part of an organisation's input tax which can be reclaimed so that the VAT charge should not be included in the cost accounts.

b. *Transport, storage and delivery charges*
   Where the purchaser has to bear these charges they form part of the cost of the goods and so should be included in the cost accounts. Where these charges are invoiced per unit or by weight (or can be easily prorated) then they would be included in the direct material cost. Often this is not practicable, or the amounts involved are small, in which case the additional charges would be allotted to production overheads.

c. *Quantity or Trade Discounts*
   These are discounts given against a list price for ordering in large quantities. For example, on a list price of £5 per unit a discount of 5% may be given for purchases over 50 units and a 10% discount for purchases of over l00. Where such discounts are available it is clearly good purchasing practice to take maximum advantage of the price reductions possible. From the cost accounting viewpoint the net price of the items is the one which should be used so that, based on the example above, the price would be £4.50 per unit if ordering in lots of over 100.

d. *Cash discount*
   This is a small percentage allowance which can be obtained by settling invoices promptly. For example, a supplier's terms may be $1\frac{1}{2}\%$ discount for settlement within seven days otherwise Net Monthly.
   The cash discount is generally considered to be a financial accounting item which would not normally be included in the cost accounts.

e. *Packing and container charges*
   Where packing or containers are charged separately the cost accounting treatment varies according to whether the containers are returnable or not.

   i. Non-returnable packing and container charges. The cost of the packing or containers is part of the purchase price of the materials and would normally be included in the direct or indirect costs as appropriate.

   ii. Returnable packing and containers where full credit is given. The normal assumption would be that containers are returned and full credit received so that the container cost would not be included in the cost accounts. In certain circumstances however, experience may show that, because of damage or losses, the organisation does not receive credit for all packing and containers charged. In such cases a suitable addition could be made to the direct material cost or, if the amount is small, a charge could be made to production overheads.

   iii. Returnable packing and containers where only a partial credit is given. The net cost of the containers (amount charged less credit received) is an addition to the material cost and would be included in the cost accounts.

16. PARETO OR ABC ANALYSIS

Detailed stock control uses time and resources and can cost a considerable amount of money. Because of this it is important that the effect is directed where it can be most cost-effective – there is little point in elaborate and costly recording and control procedures for an item of insignificant value.

It is therefore worthwhile carrying out a so-called Pareto or ABC analysis. It is often found that a few items account for a large proportion of the value, and, accordingly, should have the closest monitoring. A typical analysis of stock items could be as follows:

Class A   items 80% of value in 20% of items – close day-to-day control

Class B   items 15% of value in 30% of items – regular review

Class C   items 5% of value in 50% of items – infrequent review

Such a review can help to ensure that resources are used to maximum advantage. Detailed, selective control will be more effective than a generalised approach which treats all items identically. However, care must be taken with this approach. There are some low value items that are critical to the firm. If they are out of stock then high costs may be incurred, perhaps because of machine breakdowns and production stoppages – low value does not necessarily mean low importance.

17. SUMMARY

a. There must be a consistent, reasonably simple method of pricing issues so that production is charged a realistic figure for materials consumed.

b. The problems involved in pricing issues arise from changing purchase prices, the frequent impossibility of identifying materials with particular purchases and administrative problems.

c. The major pricing methods are First in First out (FIFO), Last in First out (LIFO), Average price and Standard price.

d. SSAP 9, Stocks and Work in Progress, and IAS 2 recommend the use of either unit (or specific) price, FIFO, or Average price.

e. Many of the pricing systems are administratively clumsy, requiring either the monitoring of batches or frequent price calculations.

f. Some of the administrative problems can be overcome by the use of a Standard price system, but there is the very real practical problem of establishing a realistic standard price. If conditions are such that frequent revisions of the standard price are necessary, many of the advantages of the system are lost.

18. POINTS TO NOTE

a. It will be apparent that there is no such thing as 'true' issue price. It is a question of judgement which system is best suited to a particular organisation.

b. The stores ledger accounts shown in this chapter are examples of the perpetual inventory system described in Chapter 4, ie, where a balance is shown after each receipt and issue.

c. Regardless of SSAP recommendations and Inland Revenue acceptability, any pricing or stock valuation system could be used for internal purposes. However, to avoid duplication of effort there is merit in using a system for internal purposes which will be acceptable as a basis of stock valuation for financial accounting purposes.

d. The issue pricing systems described in this Chapter are the most common. Other systems exist, an example of which is 'Next in First Out' (NIFO). In this system, issues are priced at the 'next' price, ie the price of items which have been ordered but not received. This price would be close to current market prices. This system is complicated and rarely used.

Student self-testing

Exercises (answers below)

1. The following information is available about a component.

Opening Stock	1st Jan	500 at £2 each
Receipts	6th Jan	160 at £2.20 each
	20th Jan	180 at £2.25 each
Issues	2 Jan	300
	16 Jan	210

Complete three separate stores ledger accounts assuming that issues are priced using:

a. LIFO

b. FIFO

c. Average Price

2. Which of the following items would be considered as part of the cost of materials taken in stores?
   a. Cash discount
   b. Trade discount
   c. VAT
   d. Freight and carriage charges
   e. Cost of non-returnable containers
   f. Cost of returnable containers

3. At what price per unit would Part No. 52Y be entered in the Stores Ledger if the following invoice was received from a supplier?

Invoice

	£
150 units Part No. 52Y @ £5 ea =	750
less 20% discount	150
	600
plus VAT @ 17.5%	105
	705
plus Packing Charges 5 non-returnable pallets	25
	730

Note: A 2.5 % discount will be given for payment in 30 days.

Solutions to exercises

1. Stores Ledger Account – LIFO

	Qty	Price £	£		Qty	Price £	£
1st Jan Bal	500	2	1,000	2 Jan Issue	300	2	600
6 Jan Rec.	160	2.20	352				
20 Jan Rec.	180	2.25	405	16 Jan Issue	[1]210		[2]452
				Bal c/f	[3]330		[4]705
	840		1,757		840		1,757

Workings: [1]160 + 50; [2]160 × £2.20 + 50 × £2; [3]180 + 150; [4]180 × £2.25 + 150 × £2.

Stores Ledger Account – FIFO

	Qty	Price £	£		Qty	Price £	£
1st Jan Bal	500	2	1,000	2 Jan Issue	300	2	600
6 Jan Rec.	160	2.20	352	16 Jan Issue	[1]210		[2]422
20 Jan	180	2.25	405				
				Bal c/f	[3]330		[4]735
	840		1,757		840		1,757

Workings: [1]200 + 10; [2]200 × £2 + 10 × £2.20; [3]150 + 180; [4]150 × £2.20 + 180 × £2.25.

Stores Ledger Account – Average price

	Qty	Price £	£		Qty	Price £	£
1st Jan Bal	500	2	1,000	2 Jan Issue	300	2	600
6 Jan Rec.	160	2.20	352	16 Jan	210	[1]2.088	439
20 Jan	180	2.25	405	Bal c/f	330	[2]2.176	718
	840		1,757		840		1,757

Workings:

$$[1]200 \times £2 + 160 \times £2.20 = 752 \text{ and } \frac{752}{360} = £2.088;$$

$$[2]150 \times £2.088 + 180 \times £2.25 = 718 \text{ and } \frac{718}{330} = £2.176.$$

2. a. Cash discount. The consensus is that these would not be deducted from the invoice price.

   b. Trade discount. The net value of materials after the trade discount would be used in the cost accounts.

c. VAT. This would not be included.

d. Freight charges. Are generally deemed to be part of the cost of obtaining materials.

e. Unreturnable containers. Classed as part of materials costs.

f. Returnable containers. The cost of returnable containers would not be included in material costs though if the containers were returnable but at a reduced value then their net cost would be included in the material costs.

3. The cost after 20% Trade Discount, is included. VAT is reclaimable so is not included. The pallets were non-returnable so the cost is included. The 2.5% discount is not included.

	£
Thus:	
150 units net cost	600
+ packing	25
	625

$\therefore$ cost per unit $= 625 \div 150 = £4.17$

Assessment section 1

EXAMINATION QUESTIONS (ANSWERS ON THE WEBSITE)

A1.1   A cost unit is:
    A   the cost per hour of operating a machine.
    B   the cost per unit of electricity consumed.
    C   a unit of product or service in relation to which costs are ascertained.
    D   a measure of work output in a standard hour.

A1.2   The process of cost apportionment is carried out so that
    A   costs may be controlled.
    B   cost units gather overheads as they pass through cost centres.
    C   whole items of cost can be charged to cost centres.
    D   common costs are shared among cost centres.

A1.3   Prime cost is
    A   all costs incurred in manufacturing a profit.
    B   the total of direct costs.
    C   the material cost of a product.
    D   the cost of operating a department.

A1.4   A cost driver is
    A   an item of production overhead.
    B   a common cost which is shared over cost centres.
    C   any cost relating to transport.
    D   an activity which generates costs.

A1.5   A trade discount is
    A   a reduction in price per unit given to some customers.
    B   a discount for early payment.
    C   a special sales promotion.
    D   the reduction in overhead costs per unit as production increases.

A1.6 There are 27,500 units of Part Number X53 on order with the suppliers and 16,250 units outstanding on existing customers' orders. If the free stock is 13,000 units, what is the physical stock?

A 1,750
B 3,250
C 14,000
D 29,250

The following data are to be used for sub-questions A 1.7 and A 1.8.

A small management consultancy has prepared the following information:

Overhead absorption rate per consulting hour	£12.50
Salary cost per consulting hour (senior)	£20.00
Salary cost per consulting hour (junior)	£15.00

The firm adds 40% to total cost to arrive at a selling price.

A1.7 Assignment number 652 took 86 hours of a senior consultant's time and 220 hours of junior time. What price should be charged for assignment no 652?

A £5,355
B £7,028
C £8,845
D £12,383

A1.8 During a period 3,000 consulting hours were charged out in the ratio of 1 senior to 3 junior hours. Overheads were exactly as budgeted. What was the total gross margin for the period?

A £34,500
B £48,300
C £86,250
D £120,750

A1.9 A component has a safety stock of 500, a re-order quantity of 3,000 and a rate of demand which varies between 200 and 700 per week. The average stock is approximately

A 2,000
B 2,300
C 2,500
D 3,500

Use the following data to answer questions A1.10 and A1.11 below

E Ltd's stock purchases during a recent week were as follows:

Day	Price per unit($)	Units Purchased
1	1.45	55
2	1.60	80
3	1.75	120
4	1.80	75
5	1.90	130

There was no stock at the beginning of the week. 420 units were issued to production during the week. The company updates its stock records after every transaction.

A1.10 Using a first in, first out (FIFO) method of costing stock issues, the value of closing stock would:

A $58.00

B $70.00

C $72.00

D $76.00

A1.11 If E Ltd changes to the weighted average method of stock valuation, the effect on closing stock value and on the profit for the week compared with the FIFO method will be:

	Closing stock value	Gross Profit
A	Higher	Higher
B	Lower	Higher
C	Lower	Lower
D	Higher	Lower

A1.12 X Ltd X ltd uses the FIFO method to charge material costs to production. Opening stock of material M at the beginning of April was 270 units valued at £4 per unit.

Movements of material M during April were as follows:

4 April   Received 30 units at £4.10 per unit

9 April   Issued 210 units

14 April Issued 80 units

22 April Received 90 units at £4.20 per unit

24 April Issued 40 units

A What was the total value of the issues to production during April?

B What was the value of closing stock at the end of April?

A1.13 The following data relate to stock item CDR345:

Ordering costs	£100 per order
Stockholding costs	£4 per unit per annum
Annual demand	5,000 units

The economic order quantity is:

A 250 units

B 354 units

C 500 units

D 1,000 units

A1.14 A paint manufacturer has a number of departments. Each department is located in a separate building on the same factory site. In mixing department the basic raw materials are mixed together in very large vessels.

These are then moved onto the colour adding department where paints of different colours are created in these vessels.

In the next department – the pouring department – the paint is poured from these vessels into litre sized tins.

The tins then go on to the labelling department prior to going on to the finished goods department.

The following statements relate to the paint manufacturer:

(i) The mixing department is a cost centre.

(ii) A suitable cost unit for the colour adding department is a litre tin of paint.

(iii) The pouring department is a profit centre.

Which statement or statements is/are correct?

A (i) only

B (i) and (ii) only

C (i) and (iii) only

D (ii) and (iii) only

The above are a selection of multiple choice questions from CIMA's Management Accounting Fundamentals, Fundamentals of Management Accounting, Operational Cost Accounting and ACCA's Financial Information for Management.

A1.15 a. Explain the meaning of:

i. continuous stocktaking, and

ii. perpetual inventory

in the context of a material control system.

b. A company operates a historic batch costing system, which is not integrated with the financial accounts, and uses the weighted average method of pricing raw material issues. A weighted average price (to 3 decimal places of a pound £) is calculated after each purchase of material.

Receipts and issues of Material X for a week were as follows:

Receipts into stock			Issues to production	
Day	Kgs	£	Day	Kgs
1	1,400	1.092.00	2	1,700
4	1,630	1,268.14	5	1,250

At the beginning of the week, stock of material X was 3,040 kgs at a cost of £0.765 per kg. Of the issues of material on Day 2, 60 kgs were returned to stock on Day 3. Of the receipts of material on Day 1, 220 kgs were returned to the supplier on Day 4. Invoices for the material receipts during the week remained unpaid at the end of the week.

Required:

i. Prepare a tabulation of the movement of stock during the week, showing the changes in the level of stock, its valuation per kilogram, and the total value of stock held.

ii. Record the week's transactions in the Material X stock account in the Cost Ledger, indicating clearly in each case the account in which the corresponding entry should be posted.

(ACCA Management Information)

A1.16 A company manufactures several products which use Material X. At the end of November the inventory account showed stock of Material X of 2,760 kgs. However, a physical count at the end of the month reported only 2,705 kgs in stock. Opening stock of material X at the beginning of November in the accounting records was 2,630 kgs at £3.12 per kg. 920 kg of Material X were purchased on credit on 10 November for £2,907.20 and a further purchase of 970 kg of the material was received on 26 November. 40 kg of the material purchased on 10 November were faulty and were returned to the supplier. Except for these returns all other Material X recorded as being issued from stock during the month was used in production.

At the beginning of November £5,650.30 was owed to the supplier for Material X purchases. During November £5,760.70 was paid to the supplier and at the end of the month £5,833.90 remained outstanding for Material X purchases.

Required:

a. Record the transactions for the month in the Material X stock account showing both quantities and value. Stock issues are made on a FIFO basis. In recording the entries in the stock account you should clearly indicate the account in which the corresponding entry would be made in the company's integrated accounting system.
b. List the possible reasons for stock discrepancies revealed by physical stock counts.
c. Outline the documents, and process, used in the ordering, and receipt, of materials from suppliers.

(ACCA Cost & Management Accounting)

A1.17 'Attributing direct costs and absorbing overhead costs to the product/ service through an activity based costing approach will result in a better understanding of the true cost of the final output.'

[Source: a recent CIMA publication on costing in a service environment]

You are required to explain and comment on the above statement.

(CIMA Cost Accounting)

A1.18 Cost must be classified to facilitate its arrangement in as flexible a manner as possible.

Required:

a. Explain the meaning of the 'classification of cost' and give some practical examples of the ways cost is classified.
b. Design a code number series for use in a costing system integrated with a financial accounting system. Detail some practical examples of the code numbers.
c. Detail four advantages of using code numbers for stock materials.

(AAT, Cost Accounting & Budgeting)

A1.19 The following information is provided concerning a particular raw material:

Average usage	1,000 kilos per day
Minimum usage	800 kilos per day
Maximum usage	1,350 kilos per day
Order quantity	9,000 kilos

The stock level is reviewed at the end of each day and an order is placed the following day if the normal re-order level has been reached. Delivery is reliably expected at the beginning of the fourth day following order.

Required:

a. From the above information calculate three normal control levels used for stock control purposes.
b. Draw a graph demonstrating the changing level of stock of the material based on the following actual usage over a 14 day period:

First five days	1,020 kilos per day
Next four days	1,200 kilos per day
Final five days	900 kilos per day

The stock at the beginning of day 1 was 6,000 kilos. Show clearly on the graph three control levels calculated in (a).

c. Contrast the actual minimum stock level over the period with the normal control level established, and comment on the difference and any action required.

(ACCA, Cost and Management Accounting 1)

A1.20 For the six months ended 31st October, an importer and distributor of one type of washing machine has the following transactions in his records. There was an opening balance of 100 units which had a value of £3,900.

Date	Bought Quantity in units	Cost per unit £
May	100	41
June	200	50
August	400	51.875

The price of £51.875 each for the August receipt was £6.125 per unit less than the normal price because of the large quantity ordered.

Date	Sold Quantity in units	Price each £
July	250	64
September	350	70
October	100	74

From the information given above and using weighted average, FIFO and LIFO methods for pricing issues, *you are required* for each method to:

a. show the stores ledger records including the closing stock balance and stock valuation;
b. prepare in columnar format, trading accounts for the period to show the gross profit using each of the three methods of pricing issues;
c. comment on which method, in the situation depicted, is regarded as the best measure of profit, and why.

(CIMA, Cost Accounting 1)

A1.21 A company uses Material Z (cost £3.50 per kilo) in the manufacture of Products A and B. The following forecast information is provided for the year ahead:

	Product A	Product B
Sales (units)	24,600	9,720
Finished goods stock increase by year end (units)	447	178
Post-production rejection rate (%)	1	2
Material Z usage (kilo per completed unit net of wastage)	1.8	3.0
Material Z wastage (%)	5	11

Additional information:

a. Average purchasing lead time for Material Z is two weeks.
b. Usage of Material Z is expected to be even over the year.
c. Annual stock holding costs are 18% of the material cost.
d. The cost of placing orders is £30 per order.
e. The re-order level for Material Z is set at the average usage in average lead time plus 1,000 kilos of safety (buffer) stock.

Required

a. State two items that would be regarded as 'stock holding costs' and explain how they may be controlled effectively.
b. Calculate for the year ahead:

  i. the required production of Products A and B (in units);
  ii. the total requirement for Material Z (in kilos);
  iii. the Economic Order Quantity for Material Z (in kilos).

c. Calculate the average stock investment (£) and the annual stock holding costs (£) for Material Z.

(ACCA Management Information)

A1.22 Point Ltd uses the economic order quantity (EOQ) model to establish the reorder quantity for raw material Y. The company holds no buffer stock. Information relating to raw material Y is as follows:

Annual usage 48,000 units
Purchase price £80 per unit
Ordering costs £120 per order
Annual holding costs 10% of the purchase price

Required:

a. Calculate:

  i. the EOQ for raw material Y, and
  ii. the total annual cost of purchasing ordering and holding stocks of raw material Y.

  The supplier has offered Point Ltd a discount of 1% on the purchase price if each order placed is for 2,000 units.

b. Calculate the total annual saving to Point Ltd of accepting this offer.
c. List FOUR examples of holding costs.

(ACCA Financial Information for Management)

EXAMINATION QUESTIONS WITHOUT ANSWERS

B1.1 a. The managing director of your organisation, a manufacturer of garden furniture, disagrees with you over the need for a costing system within your organisation. He says that the only requirement for the classification of costs is by the financial accountant into cost of sales, distribution cost and administration expense for the published accounts and anything beyond is unnecessary.

Required:
Write a report to the Managing Director stating your case as to why you believe he is wrong and specifying the following:

   i. The manner in which he has classified cost in his statement.
   ii. Four alternative classifications of cost and the ways in which they can assist management decision-making, planning and control.

(AAT Cost Accounting & Budgeting)

B1.2 a. In connection with control of materials, you are required to:

   i. explain the meaning and principles of classification;
   ii. explain the principles of coding;
   iii. state four advantages of using a coding system.

   b. A company manufactures shoes and slippers in half-sizes in the ranges:

	Sizes
Men's	6 to $9^1/_2$
Ladies'	3 to 9
Boys'	1 to $5^1/_2$
Girls'	1 to 5

The company uses a seven-digit code to identify its finished products, which, reading from left to right, is built up as follows: Digit one indicates whether the products are men's, ladies', boys' or girls'. The numbers used are:

1 – men's; 2 – ladies'; 3 – boys'; 4 – girls'

Digit two denotes type of footwear (shoes or slippers). Digit three denotes colour (5 is green; 6 is burgundy). Digit four denotes the material of the upper part of the product. Digit five denotes the material of the sole. Digits six and seven denote size.

Examples:

Code 1613275 represents a pair of men's slippers, brown suede, rubber sole, size $7^1/_2$
Code 1324195 represents a pair of men's shoes, black leather, leather sole, size $9^1/_2$.

You are required to:

Set suitable code numbers to the following, stating any assumptions you make:

i. boys' shoes, brown leather uppers, rubber soles, size 4;
ii. ladies' slippers, green felt uppers, rubber soles, size 4½;
iii. girls' shoes, burgundy leather uppers, leather soles, size 3½

(CIMA Cost Accounting 1)

B1.3   You are required to:

a. i. explain the term 'materials control' indicating the scope of its coverage within a manufacturing business;
   ii. differentiate between 'stock control' and 'store-keeping';
   iii. explain the term 'pareto (80/20) distribution'.

b. demonstrate your understanding of a. iii. above by:

i. classifying, for stock control purposes, the items shown below;
ii. drawing a graph that will enable management to understand the significance of your classification in b. i.

Stock item reference number	Annual usage (units)	Cost per unit £
7212	1,200	62.5
7213	800	150.0
7214	1,400	15.0
7215	2,000	11.4
7216	2,600	12.0
7217	5,000	3.2
7218	5,000	1.6
7219	2,000	3.0

(CIMA Cost Accounting 1)

B1.4   A large local government authority places orders for various stationery items at quarterly intervals. In respect of an item of stock coded A32, data are: annual usage 5,000 boxes; minimum order quantity 500 boxes; cost per box £2.

Usage of material is on a regular basis and on average, half of the amount purchased is held in inventory. The cost of storage is considered to be 25% of the inventory value. The average cost of placing an order is estimated at £12.5.

The chief executive of the authority has asked you to review the present situation and to consider possible ways of effecting cost savings.

You are required to:

a. tabulate the costs of storage and ordering item A32 for each level of orders from four to twelve placed per year;
b. ascertain from the tabulation the number of orders which should be placed in a year to minimise these costs;
c. produce a formula to calculate the order level which would minimise these costs – your formula should explain each constituent part

of the formula and their relationships;

d. give an example of the use of the formula to confirm the calculation in b. above;

e. calculate the percentage saving on the annual cost which could be made by using the economic order quantity system;

f. suggest two other approaches which could be introduced in order to reduce the present cost of storage and ordering of stationery.

(CIMA, Cost Accounting 2)

B1.5 On 1 January Mr G started a small business buying and selling a special yarn. He invested his savings of £40,000 in the business and, during the next six months, the following transactions occurred:

Yarn Purchases			**Yarn Sales**		
Date of Receipt	**Quantity Boxes**	**Total Cost £**	**Date of Despatch**	**Quantity Boxes**	**Total Value £**
13 January	200	7,200	10 February	500	25,000
8 February	400	15,200			
11 March	600	24,000	20 April	600	27,000
12 April	400	14,000			
15 June	500	14,000	25 June	400	15,200

The yarn is stored in premises Mr G has rented and the closing stock of yarn, counted on 30 June, was 500 boxes. Other expenses incurred, and paid in cash, during the six month period amounted to £2,300.

Required:

a. Calculate the value of the material issues during the six month period, and the value of the closing stock at the end of June, using the following methods of pricing:

   i. first in, first out,
   ii. last in, first out, and
   iii. weighted average (calculations to two decimal places only).

b. Calculate and discuss the effect each of the three methods of material pricing will have on the reported profit of the business and examine the performance of the business during the first six month period.

(ACCA Costing)

7

Labour: Remuneration methods

2. TRENDS IN EMPLOYMENT AND REMUNERATION

At present approximately one third of manual workers are paid by some form of incentive scheme. This overall percentage masks extremely wide variations from industry to industry. For example, in general engineering around 80% of workers are paid wholly or partly by some form of incentive scheme, whereas in process industries the figure is as low as 15%.

There is a general tendency (with, of course, exceptions) for larger firms to move away from direct incentive schemes to schemes such as measured day work. There is also a tendency for workers to become salaried employees which has clear costing implications as direct labour costs become more fixed in nature rather than varying with output.

Throughout most of the Western world patterns of employment are changing. There are fewer full-time permanent employees and more part-timers of whom a large proportion are women. There is less job security and more self-employment. There is a tendency for organisations to operate with a small core of full-time employees with a large pool of part-timers and/or contractors who can be called upon as required. In effect firms are operating a Just-in-Time system for labour; calling up temporary help when demand is high and reducing staff when demand falls. Although there are financial advantages to the organisation of such arrangements it is arguable that there are substantial social disadvantages through low and irregular earnings, insecurity and so on.

3. REMUNERATION METHODS

The two main categories of remuneration are:

a. Time based.

b. Related in some way or another to output or performance.

Within these two categories there are innumerable variations some of which have general applicability while others are of a local and specialised nature. Remuneration systems are frequently complex and administratively cumbersome, but because the system is the result of negotiations, disputes and agreements over the years, attempts to rationalise and simplify are frequently met with hostility and suspicion. The two major categories of remuneration together with typical variations are dealt with below. The newer forms of production organisation, such as Just-in-Time systems mean more and more workers will be paid time rates and will not have their pay dependent on individual output levels. There are two main reasons for this. First, parts are now only produced as and when required. This means that the repetitive production of components that move into stock is avoided as one of the key objectives of Just-in-Time is to eliminate all forms of stock. Secondly, what counts in JIT is the output of the group (known as a *production cell*) as a whole. As a consequence workers have to be flexible and adaptable and move from task to task according to demand. In such circumstances individual incentive schemes are of little or no value.

In addition more and more wages and salaries, traditionally classed as overheads, are now being traced to product lines and classed as direct. For example, IBM are now grouping many support functions around specific product lines so that identification of costs is more direct. This is, of course, part of the trend towards Activity Cost Management whereby there is much closer identification of people and expenditure to specific value adding activities.

4. TIME BASED SYSTEMS

Basic system

At the simplest level workers would be paid for the number of hours worked at a basic rate per hour up to, say, 40 hours per week. Time worked in addition to 40 hours would be classed as overtime and is usually paid at a higher rate, for example 'time and a quarter' (ie, $1^{1}/_{4} \times$ basic rate per hour) depending on the number of extra hours worked and when the overtime was worked.

Although workers' pay is not related to output, this does not mean that output and performance is unimportant. On the contrary, it is normal practice to monitor output and performance closely by shop floor supervision and managerial control systems so that workers are paid for actually working and not merely attending.

Advantages:

i. Simple to understand and administer.

ii. Simplifies wage negotiations in that only one rate needs to be determined unlike the continuous complex negotiations over individual rates usual in some incentive schemes.

Disadvantages:

i. No real incentive to increase output.

ii. All employees in the grade paid the same rate regardless of performance.

iii. Constant supervision may be necessary.

Most appropriate for:

i. Work where quality, safety, health care are all important, eg jig and tool making, nurses, signal operators, etc.

ii. Work where incentive schemes would be difficult or impossible to install, eg indirect labour, stores assistants, clerical work, etc.

iii. Work where the output level is not under the employees' control, eg power station workers.

High day rate system

This is a time based system which is designed to provide a strong incentive by paying rates well above normal basic time rates in exchange for above average output and performance. For its successful application it is necessary to ensure that the output levels are the result of detailed work studies and that there is agreement from the labour force and the unions involved on the required production level. A typical application of this system is on assembly line production in the car industry and in domestic appliance manufacture.

Advantages

i. It is claimed to attract higher grade workers.

ii. Provides a direct incentive without the complications of individual piecework rates.

iii. Simple to understand and administer.

Disadvantages

i. May cause other local employers to raise their rates to attract the better workers thus nullifying the original effect.

ii. Problems occur when the original target production figures are not met.

   Most appropriate for: Easily measurable output to which groups of workers contribute, eg car assembly.

Note:
The system is also called Measured Day Work and in practice such schemes may well have quite complex structures and rules.

Common bonuses found in time based systems

In addition to the time rates explained above, bonuses or extra payments are frequently made. Some common examples are:

i. Shift bonus. Where a worker agrees to work shifts, particularly where rotating shifts are used, he or she receives an extra amount.

ii. Timekeeping bonus. Where a person's timekeeping has been good over the week a bonus may be paid.

iii. Continuous working bonus. Where the plant has achieved continuous production without strikes, go slows or stoppages a weekly bonus is paid. This system appears to have had some success in one of the large car manufacturers.

Note:

Many variants exist, for example, many firms which operate a time based system pay, in addition, some form of output bonus and conversely some of the above bonuses are found in firms where the main method of remuneration is by an incentive scheme.

5. GENERAL FEATURES OF INCENTIVE SCHEMES

All incentive schemes relate payment to output in some way or another. There are innumerable variations; some schemes apply to individuals whilst others apply to groups of workers, some have a direct and immediate relationship to output whilst others are more indirect.

From a properly organised and well planned system both the firm and the employees can benefit. The employee from the extra income arising from increased production, and the firm from the reduced overheads per unit of the increased production. Unfortunately not all schemes achieve this ideal, but careful attention to the following factors will help to achieve this objective.

a. Remuneration should reflect workers' effort and performance and payment should be made without delay, preferably soon after completion of the task.

b. The scheme should be reasonably simple to assist administration and to enable employees to calculate their own bonus.

c. Performance levels should be demonstrably fair, ie they should be in reach of the average worker working reasonably hard.

d. There should be no artificial limit on earnings and earnings should be safeguarded when problems arise outside the employee's control.

e. The scheme should not be introduced until there has been full consultation and agreement with employees and unions.

f. The full implications of the scheme, performance levels, rates, etc must be considered, so that it will have a reasonable length of life. Rapid changes, particularly artificial ones to curtail earnings, destroy trust and cause problems.

6. ADVANTAGES AND DISADVANTAGES OF INCENTIVE SCHEMES

Advantages

a. Increases production thereby increasing wages but also reducing overheads per unit, particularly where there are substantial fixed overheads.

b. May enable firm to remain competitive in inflationary conditions.

c. May improve morale by ensuring that extra effort is rewarded.

d. More efficient workers may be attracted by the opportunity to earn higher wages.

Disadvantages

a. Frequently there are problems in establishing performance levels and rates with frequent and continuing disputes.

b. Some incentive schemes are complex and expensive to administer.

c. Some groups of workers, although relatively unskilled, may earn high wages through incentive schemes while others engaged on skilled work may become resentful when differentials are eroded.

7. INDIVIDUAL INCENTIVE SCHEMES

In general incentive schemes which relate to an individual worker seem to be the more usual and successful, probably because of the immediacy and direct relationship between effort and reward. The following are typical examples.

8. STRAIGHT PIECEWORK

At its most basic the worker would be paid an agreed rate per unit for the number of units produced. On occasions the number of operations would be the basis of payment or, where various types of articles are produced, a piecework time allowance per article would be sent and the worker paid for the piecework hours produced. For example, assume the data in the following Figure 7.1:

Note:
It will be seen that the piecework time produced is not equivalent to actual clock hours. Piecework time allowances are merely a device for measuring the work content of dissimilar items.

Rarely, if ever, is piecework found on its own. Usually it is accompanied by certain safeguards, typical of which are: Guaranteed day rates and in lieu bonuses.

a. *Piecework with guaranteed day rates*. If earnings from piecework fall below normal day rates then there is a guarantee that day rates would be paid.

FIGURE 7.1 Example data

Week No.

    37

Employee No.

    58107

Clock hours

    40

Output

    300 units of A. Piecework time allowance 1.8 mins/unit

    150 units of B. Piecework time allowance 1.5 mins/unit

    100 units of C. Piecework time allowance 2.2 mins/unit

Piecework rate

    20p per minute produced

Total production

    = (300 x 1.8) + (150 x 1.5) + (100 x 2.2) piecework minutes

    = 985 piecework minutes

Gross wages

    = 985 x 20p

    = £197

This is to safeguard earnings when there are delays, shortages, tool breakages, etc which make it impossible for the employee to earn bonus pay.

b. *In lieu bonuses*. Where a worker is normally covered by an incentive scheme and is transferred to ordinary day work, frequently an in lieu bonus is paid on top of normal day rates. Such a bonus is often paid to support workers (fork lift truck drivers, labourers, etc) whose work is not amenable to the incentive scheme used for the rest of the factory.

9. DIFFERENTIAL PIECEWORK

One objection to straight piecework systems is that, because a flat rate per unit is paid, the incentive effect at higher production levels declines. Differential piecework seeks to overcome this by increasing the rate progressively at various production levels, eg:

up to 100 units per day	10p/unit
101–150 units per day	12p/unit
151–200 units per day	15p/unit

Differential piecework would, of course, normally be accompanied by the usual safeguards of guaranteed day rates or in lieu bonuses.

Note:
On occasions in differential schemes the whole of the output is paid at the higher rate when the next production threshold is reached.

10. GROUP INCENTIVE SCHEMES

Although individually based incentive schemes are common and frequently successful, on occasions they are inappropriate and some form of group scheme is used. These schemes are likely to be more appropriate.

a. Where production is based on a group or gang basis, eg road surfacing, coal mining.

b. Where production is integrated and all efforts are directed toward the same end, eg all forms of production line manufacture, cars, domestic appliances, etc.

c. Where the production methods or product makes it infeasible to measure individual performance.

Any of the incentive methods (piecework, differential piecework, premium bonus systems, etc) can be used, with appropriate adaption, for group scheme. In addition because of the wider scope of a group scheme, incentives based on cost savings, delivery dates, quality norms are also used.

Apart from the choice of the incentive scheme there is the problem of how to share the bonus among the group. Whatever method is used, it must have the full agreement of the group and unions involved.

11. ADVANTAGES AND DISADVANTAGES OF GROUP SCHEMES

Advantages

a. May engender closer cooperation in the group and a team spirit.

b. Administratively simpler with far less recording of labour times, production rates, etc.

c. Support workers not directly associated with production can easily be included in the scheme.

d. Greatly reduces the number of rates to be negotiated.

e. May encourage more flexible working arrangements within the group.

Disadvantages

a. Less direct than individual schemes so may not provide the same incentive.

b. Less hardworking members of a group receive the same bonus and this may cause friction.

c. Not always easy to obtain agreement on proportions of the bonus which group members will receive.

12. INCENTIVE SCHEMES IN PRACTICE

A significant proportion of production workers are paid under some form of incentive or bonus scheme and there is no doubt that some schemes are extremely effective. Many others are not and recognition of some of the following problems will help to ensure a workable and efficient scheme.

a. An incentive scheme will not solve the problems of badly managed, poorly organised, ill-equipped factories or offices.

b. To ensure only good production is paid for, sound quality control and inspection procedures are vital.

c. All incentive schemes should be based on efficient working methods following comprehensive work studies. Notwithstanding this, it should be recognised that rate fixing is a subjective process which will only be finalised after employer/employee/union negotiations.

d. Care should be taken not to enter into sham productivity deals, ie where pay increases have been granted involving increased productivity which does not materialise.

13. PROFIT SHARING

Although this would not normally be classed as an incentive scheme, profit sharing is part of the package of benefits that an employee could receive. It can be defined as the payment to employees of a proportion of company profits. The amount received by individuals is usually related to their salary or wage level and the profit share may be given in cash or in shares of the company. In the latter case the system becomes a form of co-ownership. In most organisations profit sharing appears to be regarded as a welcome but minor bonus. However, in certain sectors of banking and financial services, profit sharing results in huge bonuses which are larger than the employees' normal salaries.

14. TRENDS IN LABOUR COSTING

In the past labour costs were a major proportion of total cost. This meant that it was worthwhile carrying out a thorough analysis of labour costs and making the necessary detailed accounting entries.

The position today is very different. Factories are highly automated and labour is a small (and reducing) proportion of total cost.

In these circumstances simpler costing systems are being used for labour with some companies eliminating direct labour accounting completely. For example, Hewlett Packard in both their US and UK factories now treat labour as part of overheads and not as a separate item of cost. This means that there are now only two elements in product costs; materials and overheads.

15. SUMMARY

a. There is a trend away from direct incentive schemes to measured day work, particularly for the larger companies.

b. In addition to a basic time based system there are high day rate or measured day work systems which aim to attract good workers by paying above average rates for above average performance.

c. Incentive schemes seek to increase production and should be, as far as possible; simple, directly related to performance, paid promptly, installed after full consultation, reasonably permanent.

d. Straight piecework pays a fixed rate per unit, whereas differential piecework pays extra amounts per unit above certain quantities; the aim being to provide greater incentive to higher output.

e. Group incentive schemes may use any of the incentive methods (piecework, premium bonus, etc) and are most suitable where a cooperative team effort is required.

f. Any form of incentive scheme must be based on proper work organisation, sound quality control and proper consultation.

g. Profit sharing may be by cash payout or share distribution. Frequently it is considered too remote to have any direct incentive effect.

h. In today's highly automated factories labour is a small and reducing element of cost. As a consequence labour costing is becoming less important and in some cases labour is not costed separately but is treated as part of overheads.

16. POINTS TO NOTE

a. Incentive schemes may increase the labour cost per unit but as long as the reduction in overhead cost per unit is sufficient, the scheme should be worthwhile.

b. Incentive schemes are not only applicable to manufacturing. The Government is attempting to introduce 'Performance Related Pay' across the Public Sector. Civil servants, local government officials, teachers and others are being targeted.

c. It is common costing practice to charge overtime wages above basic rate to overheads rather than direct wages. For example, if the basic rate is £12 per hour and overtime is paid at 'time and a quarter' then £12 per hour would be charged to direct wages and £3 per hour charged to overheads. The reasons for this is that it is generally fortuitous which particular job is done during overtime hours and which is done during normal hours and so it would be unjust to penalise the job which happened to be done during overtime.

There are circumstances where this practice is not adopted and where all wages, including the overtime premium, would be charged to direct wages. Examples include: process industries where there is continuous production of identical units and situations where overtime is worked at the request of a customer to bring forward a delivery date and the total wages can be charged to the job.

d. As production becomes more planned and organised and stocks are reduced or eliminated, as in JIT systems, direct incentive schemes become less appropriate. The main requirements for incentive schemes; repetitive production for stock, output individually determined and so on, run directly counter to the newer manufacturing philosophies.

e. Incentive schemes are widely encountered in the service sector. Examples include: commission on sales made for all types of representatives and sales assistants, fees and commissions for insurance and estate agents and so on. In some service sectors, eg home improvement selling, incomes are wholly related to sales made with no fixed element of remuneration.

f. Labour costs must not be considered in isolation. Productivity is all important. If high wage employees produce high volumes of quality products which have a ready market then the firm will be successful. Low wage levels with low productivity are no solution.

Student self-testing

Exercises (answers below)

1. Draw a graph showing the earnings per hour, for an output range of 0–400 units per hour if the worker is paid under the following wage systems:

    a. Daywork at £4 per hour

    b. Straight piecework at 2p per unit

    c. Differential piecework at 2p per unit from 0–200 units, 2.5p per unit for 201 to 250 units, 2.75p per unit for 251 to 300 units and 3p per unit for all units above 301.

2. A new incentive scheme has recently been introduced and the first period's results have been analysed. After studying the results the Managing Director has said that although he was pleased to see the increase in production he was disturbed to see that the average labour cost per unit had risen. In view of this it was his opinion that the scheme should be discontinued. You are required to reply to the Managing Director's comments.

3. A worker is paid by differential piecework. The scheme is as follows:

    | up to 50 | units per day | 50p per unit |
    | 51–70 | units per day | 60p per unit |
    | 71–80 | units per day | 65p per unit |
    | 81–100 | units per day | 70p per unit |

    His daily outputs for a five day week were 68 units, 83 units, 59 units, 94 units and 47 units. What will be his gross pay for the week?

Solutions to exercises

1. Graph of Earnings Per Hour

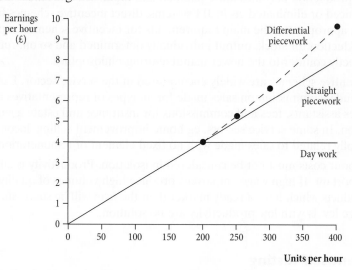

2. It is not uncommon for unit labour costs to rise on the introduction of an incentive scheme but this is not the major objective of such schemes. The main purpose of incentive schemes is to increase production (which has occurred in this case) so that the average overhead cost per unit falls. If the reduction in overhead cost per unit is greater than the increase in labour cost per unit then the scheme will be worthwhile.

3.

		£
DAY 1 68 units £(50 × .5) + (18 × .6)	=	35.80
DAY 2 83 units £(50 × .5) + (20 × .6) + (10 × .65) + (3 × .7)	=	45.60
DAY 3 59 units £(50 × .5) + (9 × .6)	=	30.40
DAY 4 94 units £(50 × .5) + (20 × .6) + (10 × .65) + (14 × .7)	=	53.30
DAY 5 47 units £(47 × .5)	=	23.50
		£188.60

8

Labour: Recording, costing and allied procedures

1. OBJECTIVES

After studying this chapter you will

● Be able to describe Time sheets, Job and Operation Cards

● Know the main steps in Wage procedures

● Understand the factors which determine wages

● Be able to describe Job Evaluation and Merit Rating

● Understand the key functions of Personnel or Human Resources Departments

● Be able to calculate Labour Turnover.

2. THE NECESSARY RECORDS

In most manufacturing companies and for many in the service sector, records of attendance time for each worker are required whatever the system of remuneration. In addition, if an incentive scheme is used, records may be required for operations, processes parts, times, quantities, sales made, enquiries handled or whatever is used as the basis for the incentive scheme.

These records form the basis of wage calculations and for such cost accounting data as: direct and indirect labour costs, overhead build-up, labour cost control. In many cases nowadays the recording is done electronically and not by using traditional forms and paperwork. The recording may be done by entries on terminals, automatic counting or weighing or by various forms of scanning using bar codes. Whatever the recording methods used the principles and objectives remain the same.

The two types of records: those for attendance and those for output are described below.

3. ATTENDANCE RECORDS

In all but the very smallest concerns this is done by the use of clock cards, one for each worker, and a time recording clock usually based at the entrance to the premises. The clock card is the basis of time recording and whatever additional time records are kept, they must be reconciled with the total attendance time recorded on the clock card by the time recording clock.

With the increased use of technology more and more recording systems are now electronic instead of mechanical but, of course, have similar objectives. Typically, electronic systems are based on the use of plastic cards with magnetic strips (akin to credit cards) which are issued to employees. Often these are known as 'swipe' cards. Electronic systems are more flexible and are almost essential where there is *flexible-time working*. This is where an employee is required to attend for a minimum number of hours each day – often within specified hours – but outside of this they may work at times to suit themselves provided they accumulate the agreed number of hours per period. Obviously, flexible-time working is more suited to clerical and administrative staff rather than production workers.

4. OUTPUT RECORDS

The records necessary must be tailored to the requirement of incentive and labour cost control systems in operation. Unnecessary recording incurs extra clerical costs and may slow down production and should be avoided. The following are typical records found in many manufacturing companies: daily and weekly time sheets, job cards, operation cards.

5. DAILY AND WEEKLY TIME SHEETS

These are records, filled in by the worker and countersigned, which show how he spent his time during the day or week. The general objective is to reconcile all the time in attendance (recorded on the clock card) with time bookings either to jobs or operations, ie direct wages, or to non-productive attendance such as a machine breakdown which would be analysed by the cost department as indirect wages.

Weekly times sheets tend to be less accurate but require less clerical effort. It really depends on whether the worker deals with numbers of small jobs, when daily time sheets would be preferred, or is employed on jobs which last a considerable time when weekly sheets may be adequate.

A typical time sheet is shown in Figure 8.1.

6. JOB CARDS

Unlike time sheets which relate to individual employees and may contain bookings relating to numerous jobs, a job card relates to a single job or batch and is likely to contain entries relating to numerous employees.

FIGURE 8.1 Time sheet

Time Sheet No.							
Enployee Name .... Clock Code .... Dept.							
Date .... Week No.							

Job No.	Start Time	Finish Time	Qty	Checker	Hrs	Rate	Extension

Analysis
Direct:
Job Nos.   £
_____   _____
_____   _____
_____   _____

Indirect:
Codes No.   £
_____   _____
Foreman's Signature   _____   _____
_____   _____

Date ....

On completion of the job it will contain a full record of the times and quantities involved in the job or batch. The use of job cards, particularly for jobs which stretch over several weeks, makes reconciliation of work time and attendance time a difficult task. These cards are difficult to incorporate directly into the wages calculation procedures.

7. OPERATION CARDS

These cards, sometimes known as piecework tickets, are provided for each operation or stage of manufacture so that each operation will have at least one card. In this way a job will have a number of operation cards and although this increases the paperwork, it does enable the operation cards to be used directly in the wage calculation procedures. A typical operation card is shown in Figure 8.2.

8. WAGES PROCEDURES

The flowchart (Figure 8.3) shows in outline a typical wages procedure from the original clock card to basic cost accounting entries.

FIGURE 8.2 Operations card (or piecework ticket)

Operation Card				

Operator's Name .... Total Batch Quantity ....

Clock No .... Start Time ....

Pay Week No. .... Date .... Stop Time ....

Part No. .... Works Order No. ....

Operation .... Special Instructions ....

Quantity Produced	No. Rejected	Good Production	Rate	£

Inspector .... Operative ....

Foreman .... Date ....

Production cannot be claimed without a properly signed card

9. LABOUR COSTING

Using job cards and/or time sheets and/or output records and the payroll, the cost department carries out a detailed analysis of all wages paid to enable the labour costs for products, operations, jobs, cost centres and departments to be established. This is done for cost ascertainment and cost control purposes. Features of various aspects of labour costing are dealt with next.

a. *Direct Wages.* That proportion of the wages of production employees directly attributable to production (ie, as ascertained from job cards and/ or time sheets) is charged to the job or operation in which engaged and the total of direct wages for the period is charged to a departmental Work-in-Progress control A/c.

Direct wages would normally exclude overtime and shift premiums. The reason for this is that such premiums, if classed as direct, would be charged only against the job(s) done during the overtime period which is unjust because it is fortuitous which jobs are done during ordinary or overtime.

In addition to employees' National Insurance (NI), UK employers have to pay to the government additional NI contributions based on the gross wages and salaries of their employees. Some employers treat these NI contributions as a direct cost and add the employer's NI to direct wages before these wages are charged to the tasks completed. Others treat the employer's NI as an indirect cost which is then included in overheads.

FIGURE 8.3 Flowchart of typical wage procedures

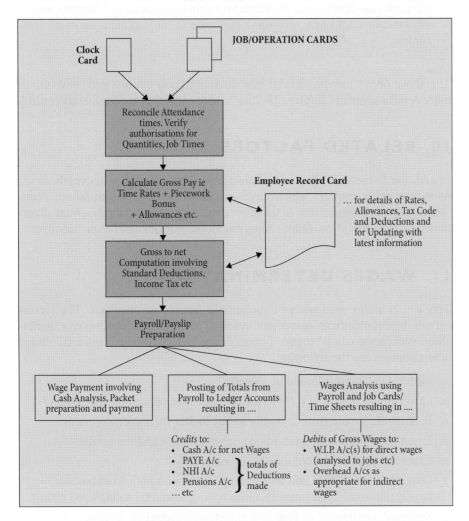

b. *Indirect wages.* The wages of such people as inspectors, stores assistants, clerks and labourers would be coded to the appropriate department to form part of the overheads of that department. In addition, the proportion of production workers' wages which cannot be classed as direct, eg idle time, overtime and shift premium would also be classified as indirect, included in overheads and subsequently absorbed into production costs via the appropriate overhead absorption rates as described in Chapter 9.

c. *Labour cost control.* The cost department activities described above provide the raw data for cost ascertainment and also for cost control purposes. Cost control at its simplest will show various comparisons, for example, direct and indirect wages, suitably analysed, compared with the same classifications for the last period for each cost centre and department and will also show various ratios. The simplest of these would be the ratio of direct to indirect wages, compared period by period for each cost centre and department. In this way trends of labour costs will be shown and may give some guidance to management on cost control.

Note:
The above points are only a brief introduction to cost control and substantially more detail is given in Chapters 23–25 on standard costing and budgetary control.

10. RELATED FACTORS

In addition to the recording and costing procedures described above, there are numerous other matters which have an impact on labour and labour costs. Some of the more important of these are dealt with below, namely – wage determination, job evaluation, merit rating, personnel policies and labour turnover.

11. WAGES DETERMINATION

This is a complex area where innumerable factors are involved. The factors vary in importance from one organisation to another and no simplistic, generalised statements can be made. Typical of the factors to be considered in wage determination are the following.

a. General economic climate of industry.

b. Government policy, ie is there a wages norm or official income policy?

c. Profitability of the firm. Is it able to pay higher than average wages?

d. Extent of unionisation and union strength locally and nationally.

e. Extent of unemployment locally and nationally.

f. Cost structure of firm and industry, eg a firm with high fixed costs of largely automatic plant may be more willing to accede to high pay claims.

g. Strategic importance of firm and industry, eg electricity industry.

h. Availability of workers with appropriate skills.

i. Extent of hazardous or dangerous working conditions.

j. Wage rates prevailing locally and nationally.

k. The productivity of the firm.

12. JOB EVALUATION

This is a technique which seeks to show in a reasonably objective manner the relative worth of jobs. It attempts to do this by analysing the content of each job under various categories, eg Training required, Degree of responsibility, Working conditions, Types of decisions involved and so on, and giving a points score for each factor. The total of the points' scores for each job is then used to establish the ranking of one job to another and, by reference to pay scales, the normal salary for the job.

Advantages

a. Makes an attempt to be objective in ranking jobs.

b. Reasonably effective within an organisation at ranking jobs, particularly relatively low level ones.

Disadvantages

a. Not suitable for ranking widely different jobs, particularly in different organisations.

b. Gives a spurious air of objectivity to job comparison. The Job Evaluation process itself contains many subjective elements.

Notes:

a. Job Evaluation studies the job not the person doing the job.

b. Job Evaluation is only one factor among many in determining the actual pay for the job.

13. MERIT RATING

Unlike job evaluation, merit rating is concerned with the individual employee. It seeks to rate an employee's performance to assist in determining whether a person should receive a merit award, promotion, demotion, etc. It does this by considering the performance and attributes of an employee under various categories, for example, initiative, attendance, accuracy, willingness, etc, etc and giving a number of points for each factor. Merit rating under various guises is frequently encountered in staff appraisal schemes, particularly in larger firms, and is considered to be of value in providing a reasonably standardised basis to the difficult task of individual appraisal.

14. THE PERSONNEL FUNCTION

Most firms of any size have a Personnel department, often called the Human Resources Department, which has responsibilities for numerous tasks concerned with the employees of the organisations. These include:

a. Advertising, recruiting and engaging labour.

b. Discharge, transfer, administration of appraisal schemes.

c. Industrial relations and union negotiations.

d. Maintenance of personnel records and provision of statistical information to Government Departments, Trade Associations, etc.

e. Provisions of information to management on such matters as absenteeism, lateness, labour turnover, normal and overtime worked, etc.

f. Staff development, training and educational schemes, including day release, apprenticeships and courses.

g. Welfare, sports and social facilities.

h. Safety and medical facilities.

i. Manpower planning and forecasting.

In general terms the Personnel function has the responsibility of providing an efficient labour force which is cost effective and keeping labour turnover to a minimum.

15. LABOUR TURNOVER

This is usually expressed as a ratio, ie

$$\frac{\text{Number of employees replaced per period}}{\text{Average total number of employees in the period}}$$

Although some labour movement is of value, high labour turnover rates destroy morale, increase costs and reduce productivity. People leave jobs for a variety of reasons, some of which are avoidable, and it is normal to analyse the reasons for leaving so as to take corrective action where possible. Typical of the reasons for labour turnover are the following:

a. Redundancy.

b. Dissatisfaction over prospects, pay, hours, conditions.

c. Lack of career structure.

d. Lack of training or day release.

e. Personal advancement.

f. Marriage, pregnancy.

g. Retirement.

h. Discharge.

i. Move from locality.

j. Changes in domestic circumstances.

16. COST OF LABOUR TURNOVER

These costs can be substantial, yet to some extent are avoidable through enlightened personnel policies and good management. The costs arise in the following areas:

a. Leaving costs, ie interviews, preparation of documentation, disruption of output.

b. Replacement costs, ie advertising, selection, personnel department procedures.

c. Training costs, ie costs of required internal and external courses.

d. Learning costs, ie slower initial production, increased scrap, tool breakages, increased accident rate, poorer service.

17. SUMMARY

a. Attendance records, often in the form of clock cards, are normally required.

b. Where incentive schemes are in operation, output records either by time sheets, job cards or piecework tickets are required.

c. Whether the recording of times, output, etc is made electronically or by using traditional paperwork the principles remain the same.

d. The main elements in the wages procedure are: time reconciliation, gross pay calculation, gross to net calculation, payroll and payslip preparation, wage payment.

e. The total of gross wages is charged to Work-in-Progress A/cs for direct wages and Overhead A/cs for indirect.

f. Overtime and shift premiums are generally classed as indirect and form part of production overheads.

g. Numerous factors determine the level of wages paid including: national and local rates, cost of living, prosperity of industry, union strength and militancy, working conditions, etc.

h. Job evaluation seeks to analyse the content of each job under various factors so as to establish the relative worth of one job to another.

i. Merit rating seeks to assess the efficiency of an individual for the purpose of bonuses, promotion, etc.

j. The personnel function is wide ranging and important and includes: engaging and discharging employees, union negotiations, staff development and training, welfare and safety.

k. Labour turnover should be monitored closely and the reasons for each employee leaving ascertained.

l. The costs of labour turnover can be high and include: engaging new labour, learning costs, training costs, lower initial productivity.

18. POINTS TO NOTE

a. Every aspect of labour relations can be critical and affect costs. The old 'scientific management' approach to labour as merely an adjunct to machinery is outmoded in modern conditions.

b. Although the principles and objectives are largely unchanged, many of the manual and paperwork procedures described in this chapter are being superseded by electronic systems. The use of computers, videos, magnetic readers, electronic counters, touch terminals and so on is becoming more and more prevalent. In general, such systems are speedier, less error-prone and automatically record processes and transmit information. However, it is worth emphasising that, in general, such systems incorporate identical principles and objectives to manual and paperwork procedures.

Student self-testing

Exercises (answers below)

1. A firm's basic rate is £8 per hour and overtime rates are time and a half for evenings and double time for weekends. The following details have been recorded on three jobs.

	Job X321 Clock Hours	Job X786 Clock Hours	Job X114 Clock Hours
Normal time	480	220	150
Evening time	102	60	80
Weekend	10	30	16

You are required to calculate the labour cost chargeable to each of the jobs in the following circumstances:

a. Where overtime is worked occasionally to meet production requirements.

b. Where the overtime is worked at the customer's request to bring forward the delivery time.

2. In practice it is unlikely that labour time and output records (eg, time sheets, piecework tickets, job cards) are perfectly accurate. Discuss the reasons for this lack of reliability and the implications for the cost accountant.

3. In order to avoid criticism for spending too long on a job some production workers have been incorrectly classifying part of the time spent actually working on jobs as waiting time. What are the implications of this practice?

Solutions to exercises

1. a. Where overtime is worked occasionally it would be normal cost accounting practice to charge the overhead premiums to production overheads and only normal time to the jobs thus:

	Job X321	Job X786	Job X114
Total hours	592	310	246
@ £8 per hour =	£4,736	£2,480	£1,968

b. Where overtime is worked by request all of the wages (including overtime premiums) would be charged to the jobs.
   Effective wage rates per hour:

Normal time	£8
Evenings	£12
Weekends	£16

	Job X321	£	Job X786	£	Job X114	£
Normal time	480 × £8 =	3,840	220 × £8 =	1,760	150 × £8 =	1,200
Evening	102 × £12 =	1,224	60 × £12 =	720	80 × £12 =	960
Weekends	10 × £16 =	160	30 × £16 =	480	16 × £16 =	256
		£5,224		£2,960		£2,416

2. Typical reasons for inaccuracies in labour records (and many other types of data used for cost accounting purposes) are:

   a. Difficulties in completing paperwork in factory conditions – lack of desks, etc.

   b. Inexperience of some production workers in clerical tasks.

   c. Delays in completing paperwork so that data are entered from memory.

   d. Deliberate falsification perhaps to improve bonuses.

   e. Poor form design. *The implications for the cost accountant are:*

      i. Job/process labour costs will be inaccurate.

      ii. The overheads absorbed (if based on labour) will be incorrect.

      iii. Sales prices if cost based will be inaccurate.

      iv. Stock and work-in-progress valuations will be incorrect.

      v. The profit figures shown in costing operating statements will differ from financial accounts based on physical stocktakes.

   f. If standard costing is used variances will be incorrect.

3. If time spent working is classified as waiting time the likely effects are:

   a. The direct costs of a job will be under-recorded.

   b. The amount of overheads will be incorrect.

   c. The amount of overheads absorbed (if based on direct labour) will be incorrect.

   d. If cost based, the job price will be incorrect.

   e. If the times involved are excessive production planning will be rendered more difficult and inaccurate.

9

Overheads

2. OVERHEAD ABSORPTION

This process was introduced in Chapter 2 from which it will be recalled that overhead absorption is the process by which overheads are included in the total cost of a product. The formal definition is:

> *A means of attributing overheads to a product or service based for example, on direct labour hours, direct labour cost or machine hours.*
>
> *Terminology*

Note:
The terminology definition given above relates to the traditional production volume based approach to overhead absorption not to an activity-based approach. The traditional approach is described first in this chapter then the changes necessary to deal with activity-based costing.

Overhead absorption becomes of greater importance when dissimilar products are made which require different production processes or for jobs which, although using identical facilities, occupy the facilities for varying length of time. It is of importance in these circumstances because the overheads absorbed into the product or job should, as far as possible, reflect the load that the product or job places upon the production facilities.

To determine the overhead to be absorbed by a cost unit it is necessary to establish an overhead absorption rate (OAR) which is calculated by using two factors; the overheads attributable to a given cost centre and the number of units of the absorption base (labour hours, machine hours, etc) that is deemed most suitable; thus:

OAR for cost centre

$$= \frac{\text{Total overheads of cost centre}}{\text{Total number of units of absorption base applicable to cost centre}}$$

The total overheads of a cost centre are established by the processes of cost allocation and cost apportionment described in Chapter 2. The various possible absorption bases are described below.

3. BASES OF ABSORPTION

The objective of the overhead absorption process is to include in the total cost of a product or service an appropriate share of the firm's total overheads. An appropriate share is generally taken to mean an amount which reflects the effort and/or time taken to produce a unit or complete a job. In the unlikely event of identical products being produced by identical processes for the whole of a period, the total overheads could be shared equally among the products. Life is rarely so simple and to cope with practical situations various absorption bases have been developed. These bases are illustrated by the following example relating to Production Cost Centre 52.

Data relating to Cost Centre 52 for period 9:	
Total overhead for period	£6,000
Total direct labour hours for period	160
Total direct wages	£1,600
Total direct material used	£3,000
Total machine hours	1,200
Total units produced	45

Using these data the following absorption rates could be calculated using the formula given in Para. 2 above.

Direct Labour hour OAR $= \dfrac{£6,000}{160\,\text{hrs}}$

$= £37.50$ overheads per labour hour

Direct Wages OAR $= \dfrac{£6,000}{£1,600}$

$= £3.75$ overheads per £ of wages or 375% of wages

$$\text{Direct Material OAR} = \frac{£6,000}{£3,000}$$

$$= £2 \text{ overheads per £ of materials or } 200\% \text{ of materials}$$

$$\text{Prime Cost OAR} = \frac{£6,000}{£4,600}$$

$$= £1.30 \text{ overheads per £ of prime cost}$$

$$\text{Machine Hour OAR} = \frac{£6,000}{1,200 \text{ hrs}}$$

$$= £5 \text{ overheads per machine hour}$$

$$\text{Cost Unit OAR} = \frac{£6,000}{45 \text{ units}}$$

$$= £133 \text{ overhead per unit produced}$$

4. USING THE CALCULATED OAR

When it has been decided what is the most appropriate rate to use for a given cost centre, the OAR is used to calculate the cost of a cost unit as in the following example.

A cost unit X has been produced in Cost Centre 52 and the following details recorded:

	Cost Unit X
Direct Materials used	£23
Direct Wages	£27.50
Direct Labour Hours	3
Machine Hours	17

Assuming that it has been decided that the Direct Labour rate is the most appropriate method to use, calculate the cost of the cost unit using the data given above.

	Cost Unit X
Direct Labour	27.50
Direct Materials	23.00
= Prime Cost	50.50
+ Overheads (3 hrs @ Labour Hour OAR of £37.5/hr)	112.50
	£163.00

In practice, as in the above example, the most appropriate OAR for a given cost centre is decided upon and used for all the cost calculations of units passing through that cost centre. Different cost centres may well have different absorption bases and the factors influencing the choice of base are given later in this chapter.

TABLE 9.1 Costs using different absorption bases

Absorption base	Direct labour hour	Direct wages	Direct material	Prime cost	Machine hour	Cost unit
OAR (from para 3)	£37.50 per hour	375% of wages	200% of materials	130% of prime cost	£5 per hour	£133 per unit
Cost Unit X data	3 labour hours	£27.50 wages	£23 materials	£50.50 prime cost	17 machine hours	1 unit
Calculation	3 × £37.50	3.75 × £27.50	2 × £23	1.3 × £50.50	17 × £5	1 × £133
Overhead absorbed by Cost Unit X	£112.50	£103.125	£46	£65.65	£85	£133

For comparative purposes the overheads which would be absorbed by cost unit X using each of the absorption bases is shown in Table 9.1.

Cost Unit X Production Data

Direct Material	£23
Direct Wages	£27.50
Direct Labour hrs	3
Machine Hours	17

Notes:

1. Although each of the bases have been used in the table, this is for illustration only. In practice one base only, that deemed most appropriate, would be used for cost calculations.

2. It will be noted that the various absorption bases produce substantially different amounts of overheads to be absorbed into the cost unit, ranging from £46 to £133.

3. The wide range of overheads possible, as shown above, emphasises the point that there is no such thing as a single, accurate cost. All costs are based on conventions and judgement.

5. CHOOSING THE APPROPRIATE ABSORPTION BASE

The factors to be considered in the choice of an appropriate base are given below, but it must be emphasised that the final choice is a matter of judgement and common sense. There are no absolute rules or formulae. What is required is an absorption basis which realistically reflects the characteristics of a given cost centre and which avoids undue anomalies.

There is general acceptance that the time based methods (Labour Hours, Machine Hours and to a lesser extent Direct Wages) are more likely to reflect the load on a cost centre and hence the incidence of overheads and so students are recommended to choose one of these methods unless there are special factors involved.

- *Direct labour hour basis*
  Most appropriate in a labour intensive cost centre and, providing the time booking system is good, easy to use. However, most production nowadays

involves substantial use of machinery so the Labour Hour method may become increasingly inappropriate.

- *Machine hour basis*

  Most appropriate in a mechanised cost centre. In such a cost centre many of the overheads are related to the machinery (power, repairs, depreciation, etc), so a machine hour rate should reflect fairly accurately the incidence of overheads.

- *Direct wages*

  This is a frequently used rate in practice and is easy to apply. Direct wages paid are related to time, but because of varying rates paid to different personnel, piecework and bonus systems, there is not an exact correlation between wages paid and time elapsed. If there was only one rate per hour paid throughout a cost centre and no form of incentive scheme, then the Direct Wages system would give identical results to the Labour Hour basis, but this is rarely the case.

- *Direct material*

  This method has little to commend and if used could lead to absurd anomalies. For example, if an identical blanking process utilised either mild steel or stainless steel sheet and the stainless was five times the price of the ordinary steel, the Direct Material Absorption method would load the stainless product with five times the overhead, even though it was produced by an identical process taking identical time.

- *Prime cost*

  Although part of Prime Cost is time related (direct wages), the inclusion of the direct material element would lead to possible anomalies as outlined above and accordingly its use is not recommended.

- *Cost unit*

  Providing all the units produced in a period were identical with identical production processes and times, then this absorption method would give accurate results. However, such circumstances are unlikely, so the times when this method can be used are very rare.

6. PREDETERMINED ABSORPTION RATES

It will be recalled from the formal definition of overhead absorption given in Para. 2 that in most cases the rates are predetermined. This simply means that the overhead absorption rate (OAR) is calculated prior to the accounting period, using estimated or budgeted figures for overheads and units of the absorption base chosen. Thus the general formula given in Para. 2 becomes

Predetermined OAR for cost centre

$$= \frac{\text{Budgeted total overheads for cost centre}}{\text{Budgeted total number of units of absorption base}}$$

The major reason for this procedure is that the actual overheads and actual number of base units are not known in total until the end of the period and the actual OAR could not be calculated until then. This would mean that product costs could not be calculated until the end of a period and clearly this would introduce unacceptable delays into such procedures as invoicing and

TABLE 9.2

Cost Centre 52 Data for Period 9		
	Budgeted	**Actual**
Overheads	£6,000	£6,312
Direct Labour Hours	160	158
Direct Wages	£1,600	£1,705
Direct Materials	£3,000	£2,947
Machine Hours	1,200	1,172
Unit Produced	45	46

estimating. This is such a major disadvantage that virtually all absorption rates used are predetermined.

7. UNDER OR OVER ABSORPTION

Using predetermined rates, overheads are absorbed into actual production throughout the accounting period. Because the predetermined rates are based on estimated production and estimated overheads, invariably, the overheads absorbed by this process do not agree with the actual overheads incurred for the period.

If the overheads absorbed are *greater* than actual overheads, this is known as *over absorption*. Conversely, if absorbed overheads are *less* than actual overheads, this is known as *under absorption*. The following example shows how to calculate the amount of overheads under or over absorbed.

Assume that the data given on Para. 3 were budgeted figures and that the actual production, overheads and other data were as shown in Table 9.2.

The predetermined overhead absorption rate for direct labour hours (which, it will be recalled, was judged the most appropriate for cost centre 52) was £37. 5 per hour.

Total overheads absorbed by actual activity of 158 labour hours = 158×37.5 = £5,925 overheads absorbed into production, but actual overheads were £6,312 thus in this example overheads were *under absorbed*.

$$\therefore \text{Under absorbed overheads} = £6,312 - 5,925$$
$$= \textbf{£387}$$

Note:
It will be observed that under (or over) absorption can arise from either actual overheads differing from budget or a difference between the actual and budgeted amount of the absorption base or a combination of these two factors.

8. DEALING WITH UNDER AND OVER ABSORPTION

The budgeted figures used for calculating the predetermined OARs are based on expected levels of production and overhead. There are many factors which cause actual results to differ from those expected and it must be realised that it is *actual costs and overheads* which determine the final profit. This means that the total of actual costs must appear in the final profit and loss account and not merely those calculated product costs which include actual prime cost plus overheads based on a predetermined OAR.

Accordingly, the amount of under absorbed overheads should be *added* to total costs before the profit is calculated and conversely the amount of over absorbed overheads should be *subtracted* from total cost.

This is now illustrated using the data from the previous paragraph relating to cost centre 52.

Actual direct material		Actual direct labour		Actual prime cost		Absorbed overheads		Calculated production cost		Under absorption		Total production cost
£2,947	+	£1,705	=	£4,652	+	£5,925	=	£10,577	+	£387	=	£10,964

P&L A/c

Notes:
a. The actual direct costs for each cost unit would of course be immediately available from the labour and material booking system for the job card.

b. The under (or over) absorption of overheads can only be established at the end of the period when actual activity or production and actual overheads are known.

c. Although eventually appearing in a Profit and Loss account or Operating Statement, the under or over absorption is sometimes put to a monthly suspense account as an intermediate stage and the net balance taken to P & L at the year end.

9. ABSORBING NON-PRODUCTION OVERHEADS

The examples of absorption bases given in the preceding paragraphs relate to production overheads. However, a significant proportion of the overheads of a typical company are non-production overheads, eg Selling and Marketing Overheads, Research and Development Overheads, Distribution Overheads, Administrative Overheads etc. These overheads also form part of the total cost of a cost unit and have to be absorbed or charged to Profit and Loss account in some fashion.

Although the absorption bases for production overheads appear to have some rationale, the methods in common use for non-production overheads unfortunately are somewhat arbitrary. The different methods used are given below, but it must be emphasised that provided a given method is used consistently by an organisation, the choice between the methods is probably not important except where costs are used as the basis of pricing. In such cases the choice of method may be very important.

Notes:
1. Conversion cost is Production cost less the cost of direct materials ie, the cost of converting materials into products.

TABLE 9.3 Typical absorption bases for non-production overheads

Types of overhead	Absorption base(s) used
Selling and Marketing	Sales value or Production cost
Research and Development	Production cost or Conversion cost or Added value
Distribution	Production cost or Sales value
Administration	Production cost or Conversion cost or Added value

2. Added value is the sales value of a product less the cost of bought out materials and services. Unlike conversion cost added value includes profit.

3. Many variations exist in practice in dealing with non-production overheads and frequently firms charge particular categories of overheads directly to the P & L A/c and do not attempt the somewhat arbitrary process of absorption. A typical example is that of Research and Development overheads.

In each case, if an absorption rate is required, the calculation would follow the pattern for predetermined OARs given in Para. 6. As an example assume that it is required to calculate an OAR for Selling and Marketing overheads and it is company policy to use Sales Value as an absorption base. The following estimated figures have been established for the period:

Estimated Selling and Marketing overheads   £25,000

Estimated total Sales Value   £280,000

$$\text{Selling and Marketing predetermined OAR} = \frac{\text{Estimated overheads}}{\text{Estimated sales value}}$$
$$= \frac{£25,000}{£280,000}$$
$$= 9\% \text{ of Sales Value.}$$

10. ABSORPTION COSTING

The process described in this chapter by which total overheads are absorbed into production naturally enough is known as *absorption costing*. The absorption of total overheads into product costs has implications for performance measurement, cost control and stock valuation and students should be aware that the process described is subject to criticism by some managers and accountants.

The criticism arises from the fact that overheads contain items, known as *fixed costs* – which do not change when the activity level changes and which would still have to be paid if there was no activity, eg rates – and items, known as *variable* costs, which vary more or less directly with activity, eg power consumption. To overcome some of the difficulties, an alternative method of costing has been developed, known as *marginal costing*, which, although using the process of absorption, excludes fixed costs from the absorption process. The explanation of fixed and variable costs and marginal costing is developed further in Chapter 19.

FIGURE 9.1 The conventional build-up of overheads

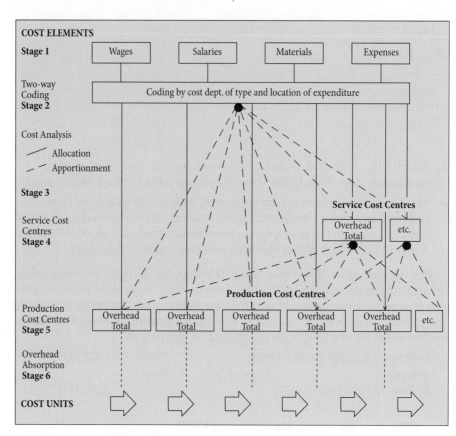

Figure 9.1 summarises the conventional method of establishing overheads and how these overheads are absorbed into production. The diagram should be studied together with the following notes.

Notes on Figure 9.1:

Stage 1 *Cost elements*

The raw data relating to Labour, Materials, Expenses are gathered from Invoices, Payroll, Goods Issued Notes and Requisitions.

Stage 2 *Coding*

All the raw cost data needs to be classified and then coded in respect of the type of expense and location. This process is fundamental to all the costing and management accounting procedures.

Stage 3 *Cost analysis*

Where discrete items of cost can be allotted to cost centres this is termed *allocation*. Where the cost has to be spread or shared over several cost centres this is known as *apportionment*. The bases of apportionment were discussed in Chapter 2.

Stage 4 *Service cost centres*

These are cost centres which provide a service to production cost centres. Examples are Maintenance, Stores and Boiler House. Their costs are built up by the usual process of allocation and primary apportionment and then their total costs are apportioned (secondary apportionment) over the production cost centres, thus forming part of production overheads which are absorbed into the cost units produced. The problems of service cost centres are dealt with in more detail below.

Stage 5 *Production cost centres*

These are the cost centres involved directly in the production process. Typical examples are, the Assembly shop, Drilling machines, Centre lathes, Spray shop.

Stage 6 *Overhead absorption*

The overheads of each production cost centre are absorbed into the costs of the units produced, usually in proportion to the time involved, ie by the Labour Hour or Machine Hour rate.

11. SERVICE COST CENTRES

Because no production cost units pass through the service cost centres, it is necessary to apportion the service department costs to the production cost centres so that all production costs (including those for the servicing departments) are absorbed into production. Typical bases for secondary apportionment, ie the apportionment of service costs to production departments are given as follows.

Service Dept.	Possible bases of Apportionment to Production Cost Centres
Maintenance	Maintenance Labour Hours
	Maintenance Wages
	Plant values
Stores	No. of Requisitions
	Weight of Materials issued
Inspection	No. of Production Employees per cost centre
	No. of Inspection Tickets
	No. of Jobs
Production Control	No. of Production Employees per cost centre
	No. of Jobs
Power Generation	Metered Usage
	Notional Capacity
	Technical Estimate
Personnel Dept.	No. of Employees per Department

Notes:

a. The basis chosen should be one that is judged to be the most equitable way of sharing the service department's costs over the departments which use the service. This may mean that a particular and unique basis of apportionment may have to be derived. It must reflect the use made of the services provided.

b. Wherever possible, service department costs should be charged directly, ie allocated. An example of this would be maintenance wages and materials. When a maintenance job is done for a department, the wages and materials used would be charged directly to the department concerned. In this way only unallocated service department costs need to be apportioned.

12. APPORTIONMENT AND ABSORPTION EXAMPLE

To illustrate and consolidate the material covered so far an example follows which shows the build-up of overheads from basic data and the calculation of suitable overhead absorption rates.

Example

Prepare an overhead analysis using the following data and calculate suitable overhead absorption rates for the Milling, Assembly and Spraying departments. The data relate to one accounting period.

	Basic data					
	Production cost centres			**Service cost centres**		
	Milling	**Assembly**	**Spraying**	**Stores**	**Maintenance**	**Totals**
No of employess	30	75	25	6	14	150
Labour hours	1,510	3,320	950	252	595	6,627
Plant and mach'y values	£225,000	£75,000	£45,000	£17,000	£85,000	£447,000
Area (m²)	7,500	10,000	3,500	500	1,000	22,500
Material requisitions	1,400	300	250		550	2,500
Maint'ce hrs (minor work)	75	30	45			150
KWH ('000)	300	70	50	10	170	600
Machine hours	8,400	1,100	300			9,800
During the period the following data were recorded:						
Indirect materials	£2,500	£1,000	£1,500	£300	£1,700	£7,000
Indirect labour	£5,250	£2,500	£2,250	£4,250	£11,750	£26,000
Major maintenance work	£18,500	£7,500	£4,500			£30,500

The following details were obtained from the accounts relating to the period.

	£
Fire Insurance	1,250
Power	4,500
Heating and Lighting	2,000
Rates	1,800
Machine depreciation	8,400
Machine insurance	850
Canteen deficit	4,250
Balance of maintenance costs (excl. major works)	17,500

Solution
Notes (to following table)

1. All apportionments follow a similar principle. For example, the total Fire and Machine Insurance of £2,100 is divided by the total plant value of £447,000 which is then multiplied, in turn, by the value of the plant in each cost centre.

2. The secondary apportionment is carried out using a net plant value of £345,000, ie less the values in stores and maintenance.

3. The additional complications which can arise with Service Depts. are dealt with below.

4. Maintenance is apportioned on Plant Values because maintenance hours are not available for the service CCs which naturally must have some maintenance.

Overhead Analysis

Overhead item	Apportionment basis	Totals £	Milling £	Assembly £	Spraying £	Stores £	Maintenance £
			Production Cost Centres			**Service Cost Centres**	
Allocated items							
Indirect material		7,000	2,500	1,000	1,500	300	1,700
Indirect labour		26,000	5,250	2,500	2,250	4,250	11,750
Major maintenance		30,500	18,500	7,500	4,500		
Apportioned items							
Fire and machine insurance	Plant values (1.)	2,100	1,056	353	212	79	400
Power	Kwh	4,500	2,250	525	375	75	1,275
Heating and lighting	Floor area	2,000	667	889	311	44	89
Rates	Floor area	1,800	600	800	280	40	80
Machine depreciation	Plant values	8,400	4,227	1,411	847	316	1,599
Canteen deficit	No of Employees	4,250	850	2,125	708	170	397
Maintenance	Plant values	17,500	8,806	2,940	1,764	658	3,332
	Totals	104,050	44,706	20,043	12,747	5,932	20,622
Secondary apportionment							
Stores	Material requisitions		3,322	712	593	−5,932	1,305
Maintenance	Plant values (2.)		14,300	4,767	2,860		−21,927
Total production dept overheads		104,050	62,328	25,522	16,200		
Overhead absorption basis			Machine hrs	Labour hrs	Labour hrs		
Overhead absorption rates			$\frac{£62,328}{8,400}$	$\frac{£25,522}{3,320}$	$\frac{£16,200}{950}$		
			= £7.42 per mach. hr.	= £7.69 per lab. hr.	= £17.05 per lab. hr.		

13. ESTABLISHING SERVICE DEPARTMENTAL COSTS

The necessity to apportion service costs has been described above. However, before this apportionment takes place, it is necessary to establish the total service department costs. This is discussed below in three differing circumstances: where service departments only do work for other departments and not each other; where some service departments do work for other service departments; and where service departments provide reciprocal services to each other as well as providing a service to production.

14. SERVICES TO NON-SERVICE DEPARTMENTS ONLY

This is the simplest situation and is somewhat unlikely. It is the position illustrated in Figure 9.1 and total service department costs are easily arrived at by the usual process of allocation and primary apportionment from the raw data, ie, Stages 1, 2 and 3 from Figure 9.1.

15. SERVICE DEPARTMENTS WORKING FOR OTHER SERVICE DEPARTMENTS

Where a service department provides a service to another service department, for example stores to maintenance, it is necessary to apportion the providing departments costs *before* that of the receiving department. In the example given, stores costs would be apportioned to maintenance (and appropriate production cost centres), then the maintenance department's costs would be apportioned between the various production cost centres. The reason for this is that the total cost of the maintenance department must include an appropriate charge for stores issue received.

16. RECIPROCAL SERVICES

A particular problem arises where two or more service departments work for each other as well as for production. For example, assume that Maintenance (M) do work for Stores (S) and Stores supply items to Maintenance. The total cost of M cannot be ascertained until the charge for S's service is known, and similarly the total cost of S cannot be found until the charge for M's work is known.

Some way has to be found to break into this circular problem so as to be able to ascertain service department costs. This can be done by three methods; continuous allotment, elimination, and using simultaneous equations. These methods will be illustrated by using the following example:

Example
A small factory has two service departments, Maintenance (M) and Stores (S) and three Production departments (P1, P2, and P3).

The service departments provide services for each other as well as for the Production departments and it has been agreed that the most appropriate bases of apportionment for service department costs are: Capital equipment values for Maintenance and number of requisitions for Stores.

The overheads applicable to each department following allocation and primary apportionment are:

Department	Overheads
M	6,800
S	2,700
P1	12,000
P2	19,500
P3	26,000
Total	£67,000

Data for apportionment of Service Department overheads

	M	S	P1	P2	P3
Capital values	£15,000	£10,000	£50,000	£76,000	£64,000
Proportion	–	5%	25%	38%	32%
No of requisitions	900	–	2,400	1,620	1,080
Proportion	15%	–	40%	27%	18%

The above data are used for each of the solution methods described below.

17. THE CONTINUOUS ALLOTMENT METHOD

The principle involved in this method is that the appropriate proportion of the costs of the first service department are allotted to the second (ie, 5% of M to S), then the appropriate proportion of the second department is allotted back to the first department (ie, 15% of S to M) and so on until the amounts allotted to and fro become insignificant.

This is now shown in the following table.

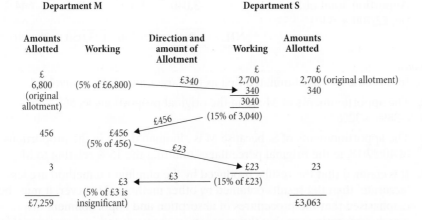

Department M			Department S	
Amounts Allotted	**Working**	**Direction and amount of Allotment**	**Working**	**Amounts Allotted**
£			£	£
6,800 (original allotment)	(5% of £6,800)	£340	2,700	2,700 (original allotment)
			340	340
			3040	
		£456 — (15% of 3,040)		
456	£456			
	(5% of 456)	£23		
3			£23	23
	£3	£3 — (15% of £23)		
	(5% of £3 is			
£7,259	insignificant)			£3,063

The notional service department overheads, ie £7,259 and £3,063 are then used in the secondary apportionment thus:

	Departments				
	M £	**S** £	**P1** £	**P2** £	**P3** £
Original Allotment	6,800	2,700	12,000	19,500	26,000
Notional Overheads for M apportioned over serviced Depts.	−7,259	363	1,815	2,758	2,323
Notional Overheads for S apportioned over serviced Depts.	459	−3,063	1,225	827	552
	NIL	NIL	£15,040	£23,085	£28,875

Note:

Amounts rounded to nearest £.
The final apportioned overheads equal the original total allotments,
ie, £15,040 + 23,085 + 28,875 = £67,000

18. THE ELIMINATION METHOD

This is a simpler method which apportions in turn service department costs to users. Once a service department's costs have been apportioned the department is eliminated from further apportionments. This means that return charges from other service departments do not arise, ie the cost effects of reciprocal servicing is ignored. The sequence in which departments are eliminated can be related to either the amounts involved or the number of departments serviced. The method is illustrated below using the data from Example 1.

	Departments				
	M £	**S** £	**P1** £	**P2** £	**P3** £
Original Allotment	6,800	2,700	12,000	19,500	26,000
Apportion Total of M (ie, £6,800) and eliminate M	−6,800	340	1,700	2,584	2,176
Apportion Total of S (ie, £2,700 + 340)		−3,040	1,430	966	644
	NIL	NIL	£15,130	£23,050	£28,820

Notes:

1. In this case M was eliminated first as the larger amount was involved.

2. The apportionments of M are in the original proportions ie, 5% −25% −38% −32%.

3. The apportionments of S, because M is eliminated, are in the proportions of 40:27:18, ie the original percentages omitting the 15% relating to M.

4. It is claimed that the results produced by the elimination method are less 'accurate' than the results obtained by other methods. However, it must be emphasised that the procedures of absorption and apportionment are merely conventions so that the concepts of accuracy and inaccuracy in this

context have doubtful validity. All that can be said is that the methods produce different results.

19. SIMULTANEOUS EQUATIONS (ALGEBRAIC METHOD)

This method utilises an equation for each service department, (in Example 1, two equations) and solves these equations by the conventional methods, as follows:

Let m = total overheads for maintenance when the stores charges have been allotted

s = total overheads for stores when maintenance charges have been allotted

$$m = 6,800 + 0.15s$$
$$\text{and } s = 2,700 + 0.05m$$

Rearranging these equations we obtain

$$m - 0.15s = 6,800 \ldots \ldots \ldots \text{Equation I}$$
$$\text{and } s - 0.05m = 2,700 \ldots \ldots \ldots \text{Equation II}$$

To solve Equations I and II it is necessary to eliminate one of the unknowns. This can be done in this example by multiplying Equation II by 20 and adding the result to Equation I thus:

$$m - 0.15s = 6,800 \ldots \ldots \ldots \text{Equation 1}$$
$$20s - m = 54,000 \ldots \ldots \ldots 20 \times \text{Equation II}$$
$$19.85s = 60,800$$
$$s = £3,63$$

Substituting the value for s in one of the equations, the value for m can be obtained. Substituting in Equation I

$$m - 0.15(3,063) = 6,800$$
$$m = £7,259$$

Having thus obtained the values for m and s, the secondary apportionment can take place as shown in the last part of Para. 17 above.

Notes:
a. In this case the values obtained for m and s correspond exactly to the values obtained by the continuous allotment method. Sometimes there is a slight discrepancy.
b. Simultaneous equations can also be solved using matrix algebra. This method is dealt with in detail in *Quantitative Techniques*, T. Lucey, Cengage Learning.

20. DEPRECIATION

Most of the items which are classified as overheads, eg rent, rates, indirect labour and materials, office expenses, electricity and heating charges, have their values externally determined; eg the landlord fixes the rent, the local authority the rates and so on. However, a major item of overhead costs, that of depreciation, has its value determined internally and so consideration of the various depreciation methods is essential for accountants. Depreciation can be formally defined as,

> **Depreciation** *Systematic allocation of the depreciable amount of an asset over its useful life (IAS 16) Normally applied to tangible assets.*
>
> *Terminology*

Note:
When intangible assets and goodwill are concerned the process is known as amortisation.

Effectively the conventions of accounting for depreciation spread the cost of a fixed asset over its life and consequently over the production involved. A further difference between depreciation and other overheads such as rates and salaries, is that it is a notional item of expense. For items such as rates, electricity and salaries an actual cash flow takes place. However, for notional items such as depreciation no cash flows occurs, the charge being merely a book-keeping entry. This does not mean that depreciation is unimportant. It would be unrealistic not to include the cost of expensive plant and buildings in the cost of a product or service and depreciation is the most practical way this can be done.

21. DEPRECIATION METHODS

There are numerous systems available each with particular characteristics, but they fall into two categories:

a. Those that are time based.

b. Those that are based on the volume produced or the level of activity.

Whatever method is used, it is necessary to establish the total amount that needs to be charged through depreciation. This amount, termed the 'net asset cost', is calculated as follows:

> Net asset cost = Purchase price + Installation + Delivery costs − Residual value.

Notes:
a. For registered organisations the purchase price is the Invoice value less VAT; for unregistered organisations it is the gross Invoice value.

b. residual value is the amount realised on disposal less disposal costs.

The three most common methods of depreciation are, the Straight Line, Reducing Balance and the Production Unit (or Hour) methods.

22. STRAIGHT LINE DEPRECIATION

This method, sometimes known as the *equal instalment* method, writes down the value of the asset by an equal amount each year. The charge per year is found by the formula:

$$\text{Depreciation charge per year} = \frac{\text{Net asset cost}}{\text{Estimated life in years}}$$

Example

The net asset cost of a power press is £38,000 and it is estimated to have a life of 10 years. What is the depreciation charge per year?

Solution

$$\text{Straight line depreciation p.a.} = \frac{£38,000}{10}$$
$$= £3,800$$

Characteristics

a. Simple to understand and calculate.

b. Charges an equal amount for depreciation over each year of the asset's life.

c. Takes no account of the volume of activity during the year.

d. Although an equal financial amount is charged each year, inflation causes this amount to have a declining impact on real values. In the example above, £3,800 charged in year 10 has only approximately 25% of the real value of the £3,800 charged in the first year, assuming a 15% inflation rate.

e. A time based method.

23. REDUCING BALANCE METHOD (ALTERNATIVELY THE DIMINISHING BALANCE METHOD)

Under this method a fixed percentage of the written down value of the asset is charged as depreciation each year. The effect of this is that decreasing amounts are charged each year in contrast with the straight line method which produces an equal charge each year. The fixed percentage to be used is the percentage which should be deducted from the written down value each year so that, over the life of the asset, the initial total installed cost is reduced to the residual value.

The percentage can be calculated by the following formula:

$$\textbf{Percentage} = \left(1 - \sqrt[n]{\frac{s}{a}}\right) \times 100$$

$$\begin{aligned} \text{where}: n &= \text{estimated life in years} \\ s &= \text{residual value} \\ a &= \text{total installed cost} \end{aligned}$$

Example

If an asset has a total installed cost of £22,500 and an estimated residual value of £2,500 and is expected to last 10 years, what is the appropriate percentage to use for depreciation under the reducing balance method?

Solution

$n = 10; s = 2,500; a = 22,500$

$$\text{Percentage} = \left(1 - \sqrt[10]{\frac{2,500}{22,500}} \times 100\right)$$

$$= 20$$

This percentage would be deducted from the written down value thus:

		Depreciation charge	
		£	£
Total installed cost	=	22,500	
Depreciation = £22,500 × 20%	=	−4,500	4,500 Year 1
		18,000	
Depreciation = £18,000 × 20%	=	−3,600	3,600 Year 2
		14,400	
Depreciation = £14,400 × 20%	=	−2,880	2,880 Year 3
		11,520	
Depreciation = £11,520 × 20%	=	−2,304	2,304 Year 4
and so on.			

Notes:

a. In practice rates are not calculated for each asset in the manner shown above. Invariably assets are classified into various categories, eg Motor Vehicles, Plant and Machinery, etc and a given percentage, usually determined by custom and practice, used for each category, eg Motor vehicles 30%, Plant 25% and so on.

b. An approximation of the percentage rate can be found by the following simple formula:

$$\frac{200}{n\%}$$

where n is the life of the asset.

Characteristics of reducing balance method

a. The depreciation charges are heavier in the earlier years and progressively decline. An argument for this is that as maintenance charges are likely to increase as the years go by, the combined depreciation/maintenance charge will even out. Unfortunately this degree of regularity is unlikely in practice.

b. The method takes no account of the level of activity.

c. Simple to understand and calculate. Within a category of assets with the same percentage, the calculation of the total depreciation charge is simply the given percentage of the total written down value regardless of the varying ages of the assets.

d. A time based method.

24. PRODUCTION UNIT METHOD

Under this method the depreciation charge is based upon the estimated number of units to be produced by the machine over its life.

$$\text{Depreciation charge p.a.} = \frac{\text{Net asset cost}}{\text{Estimated life of machine}^*} \times \text{Units produced in the year}$$

* expressed in units of production

Example

A machine with a net asset cost of £30,000 is expected to produce 240,000 units over its working life. In a given year actual production was 27,000 units. What is the depreciation charge for the year?

Solution

$$\text{Depreciation/unit} = \frac{£30,000}{240,000}$$
$$= \textbf{£0.125}$$
$$\therefore \text{Charge for year} = £0.125 \times 27,000$$
$$= \textbf{£3,375}$$

Note:
An alternative form of this method uses production hours instead of production units.

Characteristics

a. Depreciation is directly related to activity thus becoming a variable cost.
b. Only appropriate for a relatively narrow range of assets, ie those directly producing identifiable units.
c. Administratively cumbersome.
d. Ignores the depreciation effects of time.

25. OTHER DEPRECIATION METHODS

Alternative depreciation methods which are less frequently encountered are briefly described below.

Revaluation method

The depreciation charge is the difference between the value of the asset(s) at the beginning of the year and the assessed value at the year end. Used for items where normal depreciation methods are inappropriate, eg Livestock, Tools, Site Plant.

Sum of the digits

Somewhat similar in application to the reducing balance method in that decreasing amounts are charged each year.

$$\text{Depreciation charge per year} = \frac{x}{\sum r}(\text{Net asset cost})$$

where n = estimated life of asset in years
$\sum r$ = the sum of the r values $1, 2, 3, ..., n$
$= 1 + 2 + 3 + \cdots + n$

and $x = n$ for year 1;
$= n - 1$ for year 2;
$= n - 2$ for year 3
... and so on.

Example

An asset has a net asset cost of £9,000 and a life of five years. What is the first year's depreciation using the sum of the digits method?

Solution

$n = 5$ gives : $\sum r = 5 + 4 + 3 + 2 + 1 = 15$
For Year 1 : $x = n = 5$
$\therefore$ Year 1 depreciation $= \frac{5}{15} \times 9,000$
$= \textbf{£3,000}$

Repair reserve method

In this method the annual charge comprises a normal straight line depreciation charge plus an estimated maintenance cost, ie:

charge per annum

$$= \frac{\text{Net asset cost } + \text{Estimated maintenance charge over life of asset}}{\text{Estimated life}}$$

Sinking fund

This method differs fundamentally from all other methods described. The sinking fund method makes periodic investments external to the firm so that at the end of the life of the asset the realisation of the investment will produce cash equal to the cost of the asset. It will be remembered that other depreciation methods involve book-keeping entries only and no cash flow is involved. The formula is as follows:

Charge per annum $=$ Net asset cost $\times S_{\overline{n}|r}$
where $n =$ estimated life in years
$r =$ interest rate of sinking fund and
$S_{\overline{n}|r} =$ a value obtained from Sinking Fund Tables.

For example, an asset has a net asset cost of £18,000, is expected to last five years and investment opportunities exist at 8%. What is the charge per annum?

Charge per annum $=$ £18,000 $\times S_{\overline{5}|8\%}$
$=$ £18,000 $\times 0.17046$(value from Sinking Fund Tables)
$= \textbf{£3,068}$

26. PLANT REGISTER

To be able to allocate and apportion depreciation charges (however calculated) an up to date record of all assets must be kept. This is termed a *plant register.* This may be on a card index system or, more frequently nowadays, on a computer file. Typically such a record would contain the following details:

a. Plant description, serial number, supplier details including original cost.
b. Technical data relating to speeds, capacities, fuel usage, etc.
c. Location.
d. Depreciation method, estimated life and residual value, amounts written off, written down value.
e. Details of capital allowances, balancing charges or allowances.
f. Disposal details.
g. Maintenance expenditure (usually reserved for major overhauls).
h. Details of additions and enhancements.

27. OBSOLESCENCE

This may be defined as:

> *The loss of value of a non-current asset due to advances in technology or changes in market conditions for its product.*
>
> *Terminology*

There are some relationships between normal depreciation and the concept of obsolescence, but the main distinction is that obsolescence may be rapid and is usually difficult to forecast. Consequently it is not normal practice to make regular charges relating to obsolescence. Instead, when an asset is retired prematurely due to obsolescence, it is normal practice to charge the resulting loss directly to the general profit and loss account rather than to a particular product or department.

28. ASSET IN USE AFTER BEING FULLY DEPRECIATED

When the useful life of an asset is underestimated, it may arise that an asset is fully depreciated, yet still in use. In such circumstances it is usual to continue to charge depreciation so as to maintain cost comparability with previous periods and so that current costs reflect all the costs of using the asset. The excess of depreciation so charged can either be used to create a reserve against obsolescence or credited to the general profit and loss account.

It is frequently possible to judge that the original life estimate is incorrect before the asset is fully written off. In such cases a new life estimate is made with a consequent change in the depreciation charge, so obviating the problem of having an asset in use which is fully written off.

29. REPLACEMENT VALUE AND HISTORIC COST

All the preceding paragraphs have assumed that depreciation is based on the original cost of the asset. Students should be aware that there are strong arguments for basing depreciation on current replacement values, not historical cost. The reason for this is that depreciation based on replacement values more nearly approximates to real economic values which are of greater importance to decision-making management. However, the arguments for and against the use of replacement costs raise fundamental issues of accounting theory outside the scope of this book.

30. SPECIAL OVERHEAD PROBLEMS

There are some items to which special consideration should be given as to whether they form part of overheads or not.

a. *Taxation*
   Taxation is regarded as an appropriation of profit and is invariably omitted from routine cost accounting systems. However, for many decision and planning purposes the effects of taxation can be crucial so it should be included in special studies and reports where appropriate.

b. *Value Added Tax*
   Because input VAT can be claimed back it does not represent a cost, so it is never included in the cost accounts.

c. *Interest*
   Although there are some strong theoretical arguments for the inclusion of interest in the cost accounts, there are severe problems in devising a practical scheme. In general therefore interest payments or imputed interest are not included in the routine cost accounting system. However, in a similar fashion to taxation, interest should be included in cost statements and investigation reports where it may have an effect on the decision to be taken. Typical examples include: the costs of alternative actions involving different capital investment, lease or buy decisions, financing decisions, etc.

d. *Notional costs*
   This can be formally defined as:

   Notional cost: *Cost used in product evaluation, decision-making and performance measurement to reflect the use cost of resources that have no actual (observable)cost. For example notional interest for internally generated funds or notional rent for use of space.*

   Terminology

   This is a hypothetical cost which is entered in the cost accounts so as to represent a benefit enjoyed by the organisation even though no actual cost is incurred. For example, the owner occupier of premises does not pay rent, yet some accountants would consider it correct to make a notional charge to overheads equivalent to the current rents for similar properties.

   In this way cost comparability with other organisations would be possible and the firm's costs would reflect a situation closer to current economic values. This could be vital if the firm was involved in any form of cost plus pricing. Obviously any notional charge into overheads and thence product costs would have to be counterbalanced by a credit to the general profit and loss account.

31. OVERHEADS AND ACTIVITY BASED COSTING (ABC)

ABC has developed to deal with what were seen as defects in the way that conventional absorption costing absorbs support overheads into product costs. Conventionally, all overheads were absorbed on production volume (measured as labour or machine hours) even though many support overheads vary, not with production volume, but with the range and complexity of production.

When support overheads were only a small proportion of total costs the methods of absorption used probably did not matter too much. Today however the position is dramatically different. Direct costs are a declining proportion of total cost and support overheads relating to such things as technical engineering and design services, planning, tooling, data processing, etc are a major proportion of costs in many modern factories. It is therefore of considerable importance that support overheads are traced to product costs in a more realistic manner.

As already explained in Chapter 2 this is done by collecting overheads into *cost pools* and using *cost drivers* to charge the product with a suitable amount of overheads to reflect its usage of the particular support overhead. To do this means classifying overheads in a different manner.

32. OVERHEAD CLASSIFICATION USING ABC

Using traditional classification systems, variable costs are those that vary with production volume. Examples include: direct materials, power costs and so on. On the other hand Fixed costs are those that do not vary with production volume. This embraces the majority of costs, including most overheads.

Using ABC, Kaplan and Cooper advocate classifying overhead costs in a different way. They propose: *short-term variable costs*, *long-term variable costs* and *fixed costs*.

- *Short-term variable costs*
  These are costs that do vary with production volume and would be those also classified as variable under traditional methods. A typical example would be power costs. These vary in direct relationship to production volume, expressed as machine hours.
  It is suggested that short-term variable overhead costs are traced to products using production volume-related cost drivers as appropriate. Examples include: direct labour hours, machine hours, direct material cost or weight. Unlike traditional systems where only one or two absorption bases are used, ABC recognises that there could be several cost drivers whenever labour hours, machine hours and material costs are used in different proportions by products. In most organisations, there will only be a small proportion of overheads that can be classed as short-term variable costs.

- *Long-term variable costs*
  These are overhead costs which do not vary with production volume but do vary with other measures of activity, but not immediately. For example, costs for support activities such as stock handling, production scheduling,

set-ups, etc are fixed in the shorter term but vary in the longer term according to the range and complexity of the products manufactured. ABC requires these costs be traced to products by *transaction based cost drivers*.

Most support overheads can be classified as long-term variable costs and thus traced to products using appropriate cost drivers. In traditional systems most of these would be classified as fixed.

- *Fixed costs*
  Using ABC these are classified as costs which do not vary, for a given time period with any activity indicator. An example would be the salary of the Managing Director. Research by Kaplan and Cooper suggests that these are a relatively small proportion of the total costs.

33. COST POOLS AND COST DRIVERS

The key idea behind ABC is to focus attention on what factors cause or drive costs, known as *cost drivers*.

It will be recalled from Chapter 2 that a cost driver is a factor which influences the cost of an activity; for example issuing a new Purchase Order increases the cost of the Materials procurement Activity. However, there are practical problems in choosing realistic cost drivers and Cooper warns:

There are no simple rules that pertain to the selection of cost drivers. The best approach is to identify the resources that constitute a significant proportion of the products and determine their cost behaviour. If several are long-term variable costs, a transaction-based system should be considered.

If it is decided that an activity based system is required then appropriate cost drivers are chosen and the costs associated with each activity are gathered together in *cost pools* which were defined in Chapter 2.

Cost pools have some similarities to cost centres in traditional systems. Costs are pooled, or collected, on the basis of the activity that drives the costs regardless of conventional departmental boundaries. For example if the cost driver is 'number of setups' then all costs relating to the activity of setting-up will be pooled together.

Cost pools are therefore not necessarily related to departmental boundaries nor do they encompass all the activities of a single department as the cost drivers may differ for the various activities carried out within the same department. Most conventional departments do not perform a single function so that, in general, the number of activities (and consequently cost pools) is greater than the number of departments. Figure 9.2 shows typical departmental groupings and the larger number of activities carried out.

The development of ABC and the designation of cost pools and appropriate cost drivers is not merely a cost recording and cost attribution process. It is more fundamental than that and forces the organisation to ask the following important questions:

What does this department achieve?

Does, for example, the department add value or does it simply add cost? Why is it needed? Can we do without it?

What causes the activity for which the department is responsible? This question can force a reappraisal of the underlying causes of costs. As Johnson

FIGURE 9.2 Departments and activities

Typical departments	Typical major activities
Manufacturing	Drilling, Forming, Assembly etc
Engineering services	Maintenance
Quality control etc	Product and tool design
	Internal transport
	Material acquisition/storing
	Inspection
	Order processing
	Factory loading/planning/control
	Shipping
	Invoicing
	Supplier liaison
	Material scheduling/ordering
	Production control
	All aspects of management and financial accounting
	Personnel administration including hiring/training

has said 'people cannot manage costs, they can only manage the activities which cause costs'.

Focusing on the drivers which cause overheads and tracing overheads to products on the usage of cost drivers enables a higher proportion of overheads to be product related. Using traditional systems most support overheads cannot be related to products except in the most general, arbitrary way. It is this feature of ABC which, it is claimed, produces greater realism.

34. SELECTING COST DRIVERS

Ideally there should be a direct cause/effect relationship between the consumption of overheads and the chosen cost driver. There should be a causal relationship between the amount of resource use, and therefore level of cost, and the volume of the selected cost driver. The relationship is not necessarily a short-term one. This is because salaries and related personnel costs make up a significant proportion of most support overheads and these costs are not easily adjusted in the short-run, hence, Professor Kaplan's definition of 'long-run variable costs'.

The number of cost pools and cost drivers used in practice varies widely, from hundreds in some organisations to dozens in others. As always, a balance must be struck between a complicated and expensive scheme with many cost pools and cost drivers and the loss in accuracy from having a simpler, less costly system.

The number and type of cost drivers chosen will depend on numerous factors including:

a. The required accuracy of product costing. In general the greater accuracy required, the more cost drivers.

b. The extent that a given cost driver captures the actual consumption of an activity by a product. The more closely a cost driver correlates with activity use the fewer distortions in product cost and the fewer cost drivers.

c. The extent to which a cost driver can be related to many activities or cost pools. The cost pool should be homogeneous in the sense that it can fairly be represented by one cost driver. Where this is not possible the pool may need to be sub-divided and numerous cost drivers used which will, of course, make the system more complex and costly to administer.

d. The extent that one cost can be fairly applied to diverse products. For example if the cost driver, 'number of inspections' was used to trace Inspection Costs to products, distortions will be introduced if inspections take varying amounts of time for different products. If this was the case, inspection hours may be a better cost driver or there may be a need for several cost drivers to trace costs fairly.

35. COST DRIVERS USED IN PRACTICE

Naturally, the cost pools and cost drivers chosen must suit the organisation, the products or services and the objectives of the ABC system. As a consequence they will vary from organisation to organisation and there are no universally applicable examples.

Some that have been used in practice are shown in Figure 9.3 on the following page.

It should be emphasised that not all the cost drivers shown in Figure 9.3 against the various cost pools would be used within one organisation. The most appropriate one or two for each cost pool would be selected and used to trace the costs to the product.

36. EXAMPLE OF COST DRIVER CALCULATION AND USE

An organisation has introduced ABC and has separated its main activities into reasonably homogeneous cost pools. Cost drivers have been selected for each cost pool, the usage of which correlates approximately to the amount of overheads in the cost pool. These are shown below:

Cost Pool	Cost Driver
Material Procurement	No of orders
Material Handling	No of material movements
Set-ups	No of set-ups
Maintenance	No of maintenance hours
Quality control	No of inspections
Machinery (power, depreciation etc)	No of machine hours

(Note that in a traditional costing system *all* these production overheads would be absorbed on production volume measured as direct labour or machine hours. In this example, only machinery costs are deemed to be primarily driven by production volume and machine hours are considered a reasonable measure of this.)

FIGURE 9.3 Examples of cost drivers

Activity	Possible cost drivers
Customer order processing	No of orders
	No of customers
	No of orders by size
	No of customer visits
Production control	No of engineering changes
	No of machine/layout changes
	No of parts operational
	No of personnel
	No of schedule changes
	Delivery performance
	No of production batches
	No of set-ups
	No of works orders
Material planning/Inventory control	No of parts
	No of deliveries
	No of material movements
	No of stock discrepancies
	No of shortages
	No of on-time movements
	No of schedule movements
	No of receipts
	Material weight/volume
Engineering support	No of set-ups
	No of engineering changes
	No of product changes
	No of production hours
	No of defects
	No of tool changes
	No of change notices
	No of breakdowns
Inspection and quality control	No of inspections
	No of rejects
	Checking frequency
	No of parts
	No of suppliers
	No of receipts
	No of product changes
	Batch sizes
	No of customers
	General accounting
No of suppliers/customers	Frequency of despatches
	Frequency of deliveries
	No of invoices
	No of accounting reports
	No of purchase/sales orders
	No on payroll
	No of accounting changes

Example
Budgeted overheads and cost driver volumes

Cost pool	Budgeted Overhead £'000	Cost driver	Budgeted volume	Cost driver rate
Mat. Procurement	1,100	No of orders	4,500	$\frac{£1,100}{4,500}$ = £244 per order
Mat. handling	1,850	No of movements	2,750	$\frac{£1,875}{2,750}$ = £673 per move
Set-up	900	No of set-ups	525	$\frac{£900}{525}$ = £1714 per set-up
Maintenance	2,650	Maintenance hours	21,000	$\frac{£2,650}{21,000}$ = £126 per hour
Quality control	2,300	No of inspections	8,500	$\frac{£2,300}{8,500}$ = £271 per inspection
Machinery	3,600	No of machine hours	125,000	$\frac{£3,600}{125,000}$ = £28.8 per hour

The calculated cost driver rates are used to trace the appropriate amount of overheads to the product.

For example a batch of 4,200 Part No X528 had a direct cost (material and labour) of £363,500 and usage of activities as follows:

84	material orders
49	material movements
22	set-ups
610	maintenance hours
90	inspections
1,060	machine hours

What was the cost of the batch using ABC?

Solution

Cost of batch of 4,200 Part No X5288

		£
Direct Costs		363,500
Overheads	£	
84 material orders @ £244	20,496	
49 material movements @ £673	32,977	
22 set-ups @ £1,714	37,708	
610 maintenance hours @ £126	76,860	
90 inspections @ £271	24,390	
1,060 machine hours @ £28.8	30,528	222,959
Batch cost		£586,459

37. MERITS OF ABC

The following are the main claims made regarding ABC:

a. More realistic product costs are provided especially in Advanced Manufacturing Technology (AMT) factories where support overheads are a significant proportion of total costs.

b. More overheads can be traced to the product. In modern factories there are a growing number of non-factory floor activities. ABC is concerned with all activities so takes product costing beyond the traditional factory floor basis.

c. ABC recognises it is activities which cause cost, not products and it is products which consume activities.

d. ABC focuses attention on the real nature of cost behaviour and helps in reducing costs and identifying activities which do not add value to the product.

e. ABC recognises the complexity and diversity of modern production by the use of multiple cost drivers, many of which are transaction based rather than based solely on production volume.

f. ABC provides a reliable indication of long-run variable product cost which is relevant to strategic decision-making.

g. ABC is flexible enough to trace costs to processes, customers, areas of managerial responsibility, as well as products costs.

h. ABC provides useful financial measures (eg cost driver rates) and non-financial measures (eg transactions volumes).

38. PROBLEMS WITH ABC

Undoubtedly ABC removes some of the major deficiencies of traditional absorption costing but, not surprisingly, it has its own problems. These include:

- The choice of cost drivers. It is a simplistic assumption that a chosen cost driver is an adequate summary measure of complex activities.

- The assumption of a direct, linear relationship between the usage of a cost driver and the amount of overheads. Very few costs indeed are truly variable in this sense whether in the short or long term.

- The problem of common costs. It is often difficult to attribute costs to single activities; some costs support several activities.

- Tracing difficulties. It is not always apparent which product should carry the traced overhead. For example, if a set-up takes place from which a range of products benefit, which one should bear the set-up cost? Should it be the first one after the set-up or all the products which benefit?

- Complexity. A full ABC system having numerous cost pools and cost drivers is more complex and consequently more expensive to operate. This need not be a problem provided that the benefits outweigh the costs.

39. SUMMARY

a. Overheads are built up by a process of allocation and apportionment. In traditional systems they are 'shared out' over production by means of overhead absorption:

b. Overhead absorption rates (OAR) are usually predetermined and are calculated by the general formula:

$$OAR = \frac{\text{Budgeted overheads for cost centre}}{\text{Budgeted units of absorption base}}$$

c. The appropriate absorption basis to use is the one which most accurately reflects the incidence of overheads in a given cost centre.

d. Possible absorption bases include: Direct Labour hours, Direct Wages, Machine hours, Prime Cost, etc.

e. In general the most appropriate absorption bases are those based on time, particularly Direct Labour Hours and Machine Hours.

f. Because predetermined OARs are based on estimates of overheads and activity, the amount of overhead absorbed into production is unlikely to agree with the actual overheads incurred so that under or over absorption is likely to occur.

g. When absorbed overheads are greater than actual overheads, there is over absorption; when they are less there is under absorption.

h. The amount of under or over absorption is eventually charged to the Profit and Loss account or Operating Statement.

i. Non-production overheads form part of total cost and sometimes are absorbed into product costs (usually by a percentage of Production Cost) or charged directly to Profit and Loss account.

j. Where all costs, including both fixed and variable, are included in production costs the process is termed Absorption Costing. Where only variable costs are included in production costs and fixed costs are charged to Profit and Loss account each period the system is known as Marginal Costing.

k. The overheads of service departments are built up by allocation and primary apportionment and are then spread over the production departments by secondary apportionment in proportion to usage.

l. The three methods of establishing service department overheads when reciprocal servicing occurs are: continuous allotment, elimination and the use of simultaneous equations.

m. Depreciation occurs through wear and tear and the passage of time. The accounting charge known as depreciation is a way of spreading the cost of an asset over its working life.

n. The most common methods of depreciation are: straight line, reducing balance, and production unit.

o. Other depreciation methods include: revaluation, sum of the digits, sinking fund and repair reserve.

p. Obsolescence is the loss in value due to supercession. It is not normal practice to make regular charges relating to obsolescence, but to write the loss off to the general profit and loss account when it occurs.

q. Taxation and interest are not included in routine costing. They may, however, be included as part of the special information regarding a particular decision.

r. ABC collects overheads into cost pools and traces these to products using cost drivers.

s. Kaplan considers that most support overheads are long-term variable costs that vary more with product complexity and diversity than production volume.

t. Ideally cost pools should be homogeneous and should have a single cost driver that relates directly with the amount of resource use but, in practice, the choice of cost drivers is difficult.

u. ABC recognises that it is activities which cause costs and helps in reducing costs and identifying non-value added activities.

40. POINTS TO NOTE

a. Typically a product passes through several production cost centres, absorbing overheads from each one, often using a different absorption base in each cost centre, eg labour hours, machine hours as appropriate.

b. Any overheads under or over absorbed in a period must be dealt with in that period and should not be carried forward to a future period.

c. In some simple costing systems a single, factory wide OAR is calculated. This means that there is no need to accumulate overheads for various cost centres and overheads would be absorbed by the application of the one OAR for all types of work. Obviously this is easy to do but there is a loss of accuracy because the overheads absorbed do not necessarily reflect the loading or costs of the different cost centres.

d. Non-production overheads (administration, selling, research, etc) are an increasing proportion of the total costs of firms.

e. Because there are so many assumptions and conventions involved in establishing overheads, there is little point in pursuing minute accuracy over such matters as the bases of apportionment, depreciation and reciprocal service costs.

f. Although ABC has been illustrated above in the context of manufacturing it is increasingly being used by service organisations. For example, Bath University in the UK traces central cost to its academic activities using a number of cost drivers. For example: Undergraduate Full Time Equivalent Students (FTEs), Postgraduate FTEs, Overseas FTEs, Space Utilisation and so on.

Student self-testing

Exercises (answers below)

1. a. Calculate five different overhead absorption rates for cost centre 17 based on the following budgeted data.

Labour hours for period	1,400
Total direct wages for period	£3,600
Total direct materials for period	£7,500
Total machine hours for period	2,850
Total units produced for period	535
Total overheads for period	£12,900

    b. A cost unit has been produced in Cost Centre 17 and the following details recorded:

Direct materials used	£16.50
Direct wages	£17.50
Direct labour hours	$5^{1}/_{2}$
Machine hours	$8^{1}/_{2}$

    Calculate the costs of this unit using each of the absorption bases calculated in a.

    c. What basis of overhead absorption would you recommend if you are informed that Cost Centre 17 comprises a number of numerically controlled machine tools with semi-skilled operators and that over half of the cost centre's overheads relate to machine depreciation? Give reasons.

2. a. Give three reasons why over or under absorption of overheads may arise.

    b. Calculate the amount of over/under absorption of overheads (if any) given:

    Cost Centre 258 for Period 2

	Budgeted	Actual
Direct labour hours	5,600	5,925
Direct wages	£19,040	£20,450
Machine hours	3,300	3,418
Direct materials	£26,200	£28,213
Units produced	81,000	85,296
Overheads	£57,500	£61,257

    It is considered that overhead absorption based on labour hours is the most appropriate basis for Cost Centre 258.

3. Discuss the advantages and disadvantages of basing product costs on a single blanket overhead rate for the whole factory instead of separate overhead rates for the various production cost centres.

4. A blanking machine cost £20,000 and required alterations to the premises of £8,500 to install it. Its life is expected to be 12 years when it could be sold as scrap for £1,500. Calculate the depreciation charge per annum using the Straight Line method and the charge for the first year if the Reducing Balance method was used.

5. Two products X and Y are made using similar equipment and methods. The data for last period are

	X	Y
Units produced	6,000	8,000
Labour hours per unit	1	2
Machine hours per unit	4	2
Set-ups in period	15	45
Orders handled in the period	12	60
Overheads for period	£	
Relating to production set-ups	179,000	
Relating to order handling	30,000	
Relating to machine activity	55,000	
	264,000	

Calculate the overheads to be absorbed per unit of each product based on:

a. Conventional absorption costing using a labour hour absorption rate

b. An ABC approach using suitable cost drivers.

Solutions to exercises

1. a. *Overhead absorption rates*:

Basis	Calculation	Rate
Labour hours	$\dfrac{£12,900}{1,400}$	£9.21 per hour
Percentage on Wages	$\left(\dfrac{£12,900}{3,600}\right) \times 100\%$	358% of wages
Percentage on Prime Cost	$\left(\dfrac{12,900}{£3,600 + £7,500}\right) \times 100\%$	116% of Prime Cost
Machine hours Hour	$\dfrac{£12,900}{2,850}$	£4.53 per mc.
Unit	$\dfrac{£12,900}{2,850}$	£24.11 per unit

b. Prime Cost = £16.50 + 17.50 = £34.

The overheads and total cost using the various bases are as follows:

Basis	Calculation	=	Overheads £	+	Prime Cost £	=	Total Cost £
Labour hours	(5.5 × £9.21)	=	50.65	+	34	=	84.65
Percentage on wages	(358% of £17.50)	=	62.65	+	34	=	96.65
Percentage on Prime Cost	(116% of £34)	=	39.44	+	34	=	73.44
Machine Hours	(8.5 × £4.53)	=	38.50	+	34	=	72.50
Cost unit	(£24.11 × 1)	=	£24.11	+	34	=	58.11

c. In the circumstances outlined the Machine Hour Rate would generally be considered to be the most appropriate so that the cost per unit would be £72.5 and £38.50 of overheads would be recovered on this unit.

2. a. Overheads not as budgeted. Activity level not as budgeted. Changes in labour or machine efficiency.

b. *Based on labour hours*

$$OAR = \frac{£57,500}{5,600} = £10.27 \text{ hour}$$

$\therefore$ Overheads absorbed by production $= 5,925 \times £10.27 = £60,850$

$\therefore$ Under recovery $= £61,257 - £60,850 = £407$

3. The only advantage of a blanket overhead rate is that of simplicity but the disadvantages are more numerous.

a. Does not reflect the varying characteristics and times spent in various departments.

b. Products or jobs spending more time in departments or cost centres with high overheads will be under costed. Conversely where departments with lower overheads are involved the products or jobs will be over costed.

A single, blanket absorption rate is suitable when there is a single product which passes through all departments equally although it is unnecessary as total costs can be divided by total output.

4.

$$\text{Net Asset Value} = £20,000 + 8,500 - 1,500 = 27,000$$

$$\text{Depreciation charge p.a.} - \text{Straight Line} = \frac{27,000}{12} = £2,250$$

$$\text{Reducing Balance percentage} = \left(1 - \sqrt[n]{\frac{s}{a}}\right) \times 100 = \left(1 - \sqrt[12]{\frac{1,500}{28,500}}\right)$$

$$\times 100 = (1 - 0.728) \times 100 = 22\%$$

$\therefore$ First year depreciation $= 28,500 \times 22\% = £6,270$

5. a. Labour Hours

Product X = 6,000 units × 1	6,000
Product Y = 8,000 units × 2	16,000
	22,000

$$\therefore \text{Labour hour OAR} = \frac{264,000}{22,000} = £12 \text{ per hour}$$

Overheads absorbed on labour hours

		Product X	**Product Y**
Overheads absorbed	=	1 × £12 = £12	2 × £12 = £24
∴ Total overheads	=	6,000 × £12 = £72,000	8,000 × £24 = £192,000

b. Using ABC

Machine hours per period

Product X = 6,000 × 4 =	24,000
Product Y = 8,000 × 2 =	16,000
	40,000

Cost Driver Rates

$$\text{Production Set-ups} = \frac{£179,000}{60} = £2,983 \text{ per set-up}$$

$$\text{Order Handling} = \frac{£30,000}{72} = £417 \text{ per order}$$

$$\text{Machine Costs} = \frac{£55,000}{40,000} = £1.375 \text{ per hour}$$

Overheads using ABC

			Product X			**Product Y**
			£			£
Set-ups	15 × £2,983	=	44,745	45 × £2,983	=	134,235
Orders	12 × £417	=	5,004	60 × £417	=	25,020
Machine Costs	24,000 × 1.375	=	33,000	16,000 × 1.375	=	22,000
Totals			£82,749			£181,255

10

Cost accounts

1. OBJECTIVES

After studying this chapter you will

- **Understand the distinction between Integrated and Interlocking Cost Accounts**

- **Know the double entries required in Integrated and Interlocking systems**

- **Be able to reconcile the profits of cost and financial accounts**

- **Understand how JIT principles alter cost accounting**

- **Understand Backflush Accounting and its three variants.**

2. ACCOUNTING SYSTEMS FOR COSTS

Because there are no statutory requirements to maintain detailed cost records some small firms keep only traditional financial accounts and prepare cost information in an ad-hoc fashion. In all but the very smallest firm this approach is likely to be unsatisfactory and consequently the majority of firms maintain cost accounts in some form or other.

There is a vast range of systems in operation ranging from simple analysis systems to computer based accounting systems incorporating standards, variance analysis and the automatic production of control and operating statements. Invariably the systems are tailored to suit the particular firm and so will have unique features. Nevertheless there will be recognisably common aspects to most systems and the records will be maintained using proper double entry principles.

Whatever system is adopted for recording costs, it will depend on accurate coding of source data, ie items such as invoices, job tickets, time sheets and requisitions. (The principles of coding have been dealt with in Chapter 3.) Despite the variety of cost accounting systems, two particular categories are frequently encountered. These are known as *integrated cost accounts* and *interlocking cost accounts.* Descriptions of these terms follow.

Integrated cost accounts

These accounts can be defined as:

> *A set of accounting records which provides both financial and cost accounts using a common input data for all accounting purposes.*
>
> *Terminology*

This is a single, comprehensive accounting system with no division between financial and cost accounts. It follows therefore that the same bases for matters such as stock valuation and depreciation will be used and that there is no need for reconciliation between cost profit and financial profit. Financial profit will be the cost profit adjusted by any non-cost items, eg income from investments, charitable donations, etc.

Interlocking cost accounts

These accounts can be defined as:

> *Interlocking Accounts Set of accounting records where the cost and financial accounts are distinct, the two being kept continuously in agreement by the use of control accounts or reconciled by other means.*
>
> *Terminology*

This system (of which there are many variants) uses separate cost accounts which periodically are reconciled with the financial accounts. Naturally the cost accounts use the same basic data (purchases, wages, etc) as the financial accounts, but frequently adopt different bases for matters such as depreciation and stock valuation. The interlocking of the two systems is carried out by the use of control accounts in each set of accounts, ie:

> *a cost ledger control account in the financial ledger and a financial ledger control account in the cost ledger.*

3. INTEGRATED COST ACCOUNTS

Figure 10.1 shows the main flow of accounting entries in a typical integrated system. It has been kept free from the many complications and variations that occur in practice to show clearly the underlying principles. It should be studied in conjunction with the notes which follow.

Notes on integrated accounts
a. No distinction is made between 'cost accounts' and 'financial accounts'.
b. The emphasis is on functional analysis, eg selling overheads, rather than analysis by nature, eg salaries, telephone, etc.
c. If analysis by nature is required, as in a traditional nominal ledger, then the prime data needs to be coded accordingly and natural accounts kept in addition to functional accounts.
d. The traditional form of Profit and Loss account disappears to be replaced by a Costing Profit and Loss account, or, as it is frequently known, an Operating Statement.

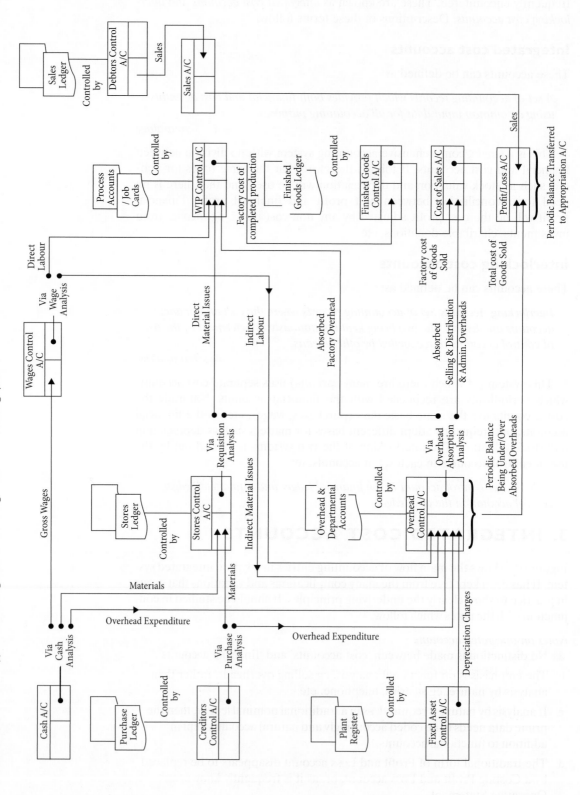

FIGURE 10.1 Typical accounting entries in an integrated cost accounting system

4. EXAMPLE OF INTEGRATED ACCOUNTS

Example

Acme Manufacturing Ltd. operate an integrated accounting system and it is required to record the following balances and transactions in the ledger accounts and prepare Final Accounts at the month's end.

Opening balance at 1st June

	£	£
Issued share capital		250,000
Reserves		65,000
Depreciation provision (plant)		38,000
Creditors control		42,750
Buildings	80,000	
Plant & Machinery (at cost)	146,500	
Bank	23,291	
Debtors	49,856	
Stocks: Raw materials	41,200	
W-I-P	24,260	
Finished Goods	30,643	
	395,750	395,750

The following information is supplied regarding the month's transactions.

	£
Purchases of raw materials	122,600
Gross wages and salaries	
Production direct wages	24,910
(including £6,800 accrued)	
Production indirect wages	6,253
Production salaries	2,985
Administration salaries	11,058
Selling and distr. salaries	6,219
Expenses	
Production control	4,286
Administration	7,017
Selling and distribution	4,935
Cash payments	
Creditors	155,296
Salaries and wages	41,025
Cash receipts – Debtors	185,473
Discounts allowed	2,100
Discounts received	
Overheads recovered	3,926
Production	28,750
Administration	18,500
Selling and distribution	10,800
Provisions	
Depreciation on plant	9,520
Bad debts	4,100

	£
Factory cost of completed production	155,000
Factory cost of goods sold	173,000
Sales	220,800
Material issues	
Production	83,621
Works maintenance	6,509

Solutions

Stores Control

Balance	41,200	WIP	83,621
Purchases	122,600	Prod Ohds	6,509
		Bal c/f	73,670
	163,800		163,800
Balance	73,670		

WIP Control

Balance	24,260	Fin Goods	155,000
Wages	24,910		
Materials	83,621		
Prod Ohds	28,750	Balance	6,541
	161,541		161,541
Balance	6,541		

Finished Goods Control

Balance	30,643	Goods Sold	173,000
Production	155,000	Balance c/f	12,643
	185,643		185,643
Balance	12,643		

Cost of Sales

Fin. Goods	173,000	P & L	202,300
Adm. Ohds	18,500		
S & D Ohds	10,800		
	202,300		202,300

Debtors Control

Balance	49,856	Cash	185,473
Sales	220,800	Discounts	2,100
		Balance	83,083
	270,656		270,656
Balance	83,083		

Creditors Control

Cash	155,296	Balance	42,750
Discounts	3,926	Purchases	122,600
Balance	22,366	Expenses	16,238
	181,588		181,588
		Balance	22,366

Wages/Salary Control

Cash	41,025	WIP	24,910
Deductions	3,600	Prod. Ohd.	6,253
		Prod. Ohd.	2,985
Accrued	6,800	Amm. Ohd.	11,058
		S & D Ohd.	6,219
	51,425		51,425
		Balance	6,800

Prodn Ohd Control

Wages	6,253		
Salaries	2,985		
Expenses	4,286	WIP	28,750
Depreciation	9,520	Under Recov.	803
Materials	6,509		
	29,553		29,553

Admin Ohd Control

Salaries	11,058		
Expenses	7,017	Cost of Sales	18,500
Over Recovery	475		
	18,500		18,500

S & D Ohd Control

Salaries	6,219		
Expenses	4,935	Cost of Sales	10,800
		Under	354
		Recovery	
	11,154		11,154
	£42,000		£42,000

Bad Debts Provision

		P & L	4,100

Wages/Salaries Deductions

		Wages	3,600

Share Capital

		Balance	250,000

Reserves

		Balance	65,000
		Profit	15,494
			80,494

Discount Allowed

Debtors	2,100	P & L	2,100

Discount Received

P & L	3,926	Creditors	3,926

Bank

Balance	23,291	Creditors	155,296
Debits	185,473	Wages	41,025
		Balance c/f	12,443
	208,764		208,764
Balance	12,443		

Buildings

Balance	80,000	

Depreciation Prov Plant

Balance c/f	47,520	Balance	38,000
		Prod. Ohd.	9,520
	47,520		47,520
		Balance	47,520

Ohd Adjustment A/c

Prod. Ohds.	803	Admin. Ohds	425
S & D Ohds.	354	P & L	732
	1,157		1,157

Sales

P & L	220,800	Debtors	220,800

Profit and Loss

Cost of Sales	202,300	Sales	220,800
Overhead adjustment	732	Discount Received	3,296
Discounts allowed	2,100		
Bad Debts Prov.	4,100		
Transfer to Reserve	15,494		
	224,726		224,726

Balance Sheet

Share Capital		250,000	Buildings		80,000
Reserves		80,494	Plant	148,500	
			less Depreciation	47,520	98,980
					178,980
Current Liabilities			Current Assets		
Creditors	22,366		Cash	12,443	
Accrued Wages	6,800		Debtors	83,083	
Deductions	3,600	32,766	less B.D.P.	4,100	91,426
			Stocks		
			Raw Matls	73,670	
			WIP	6,541	
			Fin Goods	12,643	92,854
		£363,260			£363,260

5. INTERLOCKING FINANCIAL AND COST ACCOUNTS

This system, with its many variants, is commonly encountered in practice. There are separate cost accounting and financial accounting systems in which the basic accounting data are used in the normal manner in the financial accounts and then the data and documents passed to the cost department. There the source data on costs will be reclassified into the functional analysis necessary for costing purposes, using such supplementary information as labour and machine times, production statistics, material requisitions and scrap reports.

The financial accounting system has the normal debit and credit entries within itself and in addition has a memorandum account frequently termed the Cost Ledger Control A/C. This account will have posted to it all items which are to be transferred to the cost accounting system.

In the cost ledger there will be the necessary accounts for costing purposes, eg Stores Control A/C, W-I-P Control A/C, etc and, in addition, an account which is equal and opposite to the memorandum financial account. The cost ledger account is sometimes termed the Cost Ledger Contra Account, but to avoid confusion with the memorandum cost ledger control account in the financial accounts, it is frequently called the Financial (or General) Ledger Control A/C.

The Financial Ledger Control account is an essential element of the cost ledger because it forms part of the double entry system within the ledger. It also enables the financial and cost ledgers to be interlocked because it must agree with the memorandum Cost Ledger Control account in the financial ledger. A summary of the two ledgers is shown next.

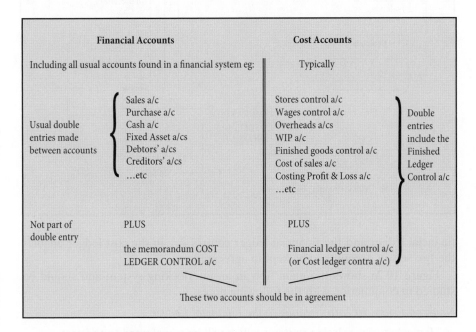

Financial Accounts		Cost Accounts	
Including all usual accounts found in a financial system eg:		Typically	
Usual double entries made between accounts	Sales a/c Purchase a/c Cash a/c Fixed Asset a/cs Debtors' a/cs Creditors' a/cs ...etc	Stores control a/c Wages control a/c Overheads a/cs WIP a/c Finished goods control a/c Cost of sales a/c Costing Profit & Loss a/c ...etc	Double entries include the Finished Ledger Control a/c
Not part of double entry	PLUS the memorandum COST LEDGER CONTROL a/c	PLUS Financial ledger control a/c (or Cost ledger contra a/c)	
	These two accounts should be in agreement		

Note:
There is no double entry connection between the Financial accounts and the Cost accounts although the use of the memorandum control account in the

FIGURE 10.2A Typical accounting entries in an interlocking system with separate financial and cost accounts

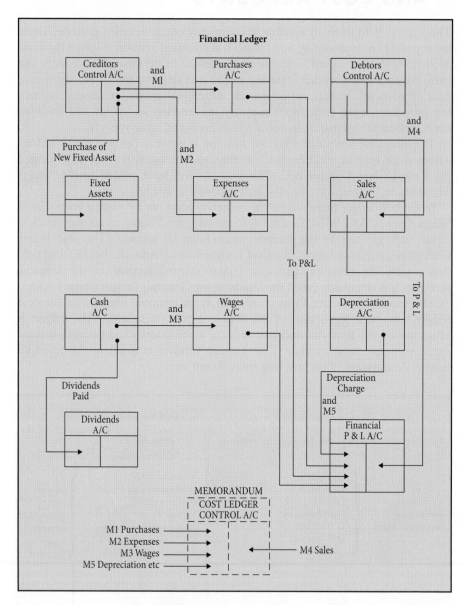

financial ledger and the financial ledger control A/c in the cost ledger enables the two sets of accounts to be kept in agreement.

Figure 10.2a shows the main flow in an interlocking system and should be studied in conjunction with the following notes.

Notes on Figure 10.2a(a) relating to the Financial Ledger

a. Typical entries relating to items which will be transferred to the cost accounts, ie wages, purchases, etc are shown as M1, M2, etc. The normal double entries are given together with the entry in the memorandum Cost Ledger Control A/c.

b. Examples of two entries are given which do not affect the cost ledger, the Purchase of a fixed asset and payment of dividends. It will be seen that for these items there is no memorandum entry.

c. Other items which appear in the financial accounts, but not in the cost accounts, include:

 i. Financial charges such as stamp duty, interest on loans, issue expenses, loss on sale of capital assets and similar financial items.

 ii. Financial income such as dividends received, interest received on loans and deposits and profits from the sales of fixed assets.

 iii. Appropriations of profit such as dividends paid, transfers to reserve and taxation.

d. Although there are no double entries spanning the cost and financial ledgers, control must be maintained over the information and documents transferred. The cost ledger control account assists this process together with batch control totals, pre-lists and documents counts.

Notes on Figure 10.2(b)

a. Comparison with Figure 10.1 will show a similar pattern of accounts in both integral and interlocking systems.

FIGURE 10.2B Typical accounting entries in an interlocking system with separate financial and cost accounts

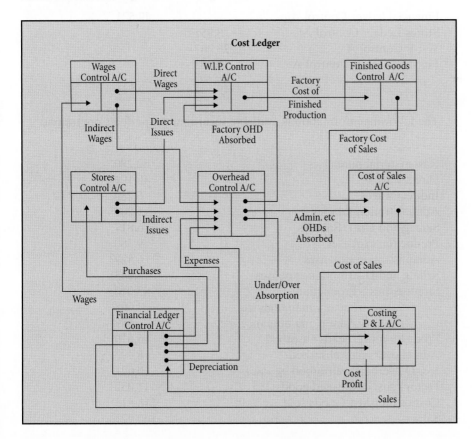

b. It will be seen that the Financial Ledger Control A/c is a necessary part of the double entry system within the cost ledger (alternative names for this account are General Ledger Control A/c or the Cost Ledger Contra A/c).

c. The balance on the Financial Ledger Control account represents the total of all the balances of the impersonal accounts in the cost ledger.

d. If work of a capital nature is carried out in the factory, this needs to be transferred to the financial accounts via the Financial Ledger Control account.

e. Periodic reconciliation of the cost and financial ledgers is necessary. This is dealt with in detail later in this chapter.

6. EXAMPLE OF ACCOUNTS USING A SEPARATE COST LEDGER

Example
Jackson Assemblies Ltd. operate interlocking financial and cost accounting systems. The following balances and data relate to their Cost Ledger and it is required to record the entries, obtain the Costing Profit and prepare a closing trial balance.

Cost Ledger Opening trial balance

	£	£
Financial ledger Control A/c		49,521
Stores Ledger Control A/c	8,951	
W-I-P Control A/c	26,367	
Finished Goods Control A/c	14,203	
	49,521	49,521

The following information is available regarding the period's operations.

	£
Raw material purchases	62,280
Direct wages	40,191
Indirect wages	6,280
Administration salaries	11,207
Selling and Distr. Salaries	6,817
Production expenses	9,380
Administration expenses	6,529
Selling and Distribution expenses	4,043
Stores issues – Production	43,010
– Factory maintenance	2,005
– Admin. maintenance	659
Production overheads absorbed	16,670
Admin overheads absorbed	18,493
S & D overheads absorbed by sales	10,621
Factory cost of finished goods	111,032
Cost of Finished Goods sold	118,815
Sales	160,921

Solution

Accounting entries in Cost Ledger

Financial Ledger Control A/c

Sales	160,921	Bal.	49,521
Bal. c/f	47,183	Purchases	62,280
		Wages	46,471
		Salaries	18,024
		Prod. exs.	9,380
		Admin exc.	6,529
		S & D exs.	4,043
		Profit	11,856
	208,104		208,104
		Bal.	47,183

Stores Ledger Control A/c

Bal.	8,951	W-I-P	43,010
F.L. control	62,280	Prod. Ohd.	2,005
		Admin Ohd.	659
		Bal c/f	25,557
	71,231		71,231
Bal.	25,557		

Finished Goods Control A/c

Bal.	14,203	Cost of Sales	118,815
W-I-P	111,032	Bal. c/f	6,420
	125,235		125,235
Bal. c/f	6,420		

Admin. Overhead Control A/c

Salaries	11,207		
Expenses	6,529	Cost of Sales	18,493
Material	659		
Ohd. adj A/c	98		
	18,493		18,493

Wages Control A/c

F.L. Control A/c	46,471	W-I-P Prod.	40,191
		Ohds	6,280
	46,471		46,471

W-I-P Control A/c

Bal.	26,367		
Issues	43,010	Fin. goods	111,032
Wages	40,191	Bal c/f	15,206
Prodn Ohds	16,670		
	126,238		126,238
Bal. c/f	15,206		

Production Overheads Control A/c

Wages	6,280	W-I-P	16,670
Exps.	9,380	Ohd adjstmt	995
		(under recovery)	
Stores	2,005		
	17,665		17,665

Selling & Distr. Overhead Control A/c

Salaries	6,817	Cost of Sales	10,621
Expenses	4,043	Ohd Adj A/c	239
	10,860		10,860

Salaries Control A/c

F.L. Control A/c	18,024	Adm. Ohds. S	11,207
		& D Ohds.	6,817
	18,024		18,024

Overhead Adjustment A/c

Prod. Ohds	995	Admin Ohds	98
S & D Ohds.	239	P & L	1,136
	1,234		1,234

Cost of Sales A/c

Admin. Ohds.	18,493		
Fin. Goods	118,815	P & L	147,929
S & D Ohds.	10,621		
	147,929		147,929

Costing P & L A/c

Cost of Sales	147,929	Sales	160,921
Ohd. Adj.	1,136		
Profit	11,856		
	160,921		160,921

Closing Trial Balance

Financial ledger Control A/c		47,183
Stores ledger Control A/c	25,557	
W-I-P Control A/c	15,206	
Finished Goods Control A/c	6,420	
	47,183	47,183

7. RECONCILIATION OF COST AND FINANCIAL ACCOUNTS

Differences can arise between the profits shown by the cost accounts and the financial accounts. Periodically these differences must be reconciled to ensure that there are no errors in either set of accounts.

Differences arise due to several factors:

a. Items appearing in financial accounts and not in cost accounts. Typical examples are: dividends received, profits and losses on sales of assets, interest paid or received, share issue and preliminary expenses, and fines paid by the company.

b. Items appearing only in the cost accounts. These are infrequent and usually relate to imputed charges for such matters as rent and interest.

c. Differences in the treatment of depreciation and different stock valuations.

The reconciliation is carried out using a memorandum reconciliation account as shown in the following example.

Example

The profit shown in the financial accounts is £18,592 and for the same period the cost accounts showed a profit of £20,496.

Comparison of the two sets of accounts revealed the following:

Stock Valuations	Cost Accounts	Financial Accounts
Raw Materials	£	£
Opening Stock	6,821	7,259
Closing Stock	5,483	5,128
Finished Goods		
Opening Stock	13,291	12,905
Closing Stock	11,430	11,131

Dividends and interest received of £552 and a loss of £1,750 on the sale of a milling machine were not entered in the cost accounts. Reconcile the profit figures.

Solution

Memorandum Reconciliation A/c

		£		£
Profit as per Financial A/cs		18,592	Profit as per cost A/cs	20,496
Stock differences				
	£		Item not credited	
Raw material – opening	438		Dividends + interest recd.	
– closing	355		Stock difference	552
Finished Goods closing	299	1,092	Finished Goods – Opening	386
Items not charged in cost accounts				
Loss on sale of machine		1,750		
		£21,434		£21,434

8. ILLUSTRATION OF INTEGRATED ACCOUNTS

To consolidate the material covered in this chapter a comprehensive example follows of a full set of accounts for one month for Acme Manufacturing Ltd who maintain a fully integrated system.

Example

Opening Balance Sheet

	£		£
Share Capital	1,000,000	Buildings (cost £600,000)	450,000
General Reserve	85,000	Plant & Machinery (cost £840,000)	585,000
P & L Appropriation	17,500	Vehicles (cost £360,000)	144,800
Debentures	400,000	Stocks – Raw Materials	102,550
Bought Ledger Control	43,250	– W-I-P	32,200
		– Finished Goods	69,250
		Sales Ledger Control	84,050
		Cash at Bank	77,900
	1,545,750		1,545,750

The transactions for the period were:

	£
Credit sales	384,500
Raw material purchases	147,000
Expense and overhead purchases	49,250
Cash from debtors	173,280
Cash to creditors	139,100
Cash drawn for wages and salaries	84,220
PAYE deductions	15,300
Works costs of goods sold	292,255
Production to Finished Goods Stock	306,405

The following allocations were made:

	Wages and Salaries	Materials	Expenses
	£	£	£
Direct costs	48,200	134,200	14,100
Production Dept's.			
Fabrication	8,300	8,520	9,800
Finishing	8,670	4,810	7,050
Service Dept's:			
Stores	3,550	13,270	3,000
Maintenance	11,600	18,450	4,350
Selling and Admin.	19,260		10,950

The following data are available from production and other records within the organisation.

	Percentage of value of Buildings	Plant	Vehicles	No of Stores (Requisitions)	Maintenance (Hours)
Production					
Fabrication Dept.	20	35	5	250	600
Finishing Dept.	30	15	15	450	300
Stores Dept.	5	15	5	–	–
Maintenance Dept.	20	25	10	250	–
Selling and Admin.	25	10	65	50	100

The depreciation rates are:

Buildings	5% p.a. on cost
Plant	10% p.a. on cost
Vehicles	20% p.a. on cost

Overheads absorbed during the period:

	£
Fabrication Dept	63,200
Finishing Dept.	43,905

Based on the above information it is required to make the appropriate ledger entries, prepare Trading and Profit and Loss accounts for the period and a closing Balance Sheet.

Solution

Ledger Accounts

Share Capital

		Bal	1,000,000

P & L Appropriation

		Bal	17,500
			52,270
			69,770

Plant and Machinery

Bal.	585,000	Depreciation	7,000
		Bal.	578,000
	585,000		585,000
Bal.	578,000		

Raw Materials Control

Bal.	102,550	W-I-P	134,200
Bought Ledger	147,000	Fabrication	8,520
		Finishing	4,810
		Stores	13,270
		Maintenance	18,450
		Bal.	70,300
	249,550		249,550
Bal.	70,300		

Finished Goods Control

Bal.	69,250	Trading A/c	292,255
W-I-P	306,405	Bal.	83,400
	375,655		375,655
Bal.	83,400		

General Reserve

		Bal.	85,000

Debentures

		Bal.	400,000

Buildings

Bal.	450,000	Depreciation	2,500
		Bal.	447,500
	450,000		450,000
Bal.	447,500		

Vehicles

Bal.	144,800	Depreciation	6,000
		Bal.	138,800
	144,800		144,800
Bal.	138,800		

WIP Control

Bal.	32,200		
Wages	48,200	Finished Goods	306,405
Materials	134,200	Bal.	29,400
Expenses	14,100		
Fabrication Ohds.	63,200		
Finishing Ohds.	43,905		
	335,805		335,805
Bal.	29,400		

Sales Ledger Control

Bal.	84,050	Bank	173,280
Sales	384,500	Bal.	295,270
Bal.	468,550		468,550
Balance	295,270		

Bank

Bal.	77,900	Bought Ledger	139,100
Sales Ledger	173,280	Wages & Salaries	84,220
		Bal.	27,860
	251,180		251,180
Bal.	27,860		

Wage & Salary Control

Bank	84,220	WIP Control	48,200
PAYE	15,360	Fabrication	8,300
		Ohds. Finishing	8,670
		Ohds. Stores	3,550
		Maintenance	11,600
		Selling &	19,260
	99,580	Admin.	99,580

Fabrication Overhead

Wages & Salaries	8,300		
Materials	8,520		
Building Deprec.	500	Absorbed Overhead	63,200
Plant Deprec.	2,450		
Vehicle Deprec.	300		
Expenses	9,800		
Ohds. Stores	5,324		
Maintenance	25,544		
Overhead Adj.	2,462		
	63,200		63,200

Stores Overhead

Wage & Salaries	3,550	Fabrication	5,324
Materials	13,270	Finishing	9,583
Building Deprec.	125	Maintenance	5,324
Plant Deprec.	1,050	S & D	1,064
Vehicle Deprec.	300		
Expenses	3,000		
	21,295		21,295

PAYE

		Wages & Salaries	15,360

Expense Control

Bought Ledger	49,250	WIP	14,100
		Fabrication	9,800
		Finishing	7,050
		Stores	3,000
		Maintenance	4,350
		S & D	10,950
	49,250		49,250

Finishing Overhead

Wages & Salaries	8,670		
Materials	4,810	Absorbed Overhead	43,905
Building Deprec.	750	Overhead Adj.	1,680
Plant Deprec.	1,050		
Vehicle Deprec.	900		
Expenses	7,050		
Stores Ohds.	9,583		
Maintenance	12,772		
	45,585		45,585

Maintenance Overhead

Wage & Salaries	11,600	Fabrication	25,544
Materials	18,450	Finishing	12,772
Building Deprec.	500	S & D	4,258
Plant Deprec.	1,750		
Vehicle Deprec.	600		
Expenses	4,350		
Stores Ohds.	5,324		
	42,574		42,574

Selling & Admin. Overheads

Wage & Salaries	11,600		
Building Deprec.	625		
Plant Deprec.	700	P & L	40,757
Vehicle Deprec.	3,900		
Expenses	10,950		
Stores Ohds.	1,064		
Maintenance	4,258		
	40,757		40,757

Overhead Adjustment A/c

Finishing Dept	1,680	Fabrication Dept	2,462
P & L A/c	782		
	2,462		2,462

Bought Ledger Control

Bank	139,100	Bal.	43,250
		Materials	147,000
Bal.	100,400	Expenses	49,250
	239,500		239,500
		Bal.	100,400

Sales

Trading A/c	384,500	Sales Ledger	384,500

Trading A/c

Cost of Sales	292,255	Sales	384,500
Gross Profit	92,245		
	384,500		384,500

P & L A/c

S & D Ohds.	40,757	Gross Profit	92,245
P & L Approp.	52,270	Overhead Adj.	782
	93,027		93,027

Closing Balance Sheet

Share Capital	1,000,000	Buildings	447,500
General Reserve	85,000	Plant & Machinery	578,000
P & L Appropriation	69,770	Vehicles	138,800
Debentures	400,000	Stocks – Raw Materials	70,300
Bought Ledger Control	100,400	– WIP	29,400
		– Finished Goods	83,400
PAYE	15,360	Sales Ledger Control	295,270
		Cash at Bank	27,860
	£1,671,530		£1,671,530

Workings

£

Depreciation – Buildings $\dfrac{5\% \times 600,000}{12}$ = 2,500

– Plant $\dfrac{10\% \times 840,000}{12}$ = 7,000

– Vehicles $\dfrac{20\% \times 360,000}{12}$ = 6,000

Apportionments

	Buildings £	Plant £	Vehicles £
Fabrication	500	2,450	300
Finishing	750	1,050	900
Stores	125	1,050	300
Maintenance	500	1,750	600
S & D	625	700	3,900
	2,500	7,000	6,000

Stores overhead apportionment (based on requisitions)

Fabrication	25%
Finishing	45%
Maintenance	25%
S & D	5%

Maintenance overhead apportionment (based on hours)

Fabrication	60%
Finishing	30%
S & D	10%

9. DEVELOPMENTS IN COST ACCOUNTING

Conventional cost accounting systems as described so far track the detailed movement of costs stage by stage. Typically this begins with the introduction of raw materials into a Stores account or Raw materials account, the subsequent issue of materials to production and the consequent entries into a Work-in-Progress account (together with labour and overhead entries). When the goods are completed, entries are made from the WIP account into the Finished Goods account.

The entries outlined above are triggered by a vast number of works tickets, documents and notes relating to material issues, parts completed, goods finished and so on. Cost accounting methods developed in this way because this was the way that production was traditionally organised and still is in many factories.

However, enormous changes have taken place in the way goods are made, materials are purchased and production is organised and, as is to be expected, changes are also occurring in cost accounting methods. The production changes are most apparent in firms using Just-in-Time Purchasing and manufacturing methods; the key features of which are:

JIT Purchasing is characterised by:

- Goods delivered immediately before demand or use.
- Increase in number of deliveries, each containing a smaller number of units.
- Goods/materials delivered in 'shop/factory ready' containers reducing materials handling.
- Long-term agreements with fewer suppliers specifying price, delivery and acceptable quality levels.
- Minimal checking by purchaser of quality and quantity of deliveries.

Frequently when JIT purchasing is adopted deliveries are made directly to the factory floor in exact accordance with production and delivery schedules.

JIT manufacturing is characterised by:

- Elimination of non-value adding activities such as storage, transport etc.
- Commitment to high quality. The target is zero defects.
- Production on demand; not for stock.
- Nil or very small raw material and WIP stocks.
- A commitment to continuous improvement.
- Simplification, space saving and reduction in lead times.

The above are fundamental developments and it is important that there are corresponding changes in the cost accounting system. This is a critical point because accounting methods must be tailored to suit the underlying operations, and not vice versa.

One important change being adopted by many firms is called *backflush accounting* or *backflush costing*.

10. BACKFLUSH ACCOUNTING OR BACKFLUSH COSTING

This is a simpler cost accounting system designed to reduce or eliminate detailed accounting entries. Instead of the detailed tracking of material movements through stores and production a backflush system focuses on the output of the firm (ie, the finished goods) and then works backwards to attribute costs between cost of goods sold and finished goods inventory and/or raw materials inventory with no separate accounting for WIP. The formal definition of back flush accounting is:

> *A method of costing, associated with a JIT production system, which applies cost to the output of a process. Costs do not mirror the flow of products through the production process, but are attached to output produced (finished goods stock and cost of sales), on the assumption that such backflushed costs are a realistic measure of the actual costs incurred.*
>
> *Terminology*

There are several variants of backflush accounting depending on the inventory accounts maintained and the number and type of *trigger points* (these determine when entries are made in the accounts). Conversion costs (labour and overheads) are recorded as in traditional systems and then applied to products at various trigger points. Normally any conversion costs not applied to products are written off immediately as expenses incurred in the period.

Figure 10.3 shows key features of three variants of backflush accounting.

FIGURE 10.3   Variants of backflush accounting

	Variant A	Variant B	Variant C
Trigger points for initiating accounting entries	1. Purchase of raw materials, components 2. Manufacture of finished goods	1. Purchase of raw materials, components 2. Sale of finished goods	Manufacture of finished goods
Inventory a/cs kept	1. Combined raw material & WIP a/c ie Raw & In-progress (RIP) a/c 2. Finished goods a/c	RIP a/c	Finished goods a/c
Main features of variants	Two trigger points Use of combined RIP a/c	Two trigger points Use of combined RIP a/c No finished goods a/c because the trigger is sales not manufacture	Simplest of all Finished goods a/c only Single trigger point Less feasible if there are significant stocks of materials and WIP

II. EXAMPLES OF BACKFLUSH ACCOUNTING

Example
The following data will be used to illustrate the three variants:

	£000
Material/component purchases for period	2,300
Conversion costs for period	1,250
Units of finished goods made	50,000
Units of finished goods sold	49,000

The standard cost of a unit of output is £70 (£45 materials, £25 conversion cost)

There are no opening stocks and for simplicity it is assumed that there are no variations from standard cost.

Required:
The backflush accounting entries using:

   i. Variant A

  ii. Variant B

 iii. Variant C

Note:
In each of the following solutions the transactions and transfers have been numbered 1, 2, 3 etc and are explained following the accounts.

Solution – Variant A

    Triggers – Purchase of materials

            – Manufacturing of finished units

RIP a/c

	£000		£000
1. Creditors	2,300	3. Finished goods	2,250
		Balance	50
	2,300		2,300
Balance	50		

Conversion Costs a/c

	£000		£000
2. Creditors	1,250	4. Finished goods	1,250

Finished Goods a/c

	£000		£000
3. RIP a/c	2,250	5. Cost of goods sold	3,430
4. Conversion cost	1,250	Balance	70
	3,500		3,500
Balance	70		

Cost of Goods Sold a/c

	£000		£000
5. Finished goods	3,430	Profit & loss a/c	3,430
	£42,000		£42,000

Notes:

1. Purchase of materials/components for period of £2,300,000

2. Conversion costs for period of £1,250,000

3. Transfer to Finished Goods A/C, materials used for production (50,000 × £45) = £2,250,000

4. Transfer to Finished Goods A/C the conversion costs of production (50,000 × £25) = £1,250,000

5. Transfer from Finished Goods A/C to Cost of Goods Sold A/C the cost of the units sold:

$$(49,000 \times £70) = £3,430,000$$

Closing stocks
It will be seen that the closing stocks are:

Raw Materials	£50,000
Finished Goods	£70,000 (ie, 1,000 × £70)
Total	£120,000

The effect of this method is that £25,000 of this period's conversion cost (1,000 × £25) is carried forward to next period in the Finished Goods balance.

Solution – Variant B

Triggers – Purchase of materials
         – Sale of finished units

RIP a/c

	£000		£000
1. Creditors	2,300	3. Cost of goods sold	2,205
		Balance	95
	2,300		2,300
Balance	2,300		
Balance	95		

Conversion costs

	£000		£000
2. Creditors	1,250	4. Cost of goods sold	1,225
		5. Period exs	25
	1,250		1,250

Cost of Goods Sold

	£000		£000
3. RIP	2,205		
4. Conv. Cost	1,225	P & L	3,430
	3,430		3,430

Period Expenses

	£000		£000
5. Conv. Cost	25	P & L	25

Notes:

1. as in Variant A

2. as above

3. Transfer to COGS of material costs in the units sold (49,000 × £45) = £2,205,000

4. Transfer to COGS of conversion costs in units sold (49,000 × £25) = £1,225,000

5. Transfer to Period Expenses of the conversion costs incurred but not attributed to units sold:

$$(1,250 - 1,225) = £25,000$$

These are charged against this periods P & L A/C.

Closing stocks
The closing stocks are:

RIP A/C £95,000

This balance comprises the £50,000 raw materials over purchased plus the materials contained in the units made but not sold, ie 1000 × £45 = £45,000. It will be seen that in this method there is no finished goods stock account and no conversion costs are carried forward in inventory valuations.

The rationales claimed for this variant are that it removes the incentive to produce for stock and it focuses attention on the overall organisational objective of producing saleable goods rather than on individual sub-unit goals such as increasing labour efficiency at a single production cost centre.

Solution – Variant C

Trigger – Manufacture of Finished units

Conversion Costs

	£000		£000
Creditors	1,250	2. Finished goods	1,250

Finished Goods A/C

	£000		£000
1. Creditors	2,250	4. Cost of goods sold	3,430
3. Con. Cost	1,250	Balance	70
	3,500		3,500
Bal	70		

Cost of Goods Sold A/C

	£000		£000
4. Finished goods	3,430	P&L	3,430

Notes:

1. Entry of material purchases for the number of units completed (50,000 × £45) = £2,250,000

2. Conversion costs for period £1,250,000

3. Transfer of conversion costs for units completed to Finished Goods (50,000 × £25) = £1,250,000

4. Transfer to COGS of the cost of the units sold (49,000 × £70) = £3,430,000

Closing stocks

Finished Goods A/C £70, 000 (ie 1,000 × £70)

In this variant the £50,000 of Raw materials purchased but not yet manufactured into finished units is not entered into the internal product costing system. For this reason this variant is only suitable where the JIT system operates with minimum raw material and WIP inventories. Where there are low inventories or there is little change in levels from period to period then the inventory valuations derived from backflush costing will not be greatly different than those from conventional systems and thus are likely to be accepted for external financial reporting.

12. SUMMARY

a. Integrated cost accounts are a single system of accounting with no divisions between financial and cost accounts.

b. Interlocking financial and cost accounts are systems in which separate financial and cost accounts are kept.

c. Separate accounts are frequently encountered and are controlled ('interlocked') by a memorandum Cost Ledger Control A/c in the financial ledger and a Financial Ledger Control A/c in the cost ledger. The Financial Ledger Control A/c in the cost ledger forms part of the double system within the cost ledger.

d. Where separate cost and financial ledgers are maintained, periodic reconciliation is necessary.

e. Cost accounting methods must suit the underlying operations especially where JIT purchasing and production are used.

f. Backflush accounting aims to streamline and simplify cost accounting and focuses on the output and then attributes costs to inventories and cost of sales.

13. POINTS TO NOTE

a. Whatever system is adopted, proper double entry standards should be maintained in the accounting system.

b. Even when the accounting system is computerised the principles shown regarding the accounting entries still apply.

c. By adopting backflush accounting and other simplifications Hewlett-Packard reduced the number of cost accounting entries from over 100,000 per period to under 10,000.

Student self-testing

Exercises (answers below)

1. A company operates interlocking financial and cost accounting book-keeping systems. The following balances and data relate to the Cost Ledger.

Cost Ledger

	£	£
Opening Balances		24,283
Financial ledger control a/c	10,652	
WIP Control a/c	9,318	
Raw Material Control a/c	4,313	
Finished Goods Control a/c	24,283	24,283

The following data concerns the period's operations.

	£
Raw material purchases	41,286
Direct wages	20,444
Indirect wages	6,135
Selling & Distribution Salaries	5,157
Admin. salaries	9,106
Admin. expenses	7,213
Production expenses	8,680
S & D expenses	5,217
Stores Issues	
– Production	36,291
– Factory maintenance	2,958
– Office maintenance	1,307
Production overhead absorbed	19,800
Admin. overhead absorbed by finished goods	17,200
S & D overheads absorbed by Sales	10,100
Factory cost of finished goods	78,280
Cost of finished goods sold	92,500
Sales	143,650

You are required to write up all the necessary accounts, prepare the Costing Profit & Loss Account and give the closing trial balance.

2. The profit shown in the financial accounts was £11,287 and for the same period the cost account showed a profit of £2,704.
Examination of the accounts showed the following differences:

	Cost Accounts £	Financial Accounts £
Depreciation	9,826	10,520
Stock Valuations Opening Stocks	27,510	25,500

	Cost Accounts £	Financial Accounts £
Closing Stocks	18,218	18,750
Profit on sale of asset	–	850
Dividends received	–	2,635
Imputed rent charge	3,250	–

Reconcile the profit figures.

3. A firm maintains separate Cost and Financial Ledgers. The opening trial balance in the Cost Ledger was as follows:

Cost Ledger – Opening Trial Balance

	£	£
Financial Ledger Control A/c		24,952
Stores Ledger Control A/c	3,916	
W-I-P Control A/c	12,521	
Finished Goods Control A/c	8,515	
	24,952	24,952

During the period sales were £37,529 and purchases, wages and overheads totalled £29,286.

At the end of the period, by coincidence, the stores ledger and W-I-P Control accounts were the same values as in the opening trial balance and the balance on the Financial Ledger Control A/C was £21,242.

What was the profit for the period and the balance on the Finished Goods Control A/C?

Solutions to exercises

1.

Raw Material Control A/c

Balance	9,318	WIP	36,291
FL control	41,286	Product ohds.	2,958
		Admin. ohds.	1,307
		Balance	10,048
	50,604		50,604
Balance	10,048		

W-I-P Control A/c

Balance	10,652	Fin. Goods	78,280
Wages	20,444		
Issues	36,291		
Overheads	19,800	Balance	8,907
	87,187		87,187
Balance	8,907		

Finished Goods Control A/c

Balance	4,313	Cost of Sales	92,500
Admin. ohds.	17,200	Balance	7,293
WIP	78,280		
	99,793		99,783
Balance	7,293		

Wages Control A/c

FL control	26,579	WIP	20,444
		Product ohds	6,135
	26,579		26,579

Product Overheads Control A/c

Wages	6,135	Ohds recovered	19,800
FL control	8,680		
Issues	2,958		
Overhead adj.	2,027		
	19,800		19,800

S & D Overhead Control A/c

FL control	5,217	Cost of Sales	10,100
Salaries	5,157	Ohd adj A/c	274
	10,374		10,374

Salaries Control A/c

FL control	14,263	Admin	9,106
		S & D	5,157
	14,263		14,263

Cost of Sales A/c

S & D ohds	10,100	P & L	102,600
Fin. Gds	92,500		
	102,600		102,600

Admin. Overheads

FL control	7,213	Fin. goods	17,200
Issues	1,307	Ohd adj a/c	426
Salaries	9,106		
	17,626		17,626

Costing P & L a/c

Cost of sales	102,600	Sales	143,650
Profit	42,377	Ohd. Adj.	1,327
	144,977		144,977

Financial Ledger Control A/c

Sales	143,650	Balance	24,283
		Purchases	41,286
		Wages	26,579
Balance c/f	26,248	Salaries	14,263
		Admin. expenses	7,213
		Prod. expenses	8,680
		S & D expenses	5,217
		Profit	42,377
	169,898		169,898
		Balance	26,248

Closing Trial Balance

Raw mat. cont.	10,048	FL control	26,248
Fin. Gds. cont.	7,293		
WIP control	8,907		
	26,248		26,248

Overhead Adjustment A/C

S & D overheads	274	Product overheads	2,027
Admin overheads	426		
P & L	1,327		
	2,027		2,027

2.

Memorandum Reconciliation A/c

	£		£
Profit as financial a/cs	11,287	Profit on Cost a/cs	2,704
Depreciation difference	694	Profit on sale of asset	850
		Dividend received	2,635
		Imputed rent charge	3,250
		Stock difference	
		(opening)	2,010
		(closing)	532
	11,981		11,981

3.

Financial Ledger Control A/c

Sales	37,529	Bal B/F	24,952
Bal B/F	21,242	Costs	29,286
		Profit	4,533
	58,771		58,771
		Balance	21,242

Closing Trial Balance

Store ledger	3,916	Financial ledger	21,242
WIP	12,521		
Finished goods	4,805		
	21,242		21,242

Assessment section 2

EXAMINATION QUESTIONS (ANSWERS ON THE WEBSITE)

The following data are to be used for sub-questions 2.1 and 2.2 below:

Budgeted Labour hours	8,500
Budgeted overheads	£148,750
Actual labour hours	7,928
Actual overheads	£146,200

A2.1 Based on the data given above, what is the labour hour overhead absorption rate?
   A £17.50 per hour
   B £17.20 per hour
   C £18.44 per hour
   D £18.76 per hour

A2.2 Based on the data given above, what is the amount of overhead under/over absorbed?
   A £2,550 under absorbed
   B £2,529 over absorbed
   C £2,550 over absorbed
   D £7,460 under absorbed

A2.3 The profit shown in the financial accounts was £158,500 but the cost accounts showed a different figure. The following stock valuations were used:

Stock valuations	Cost accounts	Financial accounts
	£	£
Opening stock	35,260	41,735
Closing stock	68,490	57,336

What was the profit in the cost accounts?

A £163,179

B £140,871

C £176,129

D £153,821

A2.4 A firm operates an integrated cost and financial accounting system. The accounting entries for an issue of Direct Materials to Production would be:

A DR work-in-progress control account; CR stores control account.

B DR finished goods account; CR stores control account.

C DR stores control account; CR work-in-progress control account.

D DR cost of sales account; CR work-in-progress control account.

A2.5 In the cost ledger the factory cost of finished production for a period was £873,190. The double entry for this is:

A Dr Cost of sales account   Cr Finished goods control account

B Dr Finished goods control account   Cr Work-in-progress control account

C Dr Costing profit and loss account Cr Finished goods control account

D Dr Work-in-progress control account Cr Finished goods control account

A firm uses job costing and recovers overheads on direct labour. Three jobs were worked on during a period, the details of which were:

	Job 1	Job 2	Job 3
	£	£	£
Opening work-in-progress	8,500	0	46,000
Material in period	17,150	29,025	0
Labour for period	12,500	23,000	4,500

The overheads for the period were exactly as budgeted, £140,000.

A2.6 Jobs 1 and 2 were the only incomplete jobs.

What was the value of closing work-in-progress?

A £81,900

B £90,175

C £140,675

D £214,425

A2.7 Job 3 was completed during the period and consisted of 2,400 identical circuit boards. The firm adds 50% to total production costs to arrive at a selling price.

What is the selling price of a circuit board?

A It cannot be calculated without more information

B £31.56

C £41.41

D £58.33

A2.8   A company absorbs overheads on machine hours which were budgeted at 11,250 with overheads of £258,750. Actual results were 10,980 hours with overheads of £254,692.
Overheads were:
A under-absorbed by £2,152
B over-absorbed by £4,058
C under-absorbed by £4,058
D over-absorbed by £2,152

A2.9   When comparing the performance of two factories, one of which is owned and the other rented, the inclusion of rent as an expense in the profit statement of the factory owned is known as the inclusion of:
A relevant cost
B a normal cost
C a notional cost
D a controllable cost

A2.10 A method of dealing with overheads involves spreading common costs over cost centres on the basis of benefit received. This is known as:
A overhead absorption
B overhead apportionment
C overhead allocation
D overhead analysis

A2.11 Over-absorbed overheads occur when:
A absorbed overheads exceed actual overheads
B absorbed overheads exceed budgeted overheads
C actual overheads exceed absorbed overheads
D budgeted overheads exceed absorbed overheads

A2.12 P Limited absorbs overheads on the basis of direct labour hours. The overhead absorption rate for the period has been based on budgeted overheads of £150,000 and 50,000 direct labour hours.
During the period, overheads of £180,000 were incurred and 60,000 direct labour hours were used.
Which of the following statements is correct?
A overhead was £30,000 over-absorbed
B overhead was £30,000 under-absorbed
C no under or over-absorption occurred
D none of the above

A2.13 A company uses the repeated distribution method to reapportion service department costs. The use of this method suggests:
A the company's overhead rates are based on estimates of cost and activity levels, rather than actual amounts.
B there are more service departments than production cost centres.
C the company wishes to avoid under- or over-absorption of overheads in its production cost centres.
D the service departments carry out work for each other.

A2.14 The management accountant's report shows that fixed production overheads were over-absorbed in the last accounting period. The combination that is certain to lead to this situation is:

Production activity   and   **Fixed overhead expenditure**

A lower than budget   D lower than budget
B higher than budget   E higher than budget
C as budgeted   F as budgeted

A2.15 Which of the following costs would be classified as production overhead cost in a food processing company (tick all that apply)?
A The cost of renting the factory building.
B The salary of the factory manager.
C The depreciation of equipment located in the materials store.
D The cost of ingredients.

A2.16 A company manufactures two products P1 and P2 in a factory divided into two cost centres, X and Y. The following budgeted data are available:

	Cost centre	
	X	Y
Allocated and apportioned fixed overhead costs	£88,000	£96,000
Direct labour hours per unit:		
Product P1	3.0	1.0
Product P2	2.5	2.0

Budgeted output is 8,000 units of each product. Fixed overhead costs are absorbed on a direct labour hour basis.
   What is the budgeted fixed overhead cost per unit for Product P2?
A £10
B £11
C £12
D £13

A2.17 A manufacturing company uses a machine hour rate to absorb production overheads, which were budgeted to be £130,500 for 9,000 machine hours. Actual overheads incurred were £128,480 and 8,800 machine hours were recorded.
   What was the total under absorption of production overheads?
A £880
B £900
C £2,020
D £2,900

A2.18 The following graph shows the wages earned by an employee during a single day:

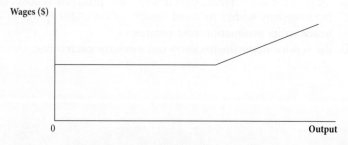

Wages ($)

0   Output

Which ONE of the remuneration systems listed below does the graph represent?

A Differential piecework.

B A flat rate per hour with a premium for overtime working.

C Straight piecework.

D Piecework with a guaranteed minimum daily wage

The above are a variety of multiple choice questions selected from CIMA's Management Accounting Fundamentals, Fundamentals of Management Accounting and ACCA's Financial Information for Management.

A2.19 (a) Identify the costs to a business arising from labour turnover.

(b) A company operates a factory which employed 40 direct workers throughout the four week period just ended. Direct employees were paid at a basic rate of £4.00 per hour for a 38 hour week. Total hours of the direct workers in the four week period were 6,528. Overtime, which is paid at a premium of 35%, is worked in order to meet general production requirements. Employee deductions total 30% of gross wages. 188 hours of direct workers' time were registered as idle.

Required:

Prepare journal entries to account for the labour costs of direct workers for the period.

(ACCA Management Information)

A2.20 A printing and publishing company has been asked to provide an estimate for the production of 100,000 catalogues, of 64 pages (32 sheets of paper) each, for a potential customer.

Four operations are involved in the production process: photography, set-up, printing and binding.

Each page of the catalogue requires a separate photographic session. Each session costs £150.

Set-up would require plates be made for each page of the catalogue. Each plate requires four hours of labour at £7 per hour and £35 of materials. Overheads are absorbed on the basis of labour hours at an hourly rate of £9.50.

In printing, paper costs £12 per thousand sheets. Material losses are expected to be 2% of input. Other printing materials will cost £7 per 500 catalogues. 1,000 catalogues are printed per hour of machine time. Labour and overhead costs incurred in printing are absorbed at a rate of £62 per machine hour.

Binding costs are recovered at a rate per machine hour. The rate is £43 per hour and 2,500 catalogues are bound per hour of machine time.

A profit margin of 10% of selling is required.

You are required to:

(a) Determine the total amount that should be quoted for the catalogue job by the printing and publishing company.

(b) Calculate the additional costs that would be charged to the job if the labour efficiency ratio achieved versus estimate in set-up is 90%.

(ACCA Management Information)

A2.21 The Utopian Hotel is developing a cost accounting system. Initially it has been decided to create four cost centres: Residential and Catering deal directly with customers while Housekeeping and Maintenance are internal service cost centres.

The following overhead details have been estimated for the next period:

	Residential £	Catering £	House-keeping £	Maintenance £	Total £
Consumable materials	14,000	23,000	27,000	9,000	73,000
Staff costs	16,500	13,000	11,500	5,500	46,500
Rent and rates					37,500
Contents insurance					14,000
Heating and Lighting					18,500
Depreciation on equipment etc					37,500
					227,000

The following information is also available:

	Residential	Catering	House-keeping	Maintenance	Total
Floor area (m^2)	2,750	1,350	600	300	5,000
Value of equipment etc	£350,000	£250,000	£75,000	£75,000	£750,000
Number of employees	20	20	15	5	60

In the period it is estimated that there will be 2,800 guest-nights and 16,000 meals will be served. Housekeeping works 70% for Residential and 30% for Catering, and Maintenance works 20% for Housekeeping, 30% for Catering and 50% for Residential.

Requirements:

a. Prepare an overhead statement showing clearly allocations and apportionments to each cost centre.
b. Calculate appropriate overhead absorption rates for Residential and Catering.
c. Calculate the under/over absorption of overheads if actual results were as follows:

Residential: 3,050 guest-nights with overheads of £144,600.
Catering: 15,250 meals with overheads of £89,250

d. Comment briefly on possible future developments in the Utopian Hotel's cost accounting system.
(CIMA Cost Accounting and Quantitative Methods)

A2.22 A company makes a range of products with total budgeted manufacturing overheads of £973,560 incurred in three production departments (A, B and C) and one service department.

Department A has 10 direct employees who each work 37 hours per week. Department B has five machines each of which is operated for 24 hours per week. Department C is expected to produce 148,000 units of final product in the budget period.

The company will operate for 48 weeks in the budget period.

Budgeted overheads incurred directly by each department are:

Production Department A	£261,745
Production Department B	£226,120
Production Department C	£93,890
Service Department D	£53,305

The balance of budgeted overheads are apportioned to departments as follows:

Production Department A	40%
Production Department B	35%
Production Department C	20%
Service Department	5%

Service Department overheads are apportioned equally to each production department.

You are required to:

a. Calculate an appropriate predetermined overhead absorption rate in each production department.
b. Calculate the manufacturing overhead cost per unit of finished product in a batch of 100 units which take nine direct labour hours in Department A and three machine hours in Department B to produce.

(ACCA Management Information)

A2.23 Limited has separate cost and financial accounting systems interlocked by control accounts in the two ledgers.

From the cost accounts, the following information was available for the period:

	£
Cost of finished goods produced	512,050
Cost of goods sold	493,460
Direct materials issued	197,750
Direct Wages	85,480
Production overheads (as per the financial accounts)	208,220
Direct material purchases	216,590

In the cost accounts, additional depreciation of £12,500 per period is charged and production overheads are absorbed at 250% of wages.

The various account balances at the beginning of the period were:

	£
Store Control	54,250
Work-in-progress control	89,100
Finished goods control	42,075

Requirements:

a. Prepare the following control accounts in the cost ledger, showing clearly the double entries between the accounts, and the closing balances:

Accounts required:

Stores control
Work-in-progress control
Finished goods control
Production overhead control

b. Explain the meaning of the balance on the production overhead control account.
c. When separate ledgers are maintained, the differing treatment of certain items may cause variations to arise between costing and financial profits. Examples of such items include stock valuations, notional expenses, and non-costing items charged in the financial accounts.

Requirement:

Briefly explain the above *three* examples and state why they may give rise to profit differences.

(CIMA Cost Accounting and Quantitative Methods)

A2.24 Having attended a CIMA course on activity based costing (ABC) you decide to experiment by applying the principles of ABC to the four products currently made and sold by your company. Details of the four products and relevant information are given below for one period:

Product	A	B	C	D
Output in units	120	100	80	120
Costs per unit	£	£	£	£
Direct material	40	50	30	60
Direct labour	28	21	14	21
Machine hours per unit	4	3	2	3

The four products are similar and are usually produced in production runs of 20 units and sold in batches of 10 units.

The production overhead is currently absorbed by using a machine hour rate, and the total of the production overhead for the period has been analysed as follows:

Machine department costs (rent, business rates, depreciation and supervision)	£10,430
Set-up costs	£5,250
Stores receiving	£3,600
Inspection/Quality control	£2,100
Materials handling and dispatch	£4,620

You have ascertained that the 'cost drivers' to be used are as listed below for the overhead costs shown:

Cost	Cost driver
Set-up costs	Number of production runs
Stores receiving	Requisitions raised
Inspection/Quality control	Number of production runs
Materials handling and dispatch	Orders executed

The number of requisitions raised on the stores was 20 for each period and the number of orders executed was 42, each order being for a batch of 10 of a product.

You are required:

a) to calculate the total costs for each product if all overhead costs are absorbed on a machine hour basis;
b) to calculate the total costs for each product, using activity based costing;
c) to calculate and list the unit product costs from your figures in (a) and (b) above, to show the differences and to comment briefly on any conclusions which may be drawn which could have profit and pricing implications.

(CIMA, Cost Accounting)

A2.25 V Ltd operates interlocking financial and cost accounts. The following balances were in the cost ledger at the beginning of a month (Month 12) of the financial year:

	Dr	Cr
Raw material stock control A/c	£28,944	
Finished goods stock control A/c	£77,168	
Financial ledger control A/c		£106,112

There is no work in progress at the end of each month.

21,600 kilos of the single raw material were in stock at the beginning of Month 12.

Purchases and issues during the month were as follows:

Purchases:
7th,	17,400 kilos at £1.35 per kilo
20th,	19,800 kilos at £1.35 per kilo

Issues:
1st,	7,270 kilos
8th,	8,120 kilos
15th,	8,080 kilos
22nd,	9,115 kilos

A weighted average price per kilo (to four decimal places of a £) is used to value issues of raw material to production. A new average price is determined after each material purchase, and issues are charged out in total to the nearest £.

Costs of labour and overhead incurred during Month 12 were £35,407. Production of the company's single product was 17,150 units.

Stocks of finished goods were:

Beginning of Month 12,	16,960 units.
End of month 12,	17,080 units.

Transfers from finished goods stock on sale of product are made on a FIFO basis.

Required:

a. Prepare the raw material stock control account, and the finished goods stock control accounts for month 12. (Show detailed working to justify the summary entries made in the accounts.)
b. Explain the purpose of the financial ledger control account.

(ACCA Cost & Management Accounting)

A2.26 WYZ Ltd has separate accounting systems for the cost and financial ledgers which are interlocked by means of control accounts in the two ledgers. The following information was available for period 7:

	£
Cost of goods sold	1,310,750
Cost of finished goods produced	1,241,500
Direct wages	173,400
Direct material issues	598,050
Direct material purchases	617,300
Production overheads (actual expenditure as per the financial accounts)	392,525

At the beginning of the period, the various account balances in the Cost Ledger were:

Account	£
Work-in-progress control	125,750
Finished goods control	94,500
Direct material stores control	48,250

In the Cost Accounts, additional production depreciation of £35,000 is charged, and production overheads were over-absorbed by £63,775 for the period.

Required:

a. Prepare the following Control Accounts in the Cost Ledger showing clearly the double entries between the accounts and the closing balances: Accounts required:

work-in-progress control
direct material stores control
finished goods control
production overhead control

b. Calculate the number of hours worked if production overheads are absorbed at the rate of £17 per labour hour, AND give possible reasons for the over-absorption of overheads in the period.

(CIMA Cost Accounting and Quantitative Methods)

A2.27 The Major Gnome Manufacturing Company has two departments – Moulding and Painting – and uses a single production overhead absorption rate based on direct labour hours. The budget and actual data for period 6 are given below:

	Direct wages £	Labour hours	Machine hours	Production overhead £
Budget				
Moulding	24,000	4,000	12,000	180,000
Painting	70,000	10,000	1,000	100,000
	94,000	14,000	13,000	280,000
Actual				
Moulding	30,000	5,000	14,000	200,000
Painting	59,500	8,500	800	95,000
	89,500	13,500	14,800	295,000

During period 6, a batch of Pixie Gnomes was made which had the following costs and times:

	Direct wages £	Labour hours	Machine hours
Moulding	726	120	460
Painting	2,490	415	38
	3,216	535	498

The direct material cost of the batch was £890.

Required:

a. Calculate the cost of the batch of Pixie Gnomes using a single company-wide overhead absorption rate on labour hours. It has been suggested that appropriate departmental overhead absorption rates may be more realistic.
b. Calculate appropriate departmental overhead absorption rates.
c. Calculate the cost of the batch of Pixie Gnomes using departmental absorption rates.
d. Briefly discuss why departmental absorption rates may be more realistic.

(CIMA Cost Accounting and Quantitative Methods)

A2.28 Sangazure Ltd manufactures many different products in a factory that has two production cost centres (T and W) and several service cost centres.

The total budgeted overhead costs (after the allocation, apportionment and reapportionment of service cost centre costs) and other information for production cost centres T and W are as follows:

Cost centre	Budgeted Overheads	Basis of overhead absorption	Budgeted activity
T	£780,000	Machine hours	16,250 Machine Hours
W	£173,400	Direct labour hours	14,450 Labour Hours

Required:

(a) Calculate the overhead absorption rates for cost centres T and W.

The prime cost of product PP, one of the products made by Sangazure Ltd, is as follows

£ per unit:

Direct material   10
Direct labour:
 Cost centre T   14
 Cost centre W   21

One unit of product PP takes 35 minutes of machine time in cost centre T. The direct labour in cost centre T is paid £7 per hour and £6 per hour in cost centre W.

(b) Calculate the total production cost for one unit of PP.

(c) Briefly explain why service cost centre costs need to be reapportioned to production cost centres. Which method of reapportionment fully recognises the work that service cost centres do for each other?

ACCA Financial Information for Management

A2.29 Phoebe Ltd manufactures many different products which pass through two production cost centres (P1 and P210). There are also two service cost centres (S1 and S2) in the factory. The following information has been extracted from the budget for the coming year.

	P1	P2	S1	S2
Allocated and apportioned production overheads	£477,550	£404,250	£132,000	£96,000
Number of employees	30	65	10	15
Total machine hours	68,000	11,400		
Total direct labour hours	4,000	14,000		

Service cost centre S1 costs are reapportioned to all other cost centres based on the number of employees. Service cost centre S2 only does work for P1 and P2 and its costs are reapportioned to these centres in the ratio 5:3 respectively.

Required:

a. Calculate:

 i. the machine hour absorption rate for cost centre P1, and
 ii. the direct labour hour absorption rate for cost.

b. Explain the difference between production overheads that have been 'allocated' and those which have been 'apportioned' to cost centres. Explain why some manufacturing companies are able to allocate electric power centres, whereas others can only apportion them.

ACCA Financial Information for Management

EXAMINATION QUESTIONS WITHOUT ANSWERS

B2.1 a. Define the term 'cost centre' and detail the factors influencing the choice of cost centres within a business.

 b. One of the cost centres in a factory is involved in the final stage of production. Budgeted fixed overhead costs for the cost centre for a period were:

Apportioned costs		£74,610	
Directly incurred costs		£98,328	

A predetermined machine hour rate is established for the absorption of fixed production overhead into product cost. Budgeted machine hours for the cost centre in the period were 1,900.

Actual overheads (apportioned and directly incurred) in the period were £173,732. The volume variance was £4,551 favourable.

Required:

Calculate for the period:

   i. the predetermined fixed overhead absorption rate
  ii. the actual machine hours
 iii. the over/under absorption of fixed overhead

  c. Explain the nature of the apportioned costs and the 'directly incurred' costs in (b) above.

(ACCA Cost & Management Accounting)

B2.2 NB Limited operates an integrated accounting system. At the beginning of October, the following balances appeared in the trial balance:

	£000	£000	£000
Freehold buildings		800	
Plant and equipment, at cost		480	
Provision for depreciation on plant and equipment			100
Stocks:			
Raw materials		400	
Work-in-process 1:			
direct materials	71		
direct wages	50		
production overhead	125	246	
Work-in-process 2			
direct materials	127		
direct wages	70		
production overhead	105	302	
Debtors		1,120	
Capital			2,200
Profit retained			220
Creditors			300
Bank			464
Sales			1,200
Cost of sales		888	
Abnormal loss		9	
Production overhead under/over absorbed			21
Administration overhead		120	
Selling distribution overhead		80	
		4,505	4,505

The transactions during the month of October were:

	£000
Raw materials purchased on credit	210
Raw materials returned to suppliers	10
Raw materials issued to:	
Process 1	136
Process 2	44
Direct wages incurred:	
Process 1	84
Process 2	130
Direct wages paid	200
Production salaries paid	170
Production expenses paid	250

	£000
Received from debtors	1,140
Paid to creditors	330
Administration overhead paid	108
Selling and distribution overhead paid	84
Sales, on credit	1,100
Cost of goods sold	844

	Direct materials £000	Direct wages £000
Abnormal loss in: Process 1	6	4
Process 2	18	6
Transfer from Process 1 to Process 2	154	94
Transfer from Process 2 to finished goods	558	140

Plant and equipment is depreciated at the rate of 20% per annum, using the straight-line basis.

Production overheads is absorbed on the basis of direct wages cost.

You are required:

a. to ascertain and state the production overhead absorption rates used for Process 1 and for Process 2;
b. to write up the ledger accounts
c. to explain the nature of abnormal losses and two possible reasons for their occurrence.

(CIMA Cost Accounting)

B2.3   a. In the context of the output from a factory or group of workers, define and distinguish 'production' and 'productivity'.

b. X Y and Z are the members of a team making metal brackets. The expected output of the team is 6,000 brackets per week, each member working a 40 hours week and being paid a basic rate of £1.75 for each hour worked. A bonus of 50% of the team's productivity index in excess of 100 is added as a percentage to the basic hourly rate.

During week No. 50, X worked 40 hours, Y 39 hours and Z 38 hours and the output for the week was 6,786 brackets.
You are required to calculate for week No. 50:

  i. the team's productivity index
  ii. the effective hourly rate paid to the operatives
  iii. the wages rate and efficiency variances of the team

c. Name the type of bonus scheme under which the members of the team are remunerated and demonstrate your understanding of the characteristics of that scheme by reference to your answers to (b).

(ACCA, Costing)

B2.4 An asset has an installed cost for £35,000, an estimated life of 10 years and an estimated scrap value of £2,000. Calculate the first year charge for depreciation using the following methods.

a. Straight line
b. Reducing balance
c. Sum of digits
d. Repair reserve where maintenance is expected to cost £18,000 over asset life.
e. Production unit where the lifetime output is estimated to be 200,000 and output in the first year estimated to be 15,000.

In addition calculate the sinking fund charge for the asset where investment opportunities exist at 12% and the asset is expected to cost £55,000 to replace in 10 years.

The value of $S_{\overline{10}|12\%}$ can be calculated using the formula $\dfrac{r}{(1+r)^n-1}$ where n is the number of years and r is the rate of interest, or alternatively tables can be used from which the value will be found to be 0.0570).

B2.5 Due to recession in its industry, which has caused a reduction in its sales, a manufacturing company is proposing to reduce by one-fifth its productive capacity, as measured in terms of the number of direct labour hours of its operators. It is considering doing this by either:

a. putting some of its operators on short time; or
b. making a number of its operators redundant through dismissal.

You are required to compare and contrast in tabular form the effects that each course of action is likely to have on the composition and level of the company's total annual:

  i. direct materials cost;
  ii. direct wages;
  iii. production overhead;
  iv. other (non-production) overhead.

(CIMA, Cost Accounting 2)

B2.6 SM Limited makes two products. Exe and Wye. For product costing purposes a single cost centre overhead rate of £3.40 per hour is used based on budgeted production overhead of £680,000 and 200,000 budgeted hours as shown below.

	Budgeted overhead	Budgeted hours
Department 1	480,000	100,000
Department 2	200,000	100,000
	£680,000	200,000

The number of hours required to manufacture each of the products is:

	Exe	Wye
Department 1	8	4
Department 2	2	6
	10	10

There was no work-in-progress or finished goods stocks at the beginning of the period of operations but at the end of the period 10,000 finished units of Exe and 5,000 finished units of Wye were in stock. There was no closing work-in-progress.

The prime cost per unit of Exe is £30. The pricing policy is to add 50% to the production cost to cover administration, selling and distribution costs and to provide what is thought to be a reasonable profit.

You are required to:

a. calculate the effect on the company's profit for the period, by using a single cost centre overhead rate compared with using departmental overhead rates;

b. show by means of a comparative statement what the price of Exe would be using (i) single cost centre overhead rate and (ii) departmental overhead rates;

c. discuss briefly whether the company should change its present policy on overhead absorption, stating reasons to support your conclusion.

(CIMA, Cost Accounting 1)

B2.7 A company re-apportions the costs incurred by two service cost centres, materials handling and inspection, to the three production cost centres of machining, finishing and assembly.

The following are the overhead costs which have been allocated and apportioned to the five cost centres:

	£000
Machining	400
Finishing	200
Assembly	100
Materials handling	100
Inspection	50

Estimates of the benefits received by each cost centre are as follows:

	Machining	Finishing	Assembly	Materials handling	Inspection
	%	%	%	%	%
Materials handling	30	25	35	–	10
Inspection	20	30	45	5	–

You are required to:

a. calculate the charge for overhead to each of the three production cost centres, including the amounts re-apportioned from the two service centres, using

   i. the continuous allotment (or repeated distribution) method, and
  ii. an algebraic method;

b. comment on whether re-apportioning service cost centre costs is generally worthwhile and suggest an alternative treatment for such costs;

c. discuss the following statement:

Some writers advocate that an under- or over-absorption of overhead should be apportioned between the cost of goods sold in the period to which it relates and to closing stocks. However, the United Kingdom practice is to treat under-or over-absorption of overhead as a period cost.
(CIMA Cost Accounting)

B2.8   You are the Cost Accountant of an industrial concern and have been given the following budgeted information regarding the four cost centres within your organisation.

	Dep't 1 £	Dep't 2 £	Maint'ce Dep't £	Canteen £	Total £
Indirect Labour	60,000	70,500	25,000	15,000	170,000
Consumables	12,000	16,000	3,000	10,000	41,000
Heat/Light					12,000
Rent and Rates					18,000
Depreciation					30,000
Supervision					24,000
Power					20,000
					315,000

You are also given the following information:

	Dep't 1	Dep't 2	Maint'ce Dep't	Canteen	Total
Floor area (m^2)	10,000	12,000	5,000	3,000	30,000
Book value of machinery in (£)	150,000	120,000	20,000	10,000	300,000
No. of employees	40	30	10		80
Kilowatt hours	4,500	4,000	1,000	500	10,000

You are also told:

   i. The canteen staff are outside contractors.
  ii. Departments 1 and 2 are production centres and the maintenance department and canteen are service cost centres.
 iii. The maintenance department provides 4,000 service hours to Department 1 and 3,000 service hours to Department 2.
 iv. That Department 1 is machine intensive and Department 2 is labour intensive.
  v. That 6,320 machine hours and 7,850 labour hours are budgeted for Departments 1 and 2 respectively for 1991.

Required:

a. An overhead cost statement showing the allocation and apportionment of overhead to the four cost centres, clearly showing the basis of apportionment.
b. Calculate the overhead absorption rates for Department 1 on the basis of the machine hours and Department 2 on the basis of labour hours.
c. On the basis that actual overheads for Department 1 turn out to be £155,000 and machine hours worked 6,000, while actual overheads for Department 2 turn out to be £156,000 and labour hours worked 7,900, calculate the under or over recovery of overheads for each department.
d. The Managing Director of your organisation suggests to you that one blanket rate rather than separate overhead absorption rates for Departments 1 and 2 based on machine hours and labour hours respectively would be more beneficial for future years.
    Draft a reply to this assertion.

(AAT Cost Accounting & Budgeting)

B2.9 The following balances were calculated for December 31st and January 31st.

	Balance at December 31st	Balance at January 31st
Stores Control A/c	54,192	51,282
W-I-P Control A/c	17,803	22,607
Finished Goods Control A/c	34,522	29,602

The following data relates to transactions in January.

	£
Material purchases	65,800
Direct labour	29,920
Indirect labour	11,860
Indirect material to production cost centres	2,790
Indirect production expenses	22,440

Production overhead is absorbed at 120% of direct wages. Prepare the three control accounts (Stores, W-I-P and Finished Goods) for January showing the production cost of goods sold and over/under absorption of production overhead.

B2.10 A company manufactures a single product from one basic raw material. The standard purchase price of the raw material is £3.50 per kilo, and standard usage is five kilos per unit of finished product. Material price variance is identified on purchase of raw material. Actual direct labour costs and production overhead absorbed are charged to units of finished product based upon weighted average costs. The production overhead absorption rate is 200% of direct labour cost.

Balances in the company's integrated accounts at the beginning of a period included:

Raw materials:
Direct materials, 5,240 kilos
Indirect materials, £1,484

Production overhead:
Accrued at the end of the previous period, £3,840

Work in Progress:
Direct material, £4,550
Direct labour and production overhead, £1,950
260 units, complete as to direct material, 50% complete as to direct labour and production overhead.

Finished goods:
1,470 units, £47,775.

Costs incurred during the period were:

Raw materials purchased:
Direct material, 7,600 kilos, £26,904
Indirect materials, £2,107.

Raw materials issued:
Direct material, 7,460 kilos.
Indirect materials, £1,963.

Production wage paid:

	Direct workers £	Indirect workers £
Gross	8,670	2,235
Employees' deductions	2,688	693
Net	5,982	1,542

The cost of the productive time of direct workers was £7,950. The balance of the wages paid to direct workers is charged to production overhead.

Other production overhead incurred: £9,252
Period sales: 1,520 units.

Production output of the single product during the period was:

Completed and transferred to finished goods stock, 1,450 units.

Closing work in progress 310 units, completed as to direct material, 60% complete as to direct labour and production overhead.

A physical stock check of the basic raw material at the end of the period revealed that 5,310 kilos remained in stock. Production overhead to be accrued totalled £4,170.

Required:

Prepare accounting entries for the period in the following accounts:

  i. raw material stock,
 ii. production wages,
iii. production overhead,
 iv. work in progress,
  v. finished goods stock.

(ACCA Cost & Management Accounting)

11

Cost accounting methods: Introduction

1. OBJECTIVES

After studying this chapter you will

- **Know what is meant by a Cost Accounting Method**

- **Be able to define Specific Order Costing and Operation/Process Costing**

- **Know that the cost accounting method used must suit the method of manufacture or the way services are supplied.**

2. WHAT IS A COST ACCOUNTING METHOD?

A cost accounting method is a system which is designed to suit the way goods are processed or manufactured or the way that services are provided. It follows therefore that each firm will have a cost accounting method which has unique features. Nevertheless there will be recognisably common features of the cost accounting systems of firms who are broadly in the same line of business.

Conversely firms employing substantially different manufacturing methods, for example a food processors and a jobbing engineering factory, will have distinctly different cost accounting methods as will the huge variety of service organisations. It must be clearly understood that whatever cost accounting method is employed, the basic costing principles relating to analysis, allocation and apportionment will be used.

3. CATEGORIES OF COST ACCOUNTING METHODS

There are two broad categories of product costing methods, namely specific order costing and continuous operation/process costing.

a. Specific order costing

This can be defined as;

The basic cost accounting method applicable where work consists of separately identifiable contracts, jobs or batches.

In most cases the job or contract is the cost unit and frequently, but not always, the jobs or contracts are different from each other. The main sub-divisions of specific order costing are

  i. Job costing

  ii. Contract costing

  iii. Batch costing

b. Continuous operation/process costing (sometimes called unit costing)
This can be defined as;

The costing method applicable where goods or services result from a sequence of continuous or repetitive operations or processes. Costs are averaged over the units produced during the period, being initially charged to the operation or process.

The key feature of this definition is that operation (or unit) costing seeks to establish the average cost per unit during a period for a number of identical cost units. The main sub-divisions of operation costing are:

i. Process costing including Joint Product and By-product Costing.

ii. Service/function costing. This type of costing although not relating to production cost units uses similar principles whereby an average cost is established per unit of service. For example, an average cost per meal supplied could be calculated for the canteen which is a service cost centre.

These categories and sub-divisions are shown in Figure 11.1.

Note to Figure 11.1:
The dotted line indicates an area of overlap between the two major categories. Although each batch is separate and identifiable and may be different from any other batch, within a given batch there will be a number of identical cost

FIGURE 11.1   Costing Methods – Categories and sub-divisions

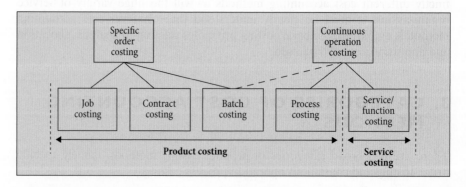

units over which the total batch costs will be averaged. Thus batch costing may have some of the characteristics of both specific order and process costing.

4. COST ACCOUNTING METHODS AND PRINCIPLES

An important difference between the principles of cost accounting in relation to Specific Order Costing and Operation Costing is that, with Operation Costing, all costs ie, Labour, Materials and Overheads are allocated or apportioned to a cost centre from which these costs are shared out over the cost units produced. This differs from Specific Order Costing where labour and materials are directly charged to a cost unit with only overheads having to be allocated or apportioned to a cost centre before sharing the costs over cost units.

5. COST ACCOUNTING METHODS AND TECHNIQUES

It must be emphasised that whatever cost accounting method is used, it can be combined with any of the cost accounting techniques if deemed appropriate. Thus, for example, a Process Costing system could utilise the technique of either, Total Absorption Costing or Marginal Costing or Standard Costing or Activity Based Costing.

6. SUMMARY

a. Cost accounting methods are designed to suit the method of manufacture or processing or the way services are supplied.

b. Whatever method is used, it will employ basic cost accounting principles relating to classification, analysis, allocation and apportionment.

c. The two main categories of cost accounting methods are: specific order costing and continuous operation (or unit) costing.

d. Specific order costing can be sub-divided into: Job Costing, Contract Costing, and Batch Costing.

e. Continuous Operation or Unit Costing can be sub-divided into: Service Costing, and Process Costing which includes Joint-Product and By-Product costing.

f. Whatever is deemed the most appropriate cost accounting technique, eg, Marginal Costing, Standard Costing etc, can be used with any of the cost accounting methods.

7. POINT TO NOTE

Different parts of the same firm may require different cost accounting methods. It is essential to relate the method to the particular activity being costed.

12

Cost accounting methods: Job and batch costing

1. OBJECTIVES

After studying this chapter you will

- **Know what the requirements are for Job Costing**

- **Understand the typical procedures necessary in a Jobbing firm**

- **Know the book-keeping entries for Job Costing**

- **Be able to design a Job Cost Card**

- **Understand Batch Costing**

- **Know how ABC principles are used in Job and Batch Costing.**

2. JOB COSTING – DEFINITION

Job costing can be defined as;

A form of specific order costing in which costs are attributed to individual jobs.
Terminology

3. PREREQUISITES FOR JOB COSTING

The main purposes of job costing are to establish the profit or loss on each job and to provide a valuation of W-I-P. To do this a considerable amount of clerical work is needed and to ensure an effective and workable system. The following requirements are necessary:

a. A sound system of production control.

b. Comprehensive works documentation. Typically this includes: works order and/or operation tickets, bill of materials and/or materials requisitions, jig and tool requisitions, etc.

c. An appropriate time booking system using either time sheets or piecework tickets.

d. A well organised basis to the costing system with clearly defined cost centres, good labour analysis, appropriate overhead absorption rates and a relevant materials issue pricing system.

4. TYPICAL PROCEDURES IN A JOBBING CONCERN

Prior to examining the cost accounting system it is necessary first to consider the typical flow of administrative procedures which ensure a job is manufactured correctly, delivered on time and charged for. An outline is shown in Figure 12.1.

FIGURE 12.1   Typical non-costing procedures in a jobbing concern

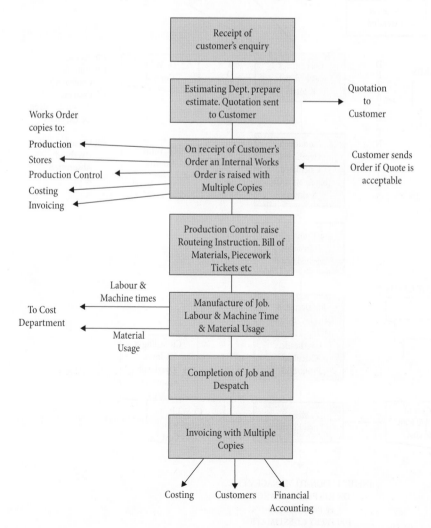

5. JOB COSTING PROCEDURES

The main objective is to charge all costs incurred to the particular job. The usual means by which this is done by creating a Job Cost Card (frequently just called the Job Card). The Job Cost Cards in total comprise the firm's

FIGURE 12.2   Outline of job costing

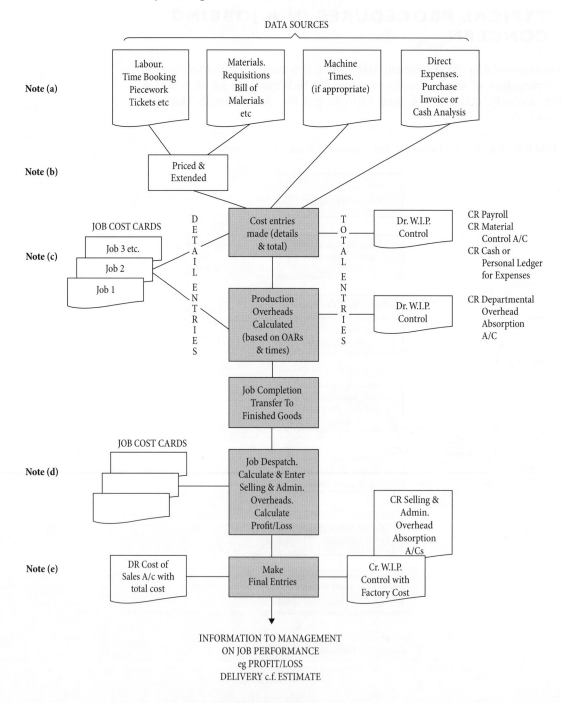

work-in-progress and the detailed entries to the job cards would be debited in total to the work-in-progress account. Figure 12.2 shows the major steps in a typical Job Costing process.

Notes on Figure 12.2:

a. The contents and origin of Labour and Material bookings have been covered in previous chapters. The machine times would be required if any of the departmental overhead absorption rates were based on the machine hour method. Direct expenses, eg royalties, tool hire, etc would be a direct charge to the job and details would be picked up either from purchase invoices or the cash book.

b. Labour time sheets and/or piecework tickets would be priced by reference to day and overtime rates, piecework and bonus rates. The materials issued would be priced using the stores record cards, employing one of the pricing systems, ie FIFO, average price, etc.

c. After the prime costs had been entered, the production departments' overheads would be calculated using the labour and/or machine times and the predetermined overhead absorption rates (OARs).

d. Until a job is despatched, it would normally be valued in the Work-in-Progress account at factory or works cost only. On despatch (or, in some systems, transfer to finished goods), the works cost would be loaded with an appropriate amount of selling and administration overheads. Any delivery costs can be charged to the job, the total cost established and the profit or loss calculated.

e. The individual Job Cost Cards will be retained and used as a basis for management information and future estimating. The closing book-keeping entries transfer the total cost of jobs despatched to cost of sales and the Factory cost is transferred from the W-I-P account (or in some systems the Finished Goods account). The amount of Selling and Administration overheads charged to jobs is credited to the overhead absorption account, so that eventually it will be possible to establish whether there has been under or over absorption of overheads.

6. ILLUSTRATION OF JOB COSTING BOOK-KEEPING

The example which follows illustrates the book-keeping entries depicted in Figure 12.2 and shows typical flows of information in a jobbing concern.

Example 1
The data below relate to a single accounting period in a jobbing engineering works.

Extracts from Job Cost Cards

	Opening W-I-P	Charged during period	Closing W-I-P
Materials	£10,620	£32,840	£12,630
Labour	15,250	53,260	16,170
Production overheads	10,830	33,520	9,260

The financial accountant supplied the following information relating to the same period:

	£
Materials purchased	39,150
Selling and admin. overheads	12,780
Production overheads	30,620
Sales	146,330

The opening stock of material was £9,200. All completed jobs are invoiced immediately to customers and you are advised that the Cost Department recover selling and administrative overheads at the rate of 10% of the cost of completed jobs.

Using the above information it is required to write up the Cost Ledger and prepare a Costing P & L A/C for the period assuming that the firm operates an interlocking system with separate financial and cost accounts.

Solution

Cost Ledger

Financial Ledger Control A/C

		Balance B/F	45,900
Sales	146,330	Purchases	39,150
		S & D	12,780
Balance C/F	53,570	Prod. ohds	30,620
		Wages	53,260
		Profit	18,190
	£199,900		£199,900
		Balance	53,570

W-I-P Control

Balance B/F	36,700		
Material	32,840	Cost of Sales	118,260
Wages	53,260	Balance	38,060
Prod. ohds.	33,520		
	156,320		156,320
Balance B/F	38,060		

Stores Control

Balance	9,200	W-I-P	32,840
F. L. control	39,150	Balance	15,510
	48,350		48,350
Balance B/F	15,510		

Production Overhead Control

F. L. control	30,620	W-I-P	33,520
Ohd. Adj.	2,900		
	33,520		33,520

Wages Control

F L control	53,260	WIP	53,260

S & D Overhead Control

FL control	12,780	Cost of Sales	11,826
		Ohd Adj	954
	12,780		12,780

Cost of Sales

W-I-P	118,260		
S & D	11,826	P & L	130,086
	130,086		130,086

Overhead Adjustment

S & D ohd	954	Prod. ohd	2,900
P & L	1,946		
	2,900		2,900

Costing P & L

Cost of Sales	130,086	Sales	146,330
Profit	18,190	Ohd. Adj	1,946
	148,276		148,276

7. JOB COST CARD

A typical job card is shown (Fig. 12.3, on the following page). It is suitable for relatively small jobs or as the summary card for larger jobs which might have supporting schedules relating to Material, Labour and Overheads.

8. BATCH COSTING

This is a form of costing which applies where a quantity of identical articles are manufactured as a batch. The most common forms of batch are:

a. where a customer orders a quantity of identical items, or

b. where an internal manufacturing order is raised for a batch of identical parts, sub-assemblies or products to replenish stocks.

In general the procedures for costing batches are similar to costing jobs. The batch would be treated as a job during manufacture and the costs collected as described previously in this chapter. On completion of the batch the cost per unit can be calculated by dividing the total batch cost by the number of good units produced. Batch costing is common in the engineering component industry, footwear and clothing manufacture and similar industries.

FIGURE 12.3 Typical job cost card

JOB COST CARD   Job No.

Customer	Customer's Order No.	Start Date
Job Description		Delivery Date
Estimate Ref.	Invoice No.	
Quoted Price	Invoice Price	Despatch Note No.

Material

Date	Req. No.	Qty	Price	Cost £	Cost p
Total C/F					

Labour

Date	Lab Anal Ref.	Cost Ctre	Hrs.	Rate	Bonus	Cost £	Cost p
Total C/F							

Overheads

M/c Hrs.	OAR	Cost £	Cost p
Total C/F			

Expenses

Date	Ref.	Description	Cost £	Cost p
Total C/F				

Job Cost Summary

	Actual £	Actual p	Estimate £	Estimate p
Direct materials B/F				
Direct Expenses B/F				
Direct Labour B/F				
= Prime Cost				
Factory Overheads B/F				
= Factory Cost				
Selling & Admin Overheads				
% on Factory Cost				
= Total Cost				
Invoice Price				
Job Profit/Loss				

Comments

Job Cost Card Completed by ....

9. ILLUSTRATION OF JOB/BATCH COSTING

The following example shows a typical cost build-up for a batch of similar parts and illustrates typical job costing procedures and the subsequent calculation of the unit cost and profit.

Example 2
A company manufacturers small assemblies to order and has the following budgeted overheads for the year, based on normal activity levels.

Department	Budgeted Overheads (£)	Overhead Absorption Base
Blanking	18,000	1,500 labour hours
Machining	43,000	2,500 machine hours
Welding	20,000	1,800 labour hours
Assembly	15,000	1,000 labour hours

Selling and Administrative overheads are 20% of Factory cost.
An order for 250 assemblies type X 128, made as Batch 5931, incurred the following costs:

Materials: £3,107
Labour: 128 hours Blanking Shop at £10/hour
452 hours Machining Shop at £11/hour
90 hours Welding Shop at £10/hour
175 hours Assembly Shop at £9/hour

£525 was paid for the hire of special X-ray equipment for testing the welds. The time booking in the machine shop was 643 machine hours.
Calculate the total cost of the batch, the unit cost and the profit per assembly if the selling price was £150/assembly.

Solution

The first step is to calculate the overhead absorption rates for the production departments.

Blanking $= \frac{£18,000}{1,500} = £12$ OAR per labour hour

Machining $= \frac{£43,000}{2,500} = £17.2$ OAR per machine hour

Welding $= \frac{£20,000}{1,800} = £11.1$ OAR per labour hour

Assembly $= \frac{£15,000}{1,000} = £15$ OAR per labour hour

Total Cost – Batch No. 5931		£
Direct Material		3,107.00
Direct Expense		525.00
	£	
Direct Labour	128 × 10	
	452 × 11	
	90 × 10	
	175 × 9	8,727.00
	= Prime Cost	£12,359.00

Production Overheads Absorption

	£	
Blanking	128 × 12	
Machining	643 × 17.2	
Welding	90 × 11.1	
Assembly	175 × 15	16,219.60
= Factory Cost		£28,578.60
+ Selling and Administrative overheads (20% of Factory Cost)	=	5,715.72
= Total Cost		£34,294.32
Total Cost/unit	$= \dfrac{£34,294.32}{250}$	= £137.18
Profit/unit	=	£12.82

10. USING ABC FOR JOB/BATCH COSTING

Overheads can be charged to jobs or batches using either traditional labour or machine hour absorption rates or by using various cost drivers in ABC systems. If all jobs or batches were much the same and placed similar loads on support activities there would be little difference in the costs calculated by either method. Such uniformity is unlikely and jobs and batches vary in the loads they place on production facilities and support activities.

As a consequence, costs calculated by traditional methods and ABC system are likely to be different. The general effect is that more complex/diverse/small quantity production will tend to be costed higher using ABC as compared to traditionally calculated costs.

The following example illustrates the general principles:

Example 3
The following details have been recorded for 4 batches made in a period

Batch	A	B	C	D
Output in units	250	60	200	120
Cost per batch	£	£	£	£
Direct Material	1,650	750	2,100	900
Direct Labour	9,200	1,520	6,880	2,400
Labour hours per batch	1,150	190	860	300

The total production overhead for the period has been analysed as follows:

	£
Machine related costs	14,600
Materials handling & despatch	6,800
Stores	8,250
Inspection/Quality control	5,850
Set-up	6,200
Engineering support	8,300
	50,000

Cost drivers have been identified for the cost pools as follows:

Cost pool	Cost driver
Machine costs	Machine hours
Materials handling	Materials movements
Stores	Requisitions raised
Inspection	No. of inspections
Set-up	No. of set-ups
Engineering support	Engineering hours

The following cost driver volumes were recorded for the batches:

Batch	A	B	C	D	Total
Machine hours per batch	520	255	610	325	1,710
Material movements	180	70	205	40	495
Requisitions	40	21	43	26	130
Inspections	18	8	13	8	47
Set-ups	12	7	16	8	43
Engineering hours	65	38	52	35	190

Required:

a. The batch and unit costs using traditional costing based on a labour hour overhead absorption rate

b. The batch and unit costs using ABC

c. Compare the costs in (a) and (b)

d. Comment on the likely position if the firm uses cost-plus pricing

Solution

a. Batch and unit costs using traditional overhead absorption based on labour hours.

$$\text{Labour hour OAR} = \frac{£50,000}{1,150 + 190 + 860 + 300} = £20 \text{ per hour}$$

Batch	A	B	C	D
Output (Units)	250	60	200	120
	£	£	£	£
Direct Material	1,650	750	2,100	900
Direct Labour	9,200	1,520	6,880	2,400
= Prime Cost	10,850	2,270	8,980	3,300
+ Overhead	23,000	3,800	17,200	6,000
(Lab. hrs × OAR)				
Total Batch Cost	33,850	6,070	26,180	9,300
Unit Cost	**135.40**	**101.17**	**130.9**	**77.50**

b. Batch and unit costs using ABC with various cost drivers.

Calculation of Cost Driver Rates

Cost Driver	Cost Pool	Cost Driver Rate
	Total number of cost driver	
Machine hours	$\frac{£14,600}{1,710}$	£8.54 per mac. Hour
Material movements	$\frac{£6,800}{495}$	£13.74 per movement
Stores	$\frac{£8,250}{130}$	£63.46 per requisition
Inspection	$\frac{£5,850}{47}$	£124.47 per inspection
Set-ups	$\frac{£6,200}{43}$	£144.19 per set-up
Engineering	$\frac{£8,300}{190}$	£43.68 per hour

Batch unit costs using ABC

Batch	A		B		C		D	
	250		60		200		120	
	£		£		£		£	
Prime cost (+ overheads)	10,850		2,270		8,980		3,300	
Machine hrs @ £8.54	(520)	4,441	(255)	2,178	(610)	5,209	(325)	2,775
Movements @ £13.74	(180)	2,473	(70)	962	(205)	2,817	(40)	550
Requisitions @ £63.46	(40)	2,538	(21)	1,333	(43)	2,729	(26)	1,650
Inspections @ £124.47	(18)	2,240	(8)	996	(13)	1,618	(8)	996
Set-ups @ £144.19	(12)	1,730	(7)	1,009	(16)	2,307	(8)	1,153
Eng. hrs @ £43.68	(65)	2,839	(38)	1,660	(52)	2,271	(35)	1,529
= Total overheads		16,261		8,138		16,951		8,653
Total Batch cost		27,111		10,408		25,931		11,953
Unit Cost		**108.44**		**173.47**		**129.65**		**99.61**

c. The unit costs compared

Batch A		Batch B		Batch C		Batch D	
Traditional	ABC	Traditional	ABC	Traditional	ABC	Traditional	ABC
£	£	£	£	£	£	£	£
135.40	108.44	101.17	173.47	130.9	129.65	77.50	99.61

It will be seen that in this example there are significant differences between the costs using the two systems. Batch C's costs are broadly the same but the costs of Batch B and D are much higher using ABC, whereas Batch A is lower.

Study of the usage of support overheads by the batches shows that Batches B and D have a higher relative usage of resources so incur greater overhead costs using ABC. Because the traditional method absorbs overheads on labour hours these differences in usage are effectively ignored. It is this feature which, it is claimed, makes product costs more realistic when ABC is used.

d. Cost-plus pricing is a pricing method where a margin (say 40%) is added to costs to produce the selling price. Cost-plus pricing is widely used in many jobbing and batch production firms.

If the firm in the example uses cost-plus pricing then the quoted selling prices will differ considerably depending on whether the traditional or ABC method was used to calculate costs. If it is accepted that the ABC costs are the more realistic then serious errors in pricing may occur if the traditional costs were used as the basis. This would mean that, based on traditional costs, Batch A would be over-priced and Batches B and D under-priced.

In effect, if pricing decisions were based on the less realistic costs then Batch A products would be subsidising Batch B and Batch D products and, in the long run, the firm would tend to receive more orders for the under-priced B and D products. This would be likely to lead to declining profits as these products place relatively higher demands on resources which should be reflected in higher prices.

11. SUMMARY

a. Job costing is employed where work is done to customer's requirements, eg in a factory or workshop.

b. For job costing to be effective there must be a good system of production control, works documentation, material and labour booking.

c. All costs incurred must be charged to the job, usually on to a job cost card.

d. The job cost cards in total form the firm's work-in progress.

e. The detail entries to the job cards would be debited in total to the Work-in-Progress account.

f. Prime costs are gathered from labour and material bookings on the shop floor and, in the case of expenses, from invoice or cash book analysis. Overheads can be charged to jobs either by the traditional methods using labour or machine hour absorption rates or by various cost driver rates using ABC. At present, overhead attribution by labour or machine hour rates is more common but this may change in the future if the use of ABC becomes more widespread.

g. Batch costing is very similar to job costing and is used where a batch of identical units are manufactured. Costs are gathered as for job costing and when the batch is completed, the total cost is divided by the number of good units made to establish the unit cost.

12. POINTS TO NOTE

a. Although job costing could be combined with any cost accounting technique, for example standard costing or marginal costing, it is normally used with the total absorption technique.

b. A realistic attitude must be taken to job costing. If there are numerous, small value jobs it is unlikely that the full process described in this chapter would be followed. Instead a General Jobbing account might be used which would be charged with the costs of small jobs and credited with the selling prices. Some loss of control and information are, however, inevitable consequences of this procedure.

Student self-testing

Exercises (answers below)

1. Batch No. X37 incurred the following costs:

Dept A	420 labour hours at £3.50
B	686 labour hours at £3.00
Direct Materials	£3,280

Factory Overheads are absorbed on labour hours and the rates are £8 per hour for Dept A and £5 per hour for Dept B. The firm uses a cost plus system for setting selling prices and expects a 25% gross profit (Sales Value minus Factory Cost).

Administration overheads are absorbed as 10% of selling price.

Assuming that 1,000 units were produced in Batch No. X37 calculate,

 a. The selling price per unit.

 b. The total amount of administrative overheads recovered by Batch No. X37.

 c. The notional net profit per unit.

2. A firm deals with a variety of jobs which are separately costed. An investigation has shown that for a number of the smaller jobs the cost of calculating the job costs represents up to $1/3$ of the total cost of the job. You are required to discuss this problem.

3. What would be the likely effects of absorbing all overheads in a firm on labour hours when some jobs contain mostly labour and little machining whilst others use many machine hours but little labour? The firm uses a cost-plus system for pricing jobs.

Solutions to exercises

1. **Labour**	**Batch Cost**	**£**	**£**
Dept A	420 × £3.50	1,470	
B	686 × £3.00	2,058	3,528
Materials			3,280
		= Prime Cost	6,808
Overheads			
Dept A	420 × £8	3,360	
B	686 × £5	3,430	6,790
		= Factory cost	13,598

∴ Factory cost should be 75% of sales value

∴ Sales value = = £18,131

∴ Admin. overheads are £18,131 × 10% = £1,813

Summary for batch	£	£
Selling Price		£18,131
– Factory Cost	13,598	
– Admin. Overheads	1,813	15,411
= Net Profit		2,720
Selling price per unit	= £18.13	
Admin. overheads recovered	= £1,813	
Net profit per unit	= £2.720	

2. This is a problem which is encountered in many aspects of cost accounting not merely the example quoted. The cost accountant must always be aware of the 'cost of costing' and relate the costs incurred in producing any form of cost information to the benefits expected from the use of such information.

    In the example cited in the question the cost accountant should investigate the uses and value obtained from the production of costs for all jobs and what would be the effect of producing individual costs only for jobs above a certain size. If such a system was adopted, costs for small jobs would be charged to a General Jobbing account which would be credited with their sales value. Although control over individual job costs would be lost if the new system was adopted, costs would be saved and a judgement must be made as to whether this cost saving would be worthwhile.

3. This is a commonly encountered problem especially when firms increase the amount of mechanisation and automation, yet do not update their costing systems. The likely effects would be:

    a. Incorrect product costs which do not reflect the actual nature of the job.

    b. As prices are based on cost the calculated selling prices will be incorrect – some too high, some too low.

    c. Because of the incorrect selling prices the firm will tend to get jobs on which it will make a loss, ie those where the prices are too low.

    d. Overhead rates and amounts under/over absorbed will be incorrect.

13

Cost accounting methods: Contract costing

1. OBJECTIVES

After studying this chapter you will

- **Know the characteristics of Contract Costing**

- **Understand how uncompleted contracts are dealt with**

- **Be able to summarise the key provisions of SSAP 9 regarding profits, losses and contract balances**

- **Know how a contractor's Balance sheet entries are derived**

- **Be able to prepare a Contract Account.**

2. WHAT IS CONTRACT COSTING?

Contract costing has many similarities to job costing and is usually applied to work which is

a. Undertaken to customer's special requirements.
b. Relatively long duration.
c. Site based, sometimes overseas.
d. Frequently of a constructional nature.

Because of the long time scale and size of many contracts, the necessity arises for intermediate valuations to be made of work done and for progress payments to be received from the client.

3. CHARACTERISTICS OF CONTRACT COSTING

Although details vary, certain characteristics are common to most contract costing systems:

a. Higher proportion of direct costs. Because of the self-contained nature of most site operations, many items normally classified as indirect can be identified specifically with a contract and/or site and thus can be charged directly, eg telephones installed on site, site power usage, site vehicles, transportation, design and planning salaries.

b. Low indirect costs. For most contracts, the only item of indirect cost would be a charge for Head Office expenses. This is usually only a small proportion of the contract cost and is absorbed normally on some overall basis, such as a percentage of total contract cost.

c. Difficulties of cost control. Because of the scale of some contracts and the size of the site there are frequently major problems of cost control concerning: material usage and losses, pilferage, labour supervision and utilisation, damage to and loss of plant and tools, vandalism, etc.

d. Surplus materials. All materials bought for a contract would be charged directly to the contract. At the end of the contract, the contract account would be credited with the cost of the materials not used and, if they were transferred directly to another contract, the new contract account debited. If they were not required immediately, the materials would be stored and the cost debited to a stock account.

4. CONTRACT PLANT

A feature of most contract work is the amount of plant used. This includes cranes, trucks, excavators, mixers and lorries. The usual ways in which plant costs are dealt with are as follows:

a. *When plant is leased.* The leasing charges are charged directly to the contract.

b. *When plant is purchased.* There are two methods in common use,

   i. charge new plant at cost to the contract for which it was purchased. When the plant is no longer required and is transferred to another contract or to base, the original contract would be credited with the second hand value of the plant. In this way the contract bears the charge for the depreciation incurred. It will be realised that this is an example of the revaluation method of depreciation.

   ii. where plant is moved frequently from contract to contract or where contracts are relatively short, a 'Plant Service Department' is created. This department organises the transfer of plant from contract to contract as required and each contract is charged a daily or weekly rental.

Note:
Whatever method is used for charging the capital costs of plant, the ordinary running costs, fuel, repairs and insurance would be charged direct to the contract.

5. PROGRESS PAYMENTS

The contract normally provides for the client to make progress payments either at specific stages of the work, eg when foundations are completed, first floor completion, or at particular agreed intervals. The basis for these interim payments is an *architect's certificate* of work satisfactorily completed. The architect's certificate shows the value of the work done at selling prices and this certificate accompanies the invoice sent to the customer. The amount paid is normally the certified value less a percentage retention which is released when the contract is fully completed and accepted by the customer.

Example I

An architect assesses the value of work done to be £265,000. The client has already paid £110,000 and the agreed retention percentage is 15%. What is the amount of the current progress payment?

Solution

$$\text{Current Payment} = \text{Value certified} - \text{Retention} - \text{Payments already made}$$
$$= £265,000 - 15\%(265,000) - 110,000$$
$$= 265,000 - 39,750 - 110,000$$
$$= \mathbf{£115,250}$$

The accounting entries for this payment when received are:

DR Bank A/C

CR Client A/C (or cash received on account)

6. PROFIT CALCULATION AND BALANCE SHEET ENTRIES FOR UNCOMPLETED CONTRACTS

The objective of contract costing is to show the profit and loss on each completed contract. However, when a contract is still in progress at the end of the financial year it is necessary to estimate the profit earned in the financial year (that is, part of the total contract profit) so as to avoid excessive fluctuations in company results from year to year. In addition, it is necessary to provide a realistic figure of the value of work-in-progress for balance sheet purposes.

While anticipated losses should be allowed for, in full, as early as possible, the attributable profit in any period is conservatively estimated to allow for unforeseen difficulties and costs. The recommended approach for estimating attributable profit for the year, and the resulting Balance Sheet entries, is given in SSAP 9, Stocks and Long-term Contracts. Key parts of the Standard are given below, followed by worked examples.

7. KEY PROVISIONS OF SSAP 9 RELATING TO PROFIT

Students are recommended to read the whole of the Standard which gives valuable guidance on all aspects of stock valuation and dealing with long-term contracts. However, key parts of the Standard dealing with long-term contracts are reproduced below, referenced by the paragraph numbers from the Standard:

What is a long-term contract? Para 22 (extract):

A contract that is required to be accounted for as long-term by this accounting standard will usually extend for a period exceeding one year. However, a duration exceeding one year is not an essential feature of a long-term contract. Some contracts with a shorter duration than one year should be accounted for as long-term contracts if they are sufficiently material to the activity of the period.

Terminology

What is turnover? Para 8:

Companies should ascertain turnover in a manner appropriate to the stage of completion of the contracts, the businesses and the industries in which they operate.

Terminology

Turnover is further explained in Appendix 1, Para 23:

Turnover (ascertained in a manner appropriate to the industry, the nature of the contracts concerned and the contractual relationship with the customer) and related costs should be recorded in the profit and loss account as contract activity progresses. Turnover may sometimes be ascertained by reference to valuation of the work carried out to date. In other cases, there may be specific points during a contract at which individual elements of work done with separately ascertainable sales values and costs can be identified and appropriately recorded as turnover (eg. because delivery or customer acceptance has taken place). This accounting standard does not provide a definition of turnover in view of the different methods of ascertaining it as outlined above. However, it does require disclosure of the means by which turnover is ascertained.

Terminology

What are the general principles for deciding upon attributable profits or losses? Paras 9, 10 and 11:

Where the business carries out long-term contracts and it is considered that their outcome can be assessed with reasonable certainty before their conclusion, the attributable profit should be calculated on a prudent basis and included in the accounts for the period under review. The profit taken up needs to reflect the proportion of the work carried out at the accounting date and to take into account any known inequalities of profitability in the various stages of a contract. The procedure to recognise profit is to include an appropriate proportion of total contract value as turnover in the profit and loss account as the contract activity progresses. The costs incurred in reaching that stage of completion are matched with this turnover, resulting in the reporting of results that can be attributed to the proportion of work completed.

Where the outcome of long-term contracts cannot be assessed with reasonable certainty before the conclusion of the contract, no profit should be reflected in the profit and loss account in respect of those contracts, although, in such circumstances, if no loss is expected it may be appropriate to show as turnover a proportion of the total contract value using a zero estimate of profit.

If it is expected that there will be a loss on a contract as a whole, all of the loss should be recognised as soon as it is foreseen (in accordance with the prudence concept). Initially, the foreseeable loss will be deducted from the work in progress figure of the particular contract, thus reducing it to net realisable value. Any loss in excess of the work in progress figure should be classified as an accrual within 'Creditors' or under 'Provisions for liabilities and charges' depending upon the circumstances. Where unprofitable contracts are of such magnitude that they can be expected to utilise a considerable part of the company's capacity for a substantial period, related administration overheads to be incurred during the period to the completion of those contracts should also be included in the calculation of the provision for losses.

Terminology

These principles are explained further in Appendix I and Para 25 and part of Para 28 are given below. Para 25:

In calculating the total estimated profit on the contract, it is necessary to take into account not only the total costs to date and the total estimated further costs to completion (calculated by reference to the same principles as were applied to cost to date) but also the estimated future costs of rectification and guarantee work, and any other future work to be undertaken under the terms of the contract. These are then compared with the total sales value of the contract. In considering future costs, it is necessary to have regard to likely increases in wages and salaries, to likely increases in the price of raw materials and to rises in general overheads, so far as these items are not recoverable from the customer under the terms of the contract.

Terminology

Para 28 (part):

The amounts to be included in the year's profit and loss account will be both the appropriate amount of turnover and the associated costs of achieving that turnover, to the extent that these amounts exceed corresponding amounts recognised in previous years.

Terminology

Thus, in memorandum form, the overall contract outcome calculation is as follows:

	£	£
Total Contract value		XX
less Costs incurred to date	XX	
Estimated costs to completion	XX	
Rectification and guarantee work	XX	
Total estimated contract costs		XX
Estimated contract profit or loss		XX

If a loss is disclosed from the above calculation then this should be provided in full in the period's accounts. If an overall profit is expected and no additional problems are foreseen then it is correct to take credit in the current period for a reasonable proportion of the overall profit. This means that some appropriate amount of turnover and related costs will appear in the firm's P&L account for the year. As will be seen from the extracts given above, the Standard does not specify how this should be done.

8. GUIDELINES ON CALCULATING INTERIM PROFITS

Various possibilities exist for estimating the profit on incomplete contracts and several options are shown below. However a prudent view must always be taken and the profit should reflect the degree of completion. If the contract is at an early stage (say, less than 30% complete) no profit should be taken. Interim profits, however calculated, should only be taken when the final contract outcome can be assessed with reasonable confidence.

Options for estimating interim profit:

a. When substantial costs have been incurred (say the contract is 30–80% complete) a formula which has traditionally been used in the construction industry is:

$$\text{Profit taken} = \frac{2}{3} \text{ or } \frac{3}{4} \text{ of the Notional profit}$$
$$\times \frac{\text{Cash received from progressive payments}}{\text{Value of work certified}}$$

where the Notional profit is Value of work certified − Cost of work certified.

b. When the contract is nearing completion (say, over 80% complete) and the eventual profit can be assessed with reasonable certainty there is no need for excessive prudence and one of the following methods may be used:

i. $\text{Profit taken} = \dfrac{\text{Progress payments to date}}{\text{Contract price}}$
$$\times \text{Estimated total profit on completion}$$

Note:
The above formula allows for the retention percentage. In the unlikely event of there being no retention by the client the formula would be:

$$\text{Profit taken} = \frac{\text{Value of work certified}}{\text{Contract price}} \times \text{Estimated total profit}$$

The above method is probably the most usual but there are other possibilities:

ii. Profit taken = Value of work certified − Cost of work certified or

iii. $\text{Profit taken} = \dfrac{\text{Cost of work done}}{\text{Estimated total cost of contract}} \times \text{Estimated total profit.}$

Example 2

At their year end Apex Developments has three contracts in progress and their details are as follows:

Contract	AP10	AP11	AP12
	£	£	£
Contract price	150,000	275,000	185,000
Costs to date	35,000	144,000	154,000
Estimated costs to completion	88,000	96,000	7,000
Value of work certified	40,000	165,000	172,000
Progress payments received	34,000	140,250	146,200
Cost of work certified	28,000	138,000	150,000

What interim profits if any, should be taken on the three contracts? (no profits have been taken so far).

Solution

First check the degree of completion and whether the contracts are expected to make a profit on completion. Only if an overall profit is expected can taking an interim profit be considered. If any contract showed an expected overall loss, this must be taken, in full, in the current accounting year in accordance with the prudence concept.

		AP10	AP11	AP12
		£	£	£
Contract price		150,000	275,000	185,000
less estimated total costs		123,000	240,000	161,000
Estimated contract profit		27,000	35,000	24,000
Approximate degree of completion				
$\dfrac{\text{Costs to date}}{\text{Total costs}}$	=	$\dfrac{35,000}{123,000}$	$\dfrac{144,000}{240,000}$	$\dfrac{154,000}{161,000}$
	=	28%	60%	96%

Thus all contracts are expected to make an overall profit on completion so taking an interim profit can be considered provided that the degree of completion justifies doing so.

Contract AP10

Only 28% complete so it would be prudent not to take any profit until more of the contract is completed.

Contract AP11

60% complete so a prudent amount of profit can be taken. As there is a retention of 15% a reasonable method of calculation would be:

$$\text{Profit taken} = \frac{2}{3} \times \text{National Profit} \times \frac{\text{Progress payments}}{\text{Value of work certified}}$$

$$= \frac{2}{3} \times (165,000 - 138,000) \times \frac{140,250}{165,000}$$

$$= \pounds 15,300$$

Note that the above figure is considerably below the difference between the value and cost of work certified, which is £27,000. This means that the amounts taken to the P & L account for turnover and cost of sales should be less than £165,000 and £138,000 respectively (this is dealt with below in Example 3).

Contract AP12
96% complete so a somewhat less prudent view can be taken of the interim profit. A reasonable calculation would be

$$\text{Profit taken} = \frac{\text{Progress payments}}{\text{Contract price}} \times \text{Estimated total prifit}$$

$$= \frac{146,200}{185,000} \times 24,000$$

$$= \textbf{£18,966}$$

It will be seen from the initial data that, in each case, there was work done but not yet certified, ie costs to date less cost of work certified. This must be carried at cost, not at sales value.

9. PROFIT AND LOSS ACCOUNT ENTRIES FOR INTERIM PROFITS

Having calculated an appropriate interim profit, as shown above, the necessary Turnover and Cost of Sales figures must be derived, for insertion in the published P & L account of the firm. The turnover and cost of sales figures are based on the formulae used for the interim profit calculations and must obviously produce the agreed profit. The methods used are demonstrated below.

Example 3
Show the amounts of turnover and cost of sales relating to the three contracts in Example 2 which will be taken to the firm's P & L account, according to the provisions of SSAP 9.

Solution

The amounts of Turnover and Cost of Sales which will be taken to the firm's P & L A/C will be those which produce the profits as already calculated above, ie:

Contract		
AP10	No Profit	
AP11	£15,300	Profit
AP12	£18,966	Profit

Contract AP 10
As no profit is to be taken on this contract there are no allocations to Turnover and Cost of Sales in the firm's P & L account.

Contract AP11
The turnover and Cost of Sales are obtained by weighting the Value and the Cost of Work certified respectively by the 2/3 proportion and the proportion

of payments made to value certified. This is merely the breakdown of the formula used to calculate the Interim profit above.

$$\text{Turnover} = \frac{2}{3} \times \text{Value of work certified} \times \frac{\text{Progress payment}}{\text{Value of work certified}}$$

$$= \frac{2}{3} \times 165{,}000 \times \frac{140{,}250}{165{,}000}$$

$$= \textbf{£93,500}$$

$$\text{Cost of Sales} = \frac{2}{3} \times \text{Cost of work certified} \times \frac{\text{Progress payments}}{\text{Value certified}}$$

$$= \frac{2}{3} \times 138{,}000 \times \frac{140{,}250}{165{,}000}$$

$$= \textbf{£78,200}$$

∴ Entries in P & L relating to Contract AP11

	£
Turnover	93,500
Cost of Sales	78,200
= Profit	15,300 as calculated.

Contract AP12

As a different formula from AP11 was used to calculate profit the calculation of Turnover and Cost of Sales is also different but is similarly based on the Interim Profit Formula used for AP12 in Example 2.

$$\text{Turnover} = \frac{\text{Progress payments}}{\text{Contract price}} \times \text{Contract price}$$

$$= \frac{146{,}200}{185{,}000} \times 185{,}000$$

$$= \textbf{£146,200}$$

$$\text{Cost of Sales} = \frac{\text{Progress payments}}{\text{Contract price}} \times \text{Estimated Total Costs}$$

$$= \frac{146{,}200}{185{,}000} \times 161{,}000$$

$$= \textbf{£127,234}$$

∴ Entries in P & L relating to contract AP12

	£
Turnover	146,200
Cost of Sales	127,234
= Profit	18,966 as calculated

Summary for the 3 contracts

	AP10	AP11 £	AP12 £	Firm's P & L A/C £
Turnover	–	93,500	146,200	239,700
Cost of Sales	–	78,200	127,234	205,434
Profit	–	15,300	18,966	34,266

Having dealt with the profit calculations and subsequent P & L account entries, we must now consider what balance sheet entries arise from incomplete contracts.

10. KEY PROVISIONS OF SSAP 9 RELATING TO BALANCE SHEET ENTRIES

Part of the Standards recommendations regarding balance sheet entries have been shown above (in Standard Para 11) and other important extracts are shown below. Para 13

In the case of long-term contracts:

(a) *long-term contract balances classified under the balance sheet heading of 'Stocks' are stated at total costs incurred, net of amounts transferred to the profit and loss account in respect of work carried out to date, less foreseeable losses and applicable payments on account. A suitable description in the financial statements would be 'at net cost, less foreseeable losses and payments on account'.*

(b) *cumulative turnover (ie, the total turnover recorded in respect of the contract in the profit and loss accounts of all accounting periods since inception of the contract) is compared with total payments on account. If turnover exceeds payments on account an 'amount recoverable on contracts' is established and separately disclosed within debtors. If payments on account are greater than turnover to date, the excess is classified as a deduction from any balance on that contract in stocks, with any residual balance in excess of cost being classified with creditors.*

In essence part (a) gives the value of net work-in-progress and part (b) shows the position when progress payments are greater or less than the value of turnover. All these terms are illustrated in the examples which follow.

11. DERIVING THE BALANCE SHEET ENTRIES

Some items which are entered into Contract accounts are conventionally treated and produce straightforward balance sheet entries. The two main items in this category are: Unused materials on site and Plant on site.

There are more difficulties however with work-in-progress and the differences between the amounts recognised as turnover and the progress payments received. SSAP 9 requires that the balances relating to long term contracts are split into two categories.

1. The costs of work done which is not yet recognised in the P & L account is shown under 'stocks' as *'Long term-contract balances'*.
2. The difference between

	£
i. amounts taken as Turnover	XX
ii. *less* Progress payments received	XX
= Net difference	XX

will be grouped with 'Debtors' as '*Amounts recoverable on long-term contracts*' if (i) is greater than (ii). Alternatively the net difference will be offset against the balances in (a) above if (ii) is greater than (i).

Thus it will be seen that various separate contract balances are calculated and then netted off to produce the final balances which appear, suitably aggregated, in the firm's published Balance Sheet.

The main stages in this process are illustrated below.

Example 4

What are the balance sheet entries for the three contracts in example 2?

(The data on the contracts and the calculations of turnover cost of sales and profit are reproduced below for convenience.)

Contract	AP10 £	AP11 £	AP12 £
Contract price	150,000	275,000	185,000
Costs to date	35,000	144,000	154,000
Estimated costs to completion	88,000	96,000	7,000
Value of work certified	40,000	165,000	172,000
Progress payments received	34,000	140,250	146,200
Cost of work certified	28,000	138,000	150,000
Calculated turnover	–	93,500	146,200
Calculated cost of sales	–	78,200	127,234
Calculated Profit	–	15,300	18,966

Solution

There are two balances to be found, as specified in Para 10 (a) and 10 (b) which may have to be netted together. These are all shown in the table below:

Contract	AP10 £	AP11 £	AP12 £	Total £
Costs incurred but not allocated to cost of sales (a) (Note 1)	35,000	65,800	26,766	127,566
Amount taken as Turnover (from Ex. 3)	–	93,500	146,200	239,700
less Progress payments	34,000	140,250	146,200	320,450
Balance (b)	(34,000)	(46,750)	–	(80,750)
Netted balance (a–b) (Note 2)	1000	19,050	26,766	46,816

Note 1:

Workings for costs incurred but not allocated to Sales.

Contract	AP10 £	AP11 £	AP12 £	Total £
Costs to date	35,000	144,000	154,000	333,000
less Cost of Sales (Ex 3)	–	78,200	127,234	205,434
= Costs incurred but not allocated to sales	35,000	65,800	26,766	127,566

Note 2:
It will be seen that for these three contracts the Progress Payments are always at least equal to the Amount taken as Turnover. According to the rules given in Para 10 this means that the two main balances ((a) and (b)) can be netted against one another.

The Balance Sheet disclosures are thus:

	AP10	AP11	AP12	Total
Stocks	£	£	£	£
Long-term contract balances	1,000	19,050	26,766	46,816

Note:
It will be seen that in this example Debtors did not arise. Debtors only arise when the Amount taken as Turnover *exceeds* the Progress Payments.

12. COMPREHENSIVE EXAMPLE

To provide further practice and to illustrate other aspects of SSAP 9 a comprehensive example follows. You are recommended to attempt the problem yourself before working through the solution.

Example 5

Nationwide Contractors Plc. at 31st December Year 8 had three contracts in progress as follows:

Contract No.	NC852 £000	NC794 £000	NC881 £000
Contract value	350	1,460	850
Costs incurred to date	165	1,100	182
Estimated future costs to complete	110	275	633
Estimated guarantee costs	–	–	95
Payments received on account	190	1,200	145
Value of work certified	212	1,125	110
Cost of work certified	165	1,070	130
Start dates (No profits have been taken so far)	30th Sep Year 7	4th Mar Year 7	1st Jan Year 8

It is required to assess whether any interim profits should be taken, to calculate the appropriate Turnover and Cost of Sales values and the Balance Sheet entries for the three contracts.

Solution
Estimated degree of completion and overall contract result

Contract No.	NC852 £000	NC794 £000	NC881 £000
Contract value	350	1,460	850
Total expected costs	275	1,375	910
Expected profit (loss)	75	85	(60)
Degree of completion	$\frac{165}{275} = 60\%$	$\frac{1,100}{1,375} = 80\%$	N.A. as all loss must be taken

Thus it will be seen that NC852 and NC794 are expected to make a profit on completion and are well advanced so it is reasonable to take an interim profit. The whole of the loss on NC881, £60,000, must be brought into account in this accounting year.

Interim Profit calculations:

Contract NC852

$$\text{Profit} = \frac{2}{3} \times \text{Notional Profit} \times \frac{\text{Payments}}{\text{Value certified}}$$

$$= \frac{2}{3} \times (212 - 165) \times \frac{190}{212}(000\text{s}) = \textbf{£28,100}$$

Contract NC794

$$\text{Profit} = \frac{2}{3} \times (1125 - 1070)(000\text{s}) = \textbf{£36,700}$$

(Because, unusually, payments received for NC794 are above the value of work certified the usual retention effect has been ignored for this contract.)

Turnover and Cost of Sales calculations:

	NC852	NC794	NC881
Turnover			
	$\frac{2}{3} \times$ Value Cert $\times \dfrac{\text{Payments}}{\text{Value Cert}}$	$\frac{2}{3} \times$ Value Certified	Value Certified
	$= \frac{2}{3} \times 212 \times \frac{190}{212}$	$= \frac{2}{3} \times 1,215$	
	$= \textbf{£126,700}$	$= \textbf{£750,000}$	$= \textbf{£110,000}$
Cost of sales			
	$\frac{2}{3} \times$ Cost Cert $\times \dfrac{\text{Payments}}{\text{Value Cert}}$	$\frac{2}{3} \times$ Cost Cert	Cost of sales to
	$= \frac{2}{3} \times 165 \times \frac{190}{212}$	$= \frac{2}{3} \times 1,070$	produce a £60,000 loss
	$= \textbf{£98,600}$	$= \textbf{£713,300}$	$= \textbf{£170,000}$

Derivation of balances for Balance Sheet.

	NC852 £000	NC794 £000	NC881 £000	Total £000
Costs to Date	165	1,100	182	1,447
less Cost of Sales	98.6	713.3	170	981.9
= Costs incurred not allocated to Sales (a)	66.4	386.7	12	465.1
Turnover	126.7	750	110	986.7
less Progress payments	190	1,200	145	1,535
Balance (b)	(63.3)	(450)	(35)	(548.3)
Netted balance (a − b)	3.1	(63.3)	(23)	(83.2)

The results can now be summarised:

Values for P & L account of Nationwide Contractors for the three incomplete contracts

	NC852 £	NC794 £	NC881 £	Total £
Turnover	126,700	750,000	110,000	986,700
less Cost of Sales	98,600	713,300	170,000	981,900
Profit (loss)	28,100	36,700	(60,000)	4,800

Contract balances for Balance Sheet

	NC852 £	NC794 £	NC881 £	Total £
Stocks				
Long-term Contract balances	3,100			3,100
With Creditors		63,300	23,000	86,600

Notes:

1. The figures have been chosen to illustrate the effect of having excess payments on account (as NC794) and a contract loss (as NC881).

2. It will be seen that there are no debtors. These can only arise when the progress payments received are less than the value taken as Turnover.

13. THE ACCOUNTING ENTRIES

A separate account will be kept for each contract with the general objective of establishing the overall contract profit or loss. To do this the following entries are required:

Contract Account

Typical Debit Entries	**Typical Credit Entries**
Debit Direct costs (Material, Labour)	Credit Plant, Materials transferred from Contract
Debit, Direct expenses (Plant hire, Sub-contractors. Architects' fees)	Credit sales value of stages/final contract value
Debit Cost of Plant bought	
Debit any materials, plant etc, transferred to contract	
Debit Head Office Charges	
Debit Interim and Final Profit	

In addition there are, of course, contra entries within the contract account relating to carry forward/brought forward items, accruals and pre-payments.

All of the above entries are shown in the following example.

14. EXAMPLE OF ACCOUNTING FOR CONTRACTS

Example 6

The following information relates to Contract 87 on the Thornley site as at the 31st December Year 1.

Contract 87 – Thornley Site
Customer – Middlethorpe Corporation

	£
Wages	42,156
Materials delivered direct to site	54,203
Materials from Main Stores	657
Materials transferred to Riverview Site	1,590
Plant purchased (at cost)	12,500
Plant transferred to Thornley	5,250
Sub-contractors charges	19,580
Site expenses (power etc)	5,086
Materials on Site 31st December	18,300
Plant on Site 31st December	14,750
Prepayments at 31st December	507
Accrued wages at 31st December	921
Sales value of stages completed	117,500
Cost of stages completed	102,300
Head Office charges are 10% of wages	
Progress payments received from client	115,000

The contract value is £550,000 and it is anticipated that there will be further costs of £375,000 (including guarantee and rectification claims). As this is the first year of the contract no profit has been taken previously.

From the above prepare the Contract Account for the year, the Balance sheet entries as at 31st December Year 1 and the opening entries for 1st January Year 2. It is company policy to take as interim profit the difference between the Sales Value and Cost of Stages completed.

Solution

CONTRACT No. 87   **CUSTOMER: Middlethorpe Corporation**
SITE: Thornley

Contract A/C

	£	£		£
SiteWages	42,156		Materials transferred out	1,590
+ accrued C/F	921	43,077	Prepayments C/D	507
Materials purchased	54,203			
Materials from Stores	657	54,860		
Plant purchased	12,500		Materials at site C/D	18,300
Plant transferred in	5,250	17,750	Plant at site C/D	14,750
Sub contractors		19,580	W-I-P C/D	7,214
Site expenses		5,086	(see note a)	
Head office Charges		4,308	Cost of stages completed	102,300
		£144,661		£144,661

CONTRACT No. 87   **CUSTOMER: Middlethorpe Corporation**
SITE: Thornley

Contract A/C

	£	£		£
Cost of stages completed		102,300		
			Sales value of stages	117,500
Profit for year (see note b)		15,200		
		117,500		117,500
1st Jan. Year 2 (see note c)				
Prepayments B/D		507		
Materials B/D		18,300	Accrued wages	921
Plant B/D		14,750		
W-I-P B/D		7,214		

Notes:

a. The total costs to date are £109,514 ie. £144,661 less items C/D and transferred out. As the cost of stages completed is £102,300 the contract balance (W-I-P) is:

	£
	109,514
less Cost of sales	102,300
= Long term contract balance	£7,214

b. Before any profit can be taken for the year it is necessary to estimate the overall project outcome to see whether a profit or loss is expected, thus: Expected contract outcome:

		£
Contract value		550,000
less Costs to date	109,514	
Future costs	375,000	484,514
Expected Overall Contract Profit		65,486

As an overall profit is expected it is reasonable to take a proportion into this year's accounts. The profit is the difference between the cost and sales value of the stages completed, as shown.

c. All the entries shown appear in the balance sheet as at 31st December Year 1 and would be aggregated with the other prepayments, accruals, stocks and work-in-progress of the firm.

   In addition a balance sheet entry arises from the personal account of the client, Middlethorpe Corporation, thus:

Middlethorpe Corporation

	£		£
		Cash (progress payments)	115,000
Sales value of	117,500	Bal C/F (ie. Debtors)	2,500
completed stages			
	117,500		117,500
1st Jan Year 2 Bal B/F	2,500		

The £2,500 balance on the Middlethorpe account would be grouped with debtors and termed 'Amounts recoverable on long-term contracts'.

Note:
That in this example a Debtor does arise because the amount taken for Turnover (£117,500) exceeds the Progress Payments (£115,000).

15. SUMMARY

a. Contract costing is akin to job costing and is used on relatively large scale, long term contracts which are frequently site based.

b. Because of the separate nature of most site work, more costs can be identified as direct, including many which are normally considered indirect.

c. If plant is purchased for use on a site, the contract account would be charged with the purchase price and credited with the second hand value of the plan on the contract completion or when the plant was transferred. In this way the plant depreciation would be charged to the appropriate contract.

d. Progress payments are made based on an architect's certificate of work done less an agreed retention percentage.

e. If a contract is uncompleted at the year end, a conservative estimate is taken of the profit for the period. SSAP 9 provides recommendations for the method of profit calculation.

f. If a loss is expected for the contract as a whole this should be allowed for, in full, as early as possible.

g. Balance sheet entries may arise in connection with uncompleted contracts for; contract balances (WIP), debtors, excess payments on account and provision for losses.

Student self-testing

Exercises (answers below)

1. Prepare columnar contract accounts for Bayes Construction Ltd who at present have two contracts in progress.
    The following details were extracted at 31st December.

Contract No.	Y282	Z650
Commencement date	1st January	1st July
	£	£
Contract price	275,000	350,000
Expenditure:		
Materials	12,680	19,280
Wages	48,643	37,218
Site expenses	6,500	8,620
Plant purchases	150,000	65,000
Materials on site 31st December	2,100	6,400
Accrued wages	4,217	2,242
Value of work certified	110,000	85,000
Cash received on work certified	93,500	63,750
Work completed but not certified	3,500	2,200

Head office charges of £22,500 are charged to contracts in proportion to their prime costs. The plant was installed at the commencement of the contracts and depreciation is calculated at 20% per annum. Both contracts have been estimated to give an overall profit on completion.

2. Site and contract work pose particular difficulties for cost control and accurate cost accounting. You are required to describe the problems which might arise and how these can be overcome or mitigated.

3. What are the arguments for and against charging individual contracts with Head Office costs?

Solutions to exercises

1.

Contract A/cs

	Y282 (£)	Z650 (£)		Y282 (£)	Z650 (£)
Wages (incl. accrued)	52,660	39,460			
Materials	12,680	19,280	Materials C/F	2,100	6,400
Site expenses	6,500	8,620	WIP C/F	3,500	2,200
Plant depreciation	30,000	6,500	Cost of work certified	108,551	75,449
Head office charges*	12,311	10,189			
	114,151	84,049		114,151	84,049
Cost of work certified	108,551	75,449	Value certified	110,000	85,000
Profit for year	1,449	9,551			
	110,000	85,000		110,000	85,000
Materials B/F	2,100	6,400	Accrued wages B/F	4,217	2,242
WIP B/F	3,500	2,200			

*Prime costs			Y282		Z650
Materials		12,680		19,280	
− Stock		2,100	10,580	6,400	12,880
+ Wages			52,660		39,460
= Prime Cost			63,240		52,340
Head Office Charges apportioned on Prime Cost			£12,311		£10,189

2. There are numerous problems associated with site and contract work, typical of which are the following:

   a. Pilferage of materials, petrol, tools, etc.

   b. Unauthorised use of equipment and vehicles.

   c. General difficulties of recording and paperwork.

   d. Wasteful use of materials, high volumes of breakages.

   e. Difficulties of supervision on dispersed sites.

   f. Wasteful labour practices, incorrect labour bookings.

It must be recognised that it is extremely difficult to eradicate these problems entirely but the following practices will help to overcome excesses.

a. Good security procedures, eg perimeter fencing, lockable stores and vehicles and so on.

b. Well motivated and competent site management.

c. On site cost clerks providing rapid information.

d. Clear, simple records and forms.

e. Simple quantity budgets for materials usage with rapid feedback of discrepancies.

3. *Arguments for charging individual contracts with a proportion of Head Office costs:*

a. The total contract cost can be calculated.

b. Head Office charges have to be recovered somewhere.

c. A net profit or loss can be calculated for each contract.

d. If prices are cost based a more realistic price can be calculated.

e. Head Office costs are inescapable and the services they represent are necessary for each contract so it is reasonable that each contract should bear a proportion.

f. Apportioned costs may obscure the real operating results of individual contracts.

g. Having a large, uncontrollable apportioned cost may be a disincentive to management.

Arguments against:

a. Any method of apportioning Head Office costs is arbitrary and thus may produce illogical results.

b. Head Office costs are not controllable at the contract level so may appear to be an unwanted burden to site management.

c. Apportioned costs may obscure the real operating results of individual contracts.

d. Having a large, uncontrollable apportioned cost may be a disincentive to site management.

14

Cost accounting methods: Operation and service costing

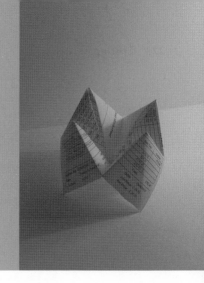

1. OBJECTIVES

After studying this chapter you will

- **Be able to define Continuous Operation/Process Costing**

- **Know what is meant by Output Costing and Service Costing**

- **Understand the uses and limitations of Unit Costs in the Public Sector**

- **Be able to give examples of Performance Measures in the Public Sector.**

2. CONTINUOUS/OPERATION PROCESS COSTING – DEFINITION

This category of cost accounting can be applied across a wide range of manufacturing and service organisations. The formal definition is repeated below:

The cost accounting method applicable where goods or services result from a sequence of continuous or repetitive operations or processes. Costs are averaged over the units produced or services supplied during the period, being initially charged to the operation or process.

Terminology

The key features of this definition are:

- continuous operations or processes
- virtually identical units of output
- total costs divided by number of units to give average cost per unit.

3. SCOPE OF CONTINUOUS OPERATION COSTING

It will be seen that operation costing is a generic term embracing a group of cost accounting methods of varying complexity. These are shown in the diagram below. Output costing and service costing are relatively simple forms of costing and are described in this chapter. Process costing and its sub-divisions are dealt with in the next chapter.

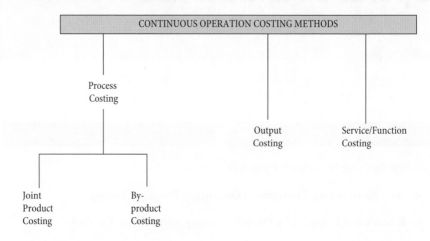

4. OUTPUT COSTING

This is a cost accounting method used where the organisation produces one product only. In consequence the whole production process is geared to the one product and is frequently highly mechanised. Typical examples of where output costing might be applied are: cement manufacture, certain dairies, mines, quarries, etc. In such circumstances cost ascertainment is a simple process, ie,

$$\text{Cost per unit (or tonne)} = \frac{\text{Total costs for period}}{\text{Number of units (or tonnage) produced in the period}}$$

Note:
Where output costing is used, partly completed units at the end of a period would normally be ignored. This is because of their relative insignificance and the fact that they would tend to even out from period to period.

5. SERVICE/FUNCTION COSTING

This is defined as:

> *Cost accounting for specific services or functions, eg, canteens, maintenance, personnel. These may be referred to as service centres, departments or functions.*

Thus, the services provided may be for sale, eg public transport, hotel accommodation restaurants, power generation, etc or they may be provided within the organisation, eg maintenance, library, stores.

A particular difficulty is to define a realistic cost unit that represents a suitable measure of the service provided. Frequently a composite cost unit is deemed the more relevant, for example, the hotel industry may use the 'occupied bed-night' as an appropriate unit for cost ascertainment and cost control. Typical cost units used in service costing are shown below.

Service	Possible Cost Units
Transport	Tonne-Mile, Passenger-Mile, Miles travelled
Hospitals	Patient-days, no. of operations
Electricity	Kilowatt-hours
Hotels	Occupied bed-nights
Restaurants	Meals served
Colleges	Full time equivalent student

Each organisation will have to determine what cost unit is most appropriate for its own purposes. Frequently if a common cost unit is agreed, valuable cost comparisons can be made between similar establishments. This is common, for example, over a wide range of local authority services, between various hospitals, between power stations and other similar organisations.

Whatever cost unit is decided upon, the calculation of the cost per unit is done in a similar fashion to output costing, ie

$$\text{Cost per service unit} = \frac{\text{Total costs per period}}{\text{No of service units supplied in the period}}$$

It will be realised that the calculation shown above is similar to the calculation of cost driver rates using ABC. Service costing with homogeneous service centres or functions and cost units that are a good measure of the service provided is a form of ABC.

Example of service costing

Information has been collected about two hospitals over the last year.

	Loamshire General	Brownton Central
Number of beds	780	500
Number of in-patients	23,472	8,165
Average stay	7½ days	*
Number of out-patient visits	216,500	63,920

*Not recorded but bed occupation percentage was 85%

Cost Breakdown

	Loamshire General		Brownton Central	
	In-patients £	Out-patients £	In-patients £	Out-patients £
Direct patient care				
Supplies, drugs etc	1,821,520	693,600	1,551,350	285,450
Medical staff	8,729,100	3,308,950	6,832,700	1,975,050
Support services	2,210,500	2,563,700	1,845,380	1,591,620
Indirect costs				
General services	3,524,470	1,721,800	1,937,410	635,600
Totals	£16,285,590	£8,288,050	£12,166,840	£4,487,720

Calculate:

a. Average length of stay in Brownton Central
b. Bed occupation percentage in Loamshire General
c. Cost per in-patient day for both hospitals
d. Cost per out-patient attendance for both hospitals and comment on the results.

Solution

a. Average stay in Brownton Central

$$\text{Potential in-patient days in a year} = 500 \text{ beds} \times 365 \text{ days}$$
$$= 182,500$$
$$85\% \text{ occupancy} = 182,500 \times 0.85$$
$$= 155,125 \text{ in-patient days.}$$
$$\text{Average stay} = \frac{155,125}{8,165}$$
$$= \textbf{19 days}$$

b. Bed occupation percentage in Loamshire General $= \dfrac{\text{Actual in-patient days}}{\text{Potential in-patient days}}$

$$= \frac{23,472 \times 7.50}{780 \times 365}\%$$
$$= \frac{176,040}{284,700}\%$$
$$= \textbf{62\%}$$

c. Costs per in-patient day $= \dfrac{\text{Costs for in-patients}}{\text{No of in-patients days}}$

	Loamshire General	Brownton Central
	£16,285,590	£12,166,840
	23,472 × 7.5	8,165 × 19
=	**£92.51**	**£78.43**

d. Cost per out-patient attendance $= \dfrac{\text{Costs for out-patients}}{\text{No of out-patients attendances}}$

	Loamshire General	Brownton Central
	£8,288,050	£4,487,720
	216,500	63,920
=	**£38.28**	**£70.21**

It will be seen that a composite cost unit (in-patient days) is used to calculate the costs. Although the calculated figures vary greatly between the hospitals it is difficult to draw any particular conclusions from this unless the hospitals catered for broadly the same type of patients, the same illnesses, were similarly equipped and so on. Brownton's inpatients had on average, a stay of 19 days while Loamshires stayed only 7 1/2 days so it is likely that there are substantial differences between the hospitals. Cost comparisons between different units or organisations are only valid if like is compared with like. The costs and occupancy percentages calculated are likely to be useful in comparing the performance within each hospital period to period. For example, Loamshire may be concerned to see a Bed-occupancy percentage of only 62% and may monitor this period by period, in order to improve the percentage. It is likely that the lower occupancy percentage is a major factor in causing the relatively high cost of £92.51 per in-patient day. This is because the fixed costs of the hospital are spread over relatively few inpatient days. If the beds were occupied more intensively then it is likely that the cost per in-patient day would fall.

6. THE USE OF UNIT COSTS IN THE PUBLIC SECTOR

Public Sector organisations cover an enormous range. Examples include: primary and secondary state education, Local Authorities, the National Health Service, Police and so on. Within these organisations there is rarely a profit figure to provide a measure of performance. Accordingly, most financial measures of performance tend to be cost-based. Costs are collected, related to some measure of throughput or output and a unit cost calculated as described above.

These unit costs have three main uses.

- *As indicators of relative efficiency*
  The Audit Commission make extensive use of unit costs to make comparisons between different establishments, local authorities and districts. Examples include comparisons of: cost per pupil in different Education Authorities, cost per patient-day at various hospitals, cost per night in police cells and so on.

- *As measures of efficiency over time*
  Unit costs allow the cost/output performance of the same organisation to be compared from year to year. They can help to indicate whether efficiency is increasing or decreasing over time so it is normal to remove the effects of inflation from the cost figures so that the underlying real performance may be seen. Various price indices may be used for removing the inflation effects but the Treasury recommended that the GDP (Gross Domestic Product) deflator should be used for all central government services in the UK including the National Health Service.

- *As an aid to cost control*
  The regular production of Unit Costs and comparison with the costs of other establishments in the same field helps to control costs and engenders a more cost-conscious attitude.

  For internal use, more detailed unit costs are often calculated which provide a sharper focus on particular costs. For example an overall unit cost per patient-day will be calculated in a hospital but this is often analysed into its component parts such as: clinicians cost per patient day, nursing costs per patient-day, administrative costs per patient-day and so on. In this way more detailed attention can be given to each element of cost.

Used as described above unit costs have certain advantages but they have a number of limitations which, in particular cases may make them less useful.

7. LIMITATIONS OF UNIT COSTS

There are four main limitations:

1. **Quality of performance is ignored.**
   This is possibly the most serious problem. A unit cost is a summary figure which gives no guidance on the quality of performance. For example comparative unit costs per metre of street cleaned say nothing about the standard of cleanliness achieved. Cost per patient day for a hospital tells us nothing about the quality of care provided, whether the patients are cured and so on.

2. **The throughput mix is likely to differ.**
   Unless the throughput mix is more or less the same, cost comparisons between different establishments will be largely meaningless. The cost of a Local Authority Children's Home catering for disturbed and delinquent children will differ greatly from those Homes catering for normal children. Like must be compared with like.

3. **Throughputs are used rather than outcomes.**
   Throughputs are numeric indicators of the level of activity. For example the number of heart by-pass operations, the number of children receiving education at a school, etc. Outcomes are the impact which the activity has on the recipient of the service and are the underlying real objectives of providing the service. For example the objective of a Surgical Department is not to carry out 4,000 by-pass operations but is to improve the quality of life for people with heart problems. In many cases in the Public Sector outcomes are not measurable so, in general, relatively easily measurable indicators of throughputs and costs are used as a proxy for real outcomes but they are not the same things.

4. **There are significant inter-regional and inter-authority differences.**
   Crude national cost comparisons ignore the fact that there are genuine in-built differences between regions. For example, some local authorities on the south coast have high proportions of retired people. Rural areas will have much higher collection costs per tonne of refuse because of the distance to be covered. Social deprivation and unemployment vary from area to area affecting health, social service and education costs so unthinking comparisons based on average unit costs have little value.

These and other problems mean that unit costs need to be used with caution and with regard to their possible limitations.

Performance measurements in the Public Sector is, of course, more comprehensive than the calculation of overall Unit Costs. This is explored below.

8. PERFORMANCE MEASUREMENT IN THE PUBLIC SECTOR

Over the last few years there has been a much greater emphasis on obtaining Value For Money (VFM) in public sector organisations such as Local Authorities, the National Health Service, Central Government Agencies and so on. The drive for VFM has led to many structural changes in the organisations in an attempt to improve efficiency and control costs.

Examples include: outside tendering for Local Authority Services such as refuse collection and street cleaning, the establishment of Trust Hospitals, the Local Management of Schools and so on. This emphasis has also led to a considerable increase in the range of cost and financial information required for control, decision-making and comparison.

As an example of the breadth of information that is now required in just one part of the Public Sector consider the following statistics suggested by the Local Authorities' Code of Practice. See Figure 14.1.

Calculation of these statistics requires a detailed cost accounting and recording system covering not merely costs but performance statistics of many types.

9. OTHER COST ACCOUNTING PROBLEMS

Merely because the calculation of unit costs is a simple process in output costing and service costing, students should not be misled into thinking that no

FIGURE 14.1   Comparative statistics suggested in the Code of Practice

For the authority's total expenditure and for each function	Net cost per 1,000 population Manpower per 1,000 population
Primary education	Pupil/teacher ratio
Secondary education	Cost per pupil
School meals	Revenue/cost ratio Pupils receiving free meals as a proportion of school roll
Children in care	As a proportion of total under 18 population Cost per child in care
Care of elderly	Residents of council homes as a proportion of total over-75s Cost per resident each week
Home helps	Contact hours per 1,000 population over 65
Police	Population per police officer Serious offences per 1,000 population
Fire	Proportion of area at high risk
Public transport	Passenger journeys per week per 1,000 population
Highways	Maintenance cost per kilometre
Housing	Rents as a proportion of total cost Management cost per dwelling Rent arrears as a percentage of year's rent income Construction cost per dwelling completed
Trading services	Revenue/gross cost ratio

other cost accounting problems exist in these industries. Many of the organisations involved are very substantial enterprises by any standard. Examples include: power stations, large area hospitals, and city passenger transport undertakings. Such organisations have all the normal problems of large scale cost collection and analysis. They need to monitor and control their costs very closely and frequently employ sophisticated budgetary control systems.

A particular problem in service organisations is caused by the high fixed cost of maintaining the total capacity which may be considerably under utilised at particular times. Examples include: electricity generation – where there is a substantial difference between peak and off peak demand, railways and bus services – where midday demand is substantially below rush hour periods, hotels – where there may be substantial differences between summer and winter or weekday and weekend demand. The cost accounting system should be comprehensive enough to show the effects of this type of demand on the costs of operation. Frequently this involves the analysis of costs into fixed and variable and the use of marginal costing techniques. These techniques are dealt with in detail later in the book.

By their nature many services are provided at one time only and if not utilised are lost forever. For example, if an airline seat is vacant on a given flight it cannot be stored for later sale. The revenue opportunity for that seat on that flight is lost forever. Similar principles apply to a range of services, eg all forms of transport, cinema and entertainment admissions, hotel accommodation, restaurant meals, power generation and so on. This increases the control problems in service industries particularly the difficulties of planning capacity levels.

10. SUMMARY

a. Operation costing is applied where continuous operations or processes produce identical units of output. Total costs are averaged over all units produced.

b. Operation costing is a general term covering the particular methods of Output Costing, Service Costing and Process Costing.

c. Output costing is used where one product only is produced. Examples include quarries and cement works.

d. Service costing is applied to organisations supplying a service or to cost centres providing internal services.

e. The cost unit to be used needs to be defined carefully. It is frequently a composite figure such as Tonne-mile or Patient-night.

f. Organisations employing output costing and service costing have all the normal problems of cost collection and analysis and frequently employ sophisticated costing techniques as part of the information service to management.

g. Unit costs can be used as measures of efficiency, for comparison and for cost control.

h. Unit costs have several limitations – quality is ignored, mix is assumed constant, throughputs are used instead of outcomes, etc so need to be used with care.

11. POINT TO NOTE

Some service organisations do not supply identical or near identical service units to customers. Examples include: Architectural/Design/Accountancy services. In such cases a form of Job costing is used.

Student self-testing

Exercises (answers below)

1. What managerial control problems arise when the facilities of a large scale service organisation are subject to substantial fluctuations in demand? How can the cost accounting system provide assistance to management in such organisations?

2. A firm operates a fleet of 20 lorries which are used for delivering goods to customers. The lorries bring back from the customers the returnable containers. Describe a simple system of cost control covering the cost of running maintenance and depreciation. What cost unit would you recommend?

Solutions to exercises

1. This is a very real practical problem which is faced by numerous service organisations. Probably the most obvious example is that of urban passenger transport. During the morning and evening rush hours there is extremely high demand yet during the day the demand falls dramatically.

   This fluctuation means that the amount of capacity which has to be provided is much greater than average usage rates. The amount and type of capacity is a critical management decision for such organisations and the cost accounting system should provide appropriate information to assist decision-making and control.

   Typical of the information to be supplied is the following:

   a. Detailed analysis of usage patterns, period by period, highlighting trends.

   b. Operating cost breakdowns clearly differentiating between fixed and variable costs.

   c. Revenue analysis showing the effects of demand patterns and projections of trends.

   d. Cost and revenue projections showing the differential effects of changes in costs, rates of inflations, tariffs, etc.

   e. Detailed budgetary control statements showing operating costs, costs of idle facilities, maintenance, etc.

   f. Cash forecasting and budgeting.

2. The costs in running a fleet of 20 lorries are substantial and a costing system is essential to maintain control.

The elements of a possible cost control system include the following:

a. Comprehensive cost classification and coding system enabling costs to be gathered, analysed and presented in various ways, eg per vehicle, repairs, running costs, labour costs and so on.

b. A regular reporting system covering each of the elements of cost/mileage travelled/tonnage carried/hours of operation showing actual against budget and highlighting trends.

c. Ad hoc reports and analyses of major items of expenditure, eg replacements, major overhauls, tyre performance, etc.

There should be an investigation into the most relevant cost unit for the particular style of operation being undertaken. It might be tonne/mile, miles travelled, operating hour or day, tonnage or some combination of such cost units.

Without knowing more details of the organisation and its operation firm recommendations are not possible.

15

Cost accounting methods: Process costing

---
1. OBJECTIVES

After studying this chapter you will

- **Know the features of Process Costing**

- **Be able to distinguish between Normal and Abnormal Losses and Abnormal Gains**

- **Understand how to calculate Equivalent Units**

- **Know how to value Work-in-Progress using either FIFO or Average Cost**

- **Be able to prepare Process Accounts with opening and closing WIP.**

2. PROCESS COSTING DEFINED

Process costing is a form of operation costing used where production follows a series of sequential processes. It is used in a variety of industries including: oil refining, food processing, paper making, chemical and drug manufacture, paint and varnish manufacture. Although details vary from one concern to another, there are common features in most process costing systems. These include:

a. Clearly defined process cost centres and the accumulation of all costs (material, labour and overheads) by the cost centres.

b. The maintenance of accurate records of units and part units produced and the cost incurred by each process.

c. The averaging of the total costs of each process over the total production of that process, including partly completed units.

d. The charging of the cost of the output of one process as the raw materials input cost of the following process.

e. Clearly defined procedures for separating costs where the process produces two or more products (ie Joint products) or where By-products arise during production. (Joint product and By-product costing are dealt with in the next chapter.)

3. CHOICE OF COST UNITS

As previously explained, the cost unit chosen should be relevant to the organisation and its product. In most cases the appropriate unit arises naturally having regard to the process and the way the product is sold and priced. Examples include:

Industry	Possible Cost Units
Brewing	Litre, gallon, barrel
Paint, Varnish	Litre, gallon
Food processing	Can, case, kilogram, tonne, litre, etc.
Oil refining	Litres or multiples, barrel

4. BASIS OF PROCESS COSTING

The basis of all process costing systems is shown in Figure 15.1.

It will be seen that material passes through the various processes gathering costs as it progresses. The diagram shows the simplest possible situation. Typical complications which occur are the costing problems associated with process losses at various stages and the valuation of partly completed units at the end of an accounting period. These are dealt with later in the chapter.

5. PROCESS LOSSES

With many forms of production the quantity, weight or volume of the process output will be less than the quantity, weight or volume of the materials input. This may be due to various reasons:

FIGURE 15.1   Process costing outline

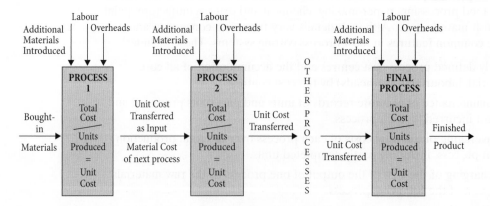

a. evaporation, residuals, ash, swarf;

b. unavoidable handling, breakage and spoilage losses;

c. withdrawal for testing and inspection.

Because of increasing material costs, careful records must be maintained of losses occurring and the resulting cost implications. If losses are in accordance with normal practice, ie standard levels, they are termed normal process losses. If they are above expectation, they are known as abnormal process losses.

6. NORMAL PROCESS LOSSES

These are unavoidable losses arising from the nature of the production process and it is therefore logical and equitable that the cost of such losses is included as part of the cost of good production. If any value can be recouped from the sale of imperfect articles or materials then this would be credited to the process account thus reducing overall cost.

Example I
A food manufacturing process has a normal wastage of 5% which can be sold as animal feedstuff at £5 tonne. In a given period the following data were recorded: Input materials 160 tonnes at £23 per tonne. Labour and overheads £2,896. Losses were at the normal level. Compute the cost per tonne.

Solution

INPUT	Tonnes	£
Materials	160	3,680
Labour and overheads		2,896
	160	6,576
less Normal loss 5%	8	40 cr
Good production	152	6,536

$$\text{Cost per tonne of good production} = \frac{6,536}{152} = £43$$

Note:
The £40 credit to the Process account will be debited to a Scrap Sales account which will eventually be credited with the actual sale. Any balance on the Scrap Sales account will be taken to P & L account.

7. ABNORMAL PROCESS LOSSES

Abnormal losses are those losses above the level deemed to be the normal loss rate for the process.

Abnormal losses cannot be foreseen and are due to such factors as: plant breakdown, industrial accidents, inefficient working or unexpected defects in materials. Conversely, unexpectedly favourable conditions might apply in a given period and actual losses may be lower than the calculated 'normal' loss. In such conditions abnormal gains would be made. The amount of abnormal loss or gain is calculated thus:

Abnormal loss (or gain) = Actual loss − Normal loss

It is an important principle, previously stated, that abnormal conditions should be excluded from routine reporting and only normal costs (which include normal process losses) charged to production. Accordingly the cost effects of abnormal losses or gains must be excluded from the Process Account. Abnormal losses or gains will be costed on the same basis as good production and therefore, like good production, will carry a share of the cost of normal losses. This is shown in the following example.

Example 2 – Abnormal loss

Assume the same data as in Example 1 except that actual production was 148 tonnes. Compute the abnormal loss and show the relevant accounts.

Solution

$$\text{Abnormal loss} = \text{Actual loss} - \text{Normal loss}$$

$$= 12 - 8$$

$$= 4 \text{ tonnes}$$

As the abnormal losses are valued at the same cost as good production (ie £43 tonne) the Process Account would be as follows.

Process A/C

	Tonnes	£		Tonnes	£
Material	160	3,680	Good production	148	6,364
Labour and		2,896	Normal losses	8	40
Overheads					
			Abnormal losses	4	172
	160	6,576		160	6,576

The other relevant accounts would be:

Abnormal losses A/C

	£		£
Process A/C	172	Scrap sales	20
		P&L	152
	172		172

Scrap sales A/C

	£		
Process A/C	40		
Abnormal losses	20		

Note:

The sale of the 4 tonnes of abnormal losses at £5 tonne is credited to the Abnormal Losses A/c. This means that only the net cost of £152 (£172 − £20) is charged to the P & L A/c.

Example 3 – Abnormal gain

Again assume the same data as Example 1 except that actual production was 155 tonnes.

Calculate the abnormal gain and show the relevant accounts.

Solution

$$\text{Abnormal gain} = \text{Actual loss} - \text{Normal loss}$$
$$= 5 - 8$$
$$= 3 \text{ tonnes}$$

These gains are valued at the same rate as good production.
The relevant accounts are as follows:

Process A/C

	Tonnes	£		Tonnes	£
Material	160	3,680	Good production	155	6,665
Labour and		2,896	Normal losses	8	40
Overheads					
Abnormal	3	129			
gains					
	163	£6,705		163	£6,705

Abnormal gains A/C

	£		£
Scrap sales A/C	15	Process A/C	129
P&L	114		
	129		129

Scrap sales A/C

	£		£
Process A/C	40	Abnormal gains	15

Notes on Example 3:

a. Although an improvement in performance has been made, the Good Production is still valued at £43 per tonne.

b. The credit to the Scrap Sales A/c of £15 is necessary so that the account only shows the effect of the 5 tonnes actually lost.

8. THE CONCEPT OF EQUIVALENT UNITS

At the end of any given period there are likely to be partly completed units. It is clear that some of the costs of the period are attributable to these units as well as those that are fully complete. To be able to spread costs equitably over part finished and fully complete units the concept of equivalent units is required. The number of equivalent units, for cost calculation purposes, is the number of equivalent fully complete units which the partly complete units (ie the W-I-P) represent.

For example, assume that in a given period production was 2,200 complete units and 600 partly complete. The partly complete units were deemed to be 75% complete.

$$\text{Total equivalent production} = \text{Completed units} + \text{Equivalent units in W-I-P}$$
$$= 2,200 + {}^3/_4 \, (600) = 2,200 + 450$$
$$= 2,650$$

The total costs for the period would be spread over the total equivalent production.

$$\text{ie} \quad \text{Cost per unit} = \frac{\text{Total costs}}{\text{Total equivalent production units}}$$

9. EQUIVALENT UNITS AND COST ELEMENTS

The above illustration of equivalent units is the simplest possible. Frequently some overall estimate of completion is not possible or desirable and it becomes necessary to consider the percentage completion of each of the cost elements; material, labour and overheads. The same principles are used to calculate equivalent units, but each cost element must be treated separately and then the cost per unit of each element is added to give the cost of a complete unit. This is shown below.

Example 4
In a given period production and cost data were as follows:

Total Costs	Materials	£5,115
	Labour	3,952
	Overheads	3,000
		£12,067

Production was 1,400 fully complete units and 200 partly complete. The degree of completion of the 200 units W-I-P was as follows:

Material	75% complete
Labour	60% complete
Overheads	50% complete

Calculate the total equivalent production, the cost per complete unit and the value of the W-I-P.

Solution

Cost Element	Equivalent Units in W-I-P	+	Fully Complete Units	=	Total Effective Production	Total costs Period £	Cost per Unit £
Material	200 × 75% = 150	+	1,400	=	1,550	5,115	3.3
Labour	200 × 60% = 120	+	1,400	=	1,520	3,952	2.6
Overheads	200 × 50% = 100	+	1,400	=	1,500	3,000	2.00
						£12,067	£7.90

From the table it will be seen that the cost of a complete unit = £7.90

$$\therefore \text{ Value of completed production} = 1,400 \times £7.90$$
$$= £11,060$$
$$\therefore \text{ Value of W-I-P} = \text{Total Costs} - \text{Value of completed production}$$
$$= £12,067 - 11,060$$
$$= £1,007$$

This can be verified by multiplying each element cost per unit by the number of equivalent units in the W-I-P of each cost element, thus:

Cost Element	No. of Equivalent Units in W-I-P	Cost per Unit	Value of WIP
Material	150	3.30	495
Labour	120	2.60	312
Overheads	100	2.00	200
			£1,007

Note on Example 4:
The way that the value of W-I-P can be cross-checked by using the cost elements or the total values should be carefully studied.

Remember:

Total cost for period = Value of completed units + Value of W-I-P

10. INPUT MATERIAL AND MATERIAL INTRODUCED

It will be recalled from Figure 15.1 that the output of one process forms the input material to the next process. The full cost of the completed units transferred forms the input material cost of the process and by its nature input material must be 100% complete.

Material introduced is extra material needed in the process and should always be shown separately from input material. Whenever there are partly completed units at the end of the period, they may contain two classifications of material, ie:

Input Material (ie previous process costs) always 100% complete.

Material Introduced which may or may not be complete.

Note:
Input material may also be described as: Units transferred, Cost of goods or units transferred or Previous process costs.

11. OPENING WORK IN PROGRESS

It follows that where there are partly completed units at the end of one period (the closing W-I-P) there will be opening work in progress at the beginning of the next period. This opening work in progress will be partially complete and will have a value brought forward from the previous period, sometimes sub-divided into the various elements of material, labour and overheads, each with a given degree of completion and value. Naturally in most practical situations there is both opening and closing work in progress and in such cases the problem arises of how to value the closing work in progress and the completed units transferred out.

There are two approaches to this problem; the *FIFO method* and the *Average cost method*.

12. FIFO METHOD OF VALUATION

Using this method it is assumed that units are dealt with on a first in–first out basis so that it is assumed that the first work done in a period is the completion of the opening W-I-P. The effect of this is that the closing W-I-P is valued at current period costs and part of the previous period's costs brought forward in the opening W-I-P valuation is attached to the cost of completed units.

13. AVERAGE COST METHOD OF VALUATION

Using this method an average unit cost is calculated using the total of the opening W-I-P valuation plus the current period costs. The effect of this is that both closing W-I-P and completed units are valued using the same average unit cost. This means that the previous period's costs (contained in the opening W-I-P valuation) influence the closing W-I-P valuation which is carried forward to the next period.

It is for this reason that it is sometimes argued that the Average Cost method makes the comparison of performance between periods more difficult than when the FIFO method is used. An alternative view is that the Average cost method is a useful device when costs fluctuate from period to period.

Neither of the valuation methods can be said to be 'incorrect' or 'correct', they are simply two different conventions which produce different answers. When costs are stable from one period to another and/or where the work-in-progress is a small proportion of throughput then the two systems produce similar results.

Examples follow which contrast the results obtained using both methods of valuation.

Example 5

Process 2 receives units from Process 1 and after carrying out work on the units transfers them to Process 3. For one accounting period the relevant data for Process 2 were as follows:

Opening W-I-P 200 units (25% complete) valued at £2,500

800 units received from Process 1 valued at £4,300

840 units were transferred to Process 3

Closing W-I-P 160 units (50% complete)

The costs for the period were £16,580 and no units were scrapped.

It is required to prepare the Process accounts for Process 2 using:

i. the FIFO method of valuation,

ii. the Average Cost method of valuation.

Solution – using FIFO method

Calculation of effective units of production

	Units
	Units
Completed units transferred out	840
+ Work contained in closing W-I-P (160 × 50%)	80
	920
− Work contained in opening W-I-P (200 × 25%)	50
∴ Effective units for period	870

$$\therefore \text{Period cost per unit} = \frac{\text{Total cost for period (ie Process costs + transfers in)}}{\text{Effective units for period}}$$

$$= \frac{£16,580 + 4,300}{870}$$

$$= £24$$

This figure is used to give the closing W-I-P valuation, ie 160 × 50% × £24 = £1,920.

The valuation of the number of complete units transferred to Process 3 is found from the balance on the process account as follows:

Process 2 Account

	Units	£		Units	£
Opening W-I-P B/F	200	2,500			
Receipts from Process 1	800	4,300	Transfers to Process 3	840	21,460
Process costs		16,580	Closing WIP C/F	160	1,920
	1,000	23,380		1,000	23,380

Note on Example 5 (FIFO METHOD):

The transfer value of £21,460 is the balance on the account and is £1,300 greater than the period cost per unit already calculated, ie £21,460 − (840 × £24) = £1,300.

This is the amount by which the opening W-I-P valuation (based on the *previous* period's costs) is greater than the current period costs, ie:

$$£2,500 − (200 × 25\% × £24) = £1,300.$$

Thus, it would be seen that only the current period cost levels, ie the £24 per unit, are carried forward to the next period in the closing W-I-P valuation.

Solution – using Average Cost method

Using this system the effective units are the transfers to the next process (840 units) plus the work contained in the closing W-I-P (80 units, ie 50% of 160 units) that is a total of 920 units.

The costs involved are the total of the opening W-I-P valuation + the valuation of units transferred in + the process 2 costs, ie:

$$£2,500 + 4,300 + 16,580 = £23,380$$

$$\therefore \text{average cost per unit} = \frac{23,380}{920}$$

$$= £25.413$$

This is used to value both the closing stock and transfers out.

$$\text{Thus Closing stock valuation} = 160 \times 50\% \times £25.413$$

$$= £2,033$$

$$\text{Transfers to Process 3} = 840 \times £25.413$$

$$= £21,347$$

The process account is as follows:

	Units	£		Units	£
Opening W-I-P B/F	200	2,500			
Receipts from	800	4,300	Transfers to	840	21,347
Process 1			Process 3		
Process costs		16,580	Closing WIP C/F	160	2,033
	1,000	23,380		1,000	23,380

Notes on Example 5 (Average Cost method):

1. It will be seen that the effect of the average cost method is, in this example, to increase the value of closing stock and reduce the value of transfers to Process 3. This is because the previous period cost levels (as contained in the opening W-I-P valuation) were higher than the current cost levels. If the previous period cost levels were lower than current levels the average cost method would cause the closing W-I-P valuations to be lower than when using the FIFO system.

2. The above example has deliberately been kept simple to show clearly the principles involved. Examples follow which show the added complications of abnormal and normal scrap and where the elements (material, labour and overheads) of the opening and closing W-I-P are involved.

It must be stressed however, that these added complications merely increase the amount of arithmetic involved, they do not alter the basic principles explained above so it is important that these are thoroughly understood before proceeding further.

Example 6
This example illustrates the treatment of opening and closing W-I-P where the W-I-P is broken down into its various elements.

The following data relate to Process Y for accounting period 2.

At the beginning of period 2 there were 800 units partly completed which had the following values:

Value

	£	% age complete
Input Material (from Process X)	8,200	100
Material Introduced	5,600	55
Labour	3,200	60
Overheads	2,400	45

During the period 4,300 units were transferred from Process X at a value of £46,500 and other costs were:

	£
Material Introduced	24,000
Labour	19,500
Overheads	18,200

At the end of the period, the closing W-I-P was 600 units which were at the following stage of completion:

Input Material	100% complete
Material Introduced	50% complete
Labour	45% complete
Overheads	40% complete

The balance of 4,500 units was transferred to Finished Goods.

Calculate the value of units transferred to Finished Goods and the value of W-I-P and prepare the Process account using:

i. the FIFO method and

ii. the Average Cost method.

Solution – Using FIFO method

As previously the first step is to calculate the effective units of production for the period. This follows identical principles to Example 5 except that in this example it is necessary to consider the four elements of the units (Input material, material introduced, labour and overheads) instead of simply the units as a whole. When the effective production is ascertained the cost per unit, for each element, can be calculated.

Calculation of effective units and cost per unit

Cost Element	Completed units	+	Equivalent units in closing W-I-P	−	Equivalent units in opening W-I-P	=	Total Effective Production (units)	Costs £	Cost per Unit £
Input material	4,500	+	600	−	800	=	4,300	46,500	10.814
Material Introduced	4,500	+	300	−	440	=	4,360	24,000	5.505
Labour	4,500	+	270	−	480	=	4,290	19,500	4.545
Overheads	4,500	+	240	−	360	=	4,380	18,200	4.155
									25.019

∴ Closing stock valuation for 600 units

			£
Input material	= 100% complete	= 600 × £10.814 =	6,488
Material introduced	= 50% complete	= 300 × £5.505 =	1,651
Labour	= 45% complete	= 270 × £4.545 =	1,227
Overheads	= 40% complete	= 240 × £4.155 =	997
			£10,363

This value is used in the Process Account in the normal way with the value of the Transfers to Finished Goods being the balance on the account.

Process Account – Process Y (FIFO)

	Units	£		Units	£
Opening W-I-P B/F	800	19,400			
Transfers in from Process X	4,300	46,500	Transfers to Fin. Goods	4,500	117,237
Material introduced		24,000	Closing WIP C/F	600	10,363
Labour		19,500			
Overheads		18,200			
	5,100	127,600		5,100	127,600

Solution – Using Average Cost method

Calculation of effective units and cost per unit

Cost Elements	Equivalent units in Closing WIP	+	Fully Complete Units	=	Total Effective Production (a)	Opening WIP Values	+	Period Costs	=	Total Cost	Cost per Unit (b)+(a)
Input Material	600 × 100% = 600	+	4,500	=	5,100	£8200	+	£46,500	=	£54,700	£10.725
Material Intro	600 × 50% = 300	+	4,500	=	4,800	5,600	+	24,000	=	29,600	6.167
Labour	600 × 45% = 270	+	4,500	=	4,770	3,200	+	19,500	=	22,700	4.759
Overheads	600 × 40% = 240	+	4,500	=	4,740	2,400	+	18,200	=	20,600	4.346
						£19,400	+	£108,200	=	£127,600	£25.997

∴ Value of completed production = 4,500 × £25.997

= **£116,987**

The value of the closing WIP can be found either by deducting the value of completed production from total costs or, more tediously, by calculating the various element values, as follows:

Value of closing WIP = Total cost − value of completed production

= £127,600 − 116,987 = **£10,613**

or this can be calculated by using the various element values, ie:

600 × £10.725	=	6,435.00
300 × £6.167	=	1,850.10
270 × £4.759	=	1,284.93
240 × £4.346	=	1,043.04
		£10,613.07

(slight rounding error)

The process account can now be completed

Process Account – Process Y (Average Cost)

	Units	£		Units	£
Opening W-I-P B/F	800	19,400			
Transfers in from Process X	4,300	46,500	Transfers to Fin. Goods	4,500	116,987
Material introduced		24,000	Closing WIP C/F	600	10,613
Labour		19,500			
Overheads		18,200			
	5,100	127,600		5,100	127,600

Example 7
This is a more complicated example which brings together the various facets of process costing covered in the chapter. It includes opening and closing W-I-P and normal and abnormal losses where the scrapped units are not fully complete.

The following data relate to Process 2 for one accounting period. Process 2 receives units from Process 1 and, after processing, transfers them to Process 3.

Opening W-I-P 600 units

	Value £	Percentage Complete
Input material	720	100
Material introduced	500	60
Labour	340	50
Overheads	270	40

Transfers in from Process 1: 4,100 units valued at 5,200.
Transfers out to Process 3: 3,500 units

	£
Materials introduced	2,956
Labour	2,200
Overheads	1,900

Closing stock 800 units at the following stage of completion

Input material	100% complete
Material introduced	60% complete
Labour	50% complete
Overheads	40% complete

400 units were scrapped at the following stage of completion

Input material	100% complete
Material introduced	100% complete
Labour	40% complete
Overheads	30% complete

The normal loss is 10% of production and the scrapped units realised 40p each.

It is required to prepare the Process Account for Process 2 using

i. the FIFO method,

ii. the Average Cost method.

Solution – Using FIFO method

The first stage is to calculate the amount of normal loss to see whether there is any abnormal loss or gain involved. The production for the period is calculated as follows:

Opening W-I-P	600 units
+ Transfers in	4,100
	4,700
− Closing W-I-P	800
∴ Production	3,900 units

∴ Normal loss is 10% of 3,900 = 390, and as the actual number scrapped were 400, there were 10 units of abnormal loss.

The calculation of effective units for cost calculation purposes follows the same principles as in Examples 5 and 6 except that the number of units of abnormal loss must be included in the total effective production because, as explained in Para 7, abnormal losses are costed on the same basis as good production.

Calculation of effective units and cost per unit

Cost Element	Completed Units	+	Equiv. Units in Closing WIP	+	Equiv. Units in Abnormal loss	−	Equiv. Units in Opening WIP	=	Total Effective Production	Costs £	Cost per Unit £
Input Material	3,500	+	800	+	10	−	600	=	3,710	5,200	1.402
Material Intro.	3,500	+	480	+	10	−	360	=	3,630	*2,800	0.771
Labour	3,500	+	400	+	4	−	300	=	3,604	2,200	0.610
Overheads	3,500	+	320	+	3	−	240	=	3,583	1,900	0.530

* This is the cost of the material introduced, £2,956, less the resale value of the normal loss, £156, ie 390 @ 40p each. The resale value of the 10 units of abnormal loss is credited to the Abnormal loss account not the process account.

The costs per unit calculated are then used to evaluate the value of the closing W-I-P and the abnormal loss

Closing W-I-P valuation

		£
Input material	800 equivalent units @ £1.402	1,121.60
Material introduced	480 equivalent units @ 0.771	370.08
Labour	400 equivalent units @ 0.612	244.80
Overheads	320 equivalent units @ 0.530	169.60
		£1,906.08
		say, **£1,906**

Abnormal loss valuation

		£
Input material	10 equivalent units @ £1.402	14.02
Material introduced	10 equivalent units @ 0.771	7.71
Labour	4 equivalent units @ 0.610	2.44
Overheads	3 equivalent units @ 0.530	1.59
		£25.76
	say,	**£26**

The process account can now be prepared.

Process 2 Account (FIFO)

	Units	£		Units	£
Opening WIP	600	1,830			
Transfers from Process 1	4,100	5,200	Normal loss	390	156
Material		2,956	Abnormal loss	10	26
Labour		2,200	Transfers to Process 3	3,500	11,998
					Balancing figure
Overheads		1,900	Closing WIP	800	1,906
	4,700	£14,086		4,700	£14,086

Solution – Using Average Cost method

Calculation of effective units and cost per unit

Cost Element	Equiv. Units in Closing WIP	+	Equiv. Units in Abnormal loss	+	Complete units	=	Effective Production	Opening WIP value £	+	Period Cost £	=	Total Costs £
Input Material	800	+	10	+	3,500	=	4,310	720	+	5,200	=	5,920
Material Intro.	480	+	10	+	3,500	=	3,990	500	+	2,800	=	3,300
Labour	400	+	4	+	3,500	=	3,904	340	+	2,200	=	2,540
Overheads	320	+	3	+	3,500	=	3,823	270	+	1,900	=	2,170

Cost per unit calculations:

Input material	$\dfrac{£5,920}{4,310}$	$= £1.374$
Material introduced	$\dfrac{£3,300}{3,990}$	$= £0.827$
Labour	$\dfrac{£2,540}{3,904}$	$= £0.651$
Overheads	$\dfrac{£2,170}{3,823}$	$= £0.568$

The various costs per unit are used to evaluate the closing W-I-P, abnormal loss and the completed production:

Closing W-I-P

Equivalent units		Cost per unit		Value
800	×	£1.374	=	£1,099.20
480	×	0.827	=	396.96
400	×	0.651	=	260.40
320	×	0.568	=	181.76
				1,938.32
				say **£1,938**

Abnormal loss

10	×	£1.374	=	£13.74
10	×	0.827	=	8.27
4	×	0.651	=	2.60
3	×	0.568	=	1.70
				£26.31
				say, **£26**

Completed production

3,500	×	£1.374	=	£4,809.00
3,500	×	0.827	=	2,894.50
3,500	×	0.651	=	2,278.50
3,500	×	0.568	=	1,988.00
				£11,970

rounded to, **£11,966** to balance

These values are used in the Process account.

Process 2 Account (Average Cost)

	Units	£		Units	£
Opening WIP	600	1,830			
			Normal loss	390	156
Transfers from Process 1	4,100	5,200	Abnormal loss	10	26
Material		2,956	Transfers to Process 3	3,500	11,966
Labour		2,200			
Overheads		1,900	Closing WIP	800	1,938
	4,700	£14,086		4,700	£14,086

Note:

If, instead of the abnormal loss, there had been an abnormal gain the treatment would be as follows for both Average cost and the FIFO methods. The total effective production would be found as in Example 6 less the number of abnormal gain units. These units would be evaluated at the cost per unit calculated and the Process account *debited* with the abnormal gain units and their value. It follows that abnormal gain units will always be fully complete whereas abnormal loss units may be partially or fully complete.

14. SUMMARY

a. Process costing is used where production follows a number of sequential processes frequently of an automatic nature.

b. The cost unit chosen should be relevant to the organisation and the product. Examples include; gallons, barrels, tonnes, kilograms.

c. Material passes through the various processes gathering costs as it progresses. The output of one process forming the input material into the next process.

d. Losses due to breakage, evaporation, machining, testing and other causes must be carefully recorded.

e. Normal process losses are unavoidable losses in production and form part of the cost of good production.

f. Abnormal losses are losses above the normal anticipated level and should be costed on the same basis as good production.

g. Abnormal gains occur when losses are below the anticipated level and should be costed on the basis as good production.

h. When partly complete units occur at the end of a period the number of equivalent units of complete production must be calculated.

i. The concept of equivalent units can also be applied to the cost elements in production; material, labour and overheads.

j. There are two methods of calculating W-I-P values; the FIFO and average cost methods.

15. POINTS TO NOTE

a. Although the calculation of the cost of W-I-P is a common examination question, in practice where the W-I-P is a small fraction of throughput, period to period, it is likely to be ignored.

b. The technique of standard costing is particularly appropriate for use in process industries. Such applications are described in Chapter 26.

Student self-testing

Exercises (answers below)

1. A firm has two processes 1 and 2.

   Material for 12,000 items was put into Process 1. There were no opening stocks and no process losses and there were transfers of 9,000 items to Process 2. The unfinished items were complete as to material and 50% complete as to labour and overhead. The costs of Process 1 were Direct Material £36,000, Direct Labour £32,000 and Overheads £8,000. Process 2 completed 7,600 items and there were 600 scrapped which was considered normal. The balance was unfinished and deemed to be 25% complete in labour and overheads. The costs for Process 2 were; Labour £28,500 and Overheads £14,000. You are required to prepare process accounts for each process.

2. Orion Ltd produce a single product which undergoes three processes. The following details relate to one period:

	Process		
	I	**II**	**III**
	£	**£**	**£**
Raw Materials (60,000 units)	80,000		
Materials Introduced	23,500	18,750	22,100
Direct Wages	15,600	12,000	13,400
Overheads allotted to Processes	3,800	4,600	3,200
Other overheads total £27,000			
Units	Units	Units	
Output in units	55,200	53,800	49,600

A normal loss of 5% of the input to each process is anticipated.
Units lost have the following scrap values:

After Process I	Nil
After Process II	£1
After Process III	£1.80

There was no opening or closing W-I-P.
Prepare ledger accounts for the period.

3. A plastic manufacturing process has a normal wastage of 8% which can be sold as scrap at £2 per Kg.
   In a given period, the following data were recorded:

Input 250 Kgs at	£7 Kg
Labour and overheads	£3,500
Actual output	225 Kgs

Show all relevant accounts.

4. In a given period the production data and costs for a process were:

Production 2,100 units fully complete

700 units partly complete

The degree of completion of the partly complete units was:

Material	80%	complete
Labour	60%	complete
Overheads	50%	complete

The costs for the period were

Material	£24,800
Labour	£16,750
Overheads	£36,200

Calculate the total equivalent production, the cost per complete unit and the value of the W-I-P.

Solutions to exercises

1.

Process 1

	Units	£		Units	£
Material input	12,000	36,000	Process 2	9,000	61,290
Labour		32,000	WIP	3,000	14,710
Overheads		8,000			
	12,000	76,000		12,000	76,000

Process 2

	Units	£		Units	£
Material input (Process 1)	9,000	61,290	Finished goods	7,600	96,892
Labour		28,500	Normal loss	600	
Overheads		14,000	WIP	800	6,898
	9,000	103,790		9,000	103,790

Working for Cost per Equivalent Units

Process 1

Units	Material	Labour	Overheads	Total
Fully complete	9,000	9,000	9,000	9,000
WIP Material	3,000			3,000
Labour (50%)		1,500		
Overheads			1,500	
Equivalent Units	12,000	10,500	10,500	12,000
Costs	£36,000	£32,000	£8,000	£76,000
Cost/Unit (complete units)	£3	£3.048	£0.762	

$$\therefore \quad \text{Cost of complete units} = 9000 \times £6.81 = £61,290$$
$$\text{Cost of W-I-P} = (3,000 \times £3) + (1,500 \times £3.048)$$
$$+ (1,500 \times £0.762) = £14,715$$
$$\text{(rounded to £14,710)}$$

Cost per Equivalent Units

Process 2

Units	Material	Labour	Overheads	Total
Fully complete	7,600	7,600	7,600	7,600
Normal Loss				600
W-I-P	800			800
Labour		200		
Overheads			200	
= Equivalent Units	8,400	7,800	7,800	9,000
Costs	£61,290	£28,500	£14,000	£103,790
Cost/Unit	£7.3	£3.654		

$$\therefore \text{Cost of complete units} = 7,600 \times £12.749 = £96,892$$
$$\text{Cost of WIP} = (800 \times £7.3) + (200 \times £3.654) + (200 \times £1.795)$$
$$= £6,930(\text{rounded to } £6,898)$$

2.

Process 1

	Units	£		Units	£	
Allotted costs	60,000	122,900	Normal loss	3,000	–	
Overheads app'd on wages		10,273	Abnormal loss	1,800		4,205
			Output to II	55,200	128,968	
	60,000	133,173		60,000	133,173	

Notes:

a.
Input	60,000 units
Normal loss (5%)	3,000
Notional output	57,000
Actual output	55,200
∴ Abnormal loss	1,800

b. The abnormal loss is costed on the same basis as good production:

$$\frac{\text{Actual costs} - \text{expected scrap credit}}{\text{Notional output}} = \frac{£133,173}{57,000} = £2.336 \text{ per unit}$$

Process 2

	Units	£		Units	£
Allotted costs		35,350	Normal loss	2,760	2,760
Overheads app'd		7,902	Output to III	53,800	173,855
Transfers from I	55,200	128,968			
Abnormal gain	1,360	4,395			
	56,560	176,615		56,560	176,615
Input	55,200	units			

a.
Normal loss (5%)	2,760
Notional output	52,440
Actual output	53,800
∴ Abnormal gain	1,360

b. The abnormal gain is costed on the same basis as good production:

$$\frac{\text{Actual costs} - \text{expected scrap credit}}{\text{Notional output}} = \frac{£172,220 - 2,760}{52,440} = £3.2315$$

Process 3

	Units	£		Units	£
Allotted costs		38,700	Normal loss	2,690	4,842
Overheads app'd		8,825	Abnormal loss	1,510	6,397
Transfers from II	53,800	173,855	Output	49,600	210,141
	53,800	221,380		53,800	221,380

Notes:

a. Input   53,800 units
    Normal loss (5%)   2,690
    Notional output   51,110
    Actual output   49,600
    ∴ Abnormal gain   1,510

b. The abnormal gain is costed on the same basis as good production per unit.

$$\frac{£221,380 - 4,842}{51,110} = £4.2367$$

Abnormal loss/Gain account

	£		£
Process I	4,205	Process II	4,395
Process III	6,397	Scrap Sales (Proc III)	2,718
Scrap sales (Proc II)	1,360		

(At the end of the year the balance on this account would be taken to the P & L account.)

Scrap Sales account

	£		£
Process II (normal)	2,760	Abnormal gains (Proc II)	1,360
Process III (normal)	4,842		
Abnormal losses (Proc III)	2,718		

(At the end of the year the balance on this account would be taken to the P & L account.)

3. Input   250 Kgs
     less Normal waste   20 Kgs
     = Normal O/P   230 Kgs
     Actual O/P   225 Kgs
     = Abnormal loss   5 Kgs

Process A/c

	Kgs	£		Kgs	£
Material	250	1,750	Good output	225	5,097
Labour		3,500	Normal loss	20	40
			Abnormal loss	5	113
	250	5,250		250	5,250

Abnormal loss A/c

Process A/c	113	P & L		113
	113			113

Scrap Sales

Process A/c	40	

4.

Cost Elements	Equivalent units in WIP	+	Complete Units	=	Total Effective Production	Total Costs £	Cost per Unit £
Material	700 × 80% = 560	+	2,100	=	2,660	24,800	9.32
Labour	700 × 60% = 420	+	2,100	=	2,520	16,750	6.65
Overheads	700 × 50% = 350	+	2,100	=	2,450	36,200	14.78
					Totals £	77,750	30.75

$\therefore$ Value of completed production = 2,100 × £30.75 = £64,575

$\therefore$ Value of WIP = Total costs − Value of completed production

= £77,750 − 64,575

= £13,175

16

Cost accounting methods:
Joint product and by-product costing

1. OBJECTIVES

After studying this chapter you will

- **Be able to distinguish between Joint products and By-products**

- **Understand the main methods of By-product Costing**

- **Know the meaning of Joint Costs, Split-off point and Subsequent costs**

- **Understand the Physical Unit and Sales Value methods of apportioning joint costs**

- **Know the Notional Sales Value method**

- **Understand the problems of dealing with joint products in Service organisations.**

2. DEFINITIONS

A joint product is the term used when two or more products arise simultaneously in the course of processing, each of which has a significant sales value in relation to each other. Examples of industries where joint products arise are as follows:

Oil Refining

- The joint products include; diesel fuel, petrol, paraffin, lubricants.

Meat processing

- The joint products include; the various grades of meat and hides.

Mining

- The joint products frequently include the recovery of several metals from the same crushing.

On the other hand a by-product is a product which arises incidentally in the production of the main product(s) and which has a relatively small sales value compared with the main product(s). Examples of by-products are:

Iron and steel manufacture

- furnace slag is sold for use in cement and brick manufacture and for road construction.

Meat trade

- bones, grease and certain offal are regarded as by-products.

Timber trade

- sawdust, small offcuts, bark are usually regarded as by-products.

After the point of separation both joint products and by-products may need further processing before they are saleable.

Note:
It will be apparent from the foregoing that clear distinctions between by-products and joint products are not possible. The exact classification of a particular item is a matter of judgement depending on the particular circumstances. What is a by-product in one factory may be termed a joint product in another.

3. BY-PRODUCT COSTING

Because by-products, by definition, have a relatively small sales value, elaborate and expensive costing systems should be avoided. The most common methods of dealing with by-products are as follows:

a. By-product net realisable value is deducted from the total cost of production.
b. Total costs (main product and by-product, if any) are deducted from Total Sales value of main and by-products.
c. By-product receipts are treated as incidental other income and transferred to general P & L account. This method is generally considered unsatisfactory except where the value is very small.
d. By-products treated as joint products. This method is most appropriate where the value of the by-product is relatively large. Details of joint product costing are dealt with in Para. 4 below.

None of the by-product costing methods is wholly satisfactory, but method (a) above probably has least disadvantages. This method is illustrated in the following example.

Example I
During a period 2,400 units of Large were produced and sold at £10 per unit. Total production costs were £17,500. Arising from the main production process 60 kgs. of Little were produced which were sold at £8 per kg.

Special packing and distribution costs of £2.20 per kg were incurred for Little. What were the net production costs and gross profit for the period?

Solution

		£	£
	Production Costs		17,500
Less	Net Realisable Value of Little	480	
		−132	348
=	Net Production Cost		17,152
	Gross Profit		£6,848
	Sales Value of Large		£24,000

4. JOINT-PRODUCT COSTING

Because joint products arise due to the inherent nature of the production process, it follows that none of the products can be produced separately. The various products become identifiable at a point known as the *'split-off point'*. Up to that stage all costs are joint costs, subsequent to the split-off point any costs incurred can be identified with specific products and they are known as 'subsequent' or 'additional processing costs'. This is shown diagrammatically in Figure 16.1.

It follows that subsequent costs after the split-off point do not pose any particular cost accounting problem because they are readily identifiable with a specific product and can be coded and charged accordingly. For product costing purposes the major problem in joint-product costing is to apportion the joint costs, ie those prior to the split-off point, on an acceptable basis.

FIGURE 16.1 Joint product costing

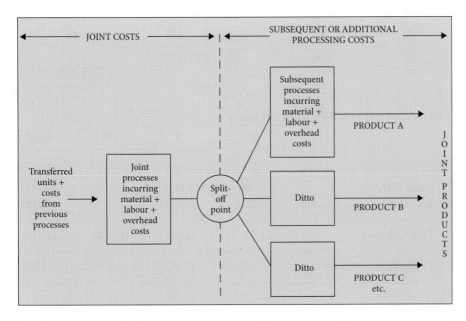

5. APPORTIONING JOINT COSTS

The commonest methods of apportioning joint costs are:

a. The physical unit basis. The joint costs are apportioned over the joint products in proportion to the physical weight or volume of the products.

b. The sales value basis. Here the joint costs are apportioned in proportion to the relative sales value of the products.

The two methods are illustrated in Example 2.

Example 2

A process produces three products, X, Y and Z. Total joint costs were £12,000 and outputs, selling prices and sales values were:

X. 200 litres sold at £25 litre giving a sale value of £5,000.

Y. 400 litres sold at £15 litre giving a sale value of £6,000.

Z. 100 litres sold at £30 litre giving a sale value of £3,000.

Apportion the joint costs and calculate the profit percentage on

i. the physical unit basis and

ii. the sales value basis.

Solution

Physical unit basis
Cost Statement

Product	Output	Apportionment	Cost Apportioned
		£	
X	200	$\frac{200}{700} \times £12,000$	3,429
Y	400	$\frac{400}{700} \times £12,000$	6,857
Z	100	$\frac{100}{700} \times £12,000$	1,714
	700		£12,000

Profit Statement on Physical Unit Basis

	X	Y	Z	Total
	£	£	£	£
Sales Value	5,000	6,000	3,000	14,000
less Apportioned Costs	3,429	6,857	1,714	12,000
Profit/(Loss)	£1,571	(£857)	£1,286	£2,000
Profit/(Loss) Percentage	31%	(14%)	43%	14%

Sales Value Basis Cost Statement

Product	Sales Value	Apportionment	Costs Apportioned
		£	
X	£5,000	$\frac{5,000}{14,000} \times £12,000$	286
Y	£6,000	$\frac{6,000}{14,000} \times £12,000$	5,143
Z	£3,000	$\frac{3,000}{14,000} \times £12,000$	2,571
	£14,000		£12,000

Profit statement on Sales Value basis

	X	Y	Z	Total
	£	£	£	£
Sales Value	5,000	6,000	3,000	14,000
less Apportioned Costs	4,286	5,143	2,571	12,000
Profit	£714	£857	£429	£2,000
Profit Percentage	14%	14%	14%	14%

Notes

a. It will be seen that the sales value basis produces the same profit percentage for each product. The method is widely used for this reason and for the assumption that the price obtained for an item is directly related to its cost.

b. The cost apportionment is made on the sales value of the products (ie, Qty × price) and not the selling price per unit.

c. It must be emphasised that whatever method is used for apportioning joint costs, it is a convention only and its accuracy cannot be tested.

6. THE NOTIONAL SALES VALUE METHOD

On occasions the products which emerge from the split-off point are not saleable without further processing. It follows therefore that, at the split-off point, sales values are not known so that joint costs cannot be apportioned until some estimate is made of a notional sales value at the split-off point.

This is done by deducting subsequent processing costs from the final sales value to arrive at a notional sales value at split-off point. This is illustrated below.

Example 3
A process with joint costs of £5,000 produces two products W and V, both of which need further processing before sale. The relevant data are as follows:

Product	Output	Subsequent Processing Costs	Final Selling Price	Final Value Sales £
W	2,000 Kgs	£1,500	£2 Kg	4,000
V	4,500 Kgs	£1,250	£1.50 Kg	6,750

Calculate the notional Sales Value at split-off point, the apportionment of joint costs, the profit on each product and the profit percentage.

Solution

Cost Statement

Product	Final Sales Value £	Subsequent Processing after Split-off £	Notional Sales Value £	Apportionment of Joint Cost	Apportioned Costs £
W	4,000	1,500	2,500	$\frac{2,500}{8,000} \times £5,000$	1,563
V	6,750	1,250	5,500	$\frac{5,500}{8,000} \times £5,000$	3,437
	£10,750	£2,750	£8,000		£5,000

Profit Statement

	W		V		Total	
	£	£	£	£	£	£
Final Sales Value		4,000		6,750		10,750
less						
Apportioned						
Costs	1,563		3,437		5,000	
Subsequent Costs	1,500	3,063	1,250	4,687	2,750	7,750
Profit		£937		£2,063		£3,000
Profit Percentage		23%		31%		28%

7. JOINT PRODUCTS IN SERVICE ORGANISATIONS

The illustrations so far in this chapter have been drawn from manufacturing industry but joint products or joint services also arise in service organisations. Wherever facilities – buildings, staff and equipment – are used in common to provide a variety of products or services then joint products may arise as in manufacturing.

Take for example, banking. Banks provide a range of financial services using, largely, a common pool of facilities. The services include: current and deposit accounts, foreign transactions, investments, insurance, trustee and taxation consultancy and so on. Although there are some identifiable costs specific to particular services, most of the costs are incurred in common for all the services so that the cost accounting system in a bank has to deal with precisely the same problems faced in, say, an oil refinery.

8. COST APPORTIONMENT AND DECISION-MAKING

The procedures outlined so far are acceptable for stock valuation and conventional profit calculation purposes, but may produce misleading information for particular types of decisions. A common type of decision is whether to sell a joint product at the split-off point or whether to incur further processing costs and sell at an enhanced price. In such circumstances, the amount of the joint costs and the method by which the joint costs are apportioned are irrelevant.

All that matters is a comparison of the increase in revenue with the increase in costs necessary to achieve that revenue. This is an example of the use of incremental costing which is important in decision-making. To illustrate this approach assume the same data as in Example 2 except that the firm has the opportunity to process further Product Y at an additional cost of £3/litre in which case the produce could be sold at £20/litre instead of £15/litre. Is this worthwhile?

		£
Incremental revenue possible = £5 litre × 400 litres =		2,000
Incremental costs necessary = £3 litres × 400 litres =		1,200
Extra Profit =		£800

The conclusion from this is that it is worthwhile incurring additional costs on a product as long as the additional sales value gained exceeds the additional costs.

9. SUMMARY

a. When two or more products arise from a process and where each has a significant sales value, they are termed joint products. When a product of relatively small value arises incidentally it is termed a by-product.

b. The most common method of by-product costing is where the net realisable value of the by-product is deducted from the total production cost.

c. The point where joint products are separately identifiable is the split-off point. Up to that point all costs are joint costs which, for product costing purposes, have to be spread over the products on a reasonable basis.

d. The main two methods of apportioning joint costs are the physical unit and the sales value bases.

e. The notional sales value basis is used where additional processing is necessary for the product to be saleable so that an actual sales value is not available at the split-off point.

f. To decide whether additional processing is worthwhile to gain extra revenue, all that is necessary is to compare the incremental costs and incremental revenue. Joint costs and methods of apportionment are irrelevant.

10. POINT TO NOTE

Processing may produce Waste–Scrap–By-Products–Joint-Products in ascending order of value. The exact classification of any given item is a matter of judgement.

Student self-testing

Exercises (answers below)

1. The following data relate to three joint products:

	A	B	C
Sales Value	£24,000	£18,000	£15,000
Selling Costs	£3,500	£4,500	£1,000
Weight (Kgs)	180	240	150

Joint costs £35,000. Calculate the profit made by each product apportioning joint costs on:

a. the sales value basis

b. the physical basis.

2. Two products, X and Y, are produced from the same material. The material costs 95p per Kg and the products appear after Process 1.

X can be sold directly but Y needs further processing in Process 2. The following data relate to one period.

Process	Materials £	Labour £	Overhead £	Total £
1	144,000	21,000	15,000	180,000
2		10,000	18,000	28,000
	£144,000	£31,000	£33,000	£208,000

Product	Kgs Sold	Closing Stock (Kgs)	Sales
X	30,000	15,000	£52,500
Y	45,000		£150,750

There were no materials on hand at the end of the period. You are required to calculate:

a. The unit price of X and its market value at split off.

b. The total joint cost to be apportioned between the two products.

c. The total cost of X and Y using the sales value method of apportionment.

3. Four joint products are produced from a refining process. In the past, no attempt has been made to apportion the joint costs and the Sales Manager obtained the best price he could for each product. The new accountant for the firm apportioned the joint costs over the products on a weight basis and found that this resulted in widely differing profit percentages. As a consequence the accountant asserted that the selling prices must be changed to take account of the cost of the products.

Discuss.

Solutions to exercises

1. Apportionment on Sales Value

Product	Sales Value £	Apportionment	Costs Apportioned £
A	24,000	$\frac{24,000}{57,000} \times £35,000 =$	14,737
B	18,000	$\frac{18,000}{57,000} \times £35,000 =$	11,053
C	15,000	$\frac{15,000}{57,000} \times £35,000 =$	9,210
	£57,000		£35,000

Profit Statement

Product	A £	B £	C £	Total £
Sales Value	24,000	18,000	15,000	57,000
less Apportioned Costs	14,737	11,053	9,210	35,000
less Selling Costs	3,500	4,500	1,000	9,000
= Profit	£5,763	£2,447	£4,790	£13,000

Apportionment on Physical Unit Basis

Product	Weight	Apportionment	Costs Apportioned
A	180	$\frac{180}{570} \times £35,000$	£11,053
B	240	$\frac{240}{570} \times £35,000$	14,737
C	150	$\frac{150}{570} \times £35,000$	9,210
	570		£35,000

Profit Statement

Product	A £	B £	C £	Total £
Sales Value	24,000	18,000	15,000	57,000
less Apportioned Costs	11,053	14,737	9,210	35,000
Selling Costs	3,500	4,500	1,000	9,000
= Profit	£9,447	(£1,237)	£4,790	£13,000

2.

$$\text{Unit price of X} = \frac{\text{Sales}}{\text{Kgs sold}} = \frac{52,500}{30,000} = £1.75$$

Market value at split off point of X is

Sales	£52,500
+ Closing Stock (15,000 × £1.75)	26,250
	£78,750

The joint costs to be apportioned are Process 1 costs which total 180,000. The notional sales value at split off point is

	£
Product X	78,750 (from above)
Product Y (150,750 – 28,000)	122,750
= Total notional sales value	£201,500

Using the values calculated above the apportionment of joint costs can be made as follows:

Product	Notional Sales Value £	Joint Costs Apportioned	£	Post Split-off Costs £	Total Costs £
X	78,750	$\frac{78,750}{201,500} \times 180,000 =$	70,347	–	70,347
Y	122,750	$\frac{122,750}{201,500} \times 180,000 =$	109,653	28,000	137,653
	201,500		£180,000	£28,000	£208,000

3. All methods of apportioning joint costs to individual joint products are arbitrary conventions totally unsuitable for any form of decision-making. The Sales Manager is acting rationally in obtaining the best price for each of the individual products. Naturally, the combined price for all the products must be greater than the total joint costs.

Assessment section 3

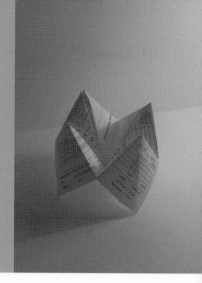

EXAMINATION QUESTIONS (ANSWERS ON THE WEBSITE)

A3.1   A company operates a process which produces three joint products –
K, P and Z. The costs of operating this process during September
amounted to £117,000.

During the month the output of the three products was

K	2,000 litres
P	4,500 litres
Z	3,250 litres

P is further processed at a cost of £9.00 per litre. The actual loss of the
second process was 10% of the input which was normal. Products K
and Z are sold without further processing.

The final selling prices of each of the products are:

K	£20.00 per litre
P	£25.00 per litre
Z	£18.00 per litre

Joint costs are attributed to products on the basis of output volume.

The profit attributed to product P was

A £6,750.
B £12,150.
C £13,500.
D £16,200.
E £18,000.

A3.2   A construction company has the following data concerning one of its
contracts:

Contract price	£2,000,000
Value certified	£1,300,000
Cash received	£1,200,000
Costs incurred	£1,050,000
Cost of work certified	£1,000,000

The profit (to the nearest £1,000) to be attributed to the contract is:
A £250,000.
B £277,000.
C £300,000.
D £950,000.
E £1,000,000.

A3.3 Process B had no opening stock. 13,500 units of raw material were transferred in at £4.50 per unit. Additional material at £1.25 per unit was added in process. Labour and overheads were £6.25 per completed unit and £2.50 per unit incomplete.

If 11,750 completed units were transferred out, what was the closing stock in Process B?
A £77,625.00.
B £14,437.50.
C £141,000.00.
D £21,000.00.

A3.4 State which of the following are characteristics of job costing:
i. homogeneous products,
ii. customer-driven production,
iii. complete production possible within a single accounting period.

A i. only
B i. and ii. only
C ii. and iii. only
D i and iii. only
E All of them

A3.5 State which of the following are characteristics of contract costing:
i. homogeneous products,
ii. customer-driven production,
iii. short timescale from commencement to completion of the cost unit.

A None of them
B i. and ii. only
C ii. and iii. only
D i and iii. only
E ii. only

A3.6 State which of the following are characteristics of service costing:
i. high levels of indirect costs as a proportion of total costs.
ii. use of composite cost units.
iii. use of equivalent units.

A i. only
B i. and ii. only
C ii. only
D ii. and iii. only
E All of them

The following information relates to questions A3.7 – A3.9.

A product is manufactured as a result of two processes, A and B. Details of process B for the month of August were as follows:

Materials transferred from process A	10,000 kg valued at £40,500
Labour costs	1,000 hours @ £5.616 per hour
Overheads	50% of labour costs
Output transferred to finished goods	8,000 kg
Closing work in progress	900 kg

Normal loss is 10% of input and losses do not have a scrap value.

Closing work in progress is 100% complete for material, and 75% complete for both labour and overheads.

A3.7 What is the value of the abnormal loss (to the nearest £)?

A Nil
B £489
C £544
D £546

A3.8 What is the value of the output (to the nearest £)?

A £39,139
B £43,488
C £43,680
D £43,977

A3.9 What is the value of the closing work in progress (to the nearest £)?

A £4,403
B £4,698
C £4,892
D £4,947

A3.10 A company undertaking long-term building contracts has a financial year end of 30 April. The following details on the purchase and use of machinery refer to contract A44, which was started on I May 2003 and is due for completion after 27 months.

1 July 2003: Machine 1 was purchased at a cost of $55,000. It is to be used throughout the contract, and will be sold for $6,400 when the contract finishes.

I October2003: Machine 2 was purchased at a cost of $28,600. The machine will be scrapped at the end of contract A44, and is not expected to have any saleable value.

If the company's policy is to charge depreciation in equal monthly amounts, the balance sheet value of machinery on contract A44 at 30 April 2004 will be:

A A $51,172
B B $52,500
C C $55,060
D D $56,500

A3.11 R Ltd makes one product, which through a single process. Details of the process account for period 1 were as follows:

	£
Material cost – 20,000 kg	26,000
Labour cost	12,000
Production overhead cost	5,700
Output	18,800 kg
Normal losses	5% of input

There was no work-in-progress at the beginning or end of the period. Process losses have no value. The cost of the abnormal loss (to the nearest £) is

A £437
B £441
C £460
D £465

A3.12 In a process where there are no work-in-progress stocks, two joint products (J and K) are created. Information (in *units*) relating to last month is as follows:

Product	Sales	Opening Stock Finished Goods	Closing Stock Finished Goods
J	6,000	100	300
K	4,000	400	200

Joint production costs last month were £110,000 and these were apportioned to joint products based on the number of units produced,

What were the joint production costs apportioned to product J for last month?

A £63,800
B £64000
C £66,000
D £68,200

A3.13 An advertising agency uses a job costing system to calculate the cost of client contracts. Contract A42 is one of several contracts undertaken in the last accounting period. Costs associated with the contract consist of

Direct materials	$ 5,500
Direct expenses	$14,500

Design staff worked 1,020 hours on contract A42, of which 120 hours were overtime. One third of these overtime hours were worked at the request of the client who wanted the contract to be completed quickly. Overtime is paid at a premium of 25 per cent of the basic rate of $24.00 per hour.

What was the prime cost of contract A42?

The above are a variety of multiple choice questions selected from CIMA's Management Accounting Fundamentals, Fundamentals of Management Accounting, Operational Cost Accounting and ACCA's Financial Information for Management.

A3.14 The following information relates to a manufacturing process for a period:

Materials costs   £16,445
Labour and overhead costs £28,596

10,000 units of output were produced by the process in the period, of which 420 failed testing and were scrapped. Scrapped units normally represent 5% of total production output. Testing takes place when production units are 60% complete in terms of labour and overheads. Materials are input at the beginning of the process. All scrapped units were sold in the period for £0.40 per unit.

Required:
Prepare the process accounts for the period including those for process scrap and abnormal losses/gains.
(ACCA Management Information)

A3.15 a. Distinguish between the cost accounting treatment of joint products and of by-products.

    b. A company operates a manufacturing process which produces joint products A and B, and by-product C. Manufacturing costs for a period total £272,926, incurred in the manufacture of:

Product   A – 16,000 kgs (selling price £6.10/kg)
                B – 53,200 kgs (selling price £7.50/kg)
                C – 2,770 kgs (selling price £0.80/kg)

Required:
Calculate the cost per kg (to 3 decimal places of a £) of Products A and B in the period, using market values to apportion joint costs.

    c. In another of the company's processes, Product X is manufacturing using raw materials P and T which are mixed in the proportions 1:2.

    d. Material purchases prices are:

        P £5.00 per kilo
        T £1.60 per kilo

Normal weight loss of 5% is expected during the process.
    In the period just ended 9,130 kilos of Product X were manufactured from 9,660 kilos of raw materials. Conversion costs in the period were £23,796. There was no work in process at the beginning or end of the period.

Required:
Prepare the Product X process account for the period.
(ACCA Management Information)

A3.16 A factory with three departments uses a single production overhead absorption rate expressed as a percentage of direct wages cost. It has been suggested that departmental overhead absorption rates would result in more accurate job costs. Set out below are the budgeted and actual data for the previous period, together with information relating to job No. 657.

| | | Hours in thousands | | | |
		Direct wages £000s	Direct labour	Machine	Production overhead £000s
Budget:					
Department:	A	25	10	40	120
	B	100	50	10	30
	C	25	25	–	75
Total:		150	85	50	225
Actual:					
Department:	A	30	12	45	130
	B	80	45	14	28
	C	30	30	–	80
Total:		140	87	59	238

During this period job No. 657 incurred the actual costs and actual times in the departments as shown below:

		Direct material £	Direct wages £	Direct labour	Machine hours
Department:	A	120	100	20	40
	B	60	60	40	10
	C	10	10	10	–

After adding production overhead to prime cost, one third is added to production cost for gross profit. This assumes that a reasonable profit is earned after deducting administration, selling and distribution costs.

You are required to:

a. calculate the current overhead absorption rate;
b. using the rate obtained in (a) above, calculate the production over-head charged to job No. 657 and state the production cost and expected gross profit on this job;
c. i. comment on the suggestion that departmental overhead absorp-tion rates would result in more accurate job costs; and
   ii. compute such rates, briefly explaining your reason for each rate;
d. using the rates calculated in (c) (ii) above, show the overhead, by department and in total, that would apply to job No. 657;
e. show the over/under absorption, by department and in total, for the period using:

   i. the current rate in your answer to (a) above, and
   ii. your suggested rates in your answer to (c) (ii) above.

(CIMA, Cost Accounting 1)

A3.17 One of the building contracts currently engaged in by a construction company commenced 15 months ago and remains unfinished. The following information relating to work on the contract has been prepared for the year just ended.

	£000
Contract price	2,100
Value of work certified at end of year	1,840
Cost of work not yet certified	35
Costs incurred:	
Opening balances	
Cost of work completed	250
Materials on site (physical stock)	10
During the year	
Materials delivered to site	512
Wages	487
Hire of plant	96
Other expenses	74
Closing balance	
Materials on site (physical stock)	18

As soon as materials are delivered to the site, they are charged to the contract account. A record is also kept of materials as they are actually used on the contract. Periodically a stock check is made and any discrepancy between book stock and physical stock is transferred to a general contract materials discrepancy account. This is absorbed back into each contract, currently at a rate of 0.4% of materials booked. The stock check at the end of the year revealed a stock shortage of £4,000.

In addition to the direct charges listed above, general overheads of the company are charged to contracts at 5% of the value of work certified. General overheads of £13,000 had been absorbed into the cost of work completed at the beginning of the year.

It has been estimated that further costs to complete the contract will be £215,000. This estimate includes the cost of materials on site at the end of the year just finished, and also a provision for rectification.

Required:

a. Explain briefly the distinguishing features of contract costing.
b. Determine the profitability of the above contract, and recommend how much profit (to the nearest £000) should be taken for the year just ended. (Provide a detailed schedule of costs.)
c. State how your recommendation in b. would be affected if the contract price was £3,500,000 (rather than £2,100,000) and if no estimate has been made of costs to completion.

(ACCA Costing)

A3.18 Acme Electronics Ltd makes specialist electronic equipment to order. There are three main departments: Preparation, Etching and Assembly. Preparation and Etching are departments which use a considerable amount of machinery, while Assembly is mainly a manual operation using simple hand tools.

For Period 7, the following budgets have been prepared:

Department	Overheads £	Activity
Preparation	165,000	3,000 machine hours
Etching	98,000	1,400 machine hours
Assembly	48,600	1,800 labour hours

During the period, an enquiry is received for 200 Control Units for which the following estimates have been made:

Total direct materials £26,500

Preparation	260 machine hours
	90 labour hours at £8 per hour
Etching	84 machine hours
	130 labour hours at £7 per hour
Assembly	180 labour hours at £6 per hour

The company adds on 20% to the factory cost to cover administration overheads.

Required:

a. Calculate the price per Control Unit which should be quoted if the company wishes to achieve 30% profit on sales.

b. At the end of Period 7 the following actual results were recorded for the Etching Department:

Actual overheads	Actual machine hours
£106,275	1,473

Determine the under/over absorption of overheads in the Etching Department.

c. Explain briefly the effect of your answer in b. on the results for the period.

(CIMA Cost Accounting and Quantitative Methods)

A3.19 The Ludford Hotel and Conference Centre is used for conference bookings and private guest bookings. Conference bookings use some bedrooms each week, the balance being available for private guest bookings.

Data have been collected relating to private guest bookings (ie non-conference bookings) which are summarised below for a 10-week period.

Week	Double rooms available for private guest bookings	Number of guests	Average stay (in nights)
1	55	198	2.1
2	60	170	2.6
3	72	462	1.4
4	80	381	3.2
5	44	83	5.6
6	62	164	3.4
7	80	348	2.6
8	54	205	1.7
9	80	442	1.8
10	24	84	3.2

Some of the costs for private guest bookings vary with the number of guests, regardless of the length of their stay, while others vary with the number of rooms available in any week.

Variable cost per guest	£17.50
Variable cost per week per room available	£56.00

The general fixed cost for private guest bookings per week is £8,100. The hotel charges £30 per person per night for accommodation for private guest bookings.

Required:

a. Calculate the total cost per guest night for private guest bookings over the 10-week period.
b. Calculate the occupancy percentage over the 10 weeks for the private guest bookings.
c. Calculate the contribution and profit for private guest bookings for the 10-week period.

(CIMA Cost Accounting and Quantitative Methods)

A3.20 Industrial Solvents Ltd mixes together three chemicals – A, B and C – in the ratio 3:2:1, to produce Allklean, a specialised anti-static fluid. The chemicals cost £8, £6 and £3.90 per litre respectively.

In a period, 12,000 litres in total were input to the mixing process. The normal process loss is 5% of input, and in the period there was an abnormal loss of 100 litres while the completed production was 9,500 litres.

There was no opening work-in-progress (WIP) and the closing WIP was 100% complete for materials and 40% complete for labour and overheads.

Labour and overheads were £41,280 in total for the period. Materials lost in production are scrapped.

Required:

a. Calculate the volume of closing WIP.
b. Prepare the mixing process account for the period, showing clearly volumes and values.
c. Briefly explain what changes would be necessary in your account if an abnormal gain were achieved in a period.

(CIMA Cost Accounting and Quantitative Methods)

A3.21 Corcoran Ltd operates several manufacturing processes. In process G, joint products (P1 and P2) are created in the ratio 5:3 by volume from the raw materials input. In this process a normal loss of 5% of the raw material input is expected, Losses have a realisable value of £5 per litre. The company holds no work in progress. The joint costs are apportioned to the joint products using the physical measure basis.
The following information relates to process G for last month:

Raw materials input	60,000 litres (at a cost of £381,000)
Abnormal gain	1,000 litres
Other costs incurred:	
Direct labour	£180,000
Direct expenses	£54,000
Production overheads 110% of direct labour cost.	

Required:

(a) Prepare the process G account for last month in which both the output volumes and values for each of the joint products are shown separately.

The company can sell product P1 for £20 per litre at the end of process G. It is considering a proposal to further process product P1 in process H in order to create product PP1. Process H has sufficient spare capacity to do this work. The further processing in process H would cost £4 per litre input from process G. In process H there would be a normal loss in volume of 10% of the input to that process. This loss has no realisable value. Product PP1 could then be sold for £26 per litre.

(b) Determine, based on financial considerations only, whether product P1 should be further processed to create product PP1.

(c) In the context of process G in Corcoran Ltd, explain the difference between 'direct expenses' and 'production overheads'

ACCA Financial Information for Management

EXAMINATION QUESTIONS WITHOUT ANSWERS

B3.1 Prepare the factory cost of Job No. 589 using the data below, where appropriate.

Justify the figures you calculate.

Job No. 589.

Direct Material issues £235.

Note:

The issues have been priced using the Average Price System as is normal in the firm but it has been brought to your notice that the replacement cost is £265.

Labour Costs

Machining	30 hours at £4 per hour basic and 4 hours at time and a half
Assembly	14 hours at £2 per hour
Finishing	8 hours at £2.5 per hour

Extract from the Overhead Analysis

	Department		
	Machining **£**	**Assembly** **£**	**Finishing** **£**
Actual overheads last year	125,296	83,781	37,530
Budgeted overheads this year	135,000	85,000	42,500
Actual labour hours last year	4,216	4,481	1,853
Budgeted labour hour this year	4,100	4,500	1,950
Machine hours last year	6,560	202	185
Budgeted machine hours this year	6,600	180	210

B3.2   The following details have been extracted from the records for a building contract which Dunbar & Company are carrying out for the Hamcaster Local Authority.

As at 31st December year 1

Cost of all work for year	£86,292
Cost of work not certified	£4,200
Value of work certified	£120,000

The client keeps a 10% retention. You are required to calculate the profit for the year using the traditional method.

Having calculated the traditional profit you are required to calculate the profit using SSAP 9 recommendations.

The following information is available in addition to that already supplied.

	£
Contract value	600,000
Estimated costs to completion	415,000
Rectification costs expected after completion	105,000

B3.3   a. The following data relates to expenditure on the estate management (building services, grounds and gardens) of two colleges.

	College Alpha	College Beta
Number of students	4,000	10,000
Total area in cubic metres	877,000	2,800,000

	College Alpha		College Beta	
	Own workforce	Contractors	Own workforce	Contractors
Cost Element	£	£	£	£
Category A (work of a periodic nature)				
1. Painting	20,000	–	–	12,000
2. Maintenance	2,000	–	4,000	14,000
Category B (irregular work)				
1. Painting	1,500	–	10,800	–
2. Maintenance	7,000	47,000	14,500	13,000
Category C (grounds and gardens)				
3. General	18,000	3,000	35,000	–
Category D (unallocated)				
4. General	10,600	–	70,000	–

Required:

  i. Tabulate the above information showing the expenditure per 1,000 cubic metres.

     Calculations should be in £s to two decimal places.

  ii. Comment briefly on your findings.

b. Contractors PLC has been engaged since 1st January Year 5 on the construction of an office for an electronics firm. The total contract price is £15m and the office block is expected to take 10 years to complete. At 31st December Year 5 site on plant was valued at £125,000 and unused materials on site were valued at £258,000. Site wages of £17,000 and direct expenses of £23,000 had been accrued. The long term contract work in progress value of the project was £653,000.

The following details apply to the contract for Year 6:

	Costs Incurred £	Cash Paid £
Site wages	150,000	153,000
Salaries	85,000	85,000
Sub-contracted work	63,000	63,000
Direct expenses	44,000	40,000

Contractors PLC absorbs production overheads into contracts on a predetermined percentage based on wages incurred. The relevant budgeted figures for Year 6 were as follows:

	£
Production overheads	990,000
Wages	2,750,000

At 31st December Year 6 site plant was valued at £97,000 and unused materials amounted to £39,000.

Contractors PLC do not consider it appropriate to account for any attributable profit until a contract is at least half-way through its total life.

Required
Prepare a contract account for the office block project for Year 6.
(AAT Cost Accounting & Budgeting)

B3.4 A change in government policy in the United Kingdom has meant that, for the first time in their history, schools are to be individually responsible for their own budgets and the use of financial resources.

Knowing that you are studying for CIMA, a family friend who is a Headmaster of a secondary school which has 1,200 boys and girls aged from 11 to 16 years has sought your advice about the financial information he ought to have to help him manage his school.

You are required, in the format of a report, to advise the Headteacher, bearing in mind the following points:

• The principles of cost accounting and financial control.
• 80% to 85% of all costs are likely to be the salaries and wages of teachers, support staff and cleaners.
• Comparisons of cost of activities, it is hoped, will be made in the future against other similar schools.
• Personal computing facilities will be available.

Note:
This question does not require special knowledge of UK schools but relates to any separately managed school which has budget responsibility.
(CIMA Cost Accounting)

B3.5   a. The standard processing loss in refining certain basic materials into an industrial cleaning compound is 15%, this scrap being sold for 50p per kg. At the beginning of Period 6, 8,000 kg of basic material was put into a process, the output of which was 7,000 kg of cleaning compound. The basic material cost 80p per kg, wages of process operators amounted to £1,200 and overhead applied to the process was £480.

      Prepare the necessary accounts to show the results of the process.

  b. The production of a product known as a Tojo requires the treatment of input units through three distinct processes at each of which refining material is added and labour and overhead costs are incurred. Work in progress at the beginning of Period 9 consists of 8,000 input units which has passed through the first process, the cost to that point being £96,000. During Period 9, refining material which cost £31,594 was put into the process and labour costs amounted to £23,940. Process Overhead is applied at the rate of 40% of process labour. 7,200 units were completed during the Period and transferred to Process 3. Of the remainder, the firm's Chief Chemist estimated that in respect of refining material, labour and overhead, half were 75% complete at the end of Period 9, and the other half 40% complete. You are required to write up Process 2 Account Period 9 showing clearly the cost to be transferred to process 3, and the value of the work in progress at the end of the period.

(ACCA Costing)

B3.6   PQR Limited produces two joint products – P and Q – together with by-product R, from a single main process (process 1). Product P is sold at the point of separation for £5 per kg whereas product Q is sold for £7 per kg after a further processing into product Q2. By-product R is sold without further processing for £1.75 per kg.

    Process 1 is closely monitored by a team of chemists who planned the output per 1,000 kg of input material to be as follows:

Product P	500kg
Product Q	350kg
Product R	100kg
Toxic Waste	50kg

The toxic waste is disposed of at a cost of £1.50 per kg, at the end of processing.

    Process 2, which is used for further processing of product Q into product Q2, has the following cost structure:

Fixed costs	£6,000 per week
Variable costs	£1.50 per kg processed

The following actual data relate to the first week of accounting period 10:

Process 1

Opening work in process	Nil
Materials input 10,000 kg costing	£15,000
Direct Labour	£10,000
Variable overhead	£4,000
Fixed overhead	£6,000

Outputs

Product P	4,800kg
Product Q	3,600kg
Product R	1,000kg
Toxic waste	600kg
Closing work-in-process	Nil

Process 2

Opening work-in-process	Nil
Input of product Q	3,600kg
Output of product Q2	3,300kg
Closing work-in-process	300kg, 50% converted.

Conversion costs were incurred in accordance with the planned cost structure.

Requirements:

a. Prepare the main process account for the first week of period 10 using the final sales value method to attribute pre-separation costs to joint products.
b. Prepare the toxic waste accounts and Process 2 Account for the first week of period 10.
c. Comment on the method used by PQR Limited to attribute pre-separation costs to its joint products.
d. Advise the management of PQR Ltd whether or not, on purely financial grounds, it should continue to process product Q into product Q2.

   i. if product Q could be sold at the point of separation for £4.30 per kg and
   ii. if 60% of the weekly fixed costs of process 2 were avoided by not processing product Q further.

(CIMA Operational Cost Accounting)

B3.7 A company operates several production processes involving the mixing of ingredients to produce bulk animal feedstuffs. One such product is mixed in two separate process operations. The information below is of the costs incurred in, and output from, Process 2 during the period just completed.

Costs incurred:	£
Transfers from Process 1	187,704
Raw materials costs	47,972
Conversion costs	63,176
Opening work in process	3,009

Production:	Units
Opening work in process	1,200
(100% complete, apart from Process 2 conversion costs which were 50% complete)	
Transfers from Process 1	112,000
Completed output	105,400
Closing work in process	1,600
(100% complete, apart from Process 2 conversion costs which were 75% complete)	

Normal wastage of materials (including product transferred from Process 1), which occurs in the early stages of Process 2 (after all materials have been added), is expected to be 5% of input. Process 2 conversion costs are all apportioned to units of good output. Wastage materials have no saleable value.

Required:

a. Prepare the Process 2 account for the period, using FIFO principles.
b. Explain how, and why, your calculations would have been different if wastage occurred at the end of the process.

(ACCA Cost & Management Accounting)

B3.8   Process costing is used by a company which has just commenced business. It makes a component in the following way. A piece of metal is stamped and formed and to this is attached one unit of material A, which is purchased. At this stage, machining and cleaning takes place. Two units of purchased material B are then attached before the whole component is spray-painted.

The consulting engineer has suggested that of the total direct labour time involved in the production process, 25% would be spent on the first operation of stamping and forming, 25% would be for the first assembly of attaching one unit of material A, $12\frac{1}{2}$ % for the machining and cleaning, 25% for the second assembly of attaching two units of material B and $12\frac{1}{2}$ % for spray-painting.

Production overhead is assumed to follow the same pattern as the labour percentage cost. All production workers are paid at the same wage rate. The following data relate to financial period 1:

		Cost £
Metal purchased	50,000 kgs	50,000
Purchases of material A	40,000 units	32,000
Purchase of material B	75,000 units	30,000
Paint used		2,144
Direct wages incurred		22,268
Production overhead incurred		10,701

Stocks at the end of period 1:

Metal	2,900 kgs
Material A	2,500 units
Material B	3,000 units
Components in process:	
Ready for the second assembly	1,500
Assembled but not painted	2,500
Completed components in finished goods	3,750

During the period 33,500 completed components were transferred to finished goods stock.

You are required:

a. to prepare a schedule which shows clearly the percentage of labour cost attributable to the component at each of the five stages of the production process;

    b. to produce a cost of production statement for period 1, showing:

        i. total production cost
       ii. equivalent production units
      iii. cost of one component (to three decimal places)
      iv. cost of completed units
       v. value of work in process at the end of period 1.

Note:

For each of (i), (ii) and (iii), show the appropriate figures for

  Metal
  Material A
  Material B
  Paint
  Direct Labour
  Production overhead

(CIMA Cost Accounting)

B3.9 a. Explain briefly the distinction between joint products and by-products.
    b. Discuss briefly the problems involved in calculating the cost of manufacture of joint products with particular reference to the apportionment of pre-separation point costs. A common method of apportioning these pre-separation point costs is by physical measurement; outline two other methods.
    c. In a process line of the JP Manufacturing Company Limited, three joint products are produced. For the month of October the following data were available:

Product	X	Y	Z
Sales price per kilogram	£5	£10	£20
Post-separation point costs	£10,000	£5,000	£15,000
Output in kilograms	2,500	1,000	1,500

Pre-separation point costs amounted to £20,000.

    The joint products are manufactured in one common process, after which they are separated and may undergo further individual processing. The pre-separation point costs are apportioned to joint products, according to weight.

You are required:

a to prepare a statement showing the estimated profit or loss for each product and in total;

b as an alternative to the costing system used in (a) above, to present a statement which will determine the maximum profit from the production of these joint products. The sales value of each product at separation point is as follows:

    X = £3   Y = £4   Z = £6

(CIMA, Cost Accounting 2)

B3.10 a. A chemical Exalete, passes through processes A and B before completion. In process B, a by-product Exaltent is produced which, after further processing in process C, is sold at a profit of 16²/₃% of selling price.

You are required, from the data given for the month of April, to prepare accounts for:

  i. processes A, B and C;
  ii. abnormal loss;
  iii. abnormal gain.

	Process		
	A	**B**	**C**
Output in units	4,200	3,800	100
Normal loss in process:			
% of input	20	5	–
	£	£	£
Scrap value of any loss in process, per unit Costs	1.5	5	–
Direct materials introduced (5,000 units)	30,000	–	–
Direct materials added	10,000	3,100	100
Direct wages incurred at £3 per hour	12,000	14,700	300
Direct expenses	7,500	1,170	–

Production overhead for the month, £72,000, is absorbed by a labour hour rate.

b. Define and explain briefly the accounting treatment of:

  i. by-products;
  ii. joint products.

(CIMA, Cost Accounting 2)

17

Planning, control and decision-making

1. OBJECTIVES

After studying this chapter you will

- **Be able to describe Planning**

- **Know the outline of long term or Corporate Planning**

- **Have been introduced to short term tactical planning and budgeting**

- **Understand the framework of control and feedback**

- **Know the principles of feed forward and target costing**

- **Be able to describe decision-making and the types of decisions**

- **Understand the role of information in decision-making.**

2. WIDER VIEW OF COST ACCOUNTING

The student who has conscientiously studied the book so far will have a good knowledge of the language and procedures of basic cost accounting. The material covered shows how data are gathered, classified, analysed and used for cost ascertainment. The rest of the book is concerned with the wider use of cost accounting information for planning, control and decision-making purposes.

It must be emphasised, however, that the existence of a sound, well organised basic cost accounting system is fundamental to whatever use is made of the information, whether for routine cost ascertainment purposes or for a one-off decision. Before considering the various ways in which cost accounting information can be of value to management, it is useful to examine some general considerations relating to planning, control and decision-making.

3. PLANNING

Planning is a primary task of management. It is concerned with the future and relies upon information from many sources, both external and internal to the organisation, for it to be successful. Information for planning includes cost and financial data and also information relating to personnel, markets, competitors, production capacities and constraints, material supplies and so on.

Planning can be defined as:

The establishment of objectives, and the formulation, evaluation and selection of the policies, strategies, tactics and action required to achieve these objectives. Planning comprises long term/strategic planning and short term operational planning. The latter usually refers to a period of one year.

Terminology

Thus it will be seen that the overall planning process covers both the long and short term and these two aspects are developed below.

4. LONG TERM STRATEGIC PLANNING

This can be defined as:

The formulation, evaluation and selection of strategies for the purpose of preparing a long-term plan of action to attain objectives. Also known as corporate planning and long range planning.

Terminology

The time span covered by a long term plan depends on the organisation, the industry in which it operates and the particular environment involved. Typically the periods involved are 3, 5, 7 or 10 years although longer periods are commonly encountered. An example is the long term plan relating to the Water Supply Industry which covers a 20-year period.

The process of long term or corporate planning is a detailed, lengthy process which in many organisations is considered an indispensable part of the management process. Figure 17.1 provides an overview of the process and shows the link with short term tactical planning.

5. CORPORATE PLANNING

Figure 17.1 shows a considerable amount of detail about CP which, in essence, is concerned with several key questions;

- What is the environment in which the organisation will have to operate in the future?
- What is the existing state of the organisation and the environment in which it operates?
- Where does the organisation want to go?
- What is the best way to get there?

The strategic or corporate plan which is developed provides the framework within which short term planning or budgeting takes place. (Note: The stages

FIGURE 17.1 Corporate planning

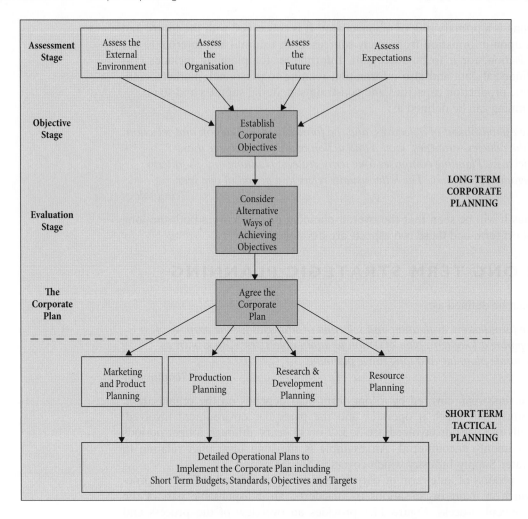

and processes in CP are developed in greater detail in *Management Accounting*, T. Lucey, Cengage Learning.)

6. SHORT TERM TACTICAL PLANNING/BUDGETING

The long term Corporate Plan serves as the longer term framework for the organisation as a whole but for operational purposes it is necessary to convert the Corporate Plan into a series of short term (usually 1 year) plans relating to sections, functions and departments. Short term tactical planning can be defined as;

Planning the utilisation of resources to achieve specific objectives in the most effective and efficient way.

Terminology

Those parts of a short-term plan to which monetary values can be attached become *budgets*.

Budget Quantitative expression of a plan for a defined period of time. It may include planned sales volume and revenues, resource quantities, costs and expenses, assets, liabilities and cash flows.

Terminology

The annual processes of short term planning and budgeting should be seen as stages in the progressive fulfilment of the Corporate Plan. The short term planning and budgeting processes steer the organisation towards the long term objectives defined in the Corporate Plan. It should be apparent that to gain the maximum advantage from short term planning and budgeting it is essential that some form of long term plan exists. Short term planning and budgeting are covered in detail in Chapter 22.

7. CONTROL

The purpose of control is to help to ensure that operations and performance conform to the plans. There are two broad elements of the control process. First, the comparison of actual and planned performance on a regular and continuing basis and secondly, the longer term process of reviewing the plan itself to see whether it needs modification in the light of the comparisons made or because of changes in the assumptions on which the plan was based, for example, new government regulations, material shortages, new competition.

It follows therefore that effective control is not possible without planning and planning without a complementary control system is pointless. In organisational systems, control is exercised by the use of information frequently, but not always, of a financial nature.

8. FEEDBACK AND CONTROL

Control in organisational systems is exercised by information feedback loops which gather information from the output side of a department, function or process which is used to govern future performance by adjusting the input side of the system.

The elements in the basic control cycle are:

a. A standard specifying the expected performance. This can be in the form of a budget, a procedure, a stock level, an output rate, a standard cost or some other target.

b. A measurement of actual performance. This should be made in an accurate, speedy, unbiased manner and using relevant units of measures. For example, time taken, £s spent, units produced, efficiency ratings and so on.

c. Comparison of a. and b. Frequently the comparison is accompanied by an analysis which attempts to isolate the reasons for any variations. A well known example of this is the accounting process of variance analysis, described in Chapters 24 to 26.

d. Feedback of deviations or variations to a control unit. In an organisational context the 'control unit' would be a manager.

e. Actions by the manager to alter performance in accordance with the plan, target or standard.

FIGURE 17.2   Control and feedback cycles

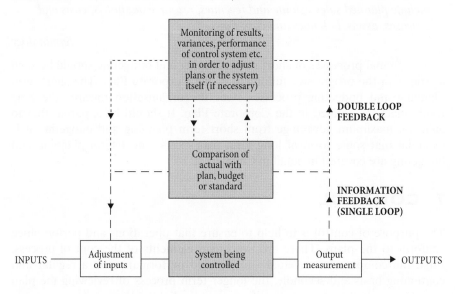

The type of feedback mentioned is feedback of relatively small variations between actual and plan so that corrective action can be taken to bring operations in line with the plan. The implication of this is that existing performance standards and plans are essentially correct and appropriate. This type of feedback, also known as single loop feedback, is the normal feedback associated with budgetary control and standard costing systems.

Students should be aware that a higher order of feedback exists, known as double loop feedback, which is designed to ensure that the plans, budgets and standards – and indeed the organisational structures and control systems themselves, are revised to meet changes in conditions.

Figure 17.2 provides an overview of feedback and control cycles.

9. FEEDFORWARD

The feedback cycle described above, ie input-process-output-monitor and compare-adjust if necessary, is relatively mechanistic but is widely used, especially at tactical levels. However, there are occasions where such a self regulatory feedback system is unable to control a process adequately and *feedforward* is used.

Feedforward is where there is monitoring at an early stage of a system or process which may indicate that an adjustment should be made to some later stage , prior to the final output. Feedforward control loops react to immediate or forthcoming dangers by making adjustments to the system in advance so as to cope with the problem in good time. In any organisation it is unlikely that pure feedforward or pure feedback control would operate in isolation. Feedback control on its own may be too slow and feedforward control too risky, so that some balance between the two is desirable.

Feedback monitors the past. Feedforward looks ahead.

Figure 17.3 shows an outline of the two types of control.

The system of *Target Costing* is an example of feedforward control.

FIGURE 17.3

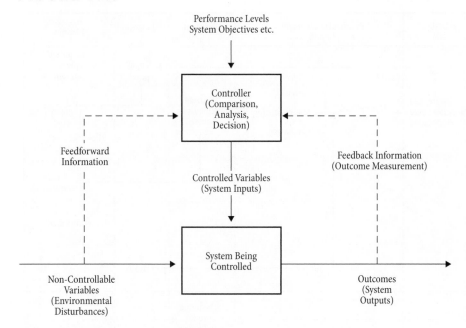

10. TARGET COSTING

A target cost is defined thus:

A product cost estimate derived by subtracting a desired profit margin from a competitive market price.

Terminology

Target costing is widely used in Japan. It is a market driven approach where market research establishes the performance requirements and target selling price required to gain the desired market share for a proposed product. The required profit margin is subtracted from the target selling price to arrive at the target cost for the product. This cost which, in the long run, must be met. Thus accounting practice is driven by the requirements of the market place.

Using the target cost approach, product designers, purchasing and manufacturing specialists work together to determine the product and process features which will enable the long-run target cost to be achieved.

Figure 17.4 outlines the whole process.

The importance of the target costing approach is that it focuses attention on the product design stage, ie prior to release to manufacturing.

Most costs are committed or locked in early in the life cycle of the product. Once the product is released to manufacturing it becomes much harder to achieve significant cost savings although some savings are possible, for example by the learning curve effect where labour costs per unit decrease as production values mount. Target costing is a practical example of *feedforward control*.

Target costing is widely used in Japan. Users include Komatsu, Olympus, Sony, Topcon and Isuzu. It is increasingly being recognised in the USA and Europe.

FIGURE 17.4

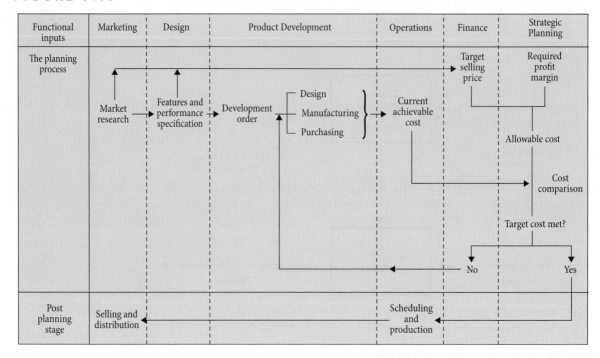

11. THE DECISION PROCESS

Decision-making is an all pervasive managerial task and because many decisions depend on financial factors it is important that the Cost Accountant is totally familiar with the processes involved and the sort of information that should be supplied to decision-makers. The stages in the overall decision process are as follows:

a. *Definition of objectives*

The decision-maker must be aware of the organisation's objectives which should, wherever possible, be quantified. If the organisation's objectives are clearly specified and are communicated widely there is less likelihood of sub-optimal decision-making taking place. This is where local or departmental objectives are pursued to the detriment of overall organisational objectives.

b. *Consideration of alternatives*

There are always various ways of achieving objectives and ideally an exhaustive list should be prepared covering all possible alternatives. However, this is a theoretical ideal which is difficult to achieve in practice.

c. *Evaluation of alternatives*

This is the process of making quantitative and financial comparisons between the various alternatives so that the ultimate decision-maker is provided with a relevant and correctly specified financial basis for the final decision. Clearly this is the stage in the decision process where the expertise of the Cost Accountant is most required so that relevant information can be supplied. What is relevant information for long and short run decision-making is dealt with later in the book.

d. *Selection of the course of action*

This is the stage where the actual choice is made by the decision-maker. Decision-making involves personal, social, psychological and political factors as well as the more objective financial and quantitative considerations. An important factor in virtually all practical decisions is the risk and uncertainty involved. This means that it is important that the information supplied by the accountant shows the effects of risk and uncertainty and the range of likely outcomes. Where uncertainty exists – which it does in virtually every situation – it can be positively misleading to provide information which shows only a single value of profit or contribution with no indication of the variabilities which may occur. Because this book is about cost accounting it naturally concentrates on financial matters. However it must be emphasised that many other factors may be of critical importance in a decision. Examples include: markets, the environment, legal factors, personal and psychological characteristics, production or service quality, reliability and so on. Decision-making is not just a consideration of financial factors.

12. LEVELS OF DECISION-MAKING

Management is involved with decision-making at all levels;

- at the *strategic level* – for example, the Board of Directors deciding to diversify the company's products or to acquire a subsidiary;
- at the *tactical level* – for example, the Sales Manager deciding upon an advertising campaign in a given region or the Production Controller deciding whether to sub-contract part of an order;
- at the *operational level* – for example, the credit Supervisor deciding to suspend deliveries to a bad payer or a work's foreman deciding which men will deal with a particular job.

Decision-making always involves a choice between alternatives. Decision-makers need information on which to base their judgement; without information, decisions are no more than inspired guesswork.

13. TYPES OF DECISIONS

Decisions range from those at the top level involving many external factors where a high degree of judgement is required to more routine internal decisions with limited scope. H.A. Simon has classified decisions into programmed and non-programmed categories.

a. Programmed decisions. These are relatively structured decisions within a clearly defined area. The decision rules are known and frequently these types of decisions can be incorporated into computer based management information systems. A typical example is a reorder decision based on usage and reorder levels in an inventory control system.

b. Non-programmed decisions. These are decisions for which decision rules and procedures cannot be devised. Generally they are non-repetitive decisions, involving many external and internal factors, frequently with high levels of risk, and requiring information from a variety of sources.

14. INFORMATION FOR DECISION-MAKING

It is important to understand that all decision-making relates to the future. It follows therefore that the decision-maker requires information regarding such things as future costs and revenues, future material supplies and prices, the likely state of the market in the future and so on. Information for decision-making must therefore be orientated towards the future and involves forecasting, estimating and extrapolation. While it is self-evident that we cannot foretell the future, it is found that past experience and records of performances, costs, etc frequently provide a sound basis for forecasting particular aspects of future operations.

However, this is only correct if future conditions are expected to be broadly similar to those in the past. If not, then an organisation's experience and records are likely to be of substantially diminished value. Information has no value in itself; its value derives from improvements in the decisions which are taken based upon the information. To enhance the value of information it must be capable of being used effectively and surveys have shown that information which has the following characteristics is more likely to be used.

- *Relevance*
  ie, appropriate to the manager's sphere of activity and to the decision in hand.
- *Timeliness*
  ie, produced and available to the manager in time for him to use. Frequently an approximate answer speedily prepared will be the most valuable.
- *Accuracy*
  ie, sufficiently accurate for it to be relied upon by the manager and sufficiently accurate for the intended purpose.
- *Understandable*
  ie, in a form readily usable by the manager. The avoidance of unexplained technical terms, the use of summaries, the use of graphical and other display methods are all ways to make information more understandable.

The types of decisions, and their information requirements, vary from level to level in the organisation. Figure 17.5 shows a summary of the main characteristics of decisions and information for the three management levels.

Figure 17.6 gives examples of decision-making at the three levels with typical information requirements.

15. SUMMARY

a. Planning is concerned with the future and consists of five stages: Setting objectives, Assessing the environment, Reviewing resources, Establishing feasible goals, and Implementation.

FIGURE 17.5 Levels of decision-making

Management Level	Decision Characteristics	Information Characteristics
Strategic	Long time horizons, large scale resources, much creativity and judgement, usually unstructured, problems difficult to define, infrequent, much uncertainty	Largely external, informal sources important, forward looking, qualitative information unimportant, instant access not vital, wide ranging, incomplete
Tactical	↕	↕
Operational	Repetitive, short timescale, small scale resources, usually structured, clear objective and decision rules, little or no discretion	Largely external, mainly historical, detailed, often quantitative, high precision, instant availability often critical, narrow in scope, comprehensive

FIGURE 17.6 Decision and information examples

Management Level	Decision Examples	Information Requirements
Strategic	Mergers and acquisitions, new product planning, capital investments, financial structuring	Market and economic forecasts, political and social trends, legislative, environmental and technological constraints and opportunities
Tactical	Pricing, capacity planning, budget preparation, purchasing contracts	Cost and sales analyses, performance measures, summaries of operations/production, budget/actual comparisons etc
Operational	Production, scheduling, maintenance, re-ordering, credit approval	Sales orders, production requirements, performance measures, customer credit status, deliveries, despatches etc

b. Effective control must be preceded by planning, and planning without complementary control is pointless.

c. Control is exercised by feedback control loops whereby information regarding the output or performance is compared to the plan or standard and adjustments made (if necessary) to the inputs.

d. The decision process includes: the definition of objectives, consideration of alternatives, evaluation of alternatives and the selection of the course of action.

e. Management are involved with decision-making at all levels, strategic, tactical and operational.

f. Decisions can be classified into programmed and non-programmed.

g. Future orientated information is necessary for decision-making.

h. Information should be relevant, timely, accurate, and in an understandable form.

16. POINT TO NOTE

Cost and financial information is an important part of the total information requirements for planning, control and decision-making, but it is not the only element. Sales, production, personnel and other information is frequently of supreme importance.

Student self-testing

Exercises (answers below)

1. The cost accounting system of the firms records the costs incurred in the past for products, departments, operations and processes. Accordingly the information contained within the cost accounting system is of no value for decision-making purposes.

    Discuss this statement.

2. Why should the problems of control be considered at the planning stage?

3. Give three examples of decision-making at each of the main management levels ie, strategic, tactical, and operational.

Solutions to exercises

1. It is true that the cost accounting system of the firm records the costs incurred in the past and it is also true, as can be inferred from the statement, that decision-making is concerned with the future. This would seem to mean that the statement is correct but this is not a realistic conclusion.

    The records and information obtained from the cost accounting system are frequently of great value in decision-making because they provide an excellent basis for judging future behaviour.

    The information obtained from the cost accounting system should not be used directly in decision-making but should be examined critically so as to serve for a guide to the future behaviour of costs, revenues, efficiencies, outputs and so on.

    It is important to realise that it is future costs and revenues which are relevant for decision-making.

2. Control is the process of ensuring that operations and performance conform, as far as practicable to the plan. If the plan has been properly developed in accordance with the objectives of the organisation then it is clearly of prime importance that a monitoring process is instituted so that actual

performance is compared with plan and, if performance is different from that planned, corrections can be made. The control mechanism should be considered and designed at the planning stage otherwise the advantages of having a planned pattern of activities is unlikely to be realised.

3. Examples of decision-making:

- at the *Strategic Level*
  major investment decisions
  acquisitions or divestments
  senior management appointments
  decisions on organisation structures
  and so on.

- at the *Tactical Level*
  pricing decisions
  middle and junior level appointments
  routine replacement decisions
  purchasing (materials, parts, etc) decisions
  production planning and scheduling
  and so on.

- at the *Operational Level*
  production and clerical appointments
  shop floor work organisation
  staff allocation
  transport decisions
  and so on.

18

Cost behaviour

1. OBJECTIVES

After studying this chapter you will

- **Know why the study of cost behaviour is important**

- **Be able to define a variable cost in linear and non-linear forms**

- **Understand the various categories of fixed costs**

- **Know the alternative cost classifications used in ABC**

- **Understand the various ways of finding cost characteristics, high/low, scatter-graphs, least squares**

- **Know how inflation affects costs**

- **Understand the problems of predicting costs.**

2. REASONS FOR THE STUDY OF COST BEHAVIOUR

If costs always remained unchanged and completely under control and if an organisation's activities and operations remained the same from period to period, then there would be little point in studying cost behaviour. Life is not as simple as that and an understanding of cost behaviour is vital for management and for accountants who advise them.

A knowledge of cost behaviour is necessary across the whole range of cost and management accounting activities, particularly in the areas of cost control, planning and decision making. Typical problems which need detailed analysis of cost behaviour before they can be solved are the following:

- 'What are the appropriate overhead costs if the throughput of the Assembly Department is increased by 15%?'
- 'Is it worthwhile to introduce second shift working to cope with a special export order?'
- 'Should we accept a large contract at less than normal selling prices if it enables us to work at full capacity?'
- 'What would be the cost effects of treating more patients as day attenders rather than as conventional in-patients?'
- 'Will it be cheaper for a Local Authority to deal with Housing Maintenance by its own Direct Service Organisation or by private sub-contractors?'

3. COST BEHAVIOUR AND THE VOLUME OF ACTIVITY

While other factors influence costs, a major influence is the level or volume of activity, and many of the reasons for studying cost behaviour relate to changes or proposed changes in the level of activity. The level of activity is expressed in many varied ways, eg tons produced, hours worked, standard hours produced, passenger/miles, invoices typed, sales, stores issues, etc, etc.

Students should also be aware that many alternative terms are used for the concept of 'level of activity', typical ones being capacity, output, volume, throughput. Activity level changes and the resulting cost changes form the basis of many practical decisions and many examination questions. The behaviour of cost in relation to changes in the level of activity is so important that it forms the basis of the accounting classifications of cost into fixed and variable costs.

4. COST BEHAVIOUR AND TIME

Normally the situations where cost behaviour is analysed for planning and decision-making are 'short run' in nature. This means that the relationship between cost and activity and the classifications of the costs themselves are most appropriate over a relatively short time span only. What is a 'relatively short time span' depends on the particular circumstances, it may be three months, six months, one year; it is unlikely to be as long as five years.

Over longer time periods unpredictable factors are bound to occur, methods will alter, technology will improve, so that predictions of cost behaviour are likely to be increasingly unreliable. In examination questions the time factor (in relation to cost behaviour!) is unlikely to be very significant, but in practice it can be a major problem.

5. PREDICTING COST BEHAVIOUR

Except in completely new circumstances where no previous experience exists, predictions about cost levels and cost behaviour in the future are likely to be based on records of past costs and their associated levels of activity. Because of this, many of the statistical techniques of forecasting and extrapolation may be of value when studying cost behaviour. Care however must be taken when using any form of forecasting technique that past conditions are indeed a guide to the future.

It is the cost behaviour in the future that is being considered and if conditions in the future are likely to be significantly different from the past, then statistical forecasting techniques will be unable to produce valid predictions. Judgement will always play a part in cost prediction, but in many cases relatively simple statistical techniques can be of great assistance. Care must also be taken to base cost predictions on the facts of particular situations and not on arbitrary, general classifications.

An example of this is the almost invariable rule, particularly in examination questions, of assuming that direct labour is a fully variable cost, whereas because of wage agreements, guaranteed daily and weekly rates, the growth of salaried works personnel, the impact of technology, etc direct labour in many organisations increasingly assumes the characteristics of a fixed cost, ie it may, within limits, be relatively unchanged with varying levels of activity.

6. VARIABLE COST DEFINITION

A variable cost can be defined as:

A cost which varies with a measure of activity.

Terminology

To this definition should be added the proviso 'in the short term' because over the longer term changing prices, methods and technology make any form of cost classification subject to change. A common assumption in accounting is that variable costs behave linearly in respect to volume changes. Naturally this is not always the case and such a simplifying assumption should only be made if it accords with the facts of the situation. This is explained in more detail below.

7. VARIABLE COST BEHAVIOUR

Numerous patterns of variable cost behaviour exist but they can be subdivided into two main groups: linear and non-linear (or curvilinear).

8. LINEAR VARIABLE COSTS

This is the simplest pattern and is where the relationship between variable cost and output can be shown as a straight line on a graph as in Figure 18.1.

FIGURE 18.1   Examples of linear variable costs

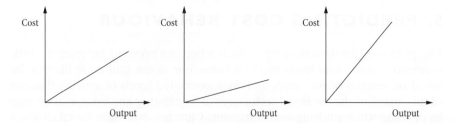

For calculations and analysis it is usually more convenient to express the linear relationship algebraically thus

$$\textbf{Cost} = \textbf{\textit{bx}}$$

where:

x = volume of output in units

b = a constant representing the variable cost per unit.

Example 1

The materials contained in each assembly Z110 are

3 Brackets @ £1.25 each

30 Screws @ £0.02 each

6 Pulleys @ £0.67 each

What is the expected variable cost of materials for producing 40 assemblies?

Solution

	Material **£**	**Cost/Assembly** **£**
	£3 × 1.25	= 3.75
	30 × 0.02	= 0.60
	6 × 0.67	= 4.02
		£8.37
Cost	= bx	
	= £8.37 × 40	
	= £334.80	

9. NON-LINEAR VARIABLE COSTS

In general where the relationship between variable cost and output can be shown as a curved line on a graph, it would be said to be *non-linear*. Many types of curves exist and two typical ones are shown in Figure 18.2.

Convex – where each extra unit of output causes a *less than proportionate* increase in cost

FIGURE 18.2 Examples of non-linear variable costs

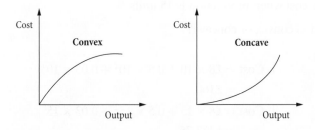

Concave – where each extra unit of output causes a *more than proportionate* increase in cost.

Convex – where each extra unit of output causes a less than proportionate increase in cost

Concave – where each extra unit of output causes a more than proportionate increase in cost.

A simple example of a cost which could result in a non-linear cost function is that of a piecework scheme for individual workers with differential rates. If the rates increased by small amounts at progressively higher output levels the graphing of wages for a number of workers would result in a concave cost function.

If the curves have particular characteristics they may be categorised as known statistical functions. One of the more common types is described below, which is known as parabola, but many other types exist. The method by which a curve is identified is by the statistical technique of curve fitting.

Note:
Other statistical functions which may represent a cost function are: simple exponential or compound interest curve, logarithmic, Gompertz, etc.

10. NON-LINEAR VARIABLE COSTS – THE PARABOLA

Where the slope of the cost function changes uniformly with changes in output (as the curves in Figure 18.2) the curve is known as a Parabola and can be expressed algebraically thus:

$$\text{Cost} = bx + cx^2 + dx^3 + \cdots px^n$$

where: x = volume of output in units

$b, c, d, \ldots p$ = constants representing the variable cost per unit.

Example 2
Analysis of cost and activity records for a project show that the variable cost can be accurately represented by the function:

$$\text{Cost} = £(bx + cx^2 + dx^3)$$

where: $b = 8$ $c = 0.5$ and $d = 0.03$.

Calculate:

i. Variable cost when production is 10 units

ii. Variable cost when production is 15 units

Is the function convex or concave?

Solution

i. $\text{Cost} = £8 \times 10 + 0.5 \times 10^2 + 0.03 \times 10^3$

$= £160$

ii. $\text{Cost} = £8 \times 15 + 0.5 \times 15^2 + 0.03 \times 15^3$

$= £333.75$

It will be seen that the increase in activity from 10 to 15 units results in more than a doubling of variable cost. This shows that there is a more than proportionate increase in the unit cost of extra production so that the function is *concave.*

Note:
It is the value of the constants which determine whether the function is convex or concave.

11. LINEAR APPROXIMATION

It is common practice in accounting, particularly under examination conditions, to make the assumption that variable costs are linear. This is often done even when the cost data are non-linear. This is shown in Figure 18.3.

Features of linear approximation
a. Convenient and greatly simplifies calculations.
b. May be reasonably accurate representation in the short run over a limited range of activity variations.
c. May encourage too ready acceptance of the view that all variable costs are linear. All variable costs do not behave linearly and accurate cost prediction in practice must rely on the analysis of cost and activity data, not upon overall blanket assumptions.

For examination purposes it can generally be assumed that, if a cost is identified as variable, it will be linear unless the context of the question clearly points to some other pattern.

12. RELATIONSHIP OF VARIABLE COST TO OTHER COSTS

Variable cost compared with accounting concept of marginal cost
Because of the assumption of linearity, variable cost equals accounting marginal cost, ie the cost of an extra unit of output is the same as the average variable cost of all output.

FIGURE 18.3

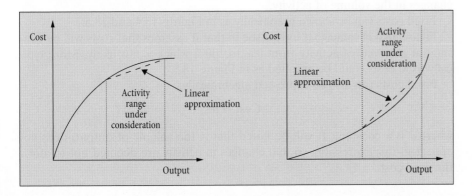

Variable cost compared with economic concept of marginal cost

The economic concept of marginal cost, ie, the cost of an additional unit, is based on non-linear functions so that at certain activity levels marginal cost is falling and at other levels it is rising, whereas the accounting concept assumes a constant variable marginal cost. The above explanation covers a wide range of activity variations, but for limited activity variations, as in a typical short-run decision, the approaches are likely to give very similar results.

13. VARIABLE COST COMPARED WITH DIRECT COSTS

Direct costs are those costs directly identifiable with a product or saleable service, whereas variable costs are determined by their behaviour in relation to changes in activity levels. Thus it will be seen that variable costs and direct costs are determined by two quite distinct principles. Some variable costs, eg material and wages, can often also be identified as direct costs.

14. EXAMPLES OF VARIABLE COSTS

Examples of costs that are frequently variable in behaviour are raw materials, sales commissions, royalties, production wages, carriage and packing costs. Care should be taken not to pigeon hole costs too readily. It is the behaviour of a cost in relation to activity that determines whether or not it is variable, not some general assumption.

15. FIXED COST – DEFINITION

A fixed cost can be defined as:

A cost which is incurred for an accounting period, and which, within certain output or turnover limits tends to be unaffected by fluctuations in the levels of activity (output or turnover).

Terminology

An alternative term for fixed costs is *period* cost.

The key parts of this definition are that fixed costs are time related and, within limits, are unaffected by changes in the level of activity. This does not mean that fixed costs do not change; rent and rates, for example, change quite frequently. The main point is that the change in the cost is not caused by changes in the volume of activity.

Fixed costs can be shown graphically as in Figures 18.4 and 18.5.

Figure 18.4 is somewhat unrealistic in that it assumes that costs will be constant at all levels of activity from 0% to 100% which is not likely. More typically fixed costs could be graphed as in Figure 18.5.

Fixed costs can also be expressed algebraically:

$$\text{Cost} = a$$

where a is a constant. It will be noted that v, the volume of output, does not appear in this expression, so that changes in activity are deemed not to affect the fixed cost.

FIGURE 18.4 Fixed cost

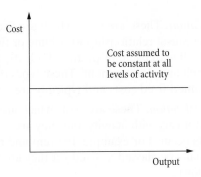

FIGURE 18.5 Fixed cost

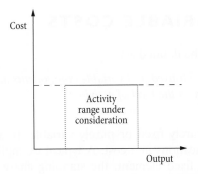

16. CATEGORIES OF FIXED COSTS

It is important not to take too superficial a view of cost classification. The accountant must look at the actual and forecast behaviour of the cost and the purpose for which it is intended so that there is a realistic approach to the classification of costs.

For planning and decision-making purposes the key point is that the classification must be *relevant for the intended purpose*. The concept of consistency of treatment which is a feature of financial accounting and cost ascertainment is not appropriate when applied to information for planning and decision-making. So that the individual characteristics of cost are not overlooked and so dealt with incorrectly it is useful to sub-divide fixed costs into five categories:

i. *The time period classification*. Those types of cost which are not likely to change significantly in the short term, usually a year. In the long term all costs may change or become avoidable.

ii. *The volume classification*. Costs which are fixed for small, but not large changes in output or capacity.

iii. *The joint classification*. Where a cost is incurred jointly with another cost and is only capable of being altered jointly. For example, if an organisation leases a showroom which has a warehouse attached then the fixed cost element applies to both parts of the asset acquired whether or not they are both wanted.

iv. *The policy classification.* These are costs which are fixed by management policy and bear no causal relationship to volume or time. They are usually items which are dealt with by appropriation budgets, eg, expenditure on advertising, research and development. These types of costs are sometimes known as programmed fixed costs and typically are reviewed annually.

v. *The avoidable classification.* These are costs which are fixed in the normal sense, ie they do not vary with activity, but they are avoidable if particular decisions or events occur. For example, the rent and rates for a branch office would normally be classed as fixed yet they are avoidable if the branch was shut down.

It will be apparent that a cost may be classed as fixed for some purposes and not others and the cost accountant must continually appraise the classification of a cost to ensure its appropriateness for the intended purpose.

17. SEMI-VARIABLE COSTS

This type of cost can be defined as;

A cost containing both fixed and variable components and which is thus partly affected by a change in the level of activity.

Terminology

Rarely is a cost purely fixed or purely variable, frequently there are elements of both classifications in a cost. A typical example would be electricity charges containing a fixed element, the standing charge, and a variable element, the cost per unit consumed.

Semi-variable costs can be shown graphically in Figure 18.6.

In each case 'a' represents the fixed element of the cost.

Semi-variable costs can also be expressed algebraically by combining the previous expressions for variable cost (Para. 8) and fixed cost (Para. 15) thus: Linear semi-variable cost:

$$\text{Cost} = a + bx$$

Non-linear semi-variable cost:

$$\text{Cost} = a + bx + cx^2 + dx^3 + \cdots + px^n$$

FIGURE 18.6 Semi-variable cost patterns

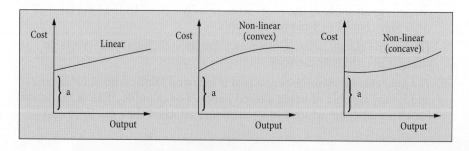

Example 3

Analysis of maintenance department costs shows that there is a fixed element of £500 per month and a variable element related to machine hours amounting to £2.25 per machine hour.

What is the expected cost for a month when the planned activity level is

i. 1,500 machine hours,
ii. 1,800 machine hours?

Solution

i. Total cost $= a + bx$

$$= £500 + 2.25(1,500)$$

$$= \textbf{£3,875}$$

ii. Total cost $= £500 + 2.25(1,800)$

$$= \textbf{£4,550}$$

Alternatively, as only the variable costs will alter between 1,500 and 1,800 hours, the second answer could be calculated as follows:

$$£3,875 + 300(2.25) = \textbf{£4,550}$$

The above example is for a clear-cut linear cost, but, even when the underlying cost pattern is non-linear, it is normal to make a linear approximation which greatly simplifies subsequent calculations.

Note:

Alternative terms for semi-variable costs are: *semi-fixed costs* and *mixed costs*.

18. ALTERNATIVE COST CLASSIFICATIONS

The classifications given above for variable, fixed and semi-variable costs are those conventionally used so must be thoroughly understood. Professor Kaplan has suggested that these are less appropriate for classifying overheads when Activity Based Costing is used. As previously explained he has suggested a three-way classification; short-term variable costs; long-term variable costs and fixed costs. Table 18.1 compares the conventional classification to those suggested by Professor Kaplan.

Kaplan's Classification for use with ABC	Comments
Short-term variable cost	
Defined as varying with production volume Typical example: Power costs	These would also be classified as variable using the conventional classification
Long-term variable cost	
Defined as varying over time, not with production volume, but some other measure of activity. Typical example: Salaries of support staff such as inspectors, engineers	Most of these would be conventionally classified as fixed
Fixed cost	
Defined as not varying, over the given period, with any activity indicator. Typical example: rates, executive salaries.	These would be conventionally classified as fixed

19. ESTABLISHING THE APPROPRIATE COST CHARACTERISTICS

So far in the examples the value of the fixed and variable elements have been provided, but in practice these characteristics have to be established. One way this can be done is by analysis of past cost and activity data. There are a number of techniques available for this purpose, three of which are dealt with below – the High/Low method, the scattergraph and the statistical technique known as the least squares method of linear regression analysis.

20. HIGH/LOW METHOD

This is a simple, crude technique which uses only the highest and lowest activity values contained in a set of data and, graphically or arithmetically, determines the rate of cost change and hence the variable cost. The variable costs so established are then used to estimate the fixed element.
   The following data will be used to illustrate the technique.

Period	Activity level (units)	Costs (£)
1.	3,200	26,980
2.	2,840	23,060
3.	2,410*	21,550
4.	3,642	29,290
5.	3,860*	28,800
6.	2,905	27,680

* It will be seen that the high/low activity points and their costs are:

2,410 units at a cost of £21,550

3,860 units at a cost of £28,800

The difference between the two points is a range of 1,450 units and £7,250. From these values the rate of cost change, ie the variable cost per unit, can be calculated thus:

$$\frac{£7,250}{1,450} = £5 \text{ per unit variable cost.}$$

From this value of variable cost the fixed element can be deduced.

Cost at 2,410 units	=	£21,500
less 2,410 × £5	=	£12,050
∴ fixed costs	=	£ 9,500

The values of the fixed and variable elements have been found above using arithmetic. The points could also be plotted on a graph and a line drawn joining the high/low points which could be extrapolated to zero units to provide an indication of the fixed element. This has been done in Figure 18.7. It will be apparent that, whether arithmetic or graphical methods are used, the high/low method is inaccurate and the results are directly affected by the extreme values which may be quite unrepresentative.

21. SCATTERGRAPH TECHNIQUE

This is simple visual technique which can be employed with as few as two previous observations, but obviously there is some gain in accuracy if a number of previous cost and activity readings are available. Figure 18.7 shows the plotting of the cost and activity data given in Para 19 above.

The estimated line of best fit has been drawn at an angle adjudged to be the best representation of the slope of the points. It should be compared with the line between the high/low points.

The dotted line is drawn to show the intersection with the cost axis and gives an estimate of the fixed cost; in this case £14,500. The slope of the line, ie the variable element, is found as follows:

cost @ zero activity = £14,500

cost @ 3,860 units = £28,800

$$\text{Thus: variable element} = \frac{28,800 - 14,500}{3,860 - 0} = £3.70$$

Thus the estimated cost function using the line of best fit is: £14,500 + £3,70x where: x equals units of activity. These values should be contrasted with

FIGURE 18.7 Scattergraph showing visual line of best fit and high and low points

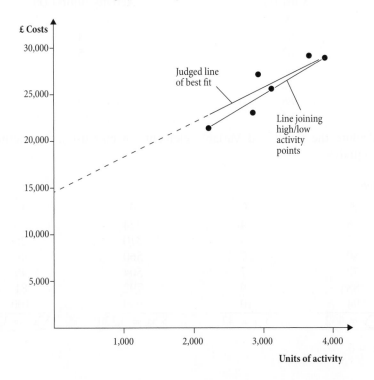

those found using the high/low method. The scattergraph technique is simple and convenient, but clearly no claims can be made for its accuracy.

22. LEAST SQUARES*

* Note: This technique is dealt with in more detail in *Quantitative Techniques*, T. Lucey, Cengage Learning. This is a statistical method for calculating a line of best fit to data and has a variety of uses including the present one of establishing a cost function. The linear cost function can be represented by

$$y = a + bx,$$
$$\text{where: } y \text{ equals cost}$$

and the other symbols are as previously defined. To find the values of the constants, a and b, two simultaneous equations need to be solved. These are:

$$\sum y = an + b\sum x \quad \text{Equation I}$$
$$\sum xy = a\sum x + b\sum x^2 \quad \text{Equation II}$$

where: n = number of pairs of cost and activity figures.
(*Note:* These equations are known as the *Normal Equations*).

The calculation will be illustrated by the following cost and activity data taken from past records.

Example 4

Cost (y) £	Activity (units) (x)
56	4
62	5
80	7
72	7
88	9
94	10

Calculate the Fixed and Variable elements of cost using the method of Least squares.

Solution

y	x	xy	x^2
56	4	224	16
62	5	310	25
80	7	560	49
72	7	504	49
88	9	792	81
94	10	940	100
$\sum y = 452$	$\sum x = 42$	$\sum xy = 3,330$	$\sum x^2 = 320$

and $n = 6$

Substituting in the equations given above we obtain

$$452 = 6a + 42b \qquad \text{I}$$
$$3{,}330 = 42a + 320b \qquad \text{II}$$

Solving in the normal manner, ie, eliminating one of the constants (in this case multiply Equation I by 7 and deduct from Equation II) we obtain:

$$3{,}330 = 42a + 320b \qquad \text{II}$$
$$3{,}164 = 42a + 294b \qquad 7 \times \text{I}$$
$$166 = 26b$$
$$\therefore b = \mathbf{6.385}$$

and substituting in either equation the value of a is found to be 30.6
∴ the linear cost function is:

$$y = \mathbf{30.6} + \mathbf{6.385}x$$

ie $\qquad y = \text{Total cost}$

$\qquad$ £30.6 = the Fixed costs

and $\quad$ £6.385 = Variable cost per unit of activity.

How is the calculated cost function used?

Assume we wish to forecast what the total cost would be when the Activity was 12 units. The required value of x, the Activity, is inserted into the cost function, thus:

$$\text{Total cost} = £30.6 + 6.385 \ (12)$$
$$= \mathbf{£107.22}$$

This represents the estimate of total cost, assuming that the past cost behavioural characteristics continue to apply. Forecasting *outside* the range of the supplied data values (ie in this example, 4–18) is known as *extrapolation*. If we wished to estimate a value within the range, say 8 units in this example, this is known as *interpolation*.

Notes

a. The above is an outline of finding the constants a and b by the method of least squares which is sometimes known as *regression analysis*.

b. The least squares method should only be applied to cost and activity data which show evidence of real correlation. Correlation and the associated Coefficient of Determination are dealt with below.

23. CORRELATION

When the value of one variable is related to another, they are said to be *correlated*. Thus, correlation means an interrelationship or association. For example, there is likely to be some correlation between the heights and weights of people.

FIGURE 18.8   Relationship between variables

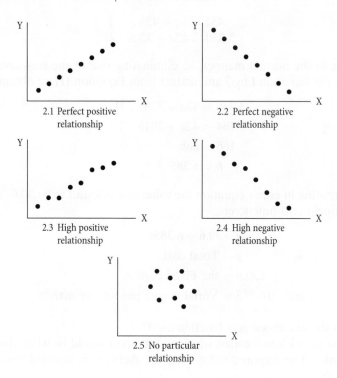

2.1 Perfect positive relationship

2.2 Perfect negative relationship

2.3 High positive relationship

2.4 High negative relationship

2.5 No particular relationship

Variables may be:

a) perfectly correlated – move in perfect unison.

b) partly correlated – some inter-relationship but not exact.

c) uncorrelated – no relationships between their movements.

The relationship between variables is shown diagrammatically in Figure 18.8.

Movement in one variable may cause movements *in the same direction* in the other variable. This is known as *positive correlation;* an example being height and weight.

Alternatively movements in one variable could cause change *in the opposite direction* in the other variable. This is known as *negative correlation.* For example if the price of an item is increased fewer will be bought. The degree of correlation can be measure by what is known as the Product Moment Coefficient of Correlation denoted by *r*. This relationship between two variables. There are several possible formulae but a practical one is:

$$r = \frac{n \sum xy - \sum x \sum y}{\sqrt{n \sum x^2 - (\sum x)^2} \times \sqrt{n \sum y^2 - (\sum y)^2}}$$

This formula is used in the following example:

Example 5

The managers of a company with 10 operating plants of similar size producing small components have observed the following pattern of expenditure on inspection and defective parts delivered to the customer.

	Inspection expenditure per 1,000 units (pence)	Defective parts per 1,000 units delivered
1	25	50
2	30	35
3	15	60
4	75	15
5	40	46
6	65	20
7	45	28
8	24	45
9	35	42
10	70	22

They are wondering how strong the relationship is between inspection expenditure and the number of faulty items delivered and to what extent they may predict the number of faulty parts delivered from a knowledge of expenditure on inspection.

Solution

First the data have to be re-arranged in ascending order of Inspection Expenditure.

X	Y	X^2	Y^2	XY
15	60	225	3,600	900
24	45	576	2,025	1,080
25	50	625	2,500	1,250
30	35	900	1,225	1,050
35	42	1,225	1,764	1,470
40	46	1,600	2,116	1,840
45	28	2,025	784	1,260
65	20	4,225	400	1,300
70	22	4,900	484	1,540
75	15	5,625	225	1,125
424	363	21,926	15,123	12,815
$\sum X$	$\sum Y$	$\sum X^2$	$\sum Y^2$	$\sum XY$

Using the formula above:

$$r = \frac{10 \times 12{,}815 - 424 \times 363}{\sqrt{(10 \times 21{,}926 - 424^2)} \times \sqrt{(10 \times 15{,}123 - 362^2)}}$$

$$= \frac{128{,}150 - 153{,}921}{\sqrt{(219{,}260 - 179{,}776)} \times \sqrt{(151{,}230 - 131{,}796)}}$$

$$= \frac{-25{,}762}{\sqrt{(39{,}484)} \times \sqrt{(19{,}461)}} = -0.93$$

Thus the correlation coefficient is −0.93 which indicates a strong negative linear association between expenditure on inspection and defective parts delivered. It will be seen that the formula automatically produces the correct sign for the coefficient.

24. COEFFICIENT OF DETERMINATION (r^2)

This measure denoted by r^2 (because it is the square of the correlation coefficient, r) measures what proportion of the variation in the actual values of one variable (y) may be predicted by changes in the value of x. In terms of Example 18.5 above what proportion of the values of Defective Parts may be predicted by changes in Inspection Expenditure.

From Example 5 the correlation coefficient was − 0.93.

Thus the Coefficient of Determination $= r^2 = (-0.93)^2 = $ **0.86**

This means that 86% of the variations in the number of defectives can be explained by variations in Inspection Expenditure leaving 14% of the variations to be explained by other factors.

Note:
To be able to draw any inferences from the coefficients r and r^2, the variables must be causally related, ie variations in one variable should be *caused* by changes in the other. Some variables may apparently move together yet this may be due to pure chance. This is known as *spurious* or *nonsense correlation*.

25. THE EFFECTS OF INFLATION

When we are trying to find the cost characteristics from past data, as shown above, a recurring problem is the effect of inflation on the costs. Over time, inflation affects all costs, both fixed and variable and to be able to get at the 'real' underlying cost characteristics the effects of inflation must be allowed for. This has to be done whatever technique of cost analysis is used, ie high/low, scattergraph, least squares or whatever.

The general principles are illustrated by the following example.

Example 6
Production and cost data have been recorded over two years thus:

	Last year	**Current year**
Production	50,000 units	54,000 units
Total costs	£1,700,000	£1,835,400

Between last year and the current year there has been 5% cost inflation.

Required:

a. Calculate the 'real' fixed and variable costs

b. Estimate what the total costs will be next year when it is expected there will be 4% cost inflation and output will be 56,000 units.

Solution

a. Eliminate the inflation effects from data supplied:

$$\text{Current year costs in 'real' terms} = \frac{\text{Current year Actual Costs}}{\text{Inflation} + 1}$$

$$= \frac{£1,835,400}{1.05}$$

$$= £1,748,000$$

Find the fixed/variable costs from the real cost and production differences

	Production Units	Costs £
Current year	54,000 units	1,748,000
Last year	50,000 units	1,700,000
Difference =	4,000 units	£48,000

$$\therefore \text{'Real' variable cost/unit} = \frac{£48,000}{4,000} = £12$$

$$\text{'Real' Fixed cost} = £1,748,000 - (54,000 \times £12) = £1.1\text{m}$$

[The actual costs in the current year are thus made up as follows:

$$(£1.1\text{m} \times 1.05) + (54,000 \times £12 \times 1.05) = £1,835,400]$$

b. Cost estimate for the next year when there is expected to be 4% cost inflation and 56,000 units output

$$= (£1.1\text{m} \times 1.05 \times 1.04) + (56,000 \times £12 \times 1.05 \times 1.04)$$

$$= £1,935,024$$

If the inflation effects between periods are not allowed for, the cost breakdown into fixed and variable cannot be accurate.

26. PAST AND FUTURE COSTS

The analysis of past cost behaviour may be of help in predicting future cost behaviour, but care should be taken with any extrapolation into the future. The past will only be a guide to the future if conditions remain more or less the same. Conditions rarely remain the same, so judgement will always be required in cost prediction. Because many factors other than changes in activity levels influence costs, eg, changes in organisation, technology, methods, climatic influences, etc, etc care should be taken not to adopt a too simplistic view of cost behaviour. On occasions no past data are available on which to base predictions. This is often the case with a new product and in such cases, or where significant changes in methods are anticipated for an existing product, cost estimates should be based on engineering and work study estimates.

The environment in which firms operate is highly volatile and change is ever present. There may be new products, new competitors, changes in methods and technology, changes in market conditions and a host of other factors.

The effect of this is that past behaviour and patterns are unlikely to be applicable in the future.

Accordingly, any form of extrapolation of the past into the future, however sophisticated it may appear, is unlikely to produce accurate results. The further into the future we are trying to forecast, the less reliance we should place on our past behaviour and results. Remember, the only thing we know for certain about the future is that it will not be the same as the past.

27. ALTERNATIVE COST PATTERNS

So far, all of the cost patterns, whether linear or non-linear, fixed, variable or semi-variable, have had regular, continuous characteristics. This is not always the case and various other patterns exist, examples of which follow.

28. STEP COSTS

These are costs which remain constant for a range of activity; then, when activity increases still further, the cost has to be increased by a significant amount. A typical example would be supervision costs. For a range of activities one supervisor will be sufficient, but there comes a point when an additional supervisor has to be appointed, so costs increase discretely. This can be shown graphically as in Figure 18.9.

There is not a simple algebraic expression which describes step costs as there is for continuous linear or non-linear functions. Analysis involving step costs can be dealt with graphically or by either of the following methods.

i. If the range of activities being considered lies within one step, eg between output levels V_1 and V_2 in Figure 18.9, then for analysis purposes the step cost can be treated as a fixed cost at level 2.

ii. Continuous approximation of step costs. Many costs in the aggregate do increase by discrete amounts so that they are strictly step costs. In many cases the steps are frequent and relatively small so that approximation by continuous functions is reasonably accurate and facilitates subsequent analysis. This can be shown as in Figure 18.10.

FIGURE 18.9   Illustration of step costs

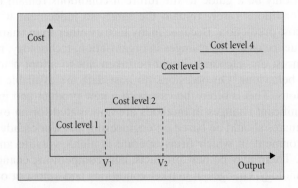

FIGURE 18.10   Continuous approximations of step costs .

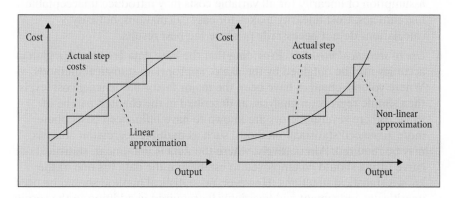

Because salaries and administrative costs comprise a large proportion of total cost in both private and public sector organisations, step costs are frequently encountered. For example, within the Education Service there are published bands which produce a stepped element in the salaries cost (which comprises about 80% of total costs). There are bands of pupil numbers which determined the number of teachers a school should have and also the salary of the head teacher. These are easily calculated step costs being based on published bands but many others exist in less obvious forms.

29. PROBLEMS OF COST BEHAVIOUR PREDICTION

It is important to be aware of the pitfalls and problems in cost prediction so that where possible they can be avoided. Typical of these are the following:

a. *Tendency to classify costs for all time.* There is a tendency to classify costs, without too much regard to their actual behaviour, as fixed or variable according to conventions. An example of this is the tendency to classify labour costs as purely variable, whereas labour costs may have a substantial fixed element. Any classification of costs into fixed and variable needs to be continually reviewed in the light of their actual behaviour and in relation to the purpose for which the classification is intended to serve.

b. *Uncritical use of historical data.* If past cost data are to be used for prediction purposes, care must be taken to ensure that they are reasonably representative and not subject to special conditions. Ideally, past cost variations which are to be used for predictions, should be those which occurred as a result of volume changes only. Many factors other than changes in volume cause cost changes (ie, technology changes, product mix changes, method and tooling changes, seasonal and climatic changes) and if past data are not adjusted to take account of non-volume factors there is the implicit assumption that the non-volume factors will act upon costs in the future in the same manner and proportions as in the past. This is a somewhat sweeping assumption.

c. *Linearity assumption.* Costs display a variety of forms and the too ready assumption of linearity for all variable costs may introduce unacceptable inaccuracies. Cost linearity makes for easy calculations, but easy calculations do not necessarily produce the best results.

d. *Use of statistical methods.* Providing that the base data are sound, a gain in accuracy may be obtained by the use of appropriate statistical methods. Where volume changes have been the major factor influencing cost levels then simple regression analysis, as described in the chapter, can be of value. Where several factors are known to have influenced costs, then more advanced statistical methods, such as multiple regression analysis may be required. Alternatively, where the data is non-linear, statistical curve fitting should be employed to establish if the data fits one of the known statistical functions. However, no statistical method should be used uncritically, judgement will invariably be required in addition to the results of the statistical exercise.

e. *Oversimplification.* Conventionally it is assumed that all variable costs vary accordingly to a single activity indicator. In a manufacturing company this is typically taken to be production volume. This is a gross over-simplification. Different costs vary with different activity indicators as previously explained when Activity Based Costing was discussed.

   Some costs vary with, (are driven by) the number of clients handled, some by the number of set-ups, others by the number of orders received or material movements or by some other cost driver. If the assumption is that all variable costs vary at the same rate accordingly to, say, production volume, it is illogical and ignores reality. In spite of this students should be aware that the assumption is frequently encountered in examination questions.

f. *Cost unit definition.* Ideally the cost units used for product and service costing and cost behaviour prediction should be standardised units; each identical with one other. In some cases this presents few problems. Each litre of beer brewed or tonne of cement produced or nuts manufactured are identical. However there are often problems especially within Service and Not-for-Profit organisations. For example, in the National Health Service 'Patient-Days' and 'Out-patient Attendances' are frequently used as cost units for internal and national comparative purposes. But patients, their illnesses, their treatments, and times taken vary considerably and make the use of such units less valid. As a consequence cost behaviour prediction becomes even more of a problem.

30. SUMMARY

a. For many accounting purposes it is vital to be able to estimate accurately the behaviour of cost in relation to changes in the level of activity.

b. Generally the situations being studied are for a limited time period and for a limited range of activity variations, ie short run.

c. Variable cost may be linear or non-linear.

d. Linear approximations of non-linear functions are frequently made.

e. Fixed or period costs are time, not activity related.

f. Semi-variable costs contain fixed and variable elements.

g. When past data are available, cost characteristics can be established visually by the scattergraph technique or by the method of regression analysis known as least squares.

h. Some cost patterns are not continuous, for example, step costs.

i. Many problems exist in accurately predicting cost behaviour and these include: inappropriate cost classifications, poor historical data, using linear approximation in inappropriate circumstances, etc.

31. POINTS TO NOTE

a. Flexible budgeting, marginal costing, cost/volume/profit analysis have as their basis, predictions about cost behaviour.

b. It has been said with some truth that in the short run all costs are fixed and in the long run all costs are variable.

c. In practice costs do not behave in regular, predictable fashions. One example is that different types of variable costs vary with different activity indicators. One cost may vary with production another with sales, another one with orders received. In examinations there is frequently the simplifying assumption that all variable costs are related to one indicator, say sales volume. This makes for simpler questions but it is not necessarily realistic.

d. On occasions it is necessary to resolve a total cost into its fixed and variable elements. This can be done, somewhat crudely, by using the scattergraph technique or by using regression analysis based on the least squares method.

Student self-testing

Exercises (answers below)

1. The behaviour of a cost can be expressed algebraically as:

$$\text{Cost} = bx + cx^2 + dx^3$$
$$\text{where } b = \text{labour hours}$$
$$c = \text{material in Kgs}$$
$$d = \text{machine hours}$$
$$\text{and } x = \text{output in units}$$

You are required to:

a. Explain what type of cost is depicted

b. Calculate the cost at output levels of 80 and 100 units when $b = 6$, $c = 0.7$ and $d = 0.04$.

2. Using the results obtained in Exercise 1 calculate the cost at 85 units using linear interpolation. What is the extent of the error caused by linear interpolation?

3. The following cost and activity data were taken from factory records.

Cost incurred £	Activity (units)
656	80
692	86
683	87
698	94
707	95
703	97
712	104

Using the least squares method of linear regression calculate the fixed and variable elements of the cost.

4. Draw a scattergraph of the data in Exercise 3 and show the calculated regression line.

Solutions to exercises

1. Cost function $= bx + cx^2 + dx^3$
   a. A non-linear variable cost of parabolic form.
   b. Cost at 80 units $= 6(80) + 0.7(80^2) + 0.04(80^3) = £25,440$
       Cost at 100 units $= 6(100) + 0.7(100^2) + 0.004(100^3) = £47,600$

2. Cost at 85 (using linear interpolation) $= £25,440 + \frac{5}{20} \times (47,600 - 25,440)$
   $= £30,980$
   The error is the difference between the linear interpolation figure of 30,980 and the value using the formula.

$$\text{Cost at } 85 = 6(85) + 0.7(85^2) + 0.04(85^3) = £30,132$$
$$\therefore \text{ Error} = £30,980 - 30,132 = \textbf{£848}$$

3. The Normal Equations:

$$\sum y = an + b \sum x$$
$$\sum xy = a \sum x + b \sum x^2$$

y	x	xy	x^2
656	80	52,480	6,400
692	86	59,512	7,396
683	87	59,421	7,596
698	94	65,612	8,836
707	95	67,165	9,025
703	97	68,191	9,409
712	104	74,048	10,816
4,851	643	446,429	59,451
$\sum y$	$\sum x$	$\sum xy$	$\sum x^2$ and $n = 7$

4,851	= 7a	+ 643b	Equation I
446,429	= 643a	+ 59,451b	Equation II

less 445,599	= 643a	+ 59,064b	Equation I × $\frac{643}{7}$
= 830	=		387b

$\therefore b = £2.145 =$ variable cost

and substituting: $4,851 = 7a + 643(2.145)$

$3,472 = 7a$

$\therefore a = £496 =$ Fixed cost

4. Scattergraph and Regression Line

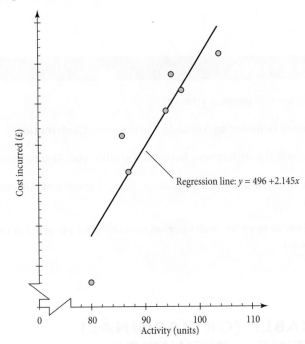

Regression line: $y = 496 + 2.145x$

19

Variable (or marginal) and absorption costing

1. OBJECTIVES

After studying this chapter you will

- **Know what is meant by Variable Costing and Contribution**

- **Understand the differences between Variable and Absorption Costing**

- **Be able to calculate stock valuations using Variable or Absorption Costing**

- **Know how to prepare multi-period variable and absorption costing statements.**

2. VARIABLE (OR MARGINAL) COSTING – DEFINITION

Variable costing, traditionally known as marginal costing, distinguishes between fixed costs and variable costs as conventionally calculated. For normal cost accounting purposes, variable cost is taken to be: direct labour, direct materials, direct expenses and the variable protion of overheads.

Variable or marginal costing is defined as:

A cost accounting method which assigns only variable costs to cost units while fixed costs are written off as period costs.

Terminology

An important feature of variable costing is the calculation of what is termed *contribution*. This is simply the difference between sales value and the variable cost of sales.

Thus:

$$\text{VARIABLE COST} = \begin{array}{c} \text{DIRECT LABOUR} \\ + \\ \text{DIRECT MATERIAL} \\ + \\ \text{DIRECT EXPENSE} \\ + \\ \text{VARIABLE OVERHEADS} \end{array}$$

$$\text{CONTRIBUTION} = \text{SALES} - \text{VARIABLE COST}$$

The term variable cost sometimes refers to the variable cost per unit and sometimes to the total variable costs of a department or batch or operation. The meaning is usually clear from the context.

Note:
Alternative names for variable costing are the *contribution approach*, *direct costing* and *marginal costing*.

3. VARIABLE COST AND MARGINAL COST

To the economist the additional cost incurred by the production of one extra unit is termed the *marginal cost*. To the accountant the additional cost is generally taken to be the average variable cost which is conventionally assumed to act in a linear fashion, ie the variable cost per unit is assumed to be constant in the short run, over the activity range being considered.

These views can be contrasted in Figure 19.1.

This difference of viewpoint regarding the additional cost per unit results in the following alternative views of a firm's total cost structure in Figure 19.2.

The economic model is an explanation of the cost behaviour of firms in general, whereas the accounting model is an attempt to provide a pragmatic basis for decision-making in a particular firm. However, it is likely that differences between the two viewpoints are more apparent than real.

A number of investigations have shown that variable costs are virtually constant per unit over the range of activity changes studied. Accordingly for short run decision-making purposes the variable cost per unit should be assumed to be constant. Thus if the variable cost per unit was £5 per unit, the total variable cost for:

FIGURE 19.1   Additional cost per unit

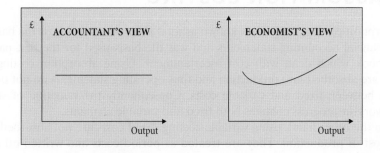

FIGURE 19.2

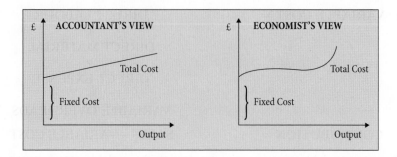

100 units would be £500

150 units would be £750

200 units would be £1,000

and so on.

Notes:

1. The assumption of linearity should only be made in appropriate conditions. Where the question or facts of the situation indicate that variable costs behave in some other way, for example, non-linearly or in a stepped fashion, then the actual behaviour pattern should be used.

2. Students should be aware that, colloquially, accountants frequently refer to the *average variable cost as the marginal cost*.

4. USES OF VARIABLE COSTING

There are two main uses for variable costing:

a. As a basis for providing information to management for planning and decision-making. It is particularly appropriate for short run decisions involving changes in volume or activity and the resulting cost changes. This is an important area of study for students and it is dealt with in detail in the following chapter.

b. It can also be used in the routine cost accounting system for the calculation of costs and the valuation of stocks. Used in this fashion, it is an alternative to total absorption costing. This facet of variable costing is dealt with below.

5. VARIABLE COSTING AND ABSORPTION COSTING

Absorption costing, sometimes known as total absorption costing, is the basis of all financial accounting statements and was the basis used for the first part of this book which dealt with cost ascertainment. Using absorption costing, all costs are absorbed into production and thus operating statements do not distinguish between fixed and variable costs. Consequently the valuation of stocks and work-in-progress contains both fixed and variable elements.

On the other hand, using variable costing, fixed costs are not absorbed into the cost of production. They are treated as period costs and written off each period in the Costing Profit and Loss account. The effect of this is that finished goods and work-in-progress are valued at variable cost only, ie the variable elements of cost, usually Prime cost plus variable overhead. At the end of a period the variable cost of sales is deducted from sales revenue to show the contribution, from which fixed costs are deducted to show net profit.

The two approaches are illustrated below using the following data:

Example I
In a period, 20,000 units of Z were produced and sold. Costs and revenues were:

	£
Sales	100,000
Production costs:	
variable	35,000
fixed	15,000
Administrative + Selling overheads:	
fixed	25,000

Prepare operating statements based on both Absorption and Variable Costing.

Solution

Operating Statements

Absorption Costing Approach		Variable Costing Approach		
	£		£	£
Sales	100,000	Sales		100,000
less Production Cost of Sales	50,000	*less* Variable cost		35,000
= Gross Profit	50,000	= Contribution		65,000
less Admin. + Selling Overheads	25,000	*less* Fixed costs		
		Production	15,000	
		Admin. S + D	25,000	40,000
= Net Profit	£25,000	= Net Profit		£25,000

The above illustration, although simple, illustrates the general characteristics of both approaches.

The key figure arising in the variable Costing statement is the Contribution of £65,000. The total amount of contribution arising from Product Z (and other products, if any) forms a pool from which fixed costs are met. Any surplus arising after fixed costs are met becomes the Net Profit.

6. CHANGES IN THE LEVEL OF ACTIVITY

When changes occur in the level of activity, the absorption costing approach may cause some confusion. In Example 1 the activity level was 20,000 units and using the absorption approach, the profit per unit and cost per unit can be calculated as follows:

	£
Selling Price per unit	5
less Total cost per unit = $\frac{£75,000}{20,000}$	3.75
Profit per unit	£1.25

If these figures were used as guides to results at any activity level other than 20,000, they would be incorrect and may mislead. For example, if the level of activity of Example 1 changed to 25,000 units, it might be assumed that the total profits would be 25,000 × £1.25 = £31,250. However, the results are likely to be as follows:

Operating Statement (Absorption approach)

	£
Sales (25,000 × £5)	125,000
less Production Cost (£35,000 × 125% + 15,000)	58,750
= Gross Profit	66,250
less Admin + Selling overheads	25,000
= Net Profit	£41,250

The difference is, of course, caused by the incorrect treatment of the fixed cost. In such circumstances the use of the variable approach presents a clearer picture. Based on the data in Example 1 the variable cost per unit and the contribution per unit is calculated as follows:

$$\text{Variable cost/unit} = \frac{\text{Variable Cost}}{\text{Quantity}} = \frac{35,000}{20,000}$$

$$= £1.75$$

$$\therefore \text{contribution/unit} = \text{Sale Price} - \text{variable cost/unit} = £5 - £1.75$$

$$= £3.25$$

If, once again, the activity is increased to 25,000 units, the expected profit would be:

$$(25,000 \text{ units} \times \text{Contribution/unit}) - \text{Fixed costs}$$
$$= (25,000 \times £3.25) - £40,000 = £41,250$$

and the operating statement on variable costing lines would be:

	£
Sales	125,000
less Variable cost (25,000 × 1.75)	43,750
= Contribution	£81,250
less Fixed costs	40,000
Net Profit	£41,250

Note:
Students will note that the variable cost and contribution per unit have been assumed to be constant and that fixed costs remain unchanged.

7. STOCKS AND VARIABLE COSTING

Although the method of presentation was different, both variable and absorption costing produced the same net profit for the data in Example 1. This was because there was no stock at the beginning or end of the period. Because the two methods differ in their valuation of stock, they produce different profit figures when stocks arise. This is illustrated below.

Example 2
Assume the same data as Example 1 except that only 18,000 of the 20,000 units produced were sold, 2000 units being carried forward as Stock to the next period. Produce operating statements based upon variable costing and absorption costing principles.

Solution

Operating Statements

Absorption Costing	£	£	Variable Costing	£	£
Sales (18,000 × £5)		90,000	Sales		90,000
less Production Cost of sales	50,000		*less* Variable cost	35,000	
– Closing stock			– closing stock		
(2,000 × £2.50)	5,000	45,000	(2,000 × £1.75)	3,500	31,500
= Gross profit		45,000	= Contribution		58,500
less Admin + Selling Overheads		25,000	*less* Fixed costs		
			Production	15,000	
			Admin S & D	25,000	40,000
= Net profit		£20,000	= Net profit		£18,500

a. The closing stock valuations using the two approaches are:

Absorption Costing = Average Production Cost (including fixed costs)
$$= \frac{£50,000}{20,000}$$
$$= £2.50$$

Variable Costing = variable costs only
$$= \frac{£35,000}{20,000}$$
$$= £1.75$$

b. By including fixed costs in stock valuation, absorption costing transfers some of this period's fixed costs into next period when they will be charged against the revenue derived from the stock carried forward (assuming it is sold). Variable costing always writes off all fixed costs in the period they are incurred.

c. In a period with increasing stocks (as the one illustrated) absorption costing will show higher profits than marginal costing. Conversely in a period of decreasing stocks variable costing will show the higher profits.

The difference is, of course, entirely due to the different treatment of fixed costs in the stock valuation.

8. TYPICAL VARIABLE COSTING STATEMENTS

Wherever marginal costing is used in the routine accounting system, similar principles to those described above will apply. Some examples of variable costing statements in typical situations follow:

a. Where Multiple Products or Multiple departments exist

Variable Costing Operating Statement				
Product or Department 1	Product or Department 2	Product or Department 3	...	Total
Sales 1 *less* Variable Cost 1 of Sales	Sales 2 *less* Variable Cost 2 of Sales	Sales 3 *less* Variable Cost 3 of Sales	etc ...	Total sales *less* Variable Cost of Sales (Total)
= Contribution 1	= Contribution 2	= Contribution 3		= Total Contribution Fixed Costs for whole organisation
				NET PROFIT

Notes:

i. Using Variable Costing no attempt is made to apportion fixed costs arbitrarily across products or departments.

ii. With such a presentation the effects of eliminating a product or department or altering the level of activity can be shown more clearly. Care must be taken in assessing the effect of a product or department elimination to ensure that any effect on fixed costs is allowed for.

b. *Process Costing*

Where variable costing is used in process accounting, the normal accounts and statements will be produced, as described in Chapter 15 except that:

i. Process accounts will contain variable costs only.

ii. Transfers from one process to another will be at variable cost.

iii. Losses, abnormal and normal, will be valued at variable cost only.

iv. All fixed costs will be written off, each period, to costing profit and loss.

9. VARIABLE COSTING OR ABSORPTION COSTING

The arguments below relate to the use of these techniques in the *routine cost accounting system* of the organisation and not to their use for decision-making or control.

Arguments for the use of variable costing in routine cost accounting:

a. Simple to operate.

b. No apportionments, which are frequently on an arbitrary basis, of fixed costs to products or departments. Many fixed costs are indivisible by their nature, eg Managing Director's Salary.

c. Where sales are constant, but production fluctuates (possibly an unlikely circumstance) variable costing shows a constant net profit whereas absorption costing shows variable amounts of profit.

d. Under or over absorption of overheads is almost entirely avoided. The usual reason for under/over absorption is the inclusion of fixed costs into overhead absorption rates and the level of activity being different from that planned.

e. Fixed costs are incurred on a time basis, eg salaries, rent rates etc and do not relate to activity. Therefore it is logical to write them off in the period they are incurred and this is done using variable costing.

f. Accounts prepared using variable costing more nearly approach the actual cash flow position.

Arguments for the use of total absorption in routine cost accounting:

a. Fixed costs are a substantial and increasing proportion of costs in modern industry. Production cannot be achieved without incurring fixed costs which thus form an inescapable part of the cost of production, so should be included in stock valuations. Variable costing may give the impression that fixed costs are somehow divorced from production.

b. Where production is constant but sales fluctuate, net profit fluctuations are less with absorption costing than with variable costing.

c. Where stock building is a necessary part of operations, eg timber seasoning, spirit maturing, firework manufacture, the inclusion of fixed costs in stock valuation is necessary and desirable. Otherwise a series of fictitious losses will be shown in earlier periods to be offset eventually by excessive profits when the goods are sold.

d. The calculation of variable cost and the concentration upon contribution may lead to the firm setting prices which are below total cost although producing some contribution. Absorption cost makes this less likely because of the automatic inclusion of fixed charges.

e. SSAP 9 (Stocks and Work in Progress) recommends the use of absorption costing for financial accounts because costs and revenues must be matched in the period when the revenue arises, not when the costs are incurred. Also it recommends that stock valuations must include production overheads incurred in the normal course of business even if such overheads are time related, ie fixed. The production overheads must be based upon normal activity levels.

10. CONCLUSIONS REGARDING VARIABLE AND ABSORPTION COSTING

No generalised, all embracing answer can be given as to which technique should be used. Having regard to all the factors, the accountant should make a judgement as to which technique is more appropriate for the requirements of a particular organisation. Although any technique can be used for internal purposes, SSAP 9 is quite clear that absorption costing must be the basis of the financial accounts. It would appear that the use of a full variable costing system in the routine cost ascertainment procedures of an organisation is relatively rare.

This does not mean that variable costing principles are unimportant. An understanding of the behaviour of costs and the implications of contribution is vital for accountants and managers. The use of variable costing principles in planning and decision-making, dealt with in the following chapter, is universal and is of considerable importance.

11. MULTI PERIOD EXAMPLE OF VARIABLE AND ABSORPTION COSTING

To bring together the various points covered in the chapter, a fully worked example is shown below.

Example 3
Stock, production and sales data for the single product of Industrial Detergents Ltd. are given in the following.

	Period 1	Period 2	Period 3	Period 4
Production (litres)	60,000	70,000	55,000	65,000
Sales (litres)	60,000	55,000	65,000	70,000
Opening Stock (litres)	–	–	15,000	5,000
Closing Stock (litres)	–	15,000	5,000	–

The financial data for an activity level of 60,000 litres per period are as follows

	Cost per litre £
Direct Material	2.50
Direct Labour	3.00
Production Overheads = 200% of direct labour	6.00
= Total cost/litre	£11.50
Selling price per litre	£18.00

Administrative overheads are fixed at £100,000 per period and half of the production overheads are fixed.

From the above information prepare operating statements on variable costing and absorption costing principles.

Solution
The first step is to establish the amount of fixed production overheads per period. The cost data shown above are based on 60,000 litres.

Labour for 60,000 litres = 60,000 × £3 = £180,000

Total production overheads = 200% × £180,000 = £360,000

$$\therefore \text{Fixed production overheads} = \frac{£360,000}{2} = £180,000$$

The variable overhead recovery rate is accordingly 100% of direct wages so that variable cost per litre can be calculated thus:

	£
Material	2.50
Labour	3.00
Variable overhead 100% of wages	3.00
	£8.50

Operating Statement using Variable Costing

		Period 1	Period 2	Period 3	Period 4
		£	£	£	£
Sales		1,080,000	990,000	1,170,000	1,260,000
Variable cost of Production	510,000	595,000	467,500	552,500	
+ opening stock			127,500	42,500	
– closing stock			127,500	42,500	
= Variable cost of Sales		510,000	467,500	552,500	595,000
Contribution		570,000	522,500	617,500	665,000
Fixed Costs (Admin & Prod'n)		280,000	280,000	280,000	280,000
Net profit		£290,000	£242,500	£337,500	£385,000

Note:
Stocks are valued at the variable cost of £8.50 per litre.

Operating Statement using Absorption Costing in Accordance with SSAP 9

		Period 1	Period 2	Period 3	Period 4
		£	£	£	£
Sales		1,080,000	990,000	1,170,000	1,260,000
Total cost of Production	690,000	805,000	632,500	747,500	
+ opening stock			172,500	57,500	
– closing stock		172,500	57,500		
= Total cost of Sales		690,000	632,500	747,500	805,000
Gross Profit		390,000	357,500	422,500	455,000
Administration Costs		100,000	100,000	100,000	100,000
Net profit		£290,000	£257,500	£322,500	£355,000
Planned activity Level		60,000	60,000	60,000	60,000
Actual activity Level		60,000	70,000	55,000	65,000
Difference		–	+ 10,000	– 5,000	+ 5,000
Overhead Over or (under) Absorption		–	+ £30,000	(£15,000)	+ £15,000

Notes:

a. Stocks are valued at full production cost including fixed production overheads, ie in this example £11.50 per litre. This represents the cost at normal activity levels in accordance with SSAP 9 recommendations.

b. The amount of over or under absorbed overhead represents the over or under recovery of fixed overheads caused when activity is above or below the planned activity level. In this example the fixed overheads are recovered at £3 per litre, eg in period 2 production was 70,000 litres as compared with 60,000 planned so the over absorption was 10,000 litres at £3 per litre = £30,000.

c. As explained in Chapters 9, the over/under absorption could be taken direct to P & L a/c or, more usually, taken to a suspense account from which the net balance at the end of the year would be written off to P & L.

d. The amount over absorbed would be deducted from total cost, the amount under absorbed would be added to total cost.

e. Because in this example, production and sales were equal over the periods concerned the profits using the two techniques can be reconciled thus:

Profits using Variable Costing

	£
Period 1	290,000
Period 2	242,500
Period 3	337,500
Period 4	385,000
	£1,255,000

Profits using Absorption Costing

	£
Period 1	290,000
Period 2	257,500
Period 3	322,500
Period 4	355,000
+ Net over absorption	30,000
	£1,255,000

f. It must be realised that in the long run both systems produce the same total profit. This is because all costs incurred will eventually be charged against sales. It is merely the timing of the sales and the differing stock valuation systems that cause profit differences from period to period.

12. SUMMARY

a. Variable costing is a costing technique where fixed and variable costs are differentiated. Only variable costs are charged to cost units and fixed costs are written off in full each period.

b. Contribution is the difference between sales and variable cost. The pool of contribution is available to cover the fixed costs and, when the fixed costs have been covered, the balance remaining is profit.

c. Variable costing can be used as the basis of the routine cost accounting system or for management decision-making.

d. Total absorption costing incorporates both fixed and variable costs into production and consequently into stock valuation. Stocks under variable costing are valued at variable cost only.

e. Because of the different methods of stock valuation the two approaches produce differing profit figures when stocks exist at the beginning or end of a period.

f. When used as a basis of the routine cost accounting system variable costing avoids the sometimes arbitrary apportionment of fixed overheads to products or departments, charges period costs when they are incurred, and is claimed to show a more realistic situation.

g. Absorption costing recognises that fixed costs are an inescapable part of production costs and consequently includes fixed elements in stock valuation. SSAP 9 recommends absorption costing principles for stock valuation.

13. POINT TO NOTE

Under examination conditions if the question emphasises the use of cost statements for planning or decision-making purposes, it is likely that a marginal cost approach is required.

Student self-testing

Exercises (answers below)

1. The following data were taken from the past records of a company at two output levels.

   The company has three departments and all fixed costs have been apportioned to the departments on the basis of sales turnover.

	Dept A £	Dept B £	Dept C £	Total £
Sales	50,000	75,000	125,000	250,000
less Costs	45,000	60,000	106,250	211,250
= Profit	5,000	15,000	18,750	38,750
Sales	60,000	90,000	150,000	300,000
less Costs	50,000	66,000	117,500	233,500
= Profit	10,000	24,000	32,500	66,500

   You are required to recast the above statements using the variable costing approach showing contribution per department and in total.

2. The following data were taken from the records of a company.

	Period 1	Period 2	Period 3
Production	30,000	38,000	27,000
Sales	30,000	27,000	38,000

	Period 1	Period 2	Period 3
Opening Stock	–		11,000
Closing Stock		11,000	

All the above in Kgs.

The firm makes a single product the financial details of which are as follows (based on a normal activity level of 30,000 Kgs)

	Cost per Kg (£)
Direct material	1.50
Direct labour	1.00
Production overheads = 300% of labour	3.00
	5.50

Selling price per Kg £9.

Administrative overheads are fixed at £25,000 and one third of the production overheads are fixed. Prepare separate operating statements on variable costing and absorption costing principles.

3. A firm has three departments and prepares operating statements using a variable costing approach as follows (£000):

	A	B	C	Total
Sales	650	480	1,420	2,550
less Marginal costs	475	220	850	1,545
= contribution	175	260	570	1,005
less Fixed costs				850
= Profit				155

Recast the above statement using a total cost approach assuming that fixed costs are apportioned on the basis of marginal costs.

Solutions to exercises

1. Assuming that the only changes in cost between the two output levels are changes in variable costs then the costs can be analysed as follows:

Dept A

$$\text{Variable} = \frac{\text{Cost change}}{\text{Sales change}} = \frac{£5,000}{£10,000} = \text{Costs per £ sales} = 50\text{p}$$

$\therefore$ Fixed costs $= 45,000 - (50,000 \times 0.5) = £20,000$

and using a similar process the analysis for the other departments is as follows:

Dept B

$$\text{Variable} = 40\text{p per £ sales}$$
$$\text{Fixed} = £30,000$$

Dept C

$$\text{Variable} = 45\text{p per £ sales}$$
$$\text{Fixed} = £50,000$$

Using the above information the Statements can be shown in Variable Costing form.

	Dept A £	Dept B £	Dept C £	Total £
Sales	50,000	75,000	125,000	250,000
less Variable Costs	25,000	30,000	56,250	111,250
= Contribution	25,000	45,000	68,750	138,750
			less Fixed costs	100,000
			= Profit	£38,750

	Dept A £	Dept B £	Dept C £	Total £
Sales	60,000	90,000	150,000	300,000
less Variable Costs	30,000	36,000	67,500	133,500
= Contribution	30,000	54,000	82,500	166,500
			less Fixed costs	100,000
			= Profit	£66,500

2. Based on the data supplied the Production overheads can be analysed into fixed and variable elements thus:

$\frac{1}{3}$ of production overheads are fixed = £1 per Kg

∴ Fixed overheads = £1 × 30,000 = £30,000 and the variable production cost is £4.50 per Kg.

Operating Statement Using Variable Costing

	Period 1 £	Period 1 £	Period 2 £	Period 2 £	Period 3 £	Period 3 £
Sales		270,000		243,000		342,000
variable Prod. Cost	135,000		171,000		121,500	
+ Opening Stock					49,500	
– Closing Stock			49,500			
= Variable Cost of Sales		135,000		121,500		171,000
= Contribution		135,000		121,500		171,000
less Fixed Costs		55,000		55,000		55,000
= Profit		£80,000		£66,500		£116,000

Note:
Stocks valued at Variable Cost.

Operating Statement Using Absorption Costing

	Period 1 £	Period 1 £	Period 2 £	Period 2 £	Period 3 £	Period 3 £
Sales		270,000		243,000		342,000
Total Cost of Prod.	165,000		209,000		148,500	
+ Opening Stock					60,500	
– Closing Stock			60,500			
= Total Cost of Sales		165,000		148,500		209,000
= Gross Profit		105,000		94,500		133,000
less Admin. Overheads		25,000		25,000		25,000
= Profit		£80,000		£69,500		£108,000
Over(under) recovery of fixed ohds.		–		8,000		(3,000)
= Profit		£80,000		£77,000		£105,000

Notes:

a. Stocks valued at total cost at the normal production level of 30,000 kgs.

b. Alternatively the over(under) recovery of fixed overheads could be reconciled at the year end.

3.

Statement Using Total Cost

£000s

	A	B	C	Total
Sales	650	480	1,420	2,550
less Total Costs	736	341	1,318	2,395
= Profit (loss)	(86)	139	102	155

Note the fixed costs of 850 were apportioned as follows:

$$\frac{\text{Fixed Costs}}{\text{Total Marginal Cost}} \times \text{Marginal cost of a dept} = \text{Fixed costs for the department.}$$

eg, Dept A

$$\frac{£850}{£1,545} \times £475 = £261 \text{ fixed costs}$$

$$£261 + £475 \text{ marginal} = £736 \text{ Total Costs}$$

20

Short-run decision-making

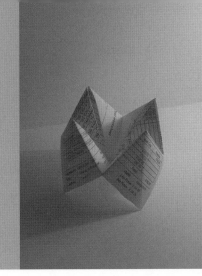

2. DECISION-MAKING

Decision-making is concerned with the future and involves a choice between alternatives. Many factors, both qualitative and quantitative, need to be considered and for many decisions financial information is a critical factor. It is therefore important that relevant information on cost and revenues is supplied. But what is relevant information? It is information about:

a. *Future costs and revenues.* It is the expected future costs and revenues that are of importance to the decision-maker. This means that past costs and revenues are only useful in so far as they provide a guide to the future. Costs already spent, known as sunk costs, are irrelevant for decision-making.

b. *Differential costs and revenues.* Only those costs and revenues which alter as a result of a decision are relevant. Where factors are common to all the alternatives being considered they can be ignored; only the differences are relevant. In many short run situations the fixed costs remain constant for each of the alternatives being considered and thus the variable costing approach showing sales, variable cost and contribution is particularly appropriate.

3. SHORT-RUN TACTICAL DECISIONS

These are decisions which seek to make the best use of existing facilities. Typically, in the short run, fixed costs remain unchanged so that the variable cost, revenue and contribution of each alternative is relevant. In these circumstances *the selection of the alternative which maximises contribution is the correct decision rule*.

In the long term (and sometimes in the short term) fixed costs do change and accordingly the differential costs must include any changes in the amount of fixed costs. Where there is a decision with no changes in fixed cost, normal variable costing principles apply. Where the situation involves changes in fixed cost a more fundamental aid to decision-making called differential costing is used. Variable costing is covered first in this chapter and then differential costing.

4. KEY FACTOR

Sometimes known as *limiting factor or principal budget factor*. This is a factor which is a binding constraint upon the organisation, ie the factor which prevents indefinite expansion or unlimited profits. It may be sales, availability of finance, skilled labour, supplies of material or lack of space. Where a single binding constraint can be identified, then the general objective of maximising contribution can be achieved by selecting the alternative which *maximises the contribution per unit of the key factor*. It will be apparent that from time to time the key factor in an organisation will change.

For example, a firm may have a shortage of orders, it overcomes this by appointing more salesmen and then finds that there is a shortage of machine capacity. The expansion of the production capacity may introduce a problem of lack of space and so on.

Note:
The 'maximising contribution per unit of the limiting factor' rule can be of value, but can only be used where there is a single binding constraint and where the constraint is continuously divisible, ie it can be altered one unit at a time. Where several constraints apply simultaneously, the simple maximising rule given above cannot be applied. This is not usually a problem for examination purposes, but real life is rarely that simple.

5. EXAMPLES OF DECISIONS WHERE VARIABLE COSTING CAN BE USED

Several typical problems in which variable costing can provide useful information for decision-making are given below. Once the general principles of variable costing are understood, they can be applied in any other similar circumstances.

The steps in analysing such problems are:

a. Check that fixed costs are expected to remain unchanged.
b. If necessary, separate out fixed and variable costs.
c. Calculate the revenue, variable costs and contribution of each of the alternatives.
d. Check to see if there is a limiting factor which will be a binding constraint and if so, calculate the contribution per unit of the limiting factor.
e. Finally, choose the alternative which maximises contribution.

The examples shown below are decisions about the acceptance of a special order, dropping a product, choice of product where a limiting factor exists, and make or buy.

6. ACCEPTANCE OF A SPECIAL ORDER

By this is meant the acceptance or rejection of an order which utilises spare capacity, but which is only available if a lower than normal price is quoted. The procedure is illustrated by the following example.

Example I
Zerocal Ltd. manufacture and market a slimming drink which they sell for 20p per can.

Current output is 400,000 cans per month which represents 80% of capacity. They have the opportunity to utilise their surplus capacity by selling their product at 13p per can to a supermarket chain who will sell it as an 'own label' product.

Total costs for the last month were £56,000 of which £16,000 were fixed costs. This represented a total cost of 14p per can.

Based on the above data should Zerocal accept the supermarket order? What other factors should be considered?

Solution

The present position is as follows

	£
Sales (400,000 × 20p) =	80,000
less Variable cost (= 10p/can)	40,000
= Contribution	40,000
less Fixed Costs	16,000
= Net profit	£24,000

On the assumption that fixed costs do not change, the special order will produce the following contribution.

	£
Sales (100,000 × 13p) =	13,000
less Variable cost (100,000 × 10p) =	10,000
= Contribution	£3,000

Thus, based on the assumptions shown the special order looks worthwhile.

However, there are several other factors which would need to be considered before a final decision is taken.

a. Will the acceptance of one order at a lower price lead other customers to demand lower prices as well?
b. Is this special order the most profitable way of using the spare capacity?
c. Will the special order lock up capacity which could be used for future, full price business?
d. Is it absolutely certain that fixed costs will not alter?

Notes:
a. Although the price of 13p is less than the total costs of 14p per can, it does provide some contribution, so may be worthwhile.
b. The process of variable cost pricing to utilise spare capacity is widely used, eg, hotels provide cheap weekend rates, railways and airlines have cheap fares for off peak periods, many manufacturers of proprietary goods produce own label products and so on.
c. The contribution from the special order can also be calculated by multiplying the quantity by the contribution per can, ie 100,000 × 3p = £3,000.

7. DROPPING A PRODUCT

If a company has a range of products one of which is deemed to be unprofitable, it may consider dropping the item from its range.

Example 2
A company produces three products for which the following operating statement has been produced:

	Product X £	Product Y £	Product Z £	Total £
Sales	32,000	50,000	45,000	127,000
Total costs	36,000	38,000	34,000	108,000
Net Profit (Loss)	(£4,000)	£12,000	£11,000	£19,000

The total costs comprise 2/3 variable 1/3 fixed.

The directors consider that as Product X shows a loss it should be discontinued.

Based on the above cost data should Product X be dropped?

What other factors should be considered?

Solution
First calculate the fixed costs, ie:

$$\frac{1}{3}(36,000) + \frac{1}{3}(38,000) + \frac{1}{3}(34,000) = £36,000 \text{ in total}$$

Rearranging the operating statement in variable costing form produces:

	Product X £	Product Y £	Product Z £	Total £
Sales	32,000	50,000	45,000	127,000
less Marginal Cost	24,000	25,333	22,667	72,000
= Contribution	£8,000	£24,667	£22,333	£55,000
less fixed costs				36,000
= Net profit				19,000

From this it will be seen that Product X produces a contribution of £8,000. Should Product X be dropped the position would be:

	£
Contribution Product Y	24,667
Contribution Product Z	22,333
Total Contribution	47,000
less Fixed Costs	36,000
= Net profit	£11,000

Thus dropping product X with an apparent loss of £4,000 reduces total profits by £8,000 which is, of course, the amount of contribution lost from Product X.

Other factors which need to be considered:

a. Although Product X does provide some contribution, it is at a low rate and alternative, more profitable products or markets should be considered.

b. The assumption above was that the fixed costs were general fixed costs which would remain even if X was dropped. If dropping X resulted in the reduction of fixed costs by more than £8,000 then the elimination would be worthwhile. However, this is unlikely.

8. CHOICE OF PRODUCT WHERE A LIMITING FACTOR EXISTS

This is where a firm has a choice between various types of products and where there is a single, binding constraint.

Example 3
A company is able to produce four products and is planning its production mix for the next period. Estimated cost, sales, and production data follow.

Product	W £		X £		Y £		Z £	
Selling Price/unit		29		36		61		51
	£		£		£		£	
Labour (@ £5/hr)	15		10		35		25	
Materials (@ £1/kg)	6	21	18	28	10	45	12	37
Contribution		£8		£8		£16		£14

Product	W	X	Y	Z
	£	£	£	£
Resources/Unit				
Labour (hours)	3	2	7	5
Materials (Kgs)	6	18	10	12
Maximum Demand (Units)	5,000	5,000	5,000	5,000

Based on the above data, which is the most appropriate mix under the two following assumptions?

a. If labour hours are limited to 50,000 in a period or

b. If material is limited to 110,000 Kgs in a period.

Solution

Wherever products have a positive contribution and there are no constraints, there is a *prima-facie* case for their production.

However, when, as in this example, constraints exist, the products **must be ranked in order of contribution per unit of the constraint** and the most profitable product mix established.

Accordingly, the contribution per unit of the inputs is calculated.

Product	W	X	Y	Z
	£	£	£	£
Contribution/Unit	8	8	16	14
Contribution/Labour Hour	2.67	4.2	29	2.8
Contribution/Kg of Mat'l	1.33	0.44	1.6	1.17

Labour hours restriction:

a. To make all the products up to the demand limit would require:
$(5,000 \times 3) + (5,000 \times 2) + (5,000 \times 7) + (5,000 \times 5) = 85,000$ labour hours but as there is a limit of 50,000 hrs in a period all the products cannot be produced up to their demand potential. Accordingly the products should be manufactured in order of attractiveness related to labour hours which is X, Z, W and finally Y.

Produce
5,000 units X using 10,000 labour hours
5,000 units Z using 25,000 labour hours
5,000 units W using 15,000 labour hours

and no units of Y which uses the total of 50,000 hours available

Materials restriction:

b. If the constraint is 110,000 kgs of material, then a similar process produces a ranking of Y, W, Z and finally X which will be noted is the opposite of the ranking produced if labour is the constraint.

When material is the constraint, the optimum production mix is:

5,000 units of Y using 50,000 Kgs material
5,000 units of W using 30,000 Kgs material

2,500 units of Z using 30,000 Kgs material
and no units of X, which uses the total of 110,000 Kgs of material.

Notes:

a. The above process of maximising contribution per unit of the limiting factor can only be used where there is a single binding constraint.

b. Most practical problems have various constraints and many more factors than the example illustrated. In such circumstances, if linearity can be assumed, linear programming* will indicate the optimum solution. An outline of the graphical method of solving Linear Programming (LP) problems is given as an appendix to this chapter.

c. In general where no constraint is identified, a reasonable decision rule is to choose the alternative which maximises contribution per £ of sales value.

*A fuller discussion of LP is given in *Quantitative Techniques*, T. Lucey, Cengage Learning.

Example 4

You have been engaged as a consultant to Acme Manufacturing Company to provide advice on the most profitable production plan for the company.

The company makes three products X, Y and Z and the appropriate data are as follows:

	Costs per unit		
	Product X	**Product Y**	**Product Z**
	£	**£**	**£**
Direct materials	15	45	30
Direct Labour Process A	36	30	45
Process B	15	18	30
Process C	18	9	36
Variable overheads	30	20	50
Fixed costs	20	20	20
Total costs	£134	£142	£211
Selling price	£150	£190	£260

The rates of pay for the direct labour are Process A £9 per hour, Process B £10 per hour and Process C £9 per hour and you are advised that the labour in Process B is in short supply and cannot be increased.

Fixed costs are recovered on a unit basis and the current production and forecasts for the three products are shown below.

	Product X Units	**Product Y** Units	**Product Z** Units
Current production	10,000	5,000	6,000
Forecast of maximum sales possible	12,000	7,000	9,000

It is required to advise the company on the most profitable mix of production showing what improvement in profitability is possible.

Solution

The total fixed costs can be ascertained from the current production levels and the cost per unit, ie:

$$(10,000 \times £20) + (5,000 \times 20) + (6,000 \times 20) = £420,000$$

The hours involved in each process for each product can be derived from the data supplied thus:

	Product X Hours	Product Y Hours	Product Z Hours
Direct Labour			
Process A (£9/hr)	4	3.33	5
Process B (£10/hr)	1.5	1.8	3
Process C (£9/hr)	2	1	4

From the above table the total number of Process B hours (the limiting factor) can be calculated using the current production figures:

$$(10,000 \times 1.5) + (5,000 \times 1.8) + (6,000 \times 3) = \textbf{42,000 hours}$$

Based on the above data a profitability statement for current production levels can be prepared.

Production (units)	Product X 10,000	Product Y 5,000	Product Z 6,000	Total 21,000
	£	£	£	£
Sales	1,500,000	950,000	1,560,000	4,010,000
less				
Variable Costs				
Direct Materials	150,000	225,000	180,000	555,000
Direct Labour A	360,000	150,000	270,000	780,000
B	150,000	90,000	180,000	420,000
C	180,000	45,000	216,000	441,000
Variable Overheads	300,000	100,000	300,000	700,000
Total variable Cost	1,140,000	610,000	1,146,000	2,896,000
= Contribution	360,000	340,000	414,000	1,114,000
			less Fixed Costs	420,000
			= Net Profit	£694,000
Contribution per unit	£36	£68	£69	
Contribution per hour of type B Labour	£24	£37.78	£23	

This means that production should be ranked in the sequence YXZ up to the limits of the sales forecast given earlier having regard to the 42,000 limit of Type B hours. This results in a production plan as follows:

Product Y	7,000 units (max)	using	12,600 hours
X	12,000 units (max)	using	18,000 hours
Z	3,800 units (balance)	using	11,400 hours
			42,000 hours

The projected profit statement is:

	Product X	Product Y	Product Z	Total
Revised Plan (units)	12,000	7,000	3,800	22,800
	£	£	£	£
Total Contribution	432,000	476,000	262,200	1,170,200
			less Fixed Costs	420,000
			= Net Profit	£750,200

The usual reservations must be expressed regarding any such production revision, for example:

a. Can the new production quantities actually be sold?

b. Will the shortfall in production of Z (6,000 − 3,800 = 2,200 units) cause problems with under utilisation of labour and machines previously used in making Product Z?

c. If customers buy combinations of the products will the reduction in availability of Product Z cause reductions in the sales of X and Y?

9. MAKE OR BUY

Frequently management are faced with the decision whether to make a particular product or component or whether to buy it in. Apart from overriding technical reasons, the decision is usually based on an analysis of the cost implications.

In general the relevant cost comparison is between the variable cost of manufacture and the buying in price. However, when manufacturing the component displaces existing production, the lost contribution must be added to the variable cost of production of the component before comparison with the buying in price. The two positions are illustrated below.

Example 5
A firm manufacturers component BK 200 and the costs for the current production level of 50,000 units are:

Costs/unit

	£
Materials	2.50
Labour	1.25
Variable overheads	1.75
Fixed overheads	3.50
TOTAL COST	£9.00

Component BK 200 could be bought in for £7.75 and, if so, the production capacity utilised at present would be unused. Assuming that there are no overriding technical considerations, should BK 200 be bought in or manufactured?

Solution
Comparison of the buying in price of £7.75 and the full cost of £9.00 suggest that the component should be bought in.

However, the correct comparison is between the VARIABLE COST of manufacture (ie, £5.50) and the buying in price of £7.75. This indicates that the component should be manufactured, not bought in.

The reason for this is that the fixed costs of £175,000 (ie, 50,000 units at £3.50) would presumably continue and, because the capacity would not be used, the fixed overheads would not be absorbed into production.

If BK 200 was bought in, overall profits would fall by £112,500, which is the difference between buying in price and the variable cost of manufacture, ie, $(£7.75 - 5.50) \times 50,000$.

Example 6

A firm is considering whether to manufacture or purchase a particular component 2,543. This would be in batches of 10,000 and the buying in price would be £6.50. The variable cost of manufacturing Component 2,543 is £4.75 per unit and the component would have to be made on a machine which was currently working at full capacity. If the component was manufactured, it is estimated that the sales of finished product FP97 would be reduced by 1,000 units. FP97 has a variable cost of £60/unit and sells for £80/unit.

Should the firm manufacture or purchase component 2,543?

Solution

A superficial view, based on the preceding example, is that because the variable cost of manufacture is substantially below the buying in price, the component should not be bought in and thus further analysis is unnecessary. However, such an approach is insufficient in this more realistic situation and the loss of contribution from the displaced product must also be considered.

Cost analysis – Component 2,543 in batches of 10,000

	£
Variable Cost of manufacture = £4.75/unit × 10,000	47,500
+ Lost contribution for FP97 = £20/unit × 1,000	20,000
	67,500
Buying in price = £6.50/unit × 10,000	65,000

∴ There is a saving of £2,500 per 10,000 batch by buying in rather than manufacture.

Note:
The lost contribution of £20,000 is an example of an opportunity costs. This is defined as the value of a benefit sacrificed in favour of an alternative course of action. This is an important principle and examples frequently occur in practice and in examination questions. Whenever there are scarce resources, there are alternative uses which must be forgone and the benefit sacrificed is the opportunity cost. Where there is no alternative use for the resource, as in Example 5, the opportunity cost is zero and it can thus be ignored.

10. DIFFERENTIAL COSTING

Differential costing is a broader and more fundamental principle than variable costing and therefore has a much wider application. Differential costing examines all the revenue and cost differences between alternatives so as to determine the most appropriate decision. Variable costing assumes that the only differences between alternatives are changes in variable costs and revenues, ie that fixed costs do not alter. Because differential costing examines all differences, it is suitable for situations where fixed costs do alter and thus becomes appropriate for both short run and long run decisions. The process by which costs are divided into fixed and variable is still necessary so as to reflect more easily changes in activity levels.

11. APPROACH USING DIFFERENTIAL COSTING

The general approach to decision-making outlined in the preceding chapters is still relevant with the proviso that even more care should be taken to iden-tify all the cost changes, both fixed and variable, because there is no assump-tion that fixed costs will remain unchanged.

A useful way of presenting differential cost statements is as follows:

Alternative A	**Alternative B**	**Difference A – B**
–	–	–
–	–	–
–	–	–

The following illustration uses this approach.

12. DIFFERENTIAL COST EXAMPLE

Example 7
A company, currently operating at full capacity, manufactures and sells sauce-pans at £2 each. Current volume is 100,000 pans per period with the following cost structure.

Operating Statement for period

	£	
Sales (100,000 at £2)		200,000
less Variable Cost		
Labour	80,000	
Material	50,000	130,000
= Contribution		70,000
Fixed Costs		30,000
= Net profit		£40,000

An opportunity has arisen to supply an additional 30,000 pans per period at £1.8 each. Acceptance of this order would incur extra fixed costs of £8,000 per period for the hire of additional machinery and the payment of an overtime premium of 20% for the extra direct labour required. Should this order by accepted? What other factors need to be considered?

Solution

Differential Cost Statement

	Present Production Level		Projected Production Level		Difference	
	100,000 Pans		130,000 Pans		30,000 Pans	
	£		£		£	
Sales		200,000		254,000		54,000
Less Variable Cost	£		£		£	
Labour	80,000		108,800		28,800	
Materials	50,000	130,000	65,000	173,800	15,000	43,800
= Contribution		70,000		80,200		10,200
less Fixed costs		30,000		38,000		8,000
= Net Profit		£40,000		£42,200		£2,200

Thus purely on the cost figures the special order would appear to be worthwhile. Additional factors that would need to be considered include:

a. Will the special order disturb the existing full price market?

b. How accurate are the projected extra costs? The additional profit is small and could easily be wiped out by slight cost increases.

c. Can administration, despatch and other service departments cope with the 30% increase in throughput without extra costs?

13. IMPLICATIONS OF DIFFERENTIAL COST

The only relevant costs for decision-making **are those which will change as a result of the decision.**

If costs are not expected to alter, then they are irrelevant to the decision. Particular examples of cost that are irrelevant are the following:

a. **Sunk costs,** ie costs which have already been incurred, are irrelevant.

b. **Book values of assets.**

c. **Cost of fully utilised resource,** ie if a limiting factor exists it will be used to the full and will therefore cost the same whatever alternative is considered. The differential cost between alternatives is therefore zero.

d. **Conventionally prepared depreciation** is not a differential cost and is therefore irrelevant.

e. **Fixed costs.** Any item which is genuinely fixed and will remain the same whichever alternative is chosen is not a differential cost and can be ignored in choosing alternatives.

f. **Committed costs.** These are costs which have to be paid as a result of past decisions. Although these are costs which will be paid in the future they are unavoidable and thus are not relevant. Naturally, a future cost which is avoidable is relevant for current decisions.

14. OPPORTUNITY COST

Opportunity cost is a factor which must be considered in decision-making. It can be defined as the value of the best alternative forgone. Although often difficult to measure, opportunity cost is of great importance because it emphasises that decisions are concerned with alternatives and that the cost of the chosen plan of action is the profit forgone from the best available alternative.

The formal definition of opportunity cost is:

The value of a benefit sacrificed when one course of action is chosen in preference to an alternative. The opportunity is represented by the foregone potential benefit from the best rejected course of action.

Terminology

Examples follow which will help to make the idea more concrete.

Example 8
A firm rents a small workshop for £50 per week, but at present does not use it. They could sub-let the workshop for £80 per week, but they are considering using it themselves for a new project.

In assessing whether the new project is worthwhile, what is the appropriate cost to use for the workshop?

Solution
The recorded historical cost of £50 is inappropriate for this purpose. If the project is initiated the firm will forgo the £80 rent they could obtain. This is the opportunity cost of the workshop and is the value to be included in the project appraisal.

Example 9
An unexpected order has been received for a product for which the labour and machine time is available and which requires three types of material A, B and C.

Material A. This material is used regularly within the firm for various products. The new order will require 1,500 kgs. The present stock is 21,000 kgs purchased at £2.50 per kg. The current replenishment price is £2.65 per kg. and it is estimated that if 1,500 kgs is used on the new order the normal stock replenishment order for A will have to be brought forward three weeks at which time it is estimated that the replenishment price will be £2.70 per kg.

Material B. 1,000 kgs of this material are in stock purchased at 85p per kg and the new order requires 800 kgs. The current replacement price is 95p per kg. This material is used on no other product and recent enquiries revealed that the material in stock could be sold at 55p per kg.

Material C. 5,000 kgs are required for the order and large quantities are in stock purchased at 18p per kg. Because of heavy usage the material is purchased weekly and the current price is 21p per kg.

What is the relevant cost for decision making purposes of each of the three materials?

Solution

Material A. Relevant Cost: £2.70 per kg
The original purchase price is irrelevant and, as it is not intended to purchase immediately, so is the current replenishment price. The relevant cost is the replenishment cost at the expected purchase time.

Material B. Relevant Cost: 55p per kg
Once again the historical purchase price is not relevant and as there is adequate in stock for current needs there is no question of replenishment. The only alternative use for the material is sale at 55p per kg.

Material C. Relevant Cost: 21p per kg
As the material will be replenished within a week the current replenishment price is relevant.

It will be noted that the recorded historical cost, which is the cost for normal cost ascertainment purposes, is not the relevant figure in any of the above examples. This is typical in decision-making and means that great care must be taken to ascertain the intended purpose for any cost which is supplied so that relevant information can be provided at all times.

15. VARIABLE COSTING AND ADVANCED MANUFACTURING TECHNOLOGY (AMT)

A number of criticisms have been made about variable costing applied to AMT factories where Just-in-Time principles are used to organise production. For example it is claimed that contribution, as conventionally calculated (ie sales – variable cost) is not a good guide to profitability because capacity factors and the rate of production are ignored. Also, variable costing treats direct labour as a variable cost whereas in many factories, in the short term, direct labour is effectively a fixed cost along with most other costs. It is because of these problems and others that alternative systems have been developed to deal with the requirements of modern factories. One of these is *throughput accounting*.

16. THROUGHPUT ACCOUNTING

Throughput accounting is a system of performance measurement and costing which traces costs to throughput time. It is claimed that it complements JIT principles and forces attention to the true determinant of profitability; the rate at which goods can be produced to satisfy customers' orders.

Throughput accounting is defined as follows:

Variable cost accounting presentation based on the definition (sales minus material and component costs. Sometimes known as super variable costing because only material costs are treated as variable.

Terminology

Throughput Accounting (TA) is based on three concepts:

Concept 1

With the exception of material costs, in the short-run, most factory costs (including direct labour) are fixed. These fixed costs can be grouped together and called Total Factory Costs (TFC).

Concept 2

With JIT, products should not be made unless there is a customer waiting for them because the ideal inventory level is zero. The effect of this is that there will be unavoidable idle capacity in some operations, except for the operation that is the bottleneck of the moment. Working on output just to increase WIP or finished goods stocks creates no profit and so would not be encouraged.

As Galloway and Waldron have stated 'If the resource cannot be exploited fully because of the bottleneck's limited capacity then letting it stand idle when it has completed the work required, costs nothing'.

This means that profit is inversely proportional to the level of inventory in the system. This can be expressed thus:

$$\text{Profit} = f\left(\frac{1}{MRT}\right)$$

where *MRT* is the manufacturing response time

Concept 3

Profitability is determined by how quickly goods can be produced to satisfy customers orders. Producing for stock does not create profits. Improving the throughput of bottleneck operations' will increase the rate at which customer demand can be met and will thus improve profitability.

Contribution in its traditional form (sales − variable costs) is not a good guide to profitability because capacity factors and the rate of production are ignored.

Using TA, product returns should be measured thus:

$$\textbf{Return per factory hour} = \frac{\textbf{Sales Price} - \textbf{Cost}}{\textbf{Time on key resource (ie the bottleneck)}}$$

Product costs are measured thus:

$$\textbf{Cost per factory hour} = \frac{\textbf{Total factory cost (TFC)}}{\textbf{Total time available on the key resource}}$$

The Returns and Cost per Factory hour are combined into the Throughput Accounting (TA) ratio thus:

$$\textbf{TA ratio} = \frac{\textbf{Return per Factory Hour (or minute)}}{\textbf{Cost per Factory Hour (or minute)}}$$

The TA ratio should be greater than 1. If it is less than 1 the product will lose money for the company and the company should consider withdrawing it from the market.

Using TA, value is not created until products are sold. Thus items made for stock produce no return and depress the TA ratio. This should encourage managers to use their limited bottleneck resource to produce products for which customer demand exists.

The TA ratio can also be considered in total terms and compares the total return from the throughput to the TFC, ie:

$$\text{Primary TA ratio} = \frac{\textbf{Return from total throughput (ie Sales – Material Costs)}}{\textbf{TFC (ie all costs other than materials)}}$$

17. BOTTLENECKS AND OVERHEAD ATTRIBUTION

A bottleneck is an activity that places a restriction on a production line or factory. A typical bottleneck being the capacity of a key machine. On occasions there may be a 'wandering' bottleneck. This means that the identified key bottleneck is not fully utilised because of a temporary limitation elsewhere, caused by poor production planning and control. If there is a wandering bottleneck the actual time on the key resource is used, not the actual time on the wandering bottleneck.

TA suggests that overheads be attributed to product costs according to their usage of bottleneck resources:

Throughput Cost = Standard minutes of throughput

(usage of bottleneck resource)

× Budgeted TFC cost per minute of bottleneck resource

Based on this, an efficiency percentage can be calculated thus:

$$\text{Efficiency \%} = \frac{\textbf{Throughput cost}}{\textbf{Actual TFC \%}}$$

This will fall below 100% if:

a. actual output is less than budgeted, eg if there was a wandering bottleneck in production or poor quality; or

b. actual factory costs exceed budget.

Labour efficiency can be measured as:

$$\text{Labour efficiency \%} = \frac{\textbf{Throughput cost}}{\textbf{total labour cost \%}}$$

18. EXAMPLES USING THROUGHPUT ACCOUNTING

The following examples illustrate various aspects of throughput accounting.

Example 10
A factory has a key resource (bottleneck) of Facility A which is available for 6,260 minutes per period.

Budgeted Factory costs and data on two products, X and Y, are shown below.

Product	Selling price/unit £	Material cost/unit £	Time in Facility A Mins
X	7	4	1
Y	7	3.50	2

Budgeted Factory costs per week

	£
Direct Labour	5,000
Indirect Labour	2,500
Power	350
Depreciation	4,500
Space costs	1,600
Engineering	700
Administration	1,000

Calculate:

- Total Factory Costs (TFC)
- Cost per Factory Minute
- Return per Factory Minute for both products
- TA ratios for both products

Solution

Total Factory Costs = Total of all costs except materials

$$= 5{,}000 + 2{,}500 + 350 + 4{,}500 + 1{,}600 + 700 + 1{,}000$$

$$= \mathbf{£15{,}650}$$

$$\text{Cost per Factory Minute} = \frac{\text{TCF}}{\text{Minutes available in bottleneck}}$$

$$= \frac{15{,}650}{6{,}260}$$

$$= \mathbf{£2.5}$$

$$\text{Return per bottleneck minute for product } X = \frac{\text{Selling price} - \text{Material cost}}{\text{Minutes in bottleneck}}$$

$$= \frac{£7 - £4}{1}$$

$$= \mathbf{£3}$$

$$\text{TA Ratio for Product } X = \frac{\text{Return per minute}}{\text{Cost per minute}}$$

$$= \frac{£3}{£2.5}$$

$$= \mathbf{£1.2}$$

$$\text{Return per bottleneck minute for Product } Y = \frac{\text{Selling price} - \text{Material cost}}{\text{Minutes in bottleneck}}$$

$$= \frac{£7 - 3.5}{2}$$

$$= \mathbf{£1.75}$$

$$\text{TA Ratio for Product } Y = \frac{\text{Return per minute}}{\text{Cost per minute}}$$

$$= \frac{£1.75}{£2.5}$$

$$= \mathbf{£0.7}$$

The TA ratios show that if we only made Product Y we would make a loss as its TA ratio is less than 1; when we make Product X we make money.

Example 11

Based on the data in Example 1 above during a week actual production was 4,750 units of Product X and 650 units of Product Y. Actual factory costs were £15,650.

Calculate:

- Throughput cost for the week
- Efficiency percentage

and comment on the possible reason(s) for the efficiency percentage calculated.

Solution

Workings

$$\text{Standard minutes of throughput for the week} = (4{,}750 \times 1) + (650 \times 2)$$
$$= \textbf{6{,}050}$$
$$\text{Throughput cost for week} = 6{,}050 \times £2.5 \text{ per min}$$
$$\text{(from Example 1)}$$
$$= \textbf{£15{,}125}$$
$$\text{Efficiency } \% = \frac{\text{Throughput cost}}{\text{Actual TFC}} \%$$
$$= \frac{£15{,}125}{£15{,}650} \%$$
$$= \textbf{96.6\%}$$

The bottleneck resource of Facility A is available for 6,260 minutes per week but produced only 6,050 standard minutes. This could be due to:

a. the presence of a 'wandering' bottleneck causing Facility A to be under-utilised; or

b. inefficiency in Facility A.

19. THROUGHPUT ACCOUNTING – CONCLUSION

It will be seen that the TA approach has certain similarities with the principle covered earlier in the chapter of maximising contribution per unit of the limiting factor.

However, there are important differences. In TA, return is defined as sales less material costs in contrast to contribution which is sales less all variable costs (material, labour and variable overheads). TA directs attention to bottlenecks and forces management to concentrate on the key elements in making profits namely; reducing inventory and the responsible time to customer demand.

Professors Kaplan and Shanks have criticised TA for its short-term emphasis but TA does appear to be helpful in JIT environments and complements the key principles of JIT.

20. PRICING DECISIONS

Decisions on pricing products or services are of great importance even though practice varies greatly. Some firms have to price products or jobs on a continuous basis, eg jobbing engineers with numerous small jobs, while others only infrequently change prices, eg a car manufacturer. Although costs are clearly of importance in setting prices they are but one factor out of many. Other considerations include: demand, competition, level of activity, legislative or regulatory restrictions and so on.

The theoretical approach to pricing is provided by what is known as marginal analysis in economics. In essence, this theory states that there are connections between price, quantity demanded and sold and total revenue. Where firms are able to pursue an independent pricing policy profit is maximised when Marginal Cost equals Marginal Revenue.

This theory is an important background to pricing but is difficult to apply in its entirety in practice mainly because it assumes perfect knowledge of all the factors involved, particularly the demand schedule, ie how many would be sold at various prices. As one would expect such information is just not available in most organisations so management have to make pricing decisions based on the imperfect information which actually is available. In many situations some form of cost-based system is used suitably adjusted to take account of what demand and other information is available.

21. COST-BASED PRICING

There are numerous cost-based pricing systems and several of the more important are examined: Full cost plus pricing, Rate of Return pricing and Variable Cost plus pricing.

Full Cost plus pricing

This system uses conventional absorption costing to find the total cost for the product or service to which is added a profit mark-up, say 30%, to arrive at a selling price. The percentage mark-up does not have to be fixed but could be altered to suit circumstances. Full Cost plus pricing is a simple, cheap method and is widely used. A key advantage is that pricing decisions can be delegated to junior management which is essential where they need to be made frequently as in jobbing firms. Its main disadvantages are that it does not explicitly consider demand and, if used inflexibly, is unlikely to produce a profit maximising price.

Rate of Return pricing

Where a firm uses the measure of performance known as Return on Capital Employed (ROCE), ie:

$$\frac{\text{Profit }\%}{\text{Capital Employed}}$$

Management may wish to know what selling price is necessary to achieve a given rate of return on the capital employed. To do this means setting a target rate of ROCE and estimating the total costs for a normal production year and the amount of capital employed.

These figures can be used in the following formula:

$$\% \text{ mark-up on cost} = \frac{\text{CapitalEmployed}}{\text{TotalAnnualCosts}} \times \frac{\text{Planned Rate of Return on}}{\text{Capital Employed}}$$

For example, assume that the planned rate of return is 15%, the Capital Employed is £8m and the estimated total annual costs are £3m. What is the required mark-up on cost?

$$\% \text{ mark-up} = \frac{£8m}{£3m} \times 15\%$$

$$= 40\%$$

Thus it will be seen that Rate of Return pricing is simply a variant of Full Cost pricing with the same advantages and disadvantages.

Variable Cost plus pricing

Instead of adding a percentage to total cost this system adds a percentage to variable cost. The system has the advantage of simplicity and of drawing attention to the importance of contribution.

Any price above variable cost does produce same contribution but it must be emphasised that overall contribution must be sufficient to cover all fixed costs and leave sufficient margin for a reasonable level of profit. Judicious use of variable pricing can increase profits. For example hotels often provide rooms at lower prices at off-peak times. The prices are above variable costs and so produce some contribution but care must be taken that lower pricing does not become the norm. Overall, prices must be set so that all costs are covered plus a reasonable level of profits.

Note:
More detail on pricing decisions is given in *Management Accounting*, T. Lucey, Cengage Learning.

22. SUMMARY

a. Decision-making is concerned with the future and with the choice between alternatives.

b. Relevant information for decision-making is concerned with future costs and revenues that will alter as a result of a decision.

c. Variable costing is most appropriate for short-run tactical decisions.

d. A key factor (or limiting factor or principal budget factor) is a binding constraint upon the organisation, eg shortage of labour, machine time or space.

e. Where a single limiting factor exists which is binding, then the decision rule is to maximise contribution per unit of the limiting factor.

f. Evaluate the sales, variable cost and contribution of the various alternatives and, if fixed costs remain unchanged, choose the alternative which maximises contribution.

g. Differential costing is a broader concept than variable costing and examines all the revenue and cost differences between alternatives.

h. The only relevant costs for decision making are those which will change as a result of the decision, ie future costs. It follows that sunk costs are irrelevant.

i. Opportunity costs are the value of the best alternative forgone and are critical for decision-making.

j. Throughput Accounting treats all costs as fixed except materials and calculates Return as Sales – Materials.

k. Returns are related to the time available on the 'bottleneck' resource. Maximising the surplus of return per minute of the bottleneck over the cost per minute maximises profit.

l. Pricing decisions should take demand into account even though such information is limited.

m. Cost-plus Systems such as Full Cost Plus and Variable Cost Plus are widely used.

23. POINTS TO NOTE

a. In practice the classification of costs into fixed and variable is extremely difficult. Cost do not behave in simple, general fashions. Some costs, eg wages, are variable in nature when activity is rising, but may become fixed when activity reduces.

b. An understanding of opportunity cost is all important for decision-making. A relevant factor in choosing any alternative is the benefit sacrificed by not choosing some other alternative.

c. Past costs are not of themselves relevant for decision-making. Their only value is that they may be of value in predicting future cost levels.

d. Always examine all the cost changes between alternatives. Do not be misled into assuming that because a cost is classified as fixed, it will always remain the same. So called 'fixed' costs can and do change quite frequently.

Student self-testing

Exercises (answers below)

1. A firm makes a single product with a marginal cost of 15p. Up to 40,000 units can be sold at 30p per unit but additional sales can only be made by reducing the selling price to 20p per unit. Fixed costs are £2,500 per period and there is a planned profit of £4,000 per period. How many units must be made and sold?

2. The following details are available regarding three products.

Product	X	Y	Z
	£	£	£
Selling Price	200	300	400
Direct Materials (£4 per Kg)	20	112	90
Direct Labour (£8 per hour)	80	44	120
Variable Overheads	40	22	60

Variable overheads are recovered at the rate of £4 per hour. Total fixed overheads are £120,000.

You are required to calculate the priority ranking of the products when the limiting factor is:

a. Sales

b. Labour

c. Materials

3. A firm makes 150,000 electric thermostats selling at £12 each. Their last operating statement was:

	£	£
Sales (150,000 × £12)		1,800,000
less Labour	650,000	
Materials	525,000	1,175,000
	= Contribution	625,000
	less Fixed Costs	450,000
	= Profit	175,000

A contract has been offered to sell an additional 50,000 thermostats at £10 each. Acceptance of this contract would increase fixed costs by £50,000 and would mean paying an overtime premium of 20% for the extra labour required. However, because of bulk purchasing a discount of 3% could be obtained for all material purchases.

Prepare a Differential Cost Statement for the above.

4. A factory has a bottleneck, Machine Z, available for 10,000 minutes per period. Two products are made and the data are

| | Per unit | | Time in Z |
Product	Selling price £	Material cost £	minutes
Mini	15	8	2
Micro	12	4	3

Total factory costs (excluding material) = £30,000

Calculate the Throughput Accounting Ratios for the products and state which earns money.

Solutions to exercises

1. Planned profit + fixed costs = contribution required.

£4,000 + 2,500 = £6,500

The first 40,000 units give (40,000 × 15p) 6,000 contribution leaving a balance of 500 which must come from the reduced price sales which have a unit contribution of 5p (20p − 15p).

Thus additional units required $= \dfrac{£500}{0.05} = 10{,}000$ units.

Thus total number of units required is $40{,}000 + 10{,}000 = 50{,}000$

2.

Contribution statement

	Product X £	Product Y £	Product Z £
Selling Price	200	300	400
– Variable Cost	140	178	270
= Contribution	60	122	130
CS ratio	30%	41%	32%
Contribution/labour hours	£6	£22.18	£8.67
Contribution/Kg material	£12	£4.35	£5.78

Priority rankings:

a. Based on sales – in order of CS ratios, Y, Z, X

b. Based on labour – in order of contribution per hr. Y, Z, X

c. Based on materials – in order of contribution per Kg X, Z, Y.

3.

Differential Cost Statement

	Existing Position £	With Additional Contract £	Difference £
Sales	1,800,000	2,300,000	500,000
less Labour	650,000	*910,000	260,000
Materials	525,000	**679,000	154,000
Variable costs	1,175,000	1,589,000	414,000
= Contribution	625,000	711,000	86,000
less Fixed costs	450,000	500,000	50,000
= Profit	175,000	211,000	36,000

* Labour Costs

$$£650{,}000 + \left(650{,}000 \times \frac{50}{150} \times 1.2\right) = £910{,}000$$

**Material Costs

$$\left(£525{,}000 + \left(525{,}000 \times \frac{50}{150}\right) \times 0.97\right) = £679{,}000$$

4. Cost per bottleneck minute $= \dfrac{£30{,}000}{10{,}000} = £3$

Return per minute:

Mini $= \dfrac{15 - 8}{2} = £3.5$; Micro $= \dfrac{12 - 4}{3} = £2.67$

$\therefore$ Throughput Accounting ratios:

Mini $= \dfrac{£3.5}{3} = 1.16$; Micro $= \dfrac{£2.67}{3} = 0.89$

Mini earns money, Micro does not.

Appendix

1. LINEAR PROGRAMMING (LP)

This subject is dealt with in detail in *Quantitative Techniques*, T. Lucey, Cengage Learning. LP is a mathematical technique concerned with the allocation of scarce resources. It is a procedure to optimise the value of some objective (for example, maximise contribution) when the factors involved are subject to constraints (for example, only 500 machine hours and 200 labour hours are available in a week). LP can be used to solve problems which:

a. can be stated in numeric terms,

b. all factors have linear relationships,

c. have one or more restrictions on the factors involved,

d. have a choice between alternatives.

2. STANDARD FORMULATION

Before attempting a solution, it is necessary to express the problem in a standard manner. This means determining the *Objective Function* and the *Constraints*. This is shown below using the following example.

A firm makes two products A and B which have a contribution of £15 and £10 per unit respectively. The production data are as follows:

	Machining Hours	Labour hours	Materials (Kgs)
	Per Unit		
Product A	4	4	1
Product B	2	6	1
Availability per week	100	180	40

It is required to determine the production plan which maximises contribution. This is a problem with two unknowns (ie, number of units A and B) with three constraints (ie, availability of machine hours, labour hours and material).

The first stage is to express the problem in the standardised format.

ie maximise: $15A + 10B$ (The objective function expressed in contribution per unit)

subject to: $4A + 2B \leq 100$ (machining hours constraint)

$\qquad 4A + 6B \leq 180$ (labour hours constraint)

$\qquad A + B \leq 40$ (materials constraint)

Because this is a problem with only two unknowns, a graphical solution is possible.

Notes on graph

a. The solution is always obtained on the edge of the feasible region and in this case is 15 units of A and 20 units of B giving a contribution of:

$$£(15 \times 15) + £(20 \times 10) = £425 \text{ TOTAL}$$

b. This solution uses the following quantities of the resources:

Machining hours	$(15 \times 4) + (20 \times 2) = 100$	(all utilised)
Labour hours	$(15 \times 4) + (20 \times 6) = 180$	(all utilised)
Material	$(15 \times 1) + (20 \times 1) = 35$	(5 Kgs spare)

GRAPHICAL LP SOLUTION

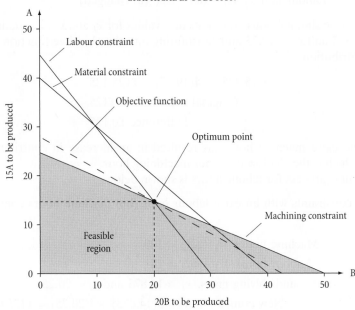

c. The materials constraint is non-binding, ie it is redundant. This can be seen from the graph as it does not touch the feasible region and also from the calculation in b. which shows that there are 5 Kgs spare.

d. Where there are more than two unknowns, graphical solution is not possible and problems have to be solved using what is known as the *Simplex method*.

The **Simplex method** is a mathematical procedure for solving LP problems where there can be any number of unknowns and constraints. The method automatically produces the optimum solution, identifies the binding constraints and, for each binding constraint, the important values known as *shadow prices* or *shadow costs*. These are values which indicate how much extra contribution would be gained if one more unit of the constraint was available. Non-binding constraints have a zero shadow price as clearly no further contribution would be gained by having additional amounts of a resource of which there is already a surplus.

When a graphical solution method is used shadow prices are not automatically available but they can be readily calculated. As an example the shadow prices of the LP graphical solution shown above will be calculated.

The solution was:	Produce $15x_1$ and $20x_2$ giving a contribution of £125.
	Constraints A and B are binding.

The problem now is to find the shadow prices of the two binding constraints, machine hours and labour hours, ie what is the valuation of one more (or less) machine hour and one more (or less) labour hour? Dealing first with machine hours, we assume that one more machine hour is available (but labour hours are constant at 180) and calculate the resulting difference in contribution, thus:

The binding constraints become:

$$\text{Machine hours } 4x_1 + 2x_2 = 101 \text{ (i.e. original } 100 + 1)$$
$$\text{Labour hours } 4x_1 + 6x_2 = 180 \text{ (unchanged)}$$

Solving these simultaneous equations new values for x_1 and x_2 are obtained: $x_1 = 15.375$ and $x_2 = 19.75$ and substituting into the objective function gives a new contribution,

$$3(15.375) + 4(19.75) = £125.125$$
$$\text{Original contribution } £125$$
$$\text{Difference } \underline{£0.125}$$

Thus one extra machine hour has resulted in an increase in contribution of **£0.125** which is the shadow price per machining hour.

A similar process for labour hours is shown below:

New constraints with an extra labour hour (but machine hours constant at 100):

$$\text{Machine hours } 4x_1 + 2x_2 = 100$$
$$\text{Labour hours } 4x_1 + 6x_2 = 181$$
$$\text{and solving gives, } x_1 = 14.875 \text{ and } x_2 = 20.25$$
$$\text{New contribution } = 3(14.875) + 4(20.25) = £125.625$$
$$\text{Original contribution } = £125$$
$$\text{Difference } = \underline{£0.625}$$
$$\text{thus shadow price per labour hour } = \textbf{£0.625}$$

The two values obtained can be verified by showing that the quantities of the binding constraints at their shadow price valuations do produce the contribution of £125 shown in the optimum solution thus:

$$100(£0.125) + 180(30.625) = £125$$

Notes:
a) Similar results would be obtained in each case if one less hour had been used in the calculations. Verify this yourself.

b) The shadow prices calculated above only apply while the constraint is binding. If, for example, more and more machining hours became available, there would eventually be so many machining hours that they would no longer be scarce and some other constraint would become binding.

Linear Programming is covered in more detail in Quantitative Techniques, *ibid.*

21

Break-even analysis

ASSUMPTIONS BEHIND C-V-P ANALYSIS

1. OBJECTIVES

After studying this chapter you will

- **Understand the uses and assumptions of Break-Even or Cost-Volume-Profit analysis**

- **Know the main CVP analysis formulae**

- **Be able to draw Traditional and Contribution Break-Even charts**

- **Know how to draw Multi-Product Profit Charts**

- **Be aware of the limitations of Break-Even and Profit charts**

- **Understand the differences between the accountant's and economist's break-even charts.**

2. BREAK-EVEN ANALYSIS

This is the term given to the study of the interrelationships between costs, volume and profit at various levels of activity. Frequently these relationships are depicted by graphs, but this is not essential.

The term break-even analysis is the one commonly used, but it is somewhat misleading as it implies that the only concern is with that level of activity which produces neither profit nor loss – the break even point – although the behaviour of costs and profits at other levels is usually of much greater significance. Because of this an alternative term, *cost-volume-profit analysis or C-V-P analysis*, is frequently used and is more descriptive.

3. USES OF C-V-P ANALYSIS

C-V-P analysis uses many of the principles of variable costing and is an important tool in short-term planning. It explores the relationship which exists between costs, revenue, output levels and resulting profit and is more relevant where the proposed changes in the levels of activity are relatively small. In these cases the established cost patterns are likely to continue, so C-V-P analysis may be useful for decision-making. Over greater changes of activity and in the longer term existing cost structures, eg the amount of fixed costs and the marginal cost per unit, are likely to change, so C-V-P analysis becomes less appropriate.

Typical short run decisions where C-V-P analysis can be useful include: choice of sales mix, pricing policies, multi-shift working, and special order acceptance.

4. ASSUMPTIONS BEHIND C-V-P ANALYSIS

Before any formulae are given or graphs drawn, the major assumptions behind C-V-P analysis must be stated. These are:

a. All costs can be resolved into Fixed and Variable elements.

b. Fixed costs will remain constant and Variable costs vary proportionately with activity.

c. Over the activity range being considered costs and revenues behave in a linear fashion.

d. That the only factor affecting costs and revenues is volume.

e. That technology, production methods and efficiency remain unchanged.

f. Particularly for graphical methods that the analysis relates to one product only or to a constant product mix.

g. There are no stock level changes or that stocks are valued at variable cost only.

It will be apparent that these are over simplifying assumptions for many practical problems. It is because of this that C-V-P analysis can only be an approximate guide for decision-making. Nevertheless, by highlighting the interaction of costs, volume, revenue and profit, useful guidance can be provided for managers making short run, tactical decisions.

5. C-V-P ANALYSIS BY FORMULA

C-V-P analysis can be undertaken by graphical means which are dealt with later in this chapter, or by simple formulae which are listed below and illustrated by examples.

a. Break-even-point (in units) $= \dfrac{\textbf{Fixed costs}}{\textbf{Contribution per unit}}$

b. Break-even point (£ sales) $= \dfrac{\textbf{Fixed costs}}{\textbf{Contribution/unit}} \times \textbf{Sales Price per unit}$

$= \textbf{Fixed Costs} \times \dfrac{1}{\textbf{CS ratio}}$

c. CS ratio: $= \dfrac{\textbf{Contribution/unit}}{\textbf{Sales Price per unit}} \times \textbf{100}$

d. Level of Sales to result in target profit (in units) $= \dfrac{\textbf{Fixed costs} + \textbf{Target Profit}}{\textbf{Contribution/unit}}$

e. Level of sales to result in target profit after tax (units)

$$= \textbf{Fixed Cost} + \dfrac{\left(\dfrac{\textbf{Target Profit}}{\textbf{1} - \textbf{Tax Rate}}\right)}{\textbf{Contribution per unit}}$$

f. Level of Sales to result in Target profit (£ sales)

$$= \dfrac{(\textbf{Fixed Cost} + \textbf{Target Profit}) \times \textbf{Sales price/unit}}{\textbf{Contribution per unit}}$$

Note:

The above formulae relate to a single product firm or one with an unvarying mix of sales. With a multi-product firm it is possible to calculate the break-even point as follows:

$$\text{Break-even-point (£ sales)} = \dfrac{\textbf{Fixed Costs} \times \textbf{Sales Value}}{\textbf{Contribution}}$$

Example 1

A company makes a single product with a sales price of £10 and a variable cost of £6. Fixed costs are £60,000 pa.

Calculate:

a. Number of units to break-even

b. Sales at break-even point

c. CS ratio

d. What number of units will need to be sold to achieve a profit of £20,000 pa

e. What level of sales will achieve a profit of £20,000 pa

f. If the taxation rate is 40% how many units will need to be sold to make a profit after tax of £20,000 pa?

g. Because of increasing costs the variable cost is expected to rise to £6.50 per unit and fixed costs to £70,000 pa. If the selling price cannot be increased what will be the number of units required to maintain a profit of £20,000 pa? (Ignore tax.)

Solution

$$\text{Contribution} = \text{Selling price} - \text{Variable cost}$$
$$= £10 - 6$$
$$= \textbf{£4}$$

a. Break-even point (units) $= \dfrac{£60,000}{£4}$
$$= £15,000$$

b. Break-even point (£ sales) $= 15,000 \times £10$
$$= £150,000$$

c. $\text{CS ratio} = \dfrac{£4 \times 100}{£10}$

$= \mathbf{40\%}$

d. $\text{Number of units for target profit} = \dfrac{60,000 + 20,000}{£4}$

$= \mathbf{20,000}$

e. $\text{Sales for target profit} = 20,000 \times £10$

$= \mathbf{£200,000}$

Alternatively, the sales for target profit can be deduced by the following reasoning. After break-even point the contribution per unit becomes net profit per unit, so that as 15,000 units were required at break-even point, 5,000 extra units would be required to make £20,000 profit,

$\therefore$ total units $= 15,000 + 5,000 = 20,000 \times £10 = £200,000$

f. $\text{Number of units for target profit after tax} = \dfrac{£60,000 + £\left(\dfrac{20,000}{1 - 0.4}\right)}{£4}$

$= \mathbf{23,333 \ units}$

g. Note that the fixed costs, variable cost and contribution have changed

$\text{No. of units for target profit} = \dfrac{£70,000 + 20,000}{£3.50}$

$= \mathbf{25,714 \ units}$

6. GRAPHICAL APPROACH

This may be preferred

a. Where a simple overview is sufficient.

b. Where there is a need to avoid a detailed, numerical approach when, for example, the recipients of the information have no accounting background. The basic chart is known as a *Break-even Chart* which can be drawn in two ways. The first is known as the *traditional approach* and the second the *contribution approach*. Whatever approach is adopted, all costs must be capable of separation into fixed and variable elements, ie semi-fixed or semi-variable costs must be analysed into their components.

7. THE TRADITIONAL BREAK-EVEN CHART

Assuming that Fixed and Variable costs have been resolved, the chart is drawn in the following way:

a. *Draw the axes*

- Horizontal showing levels of activity expressed as units of output or as percentages of total capacity.
- Vertical showing values in £s or £000s as appropriate, for costs and revenues.

b. *Draw the cost lines*

- *Fixed cost.*
  This will be a straight line parallel to the horizontal axis at the level of the Fixed costs.

- *Total cost.*
  This will start where the fixed cost line intersects the vertical axis and will be a straight line sloping upward at an angle depending on the proportion of Variable cost in total costs.

c. *Draw the revenue line*

  This will be a straight line from the point of origin sloping upwards at an angle determined by the selling price.

Example 2
A company makes a single product with a total capacity of 400,000 litres pa. Cost and sales data are as follows:

Selling price	£1 per litre
Marginal cost	£0.50 per litre
Fixed costs	£100,000

Draw a traditional break-even chart showing the likely profit at the expected production level of 300,000 litres. See Figure 21.1.

FIGURE 21.1 Traditional break-even chart

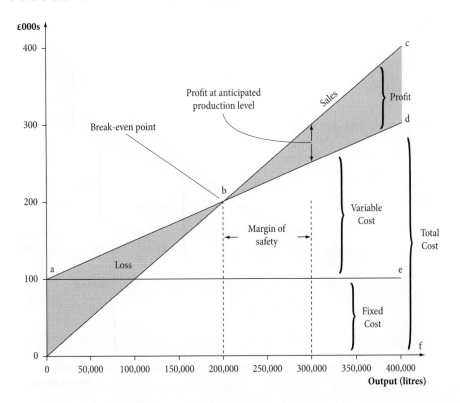

From the graph it will be seen that break-even point is at an output level of 200,000 litres and that the width of the profit wedge indicates the profit at a production level of 300,000. The profit is £50,000.

Note:
The 'margin of safety' indicated on the chart is the term given to the difference between the activity level selected and break-even point. In this case the margin of safety is 100,000 litres which in the more normal multi-product firm would be expressed in sales value.

8. THE CONTRIBUTION BREAK-EVEN CHART

This uses the same axes and data as the traditional chart. The only difference being that Variable Costs are drawn on the chart before Fixed Costs resulting in the contribution being shown as a wedge.

Example 3
Repeat Example 2 except that a contribution break-even chart should be drawn.

Notes on Figure 21.2 (following):
a. The area *c.o.e.* represents the contribution earned. There is no direct equivalent on the traditional chart.

FIGURE 21.2   Contribution break-even chart

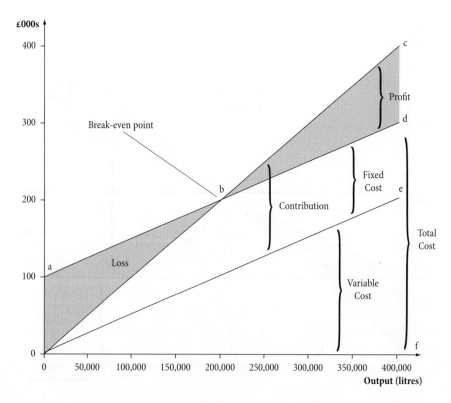

FIGURE 21.3   Alternative form of contribution break-even chart

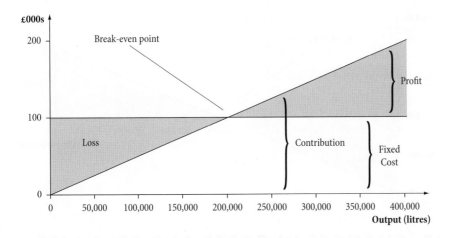

b. The area *d, a, o, f* represents total cost and is the same as the traditional chart.

c. It will be seen from the chart that the reversal of Fixed Costs and Variable Costs enables the contribution wedge to be drawn thus providing additional information.

An alternative form of the contribution break-even chart is where the net difference between sales and variable cost, ie, total contribution, is plotted against fixed costs. This is shown once again using the same data from Example 2.

Notes on Figure 21.3 (following):
a. Sales and Variable costs are not shown directly.

b. Both forms of contribution chart, Figures 21.2 and 21.3, show clearly that contribution is first used to meet fixed costs and when these costs are met the contribution becomes profit.

9. PROFIT CHART

This is another form of presentation with the emphasis on the effect on profit at varying levels of activity. It is a simpler form of chart to those illustrated so far because only a single line is drawn which enables the amount of profit or loss to be shown at various output levels. The horizontal axis is identical to the previous charts, but the vertical axis is continued below the point of origin to show losses. A contribution line is drawn from the loss at zero activity, which is equivalent to the fixed costs, through the break-even point. This type of chart is illustrated in Figure 21.4 using, once again, the data from Example 2.

Note:
Lines for Variable and Fixed Costs and Sales do not appear, merely the one summary line showing contribution at various levels of activity.

FIGURE 21.4 Profit chart

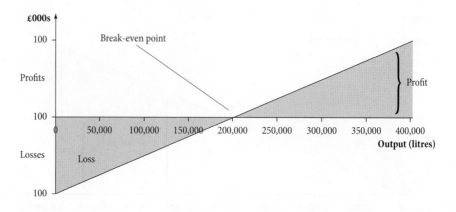

10. CHANGES IN COSTS AND REVENUES

Several of the main types of chart have been described and it should be apparent that they are all able to show cost/revenue/volume/profit relationships in a simple, effective form. It is also possible to show the effect of changes in costs and revenues by drawing additional lines on the charts. The changes are of two types:

a. Fixed cost changes. Increases or decreases in fixed costs do not change the slope of the line, but alter the point of intersection and thus the break-even point.

b. Variable cost and sales price changes. These changes alter the slope of the line thus affecting the break-even point and the shape of the profit and loss 'wedges'.

These changes are illustrated in Figures 21.5 and 21.6 using a Profit-Chart.

Note:
Figure 21.6 shows the effect of Variable cost and/or sales price changes which alter the contribution. If, say, an increase in Variable costs was exactly

FIGURE 21.5 Profit chart showing changes in fixed costs

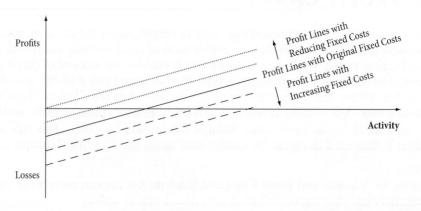

FIGURE 21.6 Profit chart showing changes in contribution ratio

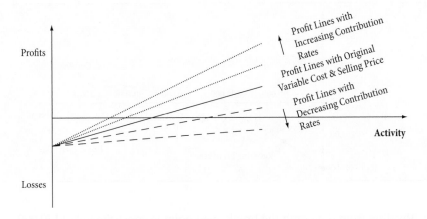

counterbalanced by an increase in sales price, the contribution would be the same and the original profit line would still be correct.

11. MULTI-PRODUCT CHART

All of the charts illustrated so far have assumed a single product. Equally they could have illustrated a given sales mix resulting in an average contribution rate equivalent to a single product. An alternative method is to plot the individual products each with their individual CS characteristics and then show the resulting overall profit line. This is shown below.

Example 4
A firm has fixed costs of £50,000 pa and has three products, the sales and contribution of which are shown below.

Product	Sales £	Contribution £	C/S ratio
X	150,000	30,000	20%
Y	40,000	20,000	50%
Z	60,000	25,000	42%

Plot the products on a profit chart and show the break-even sales.

Solution

The axes on the profit chart are drawn in the usual way and the contribution from the products, in the sequence of their CS ratio, ie Y, Z, X, drawn on the chart (Figure 21.7).

Notes:
a. The solid lines represent the contributions of the various products.
b. The dotted line represents the resulting profit of this particular sales mix and C/S ratios.

FIGURE 21.7 Multi-product profit chart

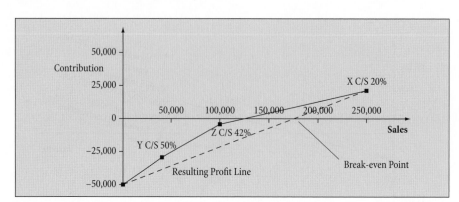

c. Reading from the graph the break-even point is approximately £170,000. The exact figure can be calculated as follows:

Product	Sales £	Contribution £
X	150,000	30,000
Y	40,000	20,000
Z	60,000	25,000
Totals	£250,000	£75,000

$$\text{overall CS ratio} = \frac{£75,000}{£250,000} \qquad = 30\%$$

$$\therefore \text{Break-even point} = \frac{\text{Fixed Costs}}{\text{CS Ratio}}$$
$$= \frac{£50,000}{0.3}$$
$$= £166,667$$

12. LIMITATIONS OF BREAK-EVEN AND PROFIT CHARTS

The various charts depicted show cost, volume and profit relationships in a simplified and approximate manner. They can be useful aids, but whenever they are used the following limitations should not be forgotten.

a. The charts are reasonable pointers to performance within normal activity ranges, say 70% to 120% of average production. Outside this relevant range the relationship depicted almost certainly will not be correct. Although it is conventional to draw the lines starting from zero activity, as they have been drawn in this chapter, relationships at the extremes of activity cannot be relied upon. A typical relevant range of activity could be shown as follows.

b. Fixed costs are likely to change at different activity levels. A stepped fixed cost line is probably the most accurate representation.

FIGURE 21.8   Break-even chart showing relevant activity range

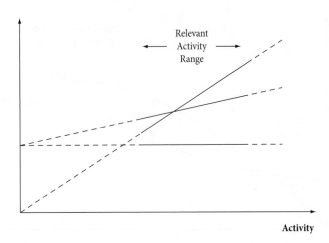

c. Variable costs and sales are unlikely to be linear. Extra discounts, overtime payments, special delivery charges, etc make it likely that variable cost and revenue lines are some form of a curve rather than a straight line.

d. The charts depict relationships which are essentially short term. This makes them inappropriate for planning purposes where the time scale stretches over several years.

e. The charts, and C-V-P analysis make the assumption that all variable costs vary accordingly to the same activity indicator, usually sales or production. This is a gross over-simplification and reduces the accuracy of the charts and C-V-P analysis.

13. THE ACCOUNTANTS' AND ECONOMISTS' VIEW OF BREAK-EVEN CHARTS

The break-even chart used by accountants has been dealt with earlier in the chapter, Figure 21.1. The chart drawn by economists is in Figure 21.9.

Notes on Figure 21.9:

a. More correctly this is a chart showing the point of profit maximisation.

b. BEP No. 2 is at the point where declining aggregate revenues equal increasing aggregate costs. BEP No. 1 is similar, but not exactly equivalent, to the single BEP shown on a typical accounting chart. The reason for the discrepancy is that the costs included in the economists' chart include an allowance for a normal level of profit, which is deemed to be an economic cost, whereas the break-even point on an accounting chart is simply the balancing of accounting costs and revenues.

c. The cost line shows economies of scale at first, then turns upwards as diminishing returns set in.

FIGURE 21.9   Economists' break-even chart

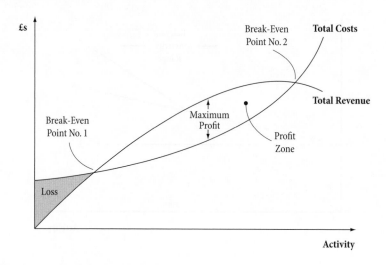

FIGURE 21.10   Accountants' and economists' chart compared

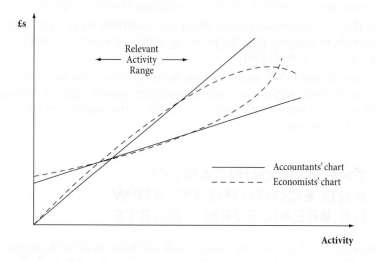

d. The revenue line curves downward on the assumption that selling prices will have to be reduced to increase sales volume.

Within the relevant activity range the differences between the economists' and accountants' chart are not great. The two types of charts are superimposed below.

14. SUMMARY

a. Break-even analysis, or more descriptively, cost-volume-profit analysis studies the relationship between costs, volume, sales and profit.

b. C-V-P analysis is most appropriate for short-run tactical decisions.

c. The major assumptions behind C-V-P analysis are that all costs are resolvable into Fixed and Variable, linearity is assumed, technology and efficiency remain constant and that volume is the only determinant of cost and revenue changes.

d. The main C-V-P formulae are

$$\text{Break-even point} = \frac{\text{Fixed costs}}{\text{Contribution per unit}}$$

$$\text{CS ratio} = \frac{\text{Contribution per unit}}{\text{Selling price per unit}}$$

e. The CS ratio is an important ratio. An alternative term is the PV ratio.

f. Break-even charts can be drawn in two different ways. The 'traditional approach' plots the fixed cost first, then variable costs, the 'contribution approach' reverses the sequence of the cost lines.

g. Profit charts plot profit against the level of activity and are simpler than break-even charts.

h. All of the charts can show the effects of varying fixed costs and/or contribution ratios.

i. Profit charts showing the contributions of various products can be drawn.

j. Break-even charts may provide a useful overview, but they have several limitations including: non-linear and stepped cost functions, difficulties of extrapolation outside normal activity levels and inappropriateness for long-term planning purposes.

k. The economist's break-even chart employs non-linear relationships and shows two break-even points.

l. Over the relevant activity range and in the short run, the accountants' and economists' charts are likely to show a similar picture.

Student self-testing

Exercises (answers below)

1. The launch of a new product is being considered and four possible output levels are being considered depending on consumer reaction. The variable costs associated with these levels are shown below.

Consumer reaction	Adverse	Average	Good	Excellent
Variable Costs (£000s)	20	30	45	70

There are fixed costs of £36,000 and the CS ratio is expected to be 60%.
You are required to calculate:

a. the profit or loss at each of the four levels.

b. the break-even point in sales value.

c. the level of sales at which a profit of £10,000 would be made.

2. The fixed costs of a company are £15,000 and the contributions from the three products are:

Contribution per unit
Product D   £5
Product E   £2.50
Product F   £3.00

The sales forecast is
Product D   1,000 units at £10 each
Product E   5,000 units at £6.50 each
Product F   2,500 units at £7 each

Assuming that the products are always sold in the same proportions you are required to:

a. Plot the above data on a Contribution Break-even Chart and

b. Show the break-even point for the company as a percentage of budgeted activity.

3. A manufacturer incurred the following costs in a period for his sole product:

	£
Labour (25% Variable)	8,000
Materials (100% Variable)	12,000
Selling Costs (10% Variable)	2,000
Other Costs (Fixed)	7,000
Total Costs	£29,000

A normal period's sales are 500 units at £70 each, but up to 650 units could be made in a period. Various alternatives are being considered:

i. Reduce the price to £63 each and sell all that could be made.
ii. Increase the price to £80 each at which price sales would be 400 units.
iii. Keep the present plan.

What is the most profitable plan? What are the CS ratios? What is the break-even point for each alternative?

4. A firm has fixed costs of £25,000 pa and has three products, the details of which are:

Product	Sales (£)	Marginal Cost (£)
A	80,000	40,000
B	130,000	90,000
C	60,000	36,000

Plot the above products on a single profit chart and show the break-even sales.

Solutions to exercises

1. CS ratio is 60% variable costs are 40% of sales. Given the variable costs, the sales for any level can be found as follows:

a. $\dfrac{\text{Variable Costs}}{0.4} = \text{Sales}$

Consumer reaction	Adverse £	Average £	Good £	Excellent £
Sales (£000s)	50	75	112.5	175
less Variable Costs	20	30	45	70
= Contribution	30	45	67.5	105
less Fixed Costs	36	36	36	36
Profit (Loss)	(6)	9	31.5	69

b. Break-even point in sales value $= \dfrac{36,000}{0.6} = £60,000$

c. Level of sales for profit of £10,000 $= \dfrac{36,000 + 10,000}{0.6} = £76,667$

2. Sales will be made in constant proportions

	Forecasted sales value £	Proportion	Variable costs £	Contribution £
Product D	10,000	0.17	5,000	5,000
E	32,500	0.54	20,000	12,500
F	17,500	0.29	10,000	7,500
	60,000	1.00	35,000	25,000

Thus overall C/S ratio $= \dfrac{25,000}{60,000} = 41.67\%$

a. & b. See graph on opposite page.

3. *Variable Costs*

	£
Labour	2,000
Material	12,000
Selling	200
	14,200

Thus cost per unit $= \dfrac{14,200}{500} = £28.4$

As the fixed costs remain the same the contributions of the three options can be considered directly.

i. Contribution $(63 - 28.4) \times 650 = £22,490$
ii. Contribution $(80 - 28.4) \times 400 = £20,640$
iii. Contribution $(70 - 28.4) \times 500 = £20,800$

Thus Option 1 is preferable, ie reduce price to 63 and sell all output.

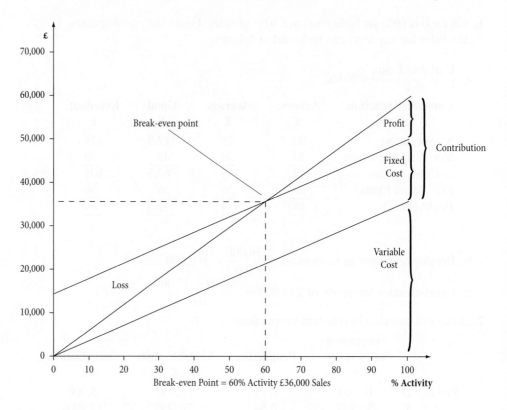

Break-even Point = 60% Activity £36,000 Sales

CS ratios

i. $= \dfrac{34.6}{63} = 55\%$

ii. $= \dfrac{51.6}{80} = 64.5\%$

iii. $= \dfrac{41.6}{70} = 59\%$

$$\text{Break-even point(units)} = \frac{\text{Fixed costs}}{\text{Contribution per unit}}$$

Option

i. $= \dfrac{4,800}{34.6} = 428$ units

ii. $= \dfrac{14,800}{51.6} = 287$ units

iii. $= \dfrac{14,800}{41.6} = 356$ units

4. Multi-Product Profit Chart

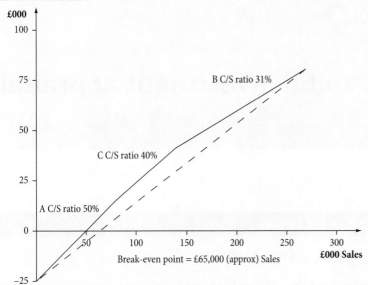

Multi-Product Profit Chart

22

Capital investment appraisal

I. OBJECTIVES

After studying this chapter you will

● **Understand the relationship of long and short-term decision-making**

● **Know why the time value of money is important**

● **Be able to use the two traditional techniques of Accounting Rate of Return and Payback**

● **Understand the principles of Discounted Cash Flow (DCF)**

● **Be able to calculate Net Present Value (NPV), Internal Rate of Return (IRR) and Discounted Payback**

● **Have been introduced to the methods of analysing risk and uncertainty.**

2. LONG RUN DECISION-MAKING

The last two chapters have been concerned with decision-making in the short run, but capital expenditure decisions are decisions where a longer term view must be taken. There are a number of similarities between short-run and long-run decision-making; for example, the choice between alternatives, the need to consider future costs and revenues, the importance of incremental changes in costs and revenues and the irrelevance of sunk costs but there is the additional requirement for investment decisions that, because of the time scale and amount of money involved, the time value of money must be considered. In addition, because of the long term nature of the investments the treatment of uncertainty and inflation becomes of even greater importance than when considering short run decisions.

3. INVESTMENT DECISIONS AND THE ACCOUNTANT

Capital expenditure decision-making is invariably a top management exercise. This is because of the scale and long term nature of the consequences of such decisions. Typically a major capital investment decision, for example, launching a new product, buying a subsidiary or new factory or similar venture, will be the subject of months or even years of investigation and analysis before the final decision is made.

The accountant's task is to gather the essential data from various sources (marketing, engineering, production, etc) from both within and external to the organisation, consider the financing and taxation implications, analyse the data using one or more of the appraisal techniques and present the decision-maker with the results of the analysis so that the decision-maker will be able to take a more informed decision.

No method or technique of investment appraisal is a panacea. All decision-making relates to the future where uncertainties abound; there may be material shortages, new competitors and products may arise, there may be strikes, changes in tastes, wars or floods – the list is endless. This means that overly sophisticated appraisal methods and pedantic, decimal point accuracy in the results presented probably serve little purpose.

It must be remembered that the accountant does not take the investment decision nor does he provide all the basic information. He performs an essential role in collating and analysing the data and presenting the results to the decision-maker.

4. THE DECISION TO INVEST

Assuming that finance is available the decision to invest will be based on three main factors.

a. The investor's beliefs about the future. Surveys have consistently shown that confidence in the future is a more important influence than such factors as marginal taxation and interest rates.

b. The alternatives available in which to invest. The various techniques covered in the rest of this chapter help to decide whether any of the alternatives being considered are worthwhile and, if so, which of the competing investment opportunities is the most favourable.

c. The investor's attitude to risk. The potential return from investment is conventionally expected to be proportional to the risk involved. The risk associated with individual projects and with combinations of projects and the decision makers attitude to risk are all key factors in investment decisions.

Numerous investment appraisal techniques are available to assist with investment decisions but, however sophisticated, they have the common characteristics that they *compare the returns expected* with the *investment required*.

The techniques covered in this book are the two 'traditional' techniques of Accounting Rate of Return and the Payback method and the two most common Discounted Cash Flow (DCF) techniques, Net Present Value and Internal Rate of Return.

5. ACCOUNTING RATE OF RETURN (ARR)

This can be defined as the ratio of average profits, after depreciation, to the capital invested. This is a basic definition only and various interpretations are possible, ie:

a. Profits may be before or after tax.

b. Capital invested may be the initial capital invested or the average capital invested over the life of the project, ie:

c. $$\frac{\textbf{Initial investment}}{2}$$

d. Capital may or may not include working capital.

Example 1
A firm is considering three projects each with an initial investment of £2,500 and a life of five years. The estimated annual profits are as follows:

After Tax and Depreciation Profits

Year	Project A £	Project B £	Project C £
1	250	500	100
2	250	450	100
3	250	100	100
4	250	100	450
5	250	100	500
	1,250	1,250	1,250

Calculate the ARR based on:

a. Initial capital invested.

b. Average capital invested.

Solution

	Project A	Project B	Project C
Average profits	$\frac{£1,250}{5}$	$\frac{£1,250}{5}$	$\frac{£1,250}{5}$
	= £250 pa	= £250 pa	= £250 pa

∴ ARR (based on initial capital of £2,500)

$$= \frac{250}{2,500} = 10\% = \frac{250}{2,500} = 10\% \quad = \frac{250}{2,500} = 10\%$$

∴ ARR (based on average capital of £1,250)

$$= \frac{250}{1,250} = 20\% = \frac{250}{1,250} = 20\% \quad = \frac{250}{1,250} = 20\%$$

6. ADVANTAGES AND DISADVANTAGES OF ARR

The only advantage that can be claimed for ARR is simplicity of calculation but the disadvantages are more numerous. Disadvantages:

a. Ignores the timings of outflows and inflows. The three projects in Example 1 are ranked equally yet there are clear differences in the timings involved.

b. Uses a measure of return the concept of accounting profit. Profit has subjective elements, is subject to accounting conventions and is not as appropriate for investment decision-making as the cash flows generated by the project.

c. There is no universally accepted method of calculating ARR.

Note:
Alternative names for the ARR are; Return on Capital Employed and Return on Investment. The use of ARR alone is not recommended.

7. PAYBACK

This is a commonly used technique which can be defined as:

> *The time required for the cash inflows from a capital investment project to equal the cash outflows.*
>
> *Terminology*

The usual decision rule is to accept the project with the shortest payback period.

Note:
particularly that Payback is based on *cash flows* not profit.

Example 2
Calculate the payback period for each of the following three projects.

	Project A		Project B		Project C	
Years	Annual Cash Flow	Cumulative Cash Flow	Annual Cash Flow	Cumulative Cash Flow	Annual Cash Flow	Cumulative Cash Flow
0	−2,000	−2,000	−2,000	−2,000	2,000	−2,000
1	+800	−1,200	+500	−1,500	+600	−1,400
2	+700	−500	+700	−800	+700	−700
3	+500	Nil	+800	Nil	+500	−200
4	−		−		+200	Nil
5	−		−		+300	+300
6	−		−		+500	+800

Payback periods:

Project A = 3 years

Project B = 3 years

Project C = 4 years

Note:

The usual investment appraisal assumptions are adopted for the above table and all subsequent examples; that Year 0 means now, Year 1 means at the end of one year, Year 2 the end of two years and so on and that a negative sign represents a cash outflow and a positive sign represents a cash inflow.

8. ADVANTAGES AND DISADVANTAGES OF PAYBACK

Advantages:

a. Simple to understand and calculate.

b. Is more objectively based because it uses project cash flows rather than accounting profits.

c. Favours quick return projects which may produce faster growth for the firm and enhance liquidity.

d. Choosing projects which payback quickest will tend to minimise time related risks. However not all risks are related merely to time elapsed.

Disadvantages:

a. Payback is a rough measure of liquidity not overall project worth. In Example 2, Project C is ranked after Project A and B even though it produces cash flows over a six-year period.

b. Payback provides only a crude measure of the timing of project cash flows. In Example 2, Project A and B are ranked equally even though there are clear differences in the timings of cash flows.

Various surveys have shown that Payback, either used by itself or in conjunction with some other technique, is the most popular appraisal technique so it is important that its strengths and weaknesses are fully understood by the student.

9. DISCOUNTED CASH FLOW (DCF)

All DCF measures use *cash flows* and make due allowance for the time value of money. These two features are expanded below:

Use of cash flows

All DCF methods use cash flows and not accounting profits. Accounting profits are invariably calculated for stewardship purposes and are period orientated thus necessitating accrual accounting with its conventions and assumptions.

For investment appraisal purposes a project orientated approach using cash flows is preferred because it is more objective and the accounting conventions regarding such matters as revenue/capital expenditure and stock valuation become largely redundant. The cash flows to be included are the *net after tax incremental cash flow effect* of the project, ie the difference in cash flow between *having* and *not having* the project.

Time value of money

There is general acceptance that any serious attempt at investment appraisal must make due allowance for the time value of money. Money has a time productivity, ie money received earlier can be put to use, for example, it can be invested to earn interest. This means that sums arising at different times cannot be compared directly, they must be reduced to equivalent values at some common date. The common date may be at any time but discounting methods typically use now, ie the present time, as the common date.

The two main DCF methods of Net Present Value (NPV) and Internal Rate of Return (IRR) are described below.

10. NET PRESENT VALUE

The NPV is the value in present day terms of the various cash inflows and outflows expected to arise at differing periods in the future. To find the NPV it is necessary first to calculate or estimate a discounting rate which is known as the cost of capital. The calculation of the cost of capital is a complex process but for the stage of studies we are concerned with the cost of capital is normally provided.

The formula for NPV is as follows:

$$NPV = \sum \frac{C_i}{(1+r)^i}$$

where

C_i is the cash flow ($+$ or $-$) at period i.

i is the period number.

r is the cost of capital.

The discount factor $\frac{1}{(1+r)i}$ can be found using a calculator but it is normal to use discount tables (see Table A). The Table shows the discount factors for discount rates ranging from 1% to 30% and for periods (usually years) from 1 to 25. For example, the discount factors for 10% for the first five years are:

$$0.909, \ 0.826, \ 0.751, \ 0.683 \text{ and } 0.621$$

Example 3

The following cash flows have been estimated for a project:

Year	0	1	2	3	4	5
	$-2,000$	$+400$	$+600$	$+700$	$+600$	$+500$

It is required to calculate the project NPV and state whether the project is acceptable assuming that the cost of capital is either:

a. 10% or

b. 20%.

Solution

a. NPV when cost of capital is 10%

$$NPV = -£2,000 + (400 \times 0.909) + (600 \times 0.826)$$
$$+ (700 \times 0.751) + (600 \times 0.683) + (500 \times 0.621)$$
$$= + £105$$

As the project NPV is positive at the cost of capital the project is acceptable (given the assumptions inherent in the basic NPV model).

b. NPV when cost of capital is 20%

$$NPV = -£2,000 + (400 \times 0.833) + (600 \times 0.694)$$
$$+ (700 \times 0.579) + (600 \times 0.482) + (500 \times 0.402)$$
$$= -£355$$

As the NPV is negative at the cost of capital the project is unacceptable (given the usual DCF assumptions).

Notes:

a. The capital investment of –£2,000 at year 0 does not need discounting because it is already in present day terms.

b. It will be seen that the higher the discounting rate the lower the NPV. In this case the higher rate (20%) makes the project unacceptable.

c. The present value of a project, if positive, can be interpreted as the potential increase in consumption made possible by the project, valued in present day terms.

11. INTERNAL RATE OF RETURN (IRR)

The IRR can be defined as the discount rate which gives zero NPV. If the answers to Example 3 are studied it will be seen that they range from a positive NPV at 10% to a negative NPV at 20%. It follows that at some discount rate between the two the NPV will be zero, ie:

Discount rate	10%	? %	20%
NPV	+105	0	−355

The value of the IRR can be found graphically or more normally, by linear interpolation thus:

$$IRR = 10\% + 10\% \times \frac{105}{460} = 12.3\%$$

where:

A is the discount rate which gives a positive NPV (ie, 10% in this example)

B is the difference between the discount rates chosen to give positive and negative NPVs (ie 20% – 10% in this example)

C is the value of positive NPV (£105 in this example)

D is the range of NPV values (from + 105 to – 355, ie a range of 460 in this example).

The IRR is used to determine whether the project is acceptable or not by comparing the calculated IRR with the cost of capital. Thus in Example 3, where two possible costs of capital were considered, the comparison is as follows:

Project IRR 12.3%

- When cost of capital is 10%, the project is *acceptable* because IRR of 12.3% is greater than the cost of capital.
- When cost of capital is 20%, the project is *not acceptable* because IRR of 12.3% is less than the cost of capital.

Notes:
a. It will be seen that both NPV and IRR give the same accept or reject decision. For most projects this is always the case but note that the ranking of a group of projects may differ using NPV as opposed to IRR.
b. For normal decision-making purposes it is sufficient to calculate either NPV or IRR and base the decision on the chosen criterion.
c. Although NPV has certain technical advantages over IRR, IRR is commonly used in practice.

12. DISCOUNTED PAYBACK

Payback, described in para 7, uses the raw project cash flows to determine how long the project will take to recoup the original investment. There are two major deficiencies with simple payback. It ignores results beyond the payback period and does not take into account timing differences within the payback period. The calculated payback period can only be a valid indicator of the time that a project will take to recoup the original investment when the project's cash flows are discounted at the cost of capital and used on the payback calculation. This is then known as *discounted payback*.

Example 4
Two projects have the following cash flows.

	X	Y
Year 0	−20,000	−20,000
1	+4,000	+4,000
2	+8,000	+4,000
3	+8,000	+4,000
4	+8,000	+8,000
5	+4,000	+12,000
6		+12,000
7		+12,000

Required:

(a) Calculate the simple payback periods.

(b) Calculate both NPVs using a 10% cost of capital.

(c) Calculate the discounted payback periods.

(d) Comment on your results.

Solution

(a) Project X pays back in three years whereas Y takes four years.

(b) The discounted cash flows are as follows:

	Cash Flows	Discounted at 10%	Cash Flows	Discounted at 10%
Year 0	−20,000	−20,000	−20,000	−20,000
1	4,000	3,636	4,000	3,636
2	8,000	6,608	4,000	3,304
3	8,000	6,008	4,000	3,004
4	8,000	5,464	8,000	5,464
5	4,000	2,484	12,000	7,452
6			12,000	6,758
7			12,000	6,156
NPV		4,200		15,784

The payback periods based on the discounted values are just under four years for *X*, ie (3,636 + 6,608 + 6,008 + 5,464) and just under five years for *Y*, ie (3,636 + 3,304 + 3,004 + 5,464 + 7,452).

(c) Both simple and discounted payback indicate that *X* is the better project. However *Y* has a much larger NPV and would be the preferred project because account is taken of the returns after the payback period.

13. COST OF CAPITAL

The cost of capital is the name given to the discount rate used in NPV calculations and for the rate against which the calculated IRR is compared. In many examination questions the cost of capital is supplied but, on occasion, it is necessary to make an estimate of its value. There are various ways of making this estimate. One frequently used method produces what is known as the *Weighted Average Cost of Capital* (WACC).

The WACC recognises that companies are complex entities and that they are funded from a number of sources. The WACC is found by calculating the average of the costs of each component of the firms finances, eg equity, preference shares, debentures and so on. The average is found by weighting the various sources by their proportionate share of the total pool of capital available.

Example 5
Multi-Source Ltd. has the following long-term sources of capital:

- 8 million £1 Ordinary Shares with a market value of £1.80 per share and an estimated cost of 18%.

- 3 million £1 Preference Shares with a market value of 80p and an estimated cost of 12%.

- £10 million of Debenture Stock with a market value of £90 per £100 nominal value and an estimated cost of 7%.

Calculate the WACC

Solution

Component	Market Value £	Proportion	Individual cost	Weighted cost
Ord Shares	8m × £1.8 = 14.4m	56%	18%	0.56 × 18% = 10.08%
Pref. Shares	3m × 80p = 2.4m	9%	12%	0.09 × 12% = 1.08%
Debentures	10m × 0.9 = 9m	35%	7%	0.35 × 7% = 2.45%
Total	25.8m	100%		13.61%

∴ The weighted average cost of capital = 13.61%. It is likely that this would be rounded up to 14% for discounting use.

Notes:

a. The proportions are based on market values not nominal values.

b. Further coverage of WACC and other methods of calculating the Cost of Capital is given in *Management Accounting* by T. Lucey, Cengage Learning.

14. RISK AND UNCERTAINTY IN INVESTMENT APPRAISAL

As pointed out earlier in the chapter it is important to make some form of appraisal of the risk and uncertainty associated with a project as well as the basic NPV or IRR calculation. This is so that the decision-maker is provided with more information about a critical aspect of the project. It can be positively misleading to produce just a single NPV value or IRR percentage when many of the factors involved in the project (eg the sales volume and price, labour rates, material prices and so on) are subject to uncertainty.

There are many approaches to the problems of assessing risk and uncertainty in project appraisal and three simple approaches (payback, sensitivity analysis and expected value) are outlined below. More sophisticated methods are discussed in detail in *Management Accounting*, ibid.

15. PAYBACK AS A MEASURE OF RISK

Payback has already been described in Para 7 as a possible way of appraising whether or not to accept a project. The technique can also be used in conjunction with NPV or IRR, to provide a simple measure of the risk associated with a project. For example if two projects both had an NPV of approximately £10,000 but one had a payback period of $4\frac{1}{2}$ years and the other six years, the former project would be preferred.

Used in this way Payback can provide some assistance in assessing time related risks but obviously factors other than elapsed time influence risk.

16. SENSITIVITY ANALYSIS

This is a technique which, although simple in principle, requires numerous calculations. It is a practical way of showing the effects of uncertainty by varying the values of key factors (eg, sales price, sales volume, rates of inflation, cost per unit) one at a time and showing the effect of the variation on the project outcome. The objective is to identify which of the factors affects the outcome the most.

For example, assume that a project (using single value estimates) has a positive NPV of £50,000 with a 15% cost of capital. Once this basic value of NPV has been obtained, the sensitivity analysis is carried out by flexing, both upwards and downwards, each of the project factors in turn. Part of the sensitivity analysis is given below relating to two of the project elements: sales price per unit and cost per unit.

Sensitivity Analysis Abstract Basic NPV Value £50,000

A Element to be varied	B Alteration from basic	C Revised NPV	D Increase/ Decrease	E Percentage change	F Sensitivity Factor (E ÷ B)
Sales price	+15	90,000	40,000	+80%	5.33
(Basic value £10	+10%	65,000	15,000	+30%	3
per unit)	−10%	32,000	−18,000	−36%	3.6
	−20%	18,000	−32,000	−64%	3.2
Cost per unit	+20%	−21,000	−71,000	−142%	7.1
(Basic value £5.5	+10%	15,000	−35,000	−70%	7
per unit)	−10%	76,000	+26,000	+52%	5.2
	−20%	94,000	+44,000	+88%	4.4

Sensitivity analysis is a useful way of identifying the most sensitive variables but it gives no indication of the likelihood of a given variation occurring and the process of flexing one factor at a time and holding others constant is almost certainly an unrealistic representation of reality where multiple and interacting changes occur.

17. EXPECTED VALUE

Expected value is a simple way of bringing some of the effects of uncertainty into the appraisal process. Expected value is the average value of an event which has several possible outcomes. The expected value or average is found by multiplying the value of each outcome by its probability. The probability of an outcome (probability could also be called the likelihood or chance of the outcome occurring) is based on the judgement of the people concerned.

For example, assume that it is required to forecast the sales for next month. The Sales Manager thinks that there is a 40% (or 0.4) chance that sales will be 10,000 units and a 60% (or 0.6) chance that they will be 13,000 units. What is the expected value of sales?

$$\text{Expected sales value} = (10,000 \times 0.4) + (13,000 \times 0.6)$$
$$= \textbf{11,800 units}.$$

Thus, the use of expected value enables the variabilities and their likelihoods, that is the uncertainties, to be incorporated into the information. Where several alternatives are being considered each of which has several outcomes the usual decision rule is to choose the option with the highest expected value.

Example 6 – Expected values in investment appraisal

Three options are being considered, each of which has several possible outcomes. The values and probabilities have been estimated as follows:

Option A Outcomes		Option B Outcomes		Option C Outcomes	
Probability	NPV £	Probability	NPV £	Probability	NPV £
0.3	8,000	0.2	4,000	0.3	2,500
0.7	11,000	0.3	7,000	0.4	9,000
		0.4	10,000	0.3	15,000
		0.1	14,000		

Required:

Calculate the expected values of the three options and recommend which should be accepted.

Solution
Expected net present values

Option A

$$(0.3 \times 8,000) + (0.7 \times 11,000) = \pounds 10,100$$

Option B

$$(0.2 \times 4,000) + (0.3 \times 7,000) \times (0.4 \times 10,000) + (0.1 \times 14,000) = \pounds 8,300$$

Option C

$$(0.3 \times 2,500) + (0.4 \times 9,000) + (0.3 \times 15,000) = \pounds 8,850$$

Thus, on the basis of Expected Net Present Value, Option A would be preferred and the options would be ranked ACB.

Notes:
(a) In each case it will be seen that the probabilities total 1 (or 100%). This shows that all outcomes have been included.

(b) The number of outcomes can vary as shown in the example but a commonly encountered situation is that shown for Option C where there are three outcomes: often termed Optimistic, Most Likely and Pessimistic.

18. POST AUDIT OF INVESTMENT DECISIONS AND APPRAISALS

The various approaches to investment appraisal covered in this chapter are aids to the process of investment decision-making and naturally take place before the actual investment decision.

Useful information can also be obtained from carrying out a post audit review after the investment decision has been taken and the project initiated. It is usual to carry out such a post audit during the life of a project and at its conclusion. Most value will be obtained when, like all forms of audit, the investment post audit is carried out by different people to those involved in the original appraisal and decision.

The objectives of the post audit are to derive information which will improve future appraisal and forecasting methods, refine the decision process and to develop and extend good practices revealed by the post audit while, hopefully, eliminating poor practice. The objective is NOT to be negative and to attach blame to individuals for judgements and decisions honestly made which turn out to be incorrect.

The various factors covered in a typical post audit include:

a. Comparison of forecast and actual results for each of the project elements, ie sales price, volume, costs, inflation and so on.

b. Review of the forecasting methods used to assess their accuracy and appropriateness.

c. Review of the sources of information used for the appraisal.

d. Review of the appraisal and analysis carried out. For example, was Payback or DCF used in an appropriate manner? Was any form of risk analysis employed?

e. Review of the unforeseen factors which arose. Could these have been foreseen by a more rigorous appraisal?

f. Review of the decision process. Was the decision reasonable in the light of the evidence available at the time? Could the decision process be improved?

19. EXTENSIONS OF BASIC INVESTMENT APPRAISAL

The contents of this chapter are merely a simple introduction to a field which is a specialisation in its own right. More advanced investment appraisal includes such matters as: dealing with inflation, the problem of combinations of projects, capital rationing, the factors governing the choice of the cost of capital and many other problems. Many of the more advanced aspects are covered in *Management Accounting* ibid.

In practice, investment appraisal is a lengthy complex task involving a range of technical specialists, a variety of forecasts and detailed study of all aspects of the proposal. Organisations do not generally rely on just one measure of appraisal, whether it be NPV, IRR, Paypack or whatever but calculate several measures in order to assess projects in more depth.

As an example of the range of factors considered in a real project and of the appraisal measures calculated consider the following outline relating to Largo resources.

FIGURE 22.1 Largo Resources Ltd

Largo Resources Ltd. (TSX VENTURE: LGO) is pleased to announce that it has received preliminary indicative terms from Investec Bank (UK) Limited ("Investec") to arrange up to 75% of the projected capital cost of developing the Maracas vanadium project (the "Project") in Bahia, Brazil. The final nature and terms of any financing will depend on the results of due diligence and prevailing market conditions and is predicated on Aker Kvaerner's ongoing feasibility study confirming the project economics set out in last month's Scoping Study prepared by Micon International Ltd. ("Micon"). The Feasibility Study for the Maracas vanadium project is scheduled for completion by June 30, 2008.

Largo President and CEO Mark Brennan commented: "we are buoyed by Investec's expression of interest and believe it supports our view of Maracas' exciting potential as a highly robust, world-class vanadium deposit."

The scoping study prepared for Largo by Micon was previously referenced in a December 10, 2007 news release. Based on an estimated initial capital investment of US$126.2 million and the milling of 14,633,000 tonnes of open pit material at a diluted grade of 1.29% vanadium pentoxide the project has a discounted payback period of 3 years and generates cashflows of US$683 million over an estimated production life of 26 years. This results in a pre-tax IRR of 40.7% and a pre-tax NPV of US$212 million at a discount rate of 10% per year.

Price forecasts for vanadium pentoxide were commissioned from CRU of London, England. The base case view of the CRU forecast is that the long-term price of vanadium pentoxide will stabilise at approximately $5.00 per lb. The open pit mine design was based on a pit shell reflecting this long-term price. The Measured and Indicated Mineral Resource at Maracas (Gulcari "A") at $5.00 per lb vanadium pentoxide consistent with a cut-off grade of 0.36% has been estimated by Micon to be 22.5 million tonnes grading 1.27% vanadium pentoxide, including a high-grade zone of 8.4 million tonnes grading 2.0% vanadium pentoxide. Based on this previously announced resource estimate, Gulcari "A" has 624 million lbs of contained vanadium pentoxide. Mineral resources that are not mineral reserves do not have demonstrated economic viability.

20. SUMMARY

a. There are similarities between short run and long run decision-making but the time value of money must be considered in long run decision-making.

b. The accountant's role in investment appraisal is to collate data, consider the financing and taxation implications, analyse the data and present the information to the decision-maker.

c. The decision to invest is based on the investor's beliefs in the future, the alternatives available and the decision-maker's attitude to risk.

d. The Accounting Rate of Return (ARR) is the ratio of average profits, after depreciation, to the capital invested.

e. Payback is the period, usually in years, in which it takes for the project's cash flows to recoup the original investment.

f. Discounted Cash Flow (DCF) techniques are based on cash flows, not profits, and take due allowance for the time value of money.

g. Net Present Value (NPV) is a DCF technique which calculates the value in present day terms of the cash inflows and outflows. If the NPV is positive at the company's cost of capital the project is acceptable.

h. Internal Rate of Return (IRR) is the discount rate which gives zero NPV. If the calculated IRR is greater than the cost of capital the project is acceptable.

i. The Weighted Average Cost of Capital is the weighted cost of the individual sources of capital.

j. Risk and uncertainty are ever present in project appraisals and the decision-maker should be provided with information about expected project risk.

k. Two simple ways of assessing risk and uncertainty are Payback and Sensitivity Analysis.

l. A post audit review is a useful way of improving forecasting, appraisal and decision methods.

21. POINTS TO NOTE

a. It will be apparent that a critical factor in investment appraisal is the quality of forecasting.

b. Arguably of more importance than the particular method of appraisal is the existence of a stream of profitable investment opportunities. These do not automatically arise – they have to be sought out and developed.

c. Regular cash flows commonly occur, for example, lease and rent payments and a short cut discounting method is possible using Present Value Annuity Factors, Table B.

For example, assume that there is a regular cash flow of £500 pa for three years and it is required to calculate the present value when the discounting rate is 10%. This could be calculated by multiplying the yearly cash flows by the separate discount factors from Table A, ie:

$$£(500 \times 0.909) + (500 \times 0.826) + (500 \times 0.751) = £1,243$$

or alternatively the annuity factor can be found from Table B for three years at 10%, ie 2.487.

$$\therefore \text{ Present value} = £500 \times 2.487 = £1,243$$

Student self-testing

Exercises (answers below)

1. The cash flows for two projects are given below:

Year		Project X	Project Y
	0	−5,000	−8,000
	1	+2,500	+1,500
	2	+1,000	+2,000
	3	+1,000	+2,500
	4	+500	+1,000
	5	+1,500	+1,000
	6	+1,000	+2,500

Calculate the Payback period for the above projects and their NPV assuming that the cost of capital is 12%.

2. Find the Internal Rates of Return of the projects in Exercise 1 using graphical methods.

3. A firm with a cost of capital of 10% has estimated that it will have to pay its Sales Manager the following amounts of commission at the end of each of the next five years:

Year	1	2	3	4	5
	£4,000	£2,000	£8,000	£3,000	£10,000

The Sales Manager would prefer to receive a regular amount at the end of each year. Calculate this amount.

Solutions to exercises

1.

		Project X		**Project Y**	
		Cash Flow	**Cumulative**	**Cash Flow**	**Cumulative**
Year	0	−5,000	−5,000	−8,000	−8,000
	1	+2,500	−2,500	+1,500	−6,500
	2	+1,000	−1,500	+2,000	−4,500
	3	+1,000	−500	+2,500	−2,000
	4	+500		+1,000	−1,000
	5	+1,500	+1,500	+1,000	−
	6	+1,000	+1,000	+2,500	+2,500

Pay Back: *Project X* = 4 years
Project Y = 5 years

NPV Calculations

Project X

$$NPV = -5{,}000 + (2{,}500 \times 0.893) + (1{,}000 \times 0.797) + (1{,}000 \times 0.712)$$
$$+ (500 \times 0.636) + (1{,}500 \times 0.567) + (1{,}000 \times 0.507)$$
$$= £417 \text{ ie, Acceptable.}$$

Project Y

$$NPV = -8{,}000 + (1{,}500 \times 0.893) + (2{,}000 \times 0.797)$$
$$+ (2{,}500 \times 0.712) + (1{,}000 \times 0.636) + (1{,}000 \times 0.567)$$
$$+ (2{,}500 \times 0.507)$$
$$= -£816 \text{ ie, Not acceptable.}$$

2.

Present Value Profile of Project X

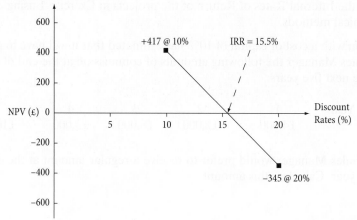

Present Value Profile of Project Y

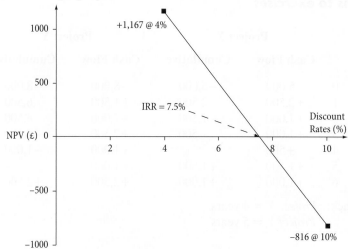

3. Present value of existing commission

$$= (4{,}000 \times 0.909) + (2{,}000 \times 0.826) + (8{,}000 \times 0.751)$$
$$+ (3{,}000 \times 0.683) + (10{,}000 \times 0.621) = \pounds19{,}555$$

Annuity factor for 5 years @ 10% = 3.791

$$\therefore \text{Regular amount} = \frac{19{,}555}{3.791} = \pounds5{,}158$$

(ie, £5,158 received annually for 5 years at 10% discount has a present value of £19,555.)

Assessment section 4

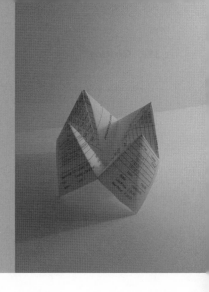

EXAMINATION QUESTIONS (ANSWERS ON WEBSITE)

A4.1 The following extract is taken from the production cost budget of S Limited:

Production (units)	2,000	3,000
Production cost (£)	11,100	12,900

The budget cost allowance for an activity level of 4,000 units is

A   £7,200
B   £14,700
C   £17,200
D   £22,200
E   none of these values.

A4.2 Z Limited manufactures a single product, the budgeted selling price and variable cost details of which are as follows:

	£
Selling price	15.00
Variable costs per unit:	
Direct materials	3.50
Direct labour	4.00
Variable overhead	2.00

Budgeted fixed overhead costs are £60,000 per annum charged at a constant rate each month. Budgeted production is 30,000 units per annum. In a month when actual production was 2,400 units and exceeded sales by 180 units, the profit reported under absorption costing was:

A   £6,660
B   £7,570
C   £7,770
D   £8,200
E   £8,400

A4.3 The actual output of 162,500 units and actual fixed costs of £87,000 were exactly as budgeted. However, the actual expenditure of £300,000 was £18,000 over budget.

What was the budgeted variable cost per unit?

A   £1.20
B   £1.85
C   £1.31
D   It cannot be calculated without more information.

A4.4 Q Limited has in stock 10,000 kg of V, a raw material which it bought for £5 per kg five years ago. This was bought for a product line which was discontinued four years ago. At present, V has no use in its existing state but could be sold as scrap for £1.50 per kg. One of the company's current products (QX) requires 2kg of a raw material which is available for £4.50 per kg. V can be modified at a cost of £1 per kg so that it may be used as a substitute for this material. However, after modification, 3kg of V is required for every unit of QX to be produced.

Q Limited has now received an invitation to tender for a product which could use V in its present state.

The relevant cost per kg of V to be included in the cost estimate for the tender is

A   £1.00
B   £1.50
C   £2.00
D   £4.50
E   £5.00

A4.5 H Limited manufactures and sells two products – J and K. Annual sales are expected to be in the ratio of J:1 K:3. Total annual sales are planned to be £420,000. Product J has a contribution to sales ratio of 40% whereas that of product K is 50%. Annual fixed costs are estimated to be £120,000.

The budgeted break-even sales value (to the nearest £1,000)

A   is £196,000
B   is £200,000
C   is £253,000
D   is £255,000
E   cannot be determined from the above data.

A4.6 Z Limited manufactures three products, the selling price and cost details of which are given below:

	Product X £	Product Y £	Product Z £
Selling price per unit	75	95	95
Costs per unit:			
Direct materials (£5/kg)	10	5	15
Direct labour (£4/kg)	16	24	20
Variable overhead	8	12	10
Fixed overhead	24	36	30

In a period when direct materials are restricted in supply, the most and the least profitable uses of direct materials are

	Most profitable	Least profitable
A	X	Z
B	Y	Z
C	X	Y
D	Z	Y
E	Y	X

A4.7 A company made 17,500 units at a total cost of £16 each. Three-quarters of the costs were variable and one quarter fixed. 15,000 units were sold at £25 each. There were no opening stocks. By how much will the profit calculated using absorption costing principles differ from the profit if marginal costing principles had been used?

A   The absorption costing profit would be £22,500 less.
B   The absorption costing profit would be £10,000 greater.
C   The absorption costing profit would be £135,000 greater.
D   The absorption costing profit would be £10,000 less.

The following information relates to questions A4.8 and A4.9.
JJ Limited manufactures a product which has a selling price of £14, a variable cost of £6 per unit. The company incurs annual fixed costs of £24,400. Annual sales demand is 8,000 units.
New production methods are under consideration, which would cause a 30% increase in fixed costs and a reduction in variable cost to £5 per unit. The new production methods would result in a superior product and would enable sales to be increased to 8,500 units per annum at a price of £15 each.

A4.8 If the change in production methods were to take place, the break-even output level would be:

A   122 units higher
B   372 units higher
C   610 units lower
D   915 units higher

A4.9 If the organisation implements the new production methods and wishes to achieve the same profit as that under the existing method, how many units would need to be produced and sold annually to achieve this?

A   7,132 units
B   8,000 units
C   8,500 units
D   9,710 units

A4.10 P Limited is considering accepting a contract. The materials required for the contract are currently held in stock at a book value of £3,000. The materials are not regularly used by the organisation and currently have a scrap value of £500. Current replacement cost for the materials is £4,500. What is the relevant cost to P Limited of using the materials on this contract?

A   £500
B   £3,500
C   £4,500
D   £5,000

A4.11 An organisation currently produces one product. The cost per unit of that product is as follows:

	£
Selling price	130
Direct materials	22
Direct labour	15
Direct expenses	3
Variable overheads	10
Total variable cost	50

Total fixed costs for the period amount of £1,600,000. How many units (to the nearest whole unit) will the organisation need to produce and sell to generate a profit of £250,000?

A   20,000
B   20,555
C   23,125
D   26,428

A4.12 The following data relate to two output levels of a department in two periods.

	Period 1	Period 2
Labour hours	14,000	18,000
Overheads	£277,500	£321,880

If there was 4% cost inflation between the two periods, what was the variable overhead rate per labour hour (to 2 decimal places) in period 1?

A   £8.00
B   £11.09
C   £17.88
D   £19.82

A4.13 After analysis, it has been found that a particular cost can be represented by the function $y = ax + bx^3$

where $y =$ total cost
        $a =$ machine hours
        $b =$ labour hours
and $x =$ standard hours produced

The cost depicted is:

A   a linear variable cost
B   a linear semi-variable cost
C   a non-linear semi-variable cost
D   a non-linear variable cost

A4.14 The following data have been extracted from the budget working papers of BL Limited:

Production volume	1,000 units	2,000 units
	£ per unit	£ per unit
Direct materials	8.00	8.00
Direct labour	7.00	7.00
Production overhead – department 1	12.00	8.40
Production overhead – department 2	8.00	4.00

The total fixed cost and variable cost per unit are:

	Total fixed cost £	Variable cost per unit £
A	7,200	15.00
B	7,200	19.80
C	8,000	23.40
D	15,200	15.00
E	15,200	19.80

A4.15 In order to utilise some spare capacity, Y Limited is preparing a quotation for a special order which requires 1,000 kgs of material R. Y Limited has 600 kgs of material R in stock (original cost £10.00 per kg). Material R is used in the company's main product Q. Each unit of Q uses 3 kgs of material R and based on an input value of £10.00 per kg of R, each unit of Q yields a contribution of £18.00.

The resale value of material R is £8.00 per kg. The present replacement price of R is £12.00 per kg. Material R is readily available in the market. The relevant cost of the 1,000 kgs of material R to be included in the quotation is:

A	£8,000
B	£10,000
C	£10,800
D	£12,000
E	£16,000

A4.16 The correlation coefficient (r) for measuring the connection between two variables (x and y) has been calculated as 0.6.

How much of the variation in the dependent variable (y) is explained by the variation in the independent variable (x)?

A	36%
B	40%
C	60%
D	64%

A4.17 A company makes a single product T and budgets to produce and sell 7,200 units each period. Cost and revenue data for the product at this level of activity are as follows.

	$ per unit
Selling price	53
Direct material cost	24
Direct labour cost	8
Other variable cost	3
Fixed cost	7
Profit	11

(a) What is the contribution to sales ratio (P/V ratio) of product T (to the nearest whole number)?

(b) The margin of safety of product T (to the nearest whole number) is what percentage of budgeted sales volume?

A4.18 Regression analysis is being used to find the line of best fit $(y = a + bx)$ from five pairs of data. The calculations have produced the following information:

$$\Sigma x = 129 \qquad \Sigma xy = 23{,}091 \quad \Sigma x^2 = 3{,}433$$
$$\Sigma y^2 = 29{,}929 \quad \Sigma y = 890$$

What is the value of 'a' in the equation for the line of best fit (to the nearest whole number)?

A 146
B 52
C 210
D 245

A4.19 Which of the following is the feasible value for a correlation coefficient?

A + 1.2
B 0
C − 1.2
D − 2.0

A4.20 A hospital's records show that the cost of carrying out health checks in the last five accounting periods have been as follows:

Period	Number of patients seen	Total cost
1	650	$17,125
2	940	17,800
3	1,260	18,650
4	990	17,980
5	1,150	18,360

Using the high-low method and ignoring inflation, the estimated cost of carrying out health checks on 850 patients in period 6 is:

A $17,515
B $17,570
C $17,625
D $17,680

A4.21

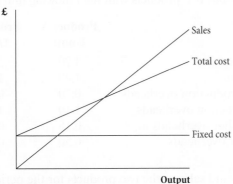

This graph is known as a:

A   semi-variable cost chart
B   conventional break-even chart
C   contribution chart
D   profit volume chart

The above are a variety of multiple choice questions drawn from CIMA's Management Accounting Fundamentals, Fundamentals of Management Accounting, Operational Cost Accounting and ACCA's Financial Information for Management.

A4.22 The transport department of the Norwest Council operates a large fleet of assorted vehicles. These vehicles are used as the need arises by the various departments of the Council. Each month a statement is prepared for the transport department comparing actual results with budget.

One of the items in the transport department's monthly statement is the cost of vehicle maintenance. This maintenance is carried out by the employees of the department. To facilitate his control the transport manager has asked that future statements should show vehicle maintenance costs analysed into fixed and variable costs. Data for the six months from January to June inclusive are given below:

	Vehicle maintenance cost £	Vehicle running hours
January	13,600	2,100
February	15,800	2,800
March	14,500	2,200
April	16,200	3,000
May	14,900	2,600
June	15,000	2,500

You are required to:

a. i. analyse the vehicle maintenance costs into fixed and variable costs, by means of a graph, based on the data given;

   ii. prove your results by utilising the least squares method;

b. discuss briefly how you would propose to calculate rates for charging out the total costs incurred to the user departments.

(CIMA, Cost Accounting 2)

A4.23 A company has two products with the following unit costs for a period:

	Product A £/unit	Product B £/unit
Direct materials	1.20	2.30
Direct labour	1.40	1.50
Variable production overheads	0.70	0.80
Fixed production overheads	1.10	1.10
Variable other overheads	0.15	0.20
Fixed other overheads	0.50	0.50

Production and sales of the two products for the period were:

	Product A 000 units	Product B 000 units
Production	250	100
Sales	225	110

Production was at normal levels. Unit costs in opening stock were the same as those for the period listed above.

Required:

a. State whether, and why, absorption or marginal costing would show a higher company profit for the period, and calculate the difference in profit depending upon which method is used.
b. Calculate the break-even sales revenue for the period (to the nearest £000) based on the above mix of sales. The selling prices of Products A and B were £5.70 and £6.90 per unit respectively.

(ACCA Management Information)

A4.24 You are the management accountant of publishing and printing company which has been asked to quote for the production of a programme for the local village fair. The work would be carried out in addition to the normal work of the company. Because of existing commitments, some weekend working would be required to complete the printing of the programme. A trainee accountant has produced the following cost estimate based upon the resources required as specified by the production manager:

		£
Direct materials – paper (book value)		5,000
– inks (purchase price)		2,400
Direct labour – skilled	250 hours @ £4.00	1,000
–unskilled	100 hours @ £3.50	350
Variable overhead	350 hours @ £4.00	1,400
Printing press depreciation	200 hours @ £2.50	500
Fixed production costs	350 hours @ £6.00	2,100
Estimating department costs		400
		13,150

You are aware that considerable publicity could be obtained for the company if you are able to win this order and the price quoted must be very competitive. The following notes are relevant to the cost estimate above:

1. The paper to be used is currently in stock at a value of £5,000. It is of an unusual colour which has not been used for some time. The replacement price of the paper is £8,000, while the scrap value of that in stock is £2,500. The production manager does not foresee any alternative use for the paper if it is not used for the village fair programmes.
2. The inks required are not held in stock. They would have to be purchased in bulk at a cost of £3,000. 80% of the ink purchased would be used in printing the programmes. No other use is foreseen for the remainder.
3. Skilled direct labour is in short supply, and to accommodate the printing of the programmes, 50% of the time required would be worked at weekends for which a premium of 25% above the normal hourly rate is paid. The normal hourly rate is £4.00 per hour.
4. Unskilled labour is presently under-utilised, and at present 200 hours per week are recorded as idle time. If the printing work is carried out at a weekend, 25 unskilled hours would have to occur at this time, both the employees concerned would be given two hours time off (for which they would be paid) in lieu of each hour worked.
5. Variable overhead represents the cost of operating the printing press and binding machines.
6. When not being used by the company, the printing press is hired to outside companies for £6.00 per hour. This earns a contribution of £3.00 per hour. There is unlimited demand for this facility.
7. Fixed production costs are those incurred by the absorbed into production, using an hourly rate based on budgeted activity.
8. The cost of the estimating department represents time spent in discussions with the village fair committee concerning the printing of its programme.

Requirements:

a. Prepare a revised cost estimate using the opportunity cost approach, showing clearly the minimum price that the company should accept for the order. Give reasons for each resource valuation in your cost estimate.
b. Explain why contribution theory is used as a basis for providing information relevant to decision-making.
c. Explain the relevance of opportunity costs in decision-making.

(CIMA Operational Cost Accounting)

A4.25 ABC Limited makes three products, all of which use the same machine which is available for 50,000 hours per period. The standard costs of the products per unit are:

	Product A £	Product B £	Product C £
Direct materials	70	40	80
Direct labour:			
Machinists (£8 per hour)	48	32	56
Assemblers (£6 per hour)	36	40	42
Total variable cost	154	112	178
Selling price per unit	200	158	224
Maximum demand (units)	3,000	2,500	5,000

Fixed costs are £300,000 per period.
ABC Limited could buy in similar quality products at the following unit prices:

A   £175
B   £140
C   £200

Requirements:

a. Calculate the deficiency in machine hours for the next period.
b. Determine which product(s) and quantities (if any) should be bought out.
c. Calculate the profit for the next period based on your recommendations in(b).

(CIMA Cost Accounting and Quantitative Methods)

A4.26 A company manufactures and markets a single product. The company's trading results for the year just ending are expected to be:

	£	£
Sales		1,476.461
Direct materials	492,326	
Direct labour	316,764	
Overheads	452,318	
		1,261,408
Profit		215,053

For the year ahead it is planned to reduce the selling price of the product by 5%. Units sold are estimated to increase by 40%.

Direct materials cost inflation is expected to be 5% in the year ahead and a 5% increase in the hourly wage rate will be payable to the direct labour force for the whole year.

Overhead expenditure in the year prior to the year just ending was £418,232.

Overhead cost inflation in the year just ending has been 5% and production and sales volumes have been 12% higher than in the previous year. The high-low method is to be used to estimate overhead expenditure for the year ahead.

Overhead cost inflation is expected to be 6% in the year ahead.

Required:

a. Prepare a statement showing the estimated trading results for the year ahead.
b. Calculate (to the nearest £000) the break-even points for each of the two years (ie year just ending and next year).
c. Comment upon the expected change in break-even point and profit.

(ACCA Cost and Management Accounting)

A4.27 A company is considering the launch of a new product, for which an investment in equipment of £150,000 would be required. The project life would be limited to five years by the expected life cycle of the product. It is expected that the equipment could be sold for £10,000 in Year 6.

Market research has indicated a 70% chance of demand for the new product being high and a 30% chance of demand being low. Cash inflows are forecast as follows:

Year	High demand £000	Low demand £000
1	60	50
2	62	50
3	65	50
4	70	50
5	70	50

If the new product is launched now, an existing product, which could otherwise be retained for a further five years, would be discontinued immediately. If retained, cash inflows of £12,000 per annum would be expected for the existing product.

The company's cost of capital (discount rate) is 15% per annum. Assume that all cash flows occur at year ends.

You are required to:

a. Calculate the expected net present value of the new product.
b. Advise the company whether to launch the new product, or to retain the existing product.

(ACCA Management Information)

A4.28 a. Your organisation has no system for authorising and controlling capital expenditure. The Managing Director has asked you, as Cost Accountant, to review the situation.

Required:

Draft a memorandum to your Board of Directors detailing an scheme for capital expenditure authorisation and control, briefly explaining each stage in your system.

b. The following information relates to two possible capital projects of which you have to select one to invest in. Both projects have an initial capital cost of £200,000 and only one can be undertaken.

Project	X	Y
Expected profits	**£**	**£**
Year 1	80,000	30,000
2	80,000	50,000
3	40,000	90,000
4	20,000	120,000
Estimated resale value at the end of Year 4	40,000	40,000

    i. Profit is calculated after deducting straight line depreciation.

    ii. The cost of capital is 16%.

Required:

For both projects calculate the following:

    i. The pay back period to one decimal place.

    ii. The accounting rate of return using average investment.

    iii. The net present value.

c. Advise the board which project in your opinion should be undertaken, giving reasons for your decision.

d. The board have looked at your proposal and you have been asked to clarify a number of issues:

    i. What is meant by the term 'cost of capital' and why is it important in coming to an investment decision?

    ii. State two ways in which risk can be taken into account when making a capital investment decision.

(AAT Cost Accounting & Budgeting)

A4.29 RJD Limited uses a standard costing system. The standard cost per unit of product D is as follows:

	£
Direct materials: 5 kg × £10/kg	50
Direct labour: 4 hr × £6/hr	24
Production overheads:	
Variable – 4 hr × £3/hr	12
Fixed	10
Standard production cost	96
Standard selling price	150

The standard fixed production overhead absorption rate was based on a budgeted activity of 10,000 units.

During period 5, production was 10,000 units as planned but sales were only 8,000 units. There was a total fixed production overhead variance of £10,000 adverse. All units were sold at £150.

There was no opening stock at the beginning of the period.

Other costs incurred during the period were in relation to selling and distribution, and administration. These were as follows:

Selling and distribution:	**Variable**	**Fixed**
	20% of sales	£60,000
Administration:		£100,000

Required:

a. Prepare a profit and loss statement for period 5 using:
   i. absorption costing;
   ii. marginal costing.
b. Prepare a reconciliation of the difference between the profit/loss under absorption costing and under marginal costing and explain the reason for the difference.
c. i. Using graph paper, prepare a profit–volume chart based on the budgeted information for period 5, indicating the break-even point and margin of safety.
   ii. Demonstrate, using the break-even formula, the accuracy of your answer to c.i. above.

(CIMA Management Accounting Fundamentals)

A4.30 Archibald Ltd manufactures and sells one product. Its budgeted profit statement for the first month of trading is as follows:

	£	£
Sales (1,200 units at £180 per unit)		216,000
Less Cost of sales:		
Production (1,800 units at £100 per unit)	180,000	
Less Closing stock (600 units at £100 per unit)	(60,000)	(120,000)
Gross profit		96,000
Less: Fixed selling and distribution costs		(41,000)
Net profit		55,000

The budget was prepared using absorption costing principles. If budgeted production in the first month had been 2,000 units then the total production cost would have been £188,000.

Required:

(a) Using the high-low method, calculate:
   (i) the variable production cost per unit; and
   (ii) the total monthly fixed production cost
(b) If the budget for the first month of trading had been prepared using marginal costing principles, calculate:
   (i) the total contribution; and
   (ii) the net profit.
(c) Explain clearly the circumstances in which the monthly profit or loss would be the same using absorption or marginal costing principles.

(ACCA Financial Information for Management)

EXAMINATION QUESTIONS WITHOUT ANSWERS

B4.1 The following cost and activity data were recorded for Department Y.

	Output (units)	
	1,800	2,400
Costs	£	£
Labour	9,000	11,400
Materials	12,600	16,800
Admin. salaries	6,000	6,000
Power	1,300	1,550
Depreciation	9,000	12,000
Rates	850	850
Indirect labour	1,460	1,460
Selling costs	6,100	7,300

You are required to:

a. Classify each type of cost with a brief explanatory note where necessary.
b. Where appropriate separate the fixed and variable elements of each cost.
c. Assuming that the pattern of cost behaviour remains the same calculate the expected cost for each item for 2,000 units.

B4.2 A distribution and marketing organisation sells three products named A, B and C in two areas which are designated as Area 1 and Area 2. The information given below is for a year.

Data:	Product A	Product B	Product C
Selling price per unit	£40	£48	£60
Purchase price per unit	£32	£36	£44
Sales, in units:			
Area 1	92,000	40,000	28,000
Area 2	30,000	40,000	40,000
Number of orders:			
Area 1	40,000	20,000	10,000
Area 2	6,000	10,000	8,000
Volume in cubic metres per unit	2.0	1.5	1.0

Costs:	Variable £	Fixed £	Basis of apportionment
Selling	188	376	Number of orders
Warehousing/ distribution	432	648	Volume sold
Advertising	270	540	Units sold
Administration	64	256	Sales value

You are required to:

a. prepare a budget for the year showing the profit or loss for each area and in total, using absorption costing:
b. prepare a budget for Area 1 only, using marginal costing and showing relevant information for each product and the total profit or loss for that area;

c. comment on the result shown in your answer to (b) above and suggest action which management ought to take.

(CIMA Cost Accounting)

B4.3   A company has the following summary trading statements reflecting performance over two accounting periods:

	Period 1	Period 2
	£000	£000
Sales	902.0	1,108.1
Variable costs	360.8	398.9
Contribution	541.2	709.2
Fixed costs	490.5	549.0
Net profit	50.7	160.2

In Period 2 selling prices were 5% higher than in Period 1 and cost inflation (affecting both variable and fixed costs) was also 5%.

At the start of Period 2 production methods were re-organised. This was the only other factor affecting costs between the two periods (apart from inflation and volume).

Requirement:

a. Calculate the percentage increase in sales volume in Period 2, compared with Period 1.

b. Calculate the increase in net profit in Period 2, compared with Period 1, due to:
   i.   volume
   ii. re-organisation of production methods (calculations should be done at Year 1 prices).

c. Calculate the sales (to the nearest £000) that were required in Period 2 in order to achieve the same net profit as Period 1.

d. State, and explain, the formula for the calculation of the break-even sales revenue for a period (figures are not required).

(ACCA Management Information)

B4.4   a. You are required, using the accountants' conventional break-even chart as a 'model', to explain how and why a break-even chart drawn by an economist would differ. Illustrative diagrams should be adjacent to your answer within your answer book and NOT on separate graph paper.

b. PM Limited owns the Premier Hotel which is on a busy main road near an international airport. The hotel has 40 rooms which are let at a rental of £35 per day.

Variable costs are £6 per room occupied per day.
Fixed costs *per month* are:

	£
Depreciation	9,000
Insurance	5,500
Maintenance	4,800
Services	2,700
Management	3,000

Business is not as good in the period October to March as it is in the period April to September. The figures below relate to the two six-monthly periods for Year 3/4

	April to September (183 days) £	October to March (182 days) £
Potential room lettings	256,200	254,800
Budgeted room lettings	218,400	165,200

You are required:

i. to calculate the budgeted room occupancy ratio to the nearest percentage figure for each six-month period;
ii. to prepare a statement showing budgeted profit or loss for each of the two six-monthly periods;
iii. to state the number of room days per month which must be let on average each month to break even;
iv. to state with reason(s) whether or not you believe the hotel should be closed during January and February because in these two particularly poor trading months the fixed costs are not covered by the receipts from letting the rooms;
v. to state briefly how you would investigate the costs for insurance and maintenance; the Manager of the hotel believes these two costs are too high and should be capable of being reduced.

(CIMA Cost Accounting)

B4.5 a. Explain how the Cost Accountant distinguishes between: (i) Scrap and, (ii) Waste, by definition and recording.

b. A Company manufacturing three different electrical components has estimated its costs and selling prices as follows:

	Product X	Product Y	Product Z
Direct Materials			
Direct Labour	£3	£4	£8
Dept. 1 (Rate £2 hour)	2	4	2
Dept. 2 (Rate £1.50 hour)	3	6	9
	8	14	19
Selling Price	15	25	40
Quantities – units	10,000	20,000	5,000

It is anticipated that 5% of products are rejected by final inspection, and transferred to a small repair department. It takes 15 minutes to repair an X, 6 minutes each Y, and 12 minutes every Z.

Operators are paid £2.40 per hour.

Overheads are budgeted as follows, and are allocated on the basis of direct labour hours:

	Variable £	Fixed £
Dept. 1	110,000	55,000
Dept. 2	130,000	65,000
Repair Dept.	550	2,750

The Management is not satisfied with the projected profit margin and have negotiated with another company who will purchase all rejected units for £3 per item for all products. The Repair Department would be closed down saving £2,000 Fixed Costs and £500 Variable Costs.

Required:

  i. Calculate the total unit cost for each product excluding any repair costs.

  ii. Calculate the total repair cost only per product for the period.

  iii. The profit projected from the information given utilising the repair dept.

  iv. The profit projected if the Management's proposal is enforced.

  v. Your report on the comparison of the alternatives and recommendation.

(AAT, Cost Accounting and Budgeting)

B4.6 Mrs Johnston has taken out a lease on a shop for a downpayment of £5,000. Additionally, the rent under the lease amounts to £5,000 per annum. If the lease is cancelled, the initial payment of £5,000 is forfeit. Mrs Johnston plans to use the shop for the sale of clothing and has estimated operations for the next 12 months as follows:

	£	£
Sales	115,000	
Less: Value added tax (VAT)	15,000	
Sales less VAT		100,000
Cost of goods sold	50,000	
Wages and wage related costs	12,000	
Rent including the downpayment	10,000	
Rates, heating, lighting and insurance	13,000	
Audit, legal and general expenses	2,000	87,000
Net profit before tax		13,000

In the figures no provision has been made for the cost of Mrs Johnston but it is estimated that one half of her time will be devoted to the business. She is undecided whether to continue with her plans because she knows that she can sub-let the shop to a friend for a monthly rent of £550 if she does not use the shop herself. You are required to:

a. i. explain and identify the 'sunk' and 'opportunity' costs in the situation depicted above;

  ii. state what decision Mrs Johnston should make according to the information given, supporting your conclusion with a financial statement;

b. explain the meaning and use of 'notional' (or 'imputed') costs and quote two supporting examples.

(CIMA, Cost Accounting 1)

B4.7 PQR Limited is an engineering company engaged in the manufacture of components and finished products.

The company is highly mechanised and each of the components and finished products requires the use of one or more types of machine in its machining department. The following costs and revenues (where appropriate) relate to a single component or unit of the finished product:

| | Components | | Finished products | |
| | A | B | C | D |
	£	£	£	£
Selling price			127	161
Direct materials	8	29	33	38
Direct wages	10	30	20	25
Variable overhead:				
Drilling	6	3	9	12
Grinding	8	16	4	12
Fixed overhead:				
Drilling	12	6	18	24
Grinding	10	20	5	15
Total cost	54	104	89	126

Notes:
1. The labour hour rate is £5 per hour.
2. Overhead absorption rates per machine hour are as follows:

| | Variable | Fixed |
	£	£
Drilling (per hour)	3	6
Grinding (per hour)	4	5

3. Components A and B are NOT used in finished products C and D. They are used in the company's other products, none of which use the drilling or grinding machines. The company does not manufacture any other components.
4. The number of machine drilling hours available is limited to 1,650 per week. There are 2,500 machine grinding hours available per week. These numbers of hours have been used to calculate the absorption rates stated above.
5. The maximum demand in units per week for each of the finished products has been estimated by the marketing director as:

Product C   250 units
Product D   500 units

6. The internal demand for components A and B each week is as follows:

Component A   50 units
Component B   100 units

7. There is no external market for components A and B.
8. PQR Limited has a contract to supply 50 units of each of its finished products to a major customer each week. These quantities are included in the maximum units of demand given in note 5 above.

Requirement:

a. Calculate the number of units of EACH finished product that PQR Limited should produce in order to maximise its profits, and the profit per week that this should yield.

b. i. The production director has now discovered that he can obtain unlimited quantities of components identical to A and B for £50 and £96 per unit respectively.

   Requirement:

   State whether this information changes the production plan of the company if it wishes to maximise its profits per week. If appropriate, state the revised production plan and the net benefit per week caused by the change to the production plan.

   ii. The solution of problems involving more than one limiting factor requires the use of linear programming.

   Requirement:

   Explain why this technique must be used in such circumstances, and the steps used to solve such a problem when using the graphical linear programming technique.

B4.8   IS Limited produces an industrial solvent by means of a process through which various ingredients are mixed and changed in form, the output being in containers of 50-litre volume which have a selling price of £15 per container.

The input ingredients cost £10 per 50-litre container; wages, which are regarded as fixed costs amount to £2,000 per week. The production rate is 60 containers per hour; theoretical production time 40 hours per week. For some time plant breakdowns have resulted in a loss of 10 hours per week on average and the production manager has suggested that preventive maintenance would reduce this idle time and the consequent lost production. Two alternatives have been suggested, viz.:

a. to have preventive maintenance carried out by a team of engineers working in the evenings, the cost being £800 per week which it is expected would reduce breakdown time to 20% of its current level;

b. to contract out the preventive maintenance to a firm which would carry out the work on Sunday mornings for a weekly fee of £300. A saving of half the breakdown time could be expected to result from this arrangement.

You are required to:

   i. prepare a statement which would assist management to decide whether to continue as at present or to adopt one or other of the two alternatives suggested;

   ii. state any other considerations management would probably have in mind in making its decision.

(ACCA, Costing)

B4.9 The opportunities afforded by the European Union have created a pleasant problem for CD Limited, which is considering concentrating its production on one of two products – 'Robroy' or 'Trigger' – both of which are currently made and sold. With the expansion in sales possible, either product can be sold in quantities which exceed the capacity of the present production facilities. Therefore, the use of subcontractors is being considered.

Sub-contractor Jason can produce up to a maximum of 10,000 units of Robroy or 8,000 units of Trigger in a year for the type of work done by Department 1. Jason's prices would be £110 for Robroy and £170 for Trigger, both prices being inclusive of the raw materials. Sub-contractor Nadira can produce up to a maximum of 6,400 units of Robroy or 4,000 units of Trigger in a year for the type of work done by Department 2. Nadira's prices would be £120 for Robroy and £154 for Trigger, both prices being inclusive of the raw materials. A market research study has shown that for more than 22,000 units of Robroy to be sold in a year, the price of the total quantity sold would need to be reduced to £270 each. If more than 18,000 units of Trigger are to be sold in a year, the price of the total quantity sold would need to be reduced to £390 each. CD Limited has stated that its standard selling prices and standard prime costs for each product for the forthcoming year are:

	Robroy		Trigger	
	Hours	**£**	**Hours**	**£**
Selling prices		300		430
Costs – Department 1:				
Direct materials		45		75
Direct wages	5	40	7.5	60
Costs – Department 2:				
Direct materials		15		20
Direct wages	7.5	75	10	100

Production overheads are to be absorbed on a direct labour hour basis and the budgeted overheads for the forthcoming year are:

	Department 1	Department 2
Fixed	£400,000	£800,000
Variable – per direct labour hour	£2.00	£2.40
Budgeted maximum labour hours available	100,000	160,000

You are required:

a) to state, with supporting calculations and estimated PROFIT figures, whether CD Limited should concentrate its resources on Robroy or Trigger if
   i) it does not use sub-contractors;
   ii) it does use sub-contractors and restricts its sales to either 22,000 units of Robroy or 18,000 units of Trigger;

b) to describe briefly one possible problem arising for each of the following situations:
  i) if your conclusion in (a)(i) above is followed;
  ii) if your conclusion in (a)(ii) above is followed;
c) to comment briefly on the usefulness of marginal costing for decision-making.

(CIMA Cost Accounting)

B4.10 A district health authority requires temporary accommodation for the training of a group of student nurses for a period of five years. The existing accommodation is both overcrowded and parts of it have been closed due to structural defects. The district estates manager has located three alternative sites which would be available namely:

i. Crystal House which can be rented at the following annual rentals:

Year	1	2	3	4	5
£	180,000	188,000	196,000	206,000	206,000

  The scheme would have annual heating cost of £150,000 per annum. The agreement also requires £24,000 to be paid with the first rental payment to cover legal and agency costs.

ii. Maxwell Building which requires £200,000 to be paid at the commencement of a lease and with an annual rental of £170,000 per annum. The annual heating costs etc. are estimated at £140,000 per annum.

iii. The Arndale Complex which would require an annual rental of £190,000 for three years rising by £15,000 thereafter. The annual heating costs are £130,000 per annum. The agreement would also require that the complex was redecorated at the end of the lease period; this would cost an estimated £120,000.

As an accounting technician employed by the health authority you are required to:

a. Compare and comment upon the cost of the three alternatives, using a discounting technique, for the five-year period. Unless otherwise stated you should assume that cash flows arise at the end of the year. The authority's notional cost of borrowing is 14% and you have been given the following information:

Year	14% Discounting Factor
1	0.877
2	0.769
3	0.675
4	0.592
5	0.519

b. Outline briefly any further information you would require before making a final decision between the three alternatives.
c. Explain what you understand by statement 'the time value of money' in relation to investment appraisal.

(AAT Public Sector Organisations & Financial Control)

23

Budgets

I. OBJECTIVES

After studying this chapter you will

- Be able to define a budget

- Understand the budget preparation process

- Know how budgets inter-relate

- Understand the distinction between fixed and flexible budgets

- Be able to calculate a flexed budget

- Understand the importance of human factors in budgeting

- Know how to prepare a Cash Budget

- Be able to describe the benefits and problems of budgeting

- Have been introduced to Zero-Based Budgeting

- Understand how Activity Based Budgeting can be used.

2. WHAT IS A BUDGET?

A budget is a quantitative expression of a plan of action prepared in advance of the period to which it relates. Budgets may be prepared for the business as a whole, for departments, for functions such as sales and production, or for financial and resource items such as cash, capital expenditure, manpower, purchases etc. The process of preparing and agreeing budgets is a means of translating the overall objectives of the organisation into detailed, feasible plans of action.

The formal definition is as follows:

budget Quantitative expression of a plan for a defined period of time. It may include planned sales volumes and revenues, resource quantities, cost and expenses, assets, liabilities and cash flows.

Terminology

3. PLANNING AND CONTROL

The budgetary process is an integral part of both planning and control. Too often budgets are associated with negative, penny-pinching control activities whereas the full process is much broader and more positive than that. Budgeting is about making plans for the future, implementing those plans and monitoring activities to see whether they conform to the plan. To do this successfully requires full top management support, cooperative and motivated middle managers and staff, and well organised reporting systems.

4. THE BENEFITS OF BUDGETING

The following benefits are those that can be derived from the full budgetary process. They do not accrue automatically, they have to be worked for. Indeed some organisations have systems of budgeting which are narrowly conceived and consequently they do not obtain the range of advantages which are possible. The benefits are dealt with under the following headings: planning and coordination, clarification of authority and responsibility, communication, control, motivation.

5. PLANNING AND COORDINATION

The formal process of budgeting works within the framework of long term, overall objectives to produce detailed operational plans for different sectors and facets of the organisation. Planning is the key to success in business and budgeting forces planning to take place. The budgeting process provides for the coordination of the activities and departments of the organisation so that each facet of the operation contributes towards the overall plan.

This is expressed in the form of a Master Budget which summarises all the supporting budgets. The budget process forces managers to think of the relationship of their function or department with others and how they contribute to the achievement of organisational objectives.

The formal definition of a Master Budget is:

Consolidates all subsidiary budgets and is normally comprised of the budgeted profit and loss statement, balance sheet and cash flow statement.

Terminology

6. CLARIFICATION OF AUTHORITY AND RESPONSIBILITY

The process of budgeting makes it necessary to clarify the responsibilities of each manager who has a budget. The adoption of a budget authorises the plans contained within it so that *management by exception* can be practised, ie a subordinate is given a clearly defined role with the authority to carry out the tasks assigned to him and when activities are not proceeding to plan, the variations are reported to a higher level. Thus the full budgetary process is an excellent example of management by exception in action.

7. COMMUNICATION

The budgetary process includes all levels of management. Accordingly it is an important avenue of communication between top and middle management regarding the firm's objectives and the practical problems of implementing these objectives and, when the budget is finalised, it communicates the agreed plans to all the staff involved. As well as vertical communication, the budgetary process requires communication between functions to ensure that coordination is achieved, for example, there must be full liaison between the sales and production functions to ensure that coordinated budgets are developed.

8. CONTROL

This aspect of budgeting is the most well known and is the aspect most frequently encountered by the ordinary staff member. The process of comparing actual results with planned results and reporting on the variations, which is the principle of budgetary control, sets a control framework which helps expenditure to be kept within agreed limits. Deviations are noted so that corrective action can be taken.

9. MOTIVATION

The involvement of lower and middle management with the preparation of budgets and the establishment of clear targets against which performance can be judged have been found to be motivating factors. However, there are many factors to be considered in relation to the human aspects of budgeting and these are dealt with in greater detail later in this chapter.

10. THE BUDGET PERIOD

Planning and therefore budgeting must be related to a specific period of time. The general process of budgeting breaks down long range plans and objectives prepared for, say, the next five years into shorter, operation periods invariably of one year. Typically these are subdivided into monthly periods for the purpose of monitoring and control.

Budgets can be prepared for any length of time and longer periods may be appropriate for particular types of budget. For example, a research and development budget may be prepared for the next three years because the long term nature of the activity makes yearly budgets less appropriate. Because of rapidly changing conditions many organisations review and modify their budgets on a rolling basis. Typically, each quarter or half year, budgets are reviewed for the following 12 months. This process is known as *continuous or rolling budgeting*.

11. LIMITING FACTOR OR KEY FACTOR OR PRINCIPAL BUDGET FACTOR

It will be recalled from Chapter 20 that the limiting factor is that factor which, at any given time, effectively limits the activities of an organisation. It may be customer demand, production capacity, shortage of labour, materials, space or finance. Because such a constraint will have a pervasive effect on all plans and budgets, the limiting factor must be identified and its effect on each of the budgets carefully considered during the budget preparation process.

Frequently the principal budget factor is customer demand, ie the company is unable to sell all the output it can produce. The limiting factor can and does change – when one constraint is removed some other limitation will occur – otherwise, of course, the organisation could expand to infinity.

12. PROFIT CENTRES AND BUDGET CENTRES

It will be recalled that a cost centre is an identifiable function or part of the organisation for which costs can be identified. A profit centre is an extension of this idea on a larger scale, where not only costs are identifiable but also profits. The formal definition is:

A part of a business accountable for costs and revenues.

Terminology

A budget centre is defined as:

A centre for which an individual budget is drawn up.

Terminology

Thus it will be apparent that a budget centre may be a cost centre, or group of cost centres or it may coincide with a profit centre. Because of its size it is likely that a typical profit centre would consist of a number of budget centres each of which would contain either a single cost centre or a group of related cost centres.

Figure 23.1 is a simplified outline of the budget preparation process. For ease of illustration it is shown as a sequential series of steps but in practice the procedure is less straightforward. There is considerable discussion and consultation, additional information is requested, revisions are made, steps are repeated and so on.

13. THE INTERRELATIONSHIP OF BUDGETS

Figure 23.2 shows the major budgets and their interrelationships for a typical manufacturing concern. In practice there would be more budgets than those shown, there would in fact be a budget for each budget centre.

FIGURE 23.1 Outline of the budgetary process

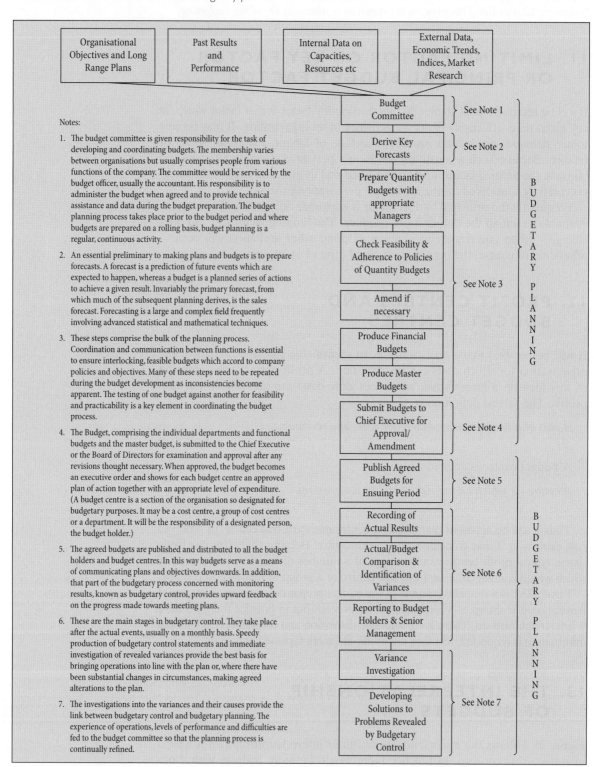

Notes:

1. The budget committee is given responsibility for the task of developing and coordinating budgets. The membership varies between organisations but usually comprises people from various functions of the company. The committee would be serviced by the budget officer, usually the accountant. His responsibility is to administer the budget when agreed and to provide technical assistance and data during the budget preparation. The budget planning process takes place prior to the budget period and where budgets are prepared on a rolling basis, budget planning is a regular, continuous activity.

2. An essential preliminary to making plans and budgets is to prepare forecasts. A forecast is a prediction of future events which are expected to happen, whereas a budget is a planned series of actions to achieve a given result. Invariably the primary forecast, from which much of the subsequent planning derives, is the sales forecast. Forecasting is a large and complex field frequently involving advanced statistical and mathematical techniques.

3. These steps comprise the bulk of the planning process. Coordination and communication between functions is essential to ensure interlocking, feasible budgets which accord to company policies and objectives. Many of these steps need to be repeated during the budget development as inconsistencies become apparent. The testing of one budget against another for feasibility and practicability is a key element in coordinating the budget process.

4. The Budget, comprising the individual departments and functional budgets and the master budget, is submitted to the Chief Executive or the Board of Directors for examination and approval after any revisions thought necessary. When approved, the budget becomes an executive order and shows for each budget centre an approved plan of action together with an appropriate level of expenditure. (A budget centre is a section of the organisation so designated for budgetary purposes. It may be a cost centre, a group of cost centres or a department. It will be the responsibility of a designated person, the budget holder.)

5. The agreed budgets are published and distributed to all the budget holders and budget centres. In this way budgets serve as a means of communicating plans and objectives downwards. In addition, that part of the budgetary process concerned with monitoring results, known as budgetary control, provides upward feedback on the progress made towards meeting plans.

6. These are the main stages in budgetary control. They take place after the actual events, usually on a monthly basis. Speedy production of budgetary control statements and immediate investigation of revealed variances provide the best basis for bringing operations into line with the plan or, where there have been substantial changes in circumstances, making agreed alterations to the plan.

7. The investigations into the variances and their causes provide the link between budgetary control and budgetary planning. The experience of operations, levels of performance and difficulties are fed to the budget committee so that the planning process is continually refined.

FIGURE 23.2   Major budgets and their relationships

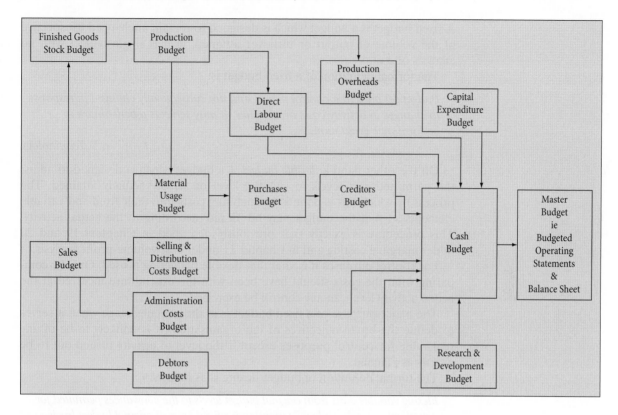

Notes on Figure 23.2:

a. There are many more relationships than depicted; for example, the capital expenditure budget depends on various factors such as the level and type of sales, the usage of machinery, the overall long term objectives of the organisation, etc.

b. Only the main functional budgets are shown. Invariably these are broken down into departmental budgets for day-to-day control purposes.

c. Because of the importance of liquidity and cash flow the cash budget frequently receives special attention. It is dealt with in Para. 21.

d. All supporting budgets contribute to the Master Budget, ie the budgeted Operating Statement (or Profit and Loss Account) and budgeted Balance Sheet. In general, the Sales Budget and the various budgets which make up the cost of sales, eg material usage, wages, salaries, overheads and so on are used to produce the budgeted Operating Statement and the budgets which deal with assets and liabilities, eg capital expenditure, cash, stock, debtors and creditors and so on make up the budgeted Balance Sheet. Naturally, there are cross relationships between them. For example, the Capital Expenditure Budget affects the amount of Fixed Assets (a balance sheet item) but also affects the budgeted Operating Statement through the depreciation charges for the new assets.

14. FIXED AND FLEXIBLE BUDGETS

A fixed budget is a budget which is designed to remain unchanged irrespective of the volume of output or turnover attained, ie it is single budget with no analysis of cost.

The formal definition of a fixed budget is:

Budget set prior to a control period and not subsequently changed in response to changes in activity costs or revenues. It may serve as a benchmark in performance evaluation.

Terminology

On the other hand a *flexible budget* is a budget which is designed to adjust the permitted cost levels to suit the level of activity actually attained. The process by which this is done is by analysing costs into their fixed and variable elements so that the budget may be 'flexed' according to the actual activity. This procedure is exactly that previously described in Chapters 19 and 20 under marginal costing and in Chapter 21 under cost-volume-profit analysis.

For control purposes it is vital that flexible budgeting is used. Only by comparing what the costs should have been with the expenditure incurred at the actual activity level can any control be exercised.

The major purpose of a fixed budget is at the planning stage when it serves to define the broad objectives of the organisation. It is unlikely to be of any real value for control purposes except if the level of activity turned out to be exactly as planned.

The formal definition of budget flexing is as follows:

Flexing variable costs from original budget levels to the allowances permitted for actual volume achieved while maintaining fixed costs at original budget levels. (Variable cost allowance = ratio of actual volume achieved to budget volume × original budget variable cost.)

Terminology

The procedures for developing a flexible budget are simple enough but the results obtained from 'flexing' a budget are only accurate if the costs behave in the ways predicted. Frequently, simplistic assumptions are made about cost behaviour which are unrealistic and potentially misleading.

Examples include:

- the frequent arbitrary assumption of cost linearity
- the assumption of continuity when the cost may actually behave in a stepped or discontinuous manner
- the often arbitrary classifications used to determine the fixed and variable elements of costs
- the fact that often all variable costs are flexed in relation to the same activity indicator (eg, sales or output) when in reality different variable costs vary in sympathy with different activity indicators. These and other problems make it necessary to treat any flexed budget with caution.

A flexible budget is essential for the control aspect of budgeting but as it is an important part of the planning process to consider what control procedures will be necessary, it is usual to carry out the required cost analyses and breakdowns at the planning stage so that the budget may be flexed in due course if this is necessary. The following examples illustrate the general principles involved in flexible budgeting.

Example 1

Ayres & Co. make a single product and have an average production of 5,000 units a month although this varies widely. The following extract from the overhead statement for the extrusion department shows the make-up of the budget and a month's actual results.

	£	Budget for Average Production of 5,000 Units £	Actual Results for January Production 4,650 Units £
Indirect Labour			
Fixed	3,000		
Variable £1/Unit	5,000	8,000	7,900
Consumables (all variable)		15,000	14,250
Variable overheads		20,000	18,200
Fixed overheads		12,500	12,500
		£55,500	£52,850

Show two budgetary control statements for January, one based on the fixed budget for 5,000 units and one based on a flexible budget for the actual level of production.

Solution

Budgetary Control Statement 1
Fixed Budget compared with Actual Results

Expense type	Fixed budget £	Actual results £	Budget variances Favourable/ (Adverse) £
Indirect Labour	8,000	7,900	100
Consumables	15,000	14,250	750
Variable overheads	20,000	18,200	1,800
Fixed overheads	12,500	12,500	–
	£55,500	£52,850	£2,650

Notes

a. The variances are the differences between budget and actual. They are favourable when actual costs are BELOW budget and adverse when ABOVE.

b. When, as in this case, the activity level is different to that planned, the comparison of actual results with a fixed budget shows little or no useful information. We see that total costs are lower than budget, but so is the activity level. What is required is the appropriate *budgeted expenditure* for the *actual production level*. This is shown below.

Budgetary Control Statement 2
Flexed Budget compared with Actual Results

Expense type	£	Flexed budget for 4,650 units £	Actual results £	Budget variances Favourable/ (Adverse) £
Indirect Labour				
Fixed	3,000			
Variable £1/unit	4,650	7,650	7,900	(250)
Consumables @ £3/unit		13,950	14,250	(300)
Variable overheads @ £4/unit		18,600	18,200	400
Fixed overheads		12,500	12,500	–
		£52,700	£52,850	£(150)

The values above in the Flexed Budget for 4,650 units are calculated as follows:

Indirect Labour This comprises a fixed element (£3,000) and a variable element at £1 per unit thus:

$$£3,000 + 4,650 \times £1 = £7,650$$

Consumables These costs are wholly variable at the rate of £3 per unit thus:

$$4,650 \times £3 = £13,950$$

Variable Overheads As the name suggests, these are fully variable at the rate of £4 per unit, thus:

$$4,650 \times £4 = £18,600$$

Fixed Overheads These overheads remain the same regardless of changes in the level of activity and will thus be the same value as in the original budget, ie £12,500.

Notes:
The above example has a number of simplifying assumptions which, although not necessarily realistic, are widely used, especially in examination questions. These assumptions include:

a. All variable costs are deemed to vary in accordance with a single activity indicator, in this case production volume.

b. The variable costs are assumed to behave in a regular, linear way.

c. Fixed costs are deemed to remain unchanged.

The next example removes some of these assumptions and includes semi-variable and non-linear costs.

Example 2

After study of planned activities, forecast cost levels and the pattern of cost behaviour the following budget has been prepared based on an anticipated activity level of 8,000 labour hours.

Nature of expense	Budgeted costs for 8,000 labour hours £	Cost classification	Cost function (x = activity level)
Direct Wages	55,500	Linear semi-variable	$£3,500 + 6.5x$
Direct Materials	84,000	Linear variable	$£10.5x$
Salaries	22,000	Fixed	$£22,000 + 0x$
Depreciation	9,500	Fixed	$£9,500 + 0x$
Other overheads	19,200	Non-linear variable	$£0.0003x^2$

Based on the above data it is required to prepare budgets for activity levels of 7,800 and 8,400 labour hours.

Solution

Expense	Cost function	Budget for activity of 7,800 hours	Budget for activity of 8,400 hours
Direct Wages	$£3,500 + 6.5x$	54,200	58,100
Direct Materials	$£10.5x$	81,900	88,200
Salaries	$£22,000 + 0x$	22,000	22,000
Depreciation	$£9,500 + 0x$	9,500	9,500
Other overheads	$£0.0003x^2$	18,252	21,168

The values in the flexed budgets for 7,800 hours and 8,400 hours are calculated by flexing or adjusting the expense according to the given cost functions thus:

Budgets for:	7,800 hours	8,400 hours
Direct Wages (semi-variable)	$£3,500 + 6.5 (7,800) = £54,200$	$£3,500 + 6.5 (8,400) = £58,100$
Direct Materials (fully variable)	$£10.5 (7,800) = £81,900$	$£10.5 (8,400) = £88,200$
Salaries (all fixed) $\therefore$ no adjustment necessary	$= £22,000$	$= £22,000$
Depreciation (all fixed) ... no adjustment necessary	$= £9,500$	$= £9,500$
Other overheads (fully variable)	$£0.0003 \times 7,800^2 = £18,252$	$£0.0003 \times 8,400^2 = £21,168$

Notes:

a. Using a flexible budget the planned expenditure level for the actual activity can be compared with the actual expenditure so highlighting discrepancies.

b. A budget analysed to fixed and variable elements can be flexed to produce realistic budgeted expenditure for any given activity level, even where the activity changes month by month.

c. A word of caution. The expenditure levels obtained by flexing the budget are only as accurate as the initial analysis into fixed and variable elements. The difficulties inherent in that analysis have been dealt with in Chapter 18.

d. For control to be effective the actual expenditure must always be compared with a realistic budget allowance and care taken with the design of control reports.

15. QUANTITY BUDGETS

As shown in Figure 23.1 an intermediate stage in the process of establishing a financial budget is the preparation of quantity budgets. These might be the number of kilograms of material required, the units to be produced, the number of units to be sold or the number of labour hours required. When the quantity budgets have been prepared and agreed the financial budgets are produced based on the appropriate quantities estimated.

An example of a quantity Production Budget follows:

Example 3
Solo Ltd make and sell one product and have estimated the following sales volumes for the next four periods.

Period 1	26,000 units
Period 2	34,000 units
Period 3	28,000 units
Period 4	22,000 units

The opening stock at the beginning of Period 1 is 2,850 units.

The management have decided that the closing stock in a period should be 10% of the sales volume expected in the next period.

Prepare Quantity Production Budgets for Periods 1, 2 and 3.

Solution

Quantity Production Budgets (units)

	Period 1	Period 2	Period 3
Closing stock	3,400	2,800	2,200
+ sales	26,000	34,000	28,000
	29,400	36,800	30,200
– opening stock	2,850	3,400	2,800
= production required	26,550	33,400	27,400

These production volumes would then form the basis of quantity budgets for labour, materials and other resources from which the financial budgets would be prepared.

16. EFFECTIVE CONTROL REPORTS

The budgetary control report is a major vehicle in the feedback process and to ensure maximum effectiveness it is important that its design, content, timing

FIGURE 23.3 Typical budgetary control report

BUDGETARY CONTROL REPORT NO.

Budget Centre .... Date Prepared ....
Budget Holder .... Budget Activity Level ....
Report Relationship Up .... Down .... Actual Activity Level ....
Accounting Period ....

Budgeted Item		Current Period			Year to Date			Trend of Variance	Significant? (Yes/No)	Comments
Code	Description	Budget	Actual	Variance	Budget	Actual	Variance			

and general impact is given careful consideration. It is actions which produce benefits while information only produces costs. In consequence it follows that a budgetary control report which is ignored or misunderstood will not lead to effective actions and so will be useless.

The key items which should be shown are:

a. The budgeted level of costs and revenues for the period and year to date.
b. The actual level of costs and revenues for the period and year to date.
c. The variances between (a) and (b) together with the trends in variances.
d. An indication of what variances are significant together with, where possible, analysis and comment which can be used to bring the variances under control. The recipients of budgetary control reports should be encouraged to make constructive criticisms of all aspects of the reporting procedure so that it is improved and made more effective.

A typical budgetary control report is shown in Figure 23.3. It should be noted that the budgeted amounts would be the flexed budget allowances appropriate to the actual level of activity achieved.

Note:
The problems of deciding what variances are significant are discussed in Chapter 26.

17. HUMAN ASPECTS OF BUDGETING

The behavioural aspects of budgeting are of supreme importance but, as with many aspects of human behaviour, they are complex, often contradictory and imperfectly understood. Considerable research has been carried out on this aspect of budgeting, but broad generalisations are difficult to make. On one point there does seem to be agreement. That is, that budgeting is not considered by participants as a neutral, objective, purely technical process which is a view adopted by many accountants. The human, subjective aspects cannot be overemphasised and these are dealt with below under the following headings: goal congruence, participation, motivation, goal definition and communication.

18. GOAL CONGRUENCE

The ideal budgeting system is one which encourages goal congruence. This simply means that the goals of individuals and groups should coincide with the goals and objectives of the organisation as a whole. This is an ideal which is difficult to achieve completely but recognition must be given to the fact that organisational objectives cannot be imposed through the budgeting system without consideration of the influences of local group and departmental objectives.

There is growing evidence that authority imposed from above is less effective than authority accepted from below and that goal congruence is enhanced when there is a more participative management style rather than the traditional style of management with its emphasis on hierarchy and authority.

19. PARTICIPATION

Budgets can be imposed by top management upon the budget holders or they may be evolved following participation of the budget holders in the budget preparation. Participation promotes common understanding regarding objectives and makes the acceptance of organisational goals by the individual much more likely. The control process is also assisted by participation of the budget holders into the investigation of solutions to the problems which arise. If people are genuinely involved they feel part of the team and become more highly motivated.

When there is genuine participation in budgeting the process becomes known as bottom-up budgeting which can be defined as *'a budgeting system in which all budget holders are given the opportunity to participate in setting their own budgets'*.

20. MOTIVATION

The whole process of budget preparation and subsequent performance evaluation by budgetary control needs to be carried out so as to motivate managers rather than create resentment and adverse reactions. If the process is designed to be participative, encourages initiative and responsibility, is not seen merely as a pressure device, then the motivation of individuals will be strengthened. An emphasis on impossible targets, over emphasis on the short run, imperfectly set and understood objectives will cause motivation to be stifled.

Research has shown that motivation is increased when the reward-penalty system of the organisation is consistent with the organisational control systems of which budgetary control is a primary example. If the control system is seen to be unconnected to the reward-penalty system (ie, promotions, salary increases, bonuses, 'perks') then the control system will be perceived to be of little importance by the managers concerned and consequently it will be ignored and so, by inference, will the organisation's objectives.

21. GOAL DEFINITION

In general, people work more efficiently when they have clearly defined targets and objectives. In a perfect world personal goals would coincide with organisational goals so that individual motivation would be at its highest and targets would be totally accepted and completely defined. Such an ideal is unattainable, but the importance of goal definition and of ensuring that individual aspirations and goals are considered is an important part of enlightened budget preparation. Clearly defined goals, agreed and accepted by the individuals concerned, will encourage goal congruence and increase motivation.

22. COMMUNICATION

The process of communication, between and across the layers in the organisation, is an important factor in all planning and control systems. If any control system, including budgetary control, is not accepted by the people who have to operate it they will hamper and obstruct the flow of information so that realistic planning and control decisions will be difficult to take.

Research has shown that frequent, up to date feedback of information to a manager regarding his performance has a motivating effect. Undue delay, inaccurate data, reports containing details of items over which the manager has no control, all reduce motivation and severely restrict the usefulness of the information system.

23. CASH BUDGETS

A cash budget is one of the most important budgets prepared in an organisation. It shows, in summary form, the expected cash receipts and expected cash payments during the budget period. Liquidity and cash flow management are key factors in the successful operation of any organisation and it is with good reason that the cash budget should receive close attention from both accountants and managers.

The cash budget shows the effect of budgeted activities – selling, buying, paying wages, investing in capital equipment and so on – on the cash flow of the organisation. Cash budgeting is a continuous activity with budgets being rolled forward as time progresses. The budgets are usually subdivided into reasonably short periods – months or weeks.

Cash budgets are prepared in order to ensure that there will be just sufficient cash in hand to cope adequately with budgeted activities. The cash budget may show that there is likely to be a deficiency of cash in some future period – in which case overdraft or loans will have to be arranged or activities curtailed – or alternatively the budget may show that there is likely to be a cash surplus, in which case appropriate investment or use for the surplus can be planned rather than merely leaving the cash idle in a current account.

24. WHAT IS IN A CASH BUDGET?

A cash budget must contain every type of cash inflow or receipt and every type of cash outflow or payment. In addition to the *amounts*, the *timings* of receipts and payments must also be forecast. Some examples of typical receipts and payments follow together with comments on the difficulties found in practice with the various items.

Typical receipts include: Cash Sales, Receipts from debtors, Sales of fixed assets, Receipts of interest and dividends, Issues of new shares and loan stock. Any fees, royalties or other income, Receipts from loan repayments and so on.

Typical payments include: All payments to creditors for stock and material purchases. Wage, salary and bonus payments. Payments for overhead and expense items. Purchase of fixed assets, Payments of dividends, interest and taxation. Loan repayments and so on.

It is of the utmost importance to realise that cash receipts and payments are *not* the same as sales and the costs of sales found in the firm's Profit and Loss Account, because:

a. not all cash receipts affect profit and loss account income, eg the issue of new shares results in a cash inflow but would not be shown in the profit and loss account.

b. not all cash payments affect the costs shown in the profit and loss account, eg the purchase of a fixed asset or the payment of VAT.

c. some profit and loss items are derived from accounting conventions and are not cash flows, eg depreciation and the loss or profit on the sale of fixed assets.

d. the timing of cash receipts and payments does not coincide with the profit and loss accounting period, eg a sale is recognised in the profit and loss account when the invoice is raised yet the cash payment from the debtor may not be received until the following period or even later.

Although there are numerous items in a typical cash budget the major flows usually result from the following: cash receipts from debtors, payments to suppliers, payments for expense items and payments for (or receipts from) major non-trading items such as the purchase (or sales) of fixed assets and tax and dividend payments (or receipts). Some guidelines for these items are given below.

25. GUIDELINES FOR CASH BUDGET PREPARATION

Establishing cash receipts from debtors:

a. Forecast the expected credit sales period by period, taking account of seasonal factors, promotions, sales trends and so on.

b. Forecast the typical payment pattern of debtors. This would usually be based on a detailed analysis of experience with the existing Sales Ledgers adjusted for any expected changes in the pattern.

c. Based on a. and b. calculate when the budgeted sales revenue will be received as cash, taking care to deduct any discounts allowed for prompt payment and making an appropriate allowance for bad debts.

d. Take care to allow for the cash receipts from the opening debtors.

Establishing cash payments to suppliers:

a. Based on the Production Quantities Budget, calculate the production quantities and material usage quantities, period by period.

b. Based on opening stock levels, the required closing stock levels and the production quantities from a. calculate the quantity and cost of material purchases, period by period.

c. Decide upon the length of credit period to be taken from suppliers and using b. calculate when the cash payments will be made to suppliers.

d. Take care to allow for the cash payments to the opening creditors.

Establishing payments for other expense items. (*Note:* These include, wages, salaries, bonuses, all types of overheads and so on.)

a. Forecasts of wages to be paid will, to some extent, depend on the Production Budget mentioned previously. Allow for any bonus payments, cost of living increases, holiday pay, the delay in settling PAYE and NI payments and so on.

b. Salaries can usually be forecast accurately but take care to allow for commissions, bonuses, part-time assistance and so on.

c. The amount and timing of many overhead items can often be forecast very accurately, eg Rates, Insurance, Electricity, Telephones, etc. Take care to exclude any non-cash items which may be included in the general term 'overheads', eg depreciation is a notional cost, and not a cash flow.

Payments and receipts of major non-trading items. These include:

a. Purchases or Sales of Fixed Assets. It is the amount and timing of the cash payment(s) or receipt(s) that is of importance for cash budgeting not the way the item is dealt with in the normal accounts. For example, the sale of a Fixed Asset for £5,000 which has a written down value of £8,000 will produce a notional loss in the normal accounts of £3,000. In the cash budget it will, of course, be shown as a cash receipt of £5,000 in the appropriate period.

b. Tax payments and dividends to be paid or received can usually be forecast accurately.

c. Similarly special transactions such as share issues, loan repayments and so on are usually known well in advance.

26. FORMAT FOR CASH BUDGETS

The typical cash budget has the general form shown below.

Cash Budget

	Period 1	Period 2	Period 3	etc
Opening Cash Balance b/f + Receipts from Debtors + Sales of Capital Items + Any Loans Received + Proceeds for Share Issues + Any other Cash Receipts	XXX	YYY	ZZZ	AAA
= Total Cash Available – Payments to Creditors – Cash Purchases – Wages and Salaries – Loan Repayments – Capital Expenditure – Dividends – Taxation – Any other cash Disbursements				
= Closing Cash Balance c/f	YYY	ZZZ	AAA	

Cash budgets are good examples of rolling budgets, ie where the process of continuous budgeting takes place whereby regularly each period (week, month, quarter as appropriate) a new future period is added to the budget while the earliest period is deleted. In this way the rolling budget is continually revised so as to reflect the most up to date position. The process of continuous budgeting could, of course, be carried out for any type of budget, not just cash budgets.

27. CASH BUDGET

Example 4

The opening cash balance on 1st Jan was expected to be £30,000. The sales budgeted were as follows:

	£
November	80,000
December	90,000
January	75,000
February	75,000
March	80,000

Analysis of records shows that debtors settle according to the following pattern:

60% within the month of sale, 25% the month following, 15% the month following.

Extracts from the Purchases budget were as follows:

December	60,000
January	55,000
February	45,000
March	55,000

All purchases are on credit and past experience shows that 90% are settled in the month of purchase and the balance settled the month after.

Wages are £15,000 per month and overheads of £20,000 per month (including £5,000 depreciation) are settled monthly.

Taxation of £8,000 has to be settled in February and the company will receive settlement of an insurance claim of £25,000 in March.

Prepare a cash budget for January, February and March.

Solution

Workings

The receipts from sales are as follows:

	January Cash
November (15% × 80,000)	£12,000
December (25% × 90,000)	22,500
January (60% × 75,000)	45,000
	£79,500

	February Cash
December (15% × 90,000)	£13,500
January (25% × 75,000)	18,750
February (60% × 75,000)	45,000
	£77,250

	March Cash
January (15% × 75,000)	£11,250
February (25% × 75,000)	18,750
March (60% × 80,000)	48,000
	£78,000

Payments for Purchases:

	January Cash
December (10% × 60,000)	£6,000
January (90% × 55,000)	49,500
	£55,500

	February Cash
January (10% × 55,000)	£5,500
February (90% × 45,000)	40,500
	£46,000

	March Cash
February (10% × 45,000)	£4,500
March (90% × 55,000)	49,500
	£54,000

Cash Budget

	January £	February £	March £
Opening balance	30,000	24,000	17,250
Receipts from sales	79,500	77,250	78,000
Insurance claim			25,000
= Total Cash Available	109,500	101,250	120,250
Payments			
Purchases	55,500	46,000	54,000
Wages	15,000	15,000	15,000
Overheads (less dep'n)	15,000	15,000	15,000
Taxation		8,000	
= Total Payments	85,500	84,000	84,000
Closing balance c/f	24,000	17,250	36,250

28. RECONCILIATION OF CASH BALANCE AND PROFITS

Organisations prepare both cash budgets and operating budgets which show the budgeted profits for each period. These two forms of statements are prepared on totally different bases; the cash budget on the practical, objective basis of measuring positive and negative cash flows whereas budgeted profits are based on the normal conventions of accounting. These include, for example, the accruals concept, the charging of cost which do not create a cash flow – eg depreciation, the distinctions between capital and revenue expenditure and so on.

It is sometimes required to reconcile the budgeted cash and profit figures and the simplest approach to this is to use the Bank Reconciliation Statement approach and commence with one of the figures, say the budgeted cash balance, and then add or subtract the various elements in the budgets so as to agree with the figure of budgeted profit.

In practice there are innumerable items which cause differences between the two figures but the following examples include the major categories:

Sales/Purchases used in profit calculation whereas actual receipts from debtors and payments to creditors used in cash budgets.

Various items in cash budgets which do not appear in profit calculations, eg, capital expenditure, taxation and dividends, increases and decreases in loans, sales or fixed assets, etc.

Notional cost items such as depreciation and imputed charges appear in profit statements but not in cash budgets.

Changes in credit policies and stock levels affect cash budgets but not profit statements.

Accruals and prepayments are normal features of profit statements but do not appear in cash budgets.

29. COMMITMENT ACCOUNTING

One problem that managers have with conventional cash and expenditure budgeting is that they do not know what level of expenditure has been committed but not yet reflected in the financial information they are presented with. This is a problem in all types of organisations but is particularly acute in Public Sector organisations where they may be strict cash limits which cannot be exceeded.

One answer to this is to have a formal system of commitment accounting where the accounting system recognises a transaction and its impact on the budget, as soon as a contract or purchase or other financial commitment is entered into. If such a system was used the information available would be more up-to-date and more relevant thus helping budgetary control.

However while such a system has appeal there are some practical problems. These include:

- Administrative problems caused by contracts and orders being amended and cancelled and the problems of year end accruals.

- The difficulty of measuring the exact amount of the commitment in any periods as many orders and contracts are only estimates and deliveries are not always in accordance with the original order or contract.

- The lack of security caused by numerous accesses to the financial information system.

Because of these and other problems a full system of commitment accounting would rarely be used. Instead many Public Sector organisations show commitments in memorandum form without making entries in the financial records.

30. FORECASTING AND BUDGETS

It will be apparent from a study of the chapter so far that forecasting is an essential part of the budgeting process. Indeed it has been said with considerable truth that the budgetary process is more a test of forecasting skill than anything else.

To establish realistic budgets it is important to forecast a wide range of factors including: sales volume and prices, wage rates and earnings, material availabilities and prices, rates of inflation, the costs of bought in services, the cost of overhead items such as rates, electricity, telephones and many other such variables. It is not sufficient merely to add a percentage on to last year's budget and hope this will produce a realistic result.

There is a wide range of forecasting techniques available ranging from simple linear regression analysis using least squares, through time series analysis, exponential smoothing systems, multiple regression analysis methods to specialised mathematical models such as Box Jenkins.

Some of the elements of forecasting have been covered in Chapter 18 but this is a vast and complex field and professional statistical and computer expertise should be sought to ensure that appropriate methods are employed. (Students requiring an introduction to quantitative and qualitative techniques of forecasting are recommended to read *Quantitative Techniques*, T. Lucey, Cengage Learning.)

A word of caution: regardless of the techniques employed or the amount of computer capacity available it is very difficult to make accurate forecasts. Indeed, numerous surveys have shown that so-called naive forecasting – where the next period is assumed to be the same as the current one – frequently produces better forecasts than those prepared by experts.

31. THE BUDGET MANUAL

As one of the objectives of budgeting is to improve communications it is important that a manual is produced so that everyone in the organisation can refer to the manual for guidance and information about the budgetary process.

The budget manual does not contain the actual budgets for the ensuing period – it is more of an instructional/information manual about the way budgeting operates in the particular organisation and the reasons for having budgeting. Contents obviously vary from organisation to organisation but the following are examples of the information such a manual should contain.

Manual contents

Foreword
- preferably by Chief Executive/Managing Director

Objectives/explanation of the budgetary process
- explanation of budgetary planning and control
- objectives of each stage of the budgetary process
- relationship to long term planning

Organisation Structures and responsibilities
- structure of the organisation showing titles, responsibilities and relationships
- titles and names of current budget holders

Main budgets and relationship
- outline of all main budgets and their accounting relationships
- explanation of key budgets (eg Master Budget, Cash Budget, Sales Budget)

Budget development
- budget committee, membership and terms of reference
- sequence of budget preparation
- timetable for budget preparation and publication

Accounting procedures
- name and terms of reference of the budget officer (usually the accountant)
- coding lists
- sample forms
- timetable for accounting procedures, production of reports, closing dates.

32. BENEFITS AND PROBLEMS OF BUDGETING

Properly planned and administered budgeting systems can bring benefits but these benefits do not automatically accrue; they have to be worked for.

Problems can arise and intending accountants should have an awareness of the factors which could prevent the organisation gaining the maximum advantage from its budgeting system.

Typical benefits of budgeting:

a. It provides clear guidelines for managers and supervisors and is the major way in which organisational objectives are translated into specific tasks and objectives related to individual managers.

b. The budgetary process is an important method of communication and coordination both vertically and horizontally.

c. Because of the 'exception principle', which is at the heart of budgetary control, management time can be saved and attention directed to areas of most concern.

d. The integration of budgets makes possible better cash and working capital management.

e. Better control of current operations is helped by regular, systematic monitoring and reporting of activities.

f. Provided there is proper participation, goal congruence is encouraged and motivation increased.

Typical problems which may arise with budgeting:

a. Variances are just as frequently due to changing circumstances and poor forecasting as due to managerial performance.

b. Budgets are developed round existing organisation structures which may be inappropriate for current conditions.

c. The existence of well documented plans may cause inertia and lack of flexibility in adapting to change.

d. Badly handled budgetary systems with undue pressure or lack of regard to behavioural factors may cause antagonism and may lower morale.

To overcome some of the problems of conventional budgeting systems and to make budgeting more effective various other approaches have been developed. Two of these zero-based budgeting and activity-based budgeting are dealt with below.

33. ZERO-BASED BUDGETING (ZBB)

ZBB is a cost-benefit approach whereby it is assumed that the cost allowance for an item is zero, and will remain so until the manager responsible justifies the existence of the cost item and the benefits the expenditure brings. In this way a questioning attitude is developed whereby each cost item and its level has to be justified in relation to the way it helps to meet objectives and how the expenditure benefits the organisation.

This is a forward looking approach as opposed to the all too common method of extrapolating past activities and costs, which is a feature of the incremental budgeting approach.

ZBB is formally defined by the CIMA thus:

*Method of budgeting that requires all costs to be specifically justified by the
benefits expected.*

Terminology

The use of ZBB was pioneered by P Phyrr in the United States and has
gained wide acceptance probably because it is a simple idea obviously based
on common sense. ZBB is concerned with the evaluation of the costs and benefits of alternatives and, implicit in the technique, is the concept of opportunity cost.

ZBB is sometimes known as priority-based budgeting. This is a descriptive
term because the approach does require explicit decisions to be made about
what priorities the organisation thinks are the most important.

34. WHERE CAN ZBB BE APPLIED?

ZBB can be applied in both profit seeking and non-profit seeking organisations. The technique gained wide publicity when the then President Carter
directed that all US government departments adopt ZBB.

In a manufacturing firm, ZBB is best applied to service and support expenditure including; finance and accounting, production planning and so on.
These activities are less easily quantifiable by conventional methods and are
more discretionary in nature. Manufacturing costs such as direct materials
and labour and production overheads can be more easily controlled by well
established methods which compare production outputs with resource inputs
rather than using ZBB.

ZBB can successfully be applied to service industries and to a wide range of
non-profit seeking organisations. For example local and central government
departments, educational establishments, hospitals and so on. ZBB could be
applied in any organisation where alternative levels of provision for each activity
are possible and the costs and benefits can be separately identified.

ZBB is concerned with alternatives and means that established activities
have to be compared with alternative uses of the same resources. ZBB takes
away the implied right of existing activities to continue to receive resources,
unless it can be shown that this is the best use of those resources.

35. IMPLEMENTING ZBB

There are several formal stages involved in implementing a ZBB system but of
greater importance is the development of an appropriate questioning attitude
by all concerned. There must be a 'value for money' approach which chal-
lenges existing practices and expenditures and searching questions must be
asked at each stage, typical of which are the following:

a. Does the activity need to be carried out at all? What would be the effects, if
   any, if it ceased?

b. How does the activity – existing or proposed – contribute to the
   organisation's objectives?

c. What is the correct level of provision? Has too much or too little been
   provided in the past?

d. What is the best way to provide the function? Have all alternative possibilities been considered?

e. How much should the activity cost? Is this expenditure worth the benefits achieved?

f. Is the activity essential or one of the frills?

and so on.

36. STAGES IN IMPLEMENTING ZBB

The overall process of implementing a ZBB system can be sub-divided into three stages thus:

a. *Definition of decision packages*
   A decision package is a comprehensive description of a facet of the organisation's activities or functions which can be individually evaluated. The decision package is specified by the managers concerned and must show details of the anticipated costs and results expected expressed in terms of tasks accomplished and benefits achieved.
   Two types of decision package are possible:

   • Mutually exclusive decision packages
      These are alternative forms of activity, tasks and expenditure to carry out the same job. The best option among the mutually exclusive packages is selected by comparing costs and benefits, and other packages are then discarded. Naturally, mutually exclusive packages would only be prepared when there are quite clearly different approaches for dealing with the same function. As an example, an organisation with a distribution problem might consider two alternative decision packages: Package 1 might be an in-house fleet of lorries, whereas Package 2 could involve contracts with independent hauliers.

   • Incremental decision packages
      These packages reflect different levels of effort in dealing with a particular activity. There will be what is known as the base package, which represents the minimum feasible level of activity, and other packages which describe higher activity levels at given costs and resulting benefits.
      As an example, a base package for a Personnel Department might provide for staff engagement and termination procedures and payroll administration. Incremental packages might include: education and training, welfare and social activities, pension administration, trade union liaison and negotiations, etc. Each package would have its costs and benefits clearly tabulated.

b. *Packages are evaluated and ranked*
   When the decision packages have been prepared, management will then rank all the packages on the basis of their benefits to the organisation. This is a process of allocating scarce resources between different activities, some of which already exist and others that are new. Minimum requirements which are essential to get the job done and activities necessary to meet legal or safety obligations will naturally receive high priority. It will be

found that the ranking process focuses management's attention on discretionary or optional activities.

Because of the large number of packages prepared throughout the organisation the ranking process can become onerous and time consuming for senior management. One way of reducing this problem is for lower level managers to rank the packages for their own budget centre and for these rankings to be consolidated, with others, at the next level up in the hierarchy. Alternatively, these could be ranked within the department and need not be referred higher.

c. *Resources allocated*
   When the overall budgeted expenditure level is decided upon the packages would be accepted in the ranked priority sequence up to the agreed expenditure level. Where the ranking of lower cost packages has been delegated to departments the proportion of the expenditure budget remaining after the more expensive packages have been ranked would be allocated to individual departments. The departments would then rank their own small packages up to their allocated expenditure level.

37. ADVANTAGES OF ZBB

a. Properly carried out, it should result in a more efficient allocation of resources to activities and departments.

b. ZBB focuses attention on value for money and makes explicit the relationship between the input of resources and the output of benefits.

c. It develops a questioning attitude and makes it easier to identify inefficient, obsolete or less cost effective operations.

d. The ZBB process leads to greater staff and management knowledge of the operations and activities of the organisation and can increase motivation.

e. It is a systematic way of challenging the status quo and obliges the organisation to examine alternative activities and existing cost behaviour patterns and expenditure levels.

38. DISADVANTAGES OF ZBB

a. It is a time consuming process which can generate volumes of paperwork especially for the decision packages.

b. There is considerable management skill required in both drawing decision packages and for the ranking process. These skills may not exist in the organisation.

c. It may encourage the wrong impression that all decisions have to be made in the budget. Circumstances change and new opportunities and threats can arise at any time and organisations must be flexible enough to deal rapidly with these circumstances when they occur.

d. ZBB is not always acceptable to staff or management or trade unions who may prefer the cosy status quo and who see the detailed examination of alternatives, costs and benefits as a threat not a challenge.

e. There are considerable problems in ranking packages and there are inevitably many subjective judgements. Political pressures within organisations also contribute to the problem of ranking different types of activity, especially where there are qualitative rather than quantitative benefits.

f. It may emphasise short term benefits to the detriment of longer term ones which in the end may be more important.

Undoubtedly the major drawback to ZBB is the amount of time the system takes. One way of obtaining the benefits of ZBB is to apply it selectively on a rolling basis throughout the organisation. This year Marketing, next year, Personnel, the year after Research and Development and so on. In this way, over a period, all activities will receive a thorough scrutiny, the benefits of which should last for years.

ZBB is particularly appropriate for non-profit making organisations where quality of service is all important. These types of organisation do not necessarily apply all the detail of ZBB but try to follow its basic philosophy by undertaking reviews of base estimates rather than using the simple incremental approach. As an example, a survey by Skousen found that 54% of UK local authorities claimed to challenge base estimates each year. The UK Government Comprehensive Spending Review 2007 includes a set of zero-based reviews of baseline expenditure in Government Departments aimed at assessing effectiveness and engendering a questioning approach.

39. ACTIVITY BASED BUDGETING (ABB)

ABB, sometimes termed Activity Cost Management, is a planning and control system which seeks to support the objective of continuous improvement. It is a development of conventional budgeting systems and is based on activity analysis techniques. It will be recalled that these were described when Activity Based Costing (ABC) was covered previously. In outline, ABC identifies the *cost drivers* (ie the activities which cause costs) and gathers costs into *cost pools*.

ABB recognises that:

a. It is activities which drive costs and the aim is to control the causes (drivers) of costs directly rather than the costs themselves. In the long-run, costs will be managed and better understood.

b. Not all activities add value so it is essential to differentiate and examine activities for their value-adding potential.

c. The majority of activities in a department are driven by demands and decisions beyond the immediate control of the budget holder. Conventional budgets, expressed in financial terms against established cost headings, ignore this causal relationship.

d. More immediate and relevant performance measures are required than are found in conventional budgeting systems. These consist exclusively of traditional financial measures which are insufficient to fulfil the objectives of continuous improvement. Additional measures are required which should focus on the factors which drive activities, the quality of the activities undertaken, the responsiveness to change and so on.

It is claimed that ABB provides a link between the organisation's strategic objectives and the objectives of individual activities.

ABB can be formally defined thus:

A method of budgeting based on an activity framework and utilising cost driver data in the budget-setting and variance feedback processes.

Terminology

40. ILLUSTRATION OF ABB

A Purchasing Department has two main activities: investigating and liaising with suppliers and issuing purchase orders. Two major cost drivers have been identified: the number of suppliers and the number of purchase orders placed.

The resources and costs of the department have largely been spread over the two main cost drivers. The balance of costs have been termed 'Department sustaining costs'. These include some general clerical costs and part of the manager's costs. Based on the activity expected for the period, cost driver volumes of 270 suppliers and 1,850 purchase orders have been forecast. Using these volumes and cost analysis, cost driver units and resource item costs have been budgeted for the department after discussion with the Departmental manager. The budget is as follows:

Budget for purchasing department

Cost drivers: Cost	No of suppliers £	No of purchase orders £	Dept sustaining cost £	Total £
Management salaries	12,000	2,000	18,000	32,000
Clerical salaries	3,000	21,500	6,500	31,000
Space costs	1,000	14,500	2,000	17,500
Consumables, travelling, etc	17,500	3,000	4,500	25,000
Information technology	3,000	8,500	1,000	12,500
Other costs	4,000	6,000	7,500	17,500
Total	40,500	55,500	39,500	135,500
Activity volumes	270	1,850	–	–
Cost/unit of cost driver	**£150**	**£30**	**£39,500**	

Notes:

a. The apportionment of costs to activities will, of course, be partly subjective. The object however is that the resource has to be justified in supporting one or more of the activities or the sustaining function. There is no place to hide the costs.

b. ABB highlights the cost of activities and thus encourages new thinking.

c. ABB enables a more focused view of cost control because the activity level is taken into account. Trends can be monitored and comparison with other organisations can be made. This is known as *benchmarking*. Benchmarking, defined earlier, is a valuable method of comparing an organisation's performance measures with other organisations in the same sector. For example, detailed Perfomance Ratio Benchmarking was undertaken in 2007

FIGURE 23.4 DHL

DHL

DHL is the global market leader in the international express and logistics industry, specialising in providing innovative and customised solutions from a single source. DHL offers expertise in express, air and ocean freight, overland transport, contract logistic solutions as well as international mail services, combined with worldwide coverage and an in-depth understanding of local markets. DHL's international network links more than 220 countries and territories worldwide. More than 300,000 employees are dedicated to providing fast and reliable services that exceed customers' expectations. DHL is a Deutsche Post World Net brand. The group generated revenues of more than €63 billion in 2006.

Employees: Over 112,000
Turnover: €13.9 billion

DHL has used ABC methodology for over 15 years and have been refining their system continually to cater for a business which deals with approximately 5 million shipments of varying sizes to and from 220 countries on a daily basis. The earliest system used was designed for a document business and was less suitable for packages and, although providing useful cost and profitability information, only provided limited information on customer profitability and there was no linkage between the costing system and management performance measures. Reviews of the methodology identified that different industry and customer profiles and specific customer behaviour had a material impact on costs. The problem was that not all of these drivers could be captured on a regular, consistent basis. Consequently attention was focused on those drivers that were recognised throughout the business and could be readily measured. It thus became easier to integrate these drivers (and their associated costs) into the performance measurement process. For further details refer to www.bellisjoneshill.co.uk/activity_based_costing/examples.htm

concerning the underwriting profitability of the top 10 motor insurance firms in the UK including: AXA, Fortis, Churchill, Royal Sun Alliance, Zurich and so on.

d. The cost driver rates £150 and £30 are used in calculating the product costs in the Activity Based Costing system.

e. The identification of activities and their costs helps to focus attention on those activities which add value and those that do not.

Activity based budgeting principles are increasingly being used in manufacturing firms, eg Siemens and Hewlett Packard, in service industries and Government departments such as the Department of Trade and Industry, Department of Health and so on. As an example consider the case of DHL who operate a world wide delivery service.

41. POSSIBLE PROBLEMS WITH ACTIVITY BASED ANALYSIS

An activity based approach may not be always suitable for month-to-month monitoring because of short-term fluctuations. If, for example, the number of purchase orders goes up by 20% in a month and resources stay the same the cost per order will decrease. However, if the increase in activity lasts long enough there is likely to be the need for more staff, overtime and so on. The inevitable variability in the cost per activity directs attention to whether resources are being used effectively and what levels may be required in the future.

There is also the need to guard against the notion that a selected cost driver provides a comprehensive basis for controlling costs. The cost levels of most activities behave in a more complex manner than can be explained by a single work load measure. Over-concentration on one performance measure can produce adverse consequences. In the Purchasing Department illustration above, the staff can decrease the cost per purchase order simply by splitting large orders into several smaller ones yet this could well have adverse longer-term effects.

42. SUMMARY

a. A budget is a quantitative expression of a plan and the full budgetary process includes planning and control.

b. Budgeting can bring a number of real advantages including coordination, clarification of responsibility, improved communication, increased control and the motivation of personnel.

c. The limiting factor (or key factor or principal budget factor) is the factor which limits the activities of the organisation. Typical limiting factors include: sales, shortage of materials or production capacity or skilled labour, lack of finance etc.

d. The budget is prepared by the budget committee having regard to the organisation's objectives and is submitted to the Board of Directors or the Chief Executive for approval. When approved it becomes an executive order.

e. When the budget is approved it is issued so that the budgetary control process can be carried out when actual results are to hand. The investigation of variances and the development of solutions to problems discovered is the key to controlling expenditure.

f. A fixed budget is a budget for a single level of activity whereas a flexible budget, because of the analysis of costs into fixed and variable elements, can be adjusted or flexed for various activity levels.

g. The attitude of the people who have to operate the budgetary system is of critical importance. Budgets are frequently seen as pressure systems imposed by top management.

h. To avoid adverse reactions from the people involved there should be full and genuine participation, clear goal definition and good communications all of which will contribute to the budgetary process being a motivating rather than a disruptive force.

i. Zero-based budgeting means that each activity starts with a nil budget. Each increment of the budget has then to be justified in terms of costs related to the benefits achieved. The idea is to contain or reduce costs especially in public sector organisations. The idea is simple and appealing but the system is cumbersome and subject to political pressure.

j. Activity Based Budgeting or Activity Cost Management means budgeting is related to activities rather than conventional departments. ABB recognises that it is activities which cause costs and is a more focused method of budgeting.

43. POINTS TO NOTE

a. A master budget is the summary of all other budgets and is expressed as a Budgeted Profit and Loss account and Balance Sheet.

b. Too much attention is paid, particularly by accountants, to the mechanics of budgeting. Of far greater importance are the behavioural aspects, ie is the process acceptable to those who have to operate it? Does it motivate them? Do they feel threatened by it?

c. Remember it is the quantities/volumes/units, etc which are budgeted and the converted into financial terms as a common measure. Money figures are not directly budgeted.

d. Budgets can be used for both planning and for control. Frequently too much attention is paid to the control aspects of budgeting and the positive planning and coordinating activities of budgetary planning are not given the attention they deserve.

e. The problems of budgetary slack are frequently encountered. This is the term used to describe the way some managers obtain a budget larger than strictly necessary so that they either can spend more liberally up to the budget or appear to be containing costs very efficiently by beating their budget. An attempt to overcome this and other problems, particularly in public sector organisations, is the use of zero-base budgeting described above.

f. Budgeting and Budgetary control are dealt with in more detail in *Management Accounting*, T. Lucey, Cengage Learning.

Student self-testing

Exercises (answers below)

1. A company produces two domestic appliances, the Starfrig and Starfreezer. The following details have been estimated:

	Year 19-1
Sales	Starfrig 40,000 @ £75 each
	Starfreezer 80,000 @ £90 each

Total costs are estimated to be:

	£
Direct materials	2,400,000
Direct Labour	4,200,000
Variable Overheads	2,100,000
Fixed Overheads	800,000

Each Starfreezer requires the same material as a Starfrig but twice as much labour. Variable overheads are absorbed on direct labour. The demand for the Starfrig has been falling and a new model, the Starfrig II is to be introduced for Year 2 incorporating a freezer compartment which will sell at £115 each.

The estimated costs of the new model are (per unit) Direct Labour £46. Variable overheads £23 and Direct Materials £25. Because of the new model fixed overheads will increase by £200,000. Sales for Year 2 are forecasted to be: Starfreezer 80,000 units Starfrig 32,000 units Starfrig II 15,000 units. You are required to prepare budgeted profit statements for Year 1 and Year 2 showing the contribution from each model.

2. A firm has produced the following budgets for two activity levels:

Expense	Budget for 5,000 units £	Budget for 6,000 units £
Wages	16,000	17,200
Materials	25,000	30,000
Salaries	22,500	23,000
Depreciation	18,000	18,000
Other Overheads	18,500	21,000

Prepare a budget for an activity level of 6,200 units.

3. A company has a cash balance of £27,000 at the beginning of March and you are required to prepare a cash budget for March, April and May having regard to the following information.

Creditors give 1 month credit

Salaries are paid in the current month Fixed costs are paid one month in arrears and include a charge for depreciation of £5,000 per month.

Credit sales are settled as follows: 40% in month of sale, 45% in next month and 12% in the following month. The balance represents bad debts.

Month	Cash Sales £	Credit Sales £	Purchases £	Salaries £	Fixed Overheads £
Jan		74,000	55,200	9,000	30,000
Feb		82,000	61,200	9,000	30,000
March	20,000	80,000	60,000	9,500	30,000
April	22,000	90,000	69,000	9,500	32,000
May	25,000	100,000	75,000	10,000	32,000

4. Contrast the preparation of conventional and Activity Based Budgets.

Solutions to exercises

1. Budgeted Profit Statement for Year 1

	Starfrig			Starfreezer	Total
Sales (units)	40,000			80,000	
	£	£	£	£	£
Sales Revenue		3,000,000		7,200,000	10,200,000
less Variable Costs					
Materials	800,000		1,600,000		
Labour	840,000		3,360,000		
Overheads	420,000	2,060,000	1,680,000	6,640,000	8,700,000
= Contribution		940,000		560,000	1,500,000
			less Fixed Costs		800,000
			= Profit		£700,000

Budgeted Profit Statement for year 2

		Starfrig 32,000		Starfrig II 15,000		Starfreezer 80,000	Total
Sales (units)	£	£	£	£	£	£	£
Sales Revenue		2,400,000		1,725,000		7,200,000	11,325,000
less Variable costs							
Materials	640,000		375,000		1,600,000		
Labour	672,000		690,000		3,360,000		
Overheads	336,000	1,648,000	345,000	1,410,000	1,680,000	6,640,000	9,698,000
= Contribution		752,000		315,000		560,000	1,627,0000
					less Fixed costs		1,000,000
					= Profit		£627,000

2. Budget for 6,200 units

Expense	Budget for 6,200 units £	Derived Cost Function
Wages	17,440	£10,000 + £1.20 unit
Materials	31,000	£5 per unit
Salaries	23,100	£20,000 + 0.50 per unit
Depreciation	18,000	Fixed
Other overheads	21,500	£6,000 + £2.50 per unit

3. **Cash Budget**

	March	April	May
Opening Balance	27,000	29,000	38,340
+ Receipts from debtors*	77,700	81,840	90,100
+ Cash sales	20,000	22,000	25,000
= Total Cash Available	124,700	132,840	153,440
− Salaries	9,500	9,500	10,000
− Fixed overheads	25,000	25,000	27,000
− Purchases	61,200	60,000	69,000
Total outlays	95,700	94,500	106,000
Balance c/f	29,000	38,340	47,440

The receipts from debtors are calculated as follows:

March	£	April	£	May	£
40% March	32,000	40% April	36,000	40% May	40,000
45% Feb	36,900	45% March	36,000	45% April	40,500
12% Jan	8,800	12% Feb	9,840	12% March	9,600
	£77,700		£81,840		£90,100

4. There are many similarities between the preparation of conventional budgets and activity based budgets. These include: consideration of organisational objectives and long term plans; the need for co-ordination, the need to consider resources and possible limiting factors.

There are however some important differences which include:

Clarification of responsibilities:
Conventional budgets are usually developed around existing Departmental Structures with their managers being responsible for budgets. Budgets based on Activities are likely to cross conventional departmental barriers thus causing potential responsibility problems.

Difficulties of cost attribution:
Especially in the development stages of activity budgeting there may be difficulties in attributing costs to activities perhaps because the cost analysis/ coding systems are more suited to gathering costs by department rather than activity.

Demand control and cost control separated:
The person designated as responsible for the cost control of an activity is not likely to be the same person who has control over the demand for the activity. This is a form of split responsibility which can cause friction.

24

Standard costing – Introduction

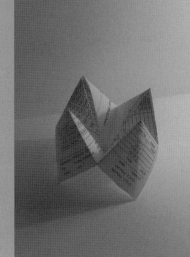

I. OBJECTIVES

After studying this chapter you will

- **Be able to define Standard Costing and Standard Cost**

- **Know how standards relate to budgets**

- **Understand how standards are set and recorded**

- **Know the advantages and disadvantages of standard costing**

- **Understand the importance of human factors in standard costing.**

2. STANDARD COSTING DEFINED

Standard costing is a technique which establishes predetermined estimates of the costs of products and services and then compares these predetermined costs with actual costs as they are incurred. The predetermined costs are known as *standard costs* and the difference between the standard cost and actual cost is known as a *variance*. The process by which the total difference between actual cost and standard cost is broken down into its different elements is known as *variance analysis*.

Standard costing in practice is a detailed process and requires considerable development work before it is a useful tool. For standard costing to be successful requires reasonable stability and the existence of repetitive work. These conditions can be found across many sectors of the economy. For example in Manufacturing, in Service Industries such as transport, computing and banking, in parts of the Public Sector (eg street cleaning, refuse disposal) and so on. Its major application in practice is in manufacturing and repetitive assembly work.

3. STANDARD COST

This can be formally defined as:

> *The planned unit cost of the products, components or services produced in a period. The standard cost may be determined on a number of bases (see standard). The main uses of standard costs are in performance measurement, control, stock valuation and in the establishment of selling prices.*
>
> *Terminology*

A standard cost is a target cost which should be attained. The build-up of a standard cost is based on sound technical and engineering studies, known production methods and layouts, work studies and work measurement, material specifications and wage and material price projections.

A standard cost is not an average of previous costs. These are likely to contain the results of past inefficiencies and mistakes. Furthermore changes in methods, technology and costs make comparisons with the past of doubtful value for control purposes.

Standards may be set using various bases as follows.

4. TYPES OF STANDARDS

There are numerous ways that standards may be developed as shown in the formal definition of a standard which follows:

> *A benchmark measure of resource usage or revenue or profit generation, set in defined conditions.*
>
> > *Standards can set on a number of bases:*

(a) on an ex ante estimate of expected performance

(b) on an ex post estimate of attainable performance

(c) on a prior period level of performance by the same organization

(d) on the level of performance achieved by comparable organizations or

(e) on the level of performance required to meet organizational objectives

> *Standards may also be set at attainable levels that assume efficient levels of operation but that include allowance for normal loss, waste and machine down time or at ideal levels that make no allowance for the above losses, and are only attainable under the most favourable conditions. The effect of different levels on staff motivation will be an important influence on the type of standards that are used.*
>
> *Terminology*

From this definition it will be seen that a standard, however it is set, provides a measurement of some resource usage, eg units, hours, minutes, kilograms and so on as appropriate. More details follow of three important types of standard:

a. *Basic standards*. These are long term standards which would remain unchanged over the years. Their sole use is to show trends over time for such items as material prices, labour rates and efficiency and the effect of changing methods. They cannot be used to highlight current efficiency or inefficiency and would not normally form part of the reporting system except as a background, statistical exercise.

The formal definition of a basic standard is: a standard established for use over a long period from which a current standard can be developed.

b. *Ideal standards.* These are based on the best possible operating conditions, ie no breakdowns, no material wastage, no stoppages or idle time, in short, perfect efficiency. Ideal standards, if used, would be revised periodically to reflect improvements in methods, materials and technology. Clearly ideal standards would be unattainable in practice and accordingly are rarely used. However, their use could be considered worthwhile for investigative and development purposes, but not for normal day-to-day control activities.

c. *Attainable standard.* This is by far the most frequently encountered standard. It is a standard based on efficient (but not perfect) operating conditions. The standard would include allowances for normal material losses, realistic allowances for fatigue, machine breakdowns, etc. It must be stressed, however, that an attainable standard must be based on a high performance level so that its achievement is possible, but has to be worked for.

Attainable standards provide a tough, but realistic target and thus can provide motivation for management. They can be used for product costing, for cost control, for stock valuation and as a basis for budgeting.

Attainable standards would be revised periodically to reflect the conditions expected to prevail during the ensuing period when the standards would apply. Unless otherwise stated, all subsequent references in this book to standards mean *attainable standards.*

Notes on the types of standard:

a. The type of standard used (basic, ideal, attainable or other type) directly affects the level of the variances which can arise and the meaning which can be attached to the variances.

b. There are real problems in determining the level of attainment in standards so it follows that, to a greater or lesser extent, all standards contain a subjective element.

c. Like budgets the setting of standards, particularly relating to price and wage levels, is dependent on forecasting skill. This means that variances can arise from both differences in efficiency levels and from forecasting errors. This fact should be remembered when interpreting any variance.

5. STANDARDS AND BUDGETS

Both standards and budgets are concerned with setting performance and cost levels for control purposes. They therefore are similar in principle although they differ in scope. Standards are a unit concept, ie they apply to particular products, to individual operations or processes or services.

Budgets are concerned with totals; they lay down cost limits for functions and departments and for the firm as a whole. As an illustration the standard material cost of the various products in a firm could be as follows:

		Standard Material Cost/Unit £	Planned Production	Total Material Cost £
Product	X321	3.50	5,000 units	17,500
Product	Y592	7.25	1,500 units	10,875
Product	Y728	1.50	2,400 units	3,600
etc	etc	etc	etc	etc
etc	etc	etc	etc	etc

Overall Total = Materials Budget = £275,000

In this way the detailed unit standards are used as the basis for developing realistic budgets. This is particularly so for direct material and direct labour costs which are more amenable to close control through standard costing whereas overheads would normally be controlled by functional and departmental budgets. Further differences are that budgets would be revised on a periodic basis, frequently as an annual exercise, whereas standards are revised only when they are inappropriate for current operating conditions. Such revisions may take place more or less frequently than budget revisions.

The accounting treatment of standards and budgets also differs. Budgets are memorandum figures and do not form part of the double entry accounting system whereas standards and the resulting variances are included. The double entry treatment of standards and variances is explained in Chapter 25.

6. SETTING STANDARDS

Realistic standards which can be used for control purposes rest on a foundation of properly organised, standardised methods and procedures and a comprehensive information system. It is little point trying to develop a standard cost for a product if the production method is not decided upon. A standard cost implies that a target or standard exists for every single element which contributes to the product: the types, usage and prices of materials and parts, the grades, rates of pay and times for the labour involved, the production methods and layouts, the tools and jigs and so on. Considerable effort is involved in establishing standard costs and keeping them up to date.

Traditionally, the standard cost for each part or product was recorded on a standard cost card and an example is given later in this chapter. With the increased usage of computers for costing purposes frequently nowadays there is no physical cost card. When a computer is used, the standard costs are recorded on a disc file and can be accessed and processed as required. Whether a computer or manual system is used, there are no differences in the principles of standard costing, although there are many differences in the method of day to day operation. The following paragraphs explain some of the detailed procedures involved in setting standards.

7. SETTING STANDARDS – MATERIALS

The materials content of a product, raw materials, sub-assemblies, piece parts, finishing materials, etc, is derived from technical and engineering specifications, frequently in the form of a Bill of Materials. The standard quantities required normally include an allowance for normal and inevitable losses in production, that is, machining loss, evaporation, and expected levels of breakages and rejections. The process of analysis is valuable in itself because savings and alternative materials and ways of using materials are frequently discovered.

The responsibility for providing material prices is that of the buying department. The prices used are not the past costs, but the forecast expected costs for the relevant budget period. The expected costs should take into account trends in material prices, anticipated changes in purchasing policies, quantity and cash discounts, carriage and packing charges and any other factor which will influence material costs.

8. SETTING STANDARDS – LABOUR

Without detailed operation and process specifications it would be impossible to establish standard labour times. The agreed methods of manufacture are the basis of setting the standard labour times. The techniques of work measurement are involved, frequently combined with work study projections based on elemental analysis when a part is not yet in production.

The labour standards must specify the exact grades of labour to be used as well as the times involved. Planned labour times are expressed in *standard hours* (or *standard minutes*). The concept of a standard hour/minute is important and can be defined as:

The amount of work achievable at standard efficiency levels, in an hour or minute.

Terminology

It will be noted that a standard hour represents a given work content. Indeed, production for a given period is frequently described as 'so many standard hours' rather than a quantity of parts. Once the times a grades of labour have been established, a forecast can be made of the relevant wage rates for the appropriate future period. This is usually done by the Personnel Department.

Note:
It must be understood that a standard hour or minute is a *measure of work content*, not a measure of time. An alternative name for a standard hour is an *output hour*.

9. SETTING STANDARDS – OVERHEADS

It will be recalled from earlier in the book how overhead absorption rates are established. These predetermined overhead absorption rates become the standards for overheads for each cost centre using the budgeted standard labour hours as the activity base. For realistic control, overheads must be analysed into their fixed and variable components and separate absorption rates calculated for both fixed and variable overheads thus:

$$\text{Standard Variable OAR} = \frac{\text{Budgeted variable overheads for cost centre}}{\text{Budgeted standard labour hours for cost centre}}$$

and

$$\text{Standard fixed OAR} = \frac{\text{Budgeted fixed overheads for cost centre}}{\text{Budgeted standard labour hours for cost centre}}$$

The level of activity adopted, expressed in standard labour hours, is the budgeted expected annual activity level which is the basis of the Master Budget. For reporting and control purposes this would be classed as 100% capacity.

10. SETTING STANDARDS – SALES PRICE AND MARGIN

Fundamental to any form of standard costing, budgeting and profit planning is the anticipated selling price for the product. The setting of the selling price is frequently a top level decision and is based on a variety of factors including: the anticipated market demand, competing products, manufacturing costs, inflation estimates and so on.

Finally, after discussion and investigation, a selling price is established at which it is planned to sell the product during the period concerned. This becomes the standard selling price. The standard sales margin is the difference between the standard cost and the standard selling price. Where a standard variable (or marginal) costing system is used, the standard contribution is calculated following the normal variable costing principles explained in Chapter 19.

Note:
Normally when 'standard cost' is mentioned it means total standard cost, ie, total absorption cost principles are used incorporating fixed and variable costs. Standard variable costing is also employed, but students should assume that total absorption cost principles are involved whenever the term standard cost is used without qualification. This nomenclature is adopted in this book. When variable costing principles are used the term *standard variable cost* is used.

11. RESPONSIBILITY FOR SETTING STANDARDS

The line managers who have to work with and accept the standards must be involved in establishing them. These managers and their superiors have the ultimate responsibility for setting the standards. Work study staff, accountants and other specialists provide technical support and information, but do not make the final decisions upon standards and performance levels.

12. THE STANDARD COST CARD

The process of setting standards results in the establishment of the standard cost for the product. The make-up of the standard cost is recorded on a standard cost card. In practice there may be numerous detail cards together with a summary card for a given product, or the standard cost details may be on a computer file. The principles, however, remain the same. A simple standard cost card is shown on the following page.

13. REVISION OF STANDARDS

To show trends and to be able to compare performance and costs between different periods, standards would be rarely changed. On the other hand, for day to day control and motivation purposes standards which reflect the most up to date position are required and consequently revisions would need to be made continually.

The above positions reflect the extremes of the situation. There is not doubt that standards which are right up to date provide a better target and are more useful for the foremen and managers concerned, but the extent and frequency of standard revision is a matter of judgement. Minor changes in rates, prices and usage are frequently ignored for a time, but their cumulative effect soon becomes significant and changes need to be made.

Prior to computer maintained standard cost files, standard cost revisions were a time consuming chore as it was necessary to ensure that all the effects of a change were recorded. For example, a change in the price of a common raw material would necessitate alterations to:

a. the standard cost cards of all products, parts and assemblies using the material;

b. any price lists, stock sheets and catalogues involving the material and products derived from the material.

Because of such factors, it is common practice for all standard costs to be revised together at regular, periodic intervals such as every 6 or 12 months, rather than on an individual, random basis.

Standard Cost Card					
PART NO: X291 **DESCRIPTION: Stub Joint** **BATCH QTY: 100**					
TOOL REF: T5983 **WORK STUDY REF: WS255** **DRAWING NO: DS92/5**					
REVISION DATE: 4/2/96 **REVISED BY: G.E.F.**					
Cost Type & Quantity	**Standard Price or Rate**	**Dept 7** £	**Dept 19** £	**Dept 15** £	**Total** £
Direct Materials					
2.5 kg PI01	£14.80 kg	£ 37.00			37.00
100 units A539	£3.75 100		£ 37.50		37.50
					74.50
Direct Labour					
Machine operation					
Grade 15					
4.8 hrs	£6.5 hr	31.20			31.20
9.2 hrs	£6.5 hr		59.80		59.80
Assembly					
Grade 8					
16.4 hrs	£5.75 hr			94.30	94.30
					185.30
Production Overhead					
Machine hour rate	£11 hr	52.80	101.20		154.00
Labour hour rate	£6hr			98.40	98.40
		121.00	198.50	192.70	252.40

Standard Cost Summary	
Direct Materials	£ 74.50
Direct Labour	185.30
Production Overheads	252.40
Standard Cost per 100	512.20

14. BEHAVIOURAL ASPECTS OF STANDARDS

The points made in the previous chapter regarding the importance of the human aspects of budgeting apply equally to standard costing. Both techniques use similar principles and both rely absolutely upon the people who have to work to the budgets and standards. Because of the detailed nature of standard costing and its involvement with foremen and production workers, communication becomes of even greater importance. Production workers frequently regard any form of performance evaluation with deep suspicion and if a cost-conscious, positive attitude is to be developed, close attention must be paid to the behavioural aspects of the system.

Appropriate participation, realistic standards, prompt and accurate reporting, no undue pressure or censure – all contribute to an acceptable system. Remember: if the system is not accepted by the people involved it will be unworkable.

15. ADVANTAGES OF STANDARD COSTING

a. Standard costing is an example of 'management by exception'. By studying the variances, management's attention is directed towards those items which are not proceeding according to plan. Management are able to delegate cost control through the standard costing system knowing that variances will be reported.

b. The process of setting, revising and monitoring standards encourages reappraisals of methods, materials and techniques so leading to cost reductions.

c. Standard costs represent what the parts and products should cost. They are not merely averages of past performances and consequently they are a better guide to pricing than historical costs. In addition, they provide a simpler basis of inventory valuation.

d. A properly developed standard costing system with full participation and involvement creates a positive, cost effective attitude through all levels of management right down to the shop floor.

16. DISADVANTAGES OF STANDARD COSTING

a. It may be expensive and time consuming to install and to keep up to date.

b. In volatile conditions with rapidly changing methods, rates and prices, standards quickly become out of date and thus lose their control and motivational effects. This can cause resentment and loss of goodwill.

c. There is research evidence to suggest that overly elaborate variances are imperfectly understood by line managers and thus they are ineffective for control purposes.

d. Standard costing concentrates only on a narrow range of financial factors but many other items are of importance, eg quality, lead times, service, customer satisfaction and so on. By ignoring these, standard costing, at best, only controls part of operations.

e. The underlying principles of standard costing, ie that a standard established prior to a period is a satisfactory measure throughout the period and that performance is acceptable if it meets this standard is alien to the spirit of JIT manufacturing. Where JIT principles are adopted there is a climate of continuous improvement and the idea of normal levels of waste and efficiency (conventionally used in standards) is not accepted because there is a drive towards zero waste and ever increasing efficiency. As a consequence it is possible that standard costing will become less useful in modern factories.

17. MOTIVATION AND STANDARDS

One of the hoped for effects of standards is that people will be motivated to achieve the targets represented by the standards. In general people are likely to be motivated by standards if they accept them and do not feel threatened by the system.

There are numerous factors which affect the way that standards motivate, or do not motivate, the people responsible for achieving the standards.

Three important factors are examined below: participation, attainment level and feedback.

Participation

Participation means that the people responsible for achieving the standards are consulted and are part of the standard setting process. Common sense would appear to suggest that people would prefer participation and that their performance would improve.

However, the empirical studies show that the position is not so straightforward. Some studies (eg Kenis, Argyris and others) found that participation improved performance whilst others (eg. Milani, Bryan and Locke) found that participation tended to lead to lower performance levels. Vroom found that participation was not suitable for certain types of people, especially those who preferred directive leadership and clear-cut unambiguous situations. In another study Brownell found that where people felt they had a large degree of control over their own destinies then there were positive effects from participation.

Thus it would appear that participation may have beneficial effects but has to be used selectively with due regard to the personalities of the people concerned.

Attainment Levels

The attainment level is the level of difficulty at which the standard is set. The various studies indicate that very difficult targets are not likely to be accepted. The person may give up and produce a performance worse than if a less demanding target had been set. Conversely if undemanding targets are set they will be achieved but the individuals are not motivated to achieve their full potential.

Hofstede conducted considerable research on the effect that targets set at different levels of difficulty have on aspiration levels (ie an individual's personal goals). In summary, he found that setting targets does not always lead to improved performance. Very loose or very tight targets were particularly ineffective and the target level which motivates the best actual performance is unlikely to be met most of the time. This means that when targets are set at a level which motivates the best performance, adverse variances will often occur. If such variances are used in a punitive fashion this is likely to make individuals press for easier targets. These may produce fewer adverse variances but at the expense of lower actual performance.

Feedback

Feedback is part of the control cycle whereby information on actual performance against budget or standard and the resulting variances is reported to the individual concerned. It has been found that prompt accurate feedback of results has a positive motivational effect. Where feedback is delayed or is not understood or is inaccurate confidence in the system is undermined and motivation reduced. Accordingly, it is of considerable importance that the costing system produces speedy, relevant feedback otherwise its effectiveness will be reduced.

18. SUMMARY

a. Standard costing compares actual costs with predetermined costs and analyses the differences, known as variances.

b. There are numerous types of standard including those based on before/ after the event performance levels, comparative standards, ideal standards and attainable standards.

c. Basic standards are long-term standards which are unchanged for long periods; ideal standards represent perfect working conditions and performances; attainable standards are standards based on high but not impossible performance levels. Attainable standards are the most common.

d. Standards relate to individual items, processes and products; budgets relate to totals.

e. Setting standards is detailed, lengthy process usually based on engineering and technical studies of times, materials and methods. Standards are set for each of the elements which make up the standard cost: labour, materials and overheads.

f. Accountants, work study engineers and other specialists provide technical advice and information, but do not set the standards. This is the responsibility of the line managers and their superiors.

g. The culmination of the standard setting process is the preparation of a standard cost card for the product showing the target cost for the following periods.

h. Difficulties arise with the too frequent revision of standards. Consequently it is common practice to revise them on a periodic basis, half yearly or yearly.

i. The behavioural aspects of standard costing, like budgeting, are all important. The system must be acceptable to the people who will have to operate it.

19. POINTS TO NOTE

a. A standard cost, like any cost, is made up from two components: the usage of materials, labour, etc and the price or rate of these elements. This cost make-up plays a significant part in variance analysis covered in the next chapter.

b. Standard costing and variance analysis are important examination topics. Because examiners are always seeking novel applications a thorough understanding of basic principles is vital for all students.

Student self-testing

Exercises (answers below)

1. 'There is a subjective element involved in the setting of all standards.' Discuss.

2. From the following data prepare the Standard Cost Card for one unit of the sole product manufactured.

   Direct Materials:
   20 Kgs 'A' @ £0.80 per Kg
   15 Kgs 'B' @ £2.49 per Kg

   Direct Labour:
   Preparation 14 hours at £3.75 per hour
   Assembly 5 hours at £2.50 per hour

The budgeted total overheads for year:

	£	Hours
Preparation dept.	88,000	21,000
Assembly dept	150,000	24,000

The fixed overheads (included in the above figures) are £25,000 and £48,000 respectively.

The standard cost card should show sub-totals for:

a. Prime cost

b. Variable production cost

c. Total production cost

3. 'Standard Costing can only be applied in factories.' Discuss.

Solutions to exercises

1. The typical build-up of a standard cost involves detailed engineering analysis of materials, methods, tools, etc and work study investigations of layouts, work flows and methods. These procedures are detailed and have the appearance of total objectivity but examination shows that there are subjective factors involved.

For example, the precise amount of material contained in a product is an objective fact but the standard cost will include an additional amount for 'normal' waste. This amount must involve judgement. Also the labour method and type of labour can be objectively determined but the rate at which labour is deemed to work is a subjective assessment. The pricing factors (eg labour rate, material price) also contain subjective factors as they relate to prices expected over the future period.

In short all standards involve some subjective elements and an awareness of this will avoid taking too pedantic a view of variances.

2.

Standard Cost Card For One Unit

		£	£
Direct Materials			
	20 Kgs A @ £0.80	16.00	
	15 Kgs B @ £2.40	36.00	52.00
Direct Labour			
Preparation	14 hrs @ £3.75	52.50	
Assembly	5 hrs @ £2.50	12.50	65.00
= Prime Cost			117.00
Variable Overheads			
Preparation	14 hrs @ £3	42.00	
Assembly	5 hrs @ £4.25	21.25	63.25
= Variable Production Cost			180.25
Fixed Overheads			
Preparation	14 hrs @ £1.19	16.67	
Assembly	5 hrs @ £2	10.00	26.67
= Total Production Cost			£206.92

3. While it is true that most applications of standard costing are in factories the technique can be more widely applied. It could be used in offices, transport undertakings, computer departments, local authorities, indeed anywhere where suitable conditions exist. These include:

   a. Some form of repetitive process or operation which is regularly carried out.

   b. Where the process has been analysed in sufficient detail for methods and times to be established with reasonable accuracy.

   c. Where it would be cost effective to monitor and control costs using a reasonably sophisticated technique such as standard costing.

25

Standard costing – Variance analysis (material, labour and overheads)

1. OBJECTIVES

After studying this chapter you will

- **Know what is meant by Variance and Analysis and its purpose**

- **Understand the relationship of variances**

- **Be able to calculate basic Material, Labour and Overhead Variances**

- **Know that there are alternative ways of calculating Overhead Variances**

- **Understand Material Mix and Yield Variances.**

2. VARIANCE ANALYSIS DEFINED

It will be recalled from the previous chapter that a variance is the difference between standard cost and actual cost. The term variance is rarely used on its own. Usually it is qualified in some way, for example; direct materials cost variance, direct labour efficiency variance and so on. The process by which the total difference between standard and actual costs is sub-divided is known as *variance analysis* which can be defined as:

> *The evaluation of performance by means of variances, whose timely reporting should maximise the opportunity for managerial action.*
>
> *Terminology*

Variances arise from differences between standard and actual quantities and/or differences between standard and actual prices. These are the *causes* of variances; the reasons for the differences have to be established by management investigation.

Note:
Variances may be *adverse*, ie where actual cost is greater than standard, or they may be *favourable*, ie where actual cost is less than standard. Alternatively they may be known as *minus* or *plus* variances respectively.

3. THE PURPOSE OF VARIANCE ANALYSIS

The only purpose of variance analysis is to provide practical pointers to the causes of off-standard performance so that management can improve operations, increase efficiency, utilise resources more effectively and reduce costs. It follows that overly elaborate variance analysis which is not understood, variances that are not acted upon and variances which are calculated too long after the event do not fulfil the central purpose of standard costing.

The types of variances which are identified must be those which fulfil the needs of the organisation. The only criterion for the calculation of a variance is its usefulness – if it is not useful for management purposes, it should not be produced.

4. RESPONSIBILITY FOR VARIANCES

Ideally, variances should be detailed enough so that responsibility can be assigned to a particular individual for a specific variance. Cost control is made much more difficult if responsibility for a variance is spread over several managers. In such circumstances it is all too easy to 'pass the buck'.

Because of the importance of this principle, standard costing and budgetary control are known in America as *responsibility accounting*. A simple example of the process of calculating variances in accordance with responsibilities is the subdivision of the direct materials cost variance, that is, the total difference in material costs between actual and standard.

This is composed of a usage component, which is usually deemed the responsibility of a foreman, and a price component which is usually deemed the responsibility of the buyer. Accordingly, a usage variance and a price variance need to be calculated to show how much of the total difference is attributable to either person. This example is at the most basic level; frequently more variances are calculated than those given above.

Note:
The assignment of clear-cut responsibilities for variances is an ideal which is difficult to achieve in practice. Interrelationships and interdependencies make the process much more complex than the basic theory.

For example, it is conventional to assume that material usage and labour efficiency variances are within the control of the departmental manager concerned. However, where a department receives inputs from another department the receiving department's operations are greatly influenced by the quality and delivery of its inputs. This is but one example of an interdependency, many others exist in a typical organisation.

5. THE RELATIONSHIP OF VARIANCES

The overall objective of variance analysis is to subdivide the total difference between budgeted profit and actual profit for the period into the detailed differences (relating to material, labour, overheads and sales) which go to make up to total difference. The particular variances which are computed in any given organisation are those which are relevant to its operations and which will aid control. Figure 25.1 on page 429 shows typical variances which are generally found useful, but it must be emphasised that relevance and appropriateness to management are the only criteria, not the fact that a variance is mentioned in textbooks and on examination papers. The chart shows a hierarchy of frequently encountered variances and should be studied carefully together with the notes which follow:

Notes to Figure 25.1:

a. Each variance and sub-variance is described in detail in the paragraphs which follow.

b. For simplicity the full title of each variance is not shown in each box. The full titles are easily derived from the chart. For example, under the *Direct Materials* Total Variance is found the *Direct Materials* Price Variance, the *Direct Materials* Usage Variance and so on.

c. The chart is arithmetically consistent, ie the total of the linked variances equals the senior variance shown. For example:

Variable Overhead Expenditure Variance

+ Variable Overhead Efficiency Variance

= Variable Overhead Variance

d. The price and quantity aspects of each variance are shown clearly on the chart and can be summarised as shown in the table below.

Cost Element	Price Variances	Quantity Variances
Direct Labour	Rate	Efficiency
Direct Materials	Price	Usage
Variable Overheads	Expenditure	Efficiency
Fixed Overheads	Expenditure	Volume

e. The *'operating profit'* variance is the difference between budgeted and actual operating profit for a period. This variance can be calculated directly and it is the sum of all variances, ie cost variances and sales variances. The operating profit variance is not entered in a ledger account because budgeted profit does not appear therein. All other variances do appear in ledger accounts. The book-keeping entries for standard costing systems are described in detail in Chapter 26.

f. The chart shows the overhead variances sub-divided into Fixed and Variable components. An alternative, and simpler, approach is not to sub-divide the overheads, in which case the overhead variances are different. Both of the approaches are illustrated later in the chapter but it must be emphasised that neither approach is 'correct' or 'incorrect' – they are merely different. It is worth repeating that the 'correct' variances are those which provide *relevant information for management*.

FIGURE 25.1 Chart of common variances

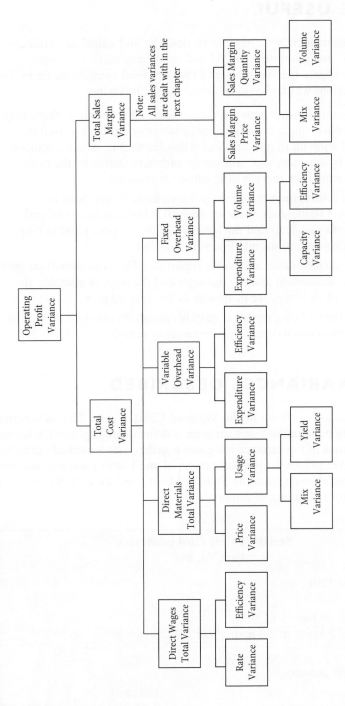

6. MAKING VARIANCE ANALYSIS MORE USEFUL

It is not sufficient merely to be able to describe and calculate variances. To make variance analysis into a useful aid to management it is necessary to probe and investigate the variances and the data used to calculate them. Typical of the questions which should be asked are the following:

a. Is there any relationship between the variances? For example, there may be pleasure in observing a favourable materials price variance caused by purchase of a job lot of material, but if this favourable variance is more than offset by adverse usage and labour variances caused by the poor quality material, then there is little cause for rejoicing.

b. Can further information than merely the variance be provided for management? Remember, variance analysis is but a means to an end. Management's task is to find the reasons for the variances and to take action to bring operations into line with the plan.

c. Is the variance significant and worth reporting? This is an important matter for both the accountant and the manager and the ways of assessing the significance of variances are dealt with in the next chapter.

d. Are the variances being reported quickly enough, to the right people, in sufficient or too much detail, with explanatory notes?

7. THE VARIANCES DESCRIBED

Each of the variances shown in the Variance Chart, Figure 25.1, is described in the following paragraphs. Each variance is defined and explained, a formula and typical causes of the variance are given together with a worked example.

The worked examples for the basic material and labour variances are based on the following abstract from the Standard Cost Card for Part No. 100X and actual results for the month of January.

Standard Cost Card (abstract) Part No. 100X	
Standard Cost/Unit	
	£
Raw Materials 50 Kgs @ £2.50/Kg	125
Direct Labour 7 hrs @ £9.50/hour	66.50
	£191.50
Actual Result for January	
Production	150 units
Direct Material Purchases	7,000 Kgs at a cost of £18,200
Opening Stock Direct Material	1,300 Kgs
Closing Stock Direct Material	850 Kgs
Wages paid (1,010 hrs)	£9,898

8. THE BASIC MATERIALS VARIANCES

This paragraph deals with the Direct Materials Total Variance, the Direct Materials Price Variance and the Direct Materials Usage Variance. A particular problem arises with Materials variances in that materials can be charged to production at either actual prices or standard prices. This affects when the price variance is calculated, ie either at the time of purchase or at the time of usage. Although both these approaches are possible, the procedure where materials are charged to production at standard price has many advantages and will be adopted in this book. This method means that variances are calculated as soon as they arise (ie a price variance when the material is purchased) and that they are more easily related to an individual's responsibility (ie a price variance would be the buyer's responsibility). Accordingly for materials variances (and ALL other variances), price variances are calculated *first* and thereafter the material is at *standard price*. The individual material variances can now be considered:

Direct Materials Total Variance – definition:

A measurement of the difference between the standard material cost of the output produced and the actual material cost incurred

(standard material cost of output produced – actual cost of material purchased)

where the quantities of material purchased and used are different, the total variance should be calculated as the sum of the usage and price variances.

Terminology

Direct Materials Price Variance – definition:

The difference between the actual price paid for purchased materials and their standard cost.

((actual quantity of material purchased × standard price)
– actual cost of material purchased).

Terminology

(This variance may be calculated at the time of purchase or the time of usage. It is generally preferable to calculate the variance at the time of purchase.)

Direct Materials Usage Variance – definition:

Measures efficiency in the use of materials by comparing standard material usage for actual production with actual material used, the difference is valued at standard cost.

(actual production × standard material per unit – actual material usage)
× standard cost per kg, litre, other).

Terminology

Formulae (when the Price Variance is extracted on purchase)

Example 1 (based on data from Para 7)

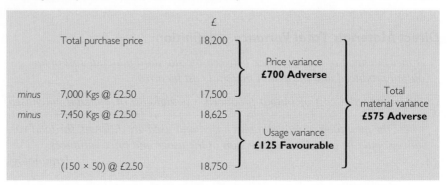

It will be seen in this case that usage was lower than planned (a gain) but the price paid was higher than planned (a loss).

Notes:

a. Although rules can be given regarding the sequence of the formula so that a minus variance is always adverse and a plus is favourable, it is easier and less error prone to determine the direction of the variance by common sense, ie if the price/usage is less than standard the variance is *favourable*, if more, then the variance is *adverse*.

b. The price variance is based on the actual quantity purchased and is extracted first. Thereafter the actual price is never used for variance calculations.

c. In the above example, the actual usage (7,450Kgs) was calculated as follows:

$$\text{Opening Stock} + \text{Purchases} - \text{Closing Stock} = \text{Usage}$$
$$\text{ie } 1,300 + 7,000 - 850 = 7,450 \text{ Kgs}$$

d. It follows from the above calculations that a price variance could arise even if there was no usage, provided that there were purchases during the period.

e. Students should note how the formulae develop from actual values (in lower case) progressively to STANDARD VALUES (in capitals). This layout is used throughout the book.

Typical causes of material variances

Price variances

a. Paying higher or lower prices than planned.

b. Losing or gaining quantity discounts by buying in smaller or larger quantities than planned.

c. Buying lower or higher quality than planned.

d. Buying substitute material due to unavailability of planned material (both (c) and (d) may affect usage variances).

Usage variances

a. Greater or lower yield from material than planned.

b. Gains or losses due to use of substitute or higher/lower quality than planned.

c. Greater or lower rate of scrap than anticipated.

Note:
As can be seen from the variance chart, Figure 25.1, the usage variance can be further divided into mix and yield variances. This is only done when useful information can be thus provided. These variances are dealt with later in the chapter.

9. LABOUR VARIANCES

This paragraph deals with the Direct Labour Total Variance, the Direct Labour Rate Variance (the 'price variance') and the Direct Labour Efficiency Variance (the 'usage' variance).

The formulae are given below and it should be noted that they follow a similar pattern to the material variances described in the previous paragraph.

These are defined as follows:

Direct Labour Total Variance – definition

Indicates the difference between the standard direct labour cost of the output which has been produced and the actual direct labour cost incurred ((standard hours produced × standard direct labour rate per hour) – (actual hours paid × actual direct labour rate per hour)).

Terminology

Direct Labour Rate Variance – definition

Indicates the actual cost of any change from the standard labour rate of remuneration ((actual hours paid × standard direct labour rate per hour) – (actual hours paid × actual direct labour rate per hour)).

Terminology

Direct Labour Efficiency Variance – definition

Indicates the standard labour cost of any change from the standard level of labour efficiency ((actual production in standard hours − actual hours worked) × standard direct labour rate per hour.)

Terminology

a. It will be seen that the second line of the rate variance and the first line of the efficiency variance are identical.

b. As with the material variances the price (rate) variance is dealt with first; thereafter all calculations use the standard rate.

c. Where appropriate records exist, an idle time variance can be calculated by multiplying the hours of idle time by the standard rate. The variance so calculated, together with the efficiency variance, forms the labour usage variance. Where no idle time variance is calculated, as in the example above, the efficiency variance is equivalent to the labour usage variance. As with labour efficiency, the effect of idle time on variable and fixed overheads can also be calculated.

Formulae

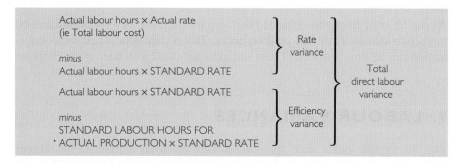

Example 2 (based on data from Para 7)

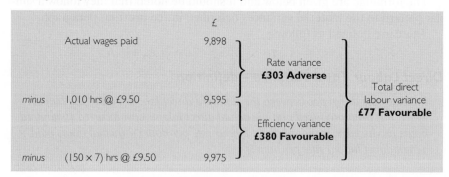

The total variance can be verified by calculating the difference between actual wages, £9,898, and the standard labour cost of the actual production, £9,975, ie:

$$£9,975 - £9,898 = £77 \textbf{ Fav}$$

In this case a higher rate was paid than planned but efficiency was better than anticipated. 1,010 actual hours were used to produce 150 units. The standard allowed was seven hours per unit; a total standard allowance of $150 \times 7 = 1,050$ hrs.

$$\therefore 40 \text{ hrs } (1,050 - 1,010) \text{ at a standard rate of £9.50 were saved,}$$

$$\text{ie a favourable efficiency variance of } 40 \times £9.50 = £380$$

Typical causes of labour variances

Rate

a. Higher rates being paid than planned due to wage award.

b. Higher or lower grade of worker being used than planned.

c. Payment of unplanned overtime or bonus.

Efficiency

a. Use of incorrect grade of labour.

b. Poor workshop organisation or supervision.

c. Incorrect materials and/or machine problems.

d. Unexpectedly favourable conditions.

10. BASIC VARIANCE ANALYSIS

So far only the basic material and labour variances have been dealt with. The illustrations have been deliberately kept simple in order to emphasise the major principles of variance analysis. There is considerable similarity between the methods of calculating all types of variance and students are advised to master the first part of this chapter before proceeding to the overhead and other variances which follow.

An important general principle which should be apparent at this stage is that *actual prices or rates are never used in variance analysis, except to calculate the price or rate variance which is always done first.*

11. INTRODUCTION TO OVERHEAD VARIANCE ANALYSIS

Before dealing with the individual variances it is necessary to recall some of the earlier material in the book. Overheads are absorbed into costs by means of predetermined overhead absorption rates (OAR) which are calculated by dividing the budgeted overheads for the period by the activity level anticipated. The activity level can be expressed in various ways (units, weight, sales, etc), but by far the most useful concept is that of the *Standard Hour*. It will be recalled that the 'Standard hour' is a unit measure of production and is the most commonly used measure of activity level. Thus:

$$\text{Total overhead absorbed} = \text{OAR} \times \text{SHP}$$

where SHP is the number of Standard Hours of Production.

Where the Standard costing system uses total absorption costing principles (ie, where both fixed and variable overheads are absorbed into production costs) the total overheads absorbed can be subdivided into Fixed Overhead Absorption Rates (FOAR) and Variable Overhead Absorption Rates (VOAR) thus:

$$\text{Fixed overheads absorbed} = \text{FOAR} \times \text{SHP}$$
$$\text{Variable overheads absorbed} = \text{VOAR} \times \text{SHP}$$
and $\quad$ Total overheads absorbed $= (\text{FOAR} + \text{VOAR}) \times \text{SHP}$.

Where standard *variable* costing is used, only variable overheads are absorbed into production costs and thus only variances relating to variable overheads arise; fixed overheads being dealt with by the budgetary control system. Thus it will be seen that overhead variance analysis is considerably simplified when standard variable costing is employed.

All the overhead variances depicted in Figure 25.1 and the Notes are described and illustrated below. First where the overheads are sub-divided into Fixed and Variable elements and then the simpler approach where overheads are considered in total.

The following data will be used for the examples:

Budget for February Department No. 82

Fixed Overheads	£11,480
Variable Overheads	£13,120
Labour Hours	3,280 hrs
Standard Hours of Production	3,280 hrs

Actual results for February Department No. 82

	£
Fixed Overheads	12,100
Variable Overheads	13,930
Actual Labour Hours (ie clock hrs)	3,150
Standard Hours Produced	3,230

Based on the budgeted figures the predetermined overhead absorption rates can be calculated:

$$\text{FOAR} = \frac{\text{Budgeted fixed overheads}}{\text{Budgeted activity level}} = \frac{£11,480}{3,280} \text{ Std. hrs} = £3.5/\textbf{hour}$$

$$\text{VOAR} = \frac{\text{Budgeted variable overheads}}{\text{Budgeted activity level}} = \frac{£13,120}{3,280} \text{ Std. hrs} = £4/\textbf{hour}$$

The total overhead absorption (OAR) is the total of the FOAR and the VOAR, ie **£7.5/hour**

Notes:
a. It will be seen that budgeted labour hours and the budgeted standard hours production are the same. This is the normal planning basis. If actual labour hours and the standard hours actually produced also were the same, then efficiency would be exactly as planned and no efficiency variances would arise. It will be seen from the data that this is not the case on this occasion.

b. It will be apparent that because absorption rates for fixed overheads have been calculated the examples will be based on total absorption costing principles.

c. The absorption base is the standard hours of production.

12. VARIABLE OVERHEAD VARIANCES

This paragraph describes the variable overhead variances: the total variance, the expenditure variance and the efficiency variance. The variances described are based on the usual assumption that variable overheads are absorbed on labour hours.

Definitions

- Variable overhead total variance The difference between the actual variable overheads incurred and the variable overheads absorbed. (This variance is simply the over or under absorption of overheads.)
- Variable overhead expenditure variance

  The difference between the actual variable overheads incurred and the allowed variable overheads based on the actual hours worked.
- Variable overhead efficiency variance

  The difference between the allowed variable overheads and the absorbed variable overhead.

Formula

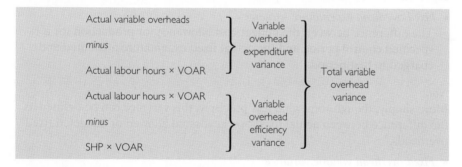

Example 3 (Based on data from para 11)

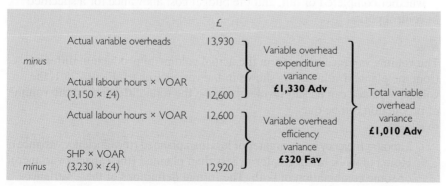

Note:
The total variance can be confirmed by calculating the difference between what variable overheads actually cost and what the actual production absorbed in variable overheads.

$$£13,930 - £12,920 = £1,010 \text{ (Adv)}$$

13. FIXED OVERHEAD VARIANCES

This paragraph describes one approach to fixed overhead variance analysis and covers the fixed overhead variance, the fixed overhead expenditure variance, the fixed overhead volume variance and its sub-variances the capacity variance and the efficiency or productivity variance. As with variable overheads the assumption is made that fixed overheads are absorbed on labour hours.

Definitions
- *Fixed overhead total variance*
  The difference between the standard cost of fixed overhead absorbed in the production achieved, whether completed or not, and the fixed overhead attributed and charged to that period.

Note:
As with the variable overhead variance, the fixed overhead variance simply represents under or over absorption.

- *Fixed overhead expenditure variance*
  The difference between the budget cost allowance for production for a specified control period and the actual fixed expenditure attributed and charged to that period.

Note:
More simply, though somewhat less precisely, this variance can be defined as the difference between actual fixed overheads and allowed or budgeted fixed overheads.

- *Fixed overhead volume variance*
  That portion of the fixed production overhead variance which is the difference between the standard cost absorbed in the production achieved, whether completed or not, and the budget cost allowance for a specified control period.

Note:
The volume variance arises from the actual volume of production differing from the planned volume. As shown in the variance chart, Figure 25.1, the volume variance can be sub-divided because the total difference in the volume of production can be due
to either:
  i. Labour efficiency being greater or less than planned (the efficiency variance).
  ii. Hours of work being greater or less than planned (the capacity variance) or some combination of both. The formal definitions of these variances follow.

- *Fixed overhead efficiency variance.*
  That portion of the fixed production overhead volume variance which is the difference between the standard cost absorbed in the production achieved, whether completed or not, and the actual direct labour hours worked (valued at the standard hourly absorption rate).

- *Fixed overhead capacity variance.*
  That portion of the fixed production overhead volume which is due to working at higher or lower capacity than standard. Capacity is often expressed in terms of average direct labour hours per day, and the variance is the difference between the budget cost allowance and the actual direct labour hours worked (valued at the standard hourly absorption rate).

The formulae for these variances are given below:

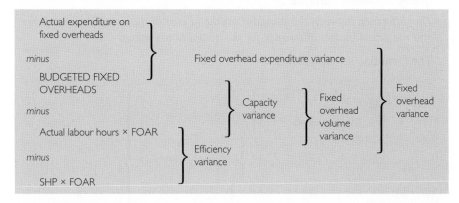

Example 4 (based on data from Para 11)

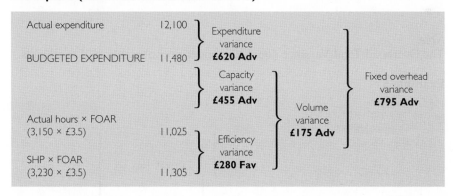

Note:
The Capacity Variance measures the Fixed Overhead effect of planned activity (ie 3,280 hours) differing from actual activity (ie 3,150 hours) thus: (3,280 − 3,150) × £3.5 per hour = £455ADV.

14. TOTAL OVERHEAD VARIANCES

As previously explained there is a simpler approach to overhead variances whereby the overheads are not sub-divided into fixed and variable elements. In such circumstances the following variances can be calculated.

Definitions

Overhead total variance

The difference between the standard overhead cost specified for the production achieved, and the actual cost incurred.

Overhead expenditure variance

The difference between budgeted and actual overhead expenditure.

Overhead efficiency variance

The difference between the standard overhead rate for the production achieved and the standard overhead rate for the actual hours taken.

Overhead volume variance

The difference between the standard overhead cost of the actual hours taken and the flexed budget allowance for the actual hours taken.

The formulae are as follows:

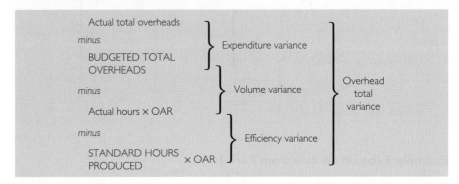

Note:
The Overhead Total Variance equals the under/over absorption of overheads.

Example 5

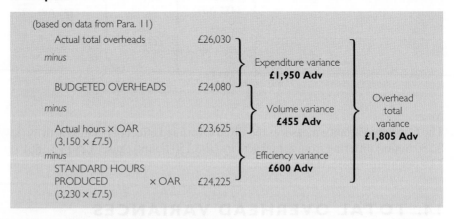

* The budgeted overheads are found from the usual process of flexing a budget, ie fixed overheads + the actual hours at the VOAR. Thus: £11,480 + (3,150 × £4) = £24,080.

It will be seen that this method is merely a summary of the variable and fixed overhead variances calculated in Examples 3 and 4. This is shown below.

	Expenditure £	Efficiency £	Capacity £	Total £
Variable overhead variances (Ex. 3)	1,330 (Adv)	320 (Fav)		1,010 (Adv)
Fixed overhead variances (Ex. 4)	620 (Adv)	280 (Fav)	455 (Adv)	795 (Adv)
Total overhead variances (Ex. 5)	1,950 (Adv)	600 (Fav)	†455 (Adv)	1,805 (Adv)

† It will be seen that what was previously entitled 'capacity variance' is directly equivalent to 'volume variance' when the Total Overhead approach is used.

15. REASONS FOR OVERHEAD VARIANCES

Overhead variances are somewhat more complex than basic labour and material variances, mainly because of the conventions of the overhead absorption process. Overhead absorption rates are calculated from estimates of expenditure and activity levels and variances arise from differences in both of these factors. In addition, because overheads are frequently absorbed into production by means of labour hours, overhead variances can also arise when labour efficiency is greater or less than planned.

Overhead variances are essentially a book balancing exercise providing an arithmetic reconciliation between standard and actual costs. Apart from the expenditure variance the calculation of the other overhead variances provides little real control information being related more to the conventions of overhead absorption than to operational reality. This aspect of overhead variances is developed in more detail in *Management Accounting*, ibid.

16. CONTROL RATIOS

The information used in calculating efficiency and volume variances – budgeted and actual labour hours and standard hours produced – can also be used to calculate various ratios which provide clear information on important aspects of the firm's operations. These ratios relate to Volume, Capacity and Efficiency and the formulae are as follows:

$$\text{Volume} = \frac{\text{Standard hours produced}}{\text{Budgeted labour hours}} \times 100$$

$$\text{Capacity ratio} = \frac{\text{Actual labour hours worked}}{\text{Budgeted labour hours}} \times 100$$

$$\text{Efficiency ratio} = \frac{\text{Standard hours produced}}{\text{Actual labour hours worked}} \times 100$$

Example

Using the data from Para 11, reproduced below, calculate the three control ratios.

Data:		
Budgeted labour hours	3,280
Actual labour hours	3,150
Standard hours produced	3,230

Solution

$$\text{Volume ratio} = \frac{3,230}{3,280} \times 100 = \mathbf{98\%}$$

$$\text{Capacity ratio} = \frac{3,150}{3,280} \times 100 = \mathbf{96\%}$$

$$\text{Efficiency ratio} = \frac{3,230}{3,150} \times 100 = \mathbf{102\%}$$

The control ratios are directly related to variances and can provide a useful relative measure rather than the absolute measure provided by variances.

The Volume ratio is equivalent to the Fixed Overhead Volume variance.

The Capacity ratio is equivalent to the Fixed Overhead Capacity variance.

The Efficiency ratio is equivalent to the Fixed and Variable Overhead and Labour Efficiency variances.

17. MORE DETAILED MATERIAL VARIANCES

The basic material variances were described earlier in the chapter. In certain circumstances it is conventional for sub-variances to be calculated, known as the *Direct Materials Mix Variance* and the *Direct Materials Yield Variance*. Typical circumstances in which such calculations are considered appropriate are those where the production process involves mixing different material inputs to make the required output. Examples include: the manufacture of fertilisers, steel, plastics, food products and so on. A feature of such processes is the existence of process losses through impurities, evaporation, breakages, machinery failures and other such factors which affect the yield from the process.

There are several methods of calculating mix and yield variances; some treat the mix variance as part of the price variance, others that there should be a combined mix/price variance, whilst another approach is that the mix and yield variances are sub-variances of the usage variance. This latter approach is illustrated in Figure 25.1 and is included in the CIMA *Terminology of Management Accounting*.

There are two alternative ways of sub-dividing the usage variance. One uses the individual standard prices of the ingredients while the other uses a weighted average price for all ingredients. For the variance calculations these prices are applied to slightly different ingredient quantities. Both methods produce the *same mix and yield variances in total*; all that differs is the amount attributed to each constituent ingredient.

For identification the methods will be termed the 'individual price' and the 'weighted average price' methods and both are defined and illustrated below using the same data for comparative purposes. The individual price method is illustrated first.

Definitions (Individual price method)

Direct Materials Mix Variance

The difference between total quantity in standard proportion, priced at the standard price and the actual quantity of material used priced at the standard price.

Direct Material Yield Variance

The difference between the standard yield of the actual material input and the actual yield, both valued at the standard material cost of the product.

18. MIX AND YIELD FORMULAE (INDIVIDUAL PRICE METHOD)

Formulae

Direct Materials Mixture Variance	=	STANDARD COST of the actual quantity of the actual mixture	*minus*	STANDARD COST of the actual quantity of the STANDARD MIXTURE

Direct Materials Yield Variance	=	STANDARD COST of the actual quantity of the STANDARD MIXTURE	*minus*	STANDARD COST of the STANDARD QUANTITY of the STANDARD MIXTURE

Notes:

a. Because the price variance is always dealt with first, the mix and yield variances use only standard prices.

b. Note how the expressions move from actual to STANDARD values and that the second part of the mix variance is the same as the first in the yield variance.

c. The yield variance measures abnormal process losses or gains.

Example 6

A fertiliser is made by mixing and processing three ingredients, P, N and Q. The standard cost data are as follows:

Ingredient	Standard Proportions	Standard cost
P	50%	£20 per tonne
N	40%	£25 per tonne
Q	10%	£42 per tonne

A standard process loss of 5% is anticipated.
In a period the output was 93.1 tonnes and the inputs were as follows:

Ingredient	Actual usage	Actual price	Actual Cost
P	49 tonnes	£16 per tonne	£784
N	43 tonnes	£27 per tonne	£1,161
Q	8 tonnes	£48 per tonne	£384
			£2,329

Calculate all relevant material variances using the individual price method.

Solution

The total variance is calculated thus:

Standard cost for 1 tonne of input

Ingredient P 0.5 tonne @ £20   = £10
N 0.4 tonne @ £25   = £10
Q 0.1 tonne @ £42   = £4.2
$$\underline{\underline{£24.2}}$$

One tonne of input at standard produces 0.95 tonnes of output so the standard cost per tonne of output is:

$$£24.2 \times \frac{100}{95} = £25.473684$$

∴ Standard cost of actual output = 93.1 × £25.473684   = £2,371.6
Actual cost of output   = £2,329
∴ Total Variance   = **£42.6 (Fav)**

The three relevant variances are: Price, Mix and Yield which are to be calculated in that order. The usage variance is merely the total of the mix and yield variances. The summary of the variance calculations is given below followed by explanatory notes.

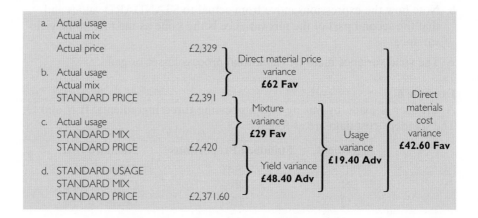

It will be seen how the factors involved, usage-mix-price, start all at actual and move stage by stage to become all at STANDARD. This is the key to remembering the method of calculation.

Notes:
a. Actual usage, actual mix, actual price is the cost given in the question, ie, £2,329.
b. The actual usage in the actual proportions is evaluated at the standard price, ie

$$£(49 \times 20) + (43 \times 25) + (8 \times 42) = £2,391$$

c. The standard mix is found by putting the actual total quantity (100 tonnes) into the standard proportions (50%, 40% and 10%), ie 50P, 40N and 10Q. These are evaluated at the standard prices and compared with the values from b.

Ingredient	Actual usage Tonnes	Total usage in standard proportions Tonnes	Difference Tonnes	Standard £	Variance £
P	49	50	+1	20	20 Fav
N	43	40	−3	25	75 Adv
Q	8	10	+2	42	84 Fav
	100	100		Total Mix Variance	29 Fav

d. The standard usage is found by working back from the actual output (93.1 tonnes) to determine what the standard total quantity of inputs should be, assuming a normal process loss of 5%.

ie Standard output quantity = 95% of standard input quantity

$$\therefore \text{ Standard input quantity} = \frac{100}{95} \times \text{actual output quantity}$$

$$= \frac{100}{95} \times 93.1$$

$$= \textbf{98 tonnes}$$

This value is pro rated in the standard proportions, calculated at the standard price and compared with the values from c. thus:

Ingredient	Total usage in standard proportions Tonnes		Standard usage for output in standard proportions Tonnes	Difference Tonnes	Standard Price £	Variance £
P	50	(98 × 50%)	49	−1	20	20 Adv
N	40	(98 × 40%)	39.2	−0.8	25	20 Adv
Q	10	(98 × 10%)	9.8	−0.2	42	8.4 Adv
	100		98	Total Yield Variance		48.4 Adv

The Mix variance plus the Yield variance equals the Usage variance, thus:

£29 FAV + 48.4 ADV = **£19.4 Adv**

If required, this latter figure can be proved by calculating the individual Usage variances for each ingredient and totalling. It will be recalled that the Material Usage variance is calculated as follows:

(Standard quantity for actual production − Actual quantity) × Standard Price

= Usage variance

This formula gives:

Ingredient

P	(49 − 49) × £20	= NIL
N	(39.2 − 43) × £25	= £95 Adv
Q	(9.8 − 8) × £42	= £75.6 Fav
	Total Usage variance =	**£19.4 Adv** as above

The alternative weighted average price method is now defined and illustrated.

19. ALTERNATIVE METHOD FOR MIX AND YIELD VARIANCES

Definitions (weighted average price method)
Direct Materials Mix Variance

> The difference between the standard quantity of inputs for the output achieved and the actual quantity used priced at the difference between individual standard prices and weighted average standard price.

Direct Materials Yield Variance

> The difference between the standard quantity of inputs for the output achieved and the actual quantity used priced at the weighted average standard price.

> Example 6 is reworked below based on these alternative definitions.

Example 6 (reworked)
The Total Variance is £42.6 ADV and the Price Variance is calculated in exactly the same manner and is, as previously, £62 Favourable.

To calculate the weighted average mix and yield variances the input quantity differences and the weighted average standard ingredient price have to be calculated.

Ingredient	Standard usage for output in std. proportions Tonnes	Actual usage Tonnes	Input differences Tonnes
P	49	49	—
N	39.2	43	−3.8
Q	9.8	8	+1.8
	98	100	−2.0

Weighted Average Standard ingredient price:
From the original data the standard cost of 1 tonne is:

Ingredient		£
P	0.5 × £20 =	10
N	0.4 × £25 =	10
Q	0.1 × £42 =	4.2
		24.2

∴ Weighted average ingredient cost is **£24.2 per tonne**.
These values are used in the variance calculations.

Mix variance:

Ingredient	Input differences Tonnes	×	Standard price less weighted average price £	=	Variance £
P	—				—
N	−3.8		(£25 − 24.2) = 0.80		3.04 Adv
Q	+1.8		(£42 − 24.2) = 17.80		32.04 Fav
			Total mix variance		**29.00** Fav

Yield variance:

Ingredient	Input differences Tonnes	×	Weighted average standard price £	=	Variance £
P	–				
N	−3.8		24.2		91.96 Adv
Q	+1.8		24.2		43.56 Fav
			Total yield variance		**48.40** Adv

Thus it will be seen that the alternative approaches produce the same total mix and yield variances but differ in the amount attributed to each ingredient. Which is the correct method?

No one method of calculating variances or any given variance is more correct than any other. The 'correct' variances are those which assist management to make the right decisions. Accordingly, management would use whichever of the above methods is deemed to provide the most relevant information if, in fact, mix and yield variances are thought to provide any useful information.

However, students should be aware that there are serious doubts about the usefulness and meaning of conventionally prepared mix and yield variances. These doubts are explored in *Management Accounting*, ibid.

20. SUMMARY

a. Variance analysis is the process of analysing the total difference between planned and actual performance into its constituent parts.

b. Variance analysis must be useful to management otherwise it is pointless.

c. Variances should be calculated in accordance with responsibilities.

d. Although there are different names, each type of variance, materials, wages and overheads, has a price element and a quantity element.

e. The relationship between variances must be considered. Variances should not be considered in isolation.

f. The basic materials variances measure the differences between actual and standard price and actual and standard usage.

g. Price variances are *always* extracted first. Thereafter all variance calculations use standard price.

h. The basic labour variances measure the difference between actual and standard wage rates and actual and standard labour efficiency.

i. An important factor in overhead absorption and overhead variance analysis is the activity level. Frequently this is measured in standard hours. A standard hour is a unit measure of production, not of time.

j. Using total absorption principles, both fixed and variable overheads are absorbed into production, so variances relating to both fixed and variable overheads will arise. Using standard marginal costing only variable overheads are absorbed into production overheads so that fixed overhead variances cannot arise.

k. Variable overhead variances reflect differences in variable overhead expenditure and labour efficiency.

l. The basic materials usage variance can be sub-divided into a mix variance and a yield variance. These variances measure differences due to mixing in non-standard proportions and to yields (ie process losses) being different to those planned.

m. The Total Cost Variance, shown in Figure 25.1, is merely the total of all the variances, ie the Direct Materials Cost Variance, the Direct Labour Cost Variance and the Variable and Fixed Overhead Variances.

21. POINTS TO NOTE

a. Variances are related to responsibilities. It follows, therefore, that a manager should only be held responsible for a variance when he has control over the resource or cost element being considered.

b. It must be stressed that variance analysis merely directs attention to the cause of off-standard performances. It does not solve the problem, nor does it establish the reasons behind the variance. These are management tasks.

c. The variance described are ones commonly found, but many others exist. It would be impossible to describe or remember all the possible variances, but of far greater importance is to understand the principles underlying variance analysis; once this is done any given variance can be calculated easily.

d. The relationships between variances must always be considered. Rarely is a single variance of great significance. Is a favourable variance offset by a larger adverse one?

e. Although budgetary control and standard costing are techniques which use the same underlying principle, an important difference is that standard costs and variances form part of the double entry system, whereas budgetary control is in memorandum form.

f. The overhead volume variances can be criticised because information which is intended for product costing purposes (ie, absorption of fixed overheads into cost units) is used as a basis for control information. Fixed overheads are based more on time than activity so that it becomes very difficult to trace responsibility for an adverse volume variance. Because of this, the fixed overhead expenditure variance is probably the most relevant fixed overhead variance for control purposes.

g. Mix and yield variances have been illustrated above using a mixture of materials. This is undoubtedly the most normal application but the principles can also be applied to circumstances where a standard mixture of resources is used to produce a product or complete a task. For example, where a gang of people of different skills is employed making a product variances using identical principles could be calculated. Also, where a mixture of products is sold, a sales mix variance, using similar principles could be calculated.

Student self-testing

Exercises (answers below)

1. The following details were extracted from the standard cost card of a component:

Raw Materials
2.82 Kgs @ £4.80 Kg

Direct Labour
Type I 6.5 hrs @ £3.75
Type II 3.85 hrs @ £4.25

During a period actual results were as follows:
Production 1,100 components.

Direct Material Purchase and usage
3,200 Kgs at a cost of £15,100

Wages Paid
Type I (7,120 hrs) £27,056
Type II (4,235) £18,210

You are required to calculate what variances have arisen.

2. The following figures relate to the Milling Department:

Budget	£
Fixed overheads	2,500
Variable overheads	1,550
Hours	650

Actual	£
Fixed overheads	2,625
Variable overheads	1,710
Clock hours	625
Standard hours produced	680

Calculate the variances using the simpler, combined overhead recovery rate approach.

3. Using the data in Exercise 2, calculate the variances relating to variable and fixed overheads.

4. The standard mix of a product is as follows:

Material	% of input	Standard cost per Kg
X	30%	£1.20
Y	50%	£2.95
Z	20%	£1.15

The standard process loss is 15% of input weight. During a period 2,450 Kgs of good output were produced from the following inputs:

Material	Input Kgs	Price per Kg
X	815	£1.25
Y	1,500	£2.90
Z	585	£1.15

You are required to calculate the relevant variances.

5. In a period results were as follows:

Output 6,250 units
Wages paid 33,680 for 10,400 hours
Material 17,059 for 3,850 Kgs.

Variances:

Labour Rate 1,720 (Adv)
Labour Efficiency 525 (Fav)
Material Price 1,400 (Fav)
Material Usage 890 (Adv)

Calculate the Standard Prime Cost per unit.

Solutions to exercises

1.

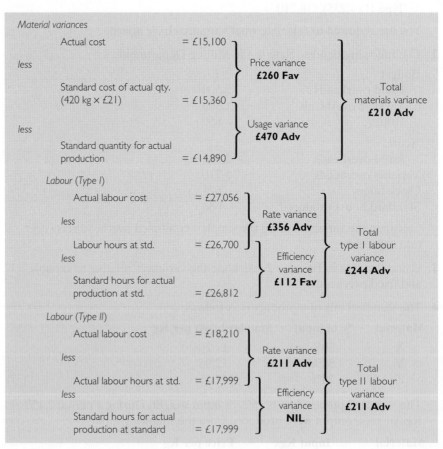

Material variances

Actual cost	= £15,100

less

Price variance **£260 Fav**

Standard cost of actual qty. (420 kg × £21)	= £15,360

less

Usage variance **£470 Adv**

Total materials variance **£210 Adv**

Standard quantity for actual production	= £14,890

Labour (Type I)

Actual labour cost	= £27,056

less

Rate variance **£356 Adv**

Labour hours at std.	= £26,700

less

Efficiency variance **£112 Fav**

Total type I labour variance **£244 Adv**

Standard hours for actual production at std.	= £26,812

Labour (Type II)

Actual labour cost	= £18,210

less

Rate variance **£211 Adv**

Actual labour hours at std.	= £17,999

less

Efficiency variance **NIL**

Total type II labour variance **£211 Adv**

Standard hours for actual production at standard	= £17,999

Note:

The two labour types could be combined but as the details are available more information is supplied if they are dealt with separately.

2. The variances to be calculated relate to overheads and, as usual, the absorption rates should be calculated using the budgeted figures.

$$\text{FOAR} = \frac{2{,}500}{650} = £3.846 \text{ per hour}$$

$$\text{VOAR} = \frac{1{,}550}{650} = £2.385 \text{ per hour}$$

and total OAR = £3.846 + £2.385 = £6.23 per hour

It will be recalled that the budgeted hours are both clock hours and standard hours produced.

The total overhead variance is:

$$\text{Actual overheads} - \text{SHP} \times (\text{FOAR} + \text{VOAR})$$

$$\text{ie, } £4{,}335 - 4{,}236 = £99 \text{ ADV}$$

This can be analysed as follows using the simpler, combined approach covered in the chapter.

3. *Variable overhead variances*

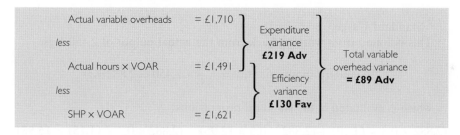

Fixed overhead variances

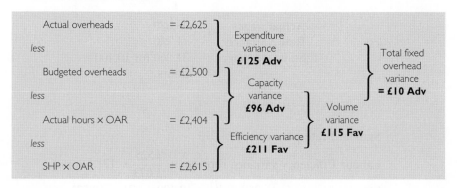

4. There are three variances to be calculated: Price, Mix and Yield:

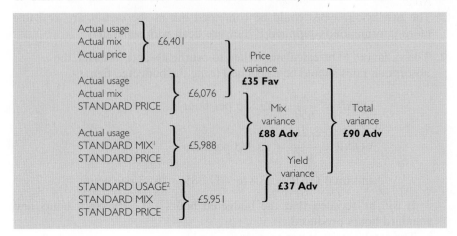

Notes:
[1] Standard mix, ie actual quantity, 2,900 Kgs into standard proportions, ie:
30%, 50% and 20%, ie:

X	30%	=	870	tonnes @ £1.20
Y	50%	=	1,450	tonnes @ £2.95
Z	20%	=	580	tonnes @ £1.15
Total			£5,988	

[2] Standard Usage.
This is found from working back from the actual output of 2,450 Kgs.

$$\therefore \text{ Standard input quantity} = \frac{100}{85} \times 2,450 = 2,882 \text{ Kgs}$$

which is evaluated in the standard proportions

$(2,882 \times 0.3 \times £1.20) + (2,882 \times 0.5 \times £2.95) + (2,882 \times 0.2 \times £1.15) = \textbf{£5,951}.$

5. *Labour*

		£
	Actual wages	33,680
less	Rate Variance	1,720
=	Standard Wages	31,960 for 10,400 hours

$\therefore$ Standard rate per hour $= £3.073$

$\therefore$ Labour Efficiency variance represents $\dfrac{£525}{3.073} = 171$ hours

$\therefore$ Standard hours for 6,250 units is $10,400 + 171 = \textbf{10,571}$

$\therefore$ Standard hours per unit $= \dfrac{10,571}{6,250} = \textbf{1.69136}$

Material

		£
	Material Cost	17,059
plus	Price Variance	1,400
	= Standard Material Cost	18,459 for 3,850 Kgs

$$\therefore \text{Standard cost per Kg} = \frac{18,459}{3,850} = £4.795$$

$$\therefore \text{Usage variance represents } \frac{£890}{4,795} = 185.6 \text{ Kgs}$$

$\therefore$ Standard usage for 6,250 units = 3,850 + 185.6 = 4,035.6 Kgs

$$\therefore \text{Standard Kgs per unit} = \frac{4,035.6}{6,250} = 0.6457$$

Standard Prime Cost/Unit

		£
Labour		
1.69136 hours @ £3.073 =		5.198
Material		
0.6457 Kgs @ £4.795 =		3.096
= Standard Prime Cost =		£8.294

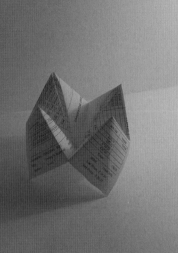

26

Standard costing – Variance analysis (sales and standard variable costs)

2. SALES MARGIN VARIANCES

The previous chapter described the various cost variances and it will be recalled that the objective of that analysis was to help management to control costs. To achieve planned profits management also wish to control sales, or more correctly, to control the profit (or margin) from sales. This is the overall objective of calculating sales margin variances. Because cost variance analysis extracts all the differences between planned and actual costs, the products are treated at standard manufacturing cost for the purpose of sales margin variance analysis. Part of Figure 25.1, Chapter 25, is given below to show the variances dealt with in this chapter.

FIGURE 26.1   Extract from Figure 25.1 Chapter 25

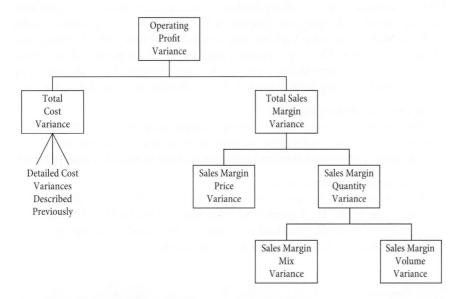

3. STANDARD SALES MARGIN

This is the difference between the standard selling price of a product and its standard cost and it is the same as the standard profit for the product.

Note:
The 'standard cost' referred to above is the 'total standard cost', ie it includes both fixed and variable costs. When fixed costs are excluded it becomes the standard variable cost and the difference between standard selling price and standard variable cost is known as the *standard sales contribution*.

4. SALES MARGIN VARIANCES – DEFINITIONS

- Total sales margin variance

  The difference between the budgeted margin from sales and the actual margin when the cost of sales is valued at the standard cost of production.
- Sales margin price variance

  That portion of the total sales margin variance which is the difference between the standard margin per unit and the actual margin per unit for the number of units sold in the period.

Note:
This is a normal price variance and could equally well be described as the 'sales turnover price variance'.

- Sales margin quantity variance
  That portion of the total sales margin variance which is the difference between the budgeted number of units sold and the actual number sold valued at the standard margin per unit.

Note:

This is a normal usage variance, analogous to the direct materials usage variance described in the previous chapter. Where more than one product is sold, the Sales Margin Quantity Variance can be subdivided into a Mix Variance and a Volume Variance. The mix variance shows the effect on profits of variations from the planned sales mixture, and the volume variance shows the effect of the unit volume varying from standard. These sub-variances are defined below.

- Sales margin mixture variance
  That portion of the sales margin quantity variance which is the difference between the actual total number of units at the actual mix and the actual total number of units at standard mix valued at the standard margin per unit.

- Sales margin volume variance
  That portion of the sales margin quantity variance which is the difference between the actual total quantity of units sold and the budgeted total number of units at the standard mix valued at the standard margin per unit. The formulae for these variances are given below.

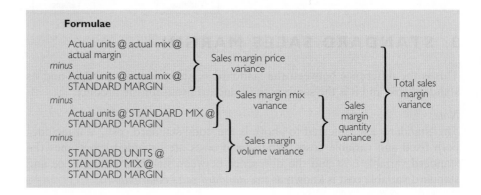

Note:

There is considerable similarity in approach between these variances and the direct materials variances shown in Example 6 in the previous chapter.

Example I

A company makes and sells three products, W, X and Y. During a period, budget and actual results were as follows:

	Budget					Actual				
	Total Sales	Unit			Budgeted Total Margin	Total Sales	Unit			Actual Total Margin
Product	£	Volume	Price	Margin	£	£	Volume	Price	Margin	£
	£		£	£				£	£	
W	5,000	500	10	2	1,000	5,500	550	10	2	1,100
X	4,500	300	15	3	900	4,000	250	16	4	1,000
Y	4,000	200	20	4	800	1,900	100	19	3	300
	13,500	1,000			£2,700	£11,400	900			£2,400

Calculate all relevant sales margin variances.

Solution

The summary of the variance calculations is shown below followed by explanatory notes.

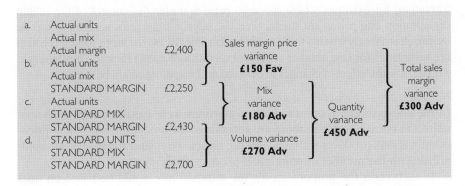

Notes:

a. This is the actual total margin achieved as shown in the question, ie

$$£(550 \times 2) + (250 \times 4) + (100 \times 3) = £2,400$$

b. This is the actual units in the actual proportions, but at the budgeted margins, ie

$$£(550 \times 2) + (250 \times 3) + (100 \times 4) = £2,250$$

c. This is the actual total number of units sold (900), but at the standard proportions, ie 50%, 30% and 20%, valued at standard margin.

$$£(450 \times 2) + (270 \times 3) + (180 \times 4) = £2,430$$

d. Finally the total budgeted margin is required. This is given in the question, ie

$$£(500 \times 2) + (300 \times 3) + (200 \times 4) = £2,700$$

The total variance can be verified by comparing the budgeted position with the actual position, ie

Total budgeted margin – Actual margin = Total sales margin variance

£2700 – 2400 = **£300 Adv**

By this stage the student should be totally familiar with the pattern of variance calculation and should be in a position to calculate an unfamiliar variance(s) from first principles. Get into the habit of cross-checking the detailed variances by calculating the total variance in the manner shown in each example in this book.

5. LIMITATIONS OF SALES MARGIN VARIANCE ANALYSIS

The purpose of all variance analysis is to aid management control. To do this variances must be relevant and within a manager's control. Because there are so many external factors involved, the control of sales volume, sales margins and sales mix is extremely difficult and it is somewhat doubtful whether full variance analysis in this area is useful.

In certain circumstances however, some of the variances may provide useful information; for example, where the sales price is under the control of the selling organisation and prices are stable, then the sales margin price variance could be useful, alternatively when a manager is responsible for two or more products which are substitutes for one another (different qualities of paint) then the mix variance would show the effect of changes in demand and therefore might be useful.

Note:

In the above example the standard proportions were based on the number of units. On occasions where there are substantial differences in the selling prices of the various products within a firm (eg bicycle tyres and tractor tyres) standardising on the number of units could product distortions.

In such cases the proportions for the standard mix would be based on sales turnover, not units. This procedure would only alter the balance between the mix and volume variances. The overall quantity variance would remain unchanged.

6. SALES VARIANCE COMPARED WITH SALES MARGIN VARIANCES

Historically variance analysis in the sales area commenced with variances based on sales turnover, ie if actual sales were above budget there was a favourable sales variance even if profits fell, perhaps because the sales of low profit items had increased. Although information on variations in sales turnover is important, nowadays it is likely to be supplied by detailed sales analyses, not through variance analysis. Management need to have information about profit performance related to sales so sales margin variances have been described.

7. STANDARD VARIABLE (OR MARGINAL) COSTING

Most standard costing systems are based on total absorption cost principles and the standards and variances described in the last two chapters are typical of such systems. Standard costing can also incorporate variable cost principles and is then termed *standard variable costing*.

It will be recalled that variable costing involves the separation of costs into those which vary with activity, termed variable costs, and those which remain unaffected by activity changes, known as fixed costs. Fixed costs are not absorbed into individual units of production and are deducted in total from the contribution (sales − variable cost) earned from units sold. Standard variable costing incorporates these principles and has the following characteristics.

a. Standards are developed in the normal manner and entered as usual on the standard cost card or computer file except that fixed costs do not appear. The standard cost card includes:

- Direct materials
- Direct labour

- Direct expenses
- Variable overheads (ie no fixed costs)

b. A standard contribution is set for each product and added to the standard variable cost. This sets the standard selling price. The standard contribution becomes the standard sales margin.

c. A budgeted profit statement is prepared for the next period with budgeted levels of sales and fixed overheads. Typically this would appear as follows:

Budgeted Profit Statement for Period

	£
Budgeted sales (Budgeted no. of units × standard selling price)	XXX
less Budgeted cost of sales	
(Budgeted no. of units × standard variable cost per unit)	XXX
= Budgeted Contribution	XXX
less Budgeted fixed costs	XXX
= Budgeted profit	XXX

d. Variance analysis is simplified because of the disappearance of the fixed overhead volume variance and its sub-variances, the capacity and volume productivity variances. All other variances are identical or very similar. The different categories are listed below.

Types of variance	Characteristics of standard variable cost variances
Direct materials Direct labour Variable overheads }	Identical to absorption standard cost variances
Fixed overheads	Only variance is the fixed overhead expenditure variance
Sales variances	With the exception that the standard sales margin is now the standard contribution, the variances are calculated in an identical manner. The new titles are: • Sales contribution variance (was sales margin variance) • Sales contribution price variance (was sales margin quantity variance) • Sales contribution quantity variance (was sales margin price variance) • Sales contribution mixture variance (was sales margin mixture variance) • Sales contribution volume variance (was sales margin volume variance)

Standard variable cost example

Example 2

The following data relate to the budget and actual results of a firm which makes and sells a single product and which employs standard variable costing.

TABLE 26.1

	Budget				Actual		
Production		10,000 units	Production				10,600 units
Sales		10,000 units	Sales				10,600 units
		£					£
Sales		18,000	Sales				180,200
less							
Standard Variable Cost	£		Actual Variable Cost		£		
– Materials	10,000		– Materials		11,600		
– Labour	60,000		– Labour		63,000		
– Var. Overhead	80,000	150,000	– Var. Overheads		83,000		157,600
= Contribution		30,000	= Contribution				22,600
less			*less*				
Fixed Costs		15,000	Fixed Costs				15,600
= Budgeted Profit		£15,000		= Actual Profit			£7,000

The Standard cost card for the product is as follows:

	£
Materials 5 Kgs @ 20p/Kg	1.00
Labour 1 hr @ £6/hour	6.00
Var. Overheads 1 hr @ £8/hour	8.00
= Standard variable cost	15.00
Standard contribution	3.00
Standard selling price	£18.00

During the period material usage was 55,000 Kgs and 41,300 labour hours were worked.

Calculate all relevant variances.

Solution

The total variance is the Operating Profit variance, ie the difference between budgeted and actual profit, ie:

$$£15,000 - £7,000 = \textbf{£8,000 Adv}$$

All other variances will in total equal the operating profit variance and will account for the difference between budgeted and actual profit.

The cost variances are as follows:

TABLE 26.2 Cost variances workings

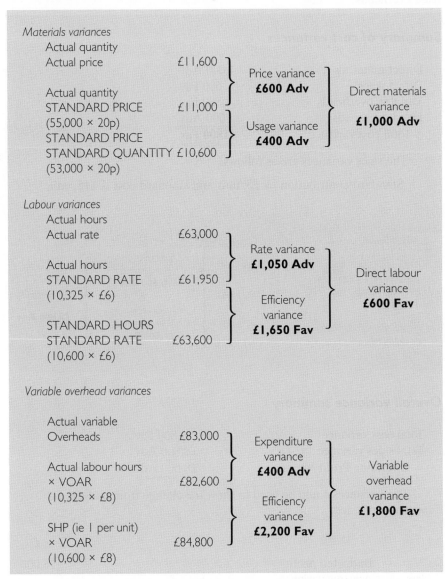

Note:
All the above variances are calculated exactly as described in the previous chapter.

Fixed overhead variance

Actual fixed overheads $-$ Budgeted fixed overheads $= £15,600 - £15,000$
$$= £600 \text{ (Adv)}$$

Note:
This is the fixed overhead expenditure variance and is the only variance for fixed overheads.

Summary of cost variances

Direct materials	1,000 Adv
Direct wages	600 Fav
Variable overheads	1,800 Fav
Fixed overheads	600 Adv
∴ Total cost variance =	**£800 Fav**

The sales variances are as follows:

Standard contribution = £3/unit and standard cost is £15/unit.

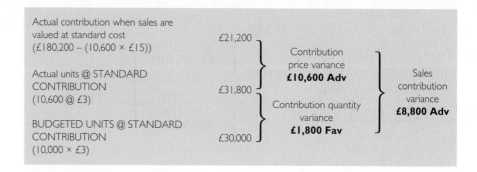

Overall variance summary

Total cost variance	800 Fav
Total sales variance	£8,800 Adv
= Operating Profit Variance	£8,000 Adv

The variances could be used to show the change from budgeted to actual profit, ie:

			£
	Budgeted profit		15,000
less	Adverse variances	£	
	Contribution price variance	10,600	
	Direct materials variance	1,000	
	Fixed overheads variance	600	12,200
			2,800
plus	Favourable variances	£	
	Contribution quantity variance	1,800	
	Direct wages variance	600	
	Variable overhead variance	1,800	4,200
	Actual profit =		£7,000

8. STANDARD COSTING IN PROCESS INDUSTRIES

Standard costing lends itself to continuous and repetitive methods of production so it follows that it can be applied most effectively in process industries. Where standard costing is used the process account is maintained **at standard cost throughout** and the problems and potential conflicts between the FIFO and average price methods are eliminated entirely.

The following example illustrates the technique.

Example 3

A company operates a standard process costing system and it is required to prepare the Process Account for Process 2, the necessary supporting expense accounts and show the variances which arise. The relevant data for Process 2 are as follows:

The opening WIP was 1,000 units which had the following element values:

	Value £	% age complete
Input material (from Process 1)	5,000	100
Material B (introduced)	1,500	50
Labour	1,800	30
Overheads	3,000	30
	£11,300	

During the period 3,800 units were received from Process 1 and 4,000 completed units were transferred to Process 3.

The closing WIP was 800 units which were at the following stages of completion:

	% age completion
Input material	100
Material B	60
Labour	40
overheads	40

The following standard costs have been established for Process 2.

	Standard Cost per unit £
Input material (std. cost Process 1)	5
Material B	3
Labour	6
Overheads	10
Total standard cost	£24

During the period actual costs for Process 2 were:

Material B	£12,350
Labour	£23,800
Overheads	£42,000

Solution

All entries in the process account are at standard cost so all that is necessary is to calculate the effective units and multiply by the appropriate standard cost to obtain the values of transfers and closing WIP.

Cost Element	Completed Units	+	Equivalent Units in Closing WIP	−	Equivalent Units in Opening WIP	=	Total Effective Units
Input Material	4,000	+	800	−	1,000	=	3,800
Material B	4,000	+	480	−	500	=	3,980
Labour	4,000	+	320	−	300	=	4,020
Overheads	4,000	+	320	−	300	=	4,020

Transfers out of completed units

$$4,000 \times £24 = £96,000$$

Closing WIP

Input Material	800 × £5	=	£4,000
Material B	480 × £3	=	£1,440
Labour	320 × £6	=	£1,920
Overheads	320 × £10	=	£3,200
			£10,560

Cost transfers to Process 2 account

Material B	3,980 × £3	=	£11,940
Labour	4,020 × £6	=	£24,120
Overheads	4,020 × £10	=	£40,200

The process account and the supporting expense accounts can now be prepared.

Process 2 A/C

	Units	£		Units	£
Opening WIP	1,000	11,300	Transfers to Process 3	4,000	96,000
Transfers from Process 1	3,800	19,000	Closing WIP	800	10,560
Material B		11,940			
Labour		24,120			
Overheads		40,200			
	4,800	106,560		4,800	106,560

Departmental Material B A/C

Stores	12,350	Process 2 A/C	11,940
		Material Variance A/C	410
	£12,350		£12,350

Departmental Wages A/C

Wages	23,800	Process 2 A/C		24,120
Labour Variance A/C	320			
	£24,120			£24,120

Departmental Overhead A/C

Overheads	42,000	Process 2 A/C	40,200
		Overhead Variance A/C	1,800
	£42,000		£42,000

Thus it will be seen that the total variances are:

Total Material Variance **£410**(**Adv**)

Total Labour Variance **£320**(**Fav**)

Total Overhead Variance **£1,800**(**Adv**)

Given the requisite data on hours, rates, usage and prices these total variances could be analysed into their sub-variances in exactly the same manner as previously described.

Note:

The Process account contains only Standard Costs. The Variances between actual and standard are dealt with in the Departmental expense accounts as shown above.

9. STANDARD COSTING IN THE PUBLIC SECTOR

As previously stated where appropriate conditions exist (ie stability and repetition) standard costing can be used in the Public Sector. It can provide more detailed control information and is probably best suited to the parts of the sector where competition has been introduced. For example, where there has been competitive tendering for Refuse Collection, Street Cleaning, Routine House Maintenance and so on.

Example 4

The Direct Service Organisation of Loamshire District Council has been awarded the street cleaning contract against competition from private firms. The contract price is £6.2 per kilometre of road and the budget and actual results for Period 1 are as follows:

Period 1

Budget	**£**	**£**
12,500 kilometres of cleaning @ £6.20 km		77,500
Direct Labour (3,200 hours @ £7)	22,400	
Direct materials (1,250 kgs @ £5)	6,250	
Variable Overheads (3,200 hrs @ £4.5)	14,400	
Fixed Overheads (3,200 @ £8)	25,600	68,650
= Budgeted surplus		8,850

Actual	£	£
11,750 kilometres cleaned @ £6.2 km		72,850
Direct Labour (3,050 hours @ £7.1)	21,655	
Direct materials (1,160 kgs @ £5)	5,800	
Variable Overheads	13,945	
Fixed Overheads	25,100	66,500
= Actual surplus		6,350

Required

a. Calculate the variances in as much detail as possible.
b. Reconcile the budgeted and actual surpluses.

Solution

a. *Sales Variances*

Sales Margin Price Variance	=	Nil
Sales Margin Quantity Variance		
= Quantity shortfall × Standard Margin		
= (12,500 − 11,750) × 0.708	=	**£531 (A)**

Note:

	£
Standard price per km =	6.20
less Standard cost (£68,650 ÷ 12,500) =	5.492
= Standard Margin =	0.708

Cost Variances

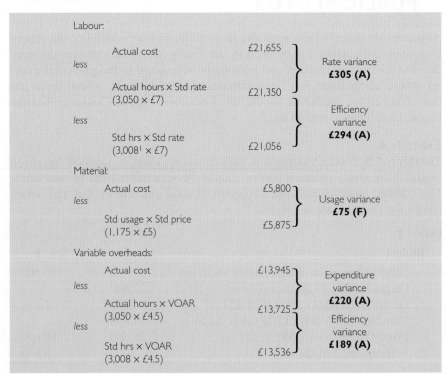

Labour:

	Actual cost	£21,655	
less			Rate variance **£305 (A)**
	Actual hours × Std rate (3,050 × £7)	£21,350	
less			Efficiency variance **£294 (A)**
	Std hrs × Std rate (3,008[1] × £7)	£21,056	

Material:

	Actual cost	£5,800	
less			Usage variance **£75 (F)**
	Std usage × Std price (1,175 × £5)	£5,875	

Variable overheads:

	Actual cost	£13,945	
less			Expenditure variance **£220 (A)**
	Actual hours × VOAR (3,050 × £4.5)	£13,725	
less			Efficiency variance **£189 (A)**
	Std hrs × VOAR (3,008 × £4.5)	£13,536	

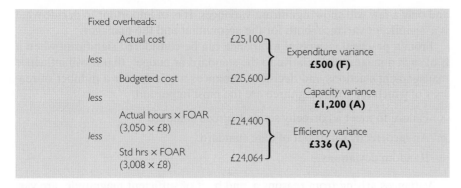

Notes:

$$\text{Standard hours required for 11,750 km} = \frac{3,200}{12,500} \times 11,750$$

$$= \mathbf{3,008}$$

$$\text{Fixed Overhead Absorption Rate} = \frac{£25,600}{3,200}$$

$$= \mathbf{£8}$$

b. *Reconciliation*

	£
Budgeted Surplus	8,850
less Sales Quantity Margin Variance	531
	8,319

Cost Variances

		ADV £	FAV £
Labour:	Rate	305	
	Efficiency	294	
Materials:	Usage		75
Var. Overheads:	Expenditure	220	
	Efficiency	189	
Fixed Overheads:	Expenditure		500
	Capacity	1,200	
	Efficiency	336	
		2,544	575
less Net Cost Variance			1,969
	= Actual Surplus		6,350

10. THE SIGNIFICANCE OF VARIANCES

Standard costing is an example of management by exception. It is hoped that the majority of items progress according to plan (ie at standard or budget) and only a few will show significant variances. It is of important to decide what is a 'significant variance' both for the accountant and the manager.

From a practical viewpoint a variance can be considered significant when it is of such a magnitude, relative to the standard or budget, that it will influence management's actions and decision. Variances may arise for a number of reasons of which the following three are the most important:

a. Failure to meet a correctly set and agreed standard.

b. An incorrectly set or out of date standard.

c. Random deviations.

Variances arising from reasons a. and b., if of sufficient magnitude, are variances which require further investigation and possibly management action. Random deviations, ie fluctuations which have arisen by chance are, by definition, uncontrollable. The problem remains of how to determine whether a variation from standard is attributable to chance and not significant or whether it is due to a controllable cause and therefore significant. The discussion on the significance of variances and setting control limits applies both to standard costing and budgetary variances.

11. STANDARD COSTS AS A RANGE

Typically a standard cost is shown as a single figure, but more correctly it should be considered as a band or range of values with the standard cost as the central value. This is illustrated by a graph (Figure 26.2) representing the times taken for a number of batches of an assembly.

If the actual result falls within the band it is considered satisfactory and the variance would not be deemed to be significant. If the actual result was outside this band it would be considered significant and would be reported and possibly a fuller investigation mounted. When used in this fashion, the range of values shown on the graph is known as a control band and the upper and lower limits known as control limits.

FIGURE 26.2   Standard Labour time for Assembly 100 X

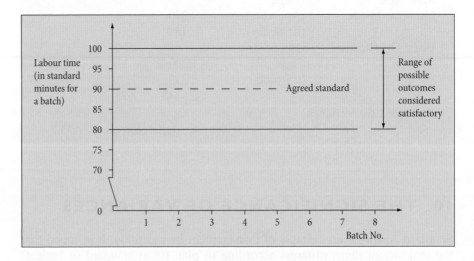

12. SETTING CONTROL LIMITS

The control limits may be set by estimation or statistical analysis.

a. *Estimation*
   This approach is the most commonly used and bases the control limits on judgement or experience. Typically a figure of $\pm 5\%$ is used and variances within this range would be deemed insignificant. Although obviously lacking any statistical rigour, this approach is practical and implicitly uses the same concepts as more rigorous methods.

b. *Statistical analysis*
   Up until now the term 'significant' has been used in a general sense. More precisely, a variance which is statistically significant is one which is of such a magnitude that it is unlikely to have arisen purely by chance. Statistical probability tests based on the properties of normal distributions can be used to determine whether differences from standard arise from chance (ie not significant) or from controllable causes (ie significant).

To set control limits which can be used to determine statistical significance is dependent upon certain statistical assumptions regarding costs and upon being able to calculate or estimate the standard deviation of the costs. (The statistical techniques alluded to above are covered in most statistics textbooks and would form part of Foundation Level Studies for all accounting students.) Based on the properties of the normal distribution, control limits at any level can be set, for example:

5% control limits are set at mean ± 1.96 standard deviations

2% control limits are set at mean ± 2.33 standard deviations

1% control limits are set at mean ± 2.57 standard deviations

0.2% control limits are set at mean ± 3.09 standard deviations

Example 5
The standard usage of a part is 120 per assembly and analysis of past usage indicates that the standard deviation of usage is four items.

a. What are the 2% control limits?
b. What is the meaning of such control limits?
c. Show the control limits graphically.

Solution

a. 2% control limits are set at the mean ± 2.33 s.d.

$$\text{ie, } 120 \pm 2.33(4)$$
$$\textbf{ie, } \mathbf{120 \pm 9.32}$$
$$\text{Upper control limit } = 120 + 9.32 = \mathbf{129.32}$$
$$\text{Lower control limit } = 120 - 9.32 = \mathbf{110.68}$$

See Figure 26.3.

b. The meaning of these control limits is that if chance alone cause variations from standard, then 98% of variances should fall within the range of the

FIGURE 26.3   Graph of control limits

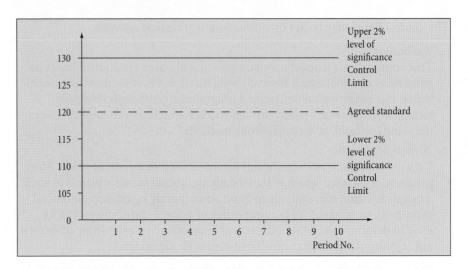

mean (standard) ± 2.33 standard deviations. If a variance falls outside these limits, ie above 129.32 or below 110.68, then the variance is said to be significant at the 2% level.

Note:
Although setting control limits by statistical means appears to be more rigorous, it must be pointed out that some of the necessary statistical assumptions regarding the cost distribution may be invalid in practice and also that the calculation or estimation of the standard deviation may be difficult.

13. VARIANCE CONTROL CHARTS

Whether the control limits are set by statistical analysis or by estimation, a variance control chart can be a useful device, particularly for the identification of trends in the variance. A series of increasing adverse variances, although still within the control limits, may point to a growing problem which perhaps may be rectified before it becomes significant. Not all variances which are significant, ie, outside the control limits, require detailed investigations. Often the cause is already known or readily ascertainable. The likely benefits of a detailed investigation must be compared with the costs involved.

14. ACCOUNTING FOR STANDARD COSTING SYSTEMS

Standard costs and the resulting variances form part of the double entry accounting system. Whether the accounting system is an integrated one or separate financial and cost records are kept, there are common features in the way standard costing is normally dealt with in the accounts.

a. Variances are isolated as early as possible, ie as near as possible to the point of occurrence or when the element of cost is charged to production by being debited to the Work-in-Progress A/c.

b. Variance accounts are maintained for each type of variance. Each period these accounts are closed down and the balances transferred to the Costing P & L account.

c. Transfers between the Work-in-Progress, Finished Goods, and Cost of Sales accounts are at standard.

d. Stocks of W.I.P., Finished Goods, and Raw Materials are the balances on the respective accounts and are automatically valued at standard. A diagram of typical entries in a standard costing system is shown in Figure 26.4.

Notes on Figure 26.4:

a. The general pattern is for the actual amount to be charged to the appropriate control account and the price (or expenditure) variance extracted at that point. The actual quantity (or hours) at the standard price (or rate) is then charged to W.I.P. where the remaining variances relating to efficiency and usage are extracted.

b. For simplicity, only the main entries have been shown on the chart. For example, issues of indirect materials would be charged to the Variable Overhead Control account at actual quantity times standard price.

c. The procedure shown on the chart means that the balances on all stock accounts, stores control, W.I.P. control and Finished Goods are at standard cost.

d. The accounting entries shown relate to unfavourable variances only. This is for clarity and obviously favourable variances do arise. The entries for favourable variances would be the reverse of those shown, eg a favourable labour efficiency variance would be DR W.I.P. CR Labour Efficiency Variance account.

e. The chart shows all variances being transferred to the P & L account at the end of a period. This is common practice, but because favourable material price, usage and labour efficiency variances relating to stocks of raw materials, WIP and finished goods mean that an unrealised profit may be taken, sometimes favourable variances are retained in the accounts until the relevant production is actually sold.

   For examination purposes this is not considered to be significant and unless the question points clearly to some other conclusion, students are recommended to close off all variance accounts each period and debit/credit as required to the Profit and Loss account.

15. EXAMPLE OF ACCOUNTS FOR STANDARD COSTING

Example 6

Dalton and company make and sell a single product, X100. The company operates a standard cost system and during a period the following details were recorded.

FIGURE 26.4 Typical accounting entries in a standard absorption costing system

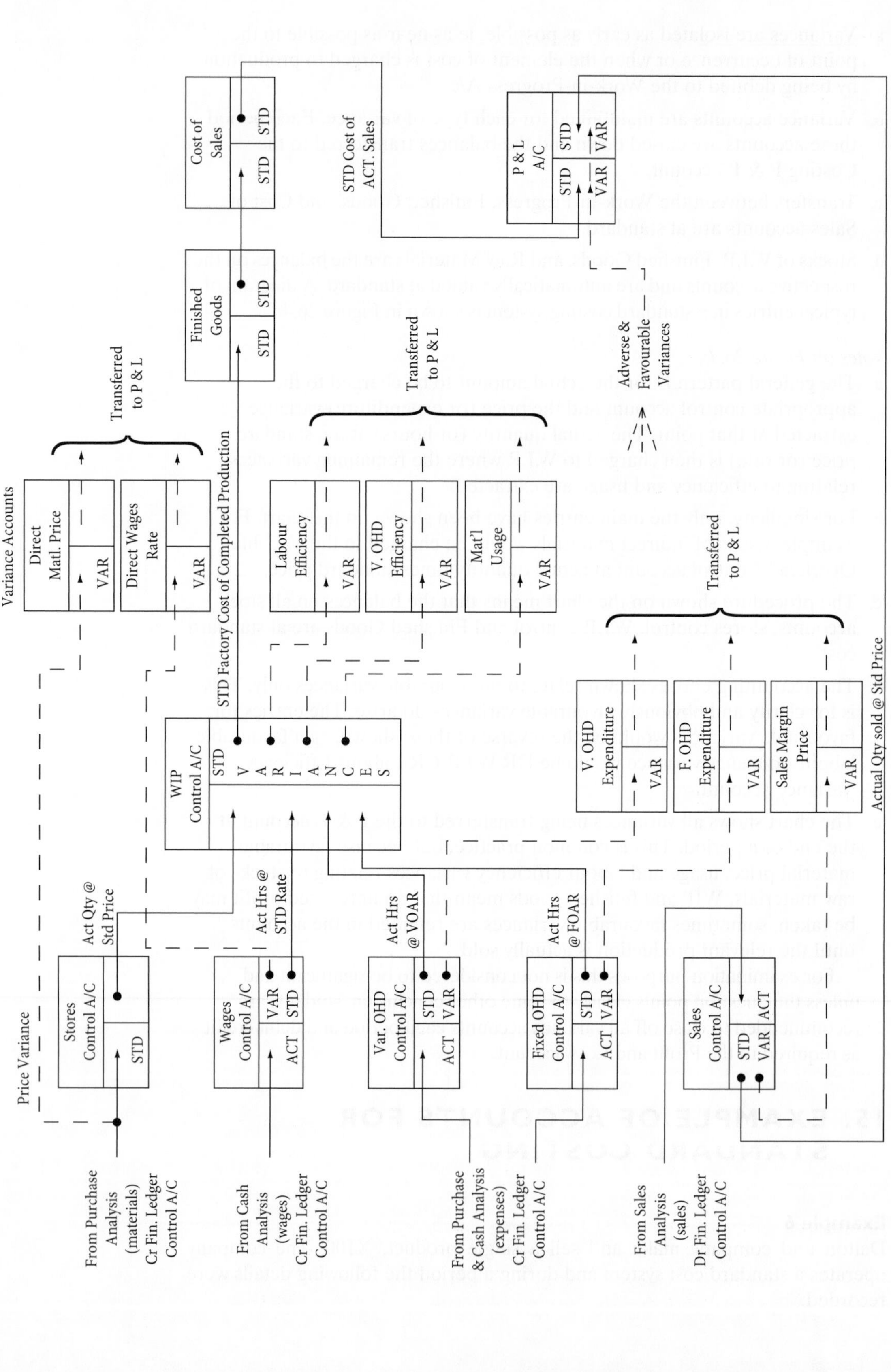

Opening trial balance

	£	£
Financial ledger control A/C		3,930
Stores control A/c (at standard)	850	
Finished Goods control A/c (at standard)	3,080	
	3,930	3,930

There was no opening W.I.P.

	Budget for period	Actual for period
Sales	1,000 units at £100 each	950 at £103
Production	1,000 units	980 units
Fixed overheads	£18,000	£17,850

The standard cost card for X100 is

	£ per unit
Direct materials (10 Kgs at £2)	20
Direct labour (6 hrs at £2.50)	15
Variable overheads (6 hrs at £4/hr)	24
Fixed overheads (6 hrs at £3/hr)	18
Total standard cost	77
Standard Profit	23
Standard Selling Price	100

During the period the following details were recorded:

	£
Purchases of materials (13,000 Kgs)	26,500
Direct wages (5,600 hours)	14,560
Variable overheads	24,192
Fixed overheads	17,850
Material issues to production were 9,810 Kgs	

Using the above information it is required to prepare all cost and variance accounts and a profit and loss account and a closing trial balance.

Solution
The first stage is to calculate the variances.

Cost variances

Material Price = (13,000 × £2) – £26,500	= £500 Adv.
Material Usage = (9,810 – (980 ×10)) × £2	= £20 Adv.
Labour Rate = (14,560 – (5,600 × £2.50))	= £560 Adv.
Labour Efficiency = (5,600 – (980 × 6)) × £2.50	= £700 Fav.
Variable Overhead Expenditure (£24,192 – (5,600 × £4))	= £1,792 Adv.
Variable Overhead Efficiency (5,600 – (980 × 6)) × £4	= £1,120 Fav.
Fixed Overhead Expenditure = £18,000 – £17,850	= £150 Fav.
Fixed Overhead Volume = 20 units × £18	= £360 Adv.

Sales margin variance

Standard sales margin = £23 and actual margin over standard cost = £26
∴ Sales margin price variance = (£26 − £23) × 950 = £2,850 Fav.

Stores Control

Balance	850	WIP	19,620
F.L. Control	26,000	Balance	7,230
	26,850		26,850
Balance	7,230		

Wages Control

F.L. Control	14,560	Labour Rate Variance	560
		WIP	14,000
	14,560		14,560

Variable Overhead Control

F.L. Control	24,192	Expens.	1,792
		Variance WIP	22,400
	24,192		24,192

Sales Control

Marg Price	2,850	F.L. Control	97,850
Variance P + L	95,000		
	97,850		97,850

Cost of Sales

Fin. Goods	73,150	P & L	73,150

Financial Ledger Control A/C

Sales	97,850	Balance	3,930
		Purch (std) (a)	26,000
		Purch Variance	500
		Wages	14,560
		Variable	24,192
Balance	12,620	Overheads Fixed	17,850
		Overheads Profit	23,438
	110,470		110,470
		Balance	12,620

Finished Goods Control

Balance	3,080	Cost of (b)	73,150
WIP	75,460	Sales	5,390
	78,540	Balance c/f	78,540

Fixed Overhead Control

F. L. Control	17,850	Volume	360
Expenditure Variance	150	WIP	17,640
	18,000		18,000

WIP Control

Wages	14,000	Materials Usage	20
Labour Efficiency	700	Var. Finished Goods (c)	75,460
Var. Materials	19,620		
Variable Overhead	22,400		
Var. Ohd. Eff.	1,120		
Variance Fixed	17,460		
Overhead			
	75,480		75,480

Variance accounts

Material Price

F. L. Control	500	P & L	500

Labour Rates

Wage Control	560	P & L	560

Variable Overhead Expenditure

Ohd. Control	1,792	P & L	1,792

Fixed Overhead Expenditure

P & L	150	Ohd. control	150

Sales Margin Price

P & L	2,850	Sales Cont	2,850

Material Usage

WIP	20	P & L	20

Labour Efficiency

P & L	700	WIP	700

Variable Overhead Efficiency

P & L	1,120	WIP	1,120

Fixed Overhead Volume

Ohd. control	360	P & L	360

Profit Statement

		£	£
	Sales (at standard)		95,000
Less	Cost of sales (at standard)		73,150
	Standard Profit on actual sales		21,850
	Sales margin price variance		2,850
			24,700
Add	Favourable cost variances		
	Fixed Overhead Expenditure	150	
	Labour Efficiency	700	
	Variable Ohd efficiency	1,120	1,970
			26,670
Less	Unfavourable cost variances		
	Materials price	500	
	Labour rate	560	
	Material usage	20	
	Fixed overhead volume	360	
	Variable Ohd expenditure	1,792	3,232
			23,438 (to Fin. Ledg. Con)

Closing Trial Balance

	£	£
Financial ledger control		12,620
Stores Control	7,230	
Finished Goods Control	5,390	
	12,620	12,620

Notes on accounts:

a. Price variance segregated so all materials carried at standard.

b. This is standard cost of 950 sales.

c. This is standard cost of 980 production.

In addition to the accounts and profit statement shown above management would also require an explanation of the difference between actual results and the original budget.

16. ACCOUNTING FOR STANDARD VARIABLE (OR MARGINAL) COSTING

This follows very similar lines to standard absorption costing as previously described. Because fixed overheads are not included in the production accounts (WIP, Finished Goods and Cost of Sales) the following differences are necessary.

a. No fixed overheads are charged to WIP, finished goods and cost of sales.

b. The valuations of all types of stock, WIP, finished goods, etc will be at standard variable cost.

c. Budgeted fixed overheads will be transferred directly from fixed overhead control to P & L, ie Cr Fixed Overhead control Dr P & L, while any balance on the Fixed overhead control in comparison to actual fixed overheads, represents the Fixed Overhead Expenditure variance.

d. The standard sales margin becomes the standard sales contribution.

17. STANDARD COSTING AND AMT

Standard costing originated in the early years of last century. It was a control system designed to serve the industrial conditions of the time and proved to be a sound management tool. Conditions, however have changed dramatically and doubts have been raised about the usefulness of standard costing in today's industrial environment.

Nowadays, world class manufacture's use computer assisted Advanced Manufacturing Technology (AMT) and Just-in-Time (JIT) production and purchasing methods. There is a constant drive for improvement and excellence, the elimination of all forms of waste, a move towards zero defects and inventories, and production according to demand rather than for stock. As a consequence of these and other developments there have been major changes in cost patterns. These can be summarised thus:

*   Direct labour now constitutes only a small proportion of costs – typically 5 – 15% in modern factories.
*   Most costs are now fixed in the short run, including labour. In many factories, materials and power costs are the only variable costs.
*   Overheads are a much higher proportion of total costs and need to be monitored and controlled much more closely than in the past.

18. PROBLEMS OF STANDARD COSTING IN AMT FACTORIES

It is argued that traditional standard costing and variance analysis is of limited value in these new circumstances. Some specific criticisms are:

a. By concentrating on a narrow range of financial factors, variance analysis ignores many other vital matters such as quality, lead times and customer satisfaction and encourages short-termism.

b. In a mainly fixed cost environment many variances are of little or no value for short-term cost control. For example, where labour costs are largely fixed, labour variances provide little information. Where overhead expenditure is unrelated to production volume, which is the case for many overheads, most overhead variances do not provide managers with realistic control information.

c. There is an over-emphasis on direct labour which is nowadays a small, and declining, proportion of total cost.

d. In traditional Standard Costing a Standard represents a target to be achieved and maintained whereas JIT has a philosophy of continuous improvement. This is best served by reporting a range of actual performance measures (eg lead and delivery times, defects found, quality and so on) over time so that trends in performance can be measured.

e. Some variances and traditional performance measures produce incorrect signals and work against AMT and JIT objectives. For example, if material price variances were used the buyer would be motivated to buy on price alone and thus avoid adverse variances. This may lead to larger inventories, poorer quality and irregular deliveries. JIT purchasing concentrates on quality, reliability and integrated deliveries not merely price.

f. Some traditional measures such as fixed overhead volume variances encourage maximising output even though this increases inventories, uses space and increases finance charges. JIT is demand led and aims to produce the required quantities only when they are actually needed. This may mean that there is idle time on occasions, which is considered preferable to producing for stock. Maximising output to move into stock does not maximise long-term profitability.

g. Much variance reporting is done weekly or even monthly. In consequence there is a significant delay between the actual event or operation and information about its performance. In fast moving JIT factories with short production cycles delays of this nature are unacceptable.

As a consequence more direct, non-financial performance measures are supplanting traditional standard costing reports and there is greater emphasis on control by production workers themselves. This is done by training workers to monitor continuously production flows, quality, set-up times, defects and so on.

In spite of the potential problems in using standard costing, properly designed systems still perform a useful role in modern organisations. As an example consider the experience of the SKF Group.

19. DEVELOPMENTS IN CONTROL AND PERFORMANCE MEASUREMENT

In order to overcome some of the deficiencies outlined above and to make control and performance measurement systems more relevant to today's needs, numerous developments are taking place. These include:

a. Standards are being revised more frequently and allowances for scrap, waste and reworks eliminated. Standards are progressively tightened in line with the JIT philosophy of continuous improvement.

b. More use of on-line data capture and computing systems to process and display information continuously in real time.

c. Labour efficiency and material quantity variances are reported immediately in physical rather than financial terms. This is speedier and the physical values (hours taken, units produced, material and component usage) have more impact on production personnel than money values.

d. A broader range of performance measures are used, most of which are non-financial. Examples include ratios and data connected with

FIGURE 26.5 SKF Group

SKF is a knowledge engineering company and a leading global supplier in the areas of bearings, seals, mechatronics, services and lubrication systems. The Group's service offer includes technical support, maintenance services, engineering consultancy and training.

The SKF business is organized into three divisions; Industrial, Automotive and Service. Each division serves a global market, focusing on its specific customer segments.

SKF has more than 100 manufacturing sites distributed all over the world and its own sales companies in 70 countries. SKF is also represented in more than 130 countries and has 15,000 distributor locations worldwide.

SKF was founded in 1907 and from the very beginning focused intensively on quality, technical development and marketing. The results of the Group's efforts in the area of research and development have led to a growing number of innovations that has created new standards and new products in the bearing world.

SKF are world class manufacturers and use Standard Cost extensively. They have tried some other concepts such as Activity Based Costing and Value Based Costing but think that the traditional way with standard costing stand up to the competition of new systems well, since the new systems often are very complicated to carry out.

The standard costing information is to be used within the following areas:

- Product Costing
- Inventory Valuation
- Variance Analysis
- Budgeting

Benchmarking is also regarded as a purpose of standard costing but this is a more general purpose.

SKF use a total currently attainable standard cost system and define 'full production cost' as all cost elements from the raw material until the product is shipped to local finished goods stock or local factory shipping terminal.

Standard costs are usually developed annually based on a number of cost and volume forecasts. As an example the cost forecast are divided into three:

- Material Cost Forecast
- External sub-contracting cost forecast
- Value-added cost forecast

When the forecasts have been prepared the costs are assigned to the production process via a two part process.

- Directly related costs: include material costs, external subcontracting costs and tooling costs
- Distributed costs: include the fixed and variable value added costs in a manufacturing channel, the set-up costs and the extra operation and sub-contracted operation costs.

Variance analysis is used mainly at the managerial rather than the operational level but it should be noted that both actuals and variances are reported. An important perceived benefit from variance analysis is that it gives an early indication of trends.

For further details refer to:

www.handels.gu.se/epc/archive/00002757/01/gbs-thesis-2002-48.pdf

Manufacturing cycle times and efficiency, In-coming quality, customer satisfaction, Delivery performance, Process times, Set-up times, Distance parts travel, No of defects and so on.

e. As discussed earlier in the book, changes in the level of many overheads are unrelated to short-term changes in production volume. These are the costs described, by Kaplan as long-run variable costs. There is a growing realisation that these types of cost are best managed in the long-term by controlling the activities which drive them.

Accordingly Activity Based Costing and Activity Based Budgeting Systems are increasingly being used in factories with AMT and JIT systems. Activity cost management is of course equally applicable to service industries and the Public Sector as well as manufacturing firms.

20. SUMMARY

a. The objective of Sales Margin Variance is to help to control the profit, ie margin, on sales.

b. The standard sales margin is the difference between the standard selling price and the standard cost of an item.

c. The total sales margin variance can be subdivided into Price and Quantity variances. Where more than one product is sold, the Quantity variance can be subdivided into Mixture and Volume variances.

d. The method of calculating the sales margin variances is similar to the methods used for calculating materials variances.

e. Standard costing can employ variable costing principles and becomes known as Standard Variable costing. Fixed costs are not absorbed into individual units of production.

f. A standard variable cost is the total of all standard variable costs. A standard contribution is added to give a standard selling price.

g. Using standard variable costing variance analysis is simplified because all fixed overhead variances disappear, except for the fixed overhead expenditure variance.

h. Material, labour and variable overhead variances are identical and, with the exception that the standard contribution becomes the sales margin, so are the sales variances.

i. Standard costing is particularly appropriate for process industries and where standard costing is employed all entries in the process account are at standard.

j. Significant variances are those which are of such a magnitude that management action will be called for.

k. The determination of what is a significant variance can be done by comparison with control limits.

l. Control limits can be set by judgement, for example plus or minus 5%, or by statistical analysis based on the properties of the normal distribution.

m. Where standard costing is used the variances form part of the double entry system.

n. Typically variances are isolated as early as possible and flows through the main accounts (WIP, Finished Goods, Process) are at standard cost.

o. The usefulness of standard costing in modern AMT factories has been questioned. Many variances are of little value when most costs are fixed and labour is a small proportion of total cost. Properly designed and used systems can however still be of value.

p. More immediate and relevant reporting on performance is required and a range of non-financial measures are used. These cover quality, process and lead times, set-up times, defects and so on. In addition cost management relating to activities is being more widely used.

21. POINTS TO NOTE

a. Variances calculated using traditional standards, as described in the last two chapters, are of value for control purposes only if the standard is still a realistic, attainable target in current conditions. If there have been uncontrollable changes in internal or external conditions then the standard may not now be a realistic one and it follows that the calculated variances will be of little or no value for control purposes and may even be misleading.

b. This is a real problem particularly in volatile conditions and one attempt to deal with this problem is to separate the traditional variances into planning variances; and operational variances.

c. Planning variances seek to explain the extent to which the original standard needs to be revised in order to reflect current conditions. In effect the original standard is brought up to date so that it is a realistic, attainable target in current conditions. Operating variances indicate the extent to which attainable targets (ie the adjusted standards) have been achieved. Operational variances are calculated after the planning variances have been derived and are thus a realistic way of assessing current performance.

d. Planning and operational variances are described more fully in *Management Accounting*, ibid.

Appendix – Summary of Variance Formulae

Basic material variances

Materials Total Variance:

(Standard Units $\times$ Standard Price) – (Actual Units $\times$ Actual Price)

Materials Price Variance:

(Standard Price – Actual Price) $\times$ Actual Quantity

Materials Usage Variance:

(Standard quantity for actual production – Actual quantity) $\times$ Standard Price

Note:

Price + Usage Variances = Total Variance

Basic labour variances

Labour Total Variance:

$$(\text{Standard labour hours produced} \times \text{Standard rate})$$
$$- (\text{Actual hours} \times \text{Actual rate})$$

Labour Rate Variance:

$$(\text{Standard rate} - \text{Actual rate}) \times \text{Actual hours}$$

Labour Efficiency Variance:

$$(\text{Standard hours produced} - \text{Actual hours}) \times \text{Standard rate}$$

Note:

$$\text{Rate} + \text{Efficiency Variances} = \text{Total Variance}$$

Overhead variances

a. The following abbreviations are used:

$$\text{SHP} = \text{Standard Hours Produced}$$
$$\text{VOAR} = \text{Variable Overhead Absorption Rate}$$
$$\text{FOAR} = \text{Fixed Overhead Absorption Rate}$$
$$\text{OAR} = \text{Total Overhead Absorption Rate (ie, Fixed + Variable)}$$

b. Overhead variances can be calculated in different ways depending on the requirements of the firm and whether the overheads have been separated into fixed and variable components. The formulae that follow show the variances which could be calculated when the overheads are sub-divided into fixed and variable components and, alternatively, when a total overhead approach is used.

Variable overhead variances

Variable Overheads Total Variance:

$$\text{Actual variable overheads} - \text{SHP} \times \text{VOAR}$$

Variable Overheads Expenditure Variance:

$$\text{Actual variable overheads} - \text{Actual hours} \times \text{VOAR}$$

Variable Overhead Efficiency Variance:

$$(\text{Actual hours} - \text{SHP}) \times \text{VOAR}$$

Note:

$$\text{Expenditure} + \text{Efficiency variances} = \text{Total variance}$$

Fixed overhead variances

Fixed Overhead Total Variance:

$$\text{Actual fixed overheads} - \text{SHP} \times \text{FOAR}$$

Fixed Overhead Capacity Variance:

$$\text{Budgeted fixed overheads} - \text{Actual hours} \times \text{FOAR}$$

Fixed Overhead Efficiency Variance:

$$(\text{Actual hours} - \text{SHP}) \times \text{FOAR}$$

Note:

1. Capacity + Efficiency variances = Volume variance
2. Volume + Expenditure variances = Total variance

Total overhead variances
(ie, including both fixed and variable)

Total Overhead Variance:

$$\text{Actual total overheads} - \text{SHP} \times \text{OAR}$$

Total Overhead Expenditure Variance:

$$\text{Actual total overhead} - \text{Budgeted total overheads}$$

Total Overhead Volume Variance:

$$\text{Budgeted total overheads} - \text{Actual hours} \times \text{OAR}$$

Total Overhead Efficiency Variance:

$$(\text{Actual hours} - \text{SHP}) \times \text{OAR}$$

Note:

Expenditure + Volume + Efficiency variances = Total variance

Material mix and yield variances
(as sub-divisions of Usage Variance)

Materials Mix Variance:

(Actual quantity in Actual proportions − Actual quantity in Standard proportions)
$\times$ Standard price

Materials Yield Variance:

(Actual quantity in Standard proportions − Standard quantity in Standard proportions)
$\times$ Standard price

Note:

$$\text{Mix} + \text{Yield variances} = \text{Usage variance}$$

Sales margin variances

Note:
for sales margin variance analysis products are valued at standard manufacturing cost.

Sales Margin Total Variance:

$$\text{Budgeted total margin } - \text{ Actual total margin}$$

Sales Margin Price Variance:

$$(\text{Actual units } \times \text{ Actual margins}) - (\text{Actual units } \times \text{ Standard margins})$$

Sales Margin Mix Variance:

$$(\text{Actual units} \times \text{Standard margins}) - (\text{Actual total units in Standard proportions} \times \text{Standard margins})$$

Sales Margin Volume Variance:

$$(\text{Actual total units in Standard proportions } - \text{ Standard total units in Standard proportions}) \times \text{ Standard margins}$$

Note:

1. Mix + Volume variances = Quantity variance
2. Price + Quantity variances = Total variance

Student self-testing

Exercises (answers below)

1. A firm makes and sells three products, A, B and C. For period 9 the budgeted and actual results were as follows:

Budget

Product	Value £	Total Sales Units	Price per Unit £	Standard Manufacturing Cost £
A	10,000	2,000	5	3.50
B	12,000	4,000	3	1.80
C	6,000	500	12	8.50
	£28,000	6,500		

Actual

Product	Total Sales Value £	Total Sales Units	Actual Margin £
A	10,500	2,100	1.35
B	12,920	3,800	1.20
C	6,844	580	3.35

Calculate all relevant sales margin variances.

2. A firm employing standard variable costing has the following actual results for a period:

Production 7,200 units

Material used	8,450 (420 Kgs)
Labour costs	35,280 (9,100 hours)
Variable overheads	34,200
Fixed costs	28,500
Direct Material Price Variance	370 (Fav)
Direct Material Usage Variance	252 (Fav)
Direct Labour Rate Variance	1,120 (Fav)
Direct Labour Efficiency Variance	1,040 (Fav)
Variable Overhead Expenditure Variance	2,350 (Adv)
Variable Overhead Efficiency Variance	910 (Fav)
Fixed Overhead Variance	500 (Adv)

Unfortunately the standard cost card has been lost together with the budget for the period but the accountant recalls that the budgeted output was 7,000 units. You are required to derive the standard cost card for the item and the budget for the period.

3. The standard labour cost of a component is £5 and a standard deviation of 20p has been estimated.
   a. Calculate the 2% control limits.

   b. In a period the output was 480 units and the labour cost was exactly on the upper 2% limit. What was the actual labour cost in the period and what was the labour cost variance?

4. A firm operates a Standard Process Costing system and three partially complete accounts are given below:

Materials A/c

Stores Control	42,800	Process A/c		44,750
	(1)			
	44,750			44,750

Wages A/c

Wages Control	21,407	Process A/c		18,480
				(2)
	21,407			21,407

Overhead A/c

Overhead Control	34,906	Process A/c		31,521
				(3)
	34,906			34,906

Required:
a. Complete the entries (1), (2), and (3).
b. Explain their meaning.
c. Where would the double entries be?

Solutions to exercises

1. The relevant variances are the Sales Margin Price, Mix and Volume Variances.

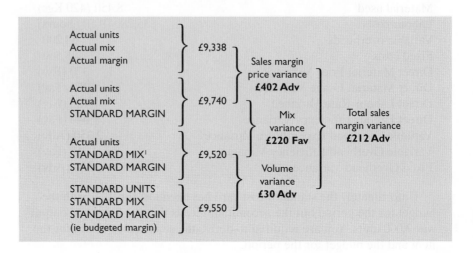

[1] Standard mix is the actual number sold (6,480) in the standard proportions, ie:

$$\frac{2,000}{6,500}, \frac{4,000}{6,500} \text{ and } \frac{500}{6,500} \text{ thus:}$$

A = 1,994 @ £1.50	=		£2,991
B = 3,988 @ £1.20	=		£4,786
C = 498 @ £3.50	=		£1,743
	=		£9,520

2. The Standard Cost Card is as follows:

Standard cost per unit	**£**
Direct Materials 0.06 Kg at £21 Kg	1.26
Direct Labour 1.3 hours at £4 hr.	5.20
= Prime Cost	6.46
+ Variable overheads 1.3 hours at £3.5 hr.	4.55
= Total Variable Cost	£11.01

Budget for period – output 7,000 units	**£**
Direct Materials	8,820
Direct Labour	36,400
Variable Overheads	31,850
= Total Variable Cost Fixed Costs	£77,070
	28,000
= Total Cost	£105,070

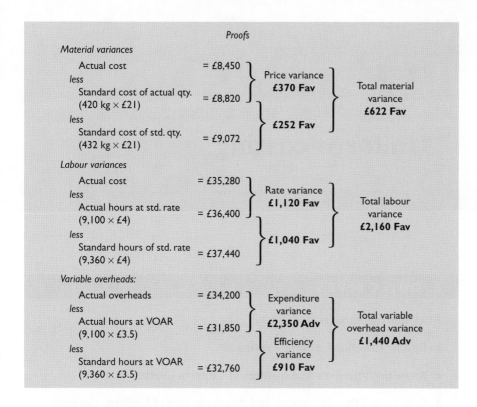

Proofs

Material variances

Actual cost	= £8,450			
less		Price variance £370 Fav		
Standard cost of actual qty. (420 kg × £21)	= £8,820		Total material variance £622 Fav	
less		£252 Fav		
Standard cost of std. qty. (432 kg × £21)	= £9,072			

Labour variances

Actual cost	= £35,280			
less		Rate variance £1,120 Fav		
Actual hours at std. rate (9,100 × £4)	= £36,400		Total labour variance £2,160 Fav	
less		£1,040 Fav		
Standard hours of std. rate (9,360 × £4)	= £37,440			

Variable overheads:

Actual overheads	= £34,200			
less		Expenditure variance £2,350 Adv		
Actual hours at VOAR (9,100 × £3.5)	= £31,850		Total variable overhead variance £1,440 Adv	
less		Efficiency variance £910 Fav		
Standard hours at VOAR (9,360 × £3.5)	= £32,760			

Fixed Overheads

$$\text{Actual} - \text{Budget} = £28,500 - 28,000 = \mathbf{£500\ Adv}$$

3. a. 2% control limits are set at the mean $\pm 2.33\ \sigma$

$\therefore \sigma = 0.20 \therefore$ control limits are £5 $\pm 2.33\ (0.20) = £5 \pm 47p$

b.
Labour cost per unit	=	£5.47
∴ Total labour cost	=	£2,625.60
Standard labour cost	=	2,400.00
∴ Labour cost variance	=	**£225.60 ADV**

4. a. Entry 1. Total material variance £1,950 FAV
Entry 2. Total labour variance £2,927 ADV
Entry 3. Total overhead variance £3,385 ADV

b. Entry 1 – This indicates that the actual material cost of £42,800 was £1,950 below the standard for the output.
Entry 2 – This indicates that the actual wages of £21,407 were £2,927 above the standard labour cost for the output.
Entry 3 – This indicates that the actual overheads of £34,906 were £3,385 above the standard overhead cost for the output.

c. The double entries would be:

For Entry 1 CR Material Variance A/c   DR Materials A/c
For Entry 2 DR Labour Variance A/c   CR Wages A/c
For Entry 3 DR Overhead Variance A/c   CR Overhead A/c

27

Uniform costing

I. OBJECTIVES

After studying this chapter you will

● **Be able to define Uniform Costing**

● **Know the objectives and features of Uniform Costing**

● **Understand the advantages and disadvantages of Uniform Costing.**

2. UNIFORM COSTING DEFINED

This can be defined as:

> *the use by several undertakings of the same costing systems, ie the same basic costing methods, principles and techniques.*

> *Terminology*

Uniform costing systems do not, in general, contain novel or advanced features. Rather they ensure that there are similar costing foundations and reports in a number of organisations. Uniform costing may be employed by members of the same group, various local authorities, or members of the same trade association. Examples of the application of uniform costing systems include: the printing, hotel and dairy industries, retail and wholesale groups with multiple outlets; local authorities.

3. OBJECTIVES

The major objectives of uniform costing are:

a. To promote uniformity of costing methods so that valid cost comparisons can be made between organisations.

b. To serve as a basis for competitive but non-destructive bidding.

c. To eliminate inefficiencies and promote good practices revealed by the cost comparisons.

d. To serve as a basis for government subsidies or grants which need similar costing systems to ensure equitable distribution.

4. FEATURES OF UNIFORM COSTING SYSTEMS

There is no hard and fast rule which determines what is a uniform costing system. However, it would be generally accepted that systems which follow agreed guidelines in the areas given below would be classed as uniform systems.

a. *Cost statements and reports.*
These should be organised and laid out in a similar fashion so that each element of cost revenue can be compared easily.

b. *Accounting periods.*
There must be agreement on whether calendar months or four-week months will be used. Invariably there will be a standard accounting calendar.

c. *Cost classification.*
An agreed classification system must be used so that similar items will be classified in the same manner by all concerned. This will avoid an item being classified by some as indirect and others as direct.

d. *Valuation basis.*
There must be agreement of the methods of valuing stocks and W.I.P. and of the methods of charging stores issues, eg will FIFO, LIFO etc be used.

e. *Asset valuation.*
These must be agreement on the basis for fixed asset valuations, eg pure historical cost or revaluation at agreed periods.

f. *Depreciation.*
Both the method (reducing balance or straight line) and the actual rates for each type of asset must be agreed.

g. *Costing principles and techniques.*
There will need to be full agreement on the methods of cost build-up and whether marginal/absorption/standard costing, or Activity Based Costing will be used.

h. *Bases of apportionment and absorption.*
When the type of system (marginal, absorption) is agreed, then there will have to be agreement on the way costs are apportioned to cost centres and on the way overheads will be absorbed into products. For example, will overheads be absorbed on units of production, labour hours, machine hours? What will be the basis of apportioning service costs to production cost centres? If ABC is used what cost pools and cost drivers will be used?

5. ADVANTAGES OF UNIFORM COSTING

a. *Cost comparability*
This is the prime advantage. Because similar principles, bases and valuations are used, genuine cost comparisons can be made between different firms or organisations.

b. *Professional expertise*
   Frequently uniform costing systems are designed by consultants or senior, experienced accountants employed by an association. In this way the systems are soundly developed to high professional standards in a manner which would be too expensive for a single organisation, particularly one operating on a small scale.

c. *Basis for data processing*
   Uniform costing systems make it easier to computerise the accounting system of the various organisations. Similar cost classifications and report layouts considerably reduce the systems and programming effort required.

d. *Staffing costs and staff flexibility*
   Because of the similar nature of the costing systems it may be possible to use lower grade staff in the separate organisations with qualified, senior personnel at headquarters. Also transferability between organisations may be facilitated.

6. DISADVANTAGES OF UNIFORM COSTING

a. *Inappropriateness to the individual organisation*
   Where members of a trade association use uniform costing, the chosen system may not suit every firm, particularly where there is a range of sizes and structures. Frequently a tailor made system would be better for particular organisations.

b. *Inflexibility*
   Uniform costing systems, like most centralised systems, are slow to adapt to changing conditions and demands upon them.

7. SUMMARY

a. Uniform costing is the use by a number of undertakings of the same costing methods, principles and techniques.

b. The major objectives are to enable cost comparisons to be made, to serve as a basis for competitive bidding and to eliminate inefficiencies.

c. The major features of uniform costing include: similar cost statements, standard accounting periods, agreed cost classifications and valuation bases and agreed costing principles and techniques.

d. The major advantages are: genuine cost comparability, high professional standards, possibly lower staff costs and greater staff interchangeability.

e. The disadvantages are: possible inappropriateness to particular organisations and possible inflexibility in relation to changing circumstances.

Student self-testing

Exercise (answer below)

1. A firm of printers is contemplating joining the uniform costing system operated by its Trade Association but the Managing Director is dubious about the advantages of becoming involved in the scheme.

Prepare a report to the Managing Director describing the advantages that the firm is likely to gain.

Solution to exercise

1. To: MANAGING DIRECTOR

From: COST ACCOUNTANT
Subject: UNIFORM COSTING SYSTEM

TERMS OF REFERENCE: To investigate and report upon the advantages to be obtained from becoming a member of the Uniform Costing System operated by the Trade Association. There are several advantages to be gained from joining the scheme of which the major ones are as follows:

a. Access to detailed cost and operating characteristics of our competitors. This will enable us to compare costs and efficiencies and may show where improvements can be made.

b. Improvement to our tendering procedures. Having an information base from which we can obtain genuinely comparable cost data should enable us to improve our bidding particularly in competitive conditions.

c. The simplified uniform system will make it easier to introduce information technology. Having agreed systems and procedures will enable us to purchase ready made application software when inevitably we introduce information technology to deal with out cost accounting systems.

Although the above are major advantages and would probably lead to an organisation joining the scheme it should be remembered that there are some disadvantages including: the fee payable, changes to existing systems and valuation methods and the fact that competitors will have access to the organisation's costs and operational data albeit in an anonymous form.

28

Cost accounting and computers

2. BACKGROUND COMPUTER KNOWLEDGE

All students taking cost accounting examinations will either be concurrently studying computers and data processing or will be exempt from the subject because of their previous studies.

Accordingly no attempt will be made in this book to explain what computers are or how they operate. The emphasis will be on highlighting some of the ways they can be used for cost accounting purposes and the resulting advantages and disadvantages. It is assumed that students are familiar with the more common terms used in data processing; for example, hardware, software, files, VDU, disc storage, terminal, online, application packages, printers, program, and so on.

Students unfamiliar with these terms or who wish to study computers and data processing in more detail are advised to consult a comprehensive book on the subject. Any questions in a cost accounting examination which involve computers are thought unlikely to require much detailed technical computer knowledge, rather it is expected that they will test understanding of the application of computers to various facets of cost accounting.

3. WHY ARE COMPUTERS USEFUL FOR COST ACCOUNTING?

Computers can be valuable tools for cost accounting purposes for the same reasons as they are for all other applications, namely, speed, accuracy, filing and retrieval abilities, calculating and decision-making capabilities, input and output facilities.

These points are expanded below:

Speed

Relative to manual methods, all aspects of computer operations (except the initial manual input of data via the keyboard) take place at very high speeds. Whether the computer is calculating an overhead variance, making an entry on a job cost file, printing an actual/budget statement or carrying out some other cost accounting task the computer does this in a minute fraction of the time it would take manually.

Accuracy

All computers incorporate inbuilt checking features which ensure for all practical purposes 100% accuracy in following a program. If a program has been thoroughly tested and produces the required output or performs the correct calculations, then this will be followed faithfully time after time after time.

On occasions computer systems do produce errors but investigations invariably show that these errors arise from such factors as errors contained in the data input or programming errors or an unforeseen combination of circumstances not allowed for in the program and not from computer malfunction.

Filing and retrieval abilities

Computer files, nowadays invariably maintained on some type of disc storage, and the associated software file handling systems, permit the rapid updating, amendment, cross-referencing and retrieval of huge volumes of data that would be virtually impossible using any manual system. Computer backing storage systems are becoming physically smaller, cheaper and permit faster access. These developments mean that accountants and managers can have more and more information readily available for instantaneous display on their terminal.

Calculating and decision making capability

Computer calculating speeds are measured in millionths of a second and are the heart of their power. In computer terms, the calculations required for cost accounting purposes are very modest yet these same calculations done manually are tedious and time-consuming. Take for example the calculations required for apportioning various items of overhead expenditure over cost centres, which is a routine but necessary task. Each calculation is simple but the overall task, including cross and down totalling, can be lengthy when done manually, yet is ideally suited to the computer where it would be done virtually instantaneously.

Allied to the calculating power of the computer is its ability to test different values or conditions and depending on the results, take different actions. It is this ability which enables the computer to make decisions and makes it qualitatively different from other machines. The speed, calculating power and decision-making ability of the computer enables the accountant to extend the scope of his analysis beyond that which would be feasible manually, except for a special once-off exercise.

As an example, manually prepared variance statements typically highlight variances above a certain value (say, £1,000) or those more than a given percentage (say ± 5%) away from standard. The computer could be programmed to do this and also to analyse the variance and its significance by statistical methods including the calculation of the standard deviation – and, where a significant variance is detected, to retrieve the history of this variance for comparison and to ascertain trends. In short, a more detailed analysis could routinely be undertaken, where required, without extra effort on the part of the accountant who would know that all truly significant variances would be highlighted so leaving more time for any personal investigations felt necessary.

This, incidentally, is the key to effective use of computers for cost accounting (or any other) purposes. They should be used, where feasible, for all forms of routine ledger keeping, calculating, searching, periodic statements, report production and so on in order that there is more time for activities requiring the human touch; for example interpretation of results, special investigations, planning, interviewing and so on.

Input and output facilities

Computers can read and search files, print results or display information on VDUs at very high speeds. With modern software, report layouts can be altered at will, results can be displayed using a range of diagrammatic and graphical displays, often in full colour, and displays can be interrogated and manipulated by the user without leaving his desk. Taken together, the various facilities provide a far more flexible and speedy service than would be possible using manual means.

4. WHAT APPLICATIONS SHOULD THE COMPUTER BE USED FOR?

Because of the dramatically falling real cost of computer systems, their increasing power and the ever growing availability of software, more and more facets of cost accounting and of other commercial tasks are worthwhile computer applications. In the early days of computers they were very expensive indeed and only a few large applications were economically worthwhile. Chip technology and miniaturisation has changed that situation dramatically.

As an example, 25 years ago a computer typically would cost £100,000 (say, 200 times the then cost of a Mini car or 100 times the annual salary of a cost clerk) yet today a machine with greater power and capacity which is infinitely more flexible and adaptable, can be purchased for £2,000 or less (a quarter of the cost of a mini car or about a month's salary for a cost clerk).

Computer power has now become much cheaper than clerical power and this fact will cause significant changes in the way that all administrative work, including cost accounting, is carried out. No longer is it necessary for all computer jobs to be high volume, repetitive tasks in order for them to be economically worthwhile. Smaller volume, more varied jobs and even one-off analyses and investigations using the 'what if' facility incorporated in much application software, have become a feasible proposition.

This means that virtually any cost accounting task is now an economic application and indeed in an increasing number of organisations – even very small ones – the desk top micro linked to disc backing storage maintains all the cost accounting records and produces all the required reports except those resulting from special one-off investigations.

Typical of the cost accounting tasks now routinely dealt with by computer is the following list, which is by no means exhaustive.

- Job and Contract Costing and associated reporting.
- Stores and material control, including issues pricing, WIP and Finished Goods valuation, EOQ calculations, etc.
- All aspects of labour costing.
- Nominal ledger including cost centre analysis, apportionments, overhead calculations.
- Budgetary Control including comparative reporting, calculation of variances.
- Standard costing including control reports, variance calculations, testing variances by statistical means.
- Cash budgeting and reporting.
- Cost accounting using either integrated or separate ledgers.
- Forecasting cost and revenue behaviour using regression analysis or more sophisticated statistical techniques.
- Fixed asset recording including depreciation calculations.

... and so on.

In addition to dealing with the above and other basic cost accounting tasks, computers are also being widely used for work which is generally regarded as Management Accounting. Examples include: investment appraisals, financial modelling, decision analysis and so on which can be grouped under the term 'Decision Support Systems'. Thus it will be seen that there are two main areas of the application of computers in organisations although there are, of course, overlaps between the categories.

- Data processing (or Transaction Processing)
- Decision Support Systems (or End user computing)

FIGURE 28.1   Computers and Information Systems

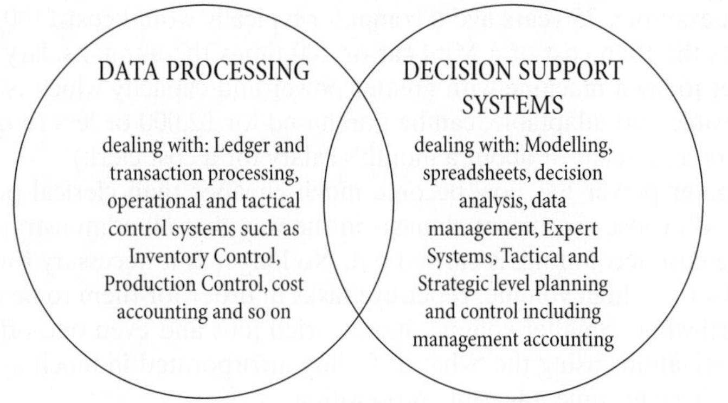

DATA PROCESSING

dealing with: Ledger and
transaction processing,
operational and tactical
control systems such as
Inventory Control,
Production Control, cost
accounting and so on

DECISION SUPPORT
SYSTEMS

dealing with: Modelling,
spreadsheets, decision
analysis, data
management, Expert
Systems, Tactical and
Strategic level planning
and control including
management accounting

These are shown in Figure 28.1

Both categories contribute to the overall Management Information System (MIS) of the organisation of which cost and management accounting information systems are a part. The two categories are developed below:

5. DATA PROCESSING SYSTEMS

These systems perform the essential role of collecting and processing the daily transactions of the organisation, hence the alternative term, transaction processing. Typically these include: all forms of ledger keeping, accounts receivable and payable, invoicing, credit control, rate demands, stock movements, cost recording and analysis, etc.

These types of systems were the first to harness the power of the computer and originally were based on centralised mainframe computers. In many cases this still applies, especially for large volume repetitive jobs, but the availability of micro and mini computers has made distributed data processing feasible and popular. Distributed data processing has many variations but in essence means that data handling and processing are carried out at or near the point of use rather than in one centralised location.

Transaction processing is substantially more significant in terms of processing time, volume of input and output than say, information production for tactical and strategic planning. Transaction processing is essential to keep the operations of the organisation running smoothly and provides the base for all other internal information support. This is shown in Figure 28.2.

6. CHARACTERISTICS OF DATA PROCESSING SYSTEMS

These systems are 'pre-specified'; that is their functions, decision rules and output formats cannot usually be changed by the end user. These systems are related directly to the structure of the organisation's data. Any change in the data they process or the functions they perform usually requires the

FIGURE 28.2 Transaction Processing as a base for MIS

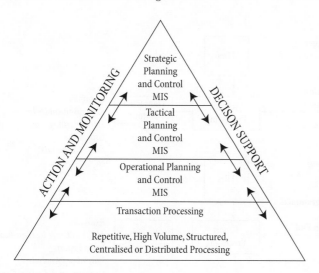

intervention of information system specialists such as system analysts and programmers.

Some data processing systems have to cope with huge volumes and a wide range of data types and output formats. As an example consider the Electricity and Gas Board Billing and Payment Handling systems, the Clearing Bank's Current Accounting Systems, the Motor Policy handling systems of a large insurer and so on. The systems and programming work required for these systems represents a major investment. For example, the development of a large scale billing system for a public utility represents something like 100 man years effort.

Of course, data processing also takes place on a more modest scale and the ready availability of application packages – ie software to deal with a particular administrative or commercial task – means that small scale users have professionally written and tested programs to deal with their routine data processing. The better packages provide for some flexibility and the user can specify – within limits – variations in output formats, data types and decision rules.

7. SCOPE OF TRANSACTION PROCESSING

Transaction processing is necessary to ensure that the day to day activities of the organisation are processed, recorded and acted upon. Files are maintained which provide both the current data for transactions, for example the amount invoiced and cash received during the month for statement preparation, and which also serve as a basis for operational and tactical control and for answering enquiries.

Transaction processing can be sub-divided into:

a. Current activity processing

b. Report processing

c. Inquiry processing

FIGURE 28.3 Sub-divisions of Transaction Processing with Inventory Control examples

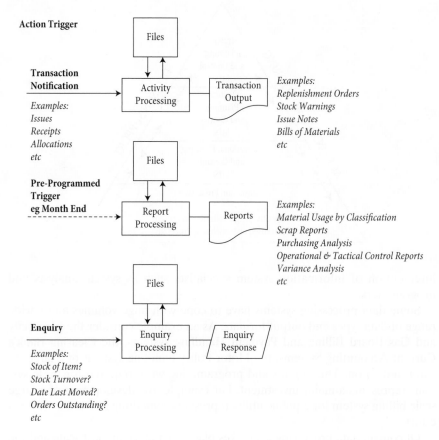

Figure 28.3 shows in outline these sub-divisions with examples of the various processing types drawn from inventory control and materials processing.

A routine data processing system is not in itself an MIS because it does not support all the management functions of the organisation nor does it have the decision focus which is the primary objective of MIS. Nevertheless it should be apparent that routine transaction processing is essential for day-to-day activities and provides the indispensable foundation upon which the organisation's MIS is built.

For example, there would be little point in developing a sophisticated flexible budgeting system complete with detailed variance analysis if the routine, but essential, cost analysis and recording system was not working perfectly.

8. DECISION SUPPORT SYSTEMS (DSS)

DSS are alternatively termed end-user computing systems. Their objective is to support managers in their work, especially decision-making. DSS tend to be used in planning, modelling, analysing alternatives and decision-making. They generally operate through terminals operated by the user who interacts with the computer system. Using a variety of tools and procedures the manager (ie the user) can develop his or her own systems to help perform his or her work more effectively. It is this active involvement and the focus on decision-making which distinguishes a DSS from a data processing system. The emphasis is on support for decision-making not an automated decision-making which is a feature of transaction processing. DSS are especially useful for semi-structured problems where problem solving is improved by interaction between the manager and the computer system. The emphasis is on small, simple models which can easily be understood and used by the manager rather than complex integrated systems which need information specialists to operate them.

The main characteristics of DSS are:

a. The computer provides support but does not replace the manager's judgement nor does it provide predetermined solutions.

b. DSS are best suited to semi-structured problems where parts of the analysis can be computerised but the decision-maker's judgement and insight is needed to control the process.

c. Where effective problem solving is enhanced by interaction between the computer and the manager.

Typical of the functions and facilities available to support managers are the following:

a. Modelling and simulation
b. Spreadsheets
c. Statistical analyses of all types
d. Forecasting
e. Non-linear and Linear programming
f. Regression analysis
g. Financial modelling
h. Sensitivity and risk analysis
i. Activity cost management.

9. SOFTWARE AND APPLICATION PACKAGES

Increasingly the decision regarding which computer system to purchase depends on the software support for the machine and the availability of application packages (ie software to deal with particular commercial and administrative tasks) either from the manufacturers of the machine or specialist software suppliers.

Because packages are becoming more flexible and are able to deal with an ever-widening range of applications, bespoke or individual programming is becoming rare. Most small, medium, and quite a few large organisations rely exclusively on bought-in packages for their work. This is in marked contrast to the earlier situation when, to own a computer, automatically meant that the organisation had to employ an number of expert (and expensive!) programmers to write unique programs.

The suppliers of packages endeavour to ensure that the package can readily be customised to suit the user's requirements. This includes the choice by the user of such things as: transaction types, data requirements, report layouts and frequency, types of calculations – including those unique to the organisation and so on. Most packages are supplied in modular form and form part of an integrated suite of packages with automatic, secure relationships and entries between the various modules.

The choice of which modules to use is, of course, under the control of the user and within a module the choice of facilities and work to be done is again under user control, usually assisted by what is termed the 'menu'. This is simply a display of options and choices from which the user can decide what the program will do next.

On occasions the manuals supplied with packages leave something to be desired but it is vital that the accountant learns about the package, how to use it, how to adapt it and how it can assist him in his work. Only by taking some effort will he or she obtain the maximum advantage from using the computer and, most importantly, remain in control of the system.

Only rarely is package designed to do cost accounting work alone. More commonly a package is designed to carry out some essential task, such as say, payroll, and costing data and reports are produced as an automatic by-product. As an example, for a payroll package the relevant cost accounting by-products could include: entries for job costs, WIP, or overheads as appropriate, labour cost analyses by type of labour/cost-centre/productive/non-productive time and so on.

Similar principles apply to the various other packages available; each would generate the routine, but essential source data on which the cost accounting system depends whether it relates to wages, materials, performance levels, waste and scrap, expenditure by cost centre and so on.

It will be realised that the same procedure is followed even when the system is dealt with by manual means. For example, a manual production control system provides data to the cost department on such matters as: output and performance levels, down time, scrap and re-work levels and so on. This data is usually transferred on a form or docket and would then be worked upon in the cost department to produce cost accounting information by pricing, extending, calculating, making ledger entries and so on. Using a computer system the transfers, calculations and ledger updating would take place automatically with total accuracy and at high speed with obvious time savings.

It would clearly be impossible to describe the detailed capabilities of all the various packages available but students are strongly advised either to gain first-hand experience of using different packages or, failing this, to study articles in the technical journals which describe the facilities available or to read the suppliers' leaflets.

One particular type of software, the spreadsheet package, is described below because of its particular usefulness for accounting and cost accounting purposes.

10. SPREADSHEET PACKAGES

Most packages are designed to deal with a single specific application, for example, stock control, sales ledger and so on, but the concept of the electronic worksheet, which is the heart of a spreadsheet package is so flexible and versatile that it can be used for innumerable tasks and applications. Once the principles have been mastered a spreadsheet package is arguably the most useful type of package available to the accountant. Undoubtably the most used spreadsheet package is Microsoft's Excel.

The basic concept of spreadsheets is that both alphabetic data (for labels, headings and titles) and numeric data can be stored and manipulated on an electronic worksheet arranged as a grid of say 64 columns, labelled alphabetically and a number of rows, say 256, which are numbered.

Each cell within the grid is referred to by its co-ordinates D3, E15, H182, etc and cell contents can be manipulated in virtually any fashion required, eg rows or columns added or subtracted, or worked upon by more complex formulae as required including any type of special calculations required by the user.

Because of the limit set by size of the display only part of the worksheet can be seen at any one time but all the data stored in the worksheet remains in the computer memory and can be recalled to the screen on the user's command, in a horizontal or vertical movement, by the process known as scrolling. A small part of a spreadsheet grid pattern is show in Figure 28.4 with the cursor in position B6.

The key feature of a spreadsheet package is its ability to change all elements in the matrix automatically when one or more of the key assumptions are changed. As an example the accountant may have prepared on the spreadsheet a series of detailed interlocking departmental operating statements culminating in an overall projected profit and loss account. If one or more of the variables (rates of pay, output levels, sales, absorption rates and so on) needs

FIGURE 28.4 Part of spreadsheet display

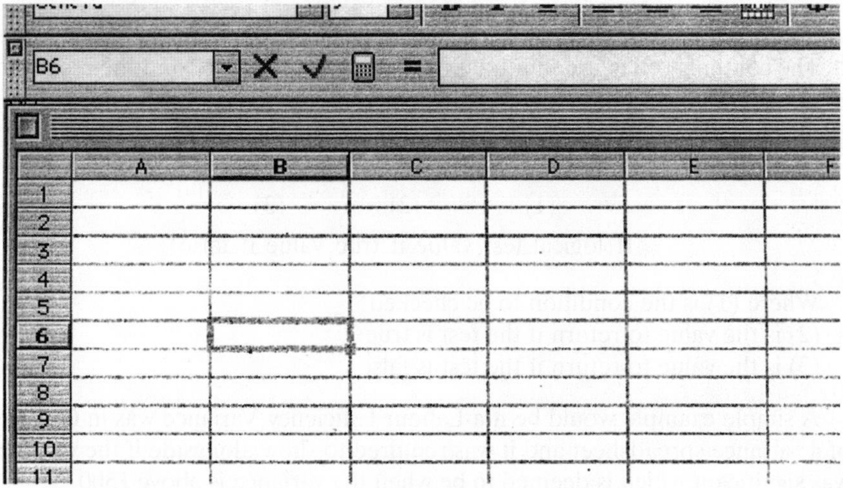

to be altered then the new value needs only to be entered once and the whole of the matrix is recalculated virtually instantaneously with all relationships, sub-totals and totals automatically catered for.

This facility allows a series of outcomes to be explored, providing answers to the 'what if' questions which are so essential to the accountant. For example, what would be the effect on profit of a change in inflation rate/cost per unit contribution margin/scrap rates or whatever factor need to be explored. Used in this way spreadsheet packages perform a modelling function and this facility is greatly expanded in the latest spreadsheet packages.

A few typical applications of spreadsheet packages are briefly described below but it must be emphasised that the potential range of applications is enormous and is only limited by the imagination of the user. Some key features and functions of spreadsheets are outlined below.

11. SPREADSHEET FEATURES

Cell contents

A cell, described above, can contain any of the following:

Values: a *number* that can be used in calculations

Text: usually *words*. Where a number which is not to be used for calculations, e.g. a Code Number, is required in a cell it must be prefixed by an apostrophe, e.g. '8932

Formulae: a powerful feature of spreadsheets. A formula refers to other cells and performs some logical, arithmetical, statistical or some other form of computation on the contents of the other cells and puts the results in the designated cell.

In Excel a formula must begin with an equals sign =.

Some examples:

In cell C20 is entered = SUM (C10:C19)

The contents of C10 through to C19 are added and the result put in C20.

In Cell D19 is entered = D6 * E12

The contents of D6 are multiplied by the contents of E12 and the result put in D19.

Logical formulae use the following structure

$$\begin{array}{ccc} (1) & (2) & (3) \end{array}$$
$$= \mathrm{If}(\mathrm{logical\_test}, \mathrm{value\_if\_true}, \mathrm{value\_if\_false})$$

Where (1) is the condition to be checked
(2) is the value to return if the test is true
(3) is the value to return if the test is false.

A simple example would be if a Labour Efficiency Variance was in Cell F20 of a variance spreadsheet and it was required to show alongside if the variance was significant which is deemed to be when the variance is above £500.

In G20 is entered = IF(F20>500, "SIGNIFICANT", "NOT SIGNIFICANT").

As another example, assume that deliveries of a component were entered in a spreadsheet as follows:

It is required to calculate the average price per unit to be inserted in D11. To do this simple statistical task, the SUMPRODUCT and SUM functions are required.

In D11 is entered = SUMPRODUCT(B5:B9,D5:D9)/SUM(D5:D9).

And the value of £11.02342 appears.

This expression multiplies the contents of B5 (the unit price) by the contents of D5 (quantity) and adds the result to B6 multiplied by D6, and so on. The grand total is divided by the sum of D5 through to D9 (the total quantity).

In addition to the above simple examples there are a vast range of other formulae dealing with databases, engineering, date and time, and statistical and financial calculations of all types.

A few typical applications of spreadsheet packages are briefly described below but it must be emphasised that the potential range of applications is enormous and is only limited by the imagination of the user.

12. SOME APPLICATIONS OF SPREADSHEETS

Monthly expenditure reports

A format, ie the layout of the report with appropriate headings, is set up initially including the necessary simple formulae for calculating variances, percentages, sub-totals, totals, etc. Various files of the data to be used on the spreadsheet display are maintained and updated each month by the current month's actual figures.

Typically the files would include: cumulative actual, monthly budget, cumulative budget, previous year cumulative. On command, the necessary budget and actuals are copied into the spreadsheet model of the monthly report. The model is then automatically recalculated producing all the necessary percentages, variances and totals. A further command prints out the completed budget report ready for distribution.

A typical layout for such a report is shown in Figure 28.5.

Cash budgets

Cash budgets are examples of routine but highly essential reports which need frequent updating to reflect current and forecast conditions, changes in credit behaviour, anticipated gains or expenditures and so on. In a similar manner to that already described the format, relationships and formulae required are set up initially and files maintained for brought forward information.

Each period (weekly, monthly, quarterly, as required) changes and up-to-date information are input and, in combination with the brought forward file data, the cash budget will be automatically projected forward by the spreadsheet program with highlighted surpluses and/or deficiencies, balances carried forward from one period to another and all the usual contents of a cash

FIGURE 28.5 Spreadsheet format for expenditure report

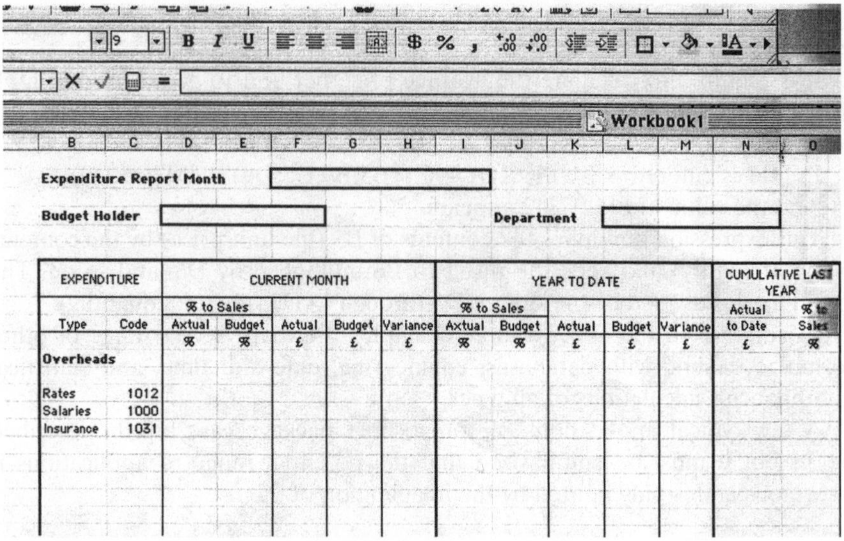

budget. The budget could be shown in both an abbreviated and detailed format and could also be displayed in a graphical form.

Figure 28.6 shows the possible output of a Summary Cash budget and a corresponding graphical display, the facility for which is increasingly being included in modern spreadsheet packages.

Maintaining standard cost records

Using traditional systems, standard costs were kept on individual cards with the standard amounts and standard prices of materials, labour and overheads extended and totalled on the card. Problems occur when there is a change in say the price of material, used in numerous components which are in turn incorporated into numbers of assemblies. A single price change might require hundreds or even thousands of amendments making standard cost revision a very lengthy and tedious manual task.

Using a spreadsheet package, after the necessary once-off initial formatting and set-up procedures, the input of a material price change – or any other change – would cause the automatic reworking of the costs of all components, assemblies and finished items containing that material. This means that costs can be updated more frequently thus making the subsequent variance analysis more useful and, where standard costs are used in estimating, may mean that selling prices are more realistic. Overall the process becomes more accurate and considerable routine clerical work is avoided.

The above brief outline of spreadsheets and typical applications is, of necessity, at a basic level. Packages are becoming ever more comprehensive and thus the possible range of applications is increasing all the time. More integrated packages are becoming available where spreadsheets, modelling, data base management and word processing facilities are all included in the same package, greatly increasing the power and flexibility.

FIGURE 28.6 Tabular and Graphical Cash budget

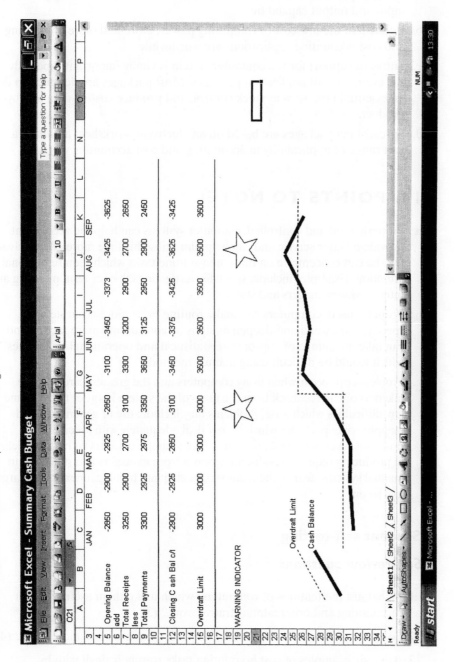

	JAN	FEB	MAR	APR	MAY	JUN	JUL	AUG	SEP
Opening Balance	-2850	-2900	-2900	-2925	-2850	-3100	-3450	-3373	-3425	-3625
add									
Total Receipts	3250	2900	2900	2700	3100	3300	3200	2900	2700	2650
less									
Total Payments	3300	2925	2925	2975	3350	3650	3125	2950	2900	2450
Closing Cash Bal c/f	-2900	-2925	-2850	-2850	-3100	-3450	-3375	-3425	-3625	-3425
Overdraft Limit	3000	3000	3000	3000	3000	3500	3500	3500	3500	3500
WARNING INDICATOR									

Overdraft Limit

Cash Balance

539

13. SUMMARY

a. Computers are useful for cost accounting purposes and accounting because of their speed, accuracy, filing and retrieval abilities, calculating power and input and output capabilities.

b. Because of the low cost of computing power, more and more accounting and cost accounting applications are worthwhile.

c. Software support for the computer system is vitally important especially the availability of application packages. Most packages are designed to do an essential task, such as stock control, and produce costing data as a by-product.

d. Spreadsheet packages are based on an electronic worksheet and have a vast range of applicability in accounting and cost accounting work.

14. POINTS TO NOTE

a. Properly used and controlled, computer systems can help the accountant provide a better service and can help him utilise his time more effectively so that he can concentrate on those non-routine tasks which require personal attention. Examples include: special investigations, longer term planning and interviewing managers and staff.

b. Properly used, computers can make routine tasks more accurate and speedy, can extend and deepen analysis by considering more factors and can take advantage of appropriate statistical and operational techniques which would be difficult using manual methods.

c. Problems can occur when using computers and the greatest care must be taken to obtain feedback from the users of the system in order to overcome any difficulties which arise. Problems may include: use of generalised and inappropriate packages which do not deal adequately with specialised problems, over-abundant printouts which swamp managers with paper, delays in producing required results, antagonism from managers and staff used to manual systems, fear of the unknown, inadequate training, unexplained jargon and so on.

Student self-testing

Self-review questions

1. What are the features of computers- which make them useful for cost accounting and other administrative work? (3)

2. Why is it now worthwhile to use computers for more and more tasks? (4)

3. Give six examples of cost accounting tasks routinely dealt with by computer. (4)

4. What are the features of Data Processing systems? (5)

5. What are the key elements in Decision Support Systems? (8)

6. What is the advantage of application packages? (9)

7. Why do most packages produce cost accounting information as a by-product? (9)

8. What is a spread sheet package? (10)

9. What type of tasks can spreadsheet package deal with? (10)

10. How could a spreadsheet package deal with the production of a cash budget? (11)

Exercises (with answers below)

1. Describe the ways computers could assist with the cost accounting tasks associated with overheads.

2. Give six areas in which the 'what if' facility available in spreadsheet and other packages could be useful to the cost accountant.

Solutions to exercises

1. Some of the overhead tasks which the computer could assist with are:

Accumulation of overheads expenditure by type of expenditure and location.

Apportionment over cost centres and departments of general overhead items eg, rates.

Statistical analysis of overhead expenditure for separation of fixed and variable elements, forecasting and decision analysis Budget preparation.

Budgetary control report production, calculation and updating of OAR's overhead analysis for monthly operating statements.

2. Six areas where 'what if' facility could be used.

Exploration of different assumptions for budget preparation.

Liquidity and cash budget statements.

Product cost calculations with different material/labour and other costs.

Testing effect on OARs of varying inflation rates/cost levels and so on.

All forms of decision analysis utilising different assumptions/costs.

Revenue and cost forecasting using different growth rates/inflation/costs.

Assessment section 5

EXAMINATION QUESTIONS (ANSWERS ON WEBSITE)

A5.1   F Limited has the following budget and actual data:

Budget fixed overhead cost	£100,000
Budget production (units)	20,000
Actual fixed overhead cost	£110,000
Actual production (units)	19,500

The fixed overhead volume variance
A is £500 adverse.
B is £2,500 adverse.
C is £10,000 adverse.
D is £17,500 adverse.
E cannot be calculated from the data given.

A5.2   J Limited operates a standard cost accounting system. The following information has been extracted from its standard cost card and budgets:

Budgeted sales volume	5,000 units
Budgeted selling price	£10.00 per unit
Standard variable cost	£5.60 per unit
Standard total cost	£7.50 per unit

If it used a standard marginal cost accounting system and its actual sales were 4,500 units at a selling price of £12.00, its sales volume variance would be:

A   £1,250 adverse.
B   £2,200 adverse.
C   £2,250 adverse.
D   £3,200 adverse.
E   £5,000 adverse.

A5.3   When a standard cost bookkeeping system is used and the actual price paid for raw materials exceeds the standard price, the double entry to record this is:

A debit raw material control account, credit raw material price variance account.

B debit work-in-progress control account, credit raw material price variance account.

C debit creditor for raw materials, credit raw material price variance account.

D debit raw material price variance account, credit raw material control account.

E debit raw material price variance account, credit work-in-progress account.

A5.4   T plc uses a standard costing system, with its material stock account being maintained at standard costs. The following details have been extracted from the standard cost card in respect of direct materials:

$$8 \text{ kg @ } £0.80/\text{kg} = £6.40 \text{ per unit}$$

Budgeted production in April 1995 was 850 units.

The following details relate to actual materials purchased and issued to production during April 1995 when actual production was 870 units:

Materials purchased	8,200 kg costing £6,888
Materials issued to production	7,150 kg

Which of the following correctly states the material price and usage variances to be reported?

	Price	**Usage**
A	£286 (A)	£152 (A)
B	£286 (A)	£280 (A)
C	£286 (A)	£294 (A)
D	£328 (A)	£152 (A)
E	£328 (A)	£280 (A)

A5.5   The following details have been extracted from the debtor collection records of C Limited:

Invoices paid in the month after sale 60%
Invoices paid in the second month after sale 25%
Invoices paid in the third month after sale 12%
Bad debts 3%
Invoices are issued on the last day of each month.

Customers paying in the month after sale are entitled to deduct a 2% settlement discount.

Credit sales values for June to September 1995 are budgeted as follows:

June	**July**	**August**	**September**
£35,000	£40,000	£60,000	£45,000

The amount budgeted to be received from credit sales in September 1995 is

A   £47,280   B   £47,680   C   £48,850   D   £49,480   E   £50,200

A5.6 In a period, 11,280 kilograms of material were used at a total standard cost of £46,248. The material usage variance was £492 adverse. What was the standard allowed weight of material for the period?

    A 11,520 kgs B 11,280 kgs   C 11,394 kgs D 11,160 kgs

A5.7 PQ Limited operates a standard costing system for its only product. The standard cost card is as follows:

Direct materials (4 kg @ £2/kg)	£8.00
Direct labour (4 hours @ £4/hour)	£16.00
Variable overhead (4 hours @ £3/hour)	£12.00
Fixed overhead (4 hours @ £5/hour)	£20.00

Fixed overheads are absorbed on the basis of labour hours. Fixed overhead costs are budgeted at £120,000 per annum rising at a constant rate during the year. Activity in period 3 of 1995 is budgeted to be 10% of total activity for the year. Actual production during period 3 was 500 units, with actual fixed overhead costs incurred being £9,800 and actual hours worked being 1,970.

The fixed overhead expenditure variance for period 3 of 1995 was

    A £2,200(F) B £200(F) C £50(F)   D £200(A) E £2,200(A)

A5.8 ABC Limited uses standard costing. It purchases a small component for which the following data are available:

Actual purchase quantity	6,800 units
Standard allowance for actual production	5,440 units
Standard price	85p./unit
Purchase price variance (ADVERSE)	(£544)

What was the actual purchase price per unit?

    A 75p.   B 77p.   C 93p.   D 95p.

A5.9 During a period 17,500 labour hours were worked at a standard cost of £6.50 per hour. The labour efficiency variance was £7,800 favourable. How many standard hours were produced?

    A 1,200   B 16,300   C 17,500   D 18,700

A5.10 AB Limited is currently preparing its production budget for product Z for the forthcoming year. The sales director has confirmed that he requires 120,000 units of product Z. Opening stock is estimated to be 13,000 units and the company wishes to reduce stock at the end of the year by 50 per cent. How many units of product Z will need to be produced?

    A 113,500 units
    B 120,000 units
    C 126,500 units
    D 133,000 units

The following information relates to questions A5.11, A5.12 and A5.13.

PP Limited has prepared the following standard cost information for one unit of Product X.

Direct materials	2 kg @ £13/kg	£26.00
Direct labour	3.3 hours @ £4/hour	£13.20
Fixed overheads	4 hours @ £2.50	£10.00

The fixed overheads are based on budgeted expenditure of £180,000 and budgeted activity of 72,000 hours.

Actual results for the period were recorded as follows:

Production	12,000 units
Materials – 26,400 kg	£336,600
Labour – 40,200 hours	£168,840
Fixed Overheads	£160,000

All the materials were purchased and used during the period.

A5.11 The direct material price and usage variances are:

	Material price	Material usage
A	£6,600(F)	£31,200(A)
B	£6,600(F)	£31,200(F)
C	£31,200(F)	£6,600(A)
D	£31,200(A)	£6,600(A)

A5.12 The direct labour rate and efficiency variances are:

	Labour rate	Labour efficiency
A	£8,040(A)	£2,400(A)
B	£8,040(A)	£2,400(F)
C	£8,040(F)	£2,400(A)
D	£8,040(F)	£2,400(F)

A5.13 The total fixed production overhead variance is:

A £20,000(F)
B £20,000(A)
C £40,000(A)
D £40,000(F)

A5.14 Z PLC uses a standard costing system and has the following labour cost standard in relation to one of its products:

4 hours of skilled labour @ £12.00 per hour = £48.00 per unit

During April 2000, 3,350 of these products were made which was 150 units fewer than budgeted. The labour cost incurred was £159,786 and the number of direct labour hours worked was 13,450.

The direct labour variances for the month were:

	Rate	Efficiency
A	£1,608 (F)	£600 (A)
B	£1,608 (F)	£600 (F)
C	£1,614 (F)	£594 (A)
D	£1,614 (F)	£600 (A)
E	£1,680 (F)	£6,600 (F)

A5.15 J Limited uses a standard costing system and has the following data relating to one of its products:

	£ Per unit	£ Per unit
Selling price		27.00
Variable costs	12.00	
Fixed costs	9.00	
		21.00
Profit per unit		6.00

Budgeted sales for April 2000 were 800 units, but the actual sales were 850 units. The revenue earned from these sales was £22,440.

If a profit reconciliation statement were to be drawn up using marginal costing principles, the sales variances would be:

	Price	Volume
A	£480 (A)	£300 (F)
B	£480 (A)	£750 (F)
C	£510 (A)	£720 (F)
D	£510 (A)	£300 (F)
E	£510 (A)	£750 (F)

The following Information relates to questions A5.16 and A5.17

A company manufactures and sells two products (X and Y) which have contributions per unit of £8 and £20 respectively. The company aims to maximise profit. Two materials (G and H) are used in the manufacture of each product. Each material is in short supply — 1,000 kg of G and 1,800 kg of H are available next period. The company holds no stocks and it can sell all the units produced.

The management accountant has drawn the following graph accurately showing the constraints for materials G and H.

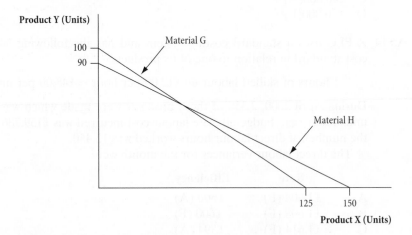

A5.16 What is the amount (in kg) of material G and material H used in each unit of product Y?

	Material G	Material H
A	10	20
B	10	10
C	20	20
D	20	10

A5.17 What is the optimal mix of production (in units) for the next period?

	Product X	Product Y
A	0	90
B	50	60
C	60	50
D	125	0

A5.18 In a standard cost bookkeeping system, when the actual material usage has been greater than the standard material usage, the double entry to record this is

A	Debit the material usage variance account	Credit the raw material control account
B	Credit the material usage variance account	Debit the raw material control account
C	Debit the material usage variance account	Credit the work-in-progress account
D	Credit the material usage variance account	Debit the work-in-progress account

A5.19 When calculating the material purchases budget, the quantity to be purchased equals

A material usage + materials closing stock – materials opening stock
B material usage – materials dosing stock + materials opening stock
C material usage – materials closing stock – materials opening stock
D material usage + materials closing stock + materials opening stock

A5.20 A company's budgeted sales for last month were 10,000 units with a standard selling price of £20 per unit and a contribution to sales ratio of 40%. Last month actual sales of 10,500 units with total revenue of £204,750 were achieved.
What were the sales price and sales volume contribution variances?

	Sales price variance (£)	Sales volume contribution variance (£)
A	5,250 adverse	4,000 favourable
B	5,250 adverse	4,000 adverse
C	5,000 adverse	4,000 favourable
D	5,000 adverse	4,000 adverse

A5.21 The company operates a standard absorption costing system. The standard fixed production overhead rate is £15 per hour.
The following data relate to last month:

Actual hours worked	5,500
Budgeted hours	5,000
Standard hours for actual production	4,800

What was the fixed production overhead capacity variance?
A £7,500 adverse
B £7,500 favourable
C £10,500 adverse
D £10,500 favourable

A5.22 A contract is under consideration which requires 600 labour hours to complete. There are 350 hours of spare labour capacity. The remaining hours for the contract can be found either by weekend overtime working paid at double the normal rate of pay or by diverting labour from the manufacture of product QZ. If the contract is undertaken and labour is diverted, then sales of product QZ will be lost. Product QZ takes three labour hours per unit to manufacture and makes a contribution of £12 per unit. The normal rate of pay for labour is £9 per hour
What is the total relevant cost of labour for the contract?
A £1,000
B £2,250
C £3,250
D £4,500

The above are a variety of multiple choice questions selected from CIMAs Management Accounting Fundamentals,Fundamentals of Management Accounting,Operational Cost Accounting and ACCAs Financial Information for Management.

(CIMA Cost Accounting)

A5.23 For the next period DNP Limited has prepared the following budgeted information for its three products:

	Product A	Product B	Product C
Sales volume (units)	8,750	12,500	5,000
Selling price per unit	£80	£64	£100
Variable cost per unit	£20	£23	£35
Fixed costs attributable to products (£000)	65	140	95
Apportioned general fixed costs (£000)	280	320	200

Requirement:
a. Prepare a statement showing the budgeted profit for EACH product and for DNP Limited in total.
b. Because of increased competition, consideration is being given to the elimination of product C.

Requirement:

Prepare a statement showing the budgeted profit for products A and B and DNP Limited in total, assuming that product C is eliminated and that the sales of products A and B remain the same and that general fixed costs fall by 10%.

c. Comment on the position revealed by your two statements.

(CIMA Cost Accounting and Quantitative Methods)

A5.24 XYZ Limited has the following forecast sales at list price for the nine months to 29 February 1996:

June	£40,000	September	£48,000	December	£44,000
July	£44,000	October	£40,000	January	£42,000
August	£50,000	November	£45,000	February	£50,000

60% of the company's sales are on credit, payable in the month after sale. Cash sales attract a 5% discount off list price.

Purchases amount to 40% of selling price, and these are paid for two months after delivery.

Stock is maintained at a level equal to 50% of the following month's sales except that in November stock is to be increased by £2,000 (at cost prices) to ensure that XYZ Limited has a safety stock during the period when its major supplier shuts down. This safety stock will be released in March.

Wages comprise a fixed sum of £2,000 per month plus a variable element equal to 10% of sales; these are payable in the month they are incurred.

Fixed costs amount to £7,500 per month, payable one month in arrears, of which £1,500 is depreciation.

XYZ Limited has capital expenditure/receipts scheduled as follows:

Acquisitions:	£
September	15,000
November	10,000
February	4,000
Disposal:	£
October	8,000

Corporation tax, payable in November, amounts to £44,000.

The bank balance on 1 September 1995 is expected to be £5,000.

Requirements:

a. Prepare a cashflow forecast for XYZ Limited for EACH of the six months from September 1995 to February 1996, using a row and column format.

b. Explain clearly,using your answer to (a) above, how a spreadsheet may be used to assist in the preparation of cash forecasts.

c. Explain how a cash forecast is an example of both feedforward and feedback control mechanisms.

(CIMA Operational Cost Accounting)

A5.25 You have been appointed as the management accountant of the DL Hospital Trust, a newly-formed organisation with specific responsibility for providing hospital services to its local community. The hospital trust is divided into a number of specialist units: one of these, unit H, specialises in the provision of a particular surgical operation.

Although the trust does not have profit maximisation as its objective, it is concerned to control its costs and to provide a value-for-money service. To achieve this, it engages teams of specialist staff on a sub-contract basis and pays them an hourly rate based upon the direct hours attributable to the surgical operation being carried out.

Surgical team fees (ie labour costs) are collected and attributed to each surgical operation, whereas overhead costs are collected and attributed to surgical operations using absorption rates. These absorption rates are based on the surgical team fees. For the year ended 31 December 1993, these rates were:

Variable overhead   62.5% of surgical team fees; and
Fixed overhead   87.5% of surgical team fees.

Each surgical operation is expected to take ten hours to complete, and the total fees of the team for each operation are expected to be £2,000.

The budget for the year ended 31 December 1993 indicated that a total of 20 such surgical operations were expected to be performed each month, and that the overhead costs were expected to accrue evenly throughout the year.

During November 1993 there were 22 operations of this type completed. These took a total of 235 hours and the total surgical team fees amounted to £44,400.

Overhead costs incurred in unit H in November 1993 amounted to:

Variable overhead	£28,650
Fixed overhead	£36,950

Requirements:

a. Prepare a statement which reconciles the original budget cost and the actual cost for this type of operation within unit H for the month of November 1993, showing the analysis of variances in as much detail as possible from the information given.

b. Distinguish between the use of budgetary control and standard costing as a means of cost control in service-based organisations.

Explain clearly the arguments in favour of using BOTH of these methods simultaneously.

c. The DL Hospital Trust has been preparing its budget for 19994, and the finance director has questioned the appropriateness of using surgical team fees as the basis of attributing overhead costs to operations.

Requirement:

Write a brief report to her explaining the arguments for and against the use of this method.

(CIMA Operational Cost Accounting)

A5.26 The following profit reconciliation statement has been prepared by the management accountant of ABC Limited for March 1995:

	£
Budgeted profit	30,000
Sales volume profit variance	5,250 A
Selling price variance	6,375 F
	31,125

Cost variances:		A	F
		£	£
Material:	price	1,985	
	usage		400
Labour:	rate		9,800
	efficiency	4,000	
Variable overhead:	expenditure		1,000
	efficiency	1,500	
Fixed overhead:	expenditure		500
	volume	24,500	
		31,985	11,700

	20,285 A
Actual profit	10,840

The standard cost card for the company's only product is as follows:

		£
Materials	5 litres @ £0.20	1.00
Labour	4 hours @ £4.00	16.00
Variable overhead	4 hours @ £1.50	6.00
Fixed overhead	4 hours @ £3.50	14.00
		37.00
Standard profit		3.00
Standard selling price		40.00

The following information is also available:
(1) There was no change in the level of finished goods stock during the month.
(2) Budgeted production and sales volumes for March 1995 were equal.
(3) Stocks of materials, which are valued at standard price, decreased by 800 litres during the month.
(4) The actual labour rate was £0.28 lower than the standard hourly rate.

Requirements:
a. Calculate the following:
   i. the actual production/sales volume,
   ii. the actual number of hours worked,
   iii. the actual quantity of materials purchased,
   iv. the actual variable overhead cost incurred,
   v. the actual fixed overhead cost incurred.

b. ABC Limited uses a standard costing system whereas other organisations use a system of budgetary control.

Requirement:

Explain the reasons why a system of budgetary control is often preferred to the use of standard costing in non-manufacturing environments.

(CIMA Operational Cost Accounting)

A5.27 B Limited operates an integrated accounting system and the following details given relate to one year.

You are required from the details given to:

a. enter in the appropriate ledger accounts the transactions for the year;
b. prepare a profit and loss account for the year; and
c. prepare a balance sheet as at the end of the year.

Trial balance at beginning of the year:	£000's	£000's
Capital	–	1,000
Reserves	–	200
Creditors	–	150
Expense creditors	–	20
Freehold buildings, at cost	500	–
Plant and machinery, at cost	300	–
Provision for depreciation of plant and machinery	–	100
Stock of: raw materials	220	–
work-in-progress	40	–
finished goods	60	–
Debtors	200	–
Bank	150	–
	1,470	1,470

The following data for the year are given:

		£000's
Materials:	purchased on credit	990
	returned to suppliers	40
	issued to production	850
Production:	wages incurred	250
	salaries	60
	expenses incurred	320
Carriage inwards		45
Provision for depreciation of plant and machinery		50
Production: Overhead absorbed		425
Production, at standard cost		1,600
Administration:	salaries	100
	expenses incurred	260
	overhead absorbed in finished goods	380
Selling and distribution:	salaries	80
	expenses incurred	120
	absorbed in cost of sales	210

		£000's
Finished goods sold		2,000
Sales on credit		2,500
Sales returns		60
Variance:	direct material:	
	price (adverse)	35
	usage (favourable)	20
	direct wages rate (favourable)	15
	direct labour efficiency (favourable)	30
	production overhead:	
	expenditure (adverse)	25
	efficiency (favourable)	40
Abnormal loss of raw material stock, insurance claim agreed and cash received		60
New machinery purchased, paid by cheque		50
Paid:	creditors	895
	expense creditors	730
Cash discount received from trade creditors		25
Paid wages and salaries		425
Deduction from wages and salaries		50
Received cheques from debtors		2,350
Cash discount allowed		35
Bad debts written off		25

All 'price' variances (ie direct material price, direct wages rate, production overhead expenditure) are recorded in the relevant expenditure accounts; 'quantity' variances (ie direct material usage, direct labour efficiency, production overhead efficiency) are recorded in the work-in-progress account.

(CIMA, Cost Accounting 2)

A5.28 A hotel is currently operating at a 55% occupancy level. The hotel's management has traditionally used flexed budget information in the format shown below. The figures given below are for the current year and management intends to use them as the basis for next year's budget.

Occupancy level	55%	75%	85%
Accommodation:	£	£	£
Room-cleaning costs	481,800	657,000	744,600
Establishment costs	363,170	477,050	533,990
Sports facilities:			
Recreational facilities cost	180,675	246,375	279,225
Equipment costs	100,000	100,000	100,000

The hotel management expects all variable costs to increase by 3.5% next year. This increase has not been incorporated into the above figures. The hotel's management team has identified a new market, luxury weekend breaks, that it believes will increase the operating level to 80% occupancy for the next year.

The new luxury weekend breaks venture will require an investment in the existing hotel to bring it up to a luxury standard. The cost in relation to upgrading the rooms and the sports facilities is expected to be £50,000 and £75,000 respectively. The management's policy is that the cost of upgrading the rooms and sporting facilities will be charged against profits over the next five years. The amounts to be charged annually are £10,000 for the upgrading for the rooms and £15,000 for the upgrading of the sports facilities.

You have recently been appointed as the management accountant for the hotel.

Requirements:
a. Comment on the format currently used by the hotel management team for the presentation of the budget information.
b. Prepare in a more appropriate format the flexed budget statement for next year, assuming that the hotel will operate at 80% occupancy.
c. Assuming that over the next year the hotel did achieve an 80% occupancy level, prepare a report for management that compares budget and actual expenditure, calculates appropriate variances and suggests reasons why the variances could have occurred.

Actual expenditure:	£
Room-cleaning costs	727,560
Establishment costs	529,258
Recreational facilities costs	275,640
Equipment costs	115,000

Note:
All fixed costs actually incurred were as budgeted. The annual charge for upgrading was as expected.

d. Briefly discuss two problems which may arise from higher occupancy levels arising from the luxury weekend breaks and the upgraded sporting facilities.

(CIMA Management Accounting Fundamentals)

A5.29 The following information is an extract from the forecasts of ABC Limited for the next three periods:

	Period 1 (£000)	Period 2 (£000)	Period 3 (£000)
Sales	432	357	330
Production cost of sales	281	198	174
Stocks at period end (valued at production cost)	47	53	25
Debtors at period end	710	684	593
Creditors at period end	210	225	192
Administrative overheads	84	91	78
Depreciation included in production costs and administrative overheads	29	32	26

The cash balance at the start of Period 2 is forecast to be £85,000. All purchases and sales are on credit and no bad debts are expected.

Requirements:
a. Prepare a columnar cash budget for each of the Periods 2 and 3.
b. Briefly discuss the advantages of preparing cash budgets
(CIMA Cost Accounting and Quantitative Methods)

A5.30 Data from the October 1999 standard cost card of product Wye, the only product of Exe PLC, is as follows:

Direct materials	4 kg @ £2.50 per kg	10.00
Direct labour	3 hours @ £6.00 per hour	18.00
Variable overhead	3 hours @ £4.00 per hour	12.00
Fixed overhead		20.00
		60.00
Standard profit		15.00
Standard selling price		75.00

Budgeted fixed overhead cost for October 1999 was £25,000.

The operating statement for October 1999, when raw material stock levels remained unchanged, was as follows:

	£ Adverse	£ Favourable	£
Budgeted profit			17,250
Sales volume profit variance		750 Adverse	
		16,500	
Selling price variance		5,500 Favourable	
		22,000	
Cost variances:			
Direct materials			
– price	535		
– usage	375		
Direct labour			
– rate	410		
– efficiency	1,200		
Variable overhead			
– expenditure		820	
– efficiency	800		
Fixed overhead			
– expenditure		1,000	
– volume		1,000	
	3,320	2,820	500 Adverse
Actual Profit			21,500

Required:
a. Calculate:
    i. actual sales units;
    ii. actual production units;

iii. actual selling price per unit;
iv. actual material price per kg;
v. actual labour hours;
vi. actual variable overhead cost;
vii. actual fixed overhead cost.

b. Prepare a report addressed to the Operations Manager which explains the meaning and possible causes of the two most significant variances which occurred in October 1999.

(CIMA Operational Cost Accounting)

EXAMINATION QUESTIONS WITHOUT ANSWERS

B5.1 The following data and estimates are available for ABC Limited for June, July and August:

	June £	July £	August £
Sales	45,000	50,000	60,000
Wages	12,000	13,000	14,500
Overheads	8,500	9,500	9,000

The following information is available regarding direct materials:

	June £	July £	August £	September £
Opening stock	5,000	3,500	6,000	4,000
Material usage	8,000	9,000	10,000	

Notes:
(1) 10% of sales are for cash, the balance is received the following month. The amount received in June for May's sales is £29,500.
(2) Wages are paid in the month they are incurred.
(3) Overheads include £1,500 per month for depreciation. Overheads are settled the month following. £6,500 is to be paid in June for May's overheads.
(4) Purchases of direct materials are paid for in the month purchased.
(5) The opening cash balance in June is £11,750.
(6) A tax bill of £25,000 is to be paid in July.

Requirements:
a. Calculate the amount of direct material purchases in EACH of the months of June, July and August.
b. Prepare cash budgets for June, July and August.
c. Describe briefly the advantages of preparing cash budgets.

(CIMA Cost Accounting and Quantitative Methods)

B5.2 A company is preparing budgets for the year ahead for two of its raw materials that are used in various products which it manufactures. Current year material usage standards are as follows:

Kilos per thousand units of product

	Product 1	Product 2	Product 3	Product 4	Product 5
Material A	25	70	15	–	55
Material B	30	5	–	20	–

It has been decided to change standards on Material B for the following year to reflect the favourable usage variances that are occuring for that material on all products. Usage variances on Material B are 10% of standard costs.

Budgeted sales quantities for the following year are:

	Product 1	Product 2	Product 3	Product 4	Product 5
(thousand units)	600	350	1850	1200	900

Production quantities are to be budgeted in line with sales, apart from Product 5 where an increase in stock of 30% is required by the end of the budget year. Stocks of the five products at the beginning of the budget year are expected to be:

	Product 1	Product 2	Product 3	Product 4	Product 5
(thousand units)	140	80	260	180	100

Stocks of Materials A and B at the end of the budget year are to be 10% of the year's budgeted usage. Stocks at the end of the current year are expected to be:

Material A	10,030 kilos
Material B	4,260 kilos

Required:

a. Describe the benefits that can be derived from a budgeting system.

b. Prepare material usage and purchases budgets (kilos only) for each of Materials A and B for the year ahead.

c. Prepare summary journal entries for the Material A stock account for the current period.

The following additional information is provided for the current period:

Material A purchases:

116,250 kilos at a cost of £280,160

(standard purchase price = £2.40 per kilo).

Production:	Product 1	Product 2	Product 3	Product 4	Product 5
(thousand units)	580	330	1900	1200	800

Material A usage has been at standard.

(ACCA Cost & Management Accounting 1)

B5.3 a. What do you understand by the term 'limiting factor' when considering production budgets?
      b. A company manufactures three products A, B and C with the following annual production budget:

	A	B	C
Unit of output	6,000	3,000	5,000
Machine hours per output unit	3	4	2
	£	£	£
Direct materials	40,000	36,000	30,000
Direct labour	17,850	18,600	16,300
Direct expense	2,150	3,400	3,700
Variable Overhead	6,000	8,000	4,000
Unit selling price	17.50	32	16

Production is restricted by a storage of materials common to all three products, this shortage is expected to last for a further two years and the factory is operating below full capacity. Fixed overhead for the year is estimated at £42,000 and is apportioned to each product on the basis of machine hours used. Prepare a statement showing, in terms of the limiting factor, the profitability of each product, and calculate the effect on contribution if production is concentrated on the product showing the highest profitability.

(CIPFA, Management Accounting)

B5.4 Budgetary control is the establishment of budgets relating the responsibilities of executives to the requirements of policy, and the continuous comparison of actual, with budgeted results, either to secure by individual action the objective of that policy or to provide a basis for its revision. In the above statement explain what is meant by:
      a. Responsibilities of executives.
      b. Requirements of a policy.
      c. Continuous comparison.
      d. A basis for its (policy) revision.

(AAT, Cost Accounting and Budgeting)

B5.5 *You are required to:*
      a. compare the operation of fixed budgets (or cash limits) within public sector organisations or local government authorities with the budgeting procedures normally used in commercial organisations, listing three advantages and three disadvantages from the public sector or local government point of view;
      b. explain the use of a budget manual and give an indication of the likely contents. Your explanation must be related to one of the following:
         i. a private sector organisation;
         ii. a public sector organisation;
         iii. a local government authority.

(CIMA, Cost Accounting)

B5.6   NAB Limited has produced the following figures relating to production for the week ended 21 May:

	Production (in units)	
	Budgeted	**Actual**
Product A	400	400
Product B	400	300
Product C	100	140

Standard production times were:

	Standard hours per unit
Product A	5.0
Product B	2.5
Product C	1.0

During the week 2,800 hours were worked on production.

You are required:

a.   i. to calculate the production volume ratio and the efficiency ratio for the week ended 21 May:

   ii. to explain the significance of the two ratios you have calculated and to state which variances may be related to each of the ratios;

b. to explain the three measures of capacity referred to in the following statement: During the recent recession, increased attention was paid to 'practical capacity' and 'budgeted capacity' because few manufacturing companies could anticipate working again at 'full capacity'.

(CIMA Cost Accounting)

B5.7   PQ Limited has two production departments – machining and assembly. Two of its main products are the Major and the Minor, the standard data for which are as follows:

	Per Unit	
	Major	**Minor**
Direct materials:		
Material @ £15 per kg	2.2 kgs	1.4 kgs
Direct Labour:		
Machining department @ £6 per hour	4.8 hrs	2.9 hrs
Assembly department @ £5 per hour	3.6 hrs	3.1 hrs
Machining time	3.5 hrs	0.9 hrs

The overhead rates for the period are as follows:

| **Machining department** | **Assembly department** |
| £16.00 per machine hour | £9.50 per labour hour |

Requirement:

a. Calculate the standard production cost for each product showing clearly, as a sub total, the standard prime cost.

b. During the period, actual results for labour were as follows:

	Major	**Minor**
Production	650 units	842 units
Direct labour:		
Machining department	2,990 hrs	2,480 hrs
	costing £18,239	costing £15,132
Assembly department	2,310 hrs	2,595 hrs
	costing £11,700	costing £12,975

Requirement:

Calculate the direct labour total variance and the rate and efficiency variances for each product and each department.

c. Explain briefly what information the above variances provide for management.

(CIMA Cost Accounting and Quantitative Methods)

B5.8 The following data have been collected for the month of April by a company which operates a standard absorption costing system:

		£
Actual production of product EM	600 units	
Actual costs incurred:		
Direct material E	660 metres	6,270
Direct material M	200 metres	650
Direct wages	3,200 hours	23,200
Variable production overhead		6,720
(which varies with hours worked)		
Fixed production overhead		27,000

Variances:	**£**	
Direct material price:		
Material E	330	Favourable
Material M	50	Adverse
Direct material usage:		
Material E	600	Adverse
Material M	nil	
Direct labour rate	800	Adverse
Direct labour efficiency	1,400	Adverse
Variable production overhead:		
expenditure	320	Adverse
efficiency	400	Adverse
Fixed production overhead:		
expenditure	500	Favourable
volume	2,500	Favourable

Opening and closing work-in-progress figures were identical, so can be ignored.

You are required:

a. to prepare for the month of April a statement of total standard costs for product EM;

b. to present a standard product cost sheet for one unit of product EM;
c. to calculate the number of units of product EM which were budgeted for April;
d. to state how the material and labour cost standards for product EM would originally have been determined.

(CIMA Cost Accounting)

B5.9 SK Limited makes and sells a single product 'Jay' for which the standard cost is as follows:

		£ per unit
Direct materials	4 kilograms at £12.00 per kg	48.00
Direct labour	5 hours at £7.00 per hour	35.00
Variable production overhead	5 hours at £2.00 per hour	10.00
Fixed production overhead	5 hours at £10.00 per hour	50.00
		143.00

The variable production overhead is deemed to vary with the hours worked. Overhead is absorbed into production on the basis of standard hours of production and the normal volume of production for the period just ended was 20,000 units (100,000 standard hours of production).

For the period under consideration, the actual results were:

Production of 'Jay'	18,000 units
	£
Direct materials used – 76,000 kgs at a cost of	836,000
Direct labour cost incurred – for 84,000 hours worked	604,800
Variable production overhead incurred	172,000
Fixed production overhead incurred	1,030,000

You are required:
a. to calculate and show, by element of cost, the standard cost for the output for the period;
b. to calculate and list the relevant variances in a way which reconciles the standard cost with the actual cost;

Note:
Fixed production overhead sub-variances of capacity and volume efficiency (productivity) are *not* required.

c. to comment briefly on the usefulness to management of statements such as that given in your answer to (b) above.

(CIMA Cost Accounting)

B5.10 a. JB plc operates a standard marginal cost accounting system. Information relating to product J, which is made in one of the company's departments, is given as follows.

Product J	Standard marginal product cost	Unit (£)
Direct material	6 kilograms at £4 per kg	24
Direct labour	1 hour at £7 per hour	7
Variable production overhead*		3
Total variable production cost		34

* Variable production overhead varies with units produced.
Budgeted fixed production overhead, per month: £100,000.
Budgeted production for product J: 20,000 units per month.

Actual production and costs for month 6 were as follows:

Units of J produced		**18,500**
		£
Direct materials purchased and used	113,500 kgs	442,650
Direct labour	17,800 hours	129,940
Variable production overhead incurred		58,800
Fixed production overhead incurred		104,000
		735,390

You are required:

    i. to prepare a columnar statement showing, by element of cost, the
       (I) original budget
      (II) flexed budget
     (III) actual costs
     (IV) total variances;
    ii. to sub-divide the variances for direct material and direct labour shown in your answer to (a)(i)(IV) above to be more informative for managerial purposes.

  b. Explain the meaning and use of a 'rolling forecast'.

(CIMA Cost Accounting)

B5.11 A firm operates a standard cost system and the following variances have been calculated:

	£	
Material price	350	FAV
Material usage	130	ADV
Labour rate	627	FAV
Labour efficiency	303	ADV
Variable overhead expenditure	804	FAV
Variable overhead efficiency	921	ADV
Fixed overhead expenditure	486	FAV
Fixed overhead volume	173	ADV

    (Ignore sales variances)

The opening trial balance was as follows:

	£	£
Financial ledger control A/C		6,620
Stores Control A/C (at standard)	2,150	
Finished Goods (334 units)	4,470	

There was no opening or closing WIP.

The budget and actual results for the period were as follows:

	Budget	**Actual**
Sales	4,900 units at £30	5,000 units at £30
Production	4,900 units	4,800 units
Fixed overheads	£8,500	

The following information was also available on the period's expenditure:

	£
Material purchases	23,250
Direct wages	19,480
Variable overheads	13,724
Fixed overheads	8,014

The closing stock of materials was £3,200 (at standard).

Using the above information prepare all necessary accounts and a profit and loss statement for the period clearly showing the final trial balance.

B5.12 B Ltd manufactures a single product in one of its factories. Information relating to the month just ended is as follows:

i. Standard cost per hundred:

	£
Raw materials: 15 kilos at £7 per kilo	105
Direct labour: 10 hours at £6 per hour	60
Variable production overhead: 10 hours at £5 per hour	50
	215

ii. 226,000 units of the product were completed and transferred to finished goods stock.

iii. 34,900 kilos of raw material were purchased in the month at a cost of £245,900.

iv. Direct wages were £138,545 representing 22,900 hours work.

v. Variable production overheads of £113,800 were incurred.

vi. Fixed production overheads of £196,800 were incurred.

vii. Stocks at the beginning and end of the month were:

	Opening Stock	**Closing Stock**
Raw materials	16,200 kilos	16,800 kilos
Work in progress	–	4,000 units, (complete at to raw materials but only 50% complete as to direct labour and overhead)
Finished goods	278,000 units	286,000 units

Raw materials, work in progress, and finished goods stocks are maintained at standard cost. You should assume that no stock discrepancies or losses occurred during the month just ended.

Required:
a. Prepare the cost ledger accounts relating to the above information in B Ltd's interlocking accounting system. Marginal costing principles are employed in the cost ledger.
b. Explain and contrast the different types of standards that may be set as a benchmark for performance measurement.

(ACCA Cost and Management Accounting)

B5.13 The financial and cost accounts of the MA Manufacturing Company for the year ended 30th September, have been reconciled as below.

Financial profit and loss account for the year ended 30th September

Raw materials:				
Opening stock	56,450		Cost of goods	810,000
			manufactured	
Purchases	324,560			
	381,010			
Closing stock	58,060	322,950		
Direct wages		247,320		
Production salaries		86,465		
Indirect wages		42,321		
Depreciation		50,000		
Power		10,642		
Telephone		8,742		
Rates		16,400		
Insurance		6,475		
Miscellaneous		18,325		
		809,640		
Work-in-progress:				
Opening stock	18,620			
Closing stock	18,260	360		
		810,000		
				810,000
Finished goods:			Sales	1,103,500
Opening stock	142,350			
Manufactured	810,000			
	952,350			
Closing stock	146,850	805,500		
Gross profit c/d		298,000		
		£1,103,500		£1,103,500
		£		£
Administration expenses		124,620	Gross profit b/d	298,000
Selling and distribution expenses		87,380	Discount received	1,600
Discount allowed		1,240		
Debenture interest		6,360		
Net profit c/d		80,000		
		£299,600		£299,600

Reconciliation of Financial and Cost Accounts Year ended 30th September

	£		£
Profit as per financial accounts	80,000	Profit as per cost accounts	84,550
Discounts allowed	1,240	Discount received	1,600
Debenture interest	6,360	Difference in stock valuation	
Difference in stock valuation:		Raw materials:	
Work-in-progress:		Opening	700
Closing	480	Raw materials:	
Finished goods:		Closing	750
Opening	720	Work-in-progress	
		Opening	620
		Finished goods:	
		Closing	580
	£88,800		£88,800

Data in the cost accounts include:

	£
Direct material price variance	3,120 Adverse
Direct material usage variance	1,280 Adverse
Direct labour rate variance	4,160 Favourable
Direct labour efficiency variance	4,470 Favourable
Production overhead expenditure variance	4,880 Favourable
Production overhead volume variance	1,680 Adverse

You are required, from the above data, to show the following accounts as they should appear in the cost ledger:
a. stores ledger control;
b. work-in-progress ledger control;
c. finished goods ledger control;
d. profit and loss

(CIMA Cost Accounting 2)

B5.14 A rapidly expanding medium-sized business, manufacturing and selling small electrical appliances used in household kitchens (toasters, can openers, food mixers, kettles, jugs), requires better information than is currently being provided for the control of its selling, warehousing and distribution activities. The sales director currently has responsibility for all aspects of selling, warehousing and distribution; he has a sales manager, a warehouse manager and a transport manager reporting directly to him. The home market is served by a territorial sales force and overseas sales are executed by agencies in the countries to which the appliances are exported.

The sales director has his own staff who keep budgets of sales and monitor actual results for comparison with these budgets but there is no costing information about the activities under his control other than that contained within nominal ledger accounts for the following:

Salespersons' salaries and commissions
Salespersons' expenses
Warehouse labour
Own transport, including maintenance

Hired transport
Packing materials
Overseas agencies' expenses and commissions
Advertising

The salaries of the three managers reporting to the sales director are included, with other staff, in a salaries account.

You are required, as the assistant management accountant, to write a report to the sales director showing:

a. the general principles which would be followed in planning a system for the control of the costs of the activities under his control;
b. in relation to functional budgets, a list of 20 accounts which ought to be provided from the company's chart of accounts;
c.   i. how the sales ought to be analysed, and
    ii. the way in which a computer could be useful to aid this analysis;
d. the cost and sales information that could be given to the salespersons and for what purpose.

(CIMA Cost Accounting)

Table A

PRESENT VALUE FACTORS

Present value of $£1 = (1 + r)^{-n}$ for $1\% < r < 15\%$

	Interest rates $(r)\%$								
Periods (n)	1%	2%	4%	6%	8%	10%	12%	14%	15%
1	0.990	0.980	0.962	0.943	0.926	0.909	0.893	0.877	0.870
2	0.980	0.961	0.925	0.890	0.857	0.826	0.797	0.769	0.756
3	0.971	0.942	0.889	0.840	0.794	0.751	0.712	0.675	0.658
4	0.961	0.924	0.855	0.792	0.735	0.683	0.636	0.592	0.572
5	0.951	0.906	0.822	0.747	0.681	0.621	0.567	0.519	0.497
6	0.942	0.888	0.790	0.705	0.630	0.564	0.507	0.456	0.432
7	0.933	0.871	0.760	0.665	0.583	0.513	0.452	0.400	0.376
8	0.923	0.853	0.731	0.627	0.540	0.467	0.404	0.351	0.327
9	0.914	0.837	0.703	0.592	0.500	0.424	0.361	0.308	0.284
10	0.905	0.820	0.676	0.558	0.463	0.386	0.322	0.270	0.247
11	0.0896	0.804	0.650	0.527	0.429	0.350	0.287	0.237	0.215
12	0.887	0.788	0.625	0.497	0.397	0.319	0.257	0.208	0.187
13	0.879	0.773	0.601	0.469	0.368	0.290	0.229	0.182	0.163
14	0.870	0.758	0.577	0.442	0.340	0.263	0.205	0.160	0.141
15	0.861	0.743	0.555	0.417	0.315	0.239	0.183	0.140	0.123
16	0.853	0.728	0.534	0.394	0.292	0.218	0.163	0.123	0.107
17	0.855	0.714	0.513	0.371	0.270	0.198	0.146	0.108	0.093
18	0.836	0.700	0.494	0.350	0.250	0.180	0.130	0.095	0.081
19	0.828	0.686	0.475	0.331	0.232	0.164	0.116	0.083	0.070
20	0.820	0.675	0.456	0.312	0.215	0.149	0.104	0.073	0.061
21	0.811	0.660	0.439	0.294	0.199	0.135	0.093	0.064	0.053
22	0.803	0.647	0.422	0.278	0.184	0.123	0.083	0.056	0.046
23	0.795	0.634	0.406	0.262	0.170	0.112	0.074	0.049	0.040
24	0.788	0.622	0.390	0.247	0.158	0.102	0.066	0.043	0.035
25	0.780	0.610	0.375	0.233	0.146	0.092	0.059	0.038	0.030

PRESENT VALUE FACTORS

Present value of $£1 = (1+r)^{-n}$ for $16\% < r < 30\%$

Periods (n)	Interest rates (r)%								
	16%	18%	20%	22%	24%	25%	26%	28%	30%
1	0.862	0.847	0.833	0.820	0.806	0.800	0.794	0.781	0.769
2	0.743	0.718	0.694	0.672	0.650	0.640	0.630	0.610	0.592
3	0.641	0.609	0.579	0.551	0.524	0.512	0.500	0.477	0.455
4	0.552	0.516	0.482	0.451	0.423	0.410	0.397	0.373	0.350
5	0.476	0.437	0.402	0.370	0.341	0.328	0.315	0.291	0.269
6	0.410	0.370	0.335	0.303	0.275	0.262	0.250	0.227	0.207
7	0.354	0.314	0.279	0.249	0.222	0.210	0.198	0.178	0.159
8	0.305	0.266	0.233	0.204	0.179	0.168	0.157	0.139	0.123
9	0.263	0.225	0.194	0.167	0.144	0.134	0.125	0.108	0.094
10	0.227	0.191	0.162	0.137	0.116	0.107	0.099	0.085	0.075
11	0.195	0.162	0.135	0.112	0.094	0.086	0.079	0.066	0.056
12	0.168	0.137	0.112	0.192	0.076	0.069	0.062	0.052	0.043
13	0.145	0.116	0.093	0.075	0.061	0.055	0.050	0.040	0.033
14	0.125	0.099	0.178	0.062	0.049	0.044	0.039	0.032	0.025
15	0.108	0.084	0.065	0.051	0.040	0.035	0.031	0.025	0.020
16	0.093	0.071	0.054	0.042	0.032	0.028	0.025	0.019	0.015
17	0.080	0.060	0.045	0.034	0.026	0.023	0.020	0.015	0.012
18	0.069	0.051	0.038	0.028	0.021	0.018	0.016	0.012	0.009
19	0.060	0.043	0.031	0.023	0.017	0.014	0.012	0.009	0.007
20	0.051	0.037	0.026	0.019	0.014	0.012	0.010	0.007	0.005
21	0.044	0.031	0.022	0.015	0.011	0.009	0.008	0.006	0.004
22	0.038	0.026	0.018	0.013	0.009	0.007	0.006	0.004	0.003
23	0.033	0.022	0.015	0.010	0.007	0.006	0.005	0.003	0.002
24	0.028	0.019	0.011	0.008	0.006	0.005	0.004	0.003	0.002
25	0.024	0.016	0.010	0.007	0.005	0.004	0.003	0.002	0.001

Table B

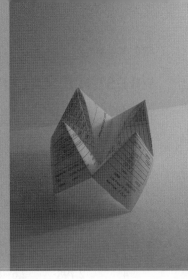

PRESENT VALUE ANNUITY FACTORS

Present value of £1 received annually for n years $\dfrac{1 - (1 + r)^{-n}}{r}$ for $1\% < r < 15\%$

Periods (n)					Interest rates (r)%				
	1%	2%	4%	6%	8%	10%	12%	14%	15%
1	0.990	0.980	0.962	0.943	0.926	0.909	0.893	0.877	0.870
2	1.970	1.942	1.886	1.833	1.783	1.736	1.690	1.647	1.626
3	2.941	2.884	2.775	2.675	2.577	2.487	2.402	2.322	2.283
4	3.902	3.808	3.610	3.465	3.312	3.170	3.037	2.914	2.855
5	4.853	4.713	4.452	4.212	3.996	3.791	3.605	3.433	3.352
6	5.795	5.601	5.242	4.917	4.623	4.355	4.111	3.889	3.784
7	6.728	6.472	6.002	5.582	5.206	4.868	4.564	4.288	4.160
8	7.652	7.325	6.733	6.210	5.747	5.335	4.968	4.639	4.487
9	8.566	8.162	7.435	6.802	6.247	5.759	5.328	4.946	4.772
10	9.471	8.983	8.111	7.360	6.710	6.145	5.650	5.216	5.019
11	10.368	9.787	8.760	7.887	7.139	6.495	5.988	5.453	5.234
12	11.255	10.575	9.385	8.384	7.536	6.814	6.194	5.660	5.421
13	12.114	11.343	9.986	8.853	7.904	7.103	6.424	5.842	5.583
14	13.004	12.106	10.563	9.295	8.244	7.367	6.628	6.002	5.724
15	13.865	12.849	11.118	9.712	8.559	7.606	6.811	6.142	5.847
16	14.718	13.578	11.652	10.106	8.851	7.824	6.974	6.265	5.954
17	15.562	14.292	12.166	10.477	9.122	8.022	7.120	6.373	6.047
18	16.328	14.992	12.659	10.828	9.372	8.201	7.250	6.467	6.128
19	17.226	15.678	13.134	11.158	9.604	8.365	7.366	6.550	6.198
20	18.046	16.351	13.590	11.470	9.818	8.514	7.469	6.623	6.259
21	18.857	17.011	14.029	11.764	10.017	8.649	7.562	6.687	6.312
22	19.660	17.658	14.451	12.042	10.201	8.772	7.645	6.743	6.369
23	20.456	18.292	14.857	12.303	10.371	8.883	7.718	6.792	6.399
24	21.243	18.914	15.247	12.550	10.529	8.985	7.784	6.815	6.434
25	22.023	19.523	15.622	12.783	10.675	9.077	7.843	6.873	6.464

PRESENT VALUE ANNUITY FACTORS

Present value of £1 received annually for n years $\dfrac{1 - (1 + r)^{-n}}{r}$ for $16\% < r < 30\%$

Periods (*n*)	Interest rates (*r*)%								
	16%	18%	20%	22%	24%	25%	26%	28%	30%
1	0.862	0.847	0.833	0.820	0.806	0.800	0.794	0.781	0.769
2	1.605	1.566	1.528	1.492	1.457	1.440	1.424	1.392	1.361
3	2.246	2.174	2.106	2.042	1.981	1.952	1.923	1.868	1.816
4	2.798	2.690	2.589	2.494	2.404	2.362	2.320	2.241	2.166
5	3.274	3.127	2.991	2.864	2.745	2.689	2.635	2.532	2.436
6	3.685	3.498	3.326	3.167	3.020	2.951	2.885	2.759	2.643
7	4.039	3.812	3.605	3.416	3.242	3.161	3.083	2.937	2.802
8	4.344	4.078	3.837	3.619	3.421	3.329	3.421	3.076	2.925
9	4.607	4.303	4.031	3.786	3.566	3.463	3.366	3.184	3.019
10	4.833	4.949	4.192	3.923	3.682	3.571	3.465	3.269	3.092
11	5.029	4.636	4.327	4.035	3.766	3.656	3.544	3.335	3.147
12	5.197	4.793	4.439	4.127	3.851	3.725	3.606	3.387	3.190
13	5.342	4.910	4.533	4.203	3.912	3.780	3.656	3.427	3.223
14	5.468	5.008	4.611	4.265	3.961	3.824	3.965	3.459	3.249
15	5.575	5.092	4.675	4.315	4.001	3.859	3.726	3.483	3.268
16	5.669	5.162	4.730	4.357	4.033	3.887	3.751	3.503	3.283
17	5.749	5.222	4.775	4.391	4.059	3.910	3.771	3.518	3.295
18	5.818	5.273	4.812	4.419	4.080	3.928	3.786	3.529	3.304
19	5.877	5.316	4.844	4.442	4.097	3.942	3.799	3.539	3.311
20	5.929	5.353	4.870	4.460	4.110	3.954	3.808	3.546	3.316
21	5.973	5.384	4.891	4.476	4.121	3.963	3.816	3.551	3.320
22	6.011	5.410	4.909	4.488	4.130	3.970	3.822	3.556	3.323
23	6.044	5.432	4.925	4.499	4.137	3.976	3.827	3.559	3.325
24	6.073	5.451	4.937	4.507	4.143	3.981	3.831	3.562	3.327
25	6.097	5.467	4.948	4.514	4.147	3.985	3.834	3.564	3.329

Examination technique

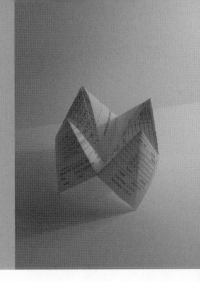

1. INTRODUCTION

If you are a genius and/or can calculate and reproduce facts and figures with the speed of a computer and/or know the examiner then there is no need for you to read this section. On the other hand if you do not fall into any of the above categories then you will stand more chance of passing your examinations first time if you study this section carefully and follow the simple rules.

2. WELL BEFORE THE EXAMINATION

No amount of examination room technique will enable you to pass unless you have prepared yourself thoroughly beforehand. The period of preparation may be years or months long. It is no use expecting to pass with a feverish last minute bout of revision. By this stage you should have worked through all of the book and you should be thoroughly familiar with your syllabus and the type of examination questions that you have been set in the past.

By the end of your study and revision you should be able to answer every question in this book.

3. IMMEDIATELY BEFORE THE EXAMINATION

a. Make sure you know exact time, date and location of examination.

b. Carefully check you travel arrangements. Leave yourself adequate time.

c. Check over your examination equipment: Calculator? Spare Battery? Pens? Pencils? Tables? Watch? Sweets? etc.

d. Check your examination number.

4. IN THE EXAMINATION ROOM

If you have followed the rules so far you are well prepared; you have all the equipment you need; you did not have to rush – you are calm and confident.
  Before you start writing

a. Carefully read the whole examination paper including the rubric.

b. Decide what questions you are going to answer.

c. Decide the sequence you will tackle the questions. Generally, answer the easiest question first.

d. Decide the time allocation for each question. In general the time allocation should be in direct proportion to the marks for each question.

e. Read the questions you have decided to answer again. Do you know exactly what the examiner is asking? Underline the key words in the question and keep these in your mind when answering.

5. DEALING WITH THE QUESTIONS

a. Make sure you plan each question first. Make a note of the main points or principles involved. If you are unable to finish the question you will gain some marks from these points.

b. Attempt all questions required and each part of each question.

c. Do not let your answer ramble on. Be as brief as possible consistent with covering all the points you know.

d. Follow a logical sequence in your answers.

e. Write neatly, underline headings and if the question asks for a particular sequence of answer then follow that sequence.

f. If diagrams, graphs or tables are required give them plenty of space, label them neatly and comprehensively, and give a key to symbols, lines etc used. A simple clear diagram showing the main points can often gain a good proportion of the marks for a question.

6. WHEN YOU HAVE FINISHED WRITING

a. Check that you have followed the examination regulations regarding examination title, examination number, candidates number and sequence of answer sheets.

b. Make sure you include all the sheets you require to be marked.

c. If you have time carefully read each and every part of each answer and check each calculation.

7. GENERAL POINTS

a. Concentrate on answering the questions set not some related topic which you happen to know something about.

b. Do not leave the examination room early. Use every minute for checking and rechecking or adding points to questions answered.

c. Always attempt every question set and every part of each question.

8. EXAMINERS' REPORTS

After every examination an Examiner's Report is prepared and you are urged to obtain a copy and thoroughly digest the contents. Much useful advice is given not only about the detail of individual questions, but about the general approach to be adopted.

Ever since examinations were invented examiners have complained, with justice, about similar problems and deficiencies. The more common ones include:

- failure to read the question
- failure to answer the question as set
- careless work, especially with calculations
- bad English
- poor writing
- poor charts/diagrams with no titles or keys
- rote learning rather than real understanding
- inadequate time planning resulting in the failure to answer all questions
- inclusion of irrelevant material
- failure to relate theory and practice.

You are strongly advised to note carefully the above list of common failings and to make sure that you are not guilty of any of them.

INDEX